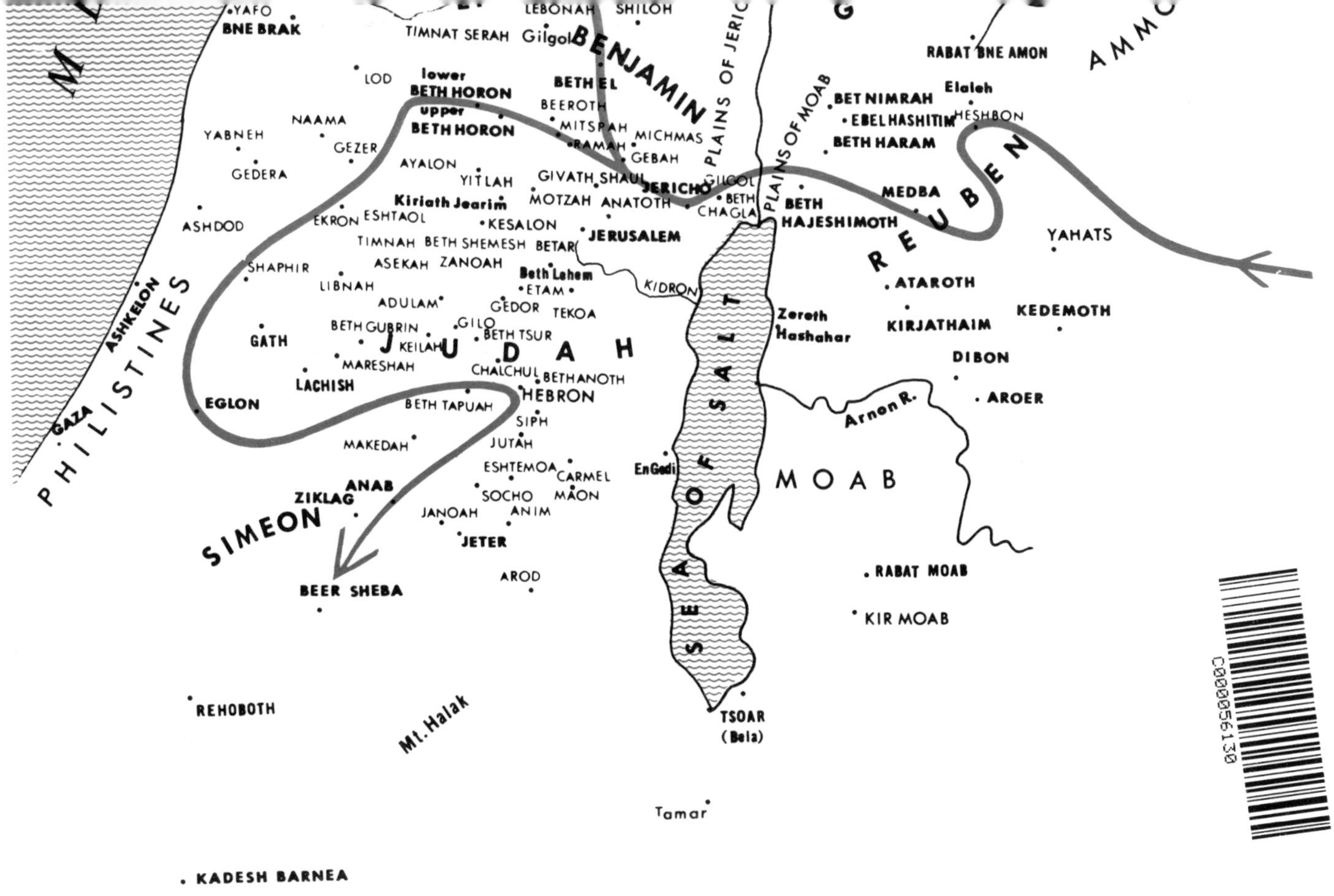

YAFO
BNE BRAK
TIMNAT SERAH
Gilgol
LEBONAH
SHILOH
BENJAMIN
PLAINS OF JERIC
RABAT BNE AMON
AMMO
LOD
lower BETH HORON
upper BETH HORON
BETH EL
BEEROTH
MITSPAH
RAMAH
MICHMAS
GEBAH
PLAINS OF MOAB
BET NIMRAH
EBEL HASHITIM
BETH HARAM
Elaleh
HESHBON
YABNEH
NAAMA
GEZER
GEDERA
AYALON
YITLAH
GIVATH SHAUL
JERICHO
GILGOL
BETH CHAGLA
BETH HAJESHIMOTH
MEDBA
REUBEN
YAHATS
ASHDOD
EKRON
ESHTAOL
Kiriath Jearim
MOTZAH
ANATOTH
KESALON
JERUSALEM
TIMNAH
BETH SHEMESH
BETAR
ASEKAH
ZANOAH
SHAPHIR
Beth Lehem
ETAM
KIDRON
ATAROTH
LIBNAH
ADULAM
GEDOR
TEKOA
Zereth Hashahar
KIRJATHAIM
KEDEMOTH
ASHKELON
PHILISTINES
GATH
BETH GUBRIN
GILO
BETH TSUR
KEILAH
JUDAH
MARESHAH
CHALCHUL
BETHANOTH
DIBON
LACHISH
HEBRON
AROER
EGLON
BETH TAPUAH
SIPH
Arnon R.
GAZA
MAKEDAH
JUTAH
ESHTEMOA
CARMEL
EnGedi
SEA OF SALT
MOAB
ANAB
ZIKLAG
SOCHO
MAON
JANOAH
ANIM
SIMEON
JETER
AROD
RABAT MOAB
BEER SHEBA
KIR MOAB
REHOBOTH
Mt. Halak
TSOAR (Bela)
Tamar
KADESH BARNEA

ISBN 0-910818-08-8

FIRST EDITION
*First Printing, 1969*

SECOND EDITION
*First Printing, 1980*
*Second Printing, 1984*
*Third Printing, 1989*
*Fourth Printing, 1992*
*Fifth Printing, 1996*
*Sixth Printing, 2002*

**The Judaica Press, Inc.**
123 Ditmas Avenue
Brooklyn, NY 11218
718-972-6200 • 800-972-6201
Fax 718-972-6204
info@judaicapress.com
**www.judaicapress.com**

*Manufactured in the United States of America*

# CONTENTS

**משה פיינשטיין**
**ר"מ תפארת ירושלים**
**בנוא יארק**

**RABBI MOSES FEINSTEIN**
**455 F. D. R. DRIVE**
**New York 2, N. Y.**
**OREGON 7-1222**

**בע"ה**

הנה ידוע ומפורסם טובא בשער בת רבים ספרי הוצאת **יודאיקא פרעסס על תנ"ך** שכבר יצא לאור על ספרי יהושע ושמואל ועכשיו בחסדי השי"ת סדרו לדפוס ג"כ על ספר שופטים והוא כולל הפירושים המקובלים בתנ"ך הנקוב בשם מקראות גדולות ועל זה הוסיפו תרגום אנגלית שהוא השפה המדוברת במדינה זו על פסוקי תנ"ך וגם תרגום לפרש"י מלה במלה עם הוספות פירושים באנגלית הנצרכים להבנת פשוטו של קרא והכל נערך ע"י תלמידי היקר הרב הגאון ר' אברהם יוסף ראזענבערג שליט"א שהוא אומן גדול במלאכת התרגום, והרבה עמל השקיע בכל פרט ופרט בדקדוק גדול, וסידר את הכל בקצור כדי להקל על הלומדים שיוכלו לעיין בנקל ואפריון נמטיה למנהל יודאיקא פרעסס מהור"ר יעקב דוד גאלדמאן שליט"א שזכה ומזכה את הרבים בלימוד התנ"ך שמעורר לומדיה לאהבה וליראה את שמו הגדול ולהאמין בו ובעבדיו הנביאים שהוא יסוד ושורש בעבודתו יתברך ואמינא לפעלא טבא יישר ויתברכו כל העוסקים בכל ברכות התורה וחכמינו ז"ל בברוך אשר יקים את דברי התורה הזאת.

וע"ז באתי עה"ח

# FOREWORD

The richness and wealth of noble thought in our divinely inspired Scriptures, encompassing the entire spectrum of the creation and of the עולם קטן, the human being, is a never ending source of delving into Nature's secrets and of refreshment of one's soul. The luxuriant vineyards of our Holy Scriptures are an inexhaustible supply of replenishment of one's personal faith and renewal of one's energy in the never ending 'מלחמת החיים', 'Battle of Life.' Never more than in today's materialistic world, when all of mankind's great scientific achievements have been harnessed to the quest for that all-elusive goal — happiness, has there been such a need for man's return to a study of the eternal, divine wisdom of the Book of Books. In the words of the prophet Amos (VIII:11) הנה ימים באים נאם ה' והשלחתי רעב בארץ, לא רעב ללחם ולא צמא למים כי אם לשמע את דברי ה'. "Behold," says the Almighty. "There are days coming when I will cause a famine to be sent in the land, not a famine for bread nor a thirst for water, but to hear the words of God."

Truly, our time, when there is no lack of physical food and drink, can be described as one in which there is felt this "religiosen drang." The spiritual revival and the search for true values is ever growing stronger, as man realizes evermore and more the futility of his efforts for happiness and the essential bankruptcy of his entire philosophy of life. He is reminded by bitter experience, of the Gaon of Vilna's maxim: כל הנאות עולם הזה כשותה מים מלוחים. "Indulgence in all physical pleasures are as one who drinks salted waters; the more one seeks to gratify his thirst, the thirstier he must become." Only in spiritual values, found in "תורת אמת", Torah of truth, can one find true happiness and true satisfaction. The Jew, indeed, before studying any sacred Book, must pronounce a blessing to Almighty God, granting him permission to study His divine wisdom. It is with this in mind that Judaica Press has approached the task of a new series of commentary and translation of the Prophets.

The volume herewith issued, inaugurates a new series of commentaries on the Books of the Prophets under the imprint of "Judaica Press," which we fervently hope will be greeted by the reading public with the response it properly deserves. We have endeavored to make this new series on the oldest of books known to mankind, unique in the following ways:

1. The Hebrew text, with the standard commentaries of Rashi and others, has been presented in its entirety, together with an English commentary containing all of Rashi's comments and the major ideas of our other great luminaries, such as Redak, Abravanel, and others including modern and contemporary commentaries.

2. Generous use has been made of pertinent Talmudic and Midrashic sources, including "Yalkut Shimoni," and also of various passages in Rashi and Ramban and other works on the Pentateuch, especially in Numbers, where the pattern of the division of the Holy Land is given.

3. In all of the commentary, there has constantly been kept in mind that the Book of Books is sacred, as the revealed word of God to His prophets. As such, any commentary misunderstanding this basic concept, has necessarily been omitted, as not being germane to an understanding of the text.

It is hoped that this work will lead to a wider dissemination of knowledge and proper perspective of historical problems.

NISON • 5740 JUDAICA PRESS
APRIL • 1980

# INTRODUCTION

BY DR. SIDNEY B. HOENIG

Joshua, the sixth book in the Bible and the first in the division of *Neviim* or Prophets, takes its name from Joshua, son of Nun, the successor of Moses and the conqueror of Canaan. Tradition ascribes the authorship of this book to Joshua himself, except for the report of the author's death.

Joshua, the Ephraimite, is not a newcomer on the Biblical scene. He had gained fame in the war against the Amalekites in the desert when he led the troops of the Israelites. He had also appeared in the Pentateuch as the faithful assistant to Moses, and as the jealous defender of the prestige of Moses in the incident of Eldad and Medad. He, too, was one of the spies sent to explore the land of Canaan. And when the spies returned, only Joshua and Caleb had the courage to face the angry Israelites and report favorably on Canaan. Joshua was designated by G-d as Moses' successor and charged with faithfulness to the Law, the conquest of Canaan and the division of the land among the tribes.

Though Joshua is the crowning figure in the book, the glory for the conquest is distinctly God's alone, in His giving Israel the Land of Canaan. The conquest is *His*. In a sense Joshua is regarded as a second Moses. His activity therefore is the fulfillment of Moses' yearning for the Promised Land. Described as the man "in whom is the spirit," tradition compares Joshua to the moon and Moses to the splendor of the sun. Many parallelisms may be found in their lives. Joshua's authority is accepted; he sanctifies Israel; there is a miraculous crossing of the Jordan; the angel speaks to him; he writes the Law on stones, etc., all in the same vein as experienced by Moses, his teacher. Hence, the Talmud also records that many ordinances such as limitation of private property rights were enacted by Joshua. Traditionally, too, he is regarded as the author of the *Alenu* (Adoration) prayer and the second section of the grace after meals (*Birkat ha-aretz*). All of these phases complement the idea of acquisition of the Land.

The book deals specifically with the conquest of Canaan, the crossing of the Jordan, the story of the spies, the punishment of Achan for taking booty, the capture of the five Kings, the various campaigns in the land, the battle at Gibeon, the destruction of *Hazor,* the allotment of the land to the different tribes in the western area as well as to the Joseph tribes in the East, and the establishment of cities of refuge. Joshua's last words of farewell are for Israel to adhere to the Torah.

Expert archaelogists have shown that the description of the conquest in 12 short chapters is a very brief extract of the event. In the many chapters are revealed the preparatory stage of terror and organized initiative.

A sensible schematic literary structure moulds the book. The book of Joshua was not written merely to provide historical and strategic information, though it displays a logical picture of the conquest from a military viewpoint and the condition of the country at that time. The scheme of the conquest basically is the pattern of observance, resulting in the fulfillment of the Promise. The conquest is preceded by circumcision, Passover celebration, revelation and dedication at Gilgal, the ban on Jericho and the reading of the Pentateuch to the whole nation. Hence it is not a strategic scheme alone but a picture of performance that we find in Joshua.

In general, the book is the realization of the promise to Abraham that his descendants would enter the Promised Land. Joshua is the first of the former prophets, linked to the Covenant, p. VIII. The Talmudic passage in Ned. 22b notes, "Had not Israel sinned, only the Pentateuch and Book of Joshua would have been given." Here there emerge the great principles of Revelation, Law execution and Land promised.

Examining then the religious teachings we note that the land is given on the conditional observance of Torah. Even the last act of Joshua is to renew the Covenant. In all, the book denotes that the Divine title to the land is manifest, though hard fighting was necessary to obtain it. The book also stresses the element of collective responsibility, similar to the story of Abraham in his battles.

Reading the book, one is conscious of a contemporary account eye witness. The phrase "unto this day" does not necessarily mean late writing. There were both national actions and local campaigns — perhaps the cities were recaptured as guerilla warfare. Because of the persistence of the Canaanites after Joshua's death, many areas had to be retaken. Traditionally then the composition by Joshua is not to be ignored.

The book is of especial interest now because of the rebuilding of Israel. One learns therein the geography of the land and its grandeurs. In Israel it is a most popular book for archaeologists and lovers of the land.

The distinct religious message in the book stresses the life of Jews as a covenant people, seeking obedience to the law and displaying Judaism as an historic religion, with God as revealed in history, contrasting it to the nature religions of the Canaanites.

Sensitive readers are concerned about the brutality shown in Joshua, but one should not forget that it is a story of a war — of a holy war. The theme is the obliteration of historically hated pagans and the battle is only in honor of God. Another point to remember is the effect of the conquest on later theology, that the land belongs to Israel "never to be uprooted." This is in accord with Ez. 39:29, and Isa. 54:17 and Mic. 4. Purified Israel is only through association with the Land, is the theme.

A most interesting question associated with the conquest is: Did the tribes settle among the Canaanites and adopt their culture; is the tradition of the wholesale destruction of the Canaanites historical? Scholars point to a distinction between the "ideal" land of Israel and the "real" land actually occupied. The ideal was from "Dan to Beersheba" and includes Tyre, Sidon etc. The warning against defection to the gods refers to those of the surrounding nations: Aram, Sidon, Moab, Ammon, the Philistines. Commentators demonstrated that the sources do not show any alliances with the Canaanites. Nowhere are the Canaanites who remained within the conquered area specified as a cause of Israelite apostasy. The view everywhere is that the Canaanites within the *real* area of Israelite settlement were destroyed. The documents that list the populations that Israel failed to evict refer not to the Canaanites who lived in the *real* land of Israel and were destroyed — but to those who lived outside it, within the *ideal* boundaries. *Garash* (expulsion), *hishmid* (destruction) and *horish* (dispossession) are mentioned again and again. There is no evidence of peaceful relations with the Canaanites. The Gibeonites, the Nethinim never mingled with Israel; they always remained an inferior caste. The *herem* status kept them apart. Moreover, never do we find the Canaanites rising within, against their conquerors. The Canaanite enclaves such as Jerusalem and Gezer were no problem.

Another point demonstrating the lack of Canaanite influence is the fact that Israel did not absorb their city-state (form). This again is explained by the fact of the *herem.* The Israelites were following a tribal federation only. The later great events consolidated the tribes, creating a strong national entity. Authority was vested in the *elders* and in the spiritual leaders, the judges — men of spirit.

The cult is that of the farmer. This does not mean a transition, for the tribes had always been half-nomads. They also tilled the soil, though not bound to a specific territory. The agricultural element in Israel's cult therefore is not less primary than the pastoral. Hence the shape of the agricultural element does not portray any Canaanite influence.

The Israelite pattern faithfully reflects Israel's non-mythological religion; it lends no support that the religion become "Canaanized on Canaan's soil." We hear nothing of idolatry during Joshua's time; it was an age of loyalty to God who revealed Himself to them on Sinai. Joshua's demand "to remove the foreign gods" (Joshua 24:23) is part of the general *ideal* and its constant warning against idolatrous practices emphasizes the continuity of the sanctity of the land of Israel. The Book of Joshua thus is most significant because *it,* above all, stresses the purity, *kedushah* of the Holy Land, the Land *of Israel.*

# INTRODUCTION

The Book of Joshua is the first of ספרי הנביאים, "Books of the Prophets," the second section of תנ"ך: Torah (Pentateuch), N'viim (Prophets), and K'tuvim (Sacred Writings), as the Bible has been divided

The Book of Joshua, moreover, occupies a unique position among all Post-Mosaic writings in that it is the only Book destined from the first to be given to Israel unconditionally, in contrast to all other subsequent writings which were transmitted as the Divine response to the sinnings of Israel: "Were it not because of Israel's sins, there would have been given to them only the Five Books of Moses (containing all the commandments) and the Book of Joshua, containing the arrangement of Eretz Israel.[2]

This book was authored by Joshua, Moses' disciple,[3] chosen by Divine command to succeed him.[4] This event took place on Sabbath afternoon on the seventh of Adar, in the year 2488 after Creation.[5] Joshua was also the author of the last eight verses of the Pentateuch.[6] He is indeed portrayed in the Talmud[7] as being equal to all Israel in the eyes of the Almighty.

There is described in the Book of Joshua the fulfillment of the Divine promise to the Patriarchs to give the land of Canaan to their descendants.[8] It commences with the miraculous manner of the crossing of the Jordan and continues through the wars of the conquest of Jericho and the entire land, culminating in the miracle of the stopping temporarily of the motion of the sun and the moon at the command of Joshua.[9] Reward and retribution are plainly visible throughout the entire Book.

The Jewish people could not be considered as having achieved the proper degree of perfection until their conquest and settlement of the Promised Land. The actualization in practice of all 613 "Mitzvot" (commandments), taught by Moses to Israel, took place only in the Land of Israel. To quote Rabbi Moses of Trani, rabbi of Safed in the latter half of the sixteenth century.

"It is possible that not all the commandments were in force during the 'generation of the wilderness' (דור המדבר), as has been noted; however, after entering the Promised Land they were committed to all the 'mitzvot', as prescribed in the Torah. This is the intent of what was said to Joshua:[10] This Book of the Torah shall not leave your mouth; you shall meditate therein day and night, in order that you observe to do all that is written in it. For from that day onward they were commanded to observe the entire Torah, as it is said: 'To do all that is written in it,' i.e. although until now they had not observed some of the commandments in the sense of being obligated to fulfill them, even some of the חובות הגוף (obligations incumbent upon the person) but henceforth they were to observe all that is written therein, (i.e. in the Torah).

Therefore, we find in the Book of Ezra,[11] when booths were constructed in observance of the holiday of Tabernacles: For the children of Israel had not done so since the days of Joshua the son of Nun. The Rabbis ask:[12] 'Is it possible that David had not constructed Sukkoth? The meaning of this phrase, however, is to compare the entry of the Jewish people into the Promised Land in the days of Joshua, with their return from exile in the days of Ezra.' It would appear that the Scripture alludes to Joshua's entry because from that time onward the people began to observe the entire Torah, as has been noted.[13]

This opinion was previously entertained by N, in the beginning of his commentary on Deuteronomy.

Even if we reject this opinion concerning חובות הגוף, there are still hundreds of "mitzvot" some of which depend for their ultimate practical fulfillment upon Eretz Israel and some upon the building of a central place of worship. This was accomplished fourteen years after entering Eretz Israel with the building of the Tabernacle at Shiloh. This was equivalent to the building of the Temple in Jerusalem. "There is no (technical) difference between Shiloh and Jerusalem..."[14]

Even the calendar, including the New Moon and the Holy Days, is inextricably bound up with a Jewish settlement in Eretz Israel.[15]

Aside from the realm of "mitzvot," it is noteworthy that even the efficacy of prayer of Joshua could have accomplished even more than that of Moses, because of the "Zechut" (merit) of the Holy Land.[16] The primacy of Eretz Israel is perhaps in no place more directly presented than in the following Talmudic passage:[17] "The Almighty wished to annihilate the world because of the wickedness of King Jehoiakim, but relented because of the righteous men of the generation. In the subsequent reign of King Zedekiah, however, the reverse was true: Zedekiah himself was righteous, turning away the wrath of the Almighty, whereas the entire generation was wicked." R comments that the righteous of the previous generation החרש והמסגר, the great Torah authorities, had all been exiled to Babylon and therefore their merit could not be counted as sufficient reason for maintaining the world. *Eretz Israel must contain righteous men to justify the existence of the world!*

Joshua, as the one who actualized all the commandments of Moses, divided the land to the individual tribes immediately upon cessation of hostilities, even before many areas had been completely subjugated. The reason is given by Maimonides, in his "opus magnum," Laws of Terumot, ch. 1: "Joshua and his count (of seventy elders) divided all of Eretz Israel to the tribes, although (parts of it) had not been conquered, lest the subsequent conquest by each tribe be considered as an individual conquest (lacking in the "Kedushah" of a communal conquest) in regard to the commandments which were in force in the Holy Land only. This division also included the designation of the six cities of refuge and the 42 cities of the Levites.[18]

Joshua's final crowning act, for which he is unique in the annals of Jewish history, is described in the final chapter, where he is instrumental in influencing Israel in entering into a covenant with the Almighty *of their own free will.* The covenant of Sinai had been accomplished through a measure of coercion,[19] but now, realizing the enormous favor shown to them by the Almighty, Israel accepted the covenant willingly, to worship Him alone and no other powers.[20] Not until 900 years later, in the days of Mordecai and Esther, would Israel go even further and accept willingly all of the 613 commandments.

The conquest of Israel, described in detail in the Book of Joshua, shows the military prowess of Joshua, and indeed, his campaign has been studied carefully to the present day by military commanders up to and including the War of Liberation in 1948. But, Joshua himself emphasizes time and again the Divine aid to Israel, without which it would have been impossible to achieve even the initial objective of conquering the walled city of Jericho. To emphasize this most strikingly, Joshua commanded the destruction of all military equipment captured in the campaign. (See Notes to Chapter 11:6)

The twenty-four chapters of Joshua fall into three broad divisions: Conquest (כבוש), Division (חלוק), and the implementation of all "mitzvot" followed by the departing instructions of Joshua (ברית). The reader is offered here a detailed outline of the Book of Joshua:

I. Conquest of Eretz Israel (I-XII).

A. Introduction (I).

1. Joshua assumes command and is given his orders (I:1-9).
2. Preparations are made to cross the Jordan (10-11).
3. Gad and Reuben repledge their aid (12-18).

B. The mission of spies to Jericho (II).
   1. The spies enter and are hidden by Rahab (1-7).
   2. Rahab exacts a promise from them (8-14).
   3. Their return to Joshua (15-24).

C. Crossing of the Jordan (III:1-V:1).
   1. Joshua orders the crossing (III:1-13).
   2. The waters of the Jordan are cut off (III:14-17).
   3. Twelve stones are taken from the river bed (IV:1-8).
   4. The crossing is completed (IV:9-19).
   5. Twelve stones are set up in Gilgal as a Memorial (IV:20-V:I).

D. The Camp at Gilgal (V:2-15).
   1. The circumcision (V:2-9).
   2. The observance of the Passover (V:10-12).
   3. Appearance of the angel (V:13-15).

E. Fall of Jericho (VI).
   1. Instructions and preparations (1-7).
   2. March around the city six days (8-14).
   3. Fall of the walls of Jericho on the seventh day (Shabat) 15-21).
   4. Rahab and her household are spared (22-27).

F. Campaign against Ai (VII:1-VIII:29).
   1. Initial defeat due to Achan's sin (VII:1-5).
   2. Joshua's prayer, discovery of Achan's sin, and his punishment (VII:6-26).
   3. Joshua's strategy (VIII:1-13).
   4. Capture and destruction of Ai (VIII:14-29).

G. An altar built on Mt. Ebal (VIII:30-35).

H. Admission of the Gibeonites (IX).
   1. Coalition formed against Israel (1-2).
   2. Gibeonites secure a treaty with Israel by ruse (3:15).
   3. The ruse is discovered (16-27).

I. Joshua's campaign in the South (X).
   1. Victory near Gibeon and the pursuit (1-15).
   2. The five kings in the cave at Makkedah (16-27).
   3. Conquest of southern Canaan (28-43).

J. Defeat of the Northern confederacy of kings and victory at the waters of Meron (XI:1-15).

K. Summary of areas conquered (XI:16-23).

L. Conclusion of history of conquest and general summary (XII).
   1. Kings conquered by Moses east of the Jordan (1-6).
   2. Thirty-one kings conquered by Joshua on western bank of Jordan (7-24).

II. Division of the land (XIII-XXI).

A. Introduction: inheritance of the eastern Trans-Jordan tribes (XIII).
   1. Command to divide the land (XIII:1-7).
   2. Survey of territory east of the Jordan (XIII:8-14).
   3. Territory of Reuben (XIII:15-23), Gad (24-28), and Manasseh (29-33).

B. Beginning of the land division (XIV).
   1. Introduction (1-5).
   2. Caleb receives possession of Hebron (6-15).

C. Lot of Judah (XV).
   1. Boundary of Judah (1-12).
   2. Caleb's and Othniel's portions (13-19).
   3. List of Judah's towns (20-63).

D. Lot of Joseph (XVI-XVII).
   1. South border of Ephraim (XVI:1-5).
   2. Northern and eastern border (6-8).
   3. Other cities held; failure to take Gezer (9-10).
   4. Division of Manasseh (XVII:1-6).
   5. Holdings of Manasseh and failure to take certain towns (7-13).
   6. Joseph demands a larger portion and Joshua's reply (14-18).

E. Lots of the remaining tribes (XVIII-XIX).
   1. Land surveyed and lots cast in Shiloh (XVIII:1-10).
   2. Lots of the remaining seven: — Benjamin (11-28), Simeon (XIX:1-9), Zebulun (10-16), Issachar (17-23), Asher (24-31), Naphtali (32-39), and Dan (40-48).
   3. Conclusion of the lot casting (49-51).

F. Cities of Refuge (XX).

G. Levitical cities from various tribes (XXI).

III. Last days of Joshua and his departing instructions (XXII-XXIV).

A. Departure of the Trans-Jordanian tribes (XXII).
   1. Eastern tribes blessed and dismissed (XXII:1-8).
   2. Building of the altar at the Jordan (9-12).
   3. Dispatching of Phinehas, and leaders from the tribes to Gad and Reuben (13-34).

B. Farewell address of Joshua (XXIII).

C. Covenant at Shechem (XXIV:1-28).
   1. Joshua reviews the mighty acts of the Lord (1-13).
   2. Joshua brings the people to accept willingly the covenant (14-28).

D. Three burials (29-33).
   1. Joshua's death and burial (29-31).
   2. Burial of Joseph (32).
   3. Eleazar's death and burial (33).

To round out the portrait of Joshua, military leader, divider of the Land of Israel, and successor to Moses the Lawgiver, we quote the "tenaim" (ordinances) promulgated by Joshua and his court. They are as follows:

1) One is permitted to pasture his flocks in privately owned forests;

2) One may gather grass (to feed livestock) in privately owned fields, except in fields of "tiltan," a species of beans to which grass is beneficial;

3) One may break off shoots (to plant or graft) except the bottom two handbreadths of an olive tree;

4) A new spring which issues forth may be used by the inhabitants of the city;

5) All tribes have the fishing rights in the Sea of Tiberias, as long as they do not spread out nets which hinder the passage of ships;

6) One may excrete behind a fence even in a field of saffron;

7) One may walk through fields after the ingathering of the grain, until the second rain, when the new seeds commence to sprout;

8) In the summer season, when the mud hardens and forms holes and ditches, making it difficult to walk on the roads, one may walk on the side of the road, even though he trespasses on private property;

9) One who strays among the vineyards, may break through the branches until he finds his way;

10) A corpse who has no known kin to bury him, must be buried in the place where he is found, even in private property.[21]

Joshua also composed the prayer of עלינו (It is incumbent upon us to praise the Lord of all etc.). He composed this prayer in gratitude for the miraculous victory over Jericho.[22] It has been incorporated into the liturgy as the closing hymn of the three daily prayers, and occupies, in addition, a central place in the majestic service of Rosh Hashanah. Joshua also composed the second blessing of the Grace After Meals.[23]

1 Meg. 7a, Baba Bathra 15a. 2 Ned. 22b. 3 Aboth, ch. 1, Rambam, introduction to "Yad". 4 Num. XXVII:18. 5 Kid. 38a. 6 Baba Bathra 15a. 7 Yoma 76a. 8 Gen. XV:18. 9 X:12. 10 Jos. 1:8. 11 Nehemiah VIII:17, included in the Book of Ezra, B. B. 15a. 12 Arachin 32b. 13 Beth Elokim, ch. 37, part 3. 14 Meg. 9b. 15 Rambam Sefer Hamitzvot, 153. 16 'Arachin 32b. 17 San. 103a. 18 XX, XXI. 19 Shab. 88a. 20 Tos. ad loc. 21 Baba Kama 80b, Rambam, Laws of Civil Damages, Ch. V. 22 Kol Bo, ch. 16, Rokeach. 23 Ber. 48b.

# ספר יהושע

## מקראות גדולות

# THE BOOK OF JOSHUA

# יהושע א

א וַיְהִי אַחֲרֵי מוֹת מֹשֶׁה עֶבֶד יְהוָה וַיֹּאמֶר יְהוָה אֶל־יְהוֹשֻׁעַ בִּן־נוּן מְשָׁרֵת מֹשֶׁה לֵאמֹר: ב מֹשֶׁה עַבְדִּי

**תרגום**

א וַהֲוָה בָּתַר דְּמִית מֹשֶׁה עַבְדָּא דַיְיָ וַאֲמַר יְיָ לִיהוֹשֻׁעַ בַּר נוּן מְשַׁמְשָׁנֵיהּ דְּמֹשֶׁה לְמֵימַר: ב מֹשֶׁה עַבְדִּי

ת״א ויהי וגו׳ מגילה לא קדושין לח תמורה טז:

**רש״י**

(א) **ויהי אחרי מות משה.** מחובר על סדר התורה המסיימת בפטירת משה וזה מחובר לה: (ב) **משה עבדי מת**. ...

**מצודת דוד**

א (א) **ויהי.** באה הוי״ו להוסיף ולחבר למה שהשלימה התורה בספור מיתת משה ואמר שאח״ז אמר ה׳ אל יהושע וגו׳: (ב) **משה עבדי מת.** ר״ל אילו היה עדיין חי לא יכולתם לעבור את הירדן כי עליו נגזר לבל יעבור:

**מצודת ציון**

א (א) **בן נון.** בן בחיר״ק כמו בן בסגו״ל ולפי שהן מלות זעירות ...

## Commentary Digest

would arise early and stay late in your study-house. He would arrange the benches and spread the mats. Since he served you with all his might, it is proper that he serve Israel and not lose his reward. Take to you Joshua the son of Nun, to fulfill what was stated: 'He who keeps the fig-tree shall eat the fruit thereof.'"[10]

*Said-saying* — This is an expression of a direct and clear prophecy, not transmitted by an intermediary. This

1. And it was after the death of Moses the servant of the Lord, that the Lord said to Joshua the son of Nun, Moses' minister, saying. 2. "Moses my servant

## Commentary Digest

### CHAPTER 1

1. *And it was after the death of Moses — "This is connected to the order of the Torah which ends with Moses' passing, and this follows it."* — R The sense of continuity of the subsequent generations is hereby manifested. Since "no one has ever arisen in Israel as Moses,"[1] Joshua and all ensuing leaders derive their authority from him. On the seventh of Nissan, immediately following the thirty day mourning period for Moses,[1*] Joshua issued his first command. — R[2]

*Joshua the son of Nun* — descended from the princely family of Ephraim, his father Nun being the son of Elishama the son of Amihud.[3] The name Joshua, in Hebrew יהושע, originates in Num. XIII:16, when Moses bestowed it upon his faithful minister and disciple, Hosea the son of Nun. The Rabbis interpret this to mean, "May the Eternal save you from the plan of the Spies."[4] Others explain that when Hosea excelled in the performance of meritorious acts, Moses added the "yud" to his name and called him Joshua.[5]

According to peshat (the simple explanation), it was customary for a king to bestow a name upon a servant whom he favored, such as Pharaoh bestowed on Joseph, and Nebuchadnezar upon Daniel, Hananiah, Mishael, and Azariah. Also, the Almighty Himself changed Abram's name to Abraham, and Sarai's to Sarah. In the same manner, Moses changed Hosea's name to Joshua.[6]

*Moses' minister* — rather than Moses' disciple. This appelation is the highest that can be bestowed upon Joshua, for "ministry of Torah is greater than its study." — E. G.[7] What service did Joshua perform for his master? He would take the pail and the bathing utensils and carry them before him to the bath-house.[8] The complete subordination of the disciple to the master renders him capable of absorbing and concentrating on his teachings.

It was by dint of Joshua's ministry to Moses and to Torah, that he achieved the position of leader after the death of his master. The Rabbis tell us that when the Almighty taught Moses the laws of inheritance, Moses considered it an opportune time to ask for his own personal needs. Said he, "If even daughters inherit, it is only proper that my *sons* inherit my honor." Replied the Holy One, Blessed be He, "He who keeps the fig-tree shall eat the fruit thereof.[9] Your sons sat and did not engage themselves in the study of the Torah, while Joshua served you and bestowed much honor upon you. Furthermore, he

מֵת וְעַתָּה קוּם עֲבֹר אֶת־הַיַּרְדֵּן הַזֶּה
אַתָּה וְכָל־הָעָם הַזֶּה אֶל־הָאָרֶץ אֲשֶׁר
אָנֹכִי נֹתֵן לָהֶם לִבְנֵי יִשְׂרָאֵל׃ ג כָּל־
מָקוֹם אֲשֶׁר תִּדְרֹךְ כַּף־רַגְלְכֶם בּוֹ לָכֶם
נְתַתִּיו כַּאֲשֶׁר דִּבַּרְתִּי אֶל־מֹשֶׁה׃
ד מֵהַמִּדְבָּר וְהַלְּבָנוֹן הַזֶּה וְעַד־הַנָּהָר
הַגָּדוֹל נְהַר־פְּרָת כֹּל אֶרֶץ הַחִתִּים וְעַד

**תרגום**

מִית וּכְעַן קוּם עִיבַר יָת יַרְדְּנָא הָדֵין אַתְּ וְכָל עַמָּא הָדֵין לְאַרְעָא דַּאֲנָא יָהֵיב לְהוֹן לִבְנֵי יִשְׂרָאֵל׃ ג כָּל אַתְרָא דְּתִתְדְּרֵיךְ פַּרְסַת רַגְלְכוֹן בֵּיהּ לְכוֹן יְהַבְתַּהּ כְּמָא דְּמַלֵּילִית עִם מֹשֶׁה׃ ד מִמַּדְבְּרָא וּלְבָנוֹנָא הָדֵין וְעַד נַהֲרָא רַבָּא נַהֲרָא פְרָת כֹּל אֲרַע חִתָּאֵי וְעַד יַמָּא רַבָּא מַעְלָנֵי שִׁמְשָׁא יְהֵא תחומכון

**רש"י**

**עבדי מת** · ואילו היה קיים בו הייתי חפץ ורבותינו דרשוהו על שלשת אלפים הלכות שנשתכחו בימי אבלו של משה בא יהושע ושאל אמר לו הקב"ה משה עבדי מת והתורה על שמו נקראת לומר לך א"א לא וטורדן במלחמה: **(ג) כל מקום אשר תדרך** · כיוצא בו נאמר למשה ושנינו בספרי אם ללמד על תחומי ארץ ישראל הרי הוא אומר מהמדבר והלבנון הזה וגו' א"כ למה נאמר כל מקום אשר תדרוך כף אף ח"ל משתכבשו את הארץ כל מה שתכבשו ומאלה לארץ יהיה קדש ויהיה שלכם: **(ד) מהמדבר והלבנון הזה** · הוא מדבר קדש מדבר צין שע"י אדום שהיה במקצוע דרומית מזרחית ודרך שם נכנסו לארץ כמ"ש והנה אנחנו בקדש (במדבר כ) ומנין שהיה בדרומית מזרחית. שנאמר והיה לכם פאת נגב ממדבר צין על ידי אדום וגו' (שם ל"ד): **ועד הנהר הגדול נהר פרת**. זו רחבה מן הדרום

**רד"ק**

לאמר לאמר לישראל שהקדוש ב"ה צוהו לעבור את הירדן כי תבטיחם בכל מקום אשר תדרוך כף רגליכם בו וגו': **(ב) קום עבור** . קום ענין זירוז וכן קום משחהו . קומו ועברו . קום התהלך: להם וגו' . לבני ישראל כמו יביאו את תרומת ה' . ותראהו את הילד: **(ג) כל מקום אשר תדרוך וגו'** . כיון שתעברו את הירדן כל מקום אשר תדרוך בו לכם יהיה כלומר אני אתן לכם כח כדי שתכבשו הכל ואח"כ זכר קצת הגבולים . ובדרש. כל מקום אשר תדרוך וגו' לרבות חוצה לארץ: **(ד) מהמדבר** · הוא מדבר סין שהוא גבול נגב: והלבנון הזה . הוא מקום ידוע בארץ ישראל ואמר הזה אע"פ שהוא מעבר הירדן לפי שהיה נראה משם להם וכן אמר משה ההר הטוב הזה והלבנון או אמר הזה על הידיעה כמו זה סיני . זה עני . לויתן זה: כל ארץ החתים . כי באותה הפאה היה יושב החתי: מבוא השמש הים הגדול . הוא מערב ארץ ישראל כמו שאמר בתורה עד הים האחרון ומה שאמר הגדול כנגד שאר הימים שבארץ ישראל

**רלב"ג**

מארץ מצרים וזה שאמר היו אלו המלחמות נעשות על ידי משה היה משיג אל אלו האומות בכללן כליון חרון לעולם מעלתו ותוקף הנפלאות הנעשות על ידו ולזה תמלא בסיחון ועוג שנלחם בהם משה שלא נשאר בהם שריד ופליט ולהיות ישראל בלתי ראויים לכמו זאת ההצלחה כמו שהתפרסם מדבר המרגלים לא זכו אל שתהיה זאת המלחמה על ידי משה ושיתה על ידי יהושע ולא היה כוחו כל כך גדול ולזה נתעלל באלו המלחמות כמו שהתבאר במה שיבוא עד שהספיד המות בינו ובין השלמת מלחמות ההם וממה שיעיד על שזה העונש השיג משה בעון ישראל מה שאמר במשנה תורה גם בי התאנף ה' בגללכם והנה הזהירו השם ית' לבלתי נטות מדרכי התורה ימין ושמאל ר"ל שלא יוסיף לדבריה ולא יגרע מהן. והנה נראה כי הנטיה לימין הוא כשיוסיף על דבריה והנטיה לשמאל כשיגרע מדבריה והזהירו גם כן שלא יתרשל מהעיון בה כי התלמוד מביא לידי מעשה בחלק המעשיי ממנה ולזה אין ראוי שיקצר האדם מלעיין בדברי' המעשיים ממנה ויחשב כי די לו שיעשה המצות המעשיות ההם כי העיון בדברי תורה בזה יתיישר בשלמות אל המעשה עם שזה יעמידהו על סוד זאת המצוה והתכלית המכוון בה ואולם העיון בחלק העיוני מהתורה שלא ייסיר למעשה

**מנחת שי**

(ג) כל מקום אשר תדרך . כל מקום כתיב בלי ה"א והמשנה תורה סוף פרשת עקב כל המקום בה"א וא' פסוק סימן והנה המקום מקום מקנה (במדבר ל"ב א'): (ד) ועד הנהר · הוא"ו בגעיא בס"ס ובדפוס ישן:

**מצודת דוד**

**ועתה** . הואיל והוא מת קום עבור וגו': (ג) **בו** . מוסב על תחלת המקרא אכל מקום: (ד) **מבוא השמש** . שהוא ברוח מבוא השמש

**מצודת ציון**

ודיקות תקל הקריאה בחיר"ק מכסגול: (ב) **קום** . הוא ענין זירוז כמו קום לך למסע (דברים י'): (ג) **תדרוך** . מל' **דרך** ענינו

## Commentary Digest

is due to its proximity to the Holy Land, according to the adage: A king's servant is like a king himself. — Y[6]

*all the land of the Hittites* — *"is included."* — R

*to the great sea westward* — *"Lengthwise from east to west."* — R The Mediterranean is identified as the great sea, since it is the largest of all the seas in and about Eretz Israel, such as the Dead Sea and the Sea of Kinnereth. — K and E.G.

has died; and now arise cross this Jordan, you and all this
nation, to the land which I give the children of Israel.
3. Every place on which the soles of your feet will tread
I have given to you, as I have spoken to Moses 4. From this
desert and Lebanon to the great river, the Euphrates, all the
land of the Hittites to

## Commentary Digest

expression is found only in reference to Moses' and Joshua's prophecies. Joshua, being Moses' disciple, attained a degree of prophecy almost equal to that of his master.[1]

2. *Moses My servant has died* — *"If he were alive, I would prefer him"* (for his victories over Sihon and Og were complete — G). *"The Rabbis interpret this passage"* as a reference not to Moses the leader, but to Moses the Lawgiver, *"concerning the* 3,000 *laws that were forgotten during the period of mourning for Moses. Joshua came and asked"* the Lord to repeat these laws to him. *"Said to him the Holy One, Blessed be He: Moses My servant has died, and the Torah is called by his name, implying to you that it is impossible"* to convey them to you. *"Go out and occupy them with martial activities."* — R[2]

3. *Every place on which — will tread — "A similar statement to this was said to Moses, concerning which we learned in Sifre*[3]*: If this verse is to teach about the boundaries of Eretz Israel, the Scripture already states: From this desert and Lebanon etc.,"* clearly defining the boundaries of the Holy Land. *"If so, why is it stated, 'Every place where your foot will tread?' Even outside of Eretz Israel."* I.e. *"After you have conquered the land, all that you will conquer outside the land, will be holy and will be yours."* — R. N delineated this command as follows: The land bounded as described, was to be conquered and restored to its original glory by destroying all vestiges of idolatry. Then, Israel was free to annex other lands if they saw fit.[3]

4. *From this desert and Lebanon* — I. e. *"the Desert of Kadesh, the Desert of Zin,* which was in the southeastern corner, through which they entered the land, as it is stated: And behold, we are in Kadesh.*[4] *Now, whence is it derived that it was in the southeast? For it is stated: And the south side shall be to you from the desert of Zin near Edom etc."*[5] — R

*to the great river, the Euphrates — "This is its width from south to North.* — R The greatness of the Euphrates

* that is near Edom

הַיָּם הַגָּדוֹל מְבוֹא הַשָּׁמֶשׁ יִהְיֶה גְּבוּלְכֶם׃
ה לֹא־יִתְיַצֵּב אִישׁ לְפָנֶיךָ כֹּל יְמֵי חַיֶּיךָ
כַּאֲשֶׁר הָיִיתִי עִם־מֹשֶׁה אֶהְיֶה עִמָּךְ לֹא
אַרְפְּךָ וְלֹא אֶעֶזְבֶךָּ׃ ו חֲזַק וֶאֱמָץ כִּי
אַתָּה תַּנְחִיל אֶת־הָעָם הַזֶּה אֶת־הָאָרֶץ
אֲשֶׁר־נִשְׁבַּעְתִּי לַאֲבוֹתָם לָתֵת לָהֶם׃
ז רַק חֲזַק וֶאֱמַץ מְאֹד לִשְׁמֹר לַעֲשׂוֹת
כְּכָל־הַתּוֹרָה אֲשֶׁר צִוְּךָ מֹשֶׁה עַבְדִּי אַל־
תָּסוּר מִמֶּנּוּ יָמִין וּשְׂמֹאול לְמַעַן תַּשְׂכִּיל

תְּחוּמְכוֹן׃ ה לָא יִתְעַתַּד אֱנָשׁ קֳדָמָךְ כָּל יוֹמֵי חַיָּיךְ כְּמָא דַהֲוָא מֵימְרִי בְּסַעֲדֵיהּ דְמֹשֶׁה כֵּן אֱהֵוֵי עִמָּךְ לָא אֶשְׁבְּקִינָךְ וְלָא אַרְחֲקִינָךְ׃ ו תְּקִיף וְעֶלָם אֲרֵי אַתְּ תַּחְסֵין יַת עַמָּא הָדֵין יַת אַרְעָא דְקַיֵּימִית לַאֲבָהַתְהוֹן לְמִתַּן לְהוֹן׃ ז לְחוֹד תְּקִיף וְעֶלָם לַחֲדָא לְמִטַּר לְמֶעְבַּד כְּכָל אוֹרַיְתָא דְפַקְדָךְ מֹשֶׁה עַבְדִּי לָא תִסְטֵי מִינַהּ לְיַמִּינָא וְלִשְׂמָאלָא בְּדִיל דְתַצְלַח

**ת"א** רק חזק וגו׳ קדושין סט, ברכות ל"ב סנהדרין מ"ט עקידה שער ט"ו:

רש"י פתח באתנח מלא ו׳ רד"ק בכל

**רש"י** לצפון: כל ארץ החתי׳ בכלל הזה: ועד הים הגדול מבוא השמש · לארכה מן המזרח למערב: (ו) חזק ואמץ · בדרך ארץ כמו שהוא אומר כי אתה תנחיל את הארץ:

**רד"ק** שהם קטנים כמו ים המלח ים כנרת: (ז) אל תסור ממנו. שב אל משה ופירושו מדרכו הטוב׳ או פירושו ממנו מספר התורה (ז) רק חזק ואמץ מאד · בתורה כמו שהוא אומר לשמור

**רלב"ג**

הוא ממה שאין ספק בו שאין ראוי שיקלר האדם בו כי הוא השלם שבפנים להישיר המעיין בו אל השלימות האינושי כמו שביארנו בביאורנו לדברי תורה. כי ההולך בדרכי התורה ומעיין בה לפי מה שאפשר הוא מושגח מאתו ית׳ ויחילו דרכיו בכל עת. ולזהו שלא יירא מהלחם בגוים ההם ואם היו חזקים מאוד אבל יהיה לבו בטוח

**מנחת שי**

(ו) חזק ואמץ כי אתה תנחיל · במקרא גדולה המ"ס נקודה בפתח ונמסר עליו ב׳ פתח ויאמר דוד ע"כ. ופסוק הוא בד"ה א׳ סוף סימן כ"ח ויאמר דויד לשלמה בנו חזק ואמץ וגו׳ ושם בד"ה מסיר עליה ב׳ פתחין וסימן חזק ואמץ אל תירא ואל. חזק ואמץ ועשה אל תירא ע"כ · וחזקו עלי דברי המסרות האלה שאינן מכוונות ותושבני לטעיות בכל המקומות ואולי דמסיר בד"ה חזק ואמץ אל תירא ואל · לא נמצא פס׳ זה במקרא והוה סליק אדעתין למימר דהוא חזק ואמץ אל תערץ ואל דלקמן בסמוך. אך בספרים המדוייקים הוא בקמץ שהוא בזקף קטן מסכימים למה שכתב עליו רד"ק במכלול דף י"ה קמץ בזקף וכל שכן חזק ואמץ כי אתה תנחיל שהוא באתנחתא · וכם"ם המדוייקים כולם שבפ׳ הם קמולים חוץ מפסוק רק חזק ואמץ מאד שהוא בפתח וזה יכשר להיות הברו דד"ה שאינו לא באתנח ולא בזקף: אשר נשבעתי לאבותם · במקצת ספרים חסר וא"ו: (ז) אל תסור ממנו · ו׳ סבירין ממנה

**מצודת דוד**

(ה) לא יתיצב · ר"ל לא יתגבר להיות נגד הקומה: לא ארפך · לא אתן לך רפיון ממני: (ו) חזק ואמץ · בהנהגת העם כראוי: (ז) רק וגו׳ · כי לולא זאת לא תועיל כלום בהנהגת העם כראוי: למען · בעבור שמירת התורה תשכיל:

**מצודת ציון**

הליכה ולעידה: (ד) והלבנון · כן שם היער ואולי גדלו בו אילני לבנה: מבוא · ענין שקיעה כמו כי בא השמש (בראשית כ"ח): (ו) ואמץ · אף הוא ענין חוזק כמו מאמץ כח (משלי כ"ד): (ז) תשכיל · ענינו הצלחה וכן ויהי דוד לכל דרכיו משכיל (שמואל א׳

## Commentary Digest

*states: For you will cause this nation to inherit the land."* — R. E G explains the terms thus: Be strong — in body, and have courage — in heart and spirit.

7. *Just be strong and very courageous* — *"in Torah, as the Scripture states: To observe and to do in accordance with all of the Torah."* — R

Just be strong in performance of mandatory precepts, and very courageous in observance of prohibitory precepts. — E G

*that you succeed* — R. K, and Z after J. Heb. תשכיל, lit. you understand. Since a successful person is thought to be wise and understanding, the term is used in this sense. — Z

the great sea westward shall be your boundary. 5. No man
shall stand up before you all the days of your life; as I was
with Moses, so shall I be with you. I will not weaken My
grasp on you nor will I abandon you. 6. Be strong and have
courage; for you will cause this nation to inherit the land
that I have sworn to their ancestors to give to them. 7. Just
be strong and very courageous to observe and do in accordance
with all of the Torah that Moses My servant has commanded
you. Do not stray therefrom right or left, in order that you
succeed

## Commentary Digest

5. *No man shall stand up before you* — although he may be as tall and mighty as Og, king of Bashan. — Y[1] The allusion to Og is arrived at since he is referred to as "man" in Deut. III:11. Malbim explains that had the Jews served the Almighty and kept His commandments out of love, this promise would have been realized. They would have taken possession of the land of Canaan without any resistance. However, since their love for the Almighty was lacking, it was necessary to wage war.[2]

Alshich divides God's promise into four parts, as follows: —

(1) *No man shall stand up before you* — You will encounter no internal opposition, such as Moses encountered from Korah, and David from Absalom.

(2) *as I was with Moses, so shall I be with you* — You will encounter no external enemies. As I was with Moses when he appeared before Pharaoh, so shall I be with you in your strife against the Canaanitish kings.

(3) *I will not weaken My grasp on you* — to leave you vulnerable to evil spiritual forces.

(4) *nor will I abandon you* — to allow your body to decay after death. This is an unusual gift bestowed upon the extremely righteous.

6. *Be strong and have courage* — In v. 7 and 9, the same admonition is repeated: "Only be strong and very courageous." The double warning is for strength and courage in study and in all areas of observance whether in peace or war.[3] The meaning of strength here is for continuous striving with all one's might toward perfection.[4] Thus, in this verse, we explain: *Be strong and have courage* — *"in worldly pursuits, as the Scripture*

בְּכֹל אֲשֶׁר תֵּלֵךְ׃ ח לֹא־יָמוּשׁ סֵפֶר
הַתּוֹרָה הַזֶּה מִפִּיךָ וְהָגִיתָ בּוֹ יוֹמָם וָלַיְלָה
לְמַעַן תִּשְׁמֹר לַעֲשׂוֹת כְּכָל־הַכָּתוּב בּוֹ
כִּי־אָז תַּצְלִיחַ אֶת־דְּרָכֶךָ וְאָז תַּשְׂכִּיל׃
ט הֲלוֹא צִוִּיתִיךָ חֲזַק וֶאֱמָץ אַל־תַּעֲרֹץ
וְאַל־תֵּחָת כִּי עִמְּךָ יְהוָה אֱלֹהֶיךָ בְּכֹל
אֲשֶׁר תֵּלֵךְ׃ י וַיְצַו יְהוֹשֻׁעַ אֶת־שֹׁטְרֵי
הָעָם לֵאמֹר׃ יא עִבְרוּ בְּקֶרֶב הַמַּחֲנֶה

קמץ בז"ק

### תרגום

בְּכָל אֲתַר דִּתְהָךְ׃ ח לָא יַעְדֵּי סִפְרָא דְאוֹרָיְתָא הָדֵין מִפּוּמָךְ וּתְהֵי הָגֵי בֵּיהּ יְמָם וְלֵילְיָא בְּדִיל דְּתִטַּר לְמֶעְבַּד כְּכָל דִּכְתִיב בֵּיהּ אֲרֵי בְכֵן תַּצְלַח יָת דַּרְכָּךְ וּבְכֵן תַּכְשַׁט׃ ט הֲלָא פַקֵידְתָּךְ תְּקֵף וְעֲלֵם לָא תִדְחַל וְלָא תִתְּבַר אֲרֵי בְסַעֲדָךְ מֵימְרָא דַיְיָ אֱלָהָךְ בְּכָל אֲתַר דִּתְהָךְ׃ י וּפַקֵיד יְהוֹשֻׁעַ יָת סַרְכֵי עַמָּא לְמֵימַר׃ יא עִבָרוּ בְּגוֹ

ת"א לא ימוש. ברכו' ל"ה סנהד' ל"ט ע"ג י"ט. מנחות כ"ט : והגית ברכו' ג פלה ט. סנהד' כו: עברו וגו'. קדושין ל"ח:

### רש"י

לעשות ככל התורה : תשכיל · תצליח : (ח) ספר התורה הזה · ספר משנה תורה היה לפניו : והגית בו · והתבוננת בו כל הגיון שבתורה בלב כד"א והגיון לבי לפניך · לבך יהגה אימה : (ט) הלא צויתיך חזק ואמץ. במלחמה כמ"ש אל תערוץ ואל תחת והיכן צוהו בימי משה שנאמר וצו את יהושע בן נון וגו' : (י) ויצו יהושע · ביום שתמו ימי בכי

### רד"ק

ואף על פי שלא זכר הספר הנה זכר התורה ובמסרה סבירין ממנה : תשכיל . פירוש תצליח וכן ת"י בדיל דתצלח וכן תרגם אונקלוס למען תשכיל בדיל דתצלח : (ח) לא ימוש . נחלקו רבותינו ז"ל בזה הפסוק י"א שהוא מצוה לכל ימי האדם ואפילו ידע כל התורה כלה ויש אומרים שהוא ברכה והנראה כי היתה מצוה ליהושע וכן לכל אדם עד שידע התורה ואחר כך ילמוד החכמות : ופי' והגית בו יומם ולילה , אחר שאמר לא ימוש הוא כפל דבר לחזק או פירוש והגית הגיון הלב כמו והגיון לבי לפניך ה' ופי' יומם ולילה לפירוש הראשון נראה שיהגה בו ביום ובלילה כל עת שימצא פנאי מעסקי מחיתו : תצליח את דרכך . חסר יו"ד הרבים מן המכתב והדומים לו כתבנו בספר מכלל בחלק הדקדוק ממנו ואמר תצליח שהוא פועל יוצא ואף על פי שאין ההצלחה ביד האדם לפי שבשמרו מצות ה' ובשכרם תבוא לו ההצלחה הרי הוא כאילו מצליח דרכו או יהיה תצליח פועל עומד ויהיה את דרכיך כמו בדרכיך :-ואז תשכיל , זה תרגם יונתן תכשט לפי שהוא קרוב לתצליח שלא לכפול את הלשון והוא קרוב לענין ההצלחה : (ט) הלא צויתיך. מלת זרוז וכן הלא שמעת בתי הלא שלחתיך והדומים להם : כי עמך ה'

### מנחת שי

וקרין ממנו מסורת פרשת לו (פ"ח) וכן לריך להגיה במסורת (שופטים י"א ל"ד) ועיין מ"ש בריש פרשת תרומה : (ח) ככל הכתוב · בקמץ חטוף לא בחולם:

### רלב"ג

בה' אשר יעדו שככר יגלה אותם : (י) ויצו יהושע את שוטרי וגו'. אחשוב שזה הענין היה אחר ששלח יהושע המרגלים והעד על זה שככר כתחבאו המרגלים ג' ימים וכאו לפי פשטי הכתובים כי ביום הד' ולמחרת היום הרביעי השכים יהושע וכל ישראל ובאו עד הירדן ולנו שם טרם יעבורו. ויתכן עוד כי ביום ההוא בעינו שלוה יהושע שוטרי העם הזה שלח המרגלים. והנה לא היה היום ההוא ממנין שלשת ימים שזכר כי הוא אמר בעוד שלשת ימים ר"ל אחר היום ההוא. והנה בתחלת היום החמישי ליום ההוא נשלמו אלו השלשת ימים והנה בעלם היום ההוא באו המרגלים לבית רחב ולנו שם הלילה ומה שאמרה ונחבאתם שמה שלשת ימים רולה לומר עד היום השלישי לנסיעתן וכן

### מצודת ציון

י"ח) כי המצליח נקרא להבריות שעושה מעשיו בהשכל : (ח) ימוש . יסור כמו לא ימושו מפיך (ישעי' נ"ט) : והגית . פעם תשמש לדבור כמו ולשוני תהגה (תהלים ל"ה) ופעם תשמש למחשבה כמו והגות לבי (שם מ"ט) : (ט) הלוא . המלה ההיא תורה לזרז ולחזק כמו הלוא שלחתיך (שופטים ו') : תערוץ ותחת. שניהם ענין פחד כמו לא תערוץ מפניהם (דברים ז') וכמו ואל תחת (שם א') : (י) שוטרי . הם הממונים להשמיע להעם דברי המושל ולהכריח על

### מצודת דוד

(ח) הזה . האמור במקרא שלפניו אשר צוך משה : למען תשמור· כי בשימוש מפיך פן תשכח מה : כי אז . כשתשמור לעשות וגו' אז תצליח : (ט) צויתיך . אני מלוה לך חזק במלחמה מול האויב ואל תירא : כי עמך ה' וגו' . ולא אמר כי עמך אני אף שה' היה

## Commentary Digest

one's intellectual capacities becomes, therefore, the greatest of all *mitzvot*. This concept is unique in Judaism, that the scholar of Torah attains a higher degree of spiritual elevation even than the "Kohen Gadol" (high priest) who enters the Holy of Holies in performance of his duties of devotion and service on Yom Kippur.[8]

9. *Did I not command you, be strong and have courage* — "in war, as it is stated: Do not fear and not be dismayed. Now, when did he command him? In Moses' time, as it is stated: [1]And command Joshua, etc." — R

10. *And Joshua commanded* — "on the day that the days of the weeping

wherever you go. 8. This book of the Torah shall not leave your mouth; you shall meditate therein day and night, in order that you observe to do all that is written in it, for then will you succeed in all your ways and then will you prosper.
9. Did I not command you, be strong and have courage, do not fear and do not be dismayed, for the Lord your G-d is with you wherever you go. 10. And Joshua commanded the officers of the nation, saying: 11. Go through the midst of the camp

## Commentary Digest

EG explains literally that through conscientious observance of the commandments, you will be given understanding and wisdom, to know how to be victorious and successful in battle.

8. *This book of the Torah shall not leave your mouth* — This is construed by some authorities as a promise and blessing, and by others as an admonition and command even to those fully conversant in all the intricacies of the Torah.[1] Maimonides[2] bases it upon the Pentateuchal command[3]: And lest they (the words of the Torah) be turned from your heart all the days of your life. And one must necessarily forget unless constant study is maintained.

*This book of the Torah* — "*The book of Deuteronomy was before him.*"[4] — R The word "This" denotes the proximity of the object mentioned, as is found in many passages. The reference to Deuteronomy rather than the entire Torah can be understood by studying the complete quotation, which reads: Rabbi Simeon ben Jochai said: The book of Deuteronomy was Joshua's banner, or insignia. At the time the Most Holy Blessed be He, revealed Himself to him, He found him sitting with the book of Deuteronomy in his hand. He said to him: Be strong, O Joshua. Be courageous, O Joshua. This book of the Torah shall not leave your mouth. Moses' blessing to the tribe of Ephraim[5] alludes to Joshua's conquest of Canaan. Therefore, this became his banner or insignia.

*And you shall meditate therein* — Heb. והגית "*Every expression of* הגיון *in the Scriptures refers to the heart, as it is stated: And the meditation of my heart* (והגיון לבי) *before you.*[6] *Your heart will meditate* (יהגה) *fear.*[7] R

In the study of the law, one must exercise his intellectual powers to their fullest extent. Since man's intellect is his greatest gift, it entails his greatest responsibility. The development of

וצוו את־העם לאמר הכינו לכם צדה כי
בעוד | שלשת ימים אתם עברים את־
הירדן הזה לבוא לרשת את־הארץ
אשר יהוה אלהיכם נתן לכם לרשתה:
יב ולראובני ולגדי ולחצי שבט המנשה
אמר יהושע לאמר: יג זכור את־הדבר
אשר צוה אתכם משה עבד־יהוה
לאמר יהוה אלהיכם מניח לכם ונתן
לכם את־הארץ הזאת: יד נשיכם טפכם

משריתא ופקידו ית
עמא למימר אתקינו
לכון זוודין ארי בסוף
תלתא יומין אתון עברין
ית ירדנא הדין למיעל
למירת ית ארעא דיי
אלהכון יהיב לכון
למירתה: יב ולשבט
ראובן ולשבט גד
ולפלגות שבטא דמנשה
אמר יהושע למימר:
יג הוו דכירין ית פתגמא
דפקיד יתכון משה
עבדא דיי למימר יי
אלהכון מניח לכון ויהב
לכון ית ארעא הדא:
יד נשיכון טפליכון
ובעירכון יתבון בארעא

## רש"י

אכל מטה: (יא) הכינו לכם צדה. כל דבר הצריך לדרך וכלי זיינם למלחמה אמר להם לתקן שאם אתה אומר במאכל ובמשתה הרי היו מסתפקים במן שבכליהם עד ט"ז בניסן וכן הוא אומר וישבות המן ממחרת. (מ"ר): בעוד שלשת ימים. בסוף שלשת ימים בעוד שתהיו

## רד"ק

אלהיך. כמו ואל משה אמר עלה אל ה' ואת יפתח ואת שמואל: (יא) הכינו לכם צדה. פי' מיני מאכלים זולתי הלחם כי עדיין הי' יורד להם המן בכל מקום שהיו נוסעי' עד ממחר' הפסח ולפי מה שאמרו חז"ל בו ביום שמת משה פסק המן אמרו הם גם כן כי בז' באדר שמת משה לקטו מן שהסתפקו בו עד ט"ז בניסן: בעוד ג' ימים. כתרגומו בסוף תלתא יומין: (יג) זכור. מקור: (יד) נשיכם טפכם. חסר וי"ו השימוש כמו שמש ירח ראובן שמעון

## רלב"ג

מאמר ויבואו ההרה וישבו שם שלשת ימים עד שבו הרודפים רוצה לומר עד היום השלישי ויהיה חסר מלת עד וכמוהו ימלאו רבים כמו שבארנו בביאורנו לדברי תורה באמרו ארבעים יכנו שהרצון בו עד ארבעים. וכן מ"ש ומושב בני ישראל וגו' שהרצון בו עד ארבע מאות ושלשים שנה וכן מה שאמר תספרו חמשים יום הרצון בו עד חמשים יום: (יא) בעוד שלשת ימים וגו'. הרצון בו זולת היום שהוא בו ואחר שיעברו אחריו שלשה ימים שלמים יהיה להם כן ולזה אמר אחר זה ויהי מקצה שלשת ימים וגו' להורות כי הרצון בזה אחר עבור שלשה ימים והנה נתאחר העני׳ עד הבקר כדי שיתפרסם לישראל עוצם המופת הזה ויראו זה בעיניהם והנה צוה לראובני ולגדי ולחצי שבט המנשה שיקיימו התנאי שהתנה להם משה בתתו להם הארץ אשר מעבר הירדן לפאת מזרח וזכר שכבר הסכימו לשמוע אל דבריו באופן שהיו שומעין

## מנחת שי

(יא) צדה. במקצת ספרים צידה מלא יו"ד וע"פ המסורת ראוי להיות חסר שזהו א' מן ג' חסרים וסימנם (בשופטים ז"ח במ"ג): (יב) ולראובני ולגדי. הרי"ש במאריך וקריאתה בשורק והאל"ף שבאמצע נחה וכמוהו רבים במ"ש (בפ' פינחס ובסוף דברים): המנשה. במאריך הה"א והמ"ם רפה במ"ש בספ' (י"ב ו,): (יד) נשיכם טפכם ומקניכם. במסרה רבתא אות ו' חסיב הדין פסוקא עם אלפ"א ביתא מן תרתין תיבותא לא נסבין וא"ו בריש תיבותא ומטעין

## מצודת דוד

המדבר ודוגמתו וישלח וגו' ואת שמואל (ש"א י"ב) והמדבר היה שמואל: (יא) וצוו וגו'. אף כי נאמר קודם שילוח המרגלים מ"מ ע"כ הלווי היה אח"ז כי ביום שהלכו המרגלים לגו ביריחו וכהר התעכבו ג' ימים ובחזירתם לגו במקומם וביום שאחריו לגו אצל הירדן וממחרת עברו הירדן: הכינו. אם כי עדיין אכלו את המן. מ"מ היה בידם מפרי האדמה אשר שהביאו להם תגרי עובדי כוכבים ואת זה צוה להכין: (יג) זכור. עליכם לזכור:

## מצודת ציון

קיומם כמו שופטים ושוטרים (שם ט"ז): (יא) צדה. מזון כמו לחם צידם (שם ט'): בעוד. תרגומו בסוף: (יד) חמשים. מזוינים כמו

## Commentary Digest

quest. The two tribes, however, offered to remain in Eretz Israel proper until after the seven years of division.[4] The half tribe of Manasseh, although not specifically mentioned, is also included in the conditional grant. Since the territory was too large for the two tribes, two families of Manasseh, the Machirites and the Gileadites, were annexed. These were probably the cattlemen who could put this land to its best use. Furthermore, since Manasseh was a large tribe, each family would have received only a

and command the nation saying: Prepare provision for yourselves, for in another three days you will cross this Jordan to come and inherit the land that the Lord your God is giving you to inherit. 12. And to the Reubenites and the Gadites and the half tribe of Manasseh, Joshua said, saying: 13. Remember the word that Moses the servant of the Lord commanded you saying: The Lord your God is giving you rest and has given you this land. 14. Your wives, your children,

## Commentary Digest

*in the mourning of Moses were ended."* — R

*the officers of the nation* — The executive (שוטרים) as distinct from the legislative and judiciary (שופטים).[2]

11. *Prepare provisions for yourselves* — *"everything necessary for the way. He told them to prepare weapons for battle. For, if you say it refers to food and drink, were they not supplied by the manna which was in their vessels until Nissan 16? For so it is stated: And the manna ceased on the morrow."* — R[3] Although the wall of Jericho fell miraculously, weapons were needed for the ensuing battle and destruction of the city. Furthermore, the miraculous sinking of the wall was not revealed to Joshua until after the crossing of the Jordan.

K explains that even though they still ate manna, this was but a substitute for bread. They purchased other foods, however, from gentile merchants. It was these foods that Joshua commanded them to prepare.

Midrashically speaking, they were commanded to prepare spiritual provisions before entering the land.[3]*

*in another three days* — lit. in yet three days, i.e. *"At the end of three days, when you will still be here three days, and afterwards you will cross."* — R

12. *And to the Reubenites and the Gadites and the half tribe of Manasseh* — In Num. XXXII, Reuben and Gad had been settled on the eastern bank of the Jordan by Moses. The privilege of settling this land was granted them in return for their promise to have their men spearhead the attack on the western side of the Jordan, Eretz Israel proper, and participate in the invasion until the land would be conquered. This involved the seven years of con-

ומקניכם ישבו בארץ אשר נתן לכם
משה בעבר הירדן ואתם תעברו
חמשים לפני אחיכם כל גבורי החיל
ועזרתם אותם: טו עד אשר־יניח יהוה
לאחיכם ככם וירשו גם־המה את־
הארץ אשר־יהוה אלהיכם נתן להם
ושבתם לארץ ירשתכם וירשתם אותה
אשר נתן לכם משה עבד יהוה בעבר
הירדן מזרח השמש: טז ויענו את־יהושע
לאמר כל אשר־צויתנו נעשה ואל־
כל־אשר תשלחנו נלך: יז ככל אשר־שמענו
אל

**תרגום**

דיהב לכון משה בעברא
דירדנא ואתון תעברון
מזרזין קדם אחוכון כל
גברי חילא ותסעדון
יתהון: טו עד דיניח יי
לאחוכון כותכון ויירתון
אף אינון ית ארעא דיי
אלהכון יהיב לכון
ותתובון לארע ירותתכון
ותירתון יתה דיהב לכון
משה עבדא דיי בעברא
דירדנא מדנח שמשא:
טז ואתיבו ית יהושע
למימר כל דפקדתנא
נעבד ולכל אתר
דתשלחננא נהך: יז בכל
דקבלנא מן משה כן
נקבל מנך לחוד יהי
מימרא

**רש"י**

כאן שלשת ימים ואחר תעברו : (יד) כל גבורי החיל · שבכם יעברו חלוצים : (טו) מזרח השמש · עבר

**מנחת שי**

בהון נסחת אחרינא דחשיב נמי טפכם נשיכם דאתם גלגים : (טו) עד אשר יניח וגו' וירשו גם המה · בס"א ישן מספרד כתוב גם הם ויש ג"כ הערה מחילוף זה במקרא אחת דפוס ישן · האמנם ע"פ המסורה נכון להיות גם המה שבמס"ר במערכת אות הגימל נמסר גם הם ד' בנביאים וסי' שם וזה אינו מן המנין *) : נתן להם · יונתן תרגם יהיב לכון ארעא שהיא קורא לכם ואין כן

הגה"ה *) בער מאיש אני . ודרכי המסורה נעלמה ממני . וכדי להקל על המעיין אעתיק לשון המסורה הנ"ל וז"ל גם הם ד' בנביאים וסימניהון וישבו גם הם בערמה · ויעלו בני יוסף גם הם · גם הם אתו ירדו שאלה · לא ישבו האופנים גם הם · עכ"ל : ובלתי ספק שהמסורה הנ"ל נדפסה בטעות והקדים המאוחר וכצ"ל ויעשו גם הם בערמה [יהושע ט' ד] ויעלו בית יוסף גם הם [שופטים א' כב] לא ישבו האופנים גם הם [יחזקאל י' טז] גם הם אתו ירדו שאולה [שם ל"א י"ז] · והא לך שהמסורת מנה הפ' דלקמן [ט' ד] בה' מהד' המנויים גם הם ובכל ספרי תנ"ך שלנו איתא גם המה וצ"ע :

**רלב"ג**

לדברי משה ושמי שיעבור על מלותו יומת כי כן יעדה התורה בהעובר על דברי הנביא וכ"ש יהושע שהיה מלך ונביא :

**מצודת דוד**

מניח . נותן לכם מקום מנוחה בזאת לכם הארץ הזאת שבעבר הזה : (טו) עד אשר יניח . עד אשר יתן ה' מקום מנוחה גם להם : וירשתם . ר"ל אז תאחזו בה מבלי מערער הואיל ותקיימו התנאי : מזרח השמש . בעבר המזרחי : (יז) רק וגו' · ר"ל לא נשמע אליך

## Commentary Digest

as an enforcement of Joshua's authority as both king and prophet.

*Only be strong and have courage*— to punish those who violate your commands and defy you, for should a king relinquish his respect, his relinquishment is invalid. — G and D "Only" is interpreted by our scholars as referring to an exception to the general rule of absolute authority and obedience to the command of a king.[3] The exclusion was to study Torah, as witnessed in the example of Amassa,[4] who tarried in fulfilling the command of David to mobilize all the soldiers, because he found them occupied in the study of Torah.[3]

CHAPTER 2

1. *And Joshua — sent — "Against my will I must say that he dispatched*

and your cattle shall settle in the land that Moses gave you on this side of the Jordan, and you, all the warriors, shall cross over armed before your brothers, and you shall help them.
15. Until the Lord gives your brothers rest as He has given you, and they too shall inherit the land that the Lord your God gives them. You will then return to the land of your inheritance which Moses the servant of the Lord gave you on this side of the Jordan towards the rising of the sun, and you will inherit it.
16. And they answered Joshua saying: All that you have commanded us we shall do and wherever you send us we shall go.
17. Just as we obeyed

## Commentary Digest

small share in Eretz Israel. Hence, we understand "the half tribe" as really but a small part of the tribe.[1]

14. *all the warriors* — *"Among you shall cross over armed."* — R

15. *toward the rising of the sun* — *"The eastern side of the Jordan.* — R The land was divided for purposes of שמיטה (the Sabbatical year) and other matters, into three general areas: Judea, Galilee, and Trans-Jordan (the eastern side of the Jordan).[2]

16. *All that you have commanded us we shall do* — Even if it were not the command of Moses your master, and as evidence, —

*and wherever you send us* — on whatever new missions you will send us, — we shall go. — A, Alshich, and M

17. *Only that the Lord your God be with you as He was with Moses* — Only then will we obey you as we obeyed your master. — Alshich and M. Even though your prophecy does not equal that of Moses, as long as you follow his way and the Lord is with you. — A

18. *that shall rebel* — *"defy your words."* — R Lest one interpret ימרה as "shall change," an expression of תמורה (change), R makes it clear that it is an expression of rebellion or defiance.

*and will not listen* — Not only one who defies your prohibitory command is liable to death, but also one who shirks his duty in the fulfillment of your mandatory command. — Azulai

*shall be put to death*—*This is the basis of the Talmudic maxim: He who rebels against the kingdom is liable to death.[3] Hence, Joshua is considered in this sense a king. G takes this passage

* See Ramban, Lev. 27:29

אֶל־מֹשֶׁה כֵּן נִשְׁמַע אֵלֶיךָ רַק יִהְיֶה יְהוָה
אֱלֹהֶיךָ עִמָּךְ כַּאֲשֶׁר הָיָה עִם־מֹשֶׁה:
יח כָּל־אִישׁ אֲשֶׁר־יַמְרֶה אֶת־פִּיךָ וְלֹא־
יִשְׁמַע אֶת־דְּבָרֶיךָ לְכֹל אֲשֶׁר־תְּצַוֶּנּוּ
יוּמָת רַק חֲזַק וֶאֱמָץ: ב א וַיִּשְׁלַח יְהוֹשֻׁעַ
בִּן־נוּן מִן־הַשִּׁטִּים שְׁנַיִם אֲנָשִׁים מְרַגְּלִים

בְּמֵימְרָא דַיְיָ אֱלָהָךְ בְּסַעְדָךְ כְּמָא דַהֲוָה בְּסַעְדֵיהּ דְמֹשֶׁה: יח כָּל גְבַר דִיסָרֵב עַל מֵימְרָךְ וְלָא יְקַבֵּל יַת פִּתְגָמָךְ לְכֹל דִתְפַקְדִנֵיהּ יִתְקְטִיל לְחוֹד תְּקַף וְעֱלַם: א וּשְׁלַח יְהוֹשֻׁעַ בַּר נוּן מִן שִׁטִּין תְּרֵין גוּבְרִין מְאַלְלִין בְּרָז לְמֵימַר אֱזִילוּ חֲזוֹ יַת ארעא

**רש"י**

מזרחי של ירדן: (יח) ימרה. יקניט את דבריך: ב (א) וישלח יהושע וגו'. על כרחי אני צ"ל שבתוך ימי אבל משה שלהם שהרי לסוף ג' ימים שתמו ימי אבל משה עברו את הירדן שמשם אנו למדים שמת משה בז' אדר כשתחה מונה ל"ג למפרע מיום שעלו מן הירדן בעשור לחודש הראשון וע"כ משנשתלחו המרגלים לא עברו את הירדן עד יום החמישי שנאמר וישבו שם שלשת ימים עד שבו הרודפים בו בלילה ויעברו ויבואו אל יהושע בן נון וישכם יהושע בבוקר ויסעו מהשטים הרי יום ד' וילינו שם טרם יעבורו נמלא שלא ופשוטו אמר להם יהושע עשו עצמכם כחרשים ועמדו על

**רד"ק**

והדומים להם: חמושים. כמו חלוצים: (יז) רק יהיה ה' אלהיך עמך. כלומר שתלך בדרך משה שיהיה ה' עמך כאשר היה עם משה: (יח) רק חזק ואמץ. דרשו רבותינו ז"ל יומת יכול אפי' לדבר עבירה ת"ל רק אכין ורקין מיעוטין הן: (א) שנים אנשים. פי' אנשים טובים ולא כאותן שהלכו בשליחות משה: **חרש** לאמור. הזהירם שילכו בשתיקה הולכים כחרשים שלא ירגישו בהם. כמו ויתחרשו כל הלילה ות"י ברז לבימר ר"ל בסתר שלחם כי לא רצה שידעו כל ישראל כדי שלא יפחדו בשלחו מרגלים והוא לא שלחם אלא לפי שידע שיצליחו בשליחותם וירחיבו לב ישראל בבשורות טובות. ובדרש חרש כמו חרס השעינם קדרות כדי שיראו קדרים ולא ירגישו בהם מהם אמרו כלי נגרות היה בידם כד"א מעשה חרש אבן ומהם פי' כמשמעו רזיהם: את הארץ וגו'. הארץ בכלל ואת יריחו בפרט לפי

**רלב"ג**

(יח) והתרו לו רק חזק ואמץ. רלה לומר שיתחזק להתנהג בכל דברי התורה כי אם ילוס לעבור על דבריה לא ישמעו אליו אלא אם היה זה לפי שעה וזה שהוא והם מחויבים לחזק התורה. או ירלה באמרו חזק ואמץ מאד שיתחזק ויתאמץ על הנהגת העם בחכילות ולא יעזוב הנהגת' כי העם לא יתכן שיהיו זולת רועה כמ"ש משה ולא תהיה עדת ה' כלאן אשר אין להם רועה: (א) ורלוי שנעיין בהתר ספק מה יקרה בענין הלווהה שלוה יהושע סוערי העם ושלהו המרגלים מה ענין אלו המרגלים והנה איך שתהיה תשובתם בבאם לא ימנעו מלבוא באהרן לרשת אותה כי כבר יעד להם יהושע כי בעוד שלשה ימים יעברו את הירדן לבא לרשת את הארץ ואם אמרנו בכבר שלח מרגלים קודם זה הנה יקשה גם כן למה לא סמך יהושע על דברי השי"ת שהבטיחו שלא יתילב איש בפניו כל ימי חייו ולמה הסכים לשלוח מרגלים עם מה שהתפרסם לו מה שהגיע מהתאחר במדבר לישראל על דבר המרגלים אשר שלח משה והנחנו אומרים בהתר זה הספק ששלוח המרגלים הוא על התר שני דרכים. הדרך הא' להקור אם יתכן שישתדל להלהם בעם

**מנחת שי**

בספרים שלנו וזהו ה' מן ה' נהם דסבירין לכם ומטעין בהו ספרי וכימנס במ"ג סדר בהעלותך על פסוק כבר אחן להם · ויותר נכון לומר דיונהן לא דק בליגתה דקרא רק במאי דסבירין איגבי והחברו מלמד עליו בפ' עד אבר יעית דסוף (פרשת דברים) דהתם נמי תרגם לכון וכן עשה בפסוק זה יהיה להם מגרשי הערים (דף' מסעי) דהוה נמי חד מן ה' להם דסבירין לכם: וירשתם אותה. בספרים מדוייקים מלא וא"ו והכי מוכח ממה שנמסר במ"ג (פ' בלק) על פסוק וזאתה החייתי: (טו) כל אשר לוויתנו · בנבילאים עם פירוש אברבנאל כתוב ככל וטעות הוא: (יז) ככל אשר שמענו · בעי"ן בגעיא לבדו: (יח) יומת · במקלת ספרים ימות והוא טעות כי הגירסא הישרה יומת כאיתא בסנהדרין סוף פרק נגמר הדין: (מ"ט)

**מצודת דוד**

רק כשיהיה ה' עמך וכו' אבל לא בזולת זה: (יח) **רק חזק**. לענוש המורדים ולא למחול על כבודך: **ב** (א) **מרגלים חרש**. מחפשים מחשבות הבריות אם נמס לבבם: **לאמר**. ר"ל וכה אמר

**מצודת ציון**

וחמושים עלו (שמות י"ג): (יח) **ימרה**. מל' מרי ומרד כמו סורר ומורה (דברים כ"א): **ב** (א) **מרגלים**. ענין חפוש כמו לחקר ולהפך ולרגל (דה"י א'

## Commentary Digest

*"is like"* חרם with a "sin" or "samech," namely pottery. *"Load yourselves with pots so that you appear as potters."* — R Another opinion explains חרש as חרש, (carpenters). They disguised themselves as potters or carpenters and they went through Jericho hawking their wares.

D explains מרגלים חרש as "spies of their thoughts," spies who were to determine the morale of the enemy.

*and see the land and Jericho* — *"Now, was Jericho not included in the generalization? Why, then, is it specified? Because it was as strong as all of them"* (the cities combined),* *it was situated on the boundary. Similarly, and there were missing of David's servants nineteen men and Asahel.*[5] *Now, was Asahel not included in the generalization? Why, then, was he specified? Because he was as strong as all of them"* (combined). *"Similarly, and King Solomon loved*

* (See also Commentary Digest below 24:11).

Moses in everything, so shall we obey you. Only that the Lord your God be with you as He was with Moses. 18. Every man that shall rebel against your words and will not listen to your commands in all that you order him shall be put to death. Only be strong and have courage.

2

1. And Joshua the son of Nun sent two men out of Shittim to spy

## Commentary Digest

*them during Moses' mourning period, for after three days following the termination of Moses' mourning period, they crossed the Jordan, for thence we deduced that Moses died on Adar 7 by counting back thirty-three days from the day they came up from the Jordan, namely, the tenth day of the first month. Now, of necessity, from the time the spies were dispatched, they did not cross the Jordan until the fifth day, as it is stated: and stayed there three days until the pursuers returned.*[1] *On that night they crossed over and came to Joshua the son of Nun,*[2] *and Joshua rose up early in the morning, and they moved from Shittim,*[3] *here is a fourth day. And they lodged there before they crossed over. Hence, they did not cross until the fifth day."* — R E. G. explains that on the very day that Moses' mourning period terminated, Joshua dispatched the spies. This was the sixth of Nissan. On that day they came to Rahab's house, and she sent them away on the eve of the seventh of Nissan. They hid on the mountain the seventh and eighth days and the night of the ninth, counting for three days. On that very night they returned to Joshua. And Joshua arose early on the morning of the ninth. They lodged[3] there the night of the tenth and on the tenth day they crossed the Jordan.

*from Shittim* — The site of Shittim was the boundary of the Jewish encampment, as it is stated: And they encamped by the Jordan — until Abel-Shittim.[3]*

*two men* — Phinehas and Caleb. See R v. 4.

*secretly* — Heb. חרש, silently. Joshua was intent upon concealing this act from the people at large, lest they lose courage upon learning that it was necessary to send spies. He wished to inform them after the spies would return with a favorable report. — K R, however, explains that the secrecy refers to their concealing their identity from the Canaanites, not from the Jews. Thus, he identifies this view with J and with Rabbi Simeon's view which appears in the Midrash.[4] *"Secretly. So did Jon. render it. He said to them: Disguise yourselves as deaf-mutes* (חרשים) *so that they will not conceal their affairs from you. Another explanation is":* חרש with a "shin"

חרש לאמר לכו ראו את־הארץ ואת־
יריחו וילכו ויבאו בית־אשה זונה ושמה
רחב וישכבו־שמה: ב ויאמר למלך
יריחו לאמר הנה אנשים באו הנה
הלילה מבני ישראל לחפר את־הארץ:

ארעא וית יריחו ואזלו ועלו לבית אתתא פונדקיתא ושמה רחב ושכיבו תמן: ב ואתאמר למלכא דיריחו למימר הא גובריא אתו הכא בליליא מבני ישראל לאללא ית ארעא:

ושלח וישלח

**רד"ק**

שהיתה עיר גדולה: זונה. כמשמעה או מוכרת מזון כמו שת"י פונדקיתא והוא בשקל טובה והאמת דעת יונתן זונה ממש כי כן דרכו במקומות לתרג' זונה פונדקית וכן שתים נשים זונות פונדקן ואף על פי שתרג' מקצתו נפקת ברא ודעתו לפי שהזונה כפונדקיתא שמפקרת עצמה לכל: וישכבו שמה. להודיע כי לא היו שם אלא לילה אחד ובאותו לילה יצאו משם: (ב) ויאמר: בפתח המ"ם כמו תשבר ותשכב ותעצר המגבה והדומים להם:

**רש"י**

עברו עד יום ה': **חרש**. כרז כך ת"י אמר להם עשו עצמכם כחרשים כדי שלא יסתירו דבריהם מפניכם ד"א חרש חרש הטעינו עצמכם קדרות כדי שתהיו נראין כקדרין: **וראו את הארץ ואת יריחו**. והלא יריחו בכלל היתה ולמה יצאת אלא שהיתה קשה כנגד כולם לפי שהיתה יושבת על הספר וכיוצא בו ויפקדו מעבדי דוד תשעה עשר איש ועשהאל והלא עשהאל בכלל היה ולמה יצא אלא שהיה קשה כנגד כולם. כיוצא בו והמלך שלמה אהב נשים נכריות רבות ואת בת פרעה. והלא בת פרעה בכלל היתה ולמה יצאת שהיה מחבבה כנגד כולם. וכלפי חטא שהחטיאה אותו יותר מכולן כך שנויה בספרי: **אשה זונה**. ת"י פונדקייתא. מוכרת מיני מזונות: (ב) **לחפר**. לרגל וכן משם חפר אוכל:

**מנחת שי**

ב (א) חרש. בס"ן ימנית וכן נדרש במדרש רות פרש' ב' ובתנחומא מלשון חרש עלים שאמרו כלי נגרות היה בידם. ועוד דרשוהו מלשון חרש שאינו שומע שאמר להם יהושע עשו עצמכם חרשים ואתם עומדים על רזיהם. ולמאן דדריש התם ובמדרש רב' ומדרש ילמדנו ריש סדר שלח לך מלשון כלי חרש בעצו עצמן קדרין והיו צווחין הרי קדירות מי שירצה יבא ויקנה דנך דרש נאמר כמ"ש בעל כלי יקר ובעל לב אהרן ונדאמרינן התם בבדיא קרי ביה חרש פי' בס"ן שבולת ויש לנו עוד ראיה שכתיב בס"ן ימנית דבמסכת דבתא (מעדנת אות הה,) דהנפה ביתא מן תרין תרין כחד ליבן (נ"ל בתרי ליבנא) תשיב בהדייהו הדש דויבנה יהושע בן נון ואידך ובקבקר חרש וגלגל (ד"ה א' ט' ט"ו) דהוא נמי בס"ן ימנות ותשיב להו נמי (שם) בהלפ"א ביתי"א מן ב' ב' מן ג' אתין עוד יש לאוכית זה מן מכלה אחרת (ערך חרש) בהומדת חרש ה' ג' מנהון מלרע וסימן מי שם פה לאדם (שמות ד' י"א) · לא תקלל חרש (ויקרא י"ט י"ד) · כמו פתן חרש · (תהלים נ"ח ה') ותרי מלעיל וסימן חרש לאמר. (דין) ובקבקר חרש וגלגל ·

**רלב"ג**

אשר הם שלוחים לרגל אותם אם לא יתכן זה כאילו תאמר שיחקרו מהעם היושב בה המעט הוא אם רב החזק הוא הרפה ומה הערים במחנים אם במבצרים והנה פרי זה הרגל הוא אם בהמבן אל המלחמה או התרחק ממנה לפי מה שיספרו המרגלים. ואולם מדרך הש' הוא לחזק לב העם הנלחמים לבד כמו שנתפרסם מענין גדעון בן יואש כי היה סומך בדברי הש"י אחר שעשה לו אות שיהיה ישועו עמו והנה הגיע מדרגתו בכוחו בש"י עד שכבר שלא הקיל שבא אליו מישראל להלחם עם מדין ולא השאיר מהם כי אם שלש מאות איש בדבר הש"י ועכ"ז לחזק לבו על דבר המלחמה צוהו הש"י שירד אל המחנה הוא ופורה נערו וישמע מה ידברו ואחר תחזקנה ידיו והנה שמע שם מה שחזק לבו לבוא בקשרי המלחמה. וכן היה בשלוח המרגלים בזה המקום כמו שנבאר ר"ל שלא היה שלחם רק לחזק לב יהושע והעם כשישמעו שנפלה אימת ישראל עליהם וכי נמוגו כל יושבי הארץ מפניהם. ואחר שהתייבש לנו זה הנה נבאר דברי זאת הפרשה לפי מנהגנו ונאמר כי מלת חרש תאמר בפנים רבים המכוון ממנה לפי מה שאראה הוא מענין אל תחרוש על רעך חורשי און

**מצודת ציון**

י"ט): **חרש**. ענינו מחשבה כמו אל תחרוש על רעך רעה (משלי ג'): **זונה**. מוכרת מזון: (ב) **הנה**. להעיר הזאת: **לחפור**. לרגל ולחפש כמו יחפרו בעמק (איוב ל"ט) ע"ש שהמחפש דבר מה בקרקע חופר בה:

## Commentary Digest

2. *men have come here* — to Jericho, a city whose gates were shut and which was barred. Furthermore, were they indeed merchants, they would have lodged outside the city wall, in order to continue on their way at dawn. — M

*this night* — unlike merchants who enter by day. — M

*to search* — Heb. לחפר lit. to dig, "*to spy. And similarly: Thence he sought* (חפר) *food.*[6] According to Alshich and M, the concept of digging is clear, since they came to delve into the inner recesses of the minds of the Canaanites. A explains that the two spies were sent to search out the land. Had they done so, they would have gone undetected. However, since they entered such a disreputable house as Rahab's, they were reported to the king of Canaan, and were forced to flee.

3. *the men who have come to you, that have entered your house* — whether they stated their intention as "having come to you," i.e. for intimacy with you, or "having come to your house" to lodge —

*for they have come to search out*

secretly, saying, Go see the land and Jericho. And they went,
and came to the house of a harlot named Rahab, and they lay
there. 2. And it was told to the king of Jericho, saying,
Behold, men have come here this night from the children of
Israel to search the land.

## Commentary Digest

*many foreign wives and Pharaoh's daughter.*[1] *Now, was Pharaoh's daughter not included in the generalization? Why, then, was she specified? Because he loved her as much as all of them"* (combined). *"And regarding the sin, since she caused him to sin more than all of them. Thus was taught in Sifre.*[2] — R Accordingly, the purpose of this mission was to see the land, but primarily Jericho, a fortified city situated on the boundary and acting as guardian for the hinterland. The victory over Jericho thus served as a psychological weapon to weaken the will to resistance of the entire land. This was Joshua's intent, e.g. not a strategic mission to determine the physical structure of the city, but the psychological makeup of its defenders. Thus, their report in v. 24, reads, Truly the Lord has delivered into our hands all the land and also the inhabitants of the country are all shattered before us. Hence, we understand their reason for choosing Rahab's house for shelter. They knew that all the kings and princes patronized her and confided their secrets to her. Accordingly, she possessed the key to the morale of the entire country. — Alshich and M

*harlot* — Heb. זונה. *"Targum Jon.,"* according to R and Z, *"renders: Innkeeper, one who sells various foodstuffs"* (מזוונות). — R The tradition is, however, that Rahab was actually a harlot,[3] perhaps operating under the guise of an innkeeper, or, according to K, J compares her to an innkeeper who invites all to avail themselves of her hospitality.

*whose name was Rahab* — a notorious harlot, the sound of whose name aroused the desire of all her acquaintances and patrons.[4] Following the fall of Jericho, she converted to Judaism, and Joshua wed her. She became the forerunner of eight prophets and priests. This is evidence that her spiritual beauty matched her physical beauty.[5]

Rahab, originating from an immoral, sinful nation, and being one of the lowest of that nation, nevertheless, repented, and became an honored member of the holy nation of Israel. Thus, she became the symbol of repentance. Her descendants, prophets and priests, who called the people to repent, pointed to the history of their ancestress as a sign of encouragement even to the most wicked who had despaired of being accepted by the Almighty. — Ginsburg

ג וַיִּשְׁלַח מֶלֶךְ יְרִיחוֹ אֶל־רָחָב לֵאמֹר הוֹצִיאִי הָאֲנָשִׁים הַבָּאִים אֵלַיִךְ אֲשֶׁר־בָּאוּ לְבֵיתֵךְ כִּי לַחְפֹּר אֶת־כָּל־הָאָרֶץ בָּאוּ: ד וַתִּקַּח הָאִשָּׁה אֶת־שְׁנֵי הָאֲנָשִׁים וַתִּצְפְּנוֹ וַתֹּאמֶר כֵּן בָּאוּ אֵלַי הָאֲנָשִׁים וְלֹא יָדַעְתִּי מֵאַיִן הֵמָּה: ה וַיְהִי הַשַּׁעַר לִסְגּוֹר בַּחֹשֶׁךְ וְהָאֲנָשִׁים יָצָאוּ לֹא יָדַעְתִּי אָנָה הָלְכוּ הָאֲנָשִׁים רִדְפוּ מַהֵר אַחֲרֵיהֶם

ג וּשְׁלַח מַלְכָּא דִירִיחוֹ לְוָת רָחָב לְמֵימַר אַפִּיקִי גֻבְרַיָא דַאֲתוֹ לְוָתִיךְ דְעַלּוּ לְבֵיתִיךְ אֲרֵי לְאַלָּלָא יַת כָּל אַרְעָא אֲתוֹ: ד וּדְבָרַת אִתְּתָא יַת תְּרֵין גֻבְרַיָא וְאַטְמָרַתְנוּן נַאֲמָרַת בְּקוּשְׁטָא אֲתוֹ לְוָתִי גֻבְרַיָא וְלָא יְדַעִית אִי מְנָן אִינוּן: ה וַהֲוָה עִדָּן לְמֵיחַד תַּרְעָא בְּקַבְלָה וְגֻבְרַיָא נְפַקוּ לָא יְדַעִית לְאָן אֲזַלוּ גֻבְרַיָא רְדוּפוּ בִּפְרִיעַ בָּתְרֵיהוֹן אֲרֵי תַדְבְּקוּנוּן:

**רש"י** קמץ בז"ק

(ד) ותצפנו· יש מקראות מדברים על הרבי' כיחיד לפי שמיהר' בהטמנת' ובמקו' לר כאילו הי' יחידי ומדרש אגדת ר' תנחומ' יש פנחס וכלב היו ופנחס עמד לפניה' ולא ראוהו שהיה מלאך ואמר ותצפנו על כלב לבדו: (ה) ויהי השער לסגור.

**רד"ק**

(ג) לחפור כמו לתור כי התר מחפש דבר: (ד) ותקח האשה: כבר לקחה אותם וצפנתם טרם הכנס שלוחי המלך לביתה כשהרגיש' שנודע הדבר למלך: ותצפנו. כל אחד לבדו כדי שלא יכירו מקומם אם יעלו לגג. ובדרש אלו שני המרגלי' היו כלב ופינחס ועמד לפניהם פינחס ולא הכירוהו ולא ראוהו לפי

**רלב"ג**

שהוא נעניין נמחשבה הרלון בזה שכבר שלח יהושע שנים אנשים מרגלים ואמשבת אנשי הארץ ר"ל שיחקרו אם נפלה אימת ישראל עליהם והם נמוגו מפניהם כי בזה יתחזק מאד לב אנשי המלחמה ולזה תמלא שהם לא רגלו הארץ ואת יריחו כי אם בזה האופן לפי שכבר באו שם בלילה ובלילה בעלמ' יצאו משם אחר שנתפרס' להם על פי רחב מחשבת הארץ ושכבר נמוגו כל יושבי הארץ מפניהם וזאת היתה ג"כ תשובתם ליהושע אמרו כי נתן השם בידינו את כל הארץ וגו' ולא היתה כוונת יהושע שירגלו הארץ באופן הראשון היה ראוי שיאמרו ליהושע שלא יכלו לרגל את הארץ כי בלילה באו ובלילה הסוא הולכתו לצאת משם ולזה הוא מבואר שהכוונה ברגול' היתה לרגל מחשבותם לבד כדי שיתחזק בזה לב אנשי המלחמה ואולי יתחזק בזה לב אנשי המלחמ' כי זה המוכך לב הוא הודעה מנו יתבאר ממנה שזה מסודר להיות כן כמו שביארנו בשני מספר מלחמות ה' ובביאורינו לספר איוב ולזה תמלא בהרבה מן האנשים שסביב העת אשר יוכלו עברות להם שישיגם פחדם מה והנה אמר להם יהושע שירגלו מחשבת אנשי הארץ בכללות וביחוד מחשבת אנשי יריחו וזהו מה שהזכירם לראות את הארץ ואת יריחו ר"ל שישאלו מחשבותם באיזה אופן שיתכן להם זה בו והנה ספר שסופר זה נמלך יריחו והסתירה אותם רחב בחכמתה למלט את נפשה ונפש בית אביה. והנה נספר אחר זה בזכרנו תועלותיה מה היה מאופן החכמה בדבריה: (ד) ותצפנו. ר"ל שצפנה כל א' מהם במקום מיוחד שאם ימצא האחד יכלל הב' והיה לה התגלות בזה לפי שכבר זכרה שהיה חשך בעת שיצאו ולזה

**מצודת דוד**

(ד) ותצפנו. כל אחד במקום מיוחד כי יותר נוח להטמין אחד אחד: האנשים. אשר תשאלו עליה': ולא ידעתי. בעת בואם: (ה) ויהי

**מצודת ציון**

(ד) ותצפנו. הסתירה אותו כמו יצפון לישרים (משלי ב'): כן. עניינו אמת כמו כן דברת (שמות י'): מאין. מאיזה מקום: (ה) אנה.

## Commentary Digest

by the report of the spies, rose up against Moses.[4] In that instance Caleb displayed his good faith. Therefore, he was chosen. "Saying" refers to Phinehas, the priest anointed for battle.[5] It was his function to recite the charge to the army when they approached their enemies.[6] He would encourage them and enjoin them to trust in the salvation of the Almighty. Hence, they were the most worthy spies, who could be trusted not to return with disheartening tales like their predecessors.[7]

*Indeed, the men came to me* — to have relations with me, for no other reasons. — A

5. *And it was time to close the gate* — of the city. — A and Z

*at darkness* — when others take shelter within the walls. — A

*that the men went out* — unlike lodgers who stay overnight. This proves that they are spies, although I knew nothing about it when I admitted them into my house. — A and M

M explains that they went out in

3. And the king of Jericho sent to Rahab, saying, Bring forth the men who have come to you, that have entered your house, for they have come to search out the entire land. 4. Now the woman had taken the two men, and had hidden *them,* and she said, Indeed the men came to me, but I did not know from where they were. 5. And it was time to close the gate, at darkness, that the men went out. I do not know where they went. Pursue after them quickly,

## Commentary Digest

*the entire land* — This was the sole purpose of their coming. — A

4. *Now the woman had taken* — prior to the entry of the king's couriers. — K

*and had hidden them* — lit. "and had hidden him" — *"Some Scriptural passages treat the plural as singular."* In this case, *"because she hastened to hide them, and"* she hid them *"in a narrow place as though they were one man. The Agadic Midrash of Rabbi Tanhuma states: They were Phinehas and Caleb, and Phinehas stood before them, yet they did not see him because he was like an angel."*[1] The Midrash proceeds to explain that the priests and prophets are compared to angels. Being the holiest and most righteous people, cleaving to the Almighty, their spiritual overpowered their physical, giving them the power to render themselves invisible. Phinehas is referred to as an angel in Judges II. He was also a priest which the prophet Malachi compares to an angel of the Lord.[1*] *"Another explanation is: And she hid him,"* i.e. *"each one by himself. And we have found the like thereof: Oil and incense make joyful the heart."*[2] (Heb. ישמח לב, sing. form.) *"And it is not written* ישמחו לב*"* (plural form), implying that each one makes the heart joyful. — R It is obvious that Joshua chose these two messengers because of their piety, especially Caleb, who had shown his good faith when he was sent by Moses to spy out the land. The Scripture conceals the identity of these spies since they committed an uncomplimentary act by entering a brothel. The rabbis, however, disclose their identity, since the harlot subsequently repented and played an important role in Jewish history.[3]

Although this Midrash is based on oral tradition, there is, nevertheless, an implication in the Scriptures that the spies were Caleb and Phinehas. In verse 1, we find the expression, חרש לאמר, silently (or secretly) saying. "Silently" refers to Caleb, who silenced the people, who, discouraged

אַחֲרֵיהֶם כִּי תַשִּׂיגוּם׃ ו וְהִיא הֶעֱלָתַם
הַגָּגָה וַתִּטְמְנֵם בְּפִשְׁתֵּי הָעֵץ הָעֲרֻכוֹת
לָהּ עַל־הַגָּג׃ ז וְהָאֲנָשִׁים רָדְפוּ אַחֲרֵיהֶם
דֶּרֶךְ הַיַּרְדֵּן עַל הַמַּעְבְּרוֹת וְהַשַּׁעַר סָגָרוּ
אַחֲרֵי כַּאֲשֶׁר יָצְאוּ הָרֹדְפִים אַחֲרֵיהֶם׃
ח וְהֵמָּה טֶרֶם יִשְׁכָּבוּן וְהִיא עָלְתָה
עֲלֵיהֶם עַל־הַגָּג׃ ט וַתֹּאמֶר אֶל־הָאֲנָשִׁים

**תרגום**

ו וְהִיא אַסְקְתִנּוּן לְאִגְּרָא וְאַטְמַרְתִּנּוּן בִּטְעוּנֵי כִתָּנָא דְסַדִּירִין לַהּ עַל אִגְּרָא׃ ז וְגֻבְרַיָּא רְדָפוּ בָּתְרֵיהוֹן אוֹרַח יַרְדְּנָא עַד מְגִזָּתָא וְתַרְעָא אֲחָדוּ בָּתַר דִּנְפַקוּ רַדְפַיָּא בָּתְרֵיהוֹן׃ ח וְאִנּוּן עַד לָא שְׁכִיבוּ וְהִיא סְלֵיקַת לְוָתְהוֹן לְאִגְּרָא׃ ט וַאֲמַרַת לְגֻבְרַיָּא יְדַעְנָא אֲרֵי יְהַב

ת״א העלתם הגגה · ברכות מ״ג שבת כ״ו:

**רד״ק** קמץ בז״ק

עומד לסגור שחשך היום: (ו) והיא העלתם הגגה ותטמנם. כבר אמר למעלה ותצפנו ועתה אמר ותטמנם להודיע איך טמנה אותם: בפשתי העץ. ר״ל שהיו עדיין הפשתן בגבעוליהם והעלתם הגגה ליבשם והטמינה אותם בתוכם ופשתי העץ כמו עצי פשתים וכן שני תולעת שני: הערוכות. הפשתים לשון נקיבות האחת פשתה והרבים פשתים כמו מן חטה חטים והיו ערוכות לה על הגג ליבשן: (ז) והאנשים רדפו אחריהם. לפי מחשבתם: על. כמו עד וכן וירכתו על צידון וכן ינהגנו על מות כמו עד מות כי הוא שתי מלות: המעברות. בשוא הבית מגיזרה מעבר בצרי ואם לא נמצא המעברות נתפשו בקמץ הבית מגזרת מעבר בקמץ: סגרו המרגלים או אנשי הבית והוא הנכון כי הם לא ירדו מהגג מפחדם להם ושם שכבו להם: אחרי וגו׳. אינו תוספת ביאור אלא אם היה אומר אחרי אשר יצאו ידמה אחר זמן והם לא אחרו לסגור השער מפחדם להם ואם היה אומר כאשר יצאו ולא אמר אחרי ידמה כי תכף בצאתם מן השער סגרו ואם היו עושין כן היו מרגישי׳ הרודפים כי המרגלי׳ נחבאים שם אלא כשהרחיקו האנשים מהשער עד שלא ירגישו בסגירת השער סגרוהו וזה טעם אחרי כאשר: (ח) והמה טרם ישכבון. טרם שישנו: עלתה עליהם. כמו אליהם כמו וילך אלקנה הרמתה על ביתו כמו אל ביתו, ודברתי על הנביאים כמו אל הנביאים, ורבים כהם כמו שכתבנו בספר מכלל:

**רש״י**

לפי שהיה כמלאך: ד״א ותלפנו כל א׳ וא׳ כפ״ע ודוגמתו מליצו שמן וקטר׳ ישמח לב ולא אמר ישמחו לב: (ו) בפשתי העץ. בגבעוליהן: (ז) על המעברות. מקום מעבר המים שהיו סבורין שחזרו לאחוריהם אל ערבות מואב והירדן מפסיק ביניהם: והשער סגרו. השוערים:

**מנחת שי**

(ד״ה שם) ועיין מ״ש בלפניה (א׳ י״ב) על אתפש: (ז) עד המעברות · יונתן שתרגם עד מגיזתא איכ״למ דפרושי קא מפרש על כמו עד וכמ״ש רד״ק והוא

**רלב״ג**

אפשר שילא האחד ונשאר השני והיא לא ידעה: (ח) והיא עלתה עליהם. ר״ל אללם כמו ועליו מטה מנשה ויבואו האנשים על הנשים:

**מצודת ציון**

לאיזה מקום: (ו) הערוכות, מלשון עריכה וסדור: (ז) על. ענינו כמו עד וכן וירכתו על לדון (בראשי׳ מט): המעברו׳. מקום מעבר הירדן: (ח) עליהם. ענינו כמו אליהם באל״ף:

**מצודת דוד**

השער. ר״ל בעת בוא זמן סגירת שער העיר כאשר חשך היום: כי תשיגום. היות זה מקרוב ילאו: (ו) ותטמנם. הוסיפה להטמינם במקום יותר נסתר: בפשתי העץ. בפשתים שהם עדיין בתוך השן והם הקנים של פשתן: הערוכות. בכדי שלא ירגישו שיש מי טמון שם: (ז) אחריהם. כן חשבו הרודפי׳ לפי דעת׳: סגרו. לפי שרלו לבקש׳ עוד בעיר לזה סגרו שומרי השער את השער שלא ילאו מעתה: (ח) והמה

## Commentary Digest

talk to them. — A and M. G renders: went up beside them.

9. *I know that the Lord has given you the land* — This is my general opinion. I have two reasons for believing this:

(1) *and that your terror is fallen upon us* — because we have become awestricken by your greatness, and —

(2) *and that all the inhabitants of the land have melted away because of you* — they are terrorstricken by the prospect of your conquest of the land, lest you destroy them. — M Others explain that Rahab converted at that time, as she expresses her belief in v. 11. At that moment, she was endowed by the Divine Spirit and she perceived that the heavenly princes of Canaan had been subdued by Michael, the great prince of Israel. This fear was transmitted to the people without their knowledge of its cause. — Azulai[1]

for you will overtake them. 6. And she had brought them up
to the roof, and she hid them with the stalks of flax, that she
had laid arranged upon the roof. 7. And the men pursued
them in the direction of the Jordan, to the fords; and as soon
as the pursuers had gone out, they shut the gate. 8. And
before they were asleep, she came up to them upon the roof.
9. And she said to the men,

## Commentary Digest

darkness without lanterns, indicating that they were fleeing.

6. *and hid them* — This verse is an explanation of the previous "and hid them," v. 4. — K Other commentators explain it as a new and better hiding place, instead of the temporary one she had previously shown them. This would serve to explain the different terms: ותצפנו and ותטמנם. — D M explains that ותצפנו means that she put them in a place where the king's messengers would be unlikely to look. ותטמנם means that she concealed them by covering them.

*with the stalks of flax* — *"With their capsules."* — R

7. *pursued them* — i.e. they *thought* they were pursuing them. — D, K, A, and M

to the fords — *"the place for crossing the water, for they thought that they had turned back towards the Plains of Moab, and the Jordan stood in between.* — R

*they shut the gate* — I.e. *"the gate-keepers."* — R and D K explains that the people of the house shut the gate of the house lest the pursuers return. — K A explains that Rahab reprimanded the gate-keepers for neglecting to shut the gate at the proper time. She blamed them for the spies' escape. Therefore, the couriers took chase immediately and locked the gate in case the spies were still hiding in the city.

*as soon as the pursuers had gone out* — I.e. shortly afterwards. Had they shut the gate immediately, they would appear suspicious, and the pursuers would suspect that the spies were hiding there. — K

8. *And before they were asleep* — Scripture tells us that even though the spies were in peril of losing their lives, should the pursuers return, or should the king send other messengers, they nevertheless had implicit trust in the Almighty and retired for the night. — K'lee Yekar, quoted by Me'am Loez. Others explain this literally. She came up upon them; i.e. upon the stalks of flax. She walked on the flax to awaken them, in the case they were sleeping. She was afraid to raise her voice, lest the pursuers overhear her. — M. L.

*came up to them* — lit. came up upon them. She came up and stood over them to remove their cover and

יהב יי לכון ית ארעא
נארי נפלת אימתכון
עלנא וארי אתברו כל
יתבי ארעא מן קדמיכון:
י ארי שמענא ית דיבש
יי ית מי ימא דסוף מן
קדמיכון במפקכון
ממצרים ודי עבדתון
לתרין מלכי אמוראה
די בעברא דירדנא
לסיחון ולעוג די גמרתון
יתהון: יא ושמענא
ואתמסי לבנא ולא
אשתארת עוד רוחא
באנש מן קדמיכון ארי
יי אלהכון הוא אלהא
דשכינתיה בשמיא
מלעילא ושליט על
ארעא מלרע: יב וכען
קיימו

ת"א כי שמענו. סוטה לד זבחים קטו: וימס לבבנו. סוטה לד. ולא קמה. זבחים קטו:

יָדַעְתִּי כִּי־נָתַן יְהוָה לָכֶם אֶת־הָאָרֶץ
וְכִי־נָפְלָה אֵימַתְכֶם עָלֵינוּ וְכִי נָמֹגוּ כָּל־
יֹשְׁבֵי הָאָרֶץ מִפְּנֵיכֶם: י כִּי שָׁמַעְנוּ אֵת
אֲשֶׁר־הוֹבִישׁ יְהוָה אֶת־מֵי יַם־סוּף
מִפְּנֵיכֶם בְּצֵאתְכֶם מִמִּצְרָיִם וַאֲשֶׁר
עֲשִׂיתֶם לִשְׁנֵי מַלְכֵי הָאֱמֹרִי אֲשֶׁר
בְּעֵבֶר הַיַּרְדֵּן לְסִיחֹן וּלְעוֹג אֲשֶׁר
הֶחֱרַמְתֶּם אוֹתָם: יא וַנִּשְׁמַע וַיִּמַּס לְבָבֵנוּ
וְלֹא־קָמָה עוֹד רוּחַ בְּאִישׁ מִפְּנֵיכֶם כִּי
יְהוָה אֱלֹהֵיכֶם הוּא אֱלֹהִים בַּשָּׁמַיִם
מִמַּעַל וְעַל־הָאָרֶץ מִתָּחַת: יב וְעַתָּה

**רש"י**

(יא) ולא קמה עוד רוח · אפילו לשכב עם אשה אמרו אין לך כל שר ונגיד שלא בא אל רחב הזונה ובת עשר שנים היתה כשיצאו ישראל ממצרים וזנתה כל מ' שנה:

**רד"ק** השבעו

(יא) ונשמע וימס לבבנו ולא קמה. כי האדם המפחד כאלו נפלה רוחו כדרך אל יפול לב אדם עליו ויונתן תרגם ולא קמה ולא

**רלב"ג**

(יא) כי ה' אלהיכם הוא אלהים, ולזה יהוא שליט על כל אשר יחפוץ ויגלה מי שהיה במערכתו שלא יוכלו בהלחמו עם ישראל או שיגלה':

**מנחת שי**

חד מן ט סבירין עד וקריין על וסימן נמסר במסרה גדולה סדר ויחי על פסוק ויברכו על לידן ועיין מ"ש בנחמיה י"ב: כאשר יצאו · י' דמטעין דסבירין אשר

**מצודת דוד**

סמרגנים: (ט) וכי נפלה וגו'. ולא נעלר כח להכנס בכם: (יא) ולא קמה וגו'. ר"ל כל איש רוחו נמוכה ושפלה: הוא אלהים. א"כ

**מצודת ציון**

(ט) אימתכם. מלשון אימה ופחד: נמוגו. נמסו: (י) הוביש. מל' יבש: החרמת'. ענין כריתה וכליון:

## Commentary Digest

existence of any other deity either in heaven or on earth. Upon this our Sages comment: Said the Holy One Blessed be He to Rahab: Your acceptance of My existence on the earth which you see is understandable. But, why did you accept My existence in heaven which you do not see? For your great faith, your descendant Ezekiel will see that which other prophets will not see, as it is stated: The heavens opened and I saw visions of God.[1] [2] M explains the sequence of the verse, thus: And we heard from a distance and our hearts melted. And there remained no spirit of bravery in any man to rise up against you when you drew near, for all know that the Lord your God He is God in heaven above and on the earth below, and who can defeat such a mighty God?

Azulai explains this passage in conjunction with the Midrashic account that when the Canaanites heard that the Israelites had fled Egypt and were headed for their country, they chopped down all the trees and destroyed all vegetation and buildings, so that the Israelites would come upon a desolate

I know that the Lord has given you the land, and that your terror is fallen upon us, and that all the inhabitants of the land have melted away because of you.
10. For we have heard how the Lord dried up the water of the Red Sea for you when you came out of Egypt; and what you did to the two kings of the Amorites that were on the other side of the Jordan, Sihon and Og, whom you completely destroyed.
11. And as soon as we heard, our hearts melted, nor did there remain anymore spirit in any man because of you, for the Lord your God He is God in heaven above and on the earth below.
12. And now,

## Commentary Digest

10. *For we have heard how the Lord dried up the waters of the Red Sea* — In these verses, there is spelled out the wondrous manner of the crossing of the Red Sea, which served to inspire terror and weakness in the nations that heard of it. No simple tide or east wind, causing a temporary lowering of the water level, could possibly have inspired such reactions as herein described.

*for you* — It would be possible to believe that Pharaoh and the Egyptians were punished because of their defiance of the Almighty, as is described in the Book of Exodus and in the Midrashim expounding those passages. From the splitting of the Red Sea, it became clear the love of God for His people Israel. — Azulai

*whom you completely destroyed* — leaving no survivors. Therefore, —

11. *And as soon as we heard, our hearts melted.* — Alshich

*nor did there remain (or arise) anymore spirit* — We speak of one who is worried as having fallen spirits. — K and D. R explains: "*And there did not remain anymore spirit — even to lie with a woman.*" This was evident to Rahab "*because, as the Rabbis said: There was neither prince or ruler who had no relations with Rahab the harlot. She was ten years old when the Israelites departed from Egypt, and she practiced harlotry for forty years.*" — R The sexual, manly impulse was absent in the face of imminent danger to one's person. Thus, רוח is explained in the sense of desire.

*for the Lord your God He is God in heaven above and on the earth below* — Here Rahab expresses her monotheistic convictions, denying the

הִשָּׁבְעוּ־נָא לִי בַּיהוָה כִּי־עָשִׂיתִי
עִמָּכֶם חָסֶד וַעֲשִׂיתֶם גַּם־אַתֶּם עִם־בֵּית
אָבִי חֶסֶד וּנְתַתֶּם לִי אוֹת אֱמֶת׃
יג וְהַחֲיִתֶם אֶת־אָבִי וְאֶת־אִמִּי וְאֶת־אַחַי
וְאֶת־אַחְוֹתַי וְאֵת כָּל־אֲשֶׁר לָהֶם
וְהִצַּלְתֶּם אֶת־נַפְשֹׁתֵינוּ מִמָּוֶת׃ יד וַיֹּאמְרוּ
לָהּ הָאֲנָשִׁים נַפְשֵׁנוּ תַחְתֵּיכֶם לָמוּת אִם
לֹא תַגִּידוּ אֶת־דְּבָרֵנוּ זֶה וְהָיָה בְּתֵת
יְהוָה לָנוּ אֶת־הָאָרֶץ וְעָשִׂינוּ עִמָּךְ חֶסֶד

אחיותי קרי

**תרגום**

קַיִימוּ כְעַן לִי בְּמֵימְרָא דַיְיָ אֲרֵי עֲבָדִית עִמְּכוֹן טִיבוּ וְתַעְבְּדוּן אַף אַתּוּן עִם בֵּית אַבָּא טִיבוּ וְתִתְּנוּן לִי אָת דִּקְשׁוֹט׃ יג וְתֵיחוּן יַת אַבָּא וְיַת אִמָּא וְיַת אַחַי וְיַת אַחְתַי וְיַת כָּל דִּילְהוֹן וּתְשֵׁיזְבוּן יַת נַפְשָׁתָנָא מִמּוֹתָא׃ יד וַאֲמַרוּ לַהּ גֻּבְרַיָּא נַפְשָׁנָא מְסִירָן חֲלַף נַפְשָׁתֵיכוֹן לִמְמָת אִם לָא תְחַוּוֹן יַת פִּתְגָּמָנָא דֵּין וִיהֵי כַּד יִתֵּן יְיָ לָנָא יַת אַרְעָא וְנַעְבֵּד עִמָּךְ טִיבוּ וּקְשׁוֹט׃

ת״א אות אמת · זוהר ויחי :

**רש״י**

(יב) אות אמת. שתעשו כשתבאו ותכבשו את העיר שתכירו

**רד״ק**

אשתארת : (יב) כי עשיתי עמכם חסד. החסד הוא הטובה שיעשה אדם עם אחר שאין לו גמול עליו והיא עשתה עמהם חסד בהחביאה אותם כי הם לא גמלוה טובה עד הנה לפיכך אמרה להם ועשיתם גם אתם עם בית אבי חסד ולא אמרה עמי כי בהחיותם אותה הוא אמת וחובה עליהם כי היא החייתה אותם ובהחיות' בית אביה היא הסד לפי' אמרו לה הם גם כן ועשינו עמך חסד ואמת אמת להחיותה וחסד להחיות בית אביה : אות אמת. האות שתתנו לי שתקיימו אותו ואל תכזבו בי : (יד) נפשנו תחתיכם למות. אנו נמסור עצמינו תחתיכם למות למי שירצה להמית אתכם : תגידו. הראשון בוי״ו כנגדה וכנגד בית אביה כי אי אפשר שלא היה שם עמה מבית אביה כי לא היתה יושבת יחידה או אפשר שאמרו כנגד בית אביה ואע״פ שלא היו שם כמו שאמרו גם כן נפשנו תחתיכם למות והשני תגידי ביו״ד כנגד' והסימ' דודי ומה היה דבר זה שאמרו לה שלא תגיד לא אמרו על דבר היות' שם בביתה שלא חשדו אותה שתגלה אותם בצאתם מביתה שהרי כסתה עליהם לשלוחי המלך אבל לאחר זמן כשבאו ישראל על העיר אי אפשר שלא נגלה הדבר כיון שאספה בית אביה לביתה אלא מה אמרו לה שלא תגיד דבר האות שיהיה להם עמה שאם תגיד יעשו גם כן האחרים שיהיה להם בית בחומה להנצל והם יטעו בדבר זה :

**מנחת שי**

בקריאה וסימנם במסורת יונה סימן א׳ (יד) : (יג) אחותי · אחיותי קרי : (יד) אם לא תגידו · קדמאה תגידו תניינא תגידי וסימן דודי והוא חד מן ו׳ וגין מתחלפים קדמאה בוא״ו תניינא ביו״ד וסימן נמסר ריש (פרשת בהעלותך) ועשינו עמך חסד ואמת · מה שכתוב במסרה גדולה עמך שפטים ועשינו עמך חסד

**רלב״ג**

(יד) אם לא תגידו. הנה התנו בזה לפי שהדבר שאלה מהם שיתנו לה אות אמת להחיות כל בית אביה והשביעה אותם על זה בה׳ והנה אם היתה מגדת דבריה׳ זה היה אפש׳ שיתערבו עם בית אביה רבים מבני יריחו ותכריחם שבועת׳ שלא להמית איש מהם כי לא יתברר להם אי זה מהם הוא מבית אביה עד שהדבר היה אפשר שימלטו בזה האופן כל יושבי יריחו או יתערבו עם כל יושבי הארץ וימלטו כלם בסבת זה

**מצודת דוד**

היכולת בידו על כולם : (יב) ועתה. הואיל והדבר ברור : חסד. היות כי עדיין לא עשיתם לי טובה מאומה : ועשיתם וגו׳. לזה גם אתם עשו חסד עם בית אבי מבלי הקדמת טובה מהם : אות אמת. סימן אמיתי למען ידעו כל ישראל לבל ישלחו בנו יד : (יד) נפשנו וגו׳. אם מי ירצה לשלוח בכם יד נמסור עצמנו למיתה בכדי להציל אתכם : את דברנו זה. את האו׳ שאתה מבקש ונתנה לך כי אם תגיד לגלות האות הרבה יעשוהו להציל עצמם : חסד ואמת. היום אתם עשית עמנו חסד אבל לפית לתשלום גמול אבל אנו נעשה עמך חסד

## Commentary Digest

no husband. She also had no children. Therefore, she begged for the preservation of her father's household. — A

*And you shall preserve alive* — that you yourselves shall not slay them —

*and you shall deliver our lives from death* — that you shall protect us from being slain by others. — She hinted also that "you will save us from a spiritual death by accepting us as proselytes. — M

14. *Our life for yours* — lit. our life instead of you to die: i.e. we will risk our lives to save you, should anyone attempt to kill you or any of your family. — K and D

*if you will not tell* — plural form to include her father's house. — K This condition was necessary lest strangers become aware of this oath and take refuge in Rahab's house posing as her relatives. In such case it would be impossible to slay anyone for fear of violating the oath. — G

I pray, swear to me by the Lord, since I have showed you
kindness, that you will also show kindness to my father's house,
and give me a true token. 13. And you shall preserve alive
my father, and my mother, and my brothers and my sisters, and
all that they have, and you shall deliver our lives from death.
14. And the men answered her, Our life for yours, if you will
not tell this our disscusion. And it shall be, when the Lord
gives us the land, that we will deal with you with kindness

## Commentary Digest

land and derive no benefit therefrom. When the Jews were forced to wander through the desert for forty years, the Canaanites replanted the trees and vegetation, and rebuilt their ruined buildings, thus restoring the land to its earlier glory. However, when Sihon and Og, the guardians of Canaan and its neighbors, fell before Israel, the Lord took away from the Canaanites their spirit of strength so that they did not again reduce the land to ruins and desolation.

12. *And now,* — before your armies cross the Jordan, and you still have the right to accept proselytes and save them from death,[1] —

*I pray, swear to me* — for one who swears to his friend cannot nullify the oath.[2]

*by the Lord* — and adding to the solemnity of the oath.[3]

*for I have shown you kindness* — One who swears to his friend to repay a kind act, cannot nullify the oath.[2] — M

*kindness* — Kindness consists of an extraordinary act, beyond the dictates of simple decency and obligation. Truth is a repayment of an obligation. Rahab's saving of the spies is an act of "chesed" (kindness), whereas sparing her life upon conquest of Jericho would merely be a repayment of her "chesed." She, therefore, interceded for her family as well, as an expression of kindness on the part of the spies. This request was honored by the spies in accordance with their promise, v. 14, "that we will deal with you with kindness and truth," i.e. we will save you as a token of truth, and your family, as a token of kindness. — K, E. G., D, and M

*a true token* — *"That you will make, so that when you come and conquer the city, that you will recognize the sign and let me live."* — R and D. A true token that you will keep and not betray me. — K

13. *And you shall preserve alive my father* — Being a harlot, she had

טו וְשַׁלְשְׁלַתִּנּוּן בְּאַטְוָנָא מִן חַרְכָּא אֲרֵי בֵיתַהּ בְּכוֹתֶל שׁוּרָא וּבְשׁוּרָא הִיא יָתְבָה׃ טז וַאֲמַרַת לְהוֹן לְטוּרָא אֱזִילוּ דִלְמָא יְעַרְעוּן בְּכוֹן רָדְפַיָּא וְתִתַּטְמְרוּן תַּמָּן תְּלָתָא יוֹמִין עַד דִּיתוּבוּן רָדְפַיָּא וּבָתַר כֵּן תְּהָכוּן לְאוֹרְחַתְכוֹן׃ יז וַאֲמַרוּ לַהּ גֻּבְרַיָּא זַכָּאִין אֲנַחְנָא מִמּוֹמָתִיךְ

ת״א בקיר החומה· ערכין לב (ברכות ת. סנהדרין כח):

וֶאֱמֶת׃ טו וַתֹּרִדֵם בַּחֶבֶל בְּעַד הַחַלּוֹן כִּי
בֵיתָהּ בְּקִיר הַחוֹמָה וּבַחוֹמָה הִיא
יוֹשָׁבֶת׃ טז וַתֹּאמֶר לָהֶם הָהָרָה לֵּכוּ פֶּן
יִפְגְּעוּ בָכֶם הָרֹדְפִים וְנַחְבֵּתֶם שָׁמָּה
שְׁלֹשֶׁת יָמִים עַד שׁוֹב הָרֹדְפִים וְאַחַר
תֵּלְכוּ לְדַרְכְּכֶם׃ יז וַיֹּאמְרוּ אֵלֶיהָ הָאֲנָשִׁים
נְקִיִּם אֲנַחְנוּ מִשְּׁבֻעָתֵךְ הַזֶּה אֲשֶׁר

### רש״י

האות ותהיוני: (טו) ותורדם בחבל בעד החלון· באותו חבל והלון היו הנואפים עולים אליה אמרה רבש״ע באלו חטאתי באלו תמחול לי: (טז) עד שוב הרדפים· נגלה בה רה״ק שישובו לסוף ג׳ ימים: (יז) נקים אנחנו · הרי אנו

### רד״ק

(טו) ותורידם בחבל. כדי שלא ירגישו השכנים אם יצאו דרך שער ביתה אם תפתח אותו בעוד לילה אחרי אשר סגרו אותו ולפיכך הורידה אותם בחבל דרך החלון וזה היה כשכלתה לדבר עמהם או אחר שישנו מעט: ובחומה היא יושבת. אף על פי שהיה לה בית בחומה היה איפשר שהיה עיקר ישיבתה בתוך העיר לפיכך אמ׳ ובחומה היא יושבת: (טז) ונחבתם שמה· חסר אל״ף נחבא או שרשו חבה בה״א כי נמצא בשורש הזה בה״א: שלשת ימים. ארז״ל מגיד ששרתה רוח הקדש על רחב שישובו לסוף שלשת ימים. שאילו לא שרתה עליה רוח הקדש מאין היא יודעת שעתידין לחזור לסוף שלשת ימים ועל דרך הפשט כי מדרך הסברה אמרה זה כי מיריחו עד הירדן יום אחד או יותר מעט וחשבה כי בין הליכתן ושובם וחפירתם וחפוש בכל הדרך יהיו שלשת ימים: שוב. בחולם: (יז) נקיים אנחנו: פי׳ בתנאי זה: הנה אנחנו באים. כלו׳ הרי אנו תולין הדבר בך לעשות האות הזה ונקים אנחנו חסר יו״ד הרבים מהמכתב והיו״ד הכתוב למ״ד הפעל ונדגש׳ כמו יו״ד ענייה והם בשקל נחתי׳ שעפים: משבועתך הזה. פי׳ מדבר שבועתך זה ואף על פי שלא ספר הכתוב שנשבעו לה כיון שאמרה להם השבעו נא

### השבעתנו

### רלב״ג

(יז) ויאמרו אליה האנשים נקיים אנחנו משבועתך. ר״ל אנחנו רוצים להיות נקיים מזאת השבועה שלא תהיה לנו למכשול ולזה אנחנו צריכין לסדר הענין באופן שנוכל להשמר בו מהמכשול בה והנה אנחנו נותנים לך אות אמת יוכר בו הבית הזה מזולתו והוא שתקשר בחלון את תקות וגו׳. והנה אין שבועתינו שנמלט ממות בית אביך אם ימלא הי זה שיהיו מהם חוץ מהבית הזה שאם נקב׳ בזה האופן הנה יהוייב שנמלט כל יושבי יריחו או כל יושבי הארץ אחר שלא יתברר לנו מי הם ממשפחתך וזה דבר לא נוכל להסכים עליו כי הוא סותר למה שצותה התורה עליו שלא תחיה כל נשמה מאלו הגוים מהמקומות הקרובים

### מנחת שי

עִמָּךְ חסד ואמת· שפטים ועמנו עִמָּךְ חסד: הכי פירושה· יהושע ועמנו עִמָּךְ ועמה עִמָּךְ מלחמה וחד פסוק סימן ואם לא תבלים ועיין מ״ב כרים (פרשת שופטים): (טז) עד שוב· בספרים מדויקים

### מצודת דוד

כל אמת מבלי תקות תשלום גמול: (טו) בעד החלון. כי שערי העיר סגרו: בקיר החומה. ופני החלון אל מחוץ לחומה: (טז) פן יפגעו. כשתלכו עתה לדרככם פן יפגעו בכם הרודפי׳ בשובם: שמה. בההר: (יז) נקיים. ר״ל רוצים אנחנו להיות נקיים מעון בטול שבועה ולזה נפרש

### מצודת ציון

(טו) בקיר. בכותל: (טז) יפגעו· ענין פגישה: ונחבתם· מל׳

## Commentary Digest

of this (Heb. הזה) your oath, i.e. the oath of חסד which is masculine and referred to by the word הזה. We only accept the oath to save you, which is truth but not the oath to save your family. Nevertheless, all those who will be with you in your house will be protected with you, but all who go out of your house will not be protected since they are not covered by an individual oath. A and M explain that the spies abrogated the first oath which Rahab had made them swear under duress at the time they were at her mercy. They did so lest her relatives mingle with other Canaanites and they would be obliged to save them all. Thus they say to Rahab. "We are free of your oath which you forced us to swear." However, they continue to make a new condition to save all members of her family who will be with her in her dwelling identified by the scarlet thread in the window.

and truth. 15. And she let them down by a rope through the window, for her house was in the town wall and she dwelt in the wall. 16. And she said to them, Go to the mountain lest the pursuers meet you; and hide yourselves there three days until the pursuers return, and afterwards you will go your way. 17. And the men said to her, We will be blameless of this your oath which

## Commentary Digest

15. *And she let them down by a rope through the window* — lit. by *the* rope.[1] *"By this very rope and window the sinners would ascend to her. She said: 'O Lord of the universe! With these have I sinned. With these forgive me.'"*[1*] — R With the very same articles wherewith she sinned, Rahab now repents through this act of kindness.

*for her house was in the town wall and she dwelt in the wall* — Rahab had a double house, one, her known residence built close to the wall, and an inner one recessed into the wall itself, which was of considerable thickness.[2] This serves to explain how she was able to let them escape undetected, and also why her home remained intact even after the wall sank into the ground.[3] Only the inner recessed house sank with the wall. — E. G. Another explanation is that she had dug a tunnel from her house through the wall by which to send away her patrons, lest they meet others and become embarrassed. — P

*and she dwelt in the wall* — A renders: and she tarried in the wall. She waited at the window in the wall to give her farewell message to the two spies.

16. *until the pursuers return* — *"There sprouted in Rahab an expression of Divine Spirit that they would return at the end of three days."*[4] — R Otherwise, she could not know when the pursuers might return. According to *peshat,* she figured that from Jericho to the Jordan was one day's journey, taking two days to go and return. Most likely, they would search for them for one day, making a total of three days. — K Y attributes this defining of a period of three days to the general rule of the righteous never enduring suffering more than three days.[5]

17. *We will be blameless* — *"We are making this matter dependent upon you to make this sign."* — R Thus, if you do not do so, we are free of guilt. Alshich explains that in reference to the two oaths which Rahab imposed upon them, one of חסד, kindness, to save her family, and one of אמת truth, to save her, they made this statement. We will be blameless

השבעתנו: יח הנה אנחנו באים בארץ
את־תקות חוט השני הזה תקשרי
בחלון אשר הורדתנו בו ואת־אביך
ואת־אמך ואת־אחיך ואת כל־בית
אביך תאספי אליך הביתה: יט והיה כל
אשר־יצא מדלתי ביתך החוצה דמו
בראשו ואנחנו נקים וכל אשר יהיה

חת' בצרי

**תרגום**

הָדָא דְקַיֶּמְתְּ עֲלָנָא:
יח הָא אֲנַחְנָא עָלִין
בְּאַרְעָא יַת תּוֹרָא דְחוּט
זְהוֹרִיתָא הָדֵין תִּקְטְרִי
בְּחַרַכָּא דְשַׁלְשֶׁלְתָּנָא
בֵיהּ וְיַת אֲבוּךְ וְיַת אִמֵּךְ
וְיַת אֲחָיְכִי וְיַת כָּל בֵּית
אֲבוּךְ תִּכְנְשִׁין לְוָתִיךְ
לְבֵיתָא: יט וִיהֵי כֹּל
דְּיִפּוֹק מִדַּשֵּׁי בֵיתִיךְ
לְבָרָא חוֹבַת קְטוֹלֵיהּ
בְּרֵישֵׁיהּ וַאֲנַחְנָא זַכָּאִין
וְכֹל דִּי יְהֵי עִמִּךְ בְּבֵיתָא

ת"א את תקות. מגילה יד:

### רש"י

תולין הדבר בך לעשות האות הזה: (יח) **את תקות חוט השני** · לשון קו וחבל: (יט) **דמו בראשו** · עון הריגתו על ראשו תהא כי הוא יגרום מיתתו: **דמו בראשנו** · עון הריגתו תהא עלינו:

### רד"ק

לי נראה שנשבעו לה כשאמרו לה נפשנו תחתיכם למות או השבעו נא לי בה' היא השבועה שהשביעה אותם והם קבלו השבועה כי אמרו לה נפשנו תחתיכם למות והדבר ההוא היא קבלת שבועה: השבעתנו. בקמץ התי"ו ומשפטו בחירק ויש אומרים כי מפני ההפסק נתחלפה התנועה ואחר שירדו אמרו לה זה ושנו התנאי ונתנו לה אות: (יח) את תקות חוט השני. פי' קו שזור ועשוי מחוטי שני וי"ת תורא דחוט זהוריתא ותרגום **שפה** לפיו סביב תורא יהא מקף לפומיה אם כן לפי דעתו פי' תקות חוט השני שפת בגד אדום ואמרו הזה **שראו** אותו בבית טרם שירדו ומה שאמרו תקשרי בחלון בעת כבוש העיר ויש פותרין תקות כמו ויכלו באפס תקוה לשון קו וחבל: הורדתנו. **בא התי"ו** בצרי במקום חירק כי יבאו זה במקום זה

### מנחת שי

מלא וא"ו ועיין מ"ש בריש פרשת ויבא: (יט) מדלתי ביתך. אין יו"ד אחר התיו:

### רלב"ג

ולא מהרחוקים אשר לא יסכימו להיות לנו למס ולזה אנחנו מבארים שאין אנחנו נקשרים להחיות כי אם הנמצאים בזה הבית: (כ) ואם תגידי את דברינו זה. באופן שימלטו אשר יושבי העיר בזה הבית כשתודיעי להם שבכר נשבענו להחיות הנמצאים בו לא תקשרנו

### מצודת דוד

הדבר היטב: (יח) **אנחנו באים.** ר"ל בעת נבוא בארץ: **הזה·** אשר הורדתנו בו: **תקשרי.** להיות לאות וסימן: **בו.** מוסב על החלון ור"ל דרך בו: (יט) **דמו בראשו.** ר"ל עון מיתתו על עצמו כי פשע בנפשו:

### מצודת ציון

מחבואה. ור"ל תסתרו במקום מחבואה: (יח) **תקות.** מלשון קו וחבל וכן נטה קו (איכה ב): **השני.** ר"ל לבוע בלבע האדומה כמו ותולעת שני. (שמות כ"ה): **תאספי.** ענין הכנסה כמו ואין איש מאסף אות'

## Commentary Digest

tory of Joshua, tied it immediately in the window, since at the time of the invasion it would be obvious that she was communicating with the enemy. — A, P, and M

22. *And they went and came to the mountain*—The wording is somewhat redundant. It would suffice to state: And they went to the mountain. The Scripture indicates that they went past the

you made us swear: 18. Behold when we come into the land,
you shall bind this line of scarlet thread in the window by which
you let us down; and you shall bring your father and your
mother, and your brothers and all your father's household
home to you. 19. And it shall be, that whosoever shall go out
of the doors of your house outside, his blood shall be upon his
head, and we will be blameless, and that whosoever shall be

## Commentary Digest

18. *Behold, when we come into the land* — lit. Behold we come into the land.

*line of scarlet thread* — Heb. תקות — *"an expression of a line (קו) or rope."* — R J renders: a border of this scarlet cloth that they saw in her house. — K

Another explanation of תקות is *hope.* The spies explained to Rahab that her only hope of remaining alive was through this thread that she was tying to her window. If she would not tie it there, she would not survive. In addition, they hinted to her that even though her sins were *crimson,* they would be forgiven, as the Prophet Isaiah states: If your sins will be like crimson, they will become white as snow (Is. 1:18).

Similarly, a tongue shaped shearing of crimson wool was hung between the horns of the goat sent to Azazel on Yom Kippur. — M. L.

19. *his blood shall be upon his head* — *"The guilt of his slaying will be upon his own head, for he will have caused his own death."* — R He is considered a suicide since he risked his life unnecessarily.

*his blood shall be upon our head* — *"The guilt of his slaying will be upon us."* — R

20. *this our discussion* — the token of the scarlet thread. — D

*of your oath* — even the second oath which we swore to you of our own free will. — M and Alshich

*which you made us swear* — which we swore at your request. — A and M If you betray our secret, not even you will be saved, surely not your family. — Alshich

21. *so be it* — or, so it is, meaning: that is the proper thing to do. — D A explains: So it is, your abrogation of the first oath is correct. With regard to the second oath, she tied the scarlet thread in the window.

*and she sent them away* — She bade them farewell. — K. D explains that since they followed her instructions in their departure, it is considered that she sent them away. P explains that she gave them permission to leave. Only then did they depart.

*and she bound the scarlet line in the window* — later when the Israelites entered Jericho. — K and D

It is also possible that Rahab, in her conviction of the impending vic-

אֹתָךְ בַּבַּיִת דָּמוֹ בְרֹאשֵׁנוּ אִם־יָד תִּהְיֶה
בּוֹ: כ וְאִם־תַּגִּידִי אֶת־דְּבָרֵנוּ זֶה וְהָיִינוּ
נְקִיִּם מִשְּׁבֻעָתֵךְ אֲשֶׁר הִשְׁבַּעְתָּנוּ:
כא וַתֹּאמֶר כְּדִבְרֵיכֶם כֶּן־הוּא וַתְּשַׁלְּחֵם
וַיֵּלֵכוּ וַתִּקְשֹׁר אֶת־תִּקְוַת הַשָּׁנִי בַּחַלּוֹן:
כב וַיֵּלְכוּ וַיָּבֹאוּ הָהָרָה וַיֵּשְׁבוּ שָׁם שְׁלֹשֶׁת
יָמִים עַד־שָׁבוּ הָרֹדְפִים וַיְבַקְשׁוּ
הָרֹדְפִים בְּכָל־הַדֶּרֶךְ וְלֹא מָצָאוּ:
כג וַיָּשֻׁבוּ שְׁנֵי הָאֲנָשִׁים וַיֵּרְדוּ מֵהָהָר
וַיַּעַבְרוּ וַיָּבֹאוּ אֶל־יְהוֹשֻׁעַ בִּן־נוּן וַיְסַפְּרוּ
לוֹ אֵת כָּל־הַמֹּצְאוֹת אוֹתָם: כד וַיֹּאמְרוּ
אֶל־יְהוֹשֻׁעַ כִּי־נָתַן יְהוָה בְּיָדֵנוּ אֶת־כָּל־

חובת קְטוֹלֵיהּ בְּרֵישָׁנָא
אִם יַד אֱנָשׁ תְּהֵי בֵיהּ:
כ וְאִם תְּחַוְיָן יַת פִּתְגָמָנָא
דֵין וּנְהֵי זַכָּאִין
מִמּוֹמָתִיךְ דְקַיֶמְתְּ עֲלָנָא:
כא וַאֲמָרַת כְּפִתְגָמֵיכוֹן
כֵּן הוּא וְשַׁלְחְתִנוּן וַאֲזָלוּ
וְקָטְרַת יַת תּוֹרָא
דְזְהוֹרִיתָא בְּחַרַכָּא:
כב וַאֲזַלוּ וְעָלוּ לְטוּרָא
וִיתִבוּ תַמָּן תְּלָתָא יוֹמִין
עַד דְתָבוּ רָדְפַיָא וּבְעוֹ
רָדְפַיָא בְּכָל אָרְחָא וְלָא
אַשְׁכָּחוּ: כג וְתָבוּ תְּרֵין
גֻבְרִין וּנְחִיתוּ מִן טוּרָא
וַעֲבָרוּ וַאֲתוֹ לְוָת יְהוֹשֻׁעַ
בַּר נוּן וְאִשְׁתְּעִיאוּ לֵיהּ
יַת כָּל דְעָרְעָא יָתְהוֹן:
כד וַאֲמָרוּ לִיהוֹשֻׁעַ אֲרֵי
מְסַר יְיָ בִּידָנָא יַת כָּל
אַרְעָא וְאַף אִתְּבָרוּ כָּל
יָתְבֵי אַרְעָא מִן קֳדָמָנָא:

ואקדים

הארץ

### רש"י

(כג) ויעברו. את הירדן:

### רד"ק

כמו יפעיל ויפעל: (יט) דמו בראשו. הוא נתחייב בדמו שלא שמר עצמו: (כא) ותשלחם. בדבור כלומר אמרה להם לכו לשלום. ותקשר. לא קשרה אותו עתה אחר שיצאו אלא ספר הכתוב כי כן עשתה כמו שצוו אותה שקשרה התקוה בחלון בעת כבוש העיר: (כג) וישובו. שבו אל הדרך כי כבר היו נחבאים בהר מפני הרודפים ובסוף ג' ימים יצאו מן המחבוא ושבו להם אל הדרך ללכת לדרכם: (כד) ויאמרו אל יהושע כי נתן ה'. זהו סוף דבריהם ממה שספרו לו כי מלת כי הוא

### רלב"ג

שבועתינו להמיותם: (כג) והנה שבו שני האנשים ביום הג' לשלוחם שהוא היום השני מהשלשה ימים שזכר יהושע במה שאמר בעוד שלשת ימים אתם עוברים את הירדן והנה ביום השלישי מאלו השלשה ימים השכים יהושע בבקר להזדרז על זאת המלאכה כי המלאכה לה' ובאו עד הירדן הוא וכל ישראל ולנו שם טרם יעברו את הירדן והנה לא עברו את הירדן בלילה ההוא אחר עבור השלשה ימים שזכר יהושע לסבות הא' כי הש"י רצה שיתפרסם זה המופת לישראל כדי שתהיה אמונת' בו יתברך וביהושע נביאו יותר חזקה ולזה חייב להמתין עבור הירדן עד בקר יום הד' והשני הוא שהש"י רצה שיהיה המופת הזה כדי להפיל אימה ופחד על כל מלכי האמורי והכנעני ולזה היה ראוי

### מצודת דוד

ואנחנו נקים. כי לא היה מהאפשר לשומרו מן המיתה: (כ) זה. הסימן והאות הזה: (כא) כן הוא. ר"ל זה הדרך הנכון: ותשלחם. לפי שהלכו אל ההר בעלתה אמר ותשלחם: ותקשור. בעת שבאו ישראל בארץ: (כד) כי נתן. במקרא שלפניו נאמר שספרו המוצאות אותם וכאשר תמו לספר אמרו הנה תכלית הדבר הוא דע כי נתן ה' וגו':

### מצודת ציון

(שופט'יט): (כג) המוצאו'. מה שקרה להם:

## Commentary Digest

*country have melted away because of us.* — as was apparent from the king of Jericho's search for us, and from Rahab's account of the demoralization of the populace. — M Of these two facts which the spies reported, it appears that the first was the more important and more conclusive, since the melting away of the people was but a preparation for the conquest, while the delivering of the land into their hand was the conquest itself. Hence, we must explain the seemingly inverted order of the Scripture. A explains thus: It is obvious to us that the Lord has delivered the land into our hands, and also, it is obvious to them, judging from the way they have

with you in the house, his blood shall be upon our head if any hand be upon him. 20. And if you tell this our discussion, then we will be blameless of your oath which you have made us swear. 21. And she said, According to your words, so be it. And she sent them away, and they departed; and she bound the scarlet line in the window. 22. And they went, and came to the mountain, and stayed there three days until the pursuers returned; and the pursuers sought them throughout all the way, but they did not find them. 23. And the two men returned and descended from the mountain, and crossed over and came to Joshua the son of Nun, and told him all that had happened to them. 24. And they said to Joshua, — For the Lord has delivered into our hands all

## Commentary Digest

mountain to scout and see whether anyone was lurking there in wait for them. Upon seeing that the coast was clear, they returned to the mountain to hide for three days as had been advised by Rahab. After the third day, they returned to the side of the mountain where they had previously been, hence the expression: and the two men returned. The expression: the two men, indicates that they remained two, having met no one on the way. — Alschich

23. *And the two men returned* — They returned from the mountain to their course. — K The Scripture emphasizes the word: "two" to indicate that they returned separately, lest the couriers of the Canaanite king recognize them as the pair of spies who fled from Rahab's house. — P

*and crossed over* — *"the Jordan."* — R

*to Joshua* — who had sent them, for the populace knew nothing of their mission. — P

24. *"— For the Lord has delivered into our hands —"* — All this has happened to us, i.e we fled from Rahab's house and were not overtaken by the Canaanites, for the Lord has delivered all the land into our hands. We had the help of Providence because the Lord has given us the land. — K. D explains: The conclusion of the entire episode is "that the Lord has delivered etc."

*and also all the inhabitants of the*

הארץ וגם־נמגו כל־ישבי הארץ
מפנינו: ג א וישכם יהושע בבקר
ויסעו מהשטים ויבאו עד־הירדן הוא
וכל־בני ישראל וילנו שם טרם יעברו:
ב ויהי מקצה שלשת ימים ויעברו
השטרים בקרב המחנה: ג ויצוו
את־העם לאמר כראתכם את ארון ברית־

**תרגום**

א וְאַקְדֵים יְהוֹשֻׁעַ בְּצַפְרָא וּנְטַלוּ מִשִּׁטִּין וַאֲתוֹ עַד יַרְדְּנָא הוּא וְכָל בְּנֵי יִשְׂרָאֵל וּבָתוּ תַמָּן קֳדָם יַעְבְּרוּן: ב וַהֲוָה מִסּוֹף תְּלָתָא יוֹמִין וַעֲבָרוּ סָרְכַיָא בְּגוֹ מַשְׁרִיתָא: ג וּפַקִידוּ יָת עַמָּא לְמֵימַר בְּמֶחֱזֵיכוֹן יָת אֲרוֹן קְיָמָא דַיְיָ אֱלָהֲכוֹן וכהניא

**רד"ק**

פעם אל הקודם: (ב) מקצה שלשת ימים. הנה ראינו בתורה כי בשנת הארבעים בחדש שבט הוכיח משה רבינו ע"ה את ישראל ובו בחדש מת או בתחלת אדר שהרי בניסן עברו ישראל את הירדן עם יהושע וכבר מת משה ועברו ימי אבלו טרם נסעם מהשטים. ואמרו רז"ל כי בשבעה באדר מת משה וראי זה מן הפסוקים אחר הקבלה כיצד חשוב אחרי ז' ימים באדר שלשים יום ימי אבל משה תמצא שנשלמו השלשים יום בשבע' בניסן ושלשה ימים שהזהירם טרם עברם את הירדן להכין צידה נמצא סוף אותן שלשת ימים הוא עשרה בניסן ובו ביום עלו מן הירדן כמו שכתוב והעם עלו מן הירדן בעשור לחדש הראשון ולא נוכל לאמר כי לא שלמו ימי האבל עד עברם את הירדן שהרי בעודם בשטים בערבות מואב שלמו ימי האבל כמו שכתוב בערבות מואב שלשים יום אבל אולי הקבלה יוכל לומר האומר כי בשבט מת משה או באדר קודם שבעה בו וכן מצינו בדברי רז"ל כי יש מהם שאמרו בז' בשבט מת משה אף על פי שסוגית התלמוד היא כי בשבעה באדר מת משה ונר' כי הקבלה נכונה כן הוא כי לא יתכן לפרש שהיו שם ימים בטלים אחרי מות משה אלא היו ימי אבלו ואחר עבור ימי אבלו צוה הקב"ה את יהושע לעבור את הירדן והנה יהי' פי' אחרי מות משה אחר עבור ימי אבלו והוא שלשים יום כי אין רוח הקדש שור' על אבל ועל עצב כמו שאמר אלישע ועתה קחו לי מנגן וגו' ואמר ביעקב אבינו ותחי רוח יעקב ותרגם אונקלוס ושרת רוח נבואה על יעקב אבוהון כי כל ימי התאבלו על יוסף לא שרתה עליו רוח הקדש והנה ביום שלשים שהוא ז' בניסן אמר הקב"ה ליהושע קום עבור ובו ביום צוה יהושע לעבור בקרב המחנה ולומר הכינו לכם צידה כי בעוד שלשת ימים אתם עוברים את הירדן והוא עשר' בניסן שעברו את הירדן כמו שכתוב ויהיה פי' מקצה שלשת ימים ביום שעברו שהוא סוף ג' ימים למה שצום הכינו לכם צידה אבל המרגלים שלחם יהושע תוך ימי אבל ושבו אל יהושע בשמנה בניסן והשכים יהושע בבקר ונסעו מהשטים בתשעה בניסן וילינו שם על שפת הירדן ובו ביום אמר יהושע אל העם התקדשו כי מחר ר"ל בעשרה בניסן יעשה ה' עמכם נפלאות. תוספ"ת כתב הרב רבי יהודה ז"ל בענין צדקתך שאומרין בשבת במנחה יש אומרים לכך אנו אומרים שלשה פסוקים של צדוק הדין לפי שנפטר משה רבינו עליו השלום במנחה בשבת ואינו כך ויש להוכיח מפרקא קמא דקדושין ע"י חשבון מכח אבלו של משה שהיו שלשים יום ובעשור לחודש אחר כי נסעו ללכת על יריחו ויריחו נלכדה בשבת וכאשר נשלך החשבון למפרע נמצא שלא מת בשבת: (ג) ויצוו את העם לאמר כראותכם וגו'. ואתם תסעו ממקומכם וגו' והלכתם

**רלב"ג**

שיהיה בעת שירצו האנשים זה המופת וזה ביום. והשלישי הוא שרצה הש"י שיתקדשו העם כדי שיהיו ראויים יותר אל שיעשה זה המופת בעבורם עם שזה הביאם לדקדק יותר בענין אלו הנפלאות כי זה ממה שיישיר' להשיג מה שהיה בהם מהפלאה והזרות ולזה הוצרך לומר שלנו שם טרם יעבורו כי יחשב לפי שיעד יהושע להם שכאשר ישלמו ג' ימים יעברו את הירדן ויבא זה לחשב שיעברו את הירדן בתחלת הלילה שאחריה ומפני זה הוצרך לבאר שלא עברו את הירדן כי אם ביום כדי שיתבאר יותר לדורות הבאים אמתת זה הספור ולזאת הסבה בעיני' צוה יהושע לשנים העשר איש שירימו להם אבן אחת לאיש על שכמו למען יהיו האבנים האלה לזכרון לבני ישראל על דבר זה המופת: (ג) והנה צוו השוטרים את העם במלות יהושע שילכו אחר ארון ברית ה' שישאוהו הכהנים הלוים והנה הוצרכו לזאת הלוואה כי בימי משה

**מצודת דוד**

ב (א) שם. אצל הירדן: (ב) שלשת ימים. וכמ"ש בעוד שלשת ימים כו' (לעיל א'): (ג) ארון ברית ה'. הארון שבו

## Commentary Digest

that "the spirit of Jacob their father revived."[4] The Targum paraphrases: the spirit of prophecy. Therefore, Joshua was incapable of receiving the divine command until the seventh of Nissan. This calculation strongly supports the tradition that Moses passed on the seventh of Adar, for had he passed away prior to that date, the command would have certainly been given earlier. — Hence, we explain: "at the end of three days," to mean: on the third day, which was the ninth of Nissan, the day preceding the crossing of the Jordan. — K[5]

3. *And they commanded the people* — they relayed Joshua's order. — G

*When you see the Ark of the covenant* — From the wording of v. 1, which begins: And *Joshua* rose up early in the morning, and continues, and *they* moved from Shittim and

the land; and also the inhabitants of the country have melted away because of us.

## 3

1. And Joshua rose up early in the morning, and they moved from Shittim and came to the Jordan, he and all the people of Israel; and they lodged before they crossed over. 2. And it was at the end of three days, that the officers went through the midst of the camp. 3. And they commanded the people, saying: When you see the Ark of the covenant of the

### Commentary Digest

melted away because of us. Alshich explains thus: No evidence is needed that the Lord has given us the land, since He promised that to you at the beginning of your reign, but also, the inhabitants of the country have melted away because of us. This we have ascertained from our conversation with Rahab.

CHAPTER 3

1. *And Joshua rose up early in the morning* — the traditional time for prayer and for general zeal. — Furthermore, the night is considered dangerous for travel, both because of natural dangers, such as wild beasts, robbers, and pits and because of evil forces which are permitted to prowl at that time. He did not start out later in the day because the zealous perform their religious duties as early as possible. — Y[1]

*and they lodged there* — Beside the Jordan. — D

*before they crossed over* — so that the miracle of the splitting of the Jordan would be witnessed both by Israel and the Canaanites, thereby sanctifying the name of the Lord. — G and M

2. *after three days* — as they had been previously informed.[1*] — D This was the tenth day of Nissan. Moses' demise occurred on the seventh of Adar. His mourning period of thirty days terminated on the seventh of Nissan. The three days of preparation ended on the tenth of Nissan when they crossed the Jordan.[2] The command for preparation could not have been given during the mourning period because the divine presence does not rest upon a prophet during sadness.[2*] This is illustrated by Elisha, who said: But now bring me a minstrel. And it was when the minstrel played, that the hand of the Lord was upon him.[3]

The Bible also tells us that when Jacob heard that Joseph was still alive,

יהוה אלהיכם והכהנים הלוים נשאים אתו ואתם תסעו ממקומכם והלכתם אחריו: ד אך רחוק יהיה ביניכם ובינו כאלפים אמה במדה אל תקרבו אליו למען אשר תדעו את הדרך אשר תלכו בה כי לא עברתם בדרך מתמול

שלשם

דכהניא לואי נטלין יתיה ואתון תטלון מאתריכון ותהכון בתרוהי: ד ברם רחיק יהי ביניכון וביניהי כתרין אלפין אמין במשחתא לא תקרבון לותיה בדיל דתידעון ית אורחא די תהכון בה ארי לא עברתון באורחא מאתמלי

ובינו* ובינו קרי

### רש"י

ג (ג) והלכתם אחריו. נשתנה המסע הזה משאר מסעות שכל זמן שמשה היה קיים היה עמוד הענן נוסע תחלה ומראה להם הדרך והארון נוסע אחר ב' דגלים עכשיו הארון נוסע תחלה: והכהנים הלוים. לפי שאלו כולם מלוי (אבי) אבי עמרם נקראו לוים כמו שפירשו רבותינו בכ"ד במ"ח מקומות (ביבמות פ"ו עמוד ב' ובבכורות ג' ובחולין כ"ד. ובתמיד כ"ז. א' בכ"ד מקומות) נקראו הכהנים לוים וזה טעמו של דבר (מ"ר): (ד) אך רחוק יהיה. כבודו של מקום הוא: ובינו. כמו ובינו ודומה לו ישמח ישראל בעושיו. ד"א ב' ארונות היו של שכינה ושל יוסף מהלכין יחד: כאלפים אמה. כדי שיהיו יכולין לילך ולהתפלל לפניו בשבת כך מפורש במדרש תנחומא לפי שידע שעתידין להיות נגיס לפני יריחו בשבת: למען אשר תדעו. מוסב על והלכתם אחריו: כי לא עברתם בדרך. לא הלכתם בענין זה עד הנה:

### רד"ק

אחריו אמרו רז"ל ת"ר כיצד עברו ישראל את הירדן בכל יום ויום היה ארון נוסע אחר שני דגלים ואותו היום נסע תחלה שנאמר הנה ארון הברית אדון כל הארץ עובר לפניכם בירדן ופרש"י ז"ל נשתנה המסע הזה משאר המסעות שכל זמן שמשה קיים היה עמוד הענן נוסע תחלה ומראה להם הדרך שנאמר ההולך לפניכם בדרך לתור לכם מקום וגו'. ובענן יומם והארון אחר שני דגלים שנאמר ונסע אוהל מועד מחנה הלוים בתוך המחנות וגומר ועכשו הארון נוסע תחלה שנאמר הנה ארון הברית וגו' עובר לפניכם בירדן כלומר מקדים לפניכם ליכנס בתוך הירדן ומה שאמר ויסעו מהר ה' דרך שלשת ימים וארון ברית ה' נוסע לפניהם ארונו של משה היה שהיו בו שברי לוחות ולשון עובר מלשון ויעביר את הכושי לישנא דאקדומי הוא ע"כ: והכהנים הלוים. עד עתה הלוים היו נושאים הארון ועתה נשאוהו הכהנים להקדישו יותר מפני הנס שנעש' לפניו עתה ואמרו רז"ל בג' מקומות נשאו הכהנים את הארון כשעברו את הירדן וכשסבבו את יריחו וכשהחזירוהו למקומו וזה היה כשהיה דוד בורח מפני אבשלום שנאמר וישב צדוק ואביתר הכהן את ארון אלהים ירושלם וכל זה להגדלת קדושתו ועוד מצינו במקום אחר בבנין הבית שהעלוהו הכהנים מעיר דוד והביאוהו לבית קדשי הקדשים ואפשר כי לפני שנתנוהו במקומו הי' שם לעולם לא מנו אלא שלש מקומות ובכלל שהחזירוהו למקומו הוא ועד עתה היה הארון נוסע אחר שני דגלים ועתה נסע תחלה: (ד) ובינו. ובינו כתיב וביניו קרי והכל אחד כי ימצא בלשון יחיד ובלשון רבים ויש בו דרש כי שני ארונות היו של יוסף ושל שכינה והיו מהלכין יחד: כאלפים אמה במדה. הכ"ף כ"ף השיעור כמו כ"ף כשש מאות איש כעשרים איש כאיפה שעורים ויתכן שהוא כ"ף האמתות לפי שאמר במדה וכמו זה הכ"ף כ"ף הדמיון כהיו' תמצאון אותו השבעה כי כיום ורוחב המי' היה אז שני' עשר מיל כנגד מחנה ישראל כמו שפירשו רז"ל ואמר להם יהושע שמשעה שיכנסו לירדן יתרחקו מן הארון אלפים אמה והטעם שצום שילכו רחוקים מן הארון

### רלב"ג

היה הנותם והסעם על פי ה' מלא תנוע' עמוד הענן יומם ועמוד האש לילה לנחותם הדרך ואולם עתה לא תהיה הליכתם בדרך בזה האופן אבל יסיו המנהיגים עתה הכהנים הלוים נושאי ארון ברית ה' על פי הנבואה ובדי שילאו כלם היה ראוי שירחקו ממנו ונזה צוו אותם שירחקו

### מנחת שי

ג (ד) בניכם ובינו. וביניו קרי (עיין רש"י ורד"ק): במדה. באתנח: ויש בו ג' ד' הב' הוא דגש קל. והמ"ם הוא להורות על ה' הידיעה שהז"ל בהמדה ודגש הדלת מורה גם הוא יורה על חסרון עפ"י שמרעו מדד. ונמסר עליו ג' דגש (ויקרא יט ל"ה) (ד"ה ב' ג' ג') ודין: למען אשר

### מצודת דוד

הלוחות שכרת ה' ברית עם ישראל בעת אשר נתנם: ואתם. ואז אתם תסעו: (ד) וביניו. ובין הארון: כאלפים. אלפים מלומדים בגל' במדה והכ"ף באה לאמיתת הדבר וכן מכרה כיום (בראשית כ"ה): למען וגו'. מוסב למקרא שלפניו לומר לכו אחר הארון למען

### מצודת ציון

ג (ד) מתמול. כמו מאתמול: שלשם. יום השלישי שלפני

## Commentary Digest

4. *But there shall be a distance — "This is respect for the Omnipresent."* — R

*between (you and) it* — "It" refers to the Holy Ark. The Masora, however, reads here: וביניו, usually a plural form. *"The same as* ובינו *and between it, and similar to this: 'Let Israel rejoice in his Maker'* (בעשיו).[3*] *Another explanation is: And between them, referring to the Holy Ark and the ark of Joseph's remains, which were travelling together."* — R This was to signify Joseph's fulfillment of all that was written in the Torah.[3**]

*just two thousand cubits* — a distance of about 1200 meters. (A meter = 39.37 in.) This is the distance one

Lord your God, and the priests the Levites bearing it, then you shall move from your place and go after it. 4. But there shall be a distance between you and it, just two thousand cubits by measure; do not come near it, that you may know the way by which you will go; for you have not passed this way before.

## Commentary Digest

(they) came to the Jordan, we are to deduce that the people followed Joshua's every act. When they saw him rise up early in the morning, they followed suit and prepared to travel. Upon seeing this, Joshua feared that they make him a supreme leader, even a demi-god, violating the pure concept of monotheism. He, therefore, ordered the officers to announce: When you see the Ark of the covenant of the Lord your God, —, then you shall move from your place etc. Do not follow my actions as indications of travel orders. Instead, follow the Ark of the Covenant of the Lord. — Alshich

*and go after it* — *"This journey differs from other journeys, for whereas previously, in the days of Moses, the pillar of cloud would lead the way, the Ark following in the very middle of the camp after two divisions"* (comprising the first six tribes had passed), *"now the Ark would travel ahead."* — R This passage can be understood by another Talmudic maxim, which reads: Three good leaders stood up for Israel: Moses, Aaron, and Miriam. Three good gifts were given for their sake, namely: the well, the cloud, and the manna. The well was given for Miriam's sake, the cloud for Aaron's sake, and the manna for Moses' sake. When Miriam died, the well was taken away. When Aaron died, the cloud was taken away. They were both returned for Moses' sake. When Moses died, they were all taken away.[1]* Hence, since this was the first journey after Moses' death, there were no clouds to guide them, and they needed the Ark for this purpose. — Azulai

*and the priests the Levites* — (R explains this verse in inverted order.) -- *"Since they are all descended from Levi, Amram's grandfather, they are called Levites, as our Sages explain in G.R.: in forty-eight places, the priests were called Levites, this being the reason for it."*[2] — R

*bearing it* — According to Maimonides,[3] only the Kohanim were permitted to carry the Ark at any time. Special dispensation was given in the wilderness to allow the Levites to carry it. N, however, is of the opinion that both Kohanim and Levites were privileged to carry the Ark, except in three instances, wherein the Kohanim were specifically commanded to carry it, this being one of them.

שְׁלֹשֶׁם: ה וַיֹּאמֶר יְהוֹשֻׁעַ אֶל־הָעָם
הִתְקַדָּשׁוּ כִּי מָחָר יַעֲשֶׂה יְהוָה
בְּקִרְבְּכֶם נִפְלָאוֹת: ו וַיֹּאמֶר יְהוֹשֻׁעַ אֶל־
הַכֹּהֲנִים לֵאמֹר שְׂאוּ אֶת־אֲרוֹן הַבְּרִית
וְעִבְרוּ לִפְנֵי הָעָם וַיִּשְׂאוּ אֶת־אֲרוֹן
הַבְּרִית וַיֵּלְכוּ לִפְנֵי הָעָם: ז וַיֹּאמֶר יְהוָה
אֶל־יְהוֹשֻׁעַ הַיּוֹם הַזֶּה אָחֵל גַּדֶּלְךָ בְּעֵינֵי
כָּל־יִשְׂרָאֵל אֲשֶׁר יֵדְעוּן כִּי כַּאֲשֶׁר הָיִיתִי

וּמִדְּקַדְמוֹהִי: ה וַאֲמַר
יְהוֹשֻׁעַ לְעַמָּא אִזְדַּמְּנוּ
אֲרֵי מְחַר יַעְבֵּד יְיָ
בֵּינֵיכוֹן פְּרִישָׁן: ו וַאֲמַר
יְהוֹשֻׁעַ לְכַהֲנַיָּא לְמֵימַר
טוּלוּ יָת אֲרוֹן קְיָמָא
וְעִבְרוּ קֳדָם עַמָּא וּנְטַלוּ
יָת אֲרוֹנָא דִקְיָמָא וַאֲזַלוּ
קֳדָם עַמָּא: ז וַאֲמַר יְיָ
לִיהוֹשֻׁעַ יוֹמָא הָדֵין
אֲשָׁרֵי לְרַבְּיוּתָךְ בְּעֵינֵי
כָּל יִשְׂרָאֵל דְּיִדְעִין אֲרֵי
כְּמָא דַהֲוָה מֵימְרִי
בְּסַעֲדֵיהּ דְּמֹשֶׁה כֵּן יְהֵי

ת״א אחל גדלך העניח כ פ״ג כס:

**רד״ק**

הכתוב אומר הטעם למען תדעו את הדרך ויש בזה דרש כי מה שצוה להם רחוק יהיה ביניכם ובינו כאלפים אמה במדה על חנותם לפני יריחו צוה להם ואמר להם יהושע עתידין אתם לעשות שם ביריחו את השבת אל תרחיקו מן הארון יותר מאלפים אמה לכל רוח ולמה כדי שיהיו רשאין לבא להתפלל לפני הארון בשבת ומ״ש במדה בפתח הבי״ת שמור׳ על הידיע׳ ר״ל במד׳ הידועה אצלם במלאכת המשכן: תדעו את הדרך. כדי שלא תכנסו בערבוביא ותראו מרחוק הארון ותלכו דרך ישרה כלכם אחרי הארון: כי לא עברתם בדרך. בדרך הזה כלומר שיבקעו לפניכם המים: (ה) התקדשו. תהיו מזומנים לעבור והכינו כליכם וכל דבריכם: מחר. בעברכם את הירדן. יעשה ה׳ בקרבכם נפלאות. והנפלאות בקיעת מי הירדן ועמוד המים נד אחד והאיך ידע יהושע זה ועדיין לא אמר לו השם היום הזה אחל גדלך עד למחר ביום עברם אלא כשאמר לו ביום שלשים של אבל משה קום עבור אמר לו כי עד שלשה ימים תעברו את הירדן ואמר לו הנפלאות שיעשה עמהם בעברם וזהו שאמר להם יהושע כי בעוד שלש׳ ימים אתם עוברים ואף על פי שלא זכר זה הכתוב כשאמר לו קום עבור והירדן היה מלא על כל גדותיו אז הבין יהושע כי לא יתכן עברם את הירדן אלא בנפלאות שיעשה עמהם: (ו) ויאמר יהושע אל הכהנים. ביום שעברו והוא בעשו׳ לחדש: (ז) כי כאשר הייתי עם משה. כי כמו שבקעתי הים לפני משה כן אבקע הירדן לפניך ובזה

**רש״י**

(ה) ויאמר יהושע. ביום השלישי ויום ג׳ של אבל היה ראשון לג׳ הימים: התקדשו. הזדמנו: כי מחר. בעברכם את הירדן: נפלאות. ת״י פרישן: (ו) ויאמר יהושע אל הכהנים. ביום המחרת: שאו את ארון הברית. עד

**מנחת שי**

תדעו. מלא תדעו בפשטא לא בזקף קטן: בלשום. בספרים מדוייקים מלא וכן

**רלב״ג**

ממנו אלפים אמה: (ו) והנה זכר אחר זה שכבר לוה יהושע אל העם שיתקדשו בעבור אלו הנפלאות שיעשה בקרבם אחר הלילה ההוא ולכהנים לוה שישאו ארון הברית ויעברו לפני העם: (ז) וזכר שכבר אמר הש״י ליהושע כי יחל לגדל אותו בעיני כל ישראל עד שהשתאל להם.

**מצודת ציון**

ביום הזה: (ז) אחל. מל׳ התחלה:

**מצודת דוד**

תדעון הדרך כי לא עברתם בה מעולם: (ה) כי מחר וגו׳ נפלאות. ולזה מהראוי להיות אז קדושים וטהורים מטומאה:
(ז) אשר ידעון. על ידי הנפלאות אשר אעשה על ידך:

## Commentary Digest

would be done in a wondrous manner. — K[2]

6. *And Joshua said to the priests* — "*on the morrow.*" — R

*Carry the Ark of the Covenant* — "*Until now the Levites carried it, but today the Priests.*" — R

7. *as I was with Moses* — in the splitting of the Red Sea, —

*so will I be with you* — in the cleaving of the Jordan. — K There is also implied here the subsequent miracle of the standing still of the sun in Gibeon and the moon in the vale of Ayalon,[3] just as had been the case with Moses, according to tradition, in his battles with Sihon and Og.[4] Alshich explains that this alludes to the subsequent miracle mentioned in v. 9, namely, that Joshua confined the entire nation between the staves of the ark, just as Moses had confined them all before the rock from which he was to extract water.[5]

5. And Joshua said to the people: Prepare yourselves, for
tomorrow the Lord will do wonders among you. 6. And
Joshua said to the priests, saying: Carry the Ark of the covenant,
and pass before the people. And they carried the Ark of the
covenant, and went before the people. 7. And the Lord
said to Joshua: This day I will begin to make you great in
the sight of all Israel, that they may know that as I was

## Commentary Digest

is permitted to walk on the Sabbath in an uninhabited area. — *"so that you be permitted to go and pray before it on the Sabbath. Thus it is explained in M.T.*[1] *for he knew that they would beseige Jericho on the Sabbath."* — R

*that you may know* — *"This is connected with, 'And go after it.'"* — R This is obviously not the reason for keeping a distance from the Ark, but for following it. Others explain that in order to facilitate following the Ark in an orderly fashion, it was necessary to keep a distance from it. — K and G According to this explanation, "that you may know" is the reason for "do not come near it."

*for you have not passed this way before* — *"You have not gone in this manner until now."* — R I.e. that the water be cloven before you. — K Others explain: You have not traveled in this manner, namely, with the Ark ahead of you. Therefore, be sure to follow. — P

5. *And Joshua said* — *"On the third day. And the thirtieth day of Moses' mourning period was the first of the three days."* — R

*Prepare yourselves* — This would usually be rendered: Sanctify yourselves. R, however, following J, considers: *"Prepare yourselves,"* the *peshat* of this passage. K elaborates: Prepare your luggage and all your possessions for the crossing of the Jordan. D follows the alternate explanation of: Sanctify and purify yourselves in anticipation of the impending wonders. This is similar to the Midrashic explanation: Joshua charged the Israelites that they separate themselves from sin, theft, and all unbecoming behavior, to be holy and pure when crossing the Jordan.[1]*

*for tomorrow* — *"when you cross the Jordan."* — R and K

*wonders* — *"J renders: wonders."* — R

Joshua had only been told that they were to cross the Jordan. However, since the river was overflowing, and it was impossible that it would subside within three days, he knew it

עם־משה אהיה עמך: ח ואתה תצוה את־הכהנים נשאי ארון־הברית לאמר כבאכם עד־קצה מי הירדן בירדן תעמדו: ט ויאמר יהושע אל־בני ישראל גשו הנה ושמעו את־דברי יהוה אלהיכם: י ויאמר יהושע בזאת תדעון כי אל חי בקרבכם והורש יוריש מפניכם את־הכנעני ואת־החתי ואת־החוי ואת־הפרזי ואת־הגרגשי והאמרי והיבוסי: יא הנה ארון הברית אדון כל־הארץ עבר לפניכם בירדן: יב ועתה קחו

לכם

**תרגום**

מימרי בסעדך: ח ואת תפקד ית כהניא נטלי ארונא דקימא למימר כמיעליכון עד קצת מי ירדנא בירדנא תקומון: ט ואמר יהושע לבני ישראל אתקריבו הלכא ושמעו ית פתגמיא דיי אלהכון: י ואמר יהושע בדא תדעון ארי אלה קים אתרעי לאשראה שכנתיה ביניכון ותרכא יתרך מן קדמיכון ית כנענאי וית חתאי וית חואי וית פריזאי וית גרגשאי ואמוראי ויבוסאי: יא הא ארון קימא דרבון כל ארעא עבר קדמיכון בירדנא: יב וכען דברו לכון תרי עסר

**ת״א** ארון הברית. סוטה לג עקרים מג כח:

**רש״י**

עכשיו כשאו הלוים והיום הכהנים: (ח) **כבאכם עד קצה מי הירדן.** כשתכנסו לפנים משפתו: **בירדן תעמדו.** עד אשר יעברו כל העם אל העבר השני: (ט) **גשו הנה.** למלט את כולם בין שני בדי ארון זה אחד מן המקומות שהחזיק מועט את המרובה: (י) **בזאת תדעון.** כמה שאתם רואים שכלכם מצומצמין כאן: (יא) **הברית אדון כל הארץ.** ברית של הקב״ה שהוא אדון כל הארץ. ואל תתמה על הה״א של הברית שהרבה מקראות מדברים כך כמו המסגרות המכונות העמק הפגרים: **עובר לפניכם.** מקדים לפניכם ליכנס לתוך הירדן: (יב) **קחו לכם**

**רד״ק**

(ח) עד קצה מי הירדן. עד קצה העבר השני שיצא ממנו ושם עמדו נושאי הארון עד שעברו כל העם ומהמקום ההוא סביבות מצב רגלי הכהנים לקחו שתים עשרה אבנים והעבירום עמם ושתים עשרה אבנים אחרות הקים יהושע במקום מצב רגלי הכהנים וכל זה קודם שעברו נושאי הארון מתוך הירדן: (ט) גשו הנה. הקריבם והקהילם לפני הארון במקו׳ שהיה שם יהושע והשמיע׳ את דברי ה׳: (י) בזאת תדעון. טעמו לפניו שהארון יעבור לפניהם ויכרתו מי הירדן ובאות הגדול הזה תדעון כי האל יתברך בקרבם ויוריש הגוים מלפניהם ובדרש כי טעמו למ״ש גשו הנה הכניסם כלם בין שני בדי הארון וזה א׳ מן המקומות שהחזיק המועט את המרובה: ואמר להם בזאת תדעון בזאת הפליאה שאתם רואים שכולכם מצומצמין בין בדי הארון וזה הדרש רחוק כי אילו היה זה הפלא היה נזכר בכתוב: (יא) הנה ארון הברית אדון כל הארץ. חסר וארון שזכר עומד במקום שנים ופירושו ארון אדון כל הארץ או חסר ברית שהרי זכר הברית ופירוש ברית אדון כל הארץ ויש מי שפירש כי על הארון הוא אומר אדון כל הארץ לפי ששכן שם הכבוד וכן נקרא שם כי שם ה׳ צבאות עליו וכן קראו שם הארון ה׳ כשהיו אומרין בנוסעו קומה ה׳ ושובה ה׳ בנוחו וכן אמר עלה אלהים בתרועה אמר על הארון ואמר אדון כל הארץ כי ע״י הארון הראה האל יתברך שהוא אדון כל הארץ והפך הטבעים כרצונו כי המים טבען להיות נגרים ועמדו נד אחד: (יב) ועתה קחו לכם. ולא אמר להם מה יעשו אלא הכין אותם טרם שיעברו ואחר שעברו

**רלב״ג**

**כי כאשר** היה עם משה כן יהיה עמו וזה אמנם יהיה **בזה האופן** שהודיעו הש״י איך יעשה זה המופת:

**מנחת שי**

נכון עפ״י המסורת דפרשת ויזה במ״ג: (יב) ועתה קחו לכם שני עשר איש, סימן קדמאה שני עשר תניינא דלקמן סימן ד׳ שנים עשר אנשים · תליתאה שנים

**מצודת דוד**

(ח) **עד קצה.** בקצהו המעברי: **בירדן תעמדו.** ולא תלכו מיד אל החרבה: (י) **בזאת.** בהפלאה ההולך ומפרש: (יא) **אדון וגו׳.** ר״ל של אדון וכו׳: (יב) **קחו לכם.** להיות הם במקום כולכם לעמוד קרוב לארון ויראו הם כי כאשר ינוחו כפות רגלי

**מצודת ציון**

(י) **והורש יוריש.** מענין גרושין. כמו ויורש מהם (במ׳ ל״ב):

## Commentary Digest

*all the earth* — "The covenant of the Holy One, Blessed be He, Who is the Lord of all the earth. Now, do not wonder about the 'he' of הברית" (the covenant which should read ברית אדון) "*for many Scriptural passages are worded in this manner, such as* המסגרות המכונות[2] *the borders of the bases, and* העמק הפגרים,[3] *the valley of the corpses.*" — R

*is crossing ahead of you*—R interprets עובר in the sense of "*preceding*

with Moses, so will I be with you. 8. And you shall command
the priests that bear the Ark of the covenant, saying, When
you come to the edge of the waters of the Jordan, you shall
stand still in the Jordan. 9. And Joshua said to the children
of Israel, Come here, and hear the words of the Lord your God.
10. And Joshua said, By this you shall know that the living
God is in your midst, and He will certainly drive out the
Canaanites, and the Hittites, and the Hivites, and the Perizzites
and the Girgashites, and the Amorites, and the Jebusites from
before you. 11. Behold, the Ark of the covenant of the Lord
of all the earth is crossing ahead of you in the Jordan.
12. And now take

## Commentary Digest

8. *When you come to the edge of the waters of the Jordan* — This would imply, upon their reaching the far western edge of the Jordan. — K and D The Rabbis, however, explain this to mean *"when you enter within its edge"* —

*you shall stand still in the Jordan* — *"until all the people cross to the other side."* — R[1]

9. *Come here* — *"He confined them all between the two staves of the Holy Ark. This is one of the instances wherein a small space contained a large quantity."* — R[1*]

10. *By this you shall know*[1*] — *"Since you see that all of you are confined here."* — R

*that the living G-d is in your midst* — Just as the Almighty is incorporeal, and is, therefore, not bound by the limits of physical space, so has He granted you spiritual status, and subordinated physical space to you. Hence, He will drive out all the nations of Canaan with their heavenly princes from before you. — Alshich. Others explain: by the manner described subsequently, of their crossing of the Jordan. — When the ark crosses before you and cleaves the waters of the Jordan, you will know that the living God is in your midst. — K and D. He emphasized, "the living God," indicating that although Moses was dead, God still lives and will live eternally. — A. M explains that by seeing the Ark preceding you, you shall know that the Lord goes out before you like a king who precedes his people.

11. *the covenant of the Lord of*

לָכֶם שְׁנֵי עָשָׂר אִישׁ מִשִּׁבְטֵי יִשְׂרָאֵל
אִישׁ־אֶחָד אִישׁ־אֶחָד לַשָּׁבֶט׃ יג וְהָיָה
כְּנוֹחַ כַּפּוֹת רַגְלֵי הַכֹּהֲנִים נֹשְׂאֵי אֲרוֹן
יְהוָה אֲדוֹן כָּל־הָאָרֶץ בְּמֵי הַיַּרְדֵּן מֵי
הַיַּרְדֵּן יִכָּרֵתוּן הַמַּיִם הַיֹּרְדִים מִלְמָעְלָה
וְיַעַמְדוּ נֵד אֶחָד׃ יד וַיְהִי בִּנְסֹעַ הָעָם
מֵאָהֳלֵיהֶם לַעֲבֹר אֶת־הַיַּרְדֵּן וְהַכֹּהֲנִים
נֹשְׂאֵי הָאָרוֹן הַבְּרִית לִפְנֵי הָעָם׃ טו וּכְבוֹא
נֹשְׂאֵי הָאָרוֹן עַד־הַיַּרְדֵּן וְרַגְלֵי הַכֹּהֲנִים

**תרגום**

עֲסַר גֻּבְרִין מִשִּׁבְטַיָּא דְיִשְׂרָאֵל גַּבְרָא חַד גַּבְרָא חַד לְשִׁבְטָא׃ יג וִיהֵי כְּמִנַּח פַּרְסַת רִגְלֵי כָּהֲנַיָּא נָטְלֵי אֲרוֹנָא דַיְיָ רִבּוֹן כָּל אַרְעָא בְּמֵי יַרְדְּנָא מֵי יַרְדְּנָא יִפְסְקוּן מַיָּא דְנָחֲתִין מִלְּעֵילָּא וִיקוּמוּן רוּקְבָא חַד׃ יד וַהֲוָה כַּד נְטַלוּ עַמָּא מִקִּרְוֵיהוֹן לְמֶעְבַּר יָת יַרְדְּנָא וְכָהֲנַיָּא נָטְלֵי אֲרוֹנָא דִקְיָמָא קֳדָם עַמָּא׃ טו וּכְמִמְטֵי נָטְלֵי אֲרוֹנָא עַד יַרְדְּנָא וְרַגְלֵי כָּהֲנַיָּא נָטְלֵי אֲרוֹנָא טְבִילָא

ת׳א והיה כנוח. סוטה שם וזבחים קיט: וכבוא נשאי הארון. סוטה לד:

**רד״ק**

העם אמר להם שירימו איש אבנו: (יג) ויעמדו נד אחד. פי׳ שלא יתפשטו הנה והנה בהסרתם ולא ישטפו אותם המקומות אבל יעמדו נד אחד כמו שירדו המים כן יעמדו אלה על אלה ולא יתפשטו ולא יצאו מגדות הירדן: (יד) הארון הברית.

**רש״י**

שני עשר איש. הכינו אותם להיות נכונים למה שאגזה אותם כשתעברו את הירדן: (יג) המים הירדים מלמעלה. למטה כדרך כל הנהרות המושכים: ויעמדו נד אחד. כשירדו המים עד מקום שנכרתו שם ולהנס יורדים משם ולמטה אלא הם מתקבלים ונגדשים ועולין למעלה כיפין ע״ג כיפין: נד. כמו כונס ככד. נד קציר. לשון גובה

**מנחת שי**

העבר איש. קדמאה איש אחד לשבט תניינא ותליתאה איש אחד אשבט: ועתה קחו לכם וגו, איש אחד לשבט. דין כתיב לשבט בלמ״ד והוא חד מן ג׳ לשבט קמצין ע״פ המסורת וסימן בסדר דברים והשנים שבפרשה הסמוכה בסימן ד׳

**רלב״ג**

(יד) והוא שכבר הודיע להם יהושע זה המופת טרם בואו ויעד להם זמן והוא שכאשר ינוחו כפות רגל׳ הכהנים נושאי הארון במי הירדן ברגע ההוא יכרתון מי הירדן וזה אמנם יהיה כשיכרתון המים היורדים מלמעלה ויעמדו נד אחד ולא ירדו ולזה היה מחויב שישוב מה שאחר המקום ההוא מהירדן הרבה כי המים אשר בו ירדו ולא יגרע להם דבר מן המים היורדים מלמעלה ולזה לא שיעמדו רגלי הכהנים בירדן עד עבור כל העם והודיעם שתכף שיסירו הכהנים רגליהם משם ישובו מי הירדן למקומן ולפי זה הזמן הוא בלתי מוגבל כי אפשר שיהיה זמן עבור העם הירדן ארוך אם יעברו בנחת או קצר אם יעברו במהירות וכן הענין בזמן הגע׳ רגלי הכהנים לירדן הנה היה זה מגדיל ענין הפלא הזה ומסיר הספק בו מהרואים אותו כי אם אמר אחד שיהושע היה יודע זמן הכר׳ הירדן וכמה מן הזמן עמד ואיך הנה אולי יבוא זה ספק מעט בענין זה המופת אבל בעבור שהוא לא נתן בזה זמן מוגבל כמו שזכרנו הנה אי אפשר לספק על זה המופת בזה האופן עם שהוא מבואר ממה שזכר מעמד המים היורדים כד אחד שזה בלתי אפשר בזולת מופת כמו שנבאר כשנאמר איך היה ענין זה המופת בזולת המופת: (טו) והנה ספר שכן היה הענין ר״ל שבבוא נושאי הארון עד הירדן ורגלי הכהנים נטבלו בקצה המים תיכף עמדו המים היורדים מלמעלה כמו כד אחד הרחק מאד מן העיר שמה אדם אשר מצד צרתן והיורדים על ים הערבה תמו נכרתו בהפסק ירידת המים מלמעלה והעם עמדו נגד יריחו:

**מצודת ציון**

(יג) נד. תל וקבוץ אחת וכן נלבו כמו נד נוזלים (שמות ט״ו):

**מצודת דוד**

(יג) והיה כנוח. מוסב למעלה לו׳ שמה יראו כאשר ינוח כפות רגלי הכהנים מיד יכרתון המים הכהנים מיד יכרתו המים: יורדים עתה מלמעלה וילכו להם: ויעמדו. המים אשר יבואו לאח״ז אל מקום הכריתה יעמדו שם נד אחד:

## Commentary Digest

15. *And when the bearers of the Ark came to the Jordan* — They did not need to step off the bank, but, immediately , —

*and the feet of the priests that bore the Ark were dipped in the edge of the water* — which overflowed the banks. — Alshich

*its banks* — Heb. גדותיו, *"an expression of a high bank."* — R

*their tents to cross the Jordan* — They left their tents with the intention of crossing the Jordan immediately. They had implicit faith in the Lord's promise to cleave the waters of the Jordan. — Alshich

*before the people* — directly before the people. They did not keep a distance of two thousand cubits as was customary on their travels. — Alshich

for yourselves twelve men from the tribes of Israel, a man
for every tribe. 13. And it shall be, when the soles of the
feet of the priests that bear the Ark of the Lord, Lord of all
the earth, rest in the waters of the Jordan, the waters of
the Jordan shall be cut off, the waters that come down from
above, shall stand in one heap. 14. And it was, when the
people moved from their tents, to cross the Jordan, and
the priests bearing the Ark of the covenant were before the
people. 15. And when the bearers of the Ark came to the
Jordan, and the feet of the priests

## Commentary Digest

*you to enter into the Jordan,"* as in Gen. XXXIII:3.[1] This is in order not to conflict with v. 8, where the Kohanim, according to tradition, did not cross the Jordan first, but only entered first and remained standing near the eastern bank of the Jordan.

The Almighty is depicted here as the Lord of all the earth, or of all the land. Lordship denotes the power to uproot inhabitants and to settle inhabitants. Here the Lord is exercising this power to drive out the Canaanites and to settle the Israelites in their place. —Y[1*] Just as the gatekeepers open the gates to admit the lord of the palace, so the Jordan would open the gates of the Holy Land to admit the King of Glory. — M

12. *take for yourselves twelve men* — *"Prepare them to be ready for that which I shall command them[1**] when you will cross the Jordan."* — R

13. *the waters that come down from above* — *"downstream, as is the manner of all flowing rivers."* — R

*shall stand in one heap* — *"When the water flows downstream to the place where it will be cut off, it will not flow down farther, but will be gathered and heaped, and will ascend to form stacks upon stacks.* — R Also, this verse informs us that the waters will not spread out to the neighboring areas, causing large scale flooding and the building up of a lake, as behind a dam, but will rise vertically, eventually to a height of many miles. — K The sight was witnessed from near and far, causing all the kings of Canaan to be faint of spirit.[2]

*heap* — Heb. נד, *"Like: He gathers like a heap* (כנד),[3] *A heap of harvest* (נד),[4] *an expression of height. In this manner Menahem (the grammarian) joined them together."* — R

14. *when the people moved from*

טְבִילָא בִּקְצַת מַיָּא
וְיַרְדְּנָא מְלֵי עַל כָּל
כֵּפוֹהִי כָּל יוֹמֵי חַצְדָא׃
טז וְקָמוּ מַיָּא דְּנַחְתִּין
מִלְעֵילָא קָמוּ רוּקְבָא חַד
רְחִיקִין לַחֲדָא מֵאָדָם
קַרְתָּא דִּבְסְטַר צָרְתָן
וּדְנַחְתִּין לְיַמָּא דְּמֵישְׁרָא
לְיַמָּא דְּמִלְחָא
שְׁלִימוּ פְּסָקוּ וְעַמָּא
עֲבַרוּ לְקֳבֵיל יְרִיחוֹ׃
יז וְקָמוּ כָּהֲנַיָּא נָטְלֵי
אֲרוֹן קְיָמָא דַּיְיָ בְּיַבֶּשְׁתָּא
בְּגוֹ יַרְדְּנָא מְתַקְנָא וְכָל

נֹשְׂאֵי הָאָרוֹן נִטְבְּלוּ בִּקְצֵה הַמָּיִם
וְהַיַּרְדֵּן מָלֵא עַל־כָּל־גְּדוֹתָיו כֹּל יְמֵי
קָצִיר׃ טז וַיַּעַמְדוּ הַמַּיִם הַיֹּרְדִים מִלְמַעְלָה
קָמוּ נֵד־אֶחָד הַרְחֵק מְאֹד בְּאָדָם הָעִיר
אֲשֶׁר מִצַּד צָרְתָן וְהַיֹּרְדִים עַל יָם
הָעֲרָבָה יָם־הַמֶּלַח תַּמּוּ נִכְרָתוּ וְהָעָם
עָבְרוּ נֶגֶד יְרִיחוֹ׃ יז וַיַּעַמְדוּ הַכֹּהֲנִים
נֹשְׂאֵי הָאָרוֹן בְּרִית־יְהוָה בֶּחָרָבָה בְּתוֹךְ

ת״א ויעמדו המים. סוטה לד (ביומא כח): תמו נכרתו. שבת לח: ויעמדו הכהנים. ברכות נד.

מאדם קרי

## רש״י

וכן הכרם מנחם: (טו) גדותיו. לשון שפה גבוה: כל ימי קציר. שימי ניסן ימי קציר הם: (טז) הרחק מאד. ממקום שעמדו שם נפסקו: מאדם העיר. כך שמה: והירדים. אותם שהיו יורדים משם ולמטה תחלה: תמו נכרתו. עברו כדרך הליכתן ככל הנחלים ההולכים אל הים עד אשר תמו: (יז) ויעמדו הכהנים. אצל שפת

## רד״ק

הברית חסר ופי׳ הארון ארון הברית: (טו) על כל גדותיו. על כל שפתיו מפה ומפה כל ימי קציר כלומר אף על פי שהיו ימי קציר היה מלא על כל גדותיו וכניסן עברו בעשור לחדש שהם ימי קציר או פירושו כי כן מנהגו להיות מלא ימי הקציר ואמר והירדן היה מלא כמשפטו להיות מלא כל ימי קציר כי בהחל ימי החום ותפש׳ השלג אשר בהרים וימלאו הנהרות וכן בדברי הימים כשעברו בני גד לדוד לעזרו הם אשר עברו את הירדן בחדש הראשון והוא מלא על כל גדותיו: (טז) הרחק מאד מאדם העיר. העיר הקרובה שם במקום שעברו היה שמה אדם ומה שאמר הרחק מאד להודיע כי לא נתפשטו המים היורדים אלא קמו זה על זה נד אחד רחוקים מן העיר כמו שהיו מתחילה: והיורדים. פירוש והמים היורדים אשר מתחת מקום הכריתה ירדו אל הים כמנהג הנחלים וקודם שעברו תמו אותם המים התחתונים כי הלכו כולם לים והעם עברו ביבשה בריוח כי לא היו מים אלא למעלה מהם שקמו נד אחד ומה שכתוב באדם וקרי מאדם הכתוב אומר כי לולי שקמו המים נד אחד והיו מתפשטין היו נכנסים באדם העיר ושוטפין העיר אף על פי שהיתה רחוקה כל כך היו המים רבים אבל עתה שקמו נד אחד

הירדן

## מנחת שי

כתובים הים אחד משבע במ״ס: (טז) באדם. מאדם קרי והוא חד מן ו׳ דכתיבין בי״ת וקרי מ״ם וסימן נמסר במ״ג מערכת אות הבי״ת. ואפשר לומר שיש בזה רמז למה שאמרו במדרש ילמדנו על נסים שנעשו לישראל בזכותו של אברהם היו הנו׳ קריעת הירדן בזכותו כדכתיב הרחק מאוד באדם זה אברהם שנאמר האדם הגדול בענקים. שוב מצאתי כדברי במסורת הברית הגדול סימן תתק״ת. ועיין עוד ברד״ק ולב אהרן ובענין המאמר עיין בכלי יקר ומסורת הברית הגדול ריש סדר שופטים: אשר מצד צרתן. בדפוס ישן הלד״י בפת״ח וכלא מאריך בתי״ו ובמכלול דף רכ״ג במאמר שמש בני ארבע אותיות כתוב כלשון הזה ובקמץ הראשונה ובפתח השלישית צָרְתָן צְרֵפַת. אבל כַּרְפַּס אַרְגָּז בגלגל פתוחים ע״כ. ובספר רב פעלים מחולף השמות ונקודה כתוב כלשון הזה צָרְתָן בקמץ ובפתח וכן משקל זה עד צָרְפַת ובתוספת ה״א ג״כ לצרפתה דו: אשר לצידון וכן משקל זה צָפְנַת פענח ע״כ. נראה מדבריו שהוא קורא אותם בקמץ רחב וכן כת׳ על בָשְׂמַת בת ישמעאל קמץ רחב ופתח ומשקלו אָסְנַת בת פוטיפרע דו: ע״כ וכן במקצת ספרים הלד״י במאריך אך בתי״ו לרתן ברוב הספרים היא קמוצה ובמסורת לרתן ב׳ בין סכות (מלאכים א ז) ודין עיין (במלכים א׳ סימן ד׳ וסימן י״ז): (יז) עד אשר תמו כל הגוי לעבר. היא פלוגתא דבני מערבאי ודבני מדנחאי דמסרי לעבור ד׳ מלאים סימן עד אשר תמו כל הגוי. ותניינא כל הגוי דסמיך ליה. ויהי כאשר תם כל העם לעבור בפרשתא דלקמן סימן ד׳ (יא). לעבור בן בליעל (נחום ב א) הכי נמסר במ״ג סדר בלק והכא. ומסרה אחריתי בנחום לעבור ד׳ מלאי׳ וסימנו ויהי כאשר תמו כל הגוי. תניינא ויהי כאשר תם כל העם לעבר. והנה גם לדוק וכל הלוים אתו וגו׳ (שמואל ב ט״ו). לא יוסיף לעבור בך בליעל. ונוסחי דיקי כמסרה בתרייתא סלקי ולדידי חזי לי דדא היא הפלוגתא דכתיבי במ״ג נחום

## מצודת דוד

(טו) בקצה המים. בעבר המזרחי: והירדן מלא. בא להגדיל הנס ולומר אף שמי הירדן מרובים הם שאפי׳ בכל ימי קציר בדרך מי הנהרות להתמעט היה הוא מלא על כל שפתיו: (טז) ויעמדו. מוסב למעלה לומר הנה עם כל רבוי המים עמדו היורדים מלמעלה אחר הכריתה וקמו נד אחד: הרחק מאוד. הנד ההוא היה רחוק מאוד מהעיר בשמה אדם העומדת בצד צרתן: והיורדים. המים שירדו קודם הכריתה לצד ים הערבה והוא ים המלח: תמו נכרתו. המים ההם תמו ממקומם ונכרתו והלכו להם ונשאר המקום חורב ויבש: (יז) ויעמדו. לא יצאו מיד מהירדן רק עמדו בעבר המערבי עד עברו כולם וכאשר לוה: הכן. ר״ל עמדו מוכן ומתוקן דרך קבע עד עברו כולם:

## מצודת ציון

(טו) גדותיו. הם שפתי הנהר סביב המים כמו והלך על כל גדותיו (ישעיה ח׳): (טז) תמו. מלשון תם והשלמה:

## Commentary Digest

Jordan was split. The word עיר perhaps is taken to mean an angel, as in Dan. IV, v. 10, 14, 20. Abraham, being a very righteous man, is referred to as an angel.

The "Kethiv" is באדם, in Adam. It tells us that were the waters not heaped up, they would have flowed into Adam. — K

*and those that descended* — "Those that had previously flowed downstream from there." — R

*were completely cut off* — "They flowed on their course like all streams

that bore the Ark were dipped in the edge of the water, and the Jordan overflows all its banks all the time of harvest.
16. And the waters which came down from above stood and rose up in one column, very far from Adam, the city which is beside Zarethan; and those that descended to the sea of the plain, the Salt Sea (Dead Sea), were completely cut off, and the people passed over opposite Jericho. 
17. And the priests that bore the Ark of the covenant of the Lord stood firm arranged on the dry land in the midst of

## Commentary Digest

*all the time of harvest* — *"for the days of Nissan are the harvest season.* — R

Even though it was the harvest season when there is no rainfall, the Jordan was overflowing its banks to make the miracle greater. It is also possible that during the spring season with the melting snows from the north, the Jordan is always at its greatest depth. — K

16. *very far* — *"From the place where they"* (the Israelites) *"stood, they"* (the waters) *"were cut off."* — R According to this, a comma should appear after "very far." "From Adam the city" describes the exact spot where the waters were cut off. K and D explain: very far from Adam the city, i.e. the waters were cut off far from Adam, and the heaped up waters kept the same distance. They did not flow any nearer to the city all the time they were standing there.

*from Adam the city* — *"So was its name."* — R Not מאדמה עיר, from Adamah, a city that is in the vicinity of Zarethan,[1] nor הרחק מאד מאד מהעיר, very very far from the city,[2] as has been suggested by some.

Evidently, R also wishes to negate the Y, which states: The cleaving of the Jordan was in his (Abraham's) merit. As it is stated: from Adam the city which is beside Zarethan. Have you ever heard of a city named Adam? It rather refers to Abraham who was called the great man (אדם) among the giants.[3] R states that according to *peshat,* it is the name of a city. To reconcile the Y with R, we may say that the Y also holds that Adam was a city, for a Biblical verse can never lose its literal sense (although its meaning may be extended by the methods of interpretation).[4] Y, however, intimates that since the city of Adam was unknown, it is unlikely that the Bible meant only to identify the place by an unknown name. We, therefore, expound the name as referring to Abraham, in whose merit the

הַיַּרְדֵּן הָכֵן וְכׇל־יִשְׂרָאֵל עֹבְרִים בֶּחָרָבָה
עַד אֲשֶׁר־תַּמּוּ כׇּל־הַגּוֹי לַעֲבוֹר אֶת־
הַיַּרְדֵּן׃ ד א וַיְהִי כַּאֲשֶׁר־תַּמּוּ כׇל־הַגּוֹי
לַעֲבוֹר אֶת־הַיַּרְדֵּן * וַיֹּאמֶר יְהוָה אֶל־
יְהוֹשֻׁעַ לֵאמֹר׃ ב קְחוּ לָכֶם מִן־הָעָם
שְׁנֵים עָשָׂר אֲנָשִׁים אִישׁ־אֶחָד אִישׁ־
אֶחָד מִשָּׁבֶט׃ ג וְצַוּוּ אוֹתָם לֵאמֹר שְׂאוּ־
לָכֶם מִזֶּה מִתּוֹךְ הַיַּרְדֵּן מִמַּצַּב רַגְלֵי
הַכֹּהֲנִים הָכִין שְׁתֵּים־עֶשְׂרֵה אֲבָנִים

תרגום

יִשְׂרָאֵל עָבְרִין בְּיַבֶּשְׁתָּא
עַד דִשְׁלִימוּ כָּל עַמָּא
לְמֶעְבַּר יָת יַרְדְּנָא׃
א וַהֲוָה כַּד שְׁלִימוּ כָל
עַמָּא לְמֶעְבַּר יָת יַרְדְּנָא
וַאֲמַר יְיָ לִיהוֹשֻׁעַ
לְמֵימַר׃ ב דַּבָּרוּ לְכוֹן מִן
עַמָּא תְּרֵי עֲסַר גֻּבְרִין
גַּבְרָא חַד גַּבְרָא חַד
מִשִּׁבְטָא׃ ג וּפַקִּידוּ
יָתְהוֹן לְמֵימַר טוּלוּ לְכוֹן
מִכָּא מִגּוֹ יַרְדְּנָא מֵאֲתַר
מֵיקַם רַגְלֵי כָּהֲנַיָּא
מִתְקְנַיָּא תַּרְתֵּי עַסְרֵי
אַבְנַיָּא וּתְעַבְרִנוּן יָתְהוֹן
עִמְּכוֹן וְתַחְתוּן יָתְהוֹן
בבית

ת״א באו לכם. סוטה לד:

* פסקא באמצע פסוק

**רד״ק**

רחקו מאדם העיר מאד כמו שהית הירדן רחוק מהעיר : (יח) בתוך הירדן הכן. מקור ר״ל מוכנים ומתוקנים כתרגומו מתקניא וכן ממצב רגלי הכהנים הכין ממקום שיהיו מוכנים ומתוקנים בו : (א) ויאמר ה׳ אל יהושע. וכבר אמר קודם ויאמר יהושע אל בני ישראל גשו הנה וכן ויקרא יהושע דבק עם ויהי כאשר תמו כל הגוי לעבור את הירדן לאמר שיאמר יהושע לבני

**רש״י**

הירדן : בתוך הירדן· וכל זמן שעמדו לא ירדו המים העליונים למטה ובתוך כך כל העם עוברים בחרבה : **הכן.** מכוונים ונכונים זה כנגד זה : **ד** (ב) **שנים עשר אנשים.** הם שנזכרים למעלה להיות נכונים:(ג) **והעברתם אותם עמכם.** כמלות משה לבנות מהם מזבח בהר עיבל ולכתוב עליהם את דברי התורה ובו ביום באו אל הר עיבל ובנו בהם את המזבח והעלו עולות ושלמים ואכלו ושתו

**מנחת שי**

ב׳ יכי) לא יוסיף (עוד) לעבר בך בליעל הע״ג דהתם פריסית בגעוי אחריני . **ד** (א) **ויהי** כאשר תמו כל הגוי לעבור את הירדן . ויאמר. פיסקא באמצעות

**רלב״ג**

(ב) ולפרסם זה המופת לוה לי״ב אים. אשר הכין מבני ישראל איש אחד איש אחד משבט שירימו להם איש אבן אחת על שכמו למען יסיה

**מצודת דוד**

**ד** (ג) **מתוך הירדן.** ל״ה להם לחזור אל קלה הירדן אחר שילאו ממנו : **ממצב.** ממקום שהכהנים ללבים מוכן ומתוקן כי נשאו

## Commentary Digest

mand is in no way identified with the previous one. There were two groups, each comprised of twelve chosen men. The first group was picked to witness the drying up of the Jordan when the priests stepped into the water, while the second group was to take stones from the place where the priests had stood. — The wording of the Scriptures supports this theory. — Azulai

3. *out of the midst of the Jordan* — He commanded them to return to the edge of the Jordan after they had crossed. — D

*and you shall carry them over with you* — "in accordance with Moses' commandment[5] to build an altar therewith on Mt. Ebal and to write upon them the words of the Torah. On that very day, they came to Mt. Ebal, built therewith the altar, and offered up burnt-offerings and peace-offerings, and they ate and drank and peeled them and came and lodged in Gilgal."[6] — R Gilgal was, for the fourteen years of conquest and subsequent division of the land, the home of the tabernacle, the spiritual center of Israel. This was a temporary home, until the tabernacle at Shiloh was dedicated. The latter stood for 369 years, subse-

the Jordan, and all Israel passed over on dry ground, until the whole nation had completely passed over the Jordan.

4

1. And it was when all the nation had completely passed over
the Jordan, the Lord spoke to Joshua, saying, 2. Take to
yourselves twelve men from the people, a man from every
tribe. 3. And command them saying, Take to yourselves from
here out of the midst of the Jordan, out of the place where
the priests' feet stood firm, twelve stones,

**Commentary Digest**

*that flow into the sea, until they were completed."* — R

17. *And the priests* — stood — *"by the bank of the Jordan."* — R

*in the midst of the Jordan* — *"and as long as they stood, the upper waters did not flow downstream, and during this time, all the people were crossing on the dry ground."* — R

*firm arranged* — *"standing precisely opposite one another."* — R

*and all Israel passed over on dry ground until the whole nation had completely passed over"* — Israel implies the descendants of Jacob, whereas the expression "nation" includes also the ערב רב, the vast multitudes of Egyptians who had accepted the Jewish faith and had wandered together with Israel in the desert.[1] It also includes the woodcutters and water drawers.[2] Hence, the Holy Ark of the Almighty waited in the Jordan until this multitude of proselytes and servants crossed on dry ground. This is analogous to the episode of Rabbi Phinehas ben Jair, who miraculously split a river for himself, for a Jew who was carrying wheat for Passover matzoth, and for an Arab merchant who was accompanying them.[3] — Alshich

CHAPTER 4

2. *twelve men* — *"They are the aforementioned,[4] who were to be prepared."* — R

*a man from every tribe* — lit. one man one man from a tribe.

K renders: The Lord had spoken to Joshua, saying, —. He explains this as referring to the command given above. 3:12. V. 4 is connected to the subordinate clause: **And it was when all the nation had completely passed over the Jordan, and the Lord had spoken . . . that Joshua called the twelve men. The verses between** are a parenthetical clause. The pause in the middle of v. 1 supports this theory.

Still others maintain that this com-

והעברתם אותם עמכם והנחתם אותם
במלון אשר תלינו בו הלילה: ד ויקרא
יהושע אל שנים העשר איש אשר
הכין מבני ישראל איש אחד איש
אחד משבט: ה ויאמר להם יהושע עברו
לפני ארון יהוה אלהיכם אל תוך הירדן
והרימו לכם איש אבן אחת על שכמו
למספר שבטי בני ישראל: ו למען
תהיה זאת אות בקרבכם כי ישאלון
בניכם מחר לאמר מה האבנים האלה
לכם: ז ואמרתם להם אשר נכרתו
מימי הירדן מפני ארון ברית יהוה
בעברו בירדן נכרתו מי הירדן והיו

בבית מבתא דתביתון
ביה בליליא: ד וקרא
יהושע לתרי עסר גברא
דאתקין מבני ישראל
גברא חד גברא חד
משבטא: ה ואמר להון
יהושע עברו קדם ארונא
דיי אלהכון לגו ירדנא
ואריםו לכון גבר אבנא
חדה על כתפיה למנין
שבטיא דבני ישראל:
ו בדיל דתהי דא את
בינכון ארי ישאלין
בניכון מחר למימר מא
אבניא האלין לכון
ז ותימרון להון די פסקו
מי ירדנא מן קדם ארון
קימא דיי במעבריה
בירדנא פסקו מי ירדנא
ויהוון אבניא האלין
לדכרנא לבני ישראל
עד

### תולדות אהרן

והעברתם אותם. סוטה לו: הרימו לכם. סוטה לד (סוטה כה): למען תהיה. סוטה לד:

### רש"י

וקפלו אותם והלו ולנו בגלגל: (ה) עברו לפני ארון וגו'. הכנסו עתה בירדן ועברו עד לפני הכהנים: (ז) והיו האבנים האלה. בגלגל לזכרון זה:

### רד"ק

האבנים ישראל קחו לכם וצוו אותם: (ה) עברו לפני ארון ה'. נראה כי יהושע עבר באחרונה את הירדן והעביר כל העם לפניו כדי שיהיו בטוחים יותר כשנשאר אחריהם שהמים יעמדו נד אחד עד שיעבור הוא וכיון שעברו כלם קרא לאותם שני' עשר איש שהכין שהיו עמו ואמר להם שיעברו לפני הארון שהיה בתוך הירדן כי העבר האח' אשר יצאו ממנו ואמר להם שירימו איש אבנו על שכמו ויעבירום עמם: (ז) בעברו בירדן. במקצת ספרים העי"ן בגעיא נקרא בקמץ רחב והוא מן החלופים:

### מנחת שי

פסוק: (ה) על שכמו למספר שבטי בני ישראל. ס"א שבטי ישראל ומוטעה הוא שזהו אחד מן ג' שבטי בני ישראל הסמוכים בקריאה וסימן נאמר במסורה גדולה כאן: (ו) למען תהיה וגו' כי ישאלון בניכם מחר לאמר. בספר אחד דפוס יען כתוב מחר את אבותם לאמר וגירסא זו אינה אלא מן המתמיהין שזהו אחד מן החלופים שיש בין פסוק זה ובין חבירו שבפרשה זו לקמן דין כתיב מחר לאמר וחבר מחר את אבותם לאמר דין כתיב כי ישאלון בניכם וחברו אשר ישאלון בניכם ואפ"ס כי אשר האלהים את מצרים. דין כתיב מה האבנים האלה לכם וחברו מה האבנים האלה: (ז) בעברו בירדן. במקצת

### מצודת דוד

רגליהם ונקחו האבנים אשר תחתיהם: (ד) אשר הכין. לעמוד קרוב לארון לראות אשר מיד כנוח רגלי הכהנים יכלתו תמים כמ"ש למטלה: (ה) אל תוך הירדן. כי כבר ילאו ממנה כאמור: (ו) אות. סימן לזכרון: מחר. ר"ל לאחר זמן:

### מצודת ציון

ד (ה) והרימו. והגביה:

## Commentary Digest

but by the Lord, and the proof is — when it passed over the Jordan, the waters of the Jordan were cut off — M

*and these stones shall be — "in Gilgal as a memorial of this."* — R These stones will also serve as a memorial for future generations who have not witnessed the miracle. — M

and you shall carry them over with you, and leave them in the lodging place, where you shall lodge this night. 4. And Joshua called the twelve men, whom he had prepared of the children of Israel, a man from every tribe. 5. And Joshua said to them, Pass before the Ark of the Lord your God into the midst of the Jordan, and lift up every man of you a stone upon his shoulder, according to the number of the tribes of the children of Israel: 6. That this may be a sign among you, that when your children ask in time to come, saying, What are these stones for you? 7. Then you shall say to them, That the waters of the Jordan were cut off before the Ark of the covenant of the Lord; when it passed over the Jordan, the waters of the Jordan were cut off;

## Commentary Digest

quently being destroyed by the Philistines. Also on this day, they received the sprinkling of the purifying waters of the red heifer.[1]

5. *Pass before the Ark etc.* — *"Enter now into the Jordan and pass until you are in front of the priests."* — R

This is according to the tradition that the priests carrying the Ark stood on the eastern side of the Jordan. K, however, explains that Joshua crossed after the entire nation, in order to assure them that the waters would remain standing. After all the people had crossed, he called the twelve men to cross the Jordan and take twelve stones from the place the priests were standing.

*every man of you a stone upon his shoulder* — to preserve the individuality of the tribes. — M

6. *That this may be a sign among you* — A sign for the generation living at that time and for their children. — M

*What are these stones for you?* — You yourselves saw the miracle. Why do you need to be reminded? — M

7. *That the waters of the Jordan were cut off before the Ark* — The waters were not cut off by our power

האבנים האלה לזכרון לבני ישראל עד־עולם: ח ויעשו־כן בני־ישראל כאשר צוה יהושע וישאו שתי־עשרה אבנים מתוך הירדן כאשר דבר יהוה אל־יהושע למספר שבטי בני־ישראל ויעברום עמם אל־המלון וינחום שם: ט ושתים עשרה אבנים הקים יהושע בתוך הירדן תחת מצב רגלי הכהנים נשאי ארון הברית ויהיו שם עד היום הזה: י והכהנים נשאי הארון עמדים בתוך הירדן עד־תם כל־הדבר אשר־צוה יהוה את־יהושע לדבר אל־העם ככל אשר־צוה משה את־יהושע וימהרו

**תרגום**

עד עלמא: ח ועבדו כן בני ישראל כמא די פקיד יהושע ונטלו תרתא עשרי אבניא מגו ירדנא כמא דמליל יי עם יהושע למנין שבטיא דבני ישראל ואעברונון עמהון לבית מבתא ואצנעונון תמן: ט ותרתא עשרי אבניא אקים יהושע בגו ירדנא באתר מיקם רגלי כהניא נטלי ארונא דקימא והוו תמן עד יומא הדין: י וכהניא נטלי ארונא קימין בגו ירדנא עד דשלים כל פתגמא דפקיד יי ית יהושע למללא עם עמא ככל דפקיד משה ית יהושע ואוחיאו עמא

ועברו

ת"א הקים יהושע. סוטה לה:

**רד"ק**

(ט) הקים יהושע. אף על פי שלא ראינו שצוהו האל על אלה האבנים אחר שעשה ידענו כי במצות האל יתברך עשה: תחת מצב. מקים מצב לא תחת רגליהם שהרי לא זזו משם עד שנעשה כל מה שהיה להם לעשות כמו שכתוב עד תם כל הדבר: (י) עד תם כל הדבר. הקמת האבנים בירדן והעברת האבני' האחרות אל המלון: אשר צוה ה' את יהושע. כמו שכתוב למעלה: ככל אשר צוה משה את יהושע. כמו שכתוב בתורה והיה ביום אשר תעברו את הירדן: וימהרו. הקמת האבנים והעברתם

**רש"י**

(ט) ושתים עשרה אבנים. אחרות הקים יהושע בתוך הירדן: (י) עד תום כל הדבר. כמו ששנינו במסכת סוטה עודם בירדן אמר להם יהושע דעו למה אתם עוברים את הירדן על מנת שתורישו את כל יושבי הארץ כו':

**מנחת שי**

ספרים העי"ן במארך [illegible] : (ח) לדבר דבר. הבית בסגול:

**רלב"ג**

זה אות בקרבכם להזכירם ענין זה המופת: (ט) וזכר עוד ששתים עשרה אבנים הקים יהושע בתוך הירדן תחת מצב רגלי הכהנים

**מצודת ציון**

(ט) תחת. במקום:

**מצודת דוד**

(ט) ושתים וגו'. אלו היו אחרים: עד היום הזה. ר"ל עד עולם כי כל קורא הפסוק הזה בזמנו אומר עד היום הזה והוא כלל גדול בדברי הנביאים: (י) לדבר אל העם. ר"ל שהם אשר לו לדבר אל העם לאמר דעו שאתם עוברים את הירדן בתנאי על מנת לגרש כל יושבי הארץ והדבר ההוא בעצמו צוה לו משה: וימהרו. בעבור כבוד הארון בעמד עד עברם:

## Commentary Digest

the place where the priests were standing, were found many large stones. Although Joshua had not been commanded to do so, he decided to take of these stones to set up a monument similar to the one he had set up in Gilgal. He did so nearby *instead* of the place where the priests had stood, i.e. as a memorial to the place where the priests had stood. He set up the stones in a large heap, one upon the other, towering over the waters of the Jordan.

*to this day* — i.e. forever. — D

10. *until everything was finished* — "*as we learned in Tractate Sotah*[1]

and these stones shall be for a memorial to the children of
Israel forever. 8. And the children of Israel did as Joshua
commanded, and took up twelve stones out of the midst of
the Jordan, as the Lord had spoken to Joshua, according to
the number of the tribes of the children of Israel, and carried
them over with them to the place where they lodged, and laid
them there. 9. And Joshua set up twelve stones in the midst of
the Jordan, in the place where the feet of the priests who bore
the Ark of the covenant stood; and they have been there to this
day. 10. And the priests that bore the Ark stood in the midst
of the Jordan, until everything was finished that the Lord
commanded Joshua to speak to the people, according to all
that Moses commanded Joshua; and the people hastened

### Commentary Digest

8. *the place where they lodged* — Gilgal.

9. *And — twelve stones — "I.e. others Joshua set up in the midst of the Jordan."* — R Although we do not find that God commanded him concerning these stones, we know that he did this according to the command of the Lord. — K For a prophet does nothing without divine instruction. — P

*in the place where — stood* — so that the feet of the priests would not sink in the water and mud. — R as quoted by A. After the original twelve stones had been removed, it became necessary to replace them to prevent the priests' feet from sinking. K, however, explains that the stones were not taken directly from the place where the priests were standing, since they stood there yet, but rather from the place next to their feet. G explains that Joshua had set up these stones before the miracle of the cleaving of the Jordan to announce to the people that in that place the Jordan would split. Accordingly, we should render: And Joshua had set up.

A renders: And Joshua set up — instead of the place where — stood. He explains that in the vicinity of

הָעָם וַיַּעֲבֹרוּ׃ יא וַיְהִי כַּאֲשֶׁר־תַּם
כָּל־הָעָם לַעֲבוֹר וַיַּעֲבֹר אֲרוֹן־יְהוָה
וְהַכֹּהֲנִים לִפְנֵי הָעָם׃ יב וַיַּעַבְרוּ בְּנֵי־
רְאוּבֵן וּבְנֵי־גָד וַחֲצִי שֵׁבֶט הַמְנַשֶּׁה
חֲמֻשִׁים לִפְנֵי בְּנֵי יִשְׂרָאֵל כַּאֲשֶׁר דִּבֶּר
אֲלֵיהֶם מֹשֶׁה׃ יג כְּאַרְבָּעִים אֶלֶף חֲלוּצֵי
הַצָּבָא עָבְרוּ לִפְנֵי יְהוָה לַמִּלְחָמָה אֶל
עַרְבוֹת יְרִיחוֹ׃ יד בַּיּוֹם הַהוּא גִּדַּל יְהוָה
אֶת־יְהוֹשֻׁעַ בְּעֵינֵי כָּל־יִשְׂרָאֵל וַיִּרְאוּ
אֹתוֹ כַּאֲשֶׁר יָרְאוּ אֶת־מֹשֶׁה כָּל־
יְמֵי חַיָּיו׃ טו וַיֹּאמֶר יְהוָה אֶל־יְהוֹשֻׁעַ לֵאמֹר׃

נַעֲבָרוּ׃ יא וַהֲוָה כַּד
שְׁלִים כָּל עַמָּא לְמֶעְבַּר
וַעֲבַר אֲרוֹנָא דַיְיָ
וְכָהֲנַיָּא קֳדָם עַמָּא׃
יב וַעֲבָרוּ בְּנֵי רְאוּבֵן
וּבְנֵי גָד וּפַלְגוּת שִׁבְטָא
דִמְנַשֶּׁה מְזָרְזִין קֳדָם בְּנֵי
יִשְׂרָאֵל כְּמָא דְמַלִּיל
עִמְּהוֹן מֹשֶׁה׃
יג כְּאַרְבְּעִין אַלְפִין מְזָרְזֵי
חֵילָא עֲבָרוּ קֳדָם עַמָּא
דַיְיָ לִקְרָבָא לְמֵישְׁרֵי
יְרִיחוֹ׃ יד בְּיוֹמָא הַהוּא
רַבִּי יְיָ יַת יְהוֹשֻׁעַ בְּעֵינֵי
כָּל יִשְׂרָאֵל וּדְחִילוּ מִנֵּיהּ
כְּמָא דַהֲווֹ דָחֲלִין מִן
מֹשֶׁה כָּל יוֹמֵי חַיּוֹהִי׃
טו וַאֲמַר יְיָ לִיהוֹשֻׁעַ
לְמֵימַר

ת״א כאשר תם. סוטה לה.

**רש״י**

(יא) **ויהי כאשר תם כל העם לעבור ויעבור ארון וגו׳**. לא כדרך שעברו האחרים אלא כמו שמפורש למטה בענין נתקו כפות רגלי הכהנים לאחוריהם אל החרבה על השפה שנכנסו בה שהיו עומדים אללה וחזרו המים לאחוריהם לילך כתמול שלשום נמלא ארון ונושאיו מלד זה וכל ישראל מלד זה נשא הארון את נושאיו ועבר: **לפני העם**. לעיני

**רד״ק**

ואחר כן עברו: (יא) ויהי כאשר תם כל העם וגו׳ לפני העם. פי׳ הארון והכהנים שהיו לפני העם קודם שתמו לעבור עברו אחרי עבור העם. או פי׳ כאשר תם כל העם לעבור המתינו על שפת הירדן עד שעבר הארון והלך לפני העם והלכו אחריו. או יהיה פי׳ לפני העם לעיני העם. ורז״ל פירשו בענין אחר כל זה הענין ופירושו עד קצה מי הירדן בירדן תעמדו בקצה אשר נכנסו ממנו ושם עמדו הכהנים והארון עד שעבר העם ופי׳שו נתקו כפות רגלי הכהנים אל החרבה אל החרבה אשר בצדם והיא השפה אשר נכנסו ממנה וחזרו לאחוריהם אל החרבה וזה שאמר ויעלו מן הירדן שעלו מן הירדן אל השפ׳ כדי שיחזרו המים למקומם קודם שיעבור הארון כדי להרא׳ להם נס אח׳ נמצאו ארון וכהני׳ מצד אחד וישראל מצד אחר והירדן מלא בניהם נשא ארון את נושאיו ועבר שנ׳ ויעבור ארון ה׳ לפני העם ואני תמה מזה הדרש מה הצריכם לזה לאלה הפסוקים כי כבר פירשנו אותם כלם לדעתנו ואפילו יהיה כדבריהם פי׳ קצה מי הירדן בשפה אשר נכנסו ממנה כאשר תם כל העם לעבור עבר הארון אחריהם ביבשה וכאשר נתקו כפות רגלי הכהנים אל החרבה מצד השני שבו המים למקומם ואנה ראו שארון מצד זה וישראל מצד זה ומה צריך לשאת ארון את נושאיו ולעבור ואם היה נס כזה לא היה הכתוב מפרש שהארון נשא את נושאיו למעלה מן המים ואפילו לפי שמפרש דבריהם כמשמעו שמפרש עד קצה מי הירדן הקצה שיצאו ממנו כמו שאנו מפרשים ומפרש ארון מצד זה וישראל מצד זה כי כלם היו מהשפה אשר יצאו ממנה אלא פי׳ מצד זה שהארון היה על שפת הירדן וישראל היו לפניו רחוקים וזהו כמצד אחר אם כן הארון שהיה אחרי העם איך אמר ויעבור לפני העם אלא נשא ארון את נושאיו ועבר לפני העם אף על פי כן מי הצריכם לזה הנס וכי קשה הוא לפרש שהמתינו אותו ישראל עד שעבר לפניהם כמו שפירשנו או פירוש לפני העם לעיני העם כמו שפירשנו והם שאמרו ידעו מה שאמרו כי דעתם רחבה מדעתנו: (יג) כארבעים אלף. הכ״ף כ״ף שיעור: (יד) גדל ה׳. שבקע הירדן לפניו כמו שבקע הים לפני משה: (טו) ויאמר

**צוה**

**רלב״ג**

ויתפרסם להם שאלו מקומם יעמדו מי הירדן נד אחד: (יא) והנה זכר שכבר מהרו העם לעבור יותר מהחוק הנהוג וידמה שכבר

**מנחת שי**

(יד) ויראו אותו. בספרי כ״י ודפוסים ישנים היו״ד במאריך והוא חד מן ד׳ חס׳ ע״פ המסורת וסימן במ״ג. (במערכת אות י׳ ועיין מ״ש שמואל א׳ ז׳ ז׳):

**מצודת דוד**

(יא) **ויעבור**. אחר שלוה יהושע להכהני׳ לעלות מן הירדן כמ״ש למטה אז עבר הארון ללכת לפני העם: (יג) **לפני ה׳**. ר״ל בשליחותו ש״מ:

**מצודת ציון**

(יג) **חלוצי**. מזוין כמו חלוצים תעברו (דברים ג׳): **ערבות**. ענינו כמו מדבר:

## Commentary Digest

had crossed, crossed now after the people.

13. *About forty thousand* — The tribes of Reuben and Gad had considerably more able-bodied men between the ages of twenty and sixty, as can be readily seen from the count in Num. XXVI. But it seems that only

and passed over. 11. And it was, when all the people had
completely passed over, that the Ark of the Lord passed over,
and the priests, *in the presence of the people.* 12. And the
children of Reuben, and the children of Gad, and half the tribe
of Manasseh, passed over armed before the children of Israel,
as Moses had spoken to them. 13. About forty thousand armed
for war passed over before the Lord to battle, to the plains
of Jericho. 14. On that day the Lord made Joshua great in
the sight of all Israel, and they feared him, as they had feared
Moses, all the days of his life. 15. And the Lord said to
Joshua, saying,

### Commentary Digest

*While they were still standing in the river bed of the Jordan, Joshua said to them: Know for what purpose you are crossing the Jordan. On the condition that you drive out all the inhabitants of the land etc."*[1] — R

*and the people hastened* — the setting up of the stones and their transfer. — K Out of respect for the Ark which waited for them to cross. — A and D. P explains that they crossed hurriedly like one who passes a tottering wall which causes the Almighty to be mindful of his sins.

11. *And it was, when all the people had completely passed over, that the Ark etc. passed over* — *"not after the manner in which the others had passed over, but as it is explained below in this episode,*[2] *the soles of the priests' feet were lifted up backwards to the dry land on the bank from which they had entered, beside which they were standing, and the waters returned backwards"* (? Tal. to their place, i.e. to the place where they were wont to flow) *"to flow as it had done heretofore. Hence, the Ark and its bearers are found to be on one side, and all Israel on the other side. The Ark picked up its bearers and passed over."* — R[3]

*in the presence of the people* — lit. before the people, *"i.e. before the eyes of the people,"* or in the presence of the people. — R According to tradition that the priests stood on the eastern side of the Jordan, we cannot interpret this passage literally, since the priests and the Ark crossed after the people, not before them. Therefore, R explains thus.

K explains that the Ark which had gone before the people before they

טז צַוֵּה אֶת־הַכֹּהֲנִים נֹשְׂאֵי אֲרוֹן הָעֵדוּת
וְיַעֲלוּ מִן־הַיַּרְדֵּן׃ יז וַיְצַו יְהוֹשֻׁעַ אֶת־
הַכֹּהֲנִים לֵאמֹר עֲלוּ מִן־הַיַּרְדֵּן׃ יח וַיְהִי
בַּעֲלוֹת הַכֹּהֲנִים נֹשְׂאֵי אֲרוֹן בְּרִית־יְהוָה
מִתּוֹךְ הַיַּרְדֵּן נִתְּקוּ כַּפּוֹת רַגְלֵי הַכֹּהֲנִים
אֶל הֶחָרָבָה וַיָּשֻׁבוּ מֵי־הַיַּרְדֵּן לִמְקוֹמָם
וַיֵּלְכוּ כִתְמוֹל־שִׁלְשׁוֹם עַל־כָּל־גְּדוֹתָיו׃
יט וְהָעָם עָלוּ מִן־הַיַּרְדֵּן בֶּעָשׂוֹר לַחֹדֶשׁ
הָרִאשׁוֹן וַיַּחֲנוּ בַּגִּלְגָּל בִּקְצֵה מִזְרַח

**תרגום**

למימר: טז פקיד ית כהניא נטלי ארונא דסהדותא ויסקון מן ירדנא: יז ופקיד יהושע ית כהניא למימר סקו מן ירדנא: יח והוה כד בעו למסק כהניא נטלי ארון קימא דיי מגו ירדנא אתנגידא פרסת רגלי כהניא ונחא על יבשתא ותבו מי ירדנא לאתריהון ואזלו כמאתמלי ומדקדמוהי על כל כיפוהי: יט ועמא סליקו מן ירדנא בעשרא לירחא קדמאה ושרו

ת"א נתקו כפות. סוטה לה: בעשור לחודש. ר"ה יג יבמות עא קדושין לח:

**רד"ק** (בעלות קרי)

ה' אל יהושע וגו' צוה את הכהנים. וכבר אמר כי כבר אמר למעלה ויעבור ארון ה' ועתה ספר היאך עבר כי הקב"ה אמר ליהושע קודם זה שיצוה את הכהנים שיעלו מן הירדן: (יח) ויהי בעלו' הכהנים. בבי"ת כתיב וקרי בכ"ף והענין אחד: וישבו מי הירדן כתמול שלשם על כל גדותיו. בא להודיע כי בשוב המים למקומם גם כן לא באו כאחד כיהיו שוטפים בירידתם ויציאתם חוץ מגדות הירדן אלא ירדו התחתונים עם קצת העליונים וכן מעט מעט עד אשר שבו כתמול שלשם ללכת על כל גדותיו: (יט) ויחנו בגלגל. והוא המלון אשר צוה ה' להניח שם האבנים ושם הקים יהושע ובו ביום שעברו באו הגלגל שנאמר במלון אשר תלינו בו הלילה ואמרו רז"ל כי יותר משישים מיל הוא הדרך שהלכו באותו היום מן הירדן ועד הגלגל וע"י נס הלכו הדרך ההוא אנשים ונשים וטף יותר משישים מיל

**רש"י**

העם: (טז) צוה את הכהנים. כאן פירש הכתוב את האמור למעלה היאך עבר ארון ה' והכהנים לפני העם וגו': ויעלו מן הירדן. ויעברו אין כתיב כאן אלא ויעלו למדנו שעל השפה שהיו עומדין אלא עלו ואי אפשר לומר שהיו עומדין אלא על שפת הירדן שבמערב שהרי נאמר למעלה נטבלו רגלי הכהנים בקצה המים ושם נאמר ויעמדו הכהנים וכל ישראל עוברים: (יח) נתקו כפות רגלי הכהנים. מן המים אל החרבה שאלמלא וישובו המים למקומם כמלא ארון מצד זה וישראל מצד זה נשא ארון את נושאיו ועבר ועל דבר זה נענש עוזא כשאחז בארון · נושאיו נשא עצמו לא כל שכן:

**מנחת שי**

(יח) ויהי בעלות. כתיב בבי"ת וק' בכ"ף והוא חד מן מלין דכתיבין בי"ת וקריין כ' וסימן במסרה רבתא. ורים הושע ורים דברי הימים: שלשם. בספרים מדוייקים מלא וכן ראוי על פי המסורת דפרשת ויאל במסרה גדולה (ל"א ה'):

**רלב"ג**

עשו זה כדי שיתבאר להם מדרגת יהושע בענין זה המופת כי אלו היה מוגבל זמן עמידת מי הירדן עד הזמן שהיה ראוי שיעברו בו העם לפי החק הנהוג. הי' ראוי כשמהרו לעבור שישובו מי הירדן כך זמן מה אחר עברם והנה ספר שתכף עבור העם עבר ארון ה' לפני העם ותכף שבו מי הירדן למקומם וזה גם כן היה במצות הש"י כדי שיתפרסם לישראל עולם זה המופת ר"ל שבכבר צוה הש"י את יהושע שיעלו הכהנים נושאי הארון שיעלו מהירדן תכף עבור העם: (יט) והנה זכר שהעם עלו מהירדן בעשור לחודש הראשון ויחנו בגלגל ושבכבר הקים יהושע שם י"ב האבנים אשר הרימו העם עשר שהכין

**מצודת ציון**

(יח) נתקו. נעתקו וסרו ממקומם:

## Commentary Digest

that this passage comes to magnify the miracle of the Ark's crossing, that even though the Jordan had returned to its previous swollen state of overflowing its banks, nevertheless, the Almighty transported the Ark across. — Iyun Jacob[5]

19. *and encamped in Gilgal* — the lodging place where the Lord had commanded Joshua to set up the stones. On the very day on which they crossed the Jordan, they arrived at Gilgal, a distance of over sixty mil.[6] Only by a miracle could a nation of that size with women and children travel that distance in one day. — K

20. *Joshua set up in Gilgal* — *"That is the lodging place where they lodged that night."* — R The stones were set up in Gilgal as a memorial of the miracle. The Bible does not state that he set them up "before the Lord" or "before the testimony" as is specified concerning the jar of manna[1]

16. Command the priests that bear the Ark of the testimony, that they come up out of the Jordan. 17. And Joshua commanded the priests, saying, Come up out of the Jordan. 18. And it was, when the priests that bore the Ark of the covenant of the Lord came up out of the midst of the Jordan, that *as soon as* the soles of the priests' feet were lifted up to the dry land, the waters of Jordan returned to their place, and flowed over all its banks, as before. 19. And the people came up out of the Jordan on the tenth day of the first month, and encamped in Gilgal, in the east border of Jericho.

## Commentary Digest

those up to the age of forty crossed the Jordan as picked troops to spearhead the invasion in Eretz Israel.[1]

*before the Lord* — before the people of the Lord. — J

16. *Command the priests* — "*Here the Scripture explains the aforementioned, how the Ark of the Lord and the priests passed over in the presence of the people etc.*" — R

*that they come up out of the Jordan* — "*that they cross, is not written here, but 'that they come up.' Hence, we deduce that they came up on the bank beside which they were standing. And it is impossible to say that they were standing beside the western bank of the Jordan, for it is stated above: The feet of the priests — were dipped in the edge of the water.*[2] *And there it is stated: And the priests — stood — and all Israel passed.*"[3] — R

18. *the soles of the priests' feet were lifted up* — "*from the water to the dry land which was beside them, and the waters returned to their place. Hence, the Ark is found to be on one side and Israel on the other side. Accordingly, the Ark lifted its bearers and passed over. And concerning this matter, Uzzah was punished when he took hold of the Ark.*[4] *If it bore its bearers, can it not be deduced by a fortiori conclusion that it can bear itself?*" — R[5] Here R presents Scriptural evidence to support the Talmudic account of the Ark's crossing the Jordan. K also agrees that the understanding of our Sages is highly superior to ours, and must, therefore, be accepted as explanation of this event.

*and flowed over all its banks as before* — They did not fall suddenly into the river bed, lest great flooding be caused. They, rather, returned slowly to their previous course and to their previous state of flowing over all the banks. — K and P. Others explain

מבני ישראל למען יהיה זה לזכרון לבני ישראל עד עולם וזה ממה שיורה כי במקום המקדש שמו אותו כמו הענין בצנצנת המן ובמטה אהרן שנתבאר בתורה שהושמו לפני משכן ה' למשמרת והנה נקבע המשכן בגלגל זמן מה כמו שיבא שכבר עשו בני ישראל שם הפסח בארבעה עשר יום לחודש ולא היה איפשר שיעשוהו שם שלא היה שם המשכן : (כ) והנה יראה שלא השמו האבנים האלה לפני העדות כמו הענין בצנצנת המן ומטה אהרן לשתי סבות האחת שלא נזכר בזה המקום זה אבל זכר שכבר הקימם יהושע בגלגל . והשנית שהוא ראוי שיהא הבדל עצום בין מופתי משה ומופת זולתו כמו שנזכר בסוף התורה ולזה אין ראוי שישתתפו אלו הדברים שהיו לזכרון לאלו המופתים במקום אחד עם שאלו האבנים יצטרך להם מקום גדול ולא יכילם המקום ההוא ועוד שכבר יהיה הבדל עצום בין צנצנת המן ומטה אהרן ובין האבנים האלה וזה כי צנצנת המן היה בו המופת מתמיד עד שמה שהיה נמס בחום השמש ישאר ויתקיים זה הזמן הארוך וכן היה הענין במטה אהרן עם השקדים שגמל ואלו הענינים גם כן מה שעושה בו המופת בעצמו ואולם האבנים לא היה בהם בעצמותם מן הזרות והפלא ולא היה מה שנעשה בו המופת אבל היו כבה באופן מה לזכר ענין זה המופת כמו שנזכר בזה המקום ולזה היה די שיהיו במקום שיהיה בו המשכן כי שם יבואו ישראל ברגלים שלש פעמים בשנה ויזכירום אלו האבנים ענין זה המופת עד עולם ולזה לא אמר בזה המקום שהקים יהושע אלו האבנים לפני השם אבל אמר שהקימם בגלגל כי די להזכיר זה המופת בזה האופן ומזה המקום יראה שאלו האבנים היו תמיד במקום משותף לכל ישראל כדי שיהיו זכרון מתמיד· לכולם כמו שנזכר פה והנה למדו רבותינו ז"ל ממה שנזכר פה בשבעה באדר מת משה וידמה שהסכימו שאותו אדר היה שלשים יום כי אז היו מקדשין החדש ע"פ הראיה ובו ביום שמת משה התחיל מספר השלשים יום שבכו אותו והנה היום· השני מניסן היה היום השלשים ולפי שמקלת היום ככלו הנה שלח או יהושע המרגלים ביום ההוא ובו ביום אמר לשוטרי ישראל כי בעוד שלשת ימים יעברו את הירדן והנה בסוף היום התשיעי לניסן לנו אלל הירדן וביום העשירי עברו את הירדן וחנו בגלגל ואולם אם היה בשנה ההיא אדר מעוברים והשבעה יום הנה יחויב שנאמר שבששה באדר מת משה ולפי שכבר אמר משה ביום ההוא בן מאה ועשרים שנה אנכי היום למדנו שבכמו היום שמת נולד והנה זכר אחר זה שזה המופת הוסיף מורך לב לכל מלכי האמורי והכנעני וכבר נתפרסם זה המופת לכולם מלד מה שראו בנכרתו מי הירדן שהיו אגלם עת מה כי כבר נכרתו מימי הירדן ממקום רגלי הכהנים עד היום וכאשר חקרו בזה מלאו שהסבה שיתה שהש"י הוביש מימי הירדן מפני בני ישראל עד עברם והנה נזכר בזה המקום שמה שעשה יהושע מאלו הדברים לפרסם זה המופת היה לפי שהוא מבשר מה לאסור יכבד לאולי מהשם ולזה ידמה שמשה לוהו בביאור איך יעשה זה כשיכרתו מי הירדן על ידו כדי שיגיע מזה לכל ישראל זה התועלת האפשרי שיגיע ממנו : והנה ראוי שנחקור בכאן בהיתר ספק מה אינו מעט יקרא בזה המופת אשר נזכר פה וזה שכבר השרישו ז"ל כי לא יתחדש במופתים דבר חדש ולזה הוקשא לרבא מה שאמר ואם בריאה יברא ה' מפני מ"ש אין כל חדש תחת השמש והיתר הספק הזה כשאמר שזה המופת היה למהר זמן פתיחת הארץ פיה וביאור זה כי זה יקרה לארץ באורך הזמנים כשיעלר בבטנה איד מה עשני כמו שנתבאר בספר האותות והמופת היה לעשות בזולת זמן מורגש מה שיעשהו הטבע בזמן ארוך וכן הענין בהתהפך המטה נחש אבל לא יחדש הש"י דבר חדש אלל הנמלאות כולם ולזה לא יתכן שיעשה מהמטה נחש ויהיה מטה ונחש יחד וכן לא תואר בעשות דבר מה שהיה מליאתו סותר עלמו כאילו תאמר עשיית מרובע הקטר שוה לצלעו או עשיית משולש מקוים ישרים שיהיו זויותיו פחות או יותר משתי זויות נצבות או עשיית אש קר ומה שדומה לזה ממה שמליאותו סותר נפשו ובהיות הענין כן והיה מטבע המים כשהיו מים בפועל שיהו מבקשים המקום השפל הנה ידמה שיהיה המופת בדברים אשר לא ייוחס לש"י לעשות זה המופת בכמו זה האופן ואם אמר אומר שכבר נתבאר בענין כבשן האש שבאו בו חנניה מישאל ועזריה ולא ניזוקו שכבר היה בלתי חם והוא אם אמרנו לו שהמופת לא היה שהוסר החום מהאש והוא אם הלא תראה שהאנשים שהשליכום שם מתו מחוזק החום אבל זה המופת היה אם בשהסיר הש"י במופת הטבע האשיי מהמקום שבאו בו חנניה וחבריו כמו שיראה מקלת דברי רבותי' ז"ל אם בשהקנה להם טבע שלא יוזקו בו מהאש כי כבר זכרו חכמי הרפואה שיש שם קלת דברים כשימשח אדם אחד אבר מאיבריו בהם לא יזיקיהו האש והמופת היה לעשות זה בזולת סבותיו כמו הענין בפתיחת הארץ ובהיות הענין כן הנה איך היה הענין בזה מי יתן והדע . ונאמר שכבר ידמה שנאמר שאין הנחת מים בלתי נגרים דבר חדש כי כבר יקרה בזה למים כשיהיה להם דבר מונע מהתנועה ואיפשר שחדש הש"י במופת באויר בסמוך למים ההם גשם ספירי עב מונע המים מהירידה או היה זה בשחדש רוח חזק שם במופת ידחה המים למקום ההוא ולא ייחס לבדת כמו הענין בקריעת ים סוף כמו שבארנו בביאורינו לדברי תורה כי הש"י הרבה אל מה שיהדר אל המלאת המופתים סבות מה ימעטו הזרות אשר בענין המופתים ההם ולזה תמלא שלוה ישעיהו בימתו דבלת תאנים על שחין חזקיה כי יש לו מבוא בזה מבוא מה ואע"פ שאי אפשר בו שירפא השחין בכמו זה הזמן המעט וכן תמלא במה שלוה אלישע לנעמן שירחץ שבע

פעמים בירדן כי הרחילה במים הקרים יש לה מבוא מה בזה כמו שהוא מפורסם אלא שלא תשלם בה הרפואה בזה האופן מזולת שיחובר לזה מופת . והנה הענין הזה בטבע כמו הענין במלאות התוריות כי הכל מסודר מהשם ית' ולזה כשיצטרך לשם ית' לשנות הטבע מלד מה שזהו יותר טוב בעת ההיא ממה שיסודר מהטבע הנה יתרחק ממנו המעט שאיפשר כי השם יתברך איננו שונה הסדור הטבעי כי הוא ברצונו וכן הענין בתורה ר"ל שכאשר יהיה יותר בעת ההיא הנטיה מדבריה הנה יהיה רשות לנביא או לב"ד לנטות מקצת דבריה אז כמו מעשה אליהו בהר הכרמל וכשיהיה זה כן הנה ראוי שיטו אז מדברי התורה היותר מעט שאיפשר ולזה תמצא במי שאחזו בולמוס שמאכילין אותו הקל תחלה . וכבר הותר זה הספק :

**ואולם** התועלות המגיעות מזה הספור הם י"ב :

**התועלת הראשון** הוא בעיון והוא שכבר תהיה הנבואה לנביא להשגחה על העם אשר הוא שלוח להם ולזה יחויב מזה שאם לא יצטרך העם שתגיע להם זאת ההודעה על יד איש אחר ראוי לנבואה מפני הגעתה להם על יד נביא יותר שלם ממנו שלא תגיע נבואה לאיש ההוא הראוי לנבואה בעניני העם ולזה ספר שלא נתנבא יהושע אלא אחר מות משה כי לא נצטרך לישראל ההודעה לזה על יד יהושע בשכבר נשלם להם זה באופן יותר שלם על יד משה :

**השני** הוא במדות והוא שראוי לתלמיד המבקש למוד השלמות האנושי מהמלמד הנאות לזה שיעמוד לפניו תמיד וישרתהו כי אז יתכן לו שילמד ממנו בכללות כל הדברים שירצה כן מהפילוסופיה העיונית או המדינית או מהענינים התוריים ולזה תמצא שאמר יהושע בהגעת הנבואה לו בשהוא משרת משה כאילו יאמר שמזה הלד הגיע לו מהשלמות מה שבעבורו היה ראוי לנבואה :

**השלישי** הוא להודיע שסבת בלתי עבור משה את הירדן היה חטאת העם וזה למדנו בעבור ב' דברים מזה הספור האחד הוא שבזה המקום שהתבאר בו שלא הסכים הש"י שיעבור משה את הירדן ולזה נתן סבה במה שלוה יהושע שיעבור את הירדן אחר היות משה מת תמלא שקרה אותו הש"י עבדו וזה ממה שיורה כי לא היה זה לו בחטאו ולזה אמר במשנה תורה גם בי התאנף ה' בגללכם וגו' ואם יקשה בעיניך מה שביארה התורה שזה היה על אשר מריתם את פי ה' לבלתי הקדישו בענין מי מריבה נאמר לך שזה לא יסתיר מ"ש גם בי התאנף ה' בגללכם וזה כי אולי היה נמשך לישראל מזאת ההקדשה מהתועלת באמונה בש"י מה שיהיו ראויים בו אל שתגיע להם ירושת הארץ בשלם שבפניהם על יד משה והשנית שכבר התבאר במה שיבא שכבר נתעלל יהושע בירושת הארץ וזה היה בסבה אחת השם למען נסות בם את ישראל השומרים הם את דרך ה' והוא מבואר שאם היה זה עושה ע"י משה היה משה משתדל בזה בתכלית יותר הלא תראה מה עשה לסיחון ולעוג שלא השאיר להם שריד במעט מהזמן :

**הרביעי** הוא במדות והוא שהוא ראוי למי שהוא טובה שישתדל בהצלחה בזריזות ולא יתעלל בזה ר"ל כי לא ידע אם הימים הבאים היו טובים כאלה או יפרידהו המות ולזה תמלא שאמר השם ליהושע וכבר היה עמו כאשר היה עם משה על שלא יתעלל איש בפניו הזהירו שיעשה זה בזריזות כדי שתשלם על ידו ירושת הארץ לישראל כי הש"י לא יקלר מלכת הטובות ביותר שלם שבפנים ואע"פ שכבר היה יהושע ידוע אלל חכמתו האלהי' שכבר יתעלל יהושע בזה הנה עכ"ז הזהירו שישתדל בזה בתכלית כי בבחירה האנושית הוא מושלת ע"ז כמו שביארנו בשלישי מספר מלחמות ה' ולזה אמר לו חזק ואמץ כי אתה תנחיל וגו' :

**החמישי** הוא להודיע כי ההתמדה בעיון בתורה התמימה והמשכן אחריה סבה אל שיצליחו דרכי האדם ושישלם בעיון שהוא סבה להצלחת דרכי האדם ולזה אמר רק חזק ואמץ מאד לשמור לעשות ככל התורה וגו' כי אז תצליח ואז תשכיל כאילו התחכם הש"י להטיב את ישראל בענין זאת הירושה באופן שיהיו ראויים אל שתגיע להם באופן שלם והנה פירשנו אמרו ואז תשכיל מענין השכל וידוע אותי שאם היה מענין ההצלחה יהיה אמרו ואז תשכיל מותר אין צורך בו :

**הששי** הוא במדות והוא שמי שיצטרך לעשות פועל א' לתועלת מה והוא איפשר שיגיעו מהפועל ההוא תועלות אחרים כשיעשהו אותו באופן מה הנה ראוי שלא יקלר מהגיע הפועל ההוא כל התועלות האפשריות וזה יהיה בשיעשהו באופן אשר יגיע ממנו שאר התועלות וכ"ש שראוי לו זה כשתהיה נמשך משאר התועלות השמר התועלת המכוון בזה הפועל באופן היותר שלם שאפשר ולזה תמלא כי יהושע כאשר הצטרך להכרית את מי הירדן למען יעברו העם בו בקלות ובזולת סכנה לחבר לזה מה שימשכו ממנו תועלות רבות ולזה הודיעם תחלה שבעוד שלשת ימים יהיה זה הפועל למען יכינו להם צידה כי ימים לידה לדרך אשר הם הולכים בה והיא הלוך לבוא לרשת את הארץ שהוא מלאכה לא ליום אחד ולא לשנים אלא לזמן ארוך עם שזה יוסיף לישראל באמונה ביהושע כשיראו הגעת מה שיראה להם בעת שהגביל אותו והודיעם כי בנוח כפות רגלי הכהנים בירדן יכרתו מימיו ושאחר עבור העם תכף יעלו הכהנים נושאי הארון מהירדן וישובו מי הירדן למקומם כי זה ממה שיישיר העם להתקרב לעבודת הש"י אשר הוא שליט בכמו אלו הנפלאות העצומות ולשמוע למלות יהושע נביאו כי זה כלו ממה שיישיר העם אל שתבוא להם ירושת הארץ באופן שלם ולפרסם זה המופת הנפלא הקים יהושע האבנים

## Commentary Digest

and Aaron's staff which had sprouted, blossomed, and borne ripe almonds.[2]

There are three reasons that the monument of stones was not placed in this holy place. They are as follows: (1) The miracles performed by Joshua the disciple should not be considered equal to those of Moses the master; (2) The monument of stones required a large area, more than the tabernacle afforded; (3) The jar of manna was a constant miracle, the preservation of a highly perishable food, which would usually melt in the sun. Likewise, Aaron's staff, its blossoms, and almonds, bore constant witness to the miracle. The monument of stones, however, was but a memorial to a miracle, no proof nor evidence thereof. It was, therefore, sufficient to place them in the vicinity of the sanctuary, not inside. — G

V. 8 tells that the twelve men placed the stones in Gilgal without arranging them in any order or formation. The Bible, therefore, tells us here that Joshua set them up to form a monument. — M The twelve men placed them there as a sign for their children. Accordingly, the stones themselves sufficed this purpose. Joshua, however, set them as a memorial for all posterity. Therefore, it was necessary to arrange them as a monument. — M

21. *When your children* — i.e. your posterity. — M. Your infants and future children. — K

*their fathers* — of future generations. — M

*What are these stones?* — Note the absence of the words, "to you." which appear in v. 6. This indicates that the two questions are not identical. The above deals with the children of those who crossed the Jordan. They themselves witnessed the miracle. They ask their parents, "What are these stones to you?" Why do you need them? You saw the Jordan dry up. Joshua instructs the parents to explain that the stones signify that we crossed the Jordan not by our own power, nor by natural forces, but by a miracle performed by the Almighty. At exactly the moment the priests' feet were dipped into the waters of the Jordan, the waters dried up before the ark of the Lord. Here, the Bible deals with future generations who are unfamiliar with the episode of the crossing of the Jordan. Innocently, they ask, "What are these stones?" Upon this, Joshua instructs the people —

22. *And you shall let your children know* — Through this monument you shall let your children know, saying, — Israel came over this Jordan on dry land — Here he does not explain the details of the miracle as above, only the fact of the cleaving of the Jordan for those who had no previous knowledge thereof. — M

Midrashically, the children ask the purpose of stones to commemorate this great event. Thereupon, the fathers reply, "Israel came over this Jordan on dry land." By the virtue of our patriarch Jacob, who was called Israel, we crossed this Jordan. The stones represent the twelve stones which he

ירחו: כ ואת שתים עשרה האבנים
האלה אשר לקחו מן־הירדן הקים
יהושע בגלגל: כא ויאמר אל־בני ישראל
לאמר אשר ישאלון בניכם מחר את־
אבותם לאמר מה האבנים האלה:
כב והודעתם את־בניכם לאמר ביבשה
עבר ישראל את־הירדן הזה: כג אשר־
הוביש יהוה אלהיכם את־מי הירדן

בגלגלא בסיפי מדנח
יריחו: כ וית תרתא עשר
אבניא האלין דנסיבו
מן ירדנא אקים יהושע
בגלגלא: כא ואמר
לבני ישראל למימר
דישאלון בניכון מחר
ית אבהתהון למימר
מה אבניא האלין:
כב ותהודעון ית בניכון
למימר ביבשתא עבר
ישראל ית ירדנא הדין:
כג דיביש יי אלהכון ית
מי ירדנא מן קדמיכון
עד

ת״א באים עברה האבנים . סוטה לה לז:

**רד״ק**

באיתו היום: (כה) אשר ישאלון בניכם הנולדים הקטנים ואשר יולדו: (כג) אשר הוביש ה׳ את מי הירדן מפניכם. דברי יהושע לבני ישראל ליוצאים ממצרים ולילודים במדבר אשר הוביש מפנינו אנחנו שיצאנו ממצרים: (כד) יראתם. לגזרת פעל כי

**רש״י**

(ב) הקים יהושע בגלגל׳ הוא המלון אשר לנו בו הלילה:

**רלב״ג**

האבנים תחת כפות רגלי הכהנים כדי שיראום כל ישראל כמו שזכרנו ולזה לשנים העשר איש אשר הכין להכין שתים עשרה האבנים להזכיר זה המופת בישראל עד עולם למען יראו תמיד אותם ויהיה זה סבה אל שיאריכו ימיהם על הארץ הטובה שהש״י נותן להם אשר הגיעו לירושתה עם שזה יהיה סבה להגיע להם ירושת הארץ באופן שלם כמו שבארנו ולא עם זה שיהיה זה המופת ביום למען יתפרסם זה המופת לכל מלכי האמורי אשר בעבר הירדן ימה ולכל מלכי הכנעני אשר על הים וימס לבבם מפני בני ישראל כי זה כלו ממה שיעזור על נצחם והגעת ירושת הארץ על ישראל בשלמות ולזאת הסבה שלח יהושע מרגלים להזק לב ישראל כשידעו שנפלה אימתם על כל הגוים ההם שהם באים להלחם עמם כמו שבארנו במה שקדם והנה זכר בזה הספור שיהושע עשה זה כאשר צוהו משה ע״ה כי משה פירשו אל שיעשה זה הענין בזה האופן השלם כמו שזכרנו במה שקדם:

השביעי והוא במדות הוא שהוא ראוי למי שירצה להציל איש מה מיד אחר שירצה עצמו בדבריו כאלו הוא הוסק שיפול האיש ההוא ביד רודפו כי בזה ימלא לו המכוון בהצלתו וזה שבכר ישמרהו רודף על דבריו ויתכן לו בתחבולות למלט הנרדף. ולזה תמצא כי כששלח המלך יריחו אל רחב הפונדקית שתוציא האנשים אליו מבני ישראל אמרה אחר שהלשינה אותם שאמת הוא זה אך לא הערת בזה כי אלו ידעה היותם מבני ישראל היתה מגלה זה למלכות ולעם כדי להפסם וספרה שכבר יצאו אחר שהגיע הסך הלילה ולא ידעה אנה הלכו ונתנה עצה שירדפו מהר אחריהם כי ישיגום וזה ממה שהראתם בהיא הוסקת שיפלו בידם ולזה האמינו יותר לדבריה ונשלמה בזה ההצלה למרגלים אשר כונה אליה:

השמיני והוא במדות הוא שראוי למי שירצה להציל איש מה בזה האופן הנזכר שישמר שלא יכזב בתחבולו׳ דבריו במה שיתכן שתשיגהו התפיסה ולזה תמצא שרחב לא אמרה שלא באו אליה האנשים מבני ישראל כי זה ממה שישיגהו בו התפיסה בקלות ויהיה זה סבה אל שלא יגיע התכלית שכונה וכאשר אמרה שכבר יצאו משם זכרה לזה מאמר יהיה לה התנצלות בו אם ימצא מאמרה זה כוזב בכל או בקצתו והוא שכבר אמרה שזה היה בעת שהיה השער לסגור בחשך ויתכן מפני החשך שנדמה לה שיצאו שניהם ולא יצא כי אם אחד או נשארו שניהם כי זה אפשר שיקרה מפני החשך:

## Commentary Digest

upon the Israelites who were born after that great event. — M

### CHAPTER 5

1. *who were on the side of the Jordan westward* — *"on the side to which the children of Israel had crossed, i.e. the west side. And previously, they had been on the east side."*—R

*until they had passed over* — The K'thib is "until we had passed over." These are the words of the author writing in the first person. — K

*that their heart melted* — just as was predicted by Joshua in the previous verse.

To connect this verse with the following, w.e explain thus: Since the kings of the Amorites were frightened because of the drying up of the Jordan's waters, Joshua was not afraid to circumcise the people and leave them vulnerable to attack. — M

*nor was there spirit in them anymore* — It was as though the spirit

20. And these twelve stones, which they took out of the Jordan, Joshua set up in Gilgal. 21. And he spoke to the children of Israel, saying, When your children ask their fathers in time to come, saying, What are these stones? 22. Then, you shall let your children know, saying, Israel came over this Jordan on dry land. 23. For the Lord your God dried up the waters of the Jordan

## Commentary Digest

placed around his head when he lodged in Bethel and experienced the dream of the ladder. — Alshich.[1] This is an illustration of the maxim: The deeds of the fathers are a sign for the children. The Midrash illustrates how the famine in Canaan which took place in Abraham's times was the forerunner of the one in the time of Jacob and his children. Abraham's descent to Egypt was likewise the forerunner of Jacob's descent to Egypt.[2] Similarly, when Jacob crossed the Jordan, he merely touched it with his staff and it was cloven before him. This miracle was the forerunner of Joshua's cleaving the Jordan.[3]

23. *For the Lord your God dried up the waters of the Jordan from before you* — both those who came out of Egypt and those who were born in the desert. — K

*which he dried up from before us* — those who came out of Egypt. — K

The underlying motive here is continuity of divine manifestation. Although Moses was the channel through whom the Almighty transmitted His law, and "there arose not in Israel again a prophet as Moses,"[4] yet the guiding hand of the Eternal continues to manifest itself in all subsequent generations. This is illustrated in this passage through the miracles performed by Joshua, the successor of Moses. The passage emphasizes the similarity of the miracles performed by master and disciple, to raise Joshua's prestige in the eyes of the people. The repetition of "the Lord your God" implies that it was the same God Who performed the miracle of drying up the waters of the Jordan Who dried up the Red Sea; there is no other.—A

24. *That all the people of the earth might know the power of the Lord, that it is mighty* — lit. the hand. The benefits to be derived from this miracle are twofold; one, that all the nations will know the power of God, and two, —

*that you might fear the Lord your God forever.* — A The fear of the Almighty's retribution will be cast on the nations who did not live at the time of the splitting of the Red Sea, and the awe of His majesty will fall

מִפְּנֵיכֶם עַד־עָבְרְכֶם כַּאֲשֶׁר עָשָׂה יְהוָה
אֱלֹהֵיכֶם לְיַם־סוּף אֲשֶׁר־הוֹבִישׁ מִפָּנֵינוּ
עַד־עָבְרֵנוּ׃ כד לְמַעַן דַּעַת כָּל־עַמֵּי הָאָרֶץ
אֶת־יַד יְהוָה כִּי חֲזָקָה הִיא לְמַעַן יְרָאתֶם
אֶת־יְהוָה אֱלֹהֵיכֶם כָּל־הַיָּמִים׃ ה א וַיְהִי
כִשְׁמֹעַ כָּל־מַלְכֵי הָאֱמֹרִי אֲשֶׁר בְּעֵבֶר
הַיַּרְדֵּן יָמָּה וְכָל־מַלְכֵי הַכְּנַעֲנִי אֲשֶׁר
עַל־הַיָּם אֵת אֲשֶׁר־הוֹבִישׁ יְהוָה אֶת־מֵי
הַיַּרְדֵּן מִפְּנֵי בְנֵי־יִשְׂרָאֵל עַד־עָבְרָנוּ

עברם קרי

**תרגום**

עַד דַּעֲבַרְתּוּן כְּמָא דַעֲבַד יְיָ אֱלָהֲכוֹן לְיַמָּא דְסוּף דִי יַבֵּשׁ מִן קֳדָמָנָא עַד דַעֲבַרְנָא׃ כד בְּדִיל דְיִדְעוּן כָּל עַמְמֵי אַרְעָא יַת גְבוּרְתָּא דַיְיָ אֲרֵי תַקִיפָא הִיא בְּדִיל דְתִדְחֲלוּן יַת יְיָ אֱלָהֲכוֹן כָּל יוֹמַיָא׃ ה א וַהֲוָה כַד שְׁמָעוּ כָּל מַלְכֵי אֱמוֹרָאֵי דִי בְעִבְרָא דְיַרְדְּנָא מַעַרְבָא וְכָל מַלְכֵי כְנַעֲנָאָה דִי עַל יַמָּא יַת דְיַבֵּשׁ יְיָ יַת מֵי יַרְדְּנָא מִן קֳדָם בְּנֵי יִשְׂרָאֵל עַד דַעֲבָרוּ

ואתמסי

**ת״א** ויהי כשמוע . וכתיב קנו : את אשר הוביש . (סוטה לב) :

**רש״י**

ה (א) **אשר בעבר** הירדן ימה . לצד שעברו בני ישראל הוא צד של מערבי ועד עכשיו היו בעבר מזרחי :

**רד״ק**

**וימם** יראתם לגזרת פעל והוא עבר במקום עתיד כמו תראו ורבים כמוהו : (א) עד עברנו . עד עברם קרי והם דברי הכותב :

**מנחת שי**

(כד) יראתם. בקמץ הרי״ש ולית כותיה כתמול. מלא (וע׳ המפ״ג הכ״ל ובמ״ש שם): ה (א) **עברנו** וימם עברם ק׳ וכן כתב רד״ק ׳ ובספר אחד כתיבת יד כתוב עליו עברם ק׳ ופליגין עליו :

**רלב״ג**

**התשיעי** והוא במדות הוא שכשיבוא הסכנה שתהיה סכנה מה לאנשים אשר ילכו אחד בהלכתם ראוי שיסדר היותם במקומו׳ **מתחלפים** כדי שאם ימלא האחד אולי ימלט השני ולזה תמצא עם שדבריו יסבלו כי אולי לא ילכו כי אם האחד ונדמה לו בהשך שילכו שניהם והנה נבאר אחד מהם אל הפתח והיא לא הרגישה ולזה יעזרום דבריה להציל את השני ולזה תמצא ברחב שלפנה לכל אחד מאלו המלאכים במקום מיוחד שאם ימלא האחד אולי ימלט השני:
**העשירי** והוא במדות הוא שראוי שלא יקצר האדם על מה שאפשר לו הצלתו כשלא יהיה כל מה שיהיה בהצלתו אבל ראוי שיתחדל להציל מה שאפשר להצילו אם רב אם מעט ולזה תמצא כי כשראתה רחב שאי אפשר לה הצלת עמה בכללם בפנים מהפנים השתדלה להציל בית אביה ואמנם ראתה שאי איפשר לה הצלת עמה בשום צד לפי שזה היה ממנה אם בתפישת המרגלים אם כשתשאל מהם זה ותבלהם בשלום והולם בתפישת המרגלים לא ישלם לה זה כי כבר יוכלו ישראל להלחם עמהם בזולת רגול הארץ לפי מה שנתפרסם לה מעוצ׳ יכלת אלהי ישראל שישנ׳ מנהג הטבע בעבור ישראל ואם תשאל מהם הצלת כל עמה הנה הוא מבוא׳ שזה לא יאות להם בשום פנים עם שיהיה עם גדול כזה בזול׳ הארץ ולזה השתדלת בהצל׳ המרגלי׳ לפי מה שאפשר לה להחיו׳ אותה ובית אביה והשביעה אותם בשם אלהי ישראל על זה טרם הפרדם ממנה:
**האחד עשר** והוא במדות הוא שהוא ראוי לאדם שיעשה כל דבריו בחכמה גם בעת הפחד יתישב במה שיעשהו שלא תשיגהו החרטה עליו ולזה תמצא במרגלי׳ איך דקדקו באלו התנאי׳ עם רחב באופ׳ שלא ישיג׳ בזה מה שתשיגהו עליו החרטה אחר זה כמו שביארנו :
**השנים עשר** הוא במדות והוא שאין ראוי להטיל קנאה בין האנשים לתת יתרון לאיש א׳ על האחר במה שהם ראוים בו על אופן אחד וגזה תמצא שבחר יהושע איש אחד למטה באופן שיהיו י״ב כמספר שבטי בני ישראל להכין האבנים שפיו מוגבלים לסיוע

**מצודת דוד**

(כד) **למען יראתם** . כמו ולמען יראתם ותחסר הוי״ו וכמוהו [illegible]

## Commentary Digest

A, and D. Y, however, quoting G.R., renders חרבות צרים as flint knives. The Rabbis explain this as an indication that previous practice was to perform the circumcision by means of sharp stones, as witness also the account in Ex. I:25, of Zipporah circumcising her son with a stone. Metal instruments were used only after the defeat of Goliath by David, as a reward to the metal protecting Goliath's forehead for giving way before the stone flung by David.[3] Cf. Maimonides, Laws of Circumcision:[4] All cutting instruments may be used... Iron is preferable, and all Israel has a custom of using a sharp knife.

*and circumcise again* — and again until they are all circumcised. — K

*the second time* — "for they had already circumcised a large assembly

from before you, until you passed over, as the Lord your God did to the Red Sea, which He dried up from before us, until we passed over: 24. That all the people of the earth might know the power of the Lord, that it is mighty: that you might fear the Lord your God forever.

## 5

1. And it came to pass, when all the kings of the Amorites, who were on the side of the Jordan westward, and all the kings of the Canaanites who were by the sea, heard that the Lord had dried up the waters of the Jordan from before the children of Israel until they had passed over,

### Commentary Digest

of life had left them, they were so frightened. — D

2. *At that time* — when they arrived at Gilgal and Joshua set up the monument. At this point the Lord orders Joshua to strengthen the observance of commandments. He started with circumcision, as is explained in v. 4. — A Furthermore, the festival of Passover was rapidly approaching. Since all those who were not circumcized in the desert would be disqualified from participating in the sacrifice of the paschal lamb, the Lord commanded him to circumcise them. The purifying waters of the red heifer had already been sprinkled upon them in anticipation of this event. — K and A[1]

*At that time* — the day following their strenuous journey from the Jordan to Gilgal. The Lord commanded them to circumcise under such trying circumstances and they eagerly obeyed. — Azulai from Eybeschutz

*Make* — or fashion, prepare. — K

*for yourself* — Joshua was charged with the performance of this precept. He was to be assisted or perhaps, represented by others since it was impossible for one person to circumcise the entire nation in four days. — K and A

*sharp knives* — Heb. חרבות צרים, "*according to Targum, sharp knives, also 'You have turned back the edge of his sword.'*[1]* *When the sharp edge is turned sideways and does not cut well. And so: 'Every weapon which will be sharpened against you.'*"[2] — R These are examples of the root צור being used to express sharpness. It is in no way related with צור a rock, or stone. This opinion is shared by K, G,

וַיִּמַּס לְבָבָם וְלֹא־הָיָה בָם עוֹד רוּחַ מִפְּנֵי בְּנֵי־יִשְׂרָאֵל׃ ב בָּעֵת הַהִיא אָמַר יְהוָה

תולדות אהרן עוד רוח זבחים קטז:

**תרגום**

וְאִתְמְסִי לִבְהוֹן וְלָא אִשְׁתְּאַרַת בְּהוֹן עוֹד רוּחַ מִן קֳדָם בְּנֵי יִשְׂרָאֵל׃ ב בְּעִידָנָא הַהִיא אֲמַר יְיָ לִיהוֹשֻׁעַ

## רד"ק

(ב) בעת ההיא. בעוד שהיו בגלגל צוה לו האל למול כדי שיעשו פסח כי בי' לחדש עברו ובג' ימים היה להם להיות נכונים לעשות הפסח ולהזות ולטבול כי טמאי מתי' היו בהם וישיהיו נמולים כלם כדי שיקריבו הפסח בי"ד וארז"ל כי בי' לחדש ביום בואם הזו כלם הזאה ראשונה שהיא הזאת ג' ובערב הפסח עשו הזאה שנייה שהיא הזאת ז' שהרי צריך בין הזאה להזאה ד' ימים ומלו באלו ד' ימים וטבלו ועשו פסחיהם בטהרה ומפני מה לא מלו הילודים במדבר ארז"ל כי מ' שנים שהיו ישראל במדבר לא נשבה להם רוח צפונית כי היכי דלא ליבדרו ענני כבוד לפי' לא מלו כי רוח צפונית רפואה למכת דם וזולתה סכנה ואמר ביומא דעיבא וביומא דשות' לא מהלינן ולא מסוכרינ' פי' אין מלין ואין מקיזין שותא הוא רוח קדים כי היא סכנה למוציא דם ואם יאמר אדם וכי כל יום ויום כשהזכר נמול אדם שמור לו רוח צפונית יש לומר הטעם כי בכל יום נושבת כמו שארז"ל ד' רוחות מנשבות בכל יום ורוח צפונית עם כל אחד מהן וברוב הימים היא לבדה גוברת על שאר הרוחות לפי' מלין בכל יום על הרוב ורוח צפונית היא המפזרת העננים כמו שכתוב רוח עברה ותטהרם ועל רוח צפונית הוא אומר כי אין יום בהיר וטהור אלא עם רוח צפונית וכן הוא אומר מצפון זהב יאתה ועם שאר הרוחות ימצאו העננים לרוב שאינן מתפזרות מפניהם ואף על פי שרוח צפונית עמהם כמו שאמרנו היא טפילה להם אבל בהיותה גוברת היא מפזרת העננים ולפי שבמדבר לא נשבה בטלו המילה ורז"ל לא אמרו טעם למה אין נשמרים עתה מלימול ביומה דשות' אבל אמרו כיון שהרגילו אינו מזיק וכן אמרו והאידנא דדשו בה רבים שומר פתאים ה' ואם יאמר אדם יכול היה הקב"ה להשיב רוח צפונית ולא יתבדרו ענני כבוד ולא תבטל מצות מילה אמת כי לא יבצר ממנו מזמה יתברך ויתע' והוא ית' המצוה על המילה לשמנה ימים הוא החריש מהם ולא הזהירם למול הילודים כל אותן שנים לפי שהמצוה אינה בטלה כי אם לא היתה בזמנה יכולה להיות אחר זמן ובעבור האריך זמן המצוה לא ישנה הקב"ה מנהג העולם כי אע"פ שמשנה מנהג העולם בקצת הנסים בקריע' ים סוף הירדן ועמיד' השמש לא יעשה כן ברוב הנסים כי אפי' בנצוח המלחמות ועזרו לאוהביו היה עושה ע"י סבה כמנהג העולם במלחמות כמו שצוה מלחמת יריחו הקפת העיר בשופרות כמו שעושין הצרים על עיר להפחידם ולתבהילם וכמו שצוה במלחמת העי שים לך אורב לעיר מאחריה כמו שהוא מנהג העולם וכן במלחמות אחרות ולא נוכל לומר כי שלא ברצון הש"י נמנעו מלימול הילודים במדבר כי לא ראינו שהוחיכם נביא על זה שלא מלו כל אותן שנים שהיו במדבר ומפני זה לא עשו גם כן פסח כי אם בשנה השנית שיצאו ממצרים לפי שהיו ערלים ומילת הזכרים אפי' מקצת מעכבת מעשות הפסח שנ' המול לו כל זכר ואז יקרב לעשותו ויש דרש כי שבט לוי מלו במדבר וסמכו זה לפסוק ובריתך ינצורו ויש לפרש ג"כ כי לפי' לא מלו כל אותן השנים לפי שנ' על פי ה' יחנו ועל פי ה' יסעו ולא היו יודעים יום נסעם ואם היו מלים הילודים והיו נוסעים יום המילה היו הנמולים בסכנה מפני הדרך וזה הוא שאמר כי לא מלו אותם בדרך כי הנה ראינו מרע"ה איחר זמן מילת בנו בעבור הדרך וזהו שאמר כי לא מלו אותם בדרך וא"ת הנה ראינו שנענש משה על עכוב המילה ההיא כמו שכתוב ויבקש המיתו לא נענש אלא לפי שלא נתעכב במדין עד מול בנו ועד חיותו כי ביום נסעו לא נסע על פי הדבור כי אע"פ שאמ' לו הקב"ה לך שוב מצרים לא אמר לו שיסע בו ביום והי' לו למול את בנו ולהתעכב עד חיותו ואח"כ ללכת מצרים במצות הבור' ועל כן הוכיחו בדרך על יד החולי ושמר לו עד שהיה במלון שיוכל למול שם ולהתעכב שם ומפני זה עשו פסח במדבר בשנה השנית כי מלו כלם לפי שלא היו בדרך כי לא נסעו כל אותה שנה כי עשו המשכן שם במדבר סיני ולא אמר כי לא מלו אלא הילודים בדרך וכל זמן שהיו במדבר סיני לא היו בדרך וזהו טעם הנכון בעיני: עשה לך. תקן והכן כמו וימהר לעשות אותו ופי' לך לעצמך שיהיה הוא המל ואחרים עמו כי לא יתכן שיהושע לבדו מל כל הערלים שהרי אמר לו חרבות צורי' ואילו היה הוא המל לבדו די היה בחרב אחד ועוד בארבעה ימים היאך היה יכול יהושע לבדו למול כל הילודים במדבר זה לא יתכן או יתכן שלא מל הוא אחד מהם אבל צוה אותם למול ואמ' לך כי עליו מוטל כי הוא היה מנהיגם ומה שאמר וימל כמו ויבן שלמה את הבית והדומים להם: חרבות צורים. כתרגומו אזמלון חריפין איזמלים חדים וכן אף תשיב צור חרבו ונסמך המתואר אל התואר כמו מי המרים בני שלשים או יהיה צורים שם זולתי תאר ויהיה פי' חרבות שיהיו להם

## רלב"ג

לזכרון לבני ישראל: (ב) בעת ההיא אמר ה' אל יהושע עד אז יבנה יהושע. הרבות צורים הרצון בו חרבות החדים והם הנעשים מהנחשת אליי"ר בלע"ז. והמנהג לוהו כדי שישיגם יהושע בזה המעט מהצער שאפשר בו כי יתכן בכמו אלו החרבות שיהיו בתכלית מהחדות ולזה תרגם יונתן אזמלון חריפין: ושוב מול את בני ישראל שנית. שב אל כלל העם וזה שכבר נמולו בלאתם ממצרים לתכלית שינחלו אז את הארץ וכאשר חטאו עונותיהם ונגזר עליהם המות ואיחור עד ארבעים שנה מירושת הארץ הוללכו עתה שנית לכמו זה הפועל ואולם שזאת

## מצודת דוד

ה (א) ולא היה וגו'. אמר בדרך הפלגה וגוזמא כאלו הלך מעמם רוח החיוני לגודל הפחד:

# Commentary Digest

4. *Now this is the reason* — lit. and this is the thing; i.e. this is the thing because of which Joshua circumcised the people, since they had not been circumcised on the way. — K D explains: And this is the reason that Joshua alone circumcised the entire nation and found no one capable of assisting him, since all the men of war who had left Egypt died on the way, and all those born in the desert were themselves uncircumcised, and had to be circumcised at this time. The difficulties involved in this interpretation are obvious: (1) Even if we grant that Joshua was the sole circumciser of all the thousands of Israel, as D explains, there were many people who left Egypt under twenty years of age, who did not die in the desert; (2) the Levites circumcised their children in the desert, and could, therefore assist Joshua in circumcising the people. A explains: And this is the reason why

that their heart melted, nor was there spirit in them anymore, because of the children of Israel. 2. At that time the Lord said

## Commentary Digest

*on the night of their departure from Egypt,*[1] *and this was the second time, for the entire forty years that they were in the desert, the north wind did not blow for them, and they did not have any day suitable for circumcision, as we learned in Jeb.*[1]* *Our Rabbis state, however, 'the second time' refers the uncovering the corona at circumcision,"* (i.e. splitting the membrane and pulling it back) *"which Abraham was not commanded to do."* — R[1]** The Talmud goes to great lengths to exonerate our forefathers for their failure to perform the rite of circumcision during their wandering in the desert. We are told that the atmospheric conditions necessary for healing the wound were absent the entire forty years. The north wind necessary for this did not blow lest the clouds of glory be dispersed. An alternate reason given is that the fatigue and weakness incurred from constant traveling made this operation dangerous. Since they were obliged to move along with the pillar of cloud, they could not wait for the wound to heal. The tribe of Levi, however, risked the consequences and practiced circumcision. This is the simple interpretation of the passage. The rabbis, however, find a superfluous expression in the words, "again" and "the second time." They expound this expression to require an additional act of circumcision, the splitting of the membrane and pulling it down to expose the corona. The act of פריעה (uncovering) was practiced by Abraham although he had not been enjoined to do so. At Moses' time, it was practiced as a part of the Oral Law. Now, it was merely given the status of Holy Writ, as no really new law could be introduced after the closing of the Torah.[1]*** The Midrash relates that in Egypt, when the Israelites were circumcised, Joshua performed the circumcision, Aaron the "uncovering," and Moses gave the wine for the blessing. — T Therefore, Joshua was honored with performing this precept the second time. Hence, the word "שנית," the second time.

3. *the hill of the foreskins — "It was given this appelation to commemorate the event, because the foreskins were made into a sort of mound, or hillock."* — R[2] Y[3] relates that the Israelites took the foreskins and the blood, and covered them with the sand of the desert, forming a hillock. This is the origin of the practice to cover the severed foreskin with earth, to which Israel is compared in the Almighty's promise to Jacob.[4] Others explain that this was a natural hill, which was given the appelation, "the hill of the foreskins," to commemorate the event of the mass circumcision. — J, K, G, and D

אל־יהושע עשה לך חרבות צרים ושוב מל את־בני־ישראל שנית: ג ויעש־לו יהושע חרבות צרים וימל את־בני ישראל אל־גבעת הערלות: ד וזה הדבר אשר־מל יהושע כל־העם היצא ממצרים הזכרים כל אנשי המלחמה מתו במדבר בדרך בצאתם ממצרים:

ליהושע עבד לך אזמלין חריפין ותוב גזר ית בני ישראל תנינות: ג ועבד ליה יהושע אזמלין חריפין וגזר ית בני ישראל בגבעתא וקרא ליה גבעת ערלתא: ד ודין פתגמא די גזר יהושע כל עמא דנפק ממצרים דכריא כל גברי מגיחי קרבא מיתו במדברא באורחא במפקהון

ה"א חרבות צורים. יבמות ע"א (ר"ה נט):

### רש"י

(ב) חרבות צרים. כתרגומו אזמלון חריפין וכן אף תשיב צור חרבו (תהלים פ"ט) כשהחריפות נהפך לאחור ואינו חותך יפה. וכן כל כלי יוצר עליך (ישעיה נ"ד): שנית. שמלו כבר בליל יציאתם ממצרים קהל גדול יחד וזו פעם שנית שכל הארבעים שנה שהיו במדבר לא נשבה להם רוח צפונית ולא היה להם יום נוח למול כמו ששנינו ביבמות. ורבותינו אמרו שנית זו פריעת מילה שלא נתנה לאברהם אבינו: (ג) גבעת הערלות. על שם המאורע נקרא שנעשה כמין גבעה: (ד) וזה הדבר. על ידי דבור מל אותם אמר להם סבורים אתם לירש את הארץ ערלים לא כך נאמר לאברהם ואתה את בריתי תשמור וגו' ונתתי לך ולזרעך אחריך את ארץ מגוריך (בראשית י"ז): כל העם היוצא. לא היה אחד מהם כאן שכלם מתו והם היו

### רד"ק

חדודים: ושוב מול את בני ישראל שנית. חזור פעם אחר פעם במחנה למול ולצותם למול ובאמרו ושוב מול אינו אומר פעם ושתי' לבד אלא כמה פעמים עד שיגמר הדבר וכן ושבתי בבית ה' ... (ד) וזה הדבר אשר מל יהושע. וזה הדבר שבעבורו מל יהושע

כי כל העם הילודים במדבר לא מלו אותם לפי' נצטווה יהושע למולם: כל אנשי המלחמה. ר"ל מבן עשרים שנה ומעלה כי אותם הם הפקודים ואותם מתו שהיו מולים וזהו שאמר כי מולים היו והטעם להודיע כי זה שלא מלו לא בעבור שנשתכחה מהם מצות מילה במצרים או התרשלו עליה כי מולים היו כל העם היוצאים ואפי' לדברי בעל הדרש שאו' שהתרשלו במילה

### רלב"ג

המלוה מבואר ...

### מנחת שי

(ב) עשה לך חרבות. ...

### מצודת דוד

(ב) ושוב מול וגו' שנית. אמר שנית כי גם בליל צאתם ממצרים נמולו כל ישראל יחד כן אמרז"ל: (ג) אל גבעת. בגבעת הערלות ונקרא בשם המקום על שם המאורע: (ד) וזה הדבר. ר"ל זה היה הסבה אשר יהושע לבד מל את כל העם ולא מלו אז זה את זה כי איך יתכן בלא ימלא בהם מי יודע למול: כל העם. ר"ל כי כל העם

### מצודת ציון

(ב) צורים. חדודים כמו צור חרבו (תהלים פ"ט): (ג) אל גבעת. בגבעת וכן ואל הארון (שמות כ"ה) ומבפנו

## Commentary Digest

*explained, that the north wind had not blown, and they were the ones who were circumcised now."* — R[4]

6. *who did not listen* — Because they did not listen, it was decreed upon them to wander for forty years in the desert, thus delaying the performance of circumcision. Hence, by performing this precept now, the children saved their parents from punishment in the hereafter. Had they failed to submit to this rite, their parents would be considered responsible for their failure to fulfill this commandment. Joshua exhorted them to accept this commandment for the sake of their deceased parents. — Azulai

7. *And their children whom he*

to Joshua, Make for yourself sharp knives, and circumcise again
the children of Israel the second time. 3. And Joshua made
for himself sharp knives, and circumcised the children of Israel
at the hill of the foreskins. 4. And this is the reason why
Joshua did circumcise: All the people that came out of Egypt,
that were males, all the men of war, had died in the desert by
the way *after* they came out of Egypt.

## Commentary Digest

Joshua circumcised, rather than each father circumcising his own son — All the people that came out of Egypt who were males, all the men of war, had died in the desert by the way — Therefore, since the fathers were dead, the fulfillment of this rite was delegated to Joshua. The Rabbis interpret דבר as "word" or "speech," expounding the passage thus: *"Through speech he circumcised them. He said to them, "Do you expect to inherit the land while being uncircumcised? Was it not thus stated to Abraham: 'And you shall keep my covenant etc. And I shall give to you and to your seed after you the land of your sojournings?' " "* — R[1]

*all the people that came out* — *"Not one of them was here, for they had all died, and they were circumcised, as it is stated: for . . . were circumcised."* — R

*all the men of war* — all those qualified for military service, i.e. from twenty to sixty years of age. — K

5. *For all the people that came out were circumcised* — Although they had neglected the rite of circumcision in Egypt according to certain authorities, on the eve of their departure they performed this precept, as the prophet Ezekiel says: and you were naked and bare.[1]* And I said to you, With your blood shall you live, etc.[2] You were naked and bare of commandments. And I said, With your blood shall you live, i.e. with the blood of the circumcision and the blood of the paschal sacrifice. Also, the prophet Zachariah[2]* says: Also you, through the blood of your covenant, I freed your prisoners from the pit where there was no water. — K[2]** The Midrash[3] relates that when the Lord commanded Moses concerning the Paschal lamb, He endowed Moses' sacrifice with the aroma of Paradise. When the people longed for a taste of this delicacy, Moses informed them that in order to partake thereof they were required to submit to circumcision. They did so and partook of the Paschal sacrifice. By this act, they found favor in the sight of the Almighty, Who thereupon redeemed them from Egypt.

*they had not circumcised* — "as I

ה כי־מלים היו כל־העם היצאים וכל־
העם הילדים במדבר בדרך בצאתם
ממצרים לא־מלו: ו כי ארבעים שנה
הלכו בני־ישראל במדבר עד־תם כל־
הגוי אנשי המלחמה היצאים ממצרים
אשר לא־שמעו בקול יהוה אשר
נשבע יהוה להם לבלתי הראותם את־
הארץ אשר נשבע יהוה לאבותם
לתת לנו ארץ זבת חלב ודבש: ז ואת־
בניהם הקים תחתם אתם מל יהושע
כי־ערלים היו כי לא־מלו אותם בדרך:
ח ויהי כאשר־תמו כל־הגוי להמול

**תרגום**

במפקהון ממצרים:
ה ארי גזירין הוו כל עמא
די נפקו וכל עמא
דאתילידו במדברא
בארחא במפקהון
ממצרים לא גזרו:
ו ארי ארבעין שנין
הליכו בני ישראל
במדברא עד דסף כל
עמא גברי מגיחי קרבא
דנפקו ממצרים דלא
קבילו למימרא דיי
דקיים יי להון בדיל דלא
לאחזיותהון ית ארעא
דקיים יי לאבהתהון
למתן לנא ארעא עבדא
חלב ודבש: ז וית
בניהון דקמו בתריהון
יתהון גזר יהושע ארי
ערלין הוו ארי לא גזרו
יתהון בארחא: ח והוה
כד שלימו כל עמא
למגזר

ת״א כי מולים היו. יבמות עא: כריתות ט.

**רד״ק**

במצרים וסמך לפסוק גם את בדם בריתך שלחתי אסיריך מבור אין מים בו וכן מה שאמר בדמיך חיי פעמים ר״ל שתי דמים דם פסח ודם מילה אעפ״כ בצאתם מלו כולם קוד' שעשו הפסח וזהו שאמר כי מולים היו כל העם היוצאים והנה אותם שהיו מבן עשרים שנה ומעלה מתו במדבר ומבן עשרים שנה ומטה נשארו מולים ולא הוצרך יהושע למול אלא הילודים במדבר שלא היו יכולי' למול בדרך כמו שפירשנו ופיר' לא מלו לא מלו אותם כי הוא פעל יוצא: (ז) הקים. אשר הקים וכן לעם עליתי

**רש״י**

מולים שנאמר כי מולים היו: (ה) לא מלו. כמו שפירשתי שלא נשבה רוח צפונית והם שמלו עכשיו: (ז) ואת בניהם הקים תחתם ואת בניהם שהקים תחתיהם. הם הילודים במדבר אותם מל יהושע:

**מנחת שי**

(ה) וכי העם הילדים. עיין מה שכתוב בירמיה סימן ט״ז: (ז) אתם מל יהושע. עיין מ״ש בסימן ז׳ ג׳:

**רלב״ג**

ספר שאחר שמלו ישבו במקומם עד שהיתה המכה וזה כולו ממנו. שיורה שאין ראוי לנמול שיעתק ממקומו עד חיות המכה:

**מצודת ציון**

ובהארץ: (ו) זבת. מל' זיבה ונטיפה:

**מצודת דוד**

היוצא ממצרים שהיו נמולים והראוים למול הלא הם מתו במדבר ואינם למול לזולתם: (ה) כי מלים היו. ר״ל כי לבד העם היוצאים היו נמולים אבל לא הילודים במדבר ולא היו הם א״כ ראוים למול: (ו) עד תום וא״כ לא היו מי מהנמולים להיות ראוי והגון למול זולתו: אשר נשבע. אשר בעבור זה נשבע ה' להם לבלתי וכו': (ז) הקים תחתם. אשר הקים תחתם: אותם מל יהושע. ולא נמולו עד אז כי ערלים היו עד הזמן ההוא כי היוצאים ממצרים לא מלו בניהם בהיותם בדרך ולא היו א״כ נמולים להיות הגון וראוי

## Commentary Digest

*rolled off* (or removed) *the stone.'"*[6] — R D explains: the reproach of the Egyptians who said, you are uncircumcised just as we are. To Israel, this was considered a stigma, as in Gen. XXXIV:14. חרפת may also be understood as "shame." The shameful beliefs of the idolatrous Egyptians would now be eliminated from among Israel, by observance of the Paschal rites, which signify the slaughter of the Egyptian lamb-deity. Also, the carnal lusts of the Egyptians would be weakened and modified by the circumcision; (G) or simply the shame of being ערל or uncircumcised like the Egyptians. — K A explains: the reproach of the Egyptians who said, Because of the lack of the Lord's ability to bring them to the land which He swore to them, He

5. For all the people that came out were circumcised, but all
the people that were born in the wilderness by the way as
they came forth out of Egypt, they had not circumcised.
6. For the children of Israel walked forty years in the
wilderness, until all the people, the men of war, that came out of Egypt, were consumed, those who did not listen to the voice of the Lord, to whom the Lord had sworn that He would not show them the land, which the Lord had sworn to their forefathers that He would give us, a land that flows with milk
and honey. 7. And their children, whom he raised up in their
stead, them Joshua circumcised, for they had not circumcised
them by the way. 8. And it was, when all the people were
finished being circumcised,

## Commentary Digest

*raised up in their stead* — lit. and their children he raised up in their stead; "*i.e. And their children whom he raised up in their stead, (they are the ones who were born in the desert) them Joshua circumcised.*" — R, J, K, and D

*for they had not circumcised them by the way* — They did not circumcise them because of the way, i.e. the strenuous traveling. — K[1]

8. *and they remained in their places* —*Lit. under them "in their places (J) and they did not besiege the city."* — R

*until they recovered* — "*from the wound.*" — R Since they were afraid to travel after the circumcision. — M

9. *have I rolled away* — "*I removed the reproach of the Egyptians who had said, "see that 'Ra-ah' is before your faces.*[2] *There is a star named 'Ra-ah'*[3] *which is a symbol of blood. We see it over you in the desert." And that is what Moses said in the desert, "Why should the Egyptians say, 'With 'Ra-ah' He took them out.'" But they did not know that that was the blood of circumcision. And when they circumcised in Joshua's time, and* that *blood came, that reproach was removed, for the vast multitude which had gone up with them were still vexing them. In this manner, Rabbi Moses the preacher expounded*" this passage.[4] — R

*have I rolled away* — Heb. גלותי — "*I have removed, like* '(גל) *Remove* (or roll away) *from me reproach and shame.*'[5] '(ויגל) *and he*

וישבו תחתם במחנה עד חיותם׃
ט ויאמר יהוה אל־יהושע היום גלותי
את־חרפת מצרים מעליכם ויקרא שם
המקום ההוא גלגל עד היום הזה׃ י ויחנו
בני־ישראל בגלגל ויעשו את־הפסח
בארבעה עשר יום לחדש בערב
בערבות יריחו׃ יא ויאכלו מעבור הארץ
ממחרת הפסח מצות וקלוי בעצם
היום

מגזר ויתבו באתריהון במשריתא עד דאתסיאו׃ ט ואמר יי ליהושע יומא דין אעדית ית חיסודי מצראי מן קדמיכון וקרא שמא דאתרא ההוא גלגלא עד יומא הדין׃ י ושרו בני ישראל בגלגלא ועבדו ית פסחא בארבעת עשרא יומא לירחא ברמשא במישרי יריחו׃ יא ואכלו מעבורא דארעא מבתר

**ת״א** ויעשו את הפסח. יבמות עא
זבחים קיח : מעבור הארץ. ר״ה
יג קדושין לז :

### רש״י

**וישבו תחתם.** באתריהון ולא נרו על העיר: **עד חיותם.** מן המכה: (ט) **גלותי** · הסירותי את חרפת מצרים שהיו אומרים ראו כי רעה נגד פניכם כוכב אחד יש ששמו רעה והוא סימן של דם רואין אנו אותו עליכם במדבר והוא שאמר משה במדבר למה יאמרו מצרים לאמר ברעה הוציאם והם אינם יודעים שהוא דם מילה וכשמלו בימי יהושע ובא אותו הדם הוסרה אותה החרפה שעדיין ערב רב שעלו עמהם היו מונים להם כך דרש ר׳ משה הדרשן : **גלותי** · הסירותי כמו גל מעלי חרפה · ויגל את האבן: (יא) **ממחרת** שאין מצות עשה דוחה את לא תעשה אלא אם כן היתה כתוב׳ בצדה ומאין היה להם ישן מה שהיו תגרי אומות מוכרים להם ומלת מעבו׳ מוכיח שהוא מן הישן כי אמר כי נקר׳ עבור הדגן שהוא משנים שעברה ושנה הבאה נקרא תבואה : **ממחרת**

### רד״ק

בעבור זה עשה ה׳ לי והדומים להם שיחסרו שי״ן או מילת **אשר** ומע׳ הקים כי הקב״ה הקים אותם תחת אבות׳ לירש הארץ **כמו** שאמר להם אתננה והם יירשוה : (ח) תחתם . במקומם כמו **שבו** איש תחתיו : היותם . הרפאם כמו וימרחו על השחין ויחי : (ט) חרפת מצרים. לפי שיצאו האבות ממצרים והיו הבנים ערלי׳ כמו המצריים והערלה חרפה כמו **שנאמר** כי חרפה **היא** לנו : גלגל . נכפלה בו הפ״א כי מן גלותי יאמרו גלל וכן **דרך** ל׳ הקדש בשמו׳ הלקוחים מן הפעל להוסיף בו אות או **לגרוע** ממנו כמו נח מן ינחמנו שמואל כי מה׳ שאלתיו וגם להפך **סדר** האותיו׳ כמו יעבץ מן עצב : (יא) ויאכלו מעבור הארץ . **מהישן** אבלו מצות וקלוי כי החדש היה אסור להם עד אחר **הקרבת** העומר בשש׳ עשר בניסן ואפילו למצות מצה אסור מן **ההדש**

### רלב״ג

(ט) היום גלותי. הסירותי מעליכם חרפת מצרים ר״ל לפי מה שאחשוב בהרפת מצרים אמונותיהם הנפסדות כי ענין הפסח היה מביא ישראל להעתיק מהאמונות ההם כמו שביארנו בפרשת בא ואמנם אמר זה כי עד עתה סרה זאת האמונה מהם לסבה שזכרנו ולזה סמך לזה שבבר עשו בם את הפסח בי״ד יום להדש ואפשר שיהיה כרצון בזה ההמשך לתאות המשגל כי המצרים היו פרוצים בעריות כמו שאמר בתורה בפרשת העריות כמעשה ארץ מצרים וגו׳ ולפי שהמילה מכוונת להחליש כח זה האבר הוא מבואר שבענין המילה תסיר מעליהם חרפת מצרים ויהיו יותר גדולי׳ בענין המשגל ואפשר שיאמר עוד שהרצון בזה שבבר הסיר מהם חרפת מצרים שהיו אומרים כי ברעה הוציאם להרוג אותם ולכלותם לא להנחילם הארץ והנה בהיותם מתאחרים במדבר ארבעים שנה היתה להם זאת החרפ׳ ואולם עתה ייעד אותם שבבר ירשו את הארץ אחר שבבר קיימו זאת המצוה ותסור מעליהם זאת החרפה והביאור הראשון הוא הנראה יותר ואם לא מצאנוהו לאחד מן הקודמי׳ אשר הגיעו אלינו את דבריהם : (יא) ויאכלו מעבור הארץ . הנה אמר זה לפי שלא הותר להם החדש עד ממחרת הפסח׳ ובזה להיה

### מנחת שי

(י) בערבות יריחו . העי׳ במאריך בספרים כ״י :

### מצודת דוד

להמול זולת יהושע : (ט) **היום גלותי** . עתה העברתי מעליכם מה שהיו המצרים מחרפים לאמר הלא הם ערלים כמותו וחרפה יחשב לישראל כמו שכתו׳ כי חרפה היא לנו (בראשי׳ ל״ד) :(י) **בערב.** אחר חלות היום קרוי ערב כי אז נוטה החמה לבית מערבי:(יא) **ממחרת**

### מצודת ציון

(ח) **תחתם.** במקומם: **חיותם.** ענינו רפואה כמו וימרחו על השחין ויחי (ישעי׳ ל״ח) : (ט) **גלותי** . מל׳ גלגל וסבוב · (יא) **מעבור .** תרגום של דגן הוא עבורא : **וקלוי.** שבלים קלוים כמו קלוי באש (ויקרא ב׳) : **בעצם היום.** ר״ל בגופו של יום כמו עד עלם היום הזה

## Commentary Digest

ently: And they ate of the *old* grain of the land on the morrow of the (preparation of the) Paschal lamb, unleavened cakes, i.e. on the eve of the Passover feast; and parched grain (i.e. fresh grain) on this very day, (i.e. the second day of Passover known in Scripture as "this very day"). According to R.T. there is a distinction between the two terms: עבור, and תבואה, the former being derived from the root עבר, to pass, since it is the grain of the past year. Not so the latter, which, being derived from the root בוא, to come, may refer to any grain which grows from the field and is gathered into the houses. K shares this opinion, differing only in the interpretation of "on this very day," which he takes to mean on the fif-

that they remained in their places in the camp, until they
recovered. 9. And the Lord said to Joshua, This day have I
rolled away the reproach of Egypt from you. And he called
the name of the place Gilgal to this day. 10. And the children
of Israel encamped in Gilgal, and they made the Passover
sacrifice on the fourteenth day of the month at evening in the
plains of Jericho. 11. And they ate of the grain of the land on the
morrow of the Passover, unleavened cakes and parched grain
on this very day.

## Commentary Digest

slaughtered them in the desert.[1] Now that they had crossed the Jordan and entered the Holy Land, the reproach was removed from them.

*Gilgal* — from גלותי.

10. *and they made the Passover sacrifice* — After they were circumcised, they were qualified to make the sacrifice. — M

*at evening* — i.e. after midday, בערב meaning literally "darkening," when the sun begins to descend toward the west.[1*]

*in the plains of Jericho* — in Gilgal, no place else, for the Paschal sacrifice could only be offered up in a public, or large, high place, not in a private, or small, high place. Since Gilgal was divinely designated as the first home of the tabernacle in the Holy Land, the Paschal sacrifice had to be offered up there. Had they not crossed the Jordan, it would have been impossible to perform this rite, since the Passover sacrifice was only to be made in the Holy Land.[1**] — Alshich

11. *on the morrow of the Passover* — in conformity with the Biblical injunction, "And bread — you shall not eat (from the new grain) until this very day (the second day of Passover) until you have brought the 'omer' etc."[2] Hence, we explain: "on the morrow of the Passover" as the day following the Passover festival, or — *"the day of the waving of the 'Omer, for first they sacrificed the 'Omer.' And from the seventh of Adar, when Moses died, whereupon the manna ceased to fall, they subsisted on the manna which was in their vessels, which they had gathered on the seventh of Adar, as it is stated: "the manna they ate forty years."[3] Now, was it not forty years less thirty days, for the beginning of the falling of the manna was on the fifteenth of Iyar?[4] Hence we deduce that in the cakes which the Israelites took with them from Egypt they perceived the taste of manna."* — R[5] Rabbeinu Tam,[6] however, explains the verse differ-

הַיּוֹם הַזֶּה: יב וַיִּשְׁבֹּת הַמָּן מִמָּחֳרָת
בְּאָכְלָם מֵעֲבוּר הָאָרֶץ וְלֹא־הָיָה עוֹד
לִבְנֵי יִשְׂרָאֵל מָן וַיֹּאכְלוּ מִתְּבוּאַת אֶרֶץ
כְּנַעַן בַּשָּׁנָה הַהִיא: יג וַיְהִי בִּהְיוֹת יְהוֹשֻׁעַ
בִּירִיחוֹ וַיִּשָּׂא עֵינָיו וַיַּרְא וְהִנֵּה־אִישׁ עֹמֵד
לְנֶגְדּוֹ וְחַרְבּוֹ שְׁלוּפָה בְּיָדוֹ וַיֵּלֶךְ יְהוֹשֻׁעַ

פִּסְחָא פַּטִּיר וּקְלִי בְּכֵן
יוֹמָא הָדֵין: יב וּפְסַק מַנָּא
מִיּוֹמָא דְּבַתְרוֹהִי
בְּמֵיכַלְהוֹן מֵעִיבוּרָא
דְאַרְעָא וְלָא הֲוָה עוֹד
לִבְנֵי יִשְׂרָאֵל מַנָּא וַאֲכַלוּ
מֵעֲלַלַת אַרְעָא דִכְנַעַן
בְּשַׁתָּא הַהִיא: יג וַהֲוָה
כַּד הֲוָה יְהוֹשֻׁעַ בִּירִיחוֹ
וּזְקַף עֵינוֹהִי וַחֲזָא וְהָא

ת״א ויהי בהיות. ערובין סג מגלה ו נדרים כו סנהדרין מד והנה איש מגלה ג י:

### רד״ק

הפסח. הוא ליל חמשה עשר בניסן ויומו כי הפסח קרב בארבעה עשר ומחרתו הוא יום חמש׳ עשר וכן בחמשה עשר יום לחדש הראשון ממחרת הפסח יצאו בני ישראל: (יב) וישבת המן ממחרת. מאותו מחרת שזכר מאותו היום פסק המן כי לא היו צריכים שהרי אכלו מעבור הארץ מצות וקלוי בחמשה עשר בניסן ולדברי רז״ל שאמרו כי עד י״ו בניסן אכלו המן יהיה פי׳ ממחרת ט״ו והוא י״ו כי אע״פ שאכלו בט״ו מצות וקלוי לא היה מספיק להם מה שמצאו מעבור הארץ ואותו היום אכלו גם מהמן ולמחרת שהוא י״ו בניסן אחר שהקריבו בו העומר והותרו בחדש מצאו הרבה מן החדש לאכול וז״ש ויאכלו מתבואת ארץ כנען בשנה ההיא: (יג) ויהי בהיות יהושע ביריחו. בגבול יריחו ומכאן סמכו ז״ל שעבורה של עיר דינו כעיר שהרי יהושע לא היה בתוך העיר ואמר בהיות יהושע ביריחו כי נסעו מהגלגל אחר שנמולו שם הערלים ועשו הפסח ובאו להם ליריחו לכבשה וחנו את פני העיר והקב״ה שלח מלאכו ליהושע כדי לחזקו לכבשה ולבשרו ונרא׳ לו כדמות איש וחרבו שלופ׳ בידו מורה על הגבודה ועל הנצוח כמו שנראה ליעקב אבינו ונאבק עמו לחזקו ולבשרו כמו שאמר לו כי שרית עם אלהים ועם אנשים ותוכל וכן בא ליהושע זה המלאך וחרבו

### רש״י

הפסח. יום הנפת העומר שהקריבו עומר תחלה ומז׳ באדר שמת משה שפסק המן היו מסתפקין עד עכשיו ממן שבכליהם שלקטו בשבעה באדר שנאמר את המן אכלו ארבעים שנה והלא מ׳ שנה חסר ל׳ יום שהרי תחלת ירידת המן בט״ו באייר אמור מעתה בחררה שהוציאו ישראל ממצרים טעמו טעם מן: (יב) ולא היה עוד לבני ישראל מן. לפיכך ויאכלו מעבור הארץ אם היה להם מן לא היו אוכלים מן התבואה שהמן היה נוח להם משל אומר לתינוק מפני מה אתה אוכל פת שעורין לפי שאין לו פת חטין לכך נאמר ולא היה עוד וגו׳: (יג) בהיות יהושע ביריחו. מכאן לעיבורה של עיר שהיא מן העיר שאי אפשר לומר בתוך יריחו: הלנו אתה.

### רלב״ג

מה שאמר בתורה ממחרת השבת יניפנו הכהן הרצון בו ממחרת הפסח והוא י״ו בניסן לא ממחר׳ שבת בראשי׳ כמו שהיו או׳ הצדוקי׳ שאם הי׳ הענין כן הנה לא ימלט הענין מחלוקת אם שנא׳ שכבר קרה אז שהיה פסח ביום השבת או בזולת יום השבת ואם היה בזול׳ יום השבת הנה ילטרך לו׳ כי טעו יהושע וישראל בזה וזה דבר בלתי אפשר ואם הי׳ בשבת הנה לא היה ראוי שייחסהו אל מה שהגא במקרה אבל ראוי שייחסהו אל מה שהוא בעלם ויאמ׳ ממחרת השבת כי הם לא עשו זה לפי זה הדע׳ מפני היות היום ההוא מחרת הפסח אבל מפני היותו ממחרת השבת ולזה הוא מבואר שמ״ש בתורה ממחרת השבת אין רצון בו שבת בראשי׳ אבל הרצון בו ממחרת הפסח כי הפסח תקרא שבת ר״ל היום החמשה עשר: (יב) וישבת המן ממחרת. הנה מצאנו בזה דעת לרבו׳ ז״ל קצת׳ אמ׳ שלא ירד המן אחר שמת משה אלא שכבר לקטו ממנו מה שהספיק להם עד זה הזמן ועשו ממנו חלות וקצת׳ אמ׳ שכבר ירד המן עד היו׳ ההוא ואחשוב שאשר הביא האו׳ שלא ירד המן אח׳ שמת משה אל זה המאמ׳ הוא היותו מרחיק היותו מסורה מהנבי׳ מופת אחר מותו ולפי שזה המופ׳ הנפלא א״א שיהי׳ על יד נביא זולת משה הוייב ממנו שלא ירד המן אחר מותו לא הסכי׳ שהי׳ נעש׳ אח׳ זה על יד יהושע ואשר נר׳ לנו לפי מה שהרבנו מענין המופתים בסוף המאמ׳ הו׳ מספר מלחמות ה׳ הוא שזה המופ׳ הנעש׳ על יד משה בענין המן נשאר עד היום הזה שאכלו מן החדש הלא תרא׳ כי מופת שמן המשח׳ היה נשאר תמיד כמו שביארנו במקומו וממה שיורה על זה הוא אומר וישבת המן ולא אומ׳ ויכלה המן וזה ממה שיורה שכבר היה יורד עד היום הזה ועוד כי בתורה כשנזכר׳ ירידת המן זכר המן אכלו עד בואם אל ארץ נושבת וזה ממה שיורה שכל זה הענין נעשה על יד משה וכבר ביארנו בספר מלחמו׳ ה׳ איך יהכן זה: (יג) ויהי בהיות יהושע ביריחו. ראוי שתדע שזה הענין היה במרא׳

### מצודת ציון

(שם כ״ג) ור״ל לא בלילה שלפניו אם כי הליל׳ הולך אחר היום:
(יב) וישבות. ענין בטול כמו שבת נוגש (ישעיה י״ד):
(יג) שלופה. חלולה מתער׳ כמו שלף וילא מגוה (איוב כ׳):

### מצודת דוד

הפסח. ממחרת יום א׳ של פסח שהוא זמן הקרבת העומר וקרבו העומר והדר אכלו: (יב) וישבות המן. אף כי מיום מיתת משה בשבעה באדר פסק המן מלירד מ״מ היו נזונים הגם ממן שבכליהם ובאכלם מעבור הארץ לא מצאו עוד: ויאכלו. התחילו לאכול: (יג) ביריחו. ר״ל בגבול יריחו: הלנו. בה״א השאלה לומר אם באת לעזור לנו מול האויב או לעזור להאויב:

## Commentary Digest

above R v. 11. Others maintain that the manna fell until this time.[3]*

*on the morrow* — of the first day of Passover. Although they ate of the old grain on the fifteenth, it did not suffice their needs. On the sixteenth, however, after the waving of the omer,' when they were permitted to eat new grain, the manna which had lasted miraculously for forty days, became consumed. — K[4]

*neither had the children of Israel manna anymore* — *"Therefore, they ate of the grain of the Land. Had they still had manna, they would not have eaten of the grain, for the*

12. And the manna ceased on the morrow when they ate of the grain of the land; neither had the children of Israel manna anymore; and they ate of the produce of the land of Canaan that year.
13. And it was when Joshua was in Jericho, that he lifted up his eyes and saw, and, behold, a man was standing opposite him with his sword drawn in his hand; and Joshua went

## Commentary Digest

teenth day of Nissan, the first day of the Passover festival. Hence, he must explain that the parched grain was old grain, otherwise it would have been forbidden until the following day. According to R. T. and K, the term ממחרת הפסח, is interpreted according to the Biblical sense which uses פסח as the fourteenth day of Nissan, when the Paschal lamb was slaughtered and sacrificed. According to R, however, it is used in the rabbinic sense which uses פסח as the name of the festival. In either case, this passage supports the Talmudic tradition that the 'omer' was offered on the morrow of the first day of the festival, as opposed to the Boethusians who claimed that it was always offered on Sunday, the morrow of the Sabbath,[1] interpreting literally the Biblical commandment in Lev. XXIII:15. — G

According to other authorities, the prohibition of new grain did not take effect until after conquest and division of the land. The reason they did not eat of the produce of the land prior to the sixteenth of Nissan, was because they still had manna to eat, as R explains in v. 12. It is probable that R mentions the manna in v. 11 to explain this opinion. Otherwise, he would have left it for v. 12. The Talmud bases the allegation that the manna ceased on the seventh of Adar on a discrepancy in the Biblical account of the manna.[2] And the children of Israel ate the manna for forty years until they came to an inhabited land; the manna they ate until they came to the outskirts of the land of Canaan. "An inhabited land" refers to the Holy Land proper. "The outskirts of the land of Canaan" refers to the plains of Moab on the eastern bank of the Jordan. To reconcile this discrepancy, the Talmud deduces that the manna ceased to fall in the plains of Moab following Moses' demise. They still partook of it, however, until they crossed the Jordan and came to Gilgal, thereby completing the forty year period.[3] It is indeed puzzling that R does not quote this Baraitha, but the aforementioned which is not exactly relevant to our topic.

12. *And the manna ceased* — See

גַּבְרָא קָאִים לְקִבְלֵיהּ וְחַרְבֵּיהּ שְׁלִיפָא בִּידֵיהּ וַאֲזַל יְהוֹשֻׁעַ לְוָתֵיהּ וַאֲמַר לֵיהּ הַלְמִסְעֲדָנָא אַתְּ אָתֵא אִם לְבַעֲלֵי דְבָבָנָא: יד וַאֲמַר לָא אֲרֵי אֲנָא מַלְאַךְ שְׁלִיחַ מִן קֳדָם יְיָ כְּעַן אֲתֵיתִי וּנְפַל יְהוֹשֻׁעַ עַל אַפּוֹהִי עַל אַרְעָא וּסְגִיד וַאֲמַר לֵיהּ מָה רִבּוֹנִי מְמַלֵּיל עִם עַבְדֵּיהּ: טו וַאֲמַר

אֵלָיו וַיֹּאמֶר לוֹ הֲלָנוּ אַתָּה אִם־לְצָרֵינוּ:
יד וַיֹּאמֶר ׀ לֹא כִּי אֲנִי שַׂר־צְבָא־יְהוָה
עַתָּה בָאתִי וַיִּפֹּל יְהוֹשֻׁעַ אֶל־פָּנָיו אַרְצָה
וַיִּשְׁתָּחוּ וַיֹּאמֶר לוֹ מָה אֲדֹנִי מְדַבֵּר אֶל־
עַבְדּוֹ: טו וַיֹּאמֶר שַׂר־צְבָא יְהוָה אֶל־
יְהוֹשֻׁעַ שַׁל־נַעַלְךָ מֵעַל רַגְלֶךָ כִּי הַמָּקוֹם

ת״א עתה באתי עירובין סג. מגלה ג. סנהדרין מד עקידה שער לה: ... קמץ בז״ק ... אשר

רש״י

הלמסעדנא אתיתא: (יד) עתה באתי. לעזרתך שאין אדם יכול להלחם עליה ולתופשה להפיל החומה אבל בימי משה רבך באתי ולא חפץ בי שנאמר אם אין פניך הולכים וגו׳: (טו) שר צבא ה׳. ישראל שהוא צבא לה׳ ומיכאל היה

רד״ק

שלופה בידו כדמות גבור מנצח והוא שאמר ליהושע ראה נתתי בידך את יריחו ואת מלכה: (יד) ויאמר לא. כלומר אינני כמו שאתה סבור איש בא להלחם אבל אני מלאך ה׳ וזהו שאמר שר צבא ה׳ שר צבאות מעל׳ ומטה כמו שנאמר על מיכאל השר הגדול ולפי גדולתו וקדושתו נקדש המקום שנראה בו ליהושע לפי׳ אמר קדש הוא: עתה באתי. בעת שראיתני מה שאין כן בבשר ודם וזה להחזיק בלבו כי מלאך הוא ויש בו דרש כי בא להפחידם על בטול תורה ועל שבטלו היום שעבר תמיד של בין

רלב״ג

הנבוא׳ ויורה על זה מ״ב תכף ויאמר ה׳ אל יהושע כי הוא רחוק הלאו׳ המלאך בהקיץ ובהבחתנב הכתובים על מנהגים׳ והנה הרצון באמרו ויהי בהיות יהושע ביריחו מחשבתו משוטטת שם איך יעשה לאחרית העם היושב בה ומפני זה נדמה לו דבר מעניני המלחמה ולזה המלאך כאלו חרבו שלופה בידו ולזאת הסבה ג״כ שאל לו במראה׳ הנבואה הלנו אתה אם לצרינו כמנהג הנלחמים וענהו כי אין הענין כמו שחשב אבל הוא שר צבא ה׳ והשר הוא הממונה להשגיח

מנחת שי

(יד) ויאמר לא כי אני. בספר אחד ישן כתיבת יד כתוב לא באלף וק׳ לו בוא״ו ודבר מתמיה הוא כי לא נמנה זה במסורת עם ט״ו דכתיבין לא וקריין לו ואולי טעה הסופר בהכנתם מאמר דעירובין פרק הדר (ס״ג) ואיתא נמי בפ״ק דמגילה (ג׳) ובסנהדרין פרק נגמר הדין (מ״ד) א״ל על איזה מהם באת א״ל עתה באתי: (טו) של נעלך. אין מאריך במלת של:

מצודת דוד

(יד) ויאמר לא, ר״ל לא באתי לעזור לאויבי ישראל כי אני שר של ישראל הקרואים צבא ה׳ ומה שלא ראיתני עד הנה הוא בעבור כי עתה באתי ולא מאז: מה אדוני מדבר. ר״ל דבר דבריך והנני לקיימם כעבד המקיים דברי האדון: (טו) קדש הוא. ומהראוי לעמוד עליו יחף:

מצודת ציון

(יד) אל פניו. לפניו ר״ל לפני העומד לנגדו: (טו) של. הסר וכן במשה של נעלך (שמות ג׳):

## Commentary Digest

requested a burial place for Sarah. These two nations were families of Canaan.[7]

13. *when Joshua was in Jericho* — *"Hence we deduce that the outskirts of a city are considered as part of the city, for it is impossible to say* (that he was actually) *inside Jericho."* — R[8] A distance of seventy cubits from a city is counted as the outskirts and is considered as part of the city. Since they had not yet taken Jericho, Joshua could not have been in the city proper. G understands this passage as a dream in which Joshua visualizes himself as actually standing within the walls of Jericho. He shares Maimonides' belief that it is impossible to perceive an angel except in a prophetic vision.[9] A, however, maintains that an angel who assumes a human form can be perceived in a conscious state.

*Are you for us* — *"Have you come to support us?"* — R from J

14. *I have now come* — *"to your aid, for no man can wage war against it* (Jericho) *and seize it, to throw down the wall. But in the time of Moses your master, I came and he did not want me, as it is stated: 'if Your presence does not go, etc.'"*[10] — R[11] Thus, we explain "No," as the angel's supplication to Joshua: Please do not reject me as your master did. Upon this request, Joshua prostrated himself, subordinating himself before the captain of the Lord's host.

15. *the captain of the Lord's host* — *"Israel, who is the Lord's host. Now,*

to him, and said to him, Are you for us, or for our adversaries? 14. And he said, No, but I am the the captain of the host of the Lord; I have now come. And Joshua fell on his face to the earth and prostrated himself, and said to him, What does my lord say to his servant? 15. And the captain of the Lord's host said to Joshua, Remove your shoe from your foot; for the place

## Commentary Digest

*manna was pleasing to them. An appriate parable is: One says to a child, why do you eat barley bread? Because he has no wheat bread. Therefore, it is stated: "Neither had the children of Israel manna anymore, etc."* " — R[1] The Rabbis conclude: If the Israelites still had that handful which they had gathered on the day that Moses passed away, (from which they ate all forty days,)[1*] they would not have wanted to eat of the produce of the land of Canaan.

With the termination of the manna, there came to an end the most significant era of Jewish history, immortalized by Jeremiah's: [1**]So said the Lord, I remember for you the affection of your youth, the love of your espousals, how you went after Me in the wilderness, in a land not sown." S.G. places the precision of the manna's daily falling from the skies for an unbroken period of forty years, excepting Sabbaths and holy days, at the very top of the roster of miracles that occurred to the Jewish people.

To commemorate this era, one jar of manna was preserved in the Mishkan.[2] "Take one jar and put therein one omerful of manna, and lay it up before the Lord to be kept for your generations." It was later hidden away when the Ark was hidden in the days of King Josiah,[3] and will be returned by the prophet Elijah when he heralds the coming of the Messiah.

*the land of Canaan* — It seems strange to continue throughout the Scriptures to call the Holy Land "the land of Canaan" especially according to the opinion in the Midrash[4] that it originally fell to the lot of Shem and his descendants[5] and Canaan was a usurper. The word "Canaan," however, does not refer to the geneological origin of the people, but should be understood as "land of commerce" ("Canaan" meaning merchant), situated as Eretz Israel is, on the trade crossroads of the East and West.[6] According to the Rabbis, the land was called "Canaan" in honor of the Girgarshites who evacuated their territory and fled to Africa in deference to the Israelites. It was also called this name in honor of the Hittites who showed great respect to Abraham when he

אֲשֶׁר אַתָּה עֹמֵד עָלָיו קֹדֶשׁ הוּא וַיַּעַשׂ
יְהוֹשֻׁעַ כֵּן: ו א וִירִיחוֹ סֹגֶרֶת וּמְסֻגֶּרֶת
מִפְּנֵי בְּנֵי יִשְׂרָאֵל אֵין יוֹצֵא וְאֵין בָּא:
ב וַיֹּאמֶר יְהוָה אֶל־יְהוֹשֻׁעַ רְאֵה נָתַתִּי
בְיָדְךָ אֶת־יְרִיחוֹ וְאֶת־מַלְכָּהּ גִּבּוֹרֵי
הֶחָיִל: ג וְסַבֹּתֶם אֶת־הָעִיר כֹּל אַנְשֵׁי
הַמִּלְחָמָה הַקֵּיף אֶת־הָעִיר פַּעַם אֶחָת
כֹּה תַעֲשֶׂה שֵׁשֶׁת יָמִים: ד וְשִׁבְעָה

מַלְאֲכָא דִשְׁלִיחַ מִן קֳדָם
יְיָ לִיהוֹשֻׁעַ שְׁרֵי סִינָךְ
מֵעַל רִגְלָךְ אֲרֵי אַתְרָא
דִי אַתְּ קָאֵים עֲלוֹהִי
קַדִישָׁא הוּא וַעֲבַד
יְהוֹשֻׁעַ כֵּן: א וִירִיחוֹ
אֲחִידָא הֲוַת בְּדַשִׁין
דְפַרְזְלָא וּמִתַּקְפָא
בְעַבְרִין דִנְחָשׁ מִן קֳדָם
בְּנֵי יִשְׂרָאֵל לֵית דְנָפֵק
מִנָהּ לְמֶעֱבַד קְרָבָא וְלֵית
דְעָלֵל בְּגַוָהּ לְמִשְׁאַל
בִּשְׁלָמָא: ב וַאֲמַר יְיָ
לִיהוֹשֻׁעַ חֲזֵי דִמְסָרִית
בִּידָךְ יַת יְרִיחוֹ וְיַת
מַלְכָּהּ גִּבָּרֵי חֵילָא:
ג וְתִסְחֲרוּן יַת קַרְתָּא כָּל
גִּבְרֵי עָבְדֵי קְרָבָא אַקִיף יַת קַרְתָּא זִמְנָא חֲדָא כְּדֵין תַּעְבֵּד שִׁיתָא יוֹמִין: ד וְשִׁבְעָא כַהֲנַיָא

ת״א ויריחו סוגרת. נדרים נו עקידה שער עו: יריחו ואת מלכה. עקידה שער עו:

### רש״י

ו (א) סגרת ומסגרת. כתרגומו אחידא בדשין דפרזלא ומתקפא בעברין דנחש: יסבון שנאמר ומיכאל שרכם:

### רד״ק

הערבים א״ל יהושע על איזה מהם באת אמר לו עתה באתי כלו׳ על בטול תורה שאתם בטלי׳ עתה מיד וילן יהושע בתוך העמק שלן בעומק׳ של הלכה וזה הדרש רחוק כי אין שעת המלחמה שעת ת״ת ועוד כי פסוק וילן יהושע הוא במלחמת העי ועוד כי כותב הדרש הזה טעה בפסוק וילן כי ב׳ פסוקים הם וילן יהושע סופו בתוך העם והפסו׳ האחר וילן יהושע בלילה ההוא בתוך העמק ויש בו דרש אחר עתה באתי עתה באתי שני פעמים אני הוא שבאתי בימי משה רבך שנא׳ הנה אנכי שולח מלאך וראה אותי ולא רצה שאלך עמו שאמר להקב״ה איני חפץ אלא בך מיד ויפל יהושע אל פניו ארצה: אל פניו. כמו על וכן אל ההרים לא אכל: (א) ויריחו סוגרת ומסוגרת. סוגרת אנשיה בתוכה שלא יצא אדם מן העיר ומסוגרת שלא יכנס אדם בתוכה ופירושו בסופו אין יוצא ואין בא או כפל סוגרת ומסוגרת לרב הסגירה כמו שאמר התרגום אחידא בדשין וכו׳: (ב) ויאמר ה׳ אל יהושע. ע״י המלאך הנראה לו והוא נקרא בשם ה׳ השולח אותו וכן מצאנו במלאך שנראה לגדעון ויאמר אליו ה׳ כי אהיה עמך ואמרו רז״ל כי שמי בקרבו א״ר שמעון בן לקיש מלמד שהקב״ה משתף שמו על כל מלאך ומלאך: גבורי החיל. פי׳ אנשי יריחו ומלכ׳ ואעפ״י שהם גבורי החיל נתתים בידך: (ג) הקיף את העיר. נכתב ביו״ד כמו אם היה בחירק. ואעפ״י שהוא בצר״י וכן ותגד לבני ישראל יגיד דבר: כה תעשה ששת ימים. אין לשאול טעם לסבות הבורא למה היתה ההקפה הזאת וטעם שבעה כהנים ושבעה שופרות ושבע הקפות ושבעה ימים וטעם ההקפה בתרועה להבהיל העם אשר בתוך העיר ותפול החומה תחתיה למען ידעו כל עמי הארץ כי ה׳ נלחם לישראל לא בחרב ובחנית ומספ׳ השבע׳ ידוע סודו אצל מביני מדע וכן שבעה מזבחות וז׳

### רלב״ג

בישר׳ הוא אשר באמלעותו יביא הש״י הנבואה לנביא מאת הש״י ואמר לו שיחלוץ נעלו מעל רגלו כדי שירגיש בענין המקום שהוא בו כי הוא קדש וענין נביאיי אלהי לא פועל דמיוני ואז הרגיש יהושע בשזאת ההשגה היא השגה נביאיי וזכר הנבואה שהגיע לו בזה המקום וקודם שיתחיל בזכרון הנבואה הביא ספר שיריחו היתה סוגרת ומסוגרת מפני בני ישראל באופן שלא יוכל אחד לצאת משם ולא ליכנס שם וזכר זה לפי שמזאת הסבה נלטרכו בהחרמת׳ לזה המופת שהייש׳ אותו אליו השם יתעלה בזאת הנבואה: (ג) והנה סבבים הש״י לעשות כל אלו המופתים עם הארון ה׳ להיישיר ישראל לשמור ולעשות ככל הכתוב בו והיו אלו המופתים בזה האופן מהזרות כדי להפיל אימה על הגוים ההם בשמעם אלו הנפלאות העלומות אשר עושה הש״י לישראל והיה זה המספר לשביעיות ר״ל שהקיפו העיר ז׳ ימים והיו שם ז׳ כהנים וז׳ שופרות היובלים וביום הז׳ הקיפו ז׳ פעמים שזכרנו כמספר הז׳ שזכרנו בתורה כמו השמטה וז׳ שמטות וז׳ שבתות שנים וז׳ ימים וז׳ פעמים וז׳ ימי הפסח וז׳ ימי סוכה והנה הסבים הש״י שיעשה זה המופת באמלעות זאת התרועה הגדולה כדי שיתעוררו ישראל ויקילו משנת תרדמתם ויתנו אל לבם ענין אלו הנפלאות העלומות למען יראו את ה׳ עם שים לתרועה הגדולה רושם

### מצודת ציון

ו (ג) הקיף. ענין סבוב כמו הקיפו עלי יחד (תהלים פ״ח): (ב) גבורי החיל. ר״ל עם שהם גבורי חיל: (ג) כה תעשה. להקיף פעם אחת ביום:

### מצודת דוד

ו (א) סגרת ומסגרת. ר״ל מעולם היתה סגורה בדלתים ובריח ועתה הוסיפו לסגרה עוד מפני ישראל ולא הניחו מי לצאת ממנה או לבא בה שלא יודע מבואת העיר:

## Commentary Digest

Although Jericho was always barred, now it was reinforced because of the children of Israel. — D

*none went out and none came in* — They allowed no one to enter or leave, lest the entrance be disclosed to the Israelites. — D

2. *And the Lord said to Joshua* — through the archangel Michael, the representative of the Almighty. — K

*the mighty warriors* — although they are mighty warriors. — D

3. *And you shall circle the city, all the men of war* — not only you with

upon which you stand is holy. And Joshua did so.

## 6

1. And Jericho had shut its gates and was barred because of the
children of Israel: none went out and none came in.
2. And the Lord said to Joshua, See, I have given into your hand Jericho
and its king, the mighty warriors.
3. And you shall circle the
city, all the men of war, go round about the city once. Thus shall
you do six days.
4. And seven

### Commentary Digest

*this was Michael, as it is said: "Michael your prince."*[1] — R This explanation should appear in v. 14. The reason it appears here is not clear. K explains that the Almighty had sent the angel to encourage Joshua upon his impending invasion of Jericho. Joshua was unaware of the ethereal state of his visitor, taking him for a soldier of flesh and blood. He queried, "Are you for us or for our enemies?" Thereupon, the angel replied, "No, I am not a mere human. I am the archangel Michael, the captain of the Lord's host of heaven and earth. I have come now, this very instant that you saw me. This is proof to you that I am an angel." The rabbis relate to us that the angel said to Joshua: "My mission here is: Now I have come,' i.e. to remind you of your neglect of the duty which is perenially "now," the intensive learning of Torah which is forever in the category of "now," never growing old. I have also a secondary reminder, to resume your daily sacrifices which you neglected to offer up yesterday evening. Upon the next occasion, that of the siege of Ai, Joshua spent the night delving in the profundities of the halachah.[1]* — A explains that the angel came to take command of the Jewish army. He said to Joshua, "Not as you think that you are the commander and I have come to help you. On the contrary, I am the commander of Israel's host, and you are my subordinate. Thereupon, Joshua prostrated himself in subordination, and asked, "What does my master say to his servant?"

*Remove your shoe from your foot* — strip your soul of its material trappings. Let not your body obstruct the cleaving of your soul to the Shechinah, and let it not hinder the conveyance of prophecy to you. — M

CHAPTER 6

1. *had shut its gates and was barred* — Heb. סגרת ומסגרת, lit. closed and closed, the second form being in the stronger conjugation. — *"according to Targum, closed with iron gates and reinforced with copper bolts."* — R

כֹּהֲנִים יִשְׂאוּ שִׁבְעָה שׁוֹפְרוֹת הַיּוֹבְלִים
לִפְנֵי הָאָרוֹן וּבַיּוֹם הַשְּׁבִיעִי תָּסֹבּוּ אֶת־
הָעִיר שֶׁבַע פְּעָמִים וְהַכֹּהֲנִים יִתְקְעוּ
בַּשּׁוֹפָרוֹת׃ ה וְהָיָה בִּמְשֹׁךְ ׀ בְּקֶרֶן הַיּוֹבֵל
בְּשָׁמְעֲכֶם אֶת־קוֹל הַשּׁוֹפָר יָרִיעוּ כָל־
הָעָם תְּרוּעָה גְדוֹלָה וְנָפְלָה חוֹמַת הָעִיר
תַּחְתֶּיהָ וְעָלוּ הָעָם אִישׁ נֶגְדּוֹ׃ ו וַיִּקְרָא
יְהוֹשֻׁעַ בִּן־נוּן אֶל־הַכֹּהֲנִים וַיֹּאמֶר אֲלֵהֶם
שְׂאוּ אֶת־אֲרוֹן הַבְּרִית וְשִׁבְעָה כֹהֲנִים
יִשְׂאוּ שִׁבְעָה שׁוֹפְרוֹת יוֹבְלִים לִפְנֵי אֲרוֹן
יְהוָה׃ ז וַיֹּאמְרוּ אֶל־הָעָם עִבְרוּ וְסֹבּוּ
אֶת־הָעִיר וְהֶחָלוּץ יַעֲבֹר לִפְנֵי אֲרוֹן
יְהוָה׃ ח וַיְהִי כֶּאֱמֹר יְהוֹשֻׁעַ אֶל־הָעָם

יסבון שבעא שופריא
דקרן דכריא קדם ארונא
וביומא שביעאה
תסחרון ית קרתא שבע
זמנין וכהניא יתקעון
בשופריא: ה ויהי
במיגד בקרן דכריא
במשמעכון ית קל
שופרא ייבבון כל עמא
יבבא רבא ויפול שורא
דקרתא ויתבלע תחותה
ויסקון עמא גבר
לקבליה: ו וקרא יהושע
בר נון לכהניא ואמר
להון טולו ית ארון קימא
דיי ושבעא כהניא
יטלון שבעא שופריא
דקרן דכריא קדם ארונא
דיי: ז ואמר לעמא
עברו ואקיפו ית קרתא
ומזרזי חילא יעברון
קדם ארונא דיי: ח נהוה
כד אמר יהושע לעמא
ושבעא כהניא נסבין
שבעא

ת"א במשוך בקרן. ר"ה כו:

בשמעכם קרי. ויאמר קרי.

ושבעה

## רש"י

(ד) היובלים. אילים: (ה) במשוך. בתקיעה אחרונה כשהאריך התוקע את הקול: תחתיה. במקומה:

## רד"ק

פרים וז' אלים והשביעי הוא הנבחר בימים ובחדשים ובשני': (ד) היובלים. האילי' ובדברי רז"ל א"ר עקיבא כשהלכתי לערביא שמעתי שהיו קורין לדכרא יובלא: (ה) במשוך. בהאריך התקיעה: בשמעכם את קול השופר. כתיב בבי"ת וקרי בכ"ף והענין א': ונפלה חומת העיר תחתיה. יש לשאול בית רחב שהיה בחומה אם נאמר כי נפל ונצלת היא ובית אביה זה לא יתכן כי אם היה גם כזה היה מספר אותו הכתוב ועוד שאמר באו בית האשה הזונה והוציאו משם את האשה ונר' כי הבית היה קיים ולא נפל אבל הנראה בעיני כי לא נפלה כל חומת העיר אלא מה שהיה מן החומה את פני העיר נגד מחנה ישראל נפל ועלו העם איש נגדו ובית רחב היתה בחומה מצד אחר שלא נפל ומ"ש תחתיה ר"ל שנבלעה במקומה תחת הארץ ונר' ממנה מעט על פני הארץ לזכרון הנס: (ז) ויאמר אל העם. כתיב בוי"ו ופי' יהושע והכהנים וקרי בלא וי"ו ופי' יהושע: (ח) ויהי כאמר. בכ"ף:

## רלב"ג

מעט בענין זה המופת כי הקול החזק יניע האויר תנועה חזקה אלא שלא יתכן שיגיע מזאת התנועה כמו זה הפועל הנפלא שתפול החומה גדולה: (ח) ויהי כאמר. בכ"ף: ויהי כאמר וגו, שבעה שופרות היובלים לפני ה'. יונתן תרגם קדם ארונא דה' וכן בשני דפוסים ישנים כתוב לפני ארון ה'

## מנחת שי

ו (ה) בשמעכם בשמעכם ק' והוא חד מן י"א מלין דכתיב בית וקרי כ"ף: (ז) ויאמרו אל העם. ויאמר קרי והוא חד מן מלין דכתיבין ו' בסוף תיבותא ולא קרינן וסימן נמסר במלכים א' י"ב במסדה

## מצודת דוד

(ד) יתקעו. בכל יום בעת יקיפו: (ה) את קול. ר"ל הקול ההוא המאריך בתקיעה נמשכת: איש נגדו. לא יצטרכו להקיף ולעלות בה כי כל החומה תפול: (ח) ויהי כאמור. ר"ל כן עשו

## מצודת ציון

(ד) היובלים. האילים כן תרגומו: (ה) במשך. בהאריך הקול: (ז) והחלוץ. הם ב"ג וב"ר וחצי שבט מנשה כולם היו מזויינים ביותר כמ"ש בהם החלוצים תעברו (דברים ג'):

## Commentary Digest

said, i.e. Joshua and the priests. — K Joshua's messengers. — Alshich

*to the people* — the entire populace. — M

*pass on* — before the armed men of the tribes of Reuben and Gad. — M

*and let the armed ones pass before the Ark* — Thus, the populace marched, followed by the armed men, who were in turn followed by the priests

priests shall bear seven trumpets of rams' horns before the Ark;
and on the seventh day you shall encircle the city seven times,
and the priests shall blow with the trumpets. 5. And it shall
be that when they make a long blast with the ram's horn, when
you hear the sound of the trumpet, all the people shall shout
a great shout; and the wall of the city shall fall down in
its place and the people shall go up, every man opposite him.
6. And Joshua the son of Nun called the priests, and said
to them, Take up the Ark of the Covenant, and let seven
priests bear seven trumpets of rams' horns before the Ark of
the Lord. 7. And he said to the people, Pass on, and encircle
the city, and let the armed ones pass before the Ark of the
Lord. 8. And it was when Joshua spoke to the people,

**Commentary Digest**

the Ark, but all the men of war shall share in the performance of this miraculous conquest. — M

4. *rams' horns* — Heb. היובלים, — R, J, and D. Said Rabbi Akiva, "When I went to Arabia, I heard them calling a ram יובלא. — K[1]

5. *a long blast* — *"with the final blast, when the blower lengthens the note."* — R This is the indication of the completion of the series of blasts. We find this practice in Ex. XIX:13: When the ram's horn sounds long, they may go up on the mount. There it was a sign of the withdrawal of the Shechinah. Hence, the custom of the long final blast on Rosh Hashanah. — Maharil, R.H.

Also on Yom Kippur it is a sign of the withdrawal of the Shechinah at the end of the ten days of judgment — Tikun Tefillah.

*in its place* — *Heb.* תחתיה, lit. *under it.* — R The wall was as thick as it was high. Therefore, being incapable of falling, it sank into the ground in the very place where it had been standing, allowing the soldiers to enter each one opposite himself.[2] Thus, J renders: And the wall of the city will fall and be swallowed under it.

K theorizes that only the wall facing the Israelite camp fell. Rahab's house, being on the other side of the wall, was unscathed. Cf. supra II:15.

6. *called the priests* — Take up the Ark of the covenant — If the blowing of the trumpets was delegated to the priests, surely the bearing of the Holy Ark. — Alshich

7. *And he said* — Kethib, And they

וְשִׁבְעָה הַכֹּהֲנִים נֹשְׂאִים שִׁבְעָה
שׁוֹפְרוֹת הַיּוֹבְלִים לִפְנֵי יְהוָה עָבְרוּ
וְתָקְעוּ בַּשּׁוֹפָרוֹת וַאֲרוֹן בְּרִית יְהוָה הֹלֵךְ
אַחֲרֵיהֶם: ט וְהֶחָלוּץ הֹלֵךְ לִפְנֵי הַכֹּהֲנִים
תֹּקְעוּ הַשּׁוֹפָרוֹת וְהַמְאַסֵּף הֹלֵךְ אַחֲרֵי
הָאָרוֹן הָלוֹךְ וְתָקוֹעַ בַּשּׁוֹפָרוֹת: י וְאֶת־
הָעָם צִוָּה יְהוֹשֻׁעַ לֵאמֹר לֹא תָרִיעוּ וְלֹא־
תַשְׁמִיעוּ אֶת־קוֹלְכֶם וְלֹא־יֵצֵא מִפִּיכֶם
דָּבָר עַד יוֹם אָמְרִי אֲלֵיכֶם הָרִיעוּ
וַהֲרֵיעֹתֶם: יא וַיַּסֵּב אֲרוֹן־יְהוָה אֶת־הָעִיר
הַקֵּף פַּעַם אֶחָת וַיָּבֹאוּ הַמַּחֲנֶה וַיָּלִינוּ בַּמַּחֲנֶה:

**תרגום**

שַׁבְעָא שׁוֹפְרַיָּא דְקַרְנֵי דִכְרַיָּא קֳדָם אֲרוֹנָא דַיְיָ עָבְרִין וְתָקְעִין בְּשׁוֹפְרַיָּא וַאֲרוֹן קְיָמָא דַיְיָ אָזֵיל בָּתְרֵיהוֹן: ט וּמְזָרְזֵי חֵילָא אָזְלִין קֳדָם כַּהֲנַיָּא תָּקְעֵי שׁוֹפְרַיָּא וְשִׁבְטָא דְבֵית דָּן אָזֵיל בָּתַר אֲרוֹנָא וְכַהֲנַיָּא אָזְלִין וְתָקְעִין בְּשׁוֹפְרַיָּא: י וְיָת עַמָּא פַּקֵּיד יְהוֹשֻׁעַ לְמֵימַר לָא תְיַבְּבוּן וְלָא תַשְׁמְעוּן יָת קָלְכוֹן וְלָא יִפּוֹק מִפּוּמְכוֹן פִּתְגָמָא עַד יוֹמָא דְאֵימַר לְכוֹן יַבִּיבוּ וּתְיַבְּבוּן: יא וְאַסְחַר אֲרוֹנָא דַיְיָ יָת קַרְתָּא אַקֵּיף זִמְנָא חֲדָא וַעֲלוּ בְּמַשְׁרִיתָא וּבָתוּ במשריתא

תוקעי קרי.

**רד״ק**

(ט) והחלוץ. פירשו בו שהם בני ראובן ובני גד וחצי שבט מנשה שעברו חלוצים לפני אחיהם: תוקעי. כן כתיב בוי״ו ופירושו אשר תקעו והקרי הוא תוקעי ומבואר הוא: והמאסף. אמר בו התרגום שבטא דדן לפי שהוא היה אחרון בדגלים כמו שנאמר עליו מאסף לכל המחנות: הלוך ותקוע. אינו אומר על המאסף שהיו תוקעים אלא כמו שאמר המתרגם וכהניא אזלין ותקעים בשופריא: (י) עד יום אמרי אליכם. יש מפרשים כמו עת כמו יום צעקתי בלילה ואין צריך רק פירושו כמשמעו הוא יום השביעי: (יא) ויסב ארון ה׳ את העיר. פירוש יהושע הסב הארון את עיר: הקף. ארון ה׳ את העיר פעם אחת וזה היה ביום הראשון וראשון לימי השבוע כך קבלו רז״ל כי ביום ז׳ שנלכדה יריחו יום שבת היה ואע״פ שהרגו ושרפו בשבת מי שצוה על השבת צוה לחלל שבת בכבישת יריחו וכן בשאר עיירות שהיו ישראל צרים עליהן ואמרו בקבלה עד רדתה ואפילו בשבת וכמו שצוה גם כן להעלות עולות

**רש״י**

(ט) והחלוץ. בני ראובן ובני גד היו עוברים לפניהם לפי שהיו בני גד גבורים ומכים בזרוע הזקה כמו שנאמר וטרף

**מנחת שי**

גם במ״ג יש הערה מחילוף זה בלא הכרע. ויש לי להכריע שכתוב לפני ה׳ מכת המסורת שבמערכת אות הלמ״ד במסרה רבתא נמסר ארון ה׳ כ״ג וזה אינו מן המנין וכן מצאתי בספרים כתיבת יד מדויקים: (ט) תקעו. תוקעי קרי: והמאסף. הה״א במאריך והמ״ם רפה וכן חברו שבסמוך: הולך. הלוך קרי:

**רלב״ג**

החזקה תחתיה אם לא יחוב׳ לזה המופת: (י) והנה לוה אותם יהושע שלא יריעו ולא ישמיעו את קולם עד היום הז׳ כדי שלא ירגישו בני העיר וישליכו אבנים מעל החומה ואעפ״י שהיה אפשר לש״י לשמרם מזה על דרך המופת הנה אין מדרך הש״י שיעשה המופתי׳ נבטלה

**מצודת ציון**

(ט) והמאסף. דגל מחנה דן נקרא מאסף ע״ש שהלכו באחרונה והיו מאספים כל הנכשלים מהמחנות שהלכו לאשונים:

**מצודת דוד**

כאשר אמר יהושע אל העם ושבעה כו׳: (ט) תקעי השופרות. חוזר על הכהנים: הלוך ותקוע. ר״ל לא עמדו הכהנים בעת

## Commentary Digest

*of your mouth* — even in a whisper. — M

*until the day I bid you shout* — i.e. the seventh day. Others render: until the time I bid you shout. — K

11. *And he* (Joshua) *caused the Ark of the Lord to circle* — K and A

*and they came to the camp* — Gilgal, as in IX:6, X:6. There is no mention of any other camp. — M

and the seven priests bearing the seven trumpets of rams' horns
passed on before (the Ark of) the Lord and blew with the
trumpets; and the Ark of the covenant of the Lord followed
them. 9. And the armed men went before the priests that
blew the trumpets, and the rear guard came after the Ark, (the
priests) going on, and blowing with the trumpets. 10. And
Joshua commanded the people, saying, You shall not shout nor
let your voice be heard, neither shall any word proceed out of
your mouth, until the day I bid you shout; then you shall shout.
11. And he caused the Ark of the Lord to circle the city, going
about it once; and they came into the camp and lodged in the
camp.

## Commentary Digest

blowing the trumpets, who preceded the Ark, which was followed by the rear guard. — M

9. *And the armed ones* — *"The children of Reuben and the children of Gad were passing before them, because the children of Gad were mighty warriors and would strike with a strong arm, as it is said: "And he tears the arm, even the crown of the head." "*[1] — R

*before the priests* — who preceded the Ark, as above v. 7. This was to fulfill Moses' command of passing before the Lord to battle.[2] The purpose of this order was to impress upon the populace that it is not the valor of the warriors that defeats the enemy, but the power of the Almighty God, Who is represented by the Ark of the covenant. — Alshich and M

*and the rear guard* — See below v. 13.

*(the priests) going on and blowing* — J, not the rear guard. — K They did not stand still while blowing the trumpets, but continued to march. — D and A

10. *And Joshua commanded the people* — after they had started marching. The people started to march before Joshua finished his instructions to them. Therefore, he continued to instruct them during the march. — A

*You shall not shout* — for joy. — M

*nor let your voice be heard* — in cry. — M

*neither shall any word proceed out*

יב וַיַּשְׁכֵּם יְהוֹשֻׁעַ בַּבֹּקֶר וַיִּשְׂאוּ
הַכֹּהֲנִים אֶת־אֲרוֹן יְהוָה׃ יג וְשִׁבְעָה
הַכֹּהֲנִים נֹשְׂאִים שִׁבְעָה שׁוֹפְרוֹת
הַיֹּבְלִים לִפְנֵי אֲרוֹן יְהוָה הֹלְכִים הָלוֹךְ
וְתָקְעוּ בַּשּׁוֹפָרוֹת וְהֶחָלוּץ הֹלֵךְ לִפְנֵיהֶם
וְהַמְאַסֵּף הֹלֵךְ אַחֲרֵי אֲרוֹן יְהוָה הוֹלֵךְ
וְתָקוֹעַ בַּשּׁוֹפָרוֹת׃ יד וַיָּסֹבּוּ אֶת־הָעִיר
בַּיּוֹם הַשֵּׁנִי פַּעַם אַחַת וַיָּשֻׁבוּ הַמַּחֲנֶה
כֹּה עָשׂוּ שֵׁשֶׁת יָמִים׃ טו וַיְהִי ׀ בַּיּוֹם
הַשְּׁבִיעִי וַיַּשְׁכִּמוּ בַּעֲלוֹת הַשַּׁחַר וַיָּסֹבּוּ
אֶת־הָעִיר כַּמִּשְׁפָּט הַזֶּה שֶׁבַע פְּעָמִים
רַק בַּיּוֹם הַהוּא סָבְבוּ אֶת־הָעִיר שֶׁבַע
פְּעָמִים׃ טז וַיְהִי בַּפַּעַם הַשְּׁבִיעִית תָּקְעוּ

בְּמַשְׁרִיתָא׃ יב וְאַקְדֵּים
יְהוֹשֻׁעַ בְּצַפְרָא וּנְטַלוּ
כַהֲנַיָא יָת אֲרוֹנָא דַיָי׃
יג וְשִׁבְעָא כַהֲנַיָא נָסִיבוּ
שִׁבְעָא שׁוֹפְרַיָא דְקֶרֶן
דִכְרַיָא קֳדָם אֲרוֹנָא דַיָי
אָזְלִין מֵיזַל וְתָקְעִין
בְּשׁוֹפְרַיָא וּמְזָרְזֵי חֵילָא
אָזְלִין קֳדָמֵיהוֹן וְשִׁבְטָא
דְבֵית דָן אָזֵיל בָּתַר
אֲרוֹנָא דַיָי וְכַהֲנַיָא אָזְלִין
וְתָקְעִין בְּשׁוֹפְרַיָא׃
יד וְאַסְחַרוּ יָת קַרְתָּא
בְּיוֹמָא תִנְיָנָא זִמְנָא חֲדָא
וְתָבוּ לְמַשְׁרִיתָא כְּדֵין
עֲבָדוּ שִׁתָּא יוֹמִין׃
טו וַהֲוָה בְּיוֹמָא שְׁבִיעָאָה
וְאַקְדִּימוּ כְּמִיסַק צַפְרָא
וְאַסְחַרוּ יָת קַרְתָּא
כְּהִלְכְתָא הָדֵין שְׁבַע
זִמְנִין לְחוּד בְּיוֹמָא הַהוּא
אַקִיפוּ יַת קַרְתָּא שְׁבַע
זִמְנִין׃ טז וַהֲוָה בְּזִמְנָא
שְׁבִיעָתָא תְּקַעוּ כַהֲנַיָא
בְּשׁוֹפְרַיָא וַאֲמַר יְהוֹשֻׁעַ
לְעַמָּא

הלוך קרי כעלות קרי

**רש"י**

זרוע אף קדקד: (יג) **והמאסף**· שבט דן הנוסע אחרון והוא מאסף את כל המתעכבים האחרונים: (טו) **ביום השביעי**· שבת היה:

**רד"ק**

בשבת: (יג) הולך ותקוע. כתיב הולך ר"ל שכמו שהיה המאסף הולך כן היו הכהנים תוקעים וקרי הלוך שהוא מקור והפירוש אחד: (טו) וישכימו בעלות השחר. כתיב בבי"ת וקרי בכ"ף: כמשפ' הזה שבע פעמים. כמשפט הזה שעשו בששת הימים והיו שבע פעמים עם ההקפה הראשונה הזאת של יום השביעי רק ביום ההוא **עשו** יותר הקפו' כי הקיפו העיר **שבע פעמי'**:

**מנחת שי**

(טו) ויהי ביום השביעי וישכימו כעלות. במקצת ספרים בעלות בבי"ת וקרי כעלות בכ"ף וכן דעת רד"ק ובספרים אחרים כתוב בכ"ף ומסר עליו כ"ף כתיב וק' ונראין עיקר שלא נזכר זה במסורת עם י"א מלין דכתיבין בי"ת וקריין כ"ף:

**מצודת דוד**

תקיעה כי אם הלכו ותקעו: (יב) **וישכם**. ביום השני: (יג) **הלוך ותקוע**. כפל הדבר לומר שלא פסקו מלתקוע: (טו) **כעלות השחר**. להיות הזמן מספיק להקיף שבעה פעמים: **רק וגו'**. ולזה הוצרכו להשכים אז יותר משאר הימים: (טז) **תקעו**· ר"ל תקיעה נמשכת וארוכה:

**מצודת ציון**

(טו) **השחר**. הוא האור הנוצץ בפאת המזרח טרם יעלה השמש: **כמשפט הזה**. ר"ל כמנהג הזה:

## Commentary Digest

rose early in order to have enough time for this observance. — M. L.

*after the same manner seven times* — i.e. upon the completion of their first circle, they had already circled the city seven times, including the six times of the preceding six days. — K They continued to circle the city, until —

*on that day they circled the city seven times.* — K and M

12. And Joshua rose early in the morning, and the priests took up the Ark of the Lord. 13. And the seven priests bearing the seven trumpets of rams' horns before the Ark of the Lord were going continuously, and they blew with the trumpets; and the armed men went before them; and the rear guard came after the Ark of the Lord, (the priests) going on and blowing with the trumpets. 14. And the second day they circled the city once, and returned to the camp; so they did six days. 15. And it was on the seventh day, that they rose early at the dawning (of the day), and they circled the city after the same manner seven times; only on that day they circled the city seven times. 16. And it was at the seventh time, the priests blew

## Commentary Digest

13. *and the rear guard* — *"the tribe of Dan that traveled last, and they would gather up all those who lingered behind."* — R The tribe of Dan is referred to as the rear guard or "gatherer" in Num. X:25.

*going on and blowing with the trumpets* — See above v. 9. K explains here: The rear guard was going along as the priests blew the trumpets.

15. *on the seventh day* — *"It was the Sabbath."* — R[1] I.e. the seventh day refers to the seventh day of the week as well as the seventh day of the circling. Even though they killed and burned on that day, He Who commanded concerning the prohibition of work on the Sabbath, likewise commanded concerning the siege of cities on the Sabbath. He sanctioned the commencement of a siege in the case of a mandatory war, and the continuation of a siege in the case of a voluntary war.[2] This is similar to the offering up of sacrifices on the Sabbath, which involves slaughtering and kindling fire. — K

*that they rose early at the dawning of the day* — On the seventh day they rose earlier than on the first six days, in order to circle the city seven times. — D Moreover, since it was the Sabbath, they were obligated to eat the Sabbath meals. They, therefore,

הכהנים בשופרות ויאמר יהושע אל־
העם הריעו כי־נתן יהוה לכם את־
העיר: יז והיתה העיר חרם היא וכל־
אשר־בה ליהוה רק רחב הזונה תחיה
היא וכל־אשר אתה בבית כי
החבאתה את־המלאכים אשר
שלחנו: יח ורק־אתם שמרו מן־החרם
פן־תחרימו ולקחתם מן־החרם ושמתם

**תרגום**

לעמא יביבו ארי יהב
יי לכון ית קרתא:
יז ותהי קרתא חרמא
היא וכל דבה קדם יי
לחוד רחב פונדקיתא
תחי היא וכל דעמה
בביתא ארי אטמרת
ית אזגדיא די שלחנא:
יח ולחוד אתון אסתמרו
מן חרמא דלמא תחרמון
ותסבון מן חרמא
ותשוון ית משריתא
דישראל לחרמא
ותעכרון

**תולדות אהרן** העיר חרם: מ״ק י״ז סנהדרין קיג:

**רש״י**

(יז) והיתה העיר חרם · הקדש כי היום שבת קודש וראוי להיות קדש שלל הנשלל בו: (יח) ועכרתם · לשון מים

**רד״ק**

(יז) והיתה העיר חרם היא וכל אשר בה. היא שלא תבנה עוד וכל אשר בה שלא יהנה אדם מכל אשר בה ונראה כי הקב״ה אמר לו כן כי יהושע לא אמר דבר כזה מלבו ואף על פי שלא זכר זה הכתוב ימצאו כמוהו רבים ורז״ל אמרו כי יהושע אמר דבר זה מרצונו ולא אמר לו הקב״ה אמר יהושע יריחו כבושה תחלה לארץ ישראל נוציאנה תרומה כאשה הזאת שמפרשת חלתה מתחלת עיסתה ועוד אמר יהושע בשבת לכדנו יריחו ושבת קדש שנאמר כי קדש היא לכם כל מה שכבשנו בה יהיה קדש שנאמר קדש לה׳ אוצר ה׳ יבא ואף עפ״י כן הקב״ה הסכים על ידו ומניין שהקב״ה הסכים על ידו שנא׳ חטא ישראל וגם עברו את בריתי והיה זה אחד מג׳ שגזרו בית דין שלמטה והסכים הקב״ה עמהם: כי החבאתה. בשני סימני נקבה כמו ישועתה עזרת׳ וכל כפל לחזק הענין כמו שפירש׳ בספר מכלל והכפל הנה לפי שהחביאה אותם יפה: (יח) שמרו מן החרם. שמרו עצמכם ושמרו איש את אחיו ומפני זה אמר חטא ישראל

**מנחת שי**

(יז) רק רחב הזונה תחיה וגו׳. כל אתנ״ע דינו להנקד בחטף פתח כג״ן שאלו רחצו מהרו יעקב אהרן ודומיהם ולפנים יש מתג וכו׳ מבטלים יש להם סימן נד״ח פירוש נגינה מקדמת׳ דגש שלאחריו. חירק שלפניו בחולם של שמוש. ושלשתם נמצאו בפסוק א׳ רק רחב הזונה תחיה היא וכל אשר אתה בבית כי החבאתה את המלאכים אשר שלחנו ודין חירק שלפניו אינו נוהג בהיותו בחולם של יסוד דוד: כגון נאצו נאפו כחשו מהרו אבל בהיותו בחולם של שמוש נוהג ומבטל החטף פתח כגון תהיה יהיה יחיה ויולאים מכלל זה ותהלך את הלוה ולשונם תהלך בארץ כי החירק בחולם של שמוש ואינו מבטל החטף פתח והספמיות מוסיפים עוד מבטל אחר כל שיש יו״ד לאחריו כגון ידעיה זרחיה שמעיה וכן ועזה ואחיו וכן רעיון ישעיה רות חוץ מן

(לספיות) באין כי׳ מבטל החטף פתח: החבאתה. בכמה ספרים האל״ף בקמץ ובספרים בפתח ומסורת עליו בלחד מהם לית ופתח באלף. וגם רד״ק בספר

**רלב״ג**

(יז) והנה לוה שיחרימו כל אשר בעיר ולא יהנו ממנו בדבר כדי שלא יטעו ישראל במה שיגיע להם מהשלל אחר זה ויייחסו אל מה שקנו משלל העיר הסיה ואולי יהיה זה סבה שיחשבו שאמונתם היתה טובה עד שגם מקניהם ונכסיהם מביאי׳ הצלחה למי שיקנם ולזאת הסבה בעינה קלל מי שיבנה יריחו עד שיגיע הבנין בהיות כל בניו חיים ולא ישאר לו בהשלמתו כי אם לעי׳ בניו וידמה שפעולות יושבי יריחו ואמונתם היו יותר מגונות מפעולות שאר יושבי הארץ ואמונתם ולזה לוה שלא ישאר מהם רושם ולא מן העיר או היה זה לתת מורך לשאר הגוי׳ עם שזאת הקללה לא היתה לפי הנבואה ולזה תמלא שכבר נתקיימה בימי אחאב אמר בימיו בנה חיאל בית האלי ולזה אותם שילינו רחב הזונה וכל אשר אתה ובמקומות שאספר בזולת מופת:

**מצודת ציון**

(יז) חרם. פעם תשמש על חרמי גבוה והקדש ופעם תשמש על כריתה ושממון: החבאתה. הסתירה: (יח) ועכרתם. מעניו

**מצודת דוד**

(יז) חרם. לאבדון וכריתה: היא וגו׳. ר״ל העיר עלמה ומה שבה מהדברים הראוים להביא לאולר ה׳: לה׳. ר״ל לשם ה׳ ולכבודו: (יח) שמרו. את עלמכם וזולתכם מלקחת מה מן החרם: פן תחרימו ולקחתם וגו׳. פן תכריתו את ישראל במה שתקחו מן החרם כי כולם יאבדו וזהו ושמתם וגו׳:

## Commentary Digest

A maintains that the Scripture relates to us the primary cause, not concerning itself with the validity of the oath. M explains that Rahab, having converted to Judaism before Israel's entry to the land of Canaan, was automatically exempt from being slain in the war against the Canaanites. Joshua exhorts the people to spare her family who may not yet have converted and her possessions that they be excluded from the consecration and curse.

18. *keep* — yourselves and one another. For disobeying this exhortation, Israel was held accountable in the episode of Achan.[4] — K

with the trumpets, and Joshua said to the people, Shout, for
the Lord has given you the city. 17. And the city shall be
devoted; it, and all that is in it, to the Lord; only Rahab the
harlot shall live, she and all that is with her in the house,
because she hid the messengers that we sent. 18. And only
you keep (yourselves) from the devoted thing, lest you make
yourselves condemned when you take of the devoted thing,
and make

## Commentary Digest

16. *and Joshua said to the people, Shout* — I.e. while the priests were still blowing the trumpets, Joshua commanded the people to shout for joy. — M. L.

*for the Lord has given you the city.* — Be joyful that the Lord is waging your battles, not that you are victorious. — M. L.

17. *And the city shall be devoted* — "*consecrated* (belonging to "Hekdesh"). *For the day was the Holy Sabbath; hence it was appropriate that the booty which was taken thereon be consecrated.*" — R[1] The city itself was to remain sacred and never be rebuilt. This was also a form of "terumah," or giving of the first fruits of victory to the Eternal, just as the first-born is to be dedicated to Him. It would appear that Joshua enacted this consecration because of a divine command. Our Rabbis, however, state that he did so of his own initiative, both the siege on the Sabbath and the consecration of the spoils. The Lord, however, agreed to this enactment, and punished the violators thereof. —K[2] G explains this enactment as a precaution against idolatry. Should the people take of the booty and succeed in any enterprise therewith, they might attribute their success to the potency of the gods of Jericho, whose very spoils insure success. A and M explain that since the city was taken miraculously without effort on the part of Israel, it was appropriate that the spoils be devoted to the Almighty and not be used by Israel.

*only Rahab the harlot shall live, she and all that is with her in the house, because she hid the messengers that we sent* — Joshua taught the people to appreciate any help given to them, and not to forget those responsible for that help, in the flush of victory. Although the promise given by the spies[3] might not have been valid, and the Jewish people might not have been bound by that promise, Rahab should be spared as an expression of gratitude for the aid rendered to the spies. — G

אֶת־מַחֲנֵה יִשְׂרָאֵל לְחֵרֶם וַעֲכַרְתֶּם
אוֹתוֹ: יט וְכֹל ׀ כֶּסֶף וְזָהָב וּכְלֵי נְחֹשֶׁת
וּבַרְזֶל קֹדֶשׁ הוּא לַיהוָה אוֹצַר יְהוָה
יָבוֹא: כ וַיָּרַע הָעָם וַיִּתְקְעוּ בַּשֹּׁפָרוֹת
וַיְהִי כִשְׁמֹעַ הָעָם אֶת־קוֹל הַשּׁוֹפָר
וַיָּרִיעוּ הָעָם תְּרוּעָה גְדוֹלָה וַתִּפֹּל
הַחוֹמָה תַּחְתֶּיהָ וַיַּעַל הָעָם הָעִירָה אִישׁ
נֶגְדּוֹ וַיִּלְכְּדוּ אֶת־הָעִיר: כא וַיַּחֲרִימוּ אֶת־
כָּל־אֲשֶׁר בָּעִיר מֵאִישׁ וְעַד־אִשָּׁה מִנַּעַר
וְעַד־זָקֵן וְעַד שׁוֹר וָשֶׂה וַחֲמוֹר לְפִי־
חָרֶב: כב וְלִשְׁנַיִם הָאֲנָשִׁים הַמְרַגְּלִים
אֶת־הָאָרֶץ אָמַר יְהוֹשֻׁעַ בֹּאוּ בֵּית־

וּתְעַכְרוּן יָתֵיהּ: יט וְכָל
כַּסְפָּא וְדַהֲבָא וּמָנֵי
נְחָשָׁא וּבַרְזְלָא קוּדְשָׁא
אִינוּן קֳדָם יְיָ לְאוֹצַר
בֵּית מַקְדְּשָׁא דַיְיָ
יִתְעֲלוּן: כ וְיַבִּיבוּ עַמָּא
וּתְקַעוּ בְּשׁוֹפְרַיָּא וַהֲוָה
כַּד שְׁמַע עַמָּא יָת קָל
שׁוֹפְרָא וְיַבִּיבוּ עַמָּא יַבָּבָא
רַבָּא וּנְפַל שׁוּרָא דְקַרְתָּא
וְאִתְבְּלַע תְּחוֹתוֹהִי
וּסְלִיק עַמָּא לְקַרְתָּא
גְּבַר לְקִבְלֵיהּ וּכְבַשׁוּ יָת
קַרְתָּא: כא וְגַמַּרוּ יָת כָּל
דִּבְקַרְתָּא מִגְּבַר וְעַד
אִתְּתָא מֵעוּלֵימָא וְעַד
סָבָא וְעַד תּוֹר וְאִמַּר
וַחֲמַר לְפִתְגַּם דְּחָרֶב:
כב וְלִתְרֵין גֻּבְרַיָּא
דְאַלִּילוּ יָת אַרְעָא אֲמַר
יְהוֹשֻׁעַ עוּלוּ לְבֵית
אתתא

ת״א כשמוע העם . ברכות נד : ותפול החומה . ברכות נד : הנערים המרגלים . (ברכות ח סנהדרין כח) :

**רד״ק**

מפני שלא נתנו עיניהם שלא יקח אדם משלל העיר דבר: פן תחרימו . פירושו ולקחתם מן החרם : (יט) אוצר ה׳ יבא ·

**האשה**

**מנחת שי**

מכלול דף ק״ע כתב שהוא בפתח ונתן טעם לדבר : (יט) אוצר ה׳ יבוא . חד מן י״ד דסבירין יבואו וקרינן יבוא ונמסר הסימן במסרה גדולה סוף פרשת במיני . ומה שתרגם יונתן יתעלון הוא למאי דסבירין : ותברו מלמד עליו שתרגם קדש הוא קודשא אינון : (כ) ויהי כשמע . במקצת ספרים הכ״ף רפה ועיין מס

**מצודת דוד**

(יט) וכל כסף וגו׳ . שהם הדברים הראוים לאוצר ה׳: (כ) וירע העם . ומוזר ומפרש כשמוע העם קול השופר כשהיא מארכת

**מצודת ציון**

השחת׳ וקלקול כמו עכרתם אותי (בראשית ל״ד) : (כ) וירע . מלשון תרועה: (כא) לפי חרב. החדוד של החרב נקרא פה בלשון המקרא:

## Commentary Digest

this, they shouted with a great shout, and the wall fell in its place. Thus the passage is exact and not repetitious. — A and Alshich

*a great shout* — Heb. תרועה, meaning a shout coming from the depths of one's soul. "A day of *Truah* shall it be for you"[3] describes the day of New Year. The Rabbis interpret the "truah" of Rosh Hashanah as applying to the blast of the Shofar.[4] Here the meaning is simply shouting, in contrast to the blasting of the shofar by the Kohanim.

The blowing of the shofar during the siege of Jericho, instead of the silver trumpets prescribed in Num. X:8, 9, 10 draws a contrast between Moses the master and Joshua the disciple, showing that even Joshua, Moses' devoted minister and outstanding disciple, was incapable of replacing the master of prophets. The silver trumpets belonged only to Moses, and on the day of his passing, were hidden away, never to be used by his successors.[4]

21. *And they completely destroyed*

the camp of Israel a ruin, and trouble it. 19. And all the
silver and gold, and vessels of copper and iron, are consecrated
to the Lord; *they* shall come into the treasury of the Lord.
20. And the people shouted, and (the priests) blew with the
trumpets; and it was when the people heard the sound of the
trumpet, that the people shouted with a great shout, and the
wall fell down in its place and the people went up into the
city, every man opposite him, and they took the city. 21. And
they completely destroyed all that was in the city, both man
and woman, young and old, and ox, and sheep, and ass,
with the edge of the sword. 22. And to the two men who
had spied out the country, Joshua said, Go into the

## Commentary Digest

*and trouble* — Heb. ועכרתם, *"an expression of turbid water* (מים עכורים)." — R *

19. *And all the silver and gold* — Things which are fit for the Lord's treasury are to be deposited therein, and all that are unfit are to be destroyed. — D and M Were they to be destroyed, their destruction would never be complete. Therefore, it was preferable to consecrate them. — A

*are consecrated* — lit. it is consecrated, referring to the entire booty of metal collectively. Likewise, they shall come, lit. it shall come. — Minhath Shai

*the treasury of the Lord* — in the sanctuary, where the spoils of Midian, donated by the captains of the thousands and hundreds, were kept.[1] — K

20. *And the people shouted, and (the priests) blew with the trumpets* — The Scripture goes on to explain that this shout took place when the people heard the sound of the trumpet. Then they shouted a great shout as had been predicted by Joshua in v. 5. — D and M Others explain that the people cried out for joy before they heard the extended blast of the trumpet. After the seventh round, when the priests blew the trumpets, Joshua informed the people that the city was already in their hands and ordered them to shout for joy, although the ban would prevent them from deriving pleasure therefrom. This was not, however, the anticipated great shout which had been predicted.[2] After the priests had blown the trumpets, and one priest blew *the trumpet* with a long blast, and the people heard

* I.e. you will stain the purity of Israel by taking from the booty. — D. S.

הָאִשָּׁה הַזּוֹנָה וְהוֹצִיאוּ מִשָּׁם אֶת־
הָאִשָּׁה וְאֶת־כָּל־אֲשֶׁר־לָהּ כַּאֲשֶׁר
נִשְׁבַּעְתֶּם לָהּ׃ כג וַיָּבֹאוּ הַנְּעָרִים
הַמְרַגְּלִים וַיֹּצִיאוּ אֶת־רָחָב וְאֶת־אָבִיהָ
וְאֶת־אִמָּהּ וְאֶת־אַחֶיהָ וְאֶת־כָּל־אֲשֶׁר־
לָהּ וְאֵת כָּל־מִשְׁפְּחוֹתֶיהָ הוֹצִיאוּ
וַיַּנִּיחוּם מִחוּץ לְמַחֲנֵה יִשְׂרָאֵל׃ כד וְהָעִיר
שָׂרְפוּ בָאֵשׁ וְכָל־אֲשֶׁר־בָּהּ רַק הַכֶּסֶף
וְהַזָּהָב וּכְלֵי הַנְּחֹשֶׁת וְהַבַּרְזֶל נָתְנוּ
אוֹצַר בֵּית־יְהוָה׃ כה וְאֶת־רָחָב הַזּוֹנָה
וְאֶת־בֵּית אָבִיהָ וְאֶת־כָּל־אֲשֶׁר־לָהּ
הֶחֱיָה יְהוֹשֻׁעַ וַתֵּשֶׁב בְּקֶרֶב יִשְׂרָאֵל
עַד הַיּוֹם הַזֶּה כִּי הֶחְבִּיאָה אֶת־
הַמַּלְאָכִים אֲשֶׁר־שָׁלַח יְהוֹשֻׁעַ לְרַגֵּל אֶת־יְרִיחוֹ׃

אִתְּתָא פוּנְדְּקִיתָא
וְאַפִּיקוּ מִתַּמָּן יָת אִתְּתָא
וְיָת כָּל דִּי לַהּ כְּמָא
דְּקַיֵּמְתּוּן לַהּ׃ כג וְעָלוּ
עוּלֵמַיָּא מְאַלְּלַיָּא
וְאַפִּיקוּ יָת רָחָב וְיָת
אֲבוּהָא וְיָת אִמַּהּ וְיָת
אֲחוּהָא וְיָת כָּל דִּי לַהּ
וְיָת כָּל זַרְעֲיָתַהָא אַפִּיקוּ
וְאַשְׁרוּנוּן מִבָּרָא
לְמַשְׁרִיתָא דְּיִשְׂרָאֵל׃
כד וְקַרְתָּא אוֹקִידוּ בְּנוּרָא
וְכָל דִּי בַהּ לְחוֹד כַּסְפָּא
וְדַהֲבָא וּמָאנֵי נְחָשָׁא
וּבַרְזְלָא יְהַבוּ בְּאוֹצַר
בֵּית מַקְדְּשָׁא דַּייָ׃
כה וְיָת רָחָב פּוּנְדְּקִיתָא
וְיָת בֵּית אֲבוּהָא וְיָת כָּל
דִּי לַהּ קַיֵּים יְהוֹשֻׁעַ
וִיתֵיבַת בְּגוֹ יִשְׂרָאֵל עַד
יוֹמָא הָדֵין אֲרֵי אַטְמָרַת
יָת אִזְגַּדַּיָּא דִּשְׁלַח
יְהוֹשֻׁעַ לְאַלָּלָא יָת
ארעא

רש"י

עכורים: (כג) ויבאו הנערים המרגלים. כאן היו צריכים זירוז ונעשו כנערים זריזים ובלילה ראשון היו כמלאכים ששמרו עצמן מן העבירה עם רחב הזונה לכך נקראו שם מלאכים ולכך נקראו אנשים מלאכים נערים:

רד"ק

באהל מועד שהיה שם הקדש משלל מדין הזהב שנתנו שרי האלפים והמאות: (כג) ויבואו הנערים. כל משרת יקרא נער ואפילו יהיה זקן כמו יהושע בן נון נער ואלו האנשים המרגלים היו נערי יהושע או נערי אחד מגדולי ישראל: מחוץ למחנה. ישראל הניחום מבחוץ למחנה עד שיתגיירו וישבו ולדת ישראל ואחר שנתגיירו ישבו בתוך ישראל כמ"ש ותשב בקרב ישראל עד היום הזה: (כה) החיה יהושע. שצוה לשמור לה השבועה שנשבעו לה המלאכים כמו שאמר רק רחב הזונה וגו'. ויש לפרש עוד החיה שנתן להם מחיה ממון או נחלה במה שיחיו וזהו שאמר ותשב בקרב ישראל וזהו הפי' הנכון ויש בו דרש כי יהושע לקח רחב לאשה וזהו החיה כי כיון שראו שיהושע לקח רחב לאשה נדבקו בבית אביה מגדולי ישראל ואף על פי

מנחת שי

שמלכתוב בשופטים סימן ז': (כג) ויצאו את רחב. בספרים הבלים מסורה חסר ו' ונכון לעשות כן לפי מ"ש בד"ה סימן ח'.

## Commentary Digest

*of Israel* — The Israelites placed them outside the camp until they would be converted to Judaism according to the prescribed ritual. Subsequently, they would be permitted to reside among the Israelites, like Rahab, as in v. 25 (K)

25. *Joshua saved alive* — by commanding the spies to keep the oath which they had sworn to her. It is also possible that he sustained them with money or property, as the Bible states: and she dwelt in the midst of Israel. The rabbis say that Joshua married Rahab, thereby saving her family Since others followed his example, and married other members of her

harlot's house, and bring out from there the woman and all that she has, as you swore to her. 23. And the young men who were spies went in, and brought out Rahab, and her father, and her mother, and her brothers, and all that she had; and they brought out all her families, and placed them outside the camp of Israel. 24. And they burnt the city with fire, and all that was in it; only the silver, and the gold, and the vessels of copper and iron, they put into the treasury of the house of the Lord. 25. But Rahab the harlot, and her father's household, and all that she had, Joshua saved alive; and she dwelt in the midst of Israel to this day; because she hid the messengers, whom Joshua sent to spy out Jericho.

## Commentary Digest

*all* — fulfilling thereby the Biblical command concerning the "seven nations" of Canaan, who were steeped in idolatry and immoral practices,[1] "You shall not spare a living soul."[2] In celebration of this victory, Joshua composed the majestic hymn, "Aleinu," which is recited thrice daily, and enjoys, in addition, a prominent position in the liturgy of Rosh Hashana.[3] This prayer emphasizes the superiority of Israel over the idolatrous nations, and the sublime concept of monotheism.

23. *And the young men who were spies went in* — The spies are referred to as young men, although Caleb had been sent by Moses during the second year of Israel's wandering in the desert, thirty-eight years prior to this date. K explains that נער in Hebrew, signifies a servant or minister, as יהושע בן נון נער,[4] although he was already over forty-two at the time. R, however, taking נערים in its literal sense, explains: *"here they needed* ***speed, and therefore acted as lively*** *young men. On the first night they were like angels, for they kept themselves from sinning with Rahab the harlot. Therefore, there they were called* מלאכים (lit. angels). *And therefore, they were called men,[5] angels,[6] and young men."* — R

*and all her families* — denoting that any relationship to Rahab, however distant, was sufficient to spare entire families. — Y[7]

*and placed them outside the camp*

כו וַיַּשְׁבַּע יְהוֹשֻׁעַ בָּעֵת הַהִיא לֵאמֹר אָרוּר הָאִישׁ לִפְנֵי יְהוָה אֲשֶׁר יָקוּם וּבָנָה אֶת־הָעִיר הַזֹּאת אֶת־יְרִיחוֹ בִּבְכֹרוֹ יְיַסְּדֶנָּה וּבִצְעִירוֹ יַצִּיב דְּלָתֶיהָ׃ כז וַיְהִי יְהוָה אֶת־יְהוֹשֻׁעַ וַיְהִי שָׁמְעוֹ בְּכָל־הָאָרֶץ׃ א ז וַיִּמְעֲלוּ בְנֵי־יִשְׂרָאֵל מַעַל בַּחֵרֶם וַיִּקַּח עָכָן בֶּן־כַּרְמִי בֶן־זַבְדִּי בֶן־זֶרַח לְמַטֵּה יְהוּדָה מִן־הַחֵרֶם וַיִּחַר־אַף

אַרְעָא׃ כו וְאוֹמֵי יְהוֹשֻׁעַ בְּעִידָנָא הַהִיא לְמֵימַר לִיט גַּבְרָא קֳדָם יְיָ דִּיקוּם וְיִבְנֵי יָת קַרְתָּא הָדָא יָת יְרִיחוֹ בְּבוּכְרֵיהּ יְשַׁכְלְלִינַהּ וּבִזְעֵיר בְּנוֹהִי יְקִים דַּשָּׁהָא׃ כז וַהֲוָה מֵימְרָא דַּיְיָ בְּסַעְדֵּיהּ דִּיהוֹשֻׁעַ וַהֲוָה שְׁמְעֵיהּ סַגִּי בְּכָל אַרְעָא׃ א וְשַׁקַּרוּ בְּנֵי יִשְׂרָאֵל שְׁקַר בְּחֶרְמָא וּנְסֵיב עָכָן בַּר כַּרְמִי בַּר זַבְדִּי בַּר זֶרַח לְשִׁבְטָא דִּיהוּדָה מִן

ת״א ויפבע יהופע . סנהדרין קיג שבועות לו : בבכרו ייסדנה . סנהדרין מב : ויהי ה׳ את יהושע . מגלה י :

רש״י

(כו) בבכירו ייסדנה ובצעירו · בתחלת יסוד שיבנה בה ימות בנו הבכור ויקברנו וילך עד שימות הצעיר בגמר המלאכה היא הצבת הדלתות :

רד״ק

אף שכתוב בשבעה אומות לא תתחתן בם אמרו כי רחב ובית אביה נכרים היו בארץ ולא היו משבעה גוים ויש מי שאומר כי כשנכנסו מרגלים ששלח יהושע ביריחו נתגיירה ועדיין לא נכנסו ישראל לארץ וכל זה למי שאמר כי כתיב לא תתחתן בם בגיותן כתיב : (כו) את העיר הזאת את יריחו. תוספת ביאור ורז״ל פירשו שלא יבנו אותה ויקראו אותה בשם עיר אחרת ז שלא יבנו עיר אחרת ויקראו שמה יריחו ומה שהחרים יהושע שלא תבנה עוד העיר כבר כתבנו הטעם בפסוק והיתה העיר חרם . והחכם הגדול רבינו משה בר מימון ז״ל פירש הטעם להיות המופת קיים שנפלה חומת עיר יריחו תחתיה כי כל מי שיראה החומה שוקעת בארץ יתבאר לו שאין זה תכונת בנין נהרס כך אבל נשתקע במופת . ובצעירו . שימותו כל בניו מהבכור ועד הצעיר תוך הזמן הזה מהוסד העיר עד הצבת דלתיה : (כז) שמעו . והנפר׳ שומע בשקל אורח :

רלב״ג

בבית כאשר נכבשו לא המרגלים : (א) וספר שכבר מעלו בני ישראל מעל בחרם וביאר שזה המעל היה שכבר לקח עכן מן החרם מזה ההשאה הרון אף על בני ישראל עם שמתו מהם בלבים ושבה איש לפני יושבי העיר וכבר יספק מספק ויאמר איך יתכן בזה בחק המשפט האלהי לענוש על חטא עכן בני ישרא׳ וכבר לותה התורה בלא ימותו האנשים כי אם איש על חטאו ימות וזה הספק בעינו יפול במה שזכרם התורה פוקד עון אבות על בנים ועוד שכבר זכרו ירמיה ויחזקאל שכבר יגיע עת שלא יאמר עוד אבות יאכלו בוסר ושיני בנים תקהינה

מנחת שי

(כו) ייסדנה הסמ״ך בדגש : ז (א) בן זבדי . הבי״ת רפה:ויחר אף ה׳ בבנ״י . בס״א כ״י ישן כתוב בישראל ויש ג״כ הערה מזה בדפוס ישן ובאלה פפריס בבנ״י

מצודת דוד

בתקיעה אז הריעו : (כו) וישבע . הארור תקרא שבועה : בבכורו ייסדנה . כאשר יניח היסוד ימות בכור בניו ויתרס ימותו במשך זמן הבנין וכשיעמיד דלתים ימית לעיר בניו ויתמו א״כ כולם : ז (א) וימעלו וגו׳ . על שלא שמרו זא״ז מעלה עליהם הכתוב כאלו

מצודת ציון

ז (א) וימעלו . ענין חטא ופשע : (ב) עם בית און . סמוך

## Commentary Digest

*tinue* (to bury all his sons) *until the youngest one dies at the finish of the work, viz. the setting up of the gates."* — R,[3] K, and D He who rebuilds that which the Almighty has destroyed, will be punished when the Almighty destroys that which he has built up. — A

27. *So the Lord was with Joshua* — to fulfill his curse, when Hiel the Bethelite disregarded it and rebuilt Jericho.[4] — A and M

*and his fame was throughout the entire land* — The Rabbis tell us that Joshua minted coins, on one side of which appeared an ox, and on the other side appeared a wild-ox, corresponding with Moses' blessing to the tribes of Joseph: His firstling ox majesty be his, and the horns of a wild-ox be his horns.[5] [6] This blessing is interpreted as referring to Joshua the military leader who destroyed the nations of Canaan.[7] After his first victory, when this blessing commenced to be realized, Joshua minted these coins.

## CHAPTER 7

1. *And the children of Israel committed a trespass in the consecrated*

26. And Joshua adjured them at that time, saying, Cursed be the man before the Lord, that rises up and builds this city, Jericho; with (the loss of) his first-born shall he lay its foundation, and with (the loss of) his youngest son shall be set up its gates. 27. So the Lord was with Joshua; and his fame was throughout the entire land.

7

1. And the children of Israel committed a trespass in the consecrated thing, for Achan the son of Carmi, the son of Zabdi, the son of Zerah, of the tribe of Judah, took of the consecrated thing; and the anger of the Lord

## Commentary Digest

family, they gave them life within the Jewish community.

The question of the permissibility of intermarriage with Canaanitish proselytes is discussed in the Talmud.[1] There were some authorities who prohibited it. According to them, the question of Rahab arises. To answer this, some claim that Rahab and her family were not of Canaanitish origin, but were sojourners in the land. Others hold that those who converted before the Israelites' invasion were acceptable. — K Still others hold that a special dispensation was granted by the Almighty for the sake of Rahab the penitent.[2] The descendants of Joshua and Rahab have already been discussed in previous chapters.

26. *And Joshua adjured them* — A curse is also referred to as an oath. — D

*this city, Jericho* — an additional explanation. Our rabbis, however, explain that it was forbidden to rebuild Jericho under another name, as well as to rebuild another city under the name Jericho. Thus, we explain: that rises up and builds this city under any name, or any city under the name of Jericho. — K[3]

One who rebuilds Jericho destroys the sunken wall, thereby obliterating the evidence of its miraculous falling. By building another city and calling it Jericho, he also created the illusion that Jericho has been rebuilt. — K from Maimonides

*with (the loss of) his first-born shall he lay its foundation, and with (the loss of) his youngest son* — "*At the beginning of the foundation which he builds therein, his first-born son will die and he will bury him, and con-*

יְהֹוָה בִּבְנֵי יִשְׂרָאֵל׃ ב וַיִּשְׁלַח יְהוֹשֻׁעַ
אֲנָשִׁים מִירִיחוֹ הָעַי אֲשֶׁר עִם־בֵּית אָוֶן
מִקֶּדֶם לְבֵית־אֵל וַיֹּאמֶר אֲלֵיהֶם לֵאמֹר
עֲלוּ וְרַגְּלוּ אֶת־הָאָרֶץ וַיַּעֲלוּ הָאֲנָשִׁים
וַיְרַגְּלוּ אֶת־הָעָי׃ ג וַיָּשֻׁבוּ אֶל יְהוֹשֻׁעַ
וַיֹּאמְרוּ אֵלָיו אַל־יַעַל כָּל־הָעָם כְּאַלְפַּיִם
אִישׁ אוֹ כִּשְׁלֹשֶׁת אֲלָפִים אִישׁ יַעֲלוּ
וְיַכּוּ אֶת־הָעָי אַל־תְּיַגַּע־שָׁמָּה אֶת־כָּל־
הָעָם כִּי מְעַט הֵמָּה׃ ד וַיַּעֲלוּ מִן־הָעָם
שָׁמָּה כִּשְׁלֹשֶׁת אֲלָפִים אִישׁ וַיָּנֻסוּ לִפְנֵי

**תרגום**

חַרְמָא וּתְקֵיף רוּגְזָא דַיְיָ בִּבְנֵי יִשְׂרָאֵל׃ ב וּשְׁלַח יְהוֹשֻׁעַ גֻּבְרִין מִירִיחוֹ לְעַי דְּעִם בֵּית אָוֶן מִמַּדְנַח לְבֵית אֵל וַאֲמַר לְהוֹן לְמֵימַר סַקוּ וְאַלִּילוּ יַת אַרְעָא וּסְלִיקוּ גֻּבְרַיָּא וְאַלִּילוּ יַת עָי׃ ג וְתָבוּ לְוַת יְהוֹשֻׁעַ וַאֲמַרוּ לֵיהּ לָא יִסַּק כָּל עַמָּא כִּתְרֵין אַלְפִין גֻּבְרָא אוֹ כִּתְלָתָא אַלְפִין גֻּבְרָא יִסְקוּן וְיִמְחוֹן יַת עָי לָא תַרְגֵּישׁ לְתַמָּן יַת כָּל עַמָּא אֲרֵי זְעִירִין אִינוּן׃ ד וּסְלִיקוּ מִן עַמָּא לְתַמָּן כִּתְלָתָא אַלְפִין גֻּבְרָא וְאַפִּיכוּ קֳדָם

**רש"י**

ז (ב) עם בית און · אצל בית און׃ מקדם לבית אל ·

**אנשי**

**רד"ק**

(ב) עם בית און. סמוך לבית און וכן עם באר לחי ראי סמוך׃ מקדם. ממזרח לבית אל ובזכרו סימנין אלו נראה כי עיר אחרת היתה ששמה עי אבל זאת היתה גדולה מהאחרת וידוע לפיכך נזכרת בכל מקום עם ה"א הידיעה ובעברי בני עמו הן יתה עיר ששמה

**מנחת שי**

(ב) בית און. הוא"ו בסגול. ורגלו. הגימ"ל דגושה׃ וירגלו. הגימ"ל דגושה׃

**רלב"ג**

וזה סותר למה שזכרה התורה מזה בחק השם יתברך ולא יתכן בכלל בעד העת ההיא יהיה נוהג השם יתברך לענוש הבנים על חטא אבותם ואחר כך ישנה מנהגו כי זה מבואר הביטול ובהיות הענין כן יהיה העיון בזה מי יתן ואדע ונאמר בכלל יותר זה הספק בשנאמר שהשם בלתי פוקד עון אבות על בנים בעלם כי זה יהיה עול אבל אפשר מזולת עול שימשך במקרה עונש מה לבנים בחט' האבות כי כמו זה לא יהיה בו עול כלל והמשל אם הטא אדם למלכות ועשהו בדין לאבוד ממונו הנה יגיע מזה עונש לבניו שיהיו עניים ולא יירשו דבר מנכסי אביהם שיהיו עתידין לירשם וכמו זה אמר הנביא אבותינו חטאו ואינם ואנחנו עונותיהם סבלנו וזה שלולי חטא היינו שרויים על אדמתינו אחרי הנקותינו מהטא ימשך ממנו שגלה מעל אדמתינו אלו היינו שם ובזה האופן יקרא שהש"י פוקד עון אבות על בנים לא בעלמות וככר יקרא באופן הה' שיגיע עונש מה לבנים על חטא אבותם וזה אמנם יהיה כשחטאו האבות והיו הבנים אוחזין מעשה אבותיהם בידיהם וזה שאם היו הם המתחילי' בזאת התכונה הפחותה הי' מספיק במוסרם עונש יותר קטן ממה שילטרך במוסר' כשהיו אבותיהם בזאת התכונה הפחות' כי אז בבא אליהן קנין הזק ולא יוסרו אלא בשישגם עונש גדול על זה ולזה יקרא ענשם יותר גדול מפני חטא האבות ולזאת הסבה תמצא ג"כ שיעדה התורה כאשר יעברו ישראל על המלות ייסרם הש"י שבע על חטאתיה' ולותה עם זה לשופטים שלא יכו הרשע כי אם כדי רשעתו במספר אלא בענין בן סורר ומורה שישפטו אותו למיתה בעבור כי שער' באחריתו יהיה נבל ויהיה סבת זה כי הש"י לא יביא אלו הייסורין על צד העונש שאם היה הענין כן היה זה העונש עול בחק הש"י ר"ל שיענש החוטא יותר מן הראוי לפי מריו אבל יביא אותם על צד התוכחה והשגחה ואין זה עול אבל הוא הנהגה להטבע המשל שאם רצה אדם לפרש בים עם שיירה מה והיה סוף השיירה ההיא לטבוע בים הנה אם יביא עליו הש"י יסורי' ימנעוהו מלכת בשיירה ההיא לא יהיה זה עונש אבל הטבה וחנינה וכן אם נסתבך אדם בעבירו' סבוך מה והי' מפני זה מוכן להמשך אחריהן אם ישלח לו הש"י יסורין יוסר בהם בהמשך אחר הרע שנשקע בו הנה הוא מבואר כי יהיה לו הטבה וחנינה ובכאן הותר זה הספק שיקרה במה שאמר' התורה שבע על חטאתיכם ומה שאמר הש"י פוקד עון אבות על בנים. ואמנם מה שנשאר מן הספק הוא מה שנזכר מענין עכן שחטא ונענשו על הטאו רבים זולתו והיה שחטא לא השיגהו עונש מהשם יתברך בענין ההוא וכבר באו בתורה סיפורים דומים לזה ונאמר בהיתר זה הספק שהקהל והקבוץ המתאחד יתכן שיקרה בו זה בזולת עול וזה שכאשר היה הקהל בכללו באופן שיהיה מושגח מהשם יתברך השגחה שלימה לא יתכן שתאונה אליו רעה וכאשר חטא אחד מבני הקהל חשוב כקהל באופן שתסור ההשגחה האלהית ממנו מצד שהוא כלו מתאחד

**מצודת ציון** **מצודת דוד**

לבית און כמו עם באר לחי ראי (בר' כ"ה)׃ תיגע מלשון יגיעה. כולם מעלו׃ (ג) אל יעל. ר"ל אין צורך בכולם׃

## Commentary Digest

3. *Do not let all the people go up.* — I.e. there is no necessity for all of them to go up. — D Moreover, let not all the people go up lest the inhabitants of Ai think that we fear them. — M. L.

*do not trouble all the people there.* — Furthermore, it is an unnecessary trouble. — M. L.

was kindled against the children of Israel. 2. And Joshua
sent men from Jericho, to Ai, which is beside Beth-aven, on
the east side of Beth-el, and spoke to them saying, Go up and
spy out the land. And the men went up and spied out Ai.
3. And they returned to Joshua, and said to him, Do not let
all the people go up; but let about two or three thousand
men go up and smite Ai; do not trouble all the people there;
for they are but few. 4. So there went up there of the people,
about three thousand men; and they fled before

## Commentary Digest

*thing, for Achan — took* — All of Israel is considered as one body, each individual a limb or organ thereof. Hence, a transgression of one, renders the entire organism vulnerable. Thus, Achan's sin was responsible for the withdrawal of divine providence from the army of Israel, causing its defeat and loss of thirty-six men. Although **these men were not actually guilty of committing the trespass, since they were in the face of danger, without the Almighty's protection** they fell in battle. — G, A, and M. D explains simply that all Israel were negligent in guarding the spoils of Jericho. Hence, they were all guilty in this trespass. See above VI:18.

2. *Ai* — Heb. העַי, with the definite article, unusual for proper nouns. It was called thusly to distinguish it from the smaller city of Ai in the land of Ammon.[1] For this very reason, it is explicitly located. — K

*beside Beth-aven* — lit. with Beth-aven. — R

*on the east side of Beth-el* — Heb. מקדם — J, R, and K. The derash is: which was previously called Beth-el. The city had originally been called Beth-el (the house of a god) since it housed a pagan temple. Rather than retain its original name which deified an idol, the Israelites changed it to Beth-aven (the house of iniquity, or idolatry), in accordance with the Biblical precept: And you shall destroy their name from that place.[2] — Y[3] Ironically, this very city was later to house one of King Jeroboam's golden calves, and because of Jewish idolatry, was derisively called Beth-aven by the prophet Hosea.[4]

אנשי העי: ה ויכו מהם אנשי העי
כשלשים וששה איש וירדפום לפני
השער עד־השברים ויכום במורד וימס
לבב־העם ויהי למים: ו ויקרע יהושע
שמלתיו ויפל על־פניו ארצה לפני ארון
יהוה עד־הערב הוא וזקני ישראל
ויעלו עפר על־ראשם: ז ויאמר יהושע
אהה אדני יהוה למה העברת העביר
את־העם הזה את־הירדן לתת אתנו

קדם אנשי עי: ה וקטלו
מנהון אנשי עי כתלתין
ושתא גברא ורדפונון
קדם תרעא עד
דתברונון ומחונון
במחתנא ואתמסי
לבא דעמא והוה
למיא: ו ובזע יהושע
לבושוהי ונפל על
אפוהי על ארעא
קדם ארונא דיי עד
רמשא הוא וסבי ישראל
ואסיקו עפרא על
רישיהון: ז ואמר יהושע
קביל בעותי יי אלהים
למא אעברתא אעברא
ית עמא הדין ית ירדנא
למממסר יתנא בידא

ה״א כשלשים וששה. ב״ב קכא סנהדרין מד: העברת העביר. סנהדרין מד: * בצ״ל ביד

**רש״י**

ממזרח לבית אל: (ה) עד השברים. עד דתברינון: (ז) ולו הואלנו. הלואי נמלכנו לשבת בעבר

**רד״ק**

עי כמו שאומר בירמיה שודדה עי: (ה) כשלשים וששה איש. ארז״ל זכות אברהם אבינו עמדה להם שם שהרי היו חייבין על החרם ולא הכו מהם אנשי העי כי אם שלשים וששה איש אלא זכר להם הקב״ה זכות אברהם שבנה שם מזבח שנאמר בית אל מים והעי מקדם ויבן שם מזבח לה׳ וכ״ף כשלשים כ״ף השיעור ויש מרז״ל שאמרו שהיא כ״ף הדמיון כי לא היו שלשים וששה אלא יאיר בן מנשה הכו ששקול כשלשים וששה איש והוא רובה של סנהדרין ויש דרש כי הקב״ה אמר ליהושע אתה תנחיל כשתהיה עמהם אבל כאן שלא היה עמהם נכשלו ואחר שהכתוב אומר הטעם כי בעבור העון של החרם נכשלו אין לנו לבקש טעם אחר: לפני השער עד השברים. חסרמ״ם השמוש ומשפטו מלפני השער כלומר מלפני השער שבאו שם בני ישראל להלחם מאותו מקום רדפום עד השברים ושם הכו השלשים וששה ונקרא המקום כן לפי שנשברו שם יונתן תרגם עד דתברינון: ויכום במורד. מקום היה לבני העי שהיה משופע ויורד ובאותו מקום הכום בנוסם: (ז) למה העברת. ה״א נקודה בצרי והעי״ן בשוא ופתח שלא כהמנהג כי המנהג הה״א בסגול והעי״ן בשוא או בסגול

**רלב״ג**

ולזה יהיה משולח ונעזב למקרים ולזאת הסבה קרה שמתו אלו השלשים וששה איש עם היותם בלתי חוטאים בזה ולא מת עכן כי לא יקרה רע מלך העדר ההשגחה האלהית תכף למי שהוא ראוי שיבואהו רע ולפי שעכן לא שם עצמו במקום הסכנה לא מת מפני העדר ההשגחה ממנו ואותם האנשים ששמו עצמם במקום סכנה מתו מהם הראויים למות לפי מערכתם אולם שיזק קבוץ המתאחד בחטא האיש האחד הוא מבואר וזה כי הקבוץ ההוא הוא כמו איש אחד והאיש ממנו הוא כמו אבר מאיברי איש ההוא וכמו

**מנחת שי**

(ז) למה. מלרע ורפה מכלול דף רצ״ו: העברת הה״א בצירי והעין בשוא ופתח שלא כמנהג רד״ק בפי׳ ומכלול דף פ״ב ושרשים ועיין מ״ש בחבקוק א. ביד האמרי להאבידנו. ג׳ פסוקים דמטעים עיין מ״ש בפ׳ דברים סימן א׳: (ט) ומה תעשה. בצירי השי״ן שלא כמנהג והוא חד מן ד׳ קמצים על פי המסורת והסימן

**מצודת ציון**

(ד) לפני. מלפני: (ה) השברים. שם המקום נקרא ע״ש המאורע על כי נשברו שם: במורד. במקום הירידה מהסר: (ז) אהה. ענין

## Commentary Digest

swer to his supplication, he was allowed to pray in this manner.[4]

*before the Ark* — This is the origin of the practice of reciting Tahanun in a reclining position in the presence of a Sefer Torah.[5]

*and they put dust upon their heads* — They mentioned the merit of Abraham who called himself "dust and ashes."[6] They said before the Almighty, The only reason our father Abraham built an altar on this site was so that his children would not fall here in battle. — Y[7]

7. *why have You at all brought this people over the Jordan* — Why have you performed such miracles to bring us across the Jordan, if it was only to deliver us into the hands of the Amorites? Why did You command us to erect a monument for our posterity if we are to be annihilated by the peoples of Canaan? — A and Azulai

Would that we had been content

the men of Ai. 5. And the men of Ai smote of them about
thirty-six men; and they chased them from before the gate to
Shebarim, and smote them in the descent; and the hearts of
the people melted, and became as water. 6. And Joshua rent
his clothing and fell to the earth upon his face before the
Ark of the Lord until the evening, he and the elders of Israel,
and they put dust upon their heads. 7. And Joshua said,
Woe, O Lord God, why have You at all brought this people
over the Jordan, to deliver us

## Commentary Digest

5. *about thirty-six men* — righteous men.[1] Although they had transgressed the ban, the prayer of Abraham, who had anticipated this battle, saved them from great loss.[2] According to one opinion, Jair the son of Manasseh alone, was the fallen one. He was equal to the thirty-six men who comprise the majority of the Sanhedrin. — K[3] This was rightly understood by Israel as a calamity of major proportions, meriting their hearts failing and the entire morale of the people being weakened. How different this is from modern concepts and value placed upon human life! Moreover, the vulnerability of the hosts of Israel was irrefutable proof of the withdrawal of divine providence, a prospect which terrified them in the face of the formidable odds of battling the seven nations of Canaan.

*from before the gate* — of Ai. — K

*to Shebarim* — a place so called because the army of Israel was broken there. — K and Z. R, after J, renders: *"until they broke them."*

*in the descent* — from Ai which was situated on a mountain. — K and Z

6. *And Joshua rent his clothing* — in mourning for the men who fell in battle. — M According to the opinion that the casualty was Jair the son of Manasseh who was equal to the majority of the Sanhedrin, Joshua was surely required to mourn, for when a scholar dies, all the people are like his relatives in regard to mourning. According to the other opinion that actually thirty-six men fell, they were also צדיקים (righteous men), or at least כשרים (pious men), for whom all are required to perform קריעה (rending the clothing).[3*]

*and fell to the earth upon his face* — Being certain of receiving an an-

בְּיַד הָאֱמֹרִי לְהַאֲבִידֵנוּ וְלוּ הוֹאַלְנוּ
וַנֵּשֶׁב בְּעֵבֶר הַיַּרְדֵּן: ח בִּי אֲדֹנָי מָה אֹמַר
אַחֲרֵי אֲשֶׁר הָפַךְ יִשְׂרָאֵל עֹרֶף לִפְנֵי
אֹיְבָיו: ט וְיִשְׁמְעוּ הַכְּנַעֲנִי וְכֹל יֹשְׁבֵי
הָאָרֶץ וְנָסַבּוּ עָלֵינוּ וְהִכְרִיתוּ אֶת־שְׁמֵנוּ
מִן־הָאָרֶץ וּמַה־תַּעֲשֵׂה לְשִׁמְךָ הַגָּדוֹל:
י וַיֹּאמֶר יְהוָה אֶל־יְהוֹשֻׁעַ קֻם לָךְ לָמָּה

דֶאֱמוֹרָאָה לְאוֹבָדוּתָנָא וְלַוֵי פוֹן דְשָׁרֵינָא וִיתֵיבְנָא בְּעִבְרָא דְיַרְדְנָא: ח בְּבָעוּ אֲדֹנָי מָה אֵימַר בָּתַר דְאַחֲזָרוּ יִשְׂרָאֵל קְדָלְהוֹן לְמֶהְפַּךְ קֳדָם בַּעֲלֵי דְבָבֵיהוֹן: ט וְיִשְׁמְעוּן כְּנַעֲנָאֵי וְכָל יָתְבֵי אַרְעָא וְיִסְתַּחֲרוּן עֲלָנָא וִישֵׁיצוּן יָת שְׁמָנָא מִן אַרְעָא וּמָה תַּעֲבֵד בְּדִיל שְׁמָךְ רַבָּא: י וַאֲמַר יְיָ לִיהוֹשֻׁעַ קוּם לָךְ לְמָה דְנַן אַתְּ רָמֵי עַל

ת״א ולו הואלנו . סנהדרין מד : לשמך הגדול . (תענית כה) : קום לך . תענית יד מגלה כב סנהדרין יא מד :

**רד״ק**

ובא כמוהו כלה בחכה העלה : (ט) ומה תעשה . בצרי השי״ן שלא כמנהג וכבר כתבנו הדומים לו בספר מכלל . ופירוש ומה תעשה לשמך הגדול שיאמרו הגוים מבלתי יכולת ה׳ והרי שמך כאילו נתמעט אצלם : (י) למה זה אתה נופל על פניך . על דרך מה תצעק אלי כלומר אינך צריך בקשה ותחינה ישמידו החרם והזכרת׳ ד״א עמדת לך במחנה ולא יצאת עמהם ואני אמרתי אשר יוציאם ואשר יביאם כי אתה תביא את בני

° הש׳ בצרי

**רש״י**

הירדן מזרחה בארץ סיחון ועוג שנכבשה כבר : (ט) ומה תעשה לשמך ׳המשותף בשמנו זהו מדרשו ופשוטו ומה תעשה לשם גבורתך שילא כבר ועתה יאמרו תשש כחו : (י) קום לך ׳ קם לך כתיב עמד לך מה שהתפללת לפני

**מנחת שי**

במסרה גדולה פרשת תולדות וירמיה סוף סימן מ׳ : (י) ויאמר ה׳ אל יהושע קם לך . מלא קם חסר וא״ו ודרשו רבותינו בירושלמי פרק סדר תעניות קם לך סיפא דאדכרת פירוש דמדכתיב חסר וא״ו דריש ביה קם לך כלומר זו היא

**רלב״ג**

שכשיחלה אבר מה מאברי האדם יזוק בו האדם ההוא בכללו כי כשיחטא איש אחד מהקבוץ ההוא יזוק בו כלל הקבוץ ובכאן הותרו כל הספקות ולזה תמלא שכאשר לוה השם יתברך ליהושע שיבוא העונש הראוי על חטא לא הספיק שיענש על יד יהושע זולת החוטא וכבר יחזק מה שאמרנו שלא הפיגם על זה מהעונש כי אם סור ההשגחה האלהית מה שאמר ולא אוסיף להיות עמכם אם לא תשמידו החרם מקרבכם ויאם החטא לכל ישראל

**מצודת ציון**

לשון לעקה ויללה כמו אהה אדוני (מלכים ב׳ ו׳) : ולו . הלואי וכן לו מתנו (במדבר י״ד) : הואלנו . ענין רלון כמו הואיל נא ולין (שופטים י״ט): (ח) בי . ענין ל׳ בקשה כמו בי אדוני (בראשית מ״ד):

**מצודת דוד**

(ז) ולו הואלנו . הלואי והיינו רולים מאז לשבת בעבר הירדן המזרחי ולא לעבור את הירדן ולא היה באה עלינו הלרה הזאת : (ח) מה אומר . אחר שהרגיש בעלמו שהרבה אמרים מול מעשה ה׳ חזר ואמר מה אומר אם לא כדבר הזה הואיל וישראל הפך עורף בנוסם ולעק מכאב לב: (ט) וישמעו. אשר האויב ירדפם: ומה תעשה לשמך. לבל יחולל באמרם מבלי יכולת ה׳ נאבדו: (י) למה זה וכו׳.

## Commentary Digest

the chain will be attached to it. So said the Most Holy, Blessed be He, "If I leave Israel as they are, they will be swallowed up among the nations. I shall, rather, incorporate My great Name in them, and they will remain alive, as it is written: And what will You do for Your great Name? — Y[6] Israel is the small key to the entire world, the guard and preserver of the whole creation. But, alas, because of their small number, they are likely to be swallowed up among the nations of the world. Therefore, the Lord attached His great name to His nation. His protection has become incorporated into the very existence of this nation. When Joshua split the Jordan, all the Canaanites were fully aware of the divine protection hovering over Israel. When the walls of Jericho sank, this impression was intensified. But, alas, when Israel turned their backs and fled from the small army of Ai, there resulted a profanation of the holy Name of God, a חלול השם. If the key is lost, the chain goes with it. If Israel is defeated, the incorporation of the great Name becomes invisible to the world, who say that His strength has weakened.[7]

10. *Get up — "The kethib is* קם לך

into the hand of the Amorites, to cause us to perish? Would that we had been content and dwelt on the other side of the Jordan! 8. Pray, Oh Lord, what shall I say, after Israel has turned their backs before their enemies? 9. For the Canaanites and all the inhabitants of the land shall hear and shall encircle us and cut off our name from the earth; and what will You do for Your great Name? 10. And the Lord said to Joshua, Get up; why

## Commentary Digest

*and dwelt on the other side of the Jordan* — The rabbis, in comparing this rather outspoken language of Joshua with the imploring tone of Moses' prayer to enter the land of Israel,[1] apply the saying of Solomon in Proverbs:[2] The poor man speaks imploringly, but the wealthy raises his voice with boldness. — Y[3] Moses, who was at the end of his life, was considered a poor man, who implored of the Lord to allow him to cross the Jordan and see the Holy Land. Joshua, on the other hand, who was at the beginning of his reign, and in whose hand was given the Holy Land to conquer and divide, was considered a wealthy man, and spoke with assurance.[4]

*Would that we had been content* "*Would that we had decided to dwell on the east side of the Jordan in the land of Sihon and Og, which has already been conquered.*" — R

8. *what shall I say, after Israel has turned their backs before their enemies?* — Joshua realizes that he has overstepped the boundaries of propriety by speaking so freely to God. He, therefore, defends his statement as being a spontaneous expression of pain upon Israel's defeat and his realization of its consequences. This is comparable to the outburst of Moses: "And from the time that I have come to Pharaoh to speak in Your name, he has harmed this people; and You have not saved Your people.[5] — D

9. *and what will You do for Your great Name?* — "*which is inherent in our name*[6] (i.e. Israel, the שר or prince of God). *This is the derash. The peshat is: What will You do for the Name of Your might which has already become famous? For now they will say, His strength has become weakened.*" — R These two interpretations may be incorporated into one by studying the beautiful parable the Rabbis use in explaining this passage. A king had a small key for his palace. Said the king, "If I leave it as it is, it will be lost. I shall, rather, make a chain for it, for if it would get lost,

זֶה אַתָּה נֹפֵל עַל־פָּנֶיךָ׃ יא חָטָא יִשְׂרָאֵל
וְגַם עָבְרוּ אֶת־בְּרִיתִי אֲשֶׁר צִוִּיתִי אוֹתָם
וְגַם לָקְחוּ מִן־הַחֵרֶם וְגַם גָּנְבוּ וְגַם כִּחֲשׁוּ
וְגַם שָׂמוּ בִכְלֵיהֶם׃ יב וְלֹא יֻכְלוּ בְּנֵי
יִשְׂרָאֵל לָקוּם לִפְנֵי אֹיְבֵיהֶם עֹרֶף יִפְנוּ
לִפְנֵי אֹיְבֵיהֶם כִּי הָיוּ לְחֵרֶם לֹא אוֹסִיף
לִהְיוֹת עִמָּכֶם אִם־לֹא תַשְׁמִידוּ הַחֵרֶם
מִקִּרְבְּכֶם׃ יג קֻם קַדֵּשׁ אֶת־הָעָם וְאָמַרְתָּ
הִתְקַדְּשׁוּ לְמָחָר כִּי כֹה אָמַר יְהוָה

על אפך: יא חטא
ישראל ואף עברו על
קימי דפקדית יתהון
ואף נסיבו מן חרמא
ואף גנבו ואף כדיבו
ואף שויאו במניהון:
יב ולא יכלון בני
ישראל למקם קדם
בעלי דבביהון קדלהון
יחזרון למיפך קדם
בעלי דבביהון ארי הוו
לחרמא לא אוסיף
למהוי מימרי בסעדכון
אם לא תשיצון חרמא
מביניכון: יג קום זמן ית
עמא ותימר אזדמנו

ת״א חטא ישראל. סנהדרין מג עקידה שער מו (ברכות יד): עברו את בריתי, סנהדרין מד: לקחו מן החרם. סנהדרין מד:

**רש״י**

ישראל ואנכי אהי׳ עמדכי הוא יעבור לפני העי׳הזה והוא ינחיל אותם אם תלך אתה לפניה׳ ינליחו. וא״ל לא ינליחו. דבר אחר קום לך בשבילך זאת להם לא אמרתי לך להקדיש שלל העיר:

**רדק**

ואסלח להם: (יא) חטא ישראל. ולא תאמר חטא בשגגה **אלא** וגם עברו בריתי כי ברית נכרתה ביני ובינם בהר סיני לעשותם כל אשר צויתים ואצום וכן הוא ויקח ספר הברית ויקרא באזני העם והם אמרו כל אשר דבר ה׳ נעשה ונשמע וצוה משה רבינו מפי הגבורה נביא מקרבך **מאחך** כמוני יקים לך ה׳ אלהיך אליו תשמעון והנה יהושע צוה אותם ואמר להם שלא יקחו משלל העיר דבר והנה עברו הברית שלקחו משלל העיר: וגם לקחו מן החרם. כל גם בא לרבות ופי׳ הנה בעבור החרם כאלו צום הנביא והוא יהושע מצוה בלא חרם ואם עברו המצוה עברו הברית כ״ש כי בידם החרם: וגם גנבו. כי לו לקחו **בפרהסיא** לא היה כל כך רע אבל כשגנבו כאילו חשבו להסתיר מהבורא: וגם כחשו. או אולי הרגיש אדם בדבר וכיחש עכן או בעבור שסופו לכחש שהרי כחש עד שבקש ממנו יהושע ואמר לו בני שים נא כבוד לה׳: וגם שמו בכליהם. וכל זה להכחיש יותר **כמו שאמר והנה טמונים**. ובדרש מה הם חמשה גם מלמד שעבר על ה׳ חומשי תורה: (יג) קדש התקדשו. **ענין זימון**:

**רלב״ג**

**באמרו** חטא ישראל מפני שזה הקבוץ היה מתאחד והנה לזה השם **יתברך** שיחקרו מי היה החוטא בגורל ויחס משפט הגורל לשם **יתברך** כאמרו בחיק יוטל את הגורל ומה׳ כל משפטו. וידמה שהיתה הטלת זה הגורל לפני ה׳ כמו הענין בהטלת הגורל על **חלוקת** הארץ כמו שנזכר בזה הספר. והנה הסכמנו שיהיה זה הענין על פי הגורל לפי שהוא דעת רז״ל ויראה שהוא האמת בעצמו שאם היה זה ע״פ נביא או שהיו נשאלים באורים ותומים

**מנחת שי**

בעמדה לך הטענה שהזכרת דהיינו מה תעשה לשמך הגדול: (יא) **אשר צויתי** אותם. יש מחלוקת בספרים אם הוא חסר וא״ו או מלא **ובמדויקים** כ״י מספרד מלא וכן נכון ע״פ המסורת דלעיל סי׳ ה׳ דנמסר אתם ו׳ חסר בסיפרא ולא **תנינא** זה בתוכם ומ״ש שם במ״ג בסוף מסרה הנזכרת והוריש ה׳ **מלפניכם** טעות הוא ז״ל והוריש אתם מלפניהם (יהושע כ״ג ה): (יב) לא **אוסיף**. **במקצת**

**מצודת דוד**

ר״ל אין צורך בתפלה כ״א לבער עובר החרם: (יא) **חטא ישראל**. אף **שהאיש** אחד חטא מ״מ על שלא שמרו זא״ז מעלה עליהם הכתוב כאלו כולם חטאו: **וגם עברו את בריתי**. בא להגדיל מעשה הנבלה הסיא לומר הלא אף אם יחטא איש לאיש לא ינקה והמה אף כי לא חטאו ועברו בריתי שעברו על החרם שהיא כשבועה: **וגם לקחו**. ר״ל אף העובר אחת משאר מצות ה׳ ענש יענש והמה גם לקחו מהחרמי גבוה חלק ה׳: **וגם גנבו**. אלו לקחו לעין כל היו עכ״פ **מבזים** כבוד המקום לכבוד ב״ו אבל המה גנבו להשמר מבני אדם ומה׳ לא יראו: **וגם כחשו**. הן לא יבוזו לגנב אם ישוב וניהם **ומודה** בה ומחזירה אבל המה גם כחשו: **וגם שמו בכליהם**. ר״ל לא יבוזו לגנב כי יגנוב למלא נפשו כי ירעב אבל המה גם שמו בכליהם **להיות** שמור לאוצר לא להוציא לשבור רעבון נפש וא״כ מעשה הנבלה הסיא כפולה ומוכפלת: (יב) **כי היו לחרם**. ר״ל היו **מסייעים** לעובר החרם במה שהעלימו עין ולא שמרו זא״ז: **החרם**: העובר החרם: (יג) **התקדשו**. להאסף לפני הארון **לדעת** בגל **מי**

**מצודת ציון**

(יא) **בריתי**. ענינו בכ״מ דבר המתקיים וגם שבועה הוא **דבר** המתקיים וחרם השבועה: **שמו**. נתנו: (יג) **קדש**. הזמן כמו **קדשו**

## Commentary Digest

on Mt. Sinai, to obey all the words of the Torah, which include heeding all prophets after Moses. — K

and they have also taken of the consecrated thing – not only were they disobedient, but they violated that which was sacred to My Name. — K

*and have also stolen* — thinking to hide from Me, denying the omnipotence of the Creator. — K

*and dissembled also* — Perhaps someone was aware of Achan's sin, and confronted him with it, or the Scripture deals with the future, when Achan was accused by Joshua. — K

*put into their vessels* — to conceal

do you fall upon your face? 11. Israel has sinned, and they have also transgressed My covenant which I commanded them; and they have also taken of the consecrated thing, and have also stolen, and also dissembled, and they have also put into their vessels. 12. And the children of Israel shall not be able to stand before their enemies; they will turn their backs before their enemies, because they have become accursed. I will not be with you anymore, if you do not destroy the consecrated thing from among you. 13. Arise, prepare the people, and say, Prepare yourselves for tomorrow; for thus says the Lord

## Commentary Digest

(It has arisen, or stayed, for you.) *That which you have prayed before Me and mentioned, has stood you in good stead.*[1] *Another explanation is: You stayed in camp, and did not go out with them, while I said: "And who will lead them out* (to battle) *and who will bring them* (back).[2]" *"For you shall bring the children of Israel — and I shall be with you."*[3] *"For he will cross before this nation and he will cause them to inherit."*[3]* *If you go before them, they will succeed, and if not, they will not succeed.*[4] *Another explanation is:* קום לך, (explaining לך as: on your account) *On your account this has befallen them. I did not tell you to consecrate the booty of the city."*[5] — R Although the Almighty enforced Joshua's ban, He was, nevertheless, displeased with it. He enforced it in honor of Joshua. — Azulai K explains the passage in this way: This is not a time for prayer but for action, i.e. destruction of the violator of the ban. Similarly, in Ex. XIV:15: And the Lord said to Moses, Why do you cry to Me? Speak to the children of Israel and let them travel forth. D follows the same interpretation.

11. *Israel has sinned* — Although one individual has committed a crime, communal responsibility and guilt must be recognized, now that they have crossed the Jordan, and entered the land of Israel.[6] Others explain: Since the people did not guard the consecrated thing, the entire nation was considered guilty. — D Lest one think that they sinned unwittingly, the Scripture continues: —

*and they have also transgressed My covenant* — into which they entered

אֱלֹהֵי יִשְׂרָאֵל חֵרֶם בְּקִרְבְּךָ יִשְׂרָאֵל לֹא
תוּכַל לָקוּם לִפְנֵי אֹיְבֶיךָ עַד־הֲסִירְכֶם
הַחֵרֶם מִקִּרְבְּכֶם׃ יד וְנִקְרַבְתֶּם בַּבֹּקֶר
לְשִׁבְטֵיכֶם וְהָיָה הַשֵּׁבֶט אֲשֶׁר־יִלְכְּדֶנּוּ
יְהוָֹה יִקְרַב לַמִּשְׁפָּחוֹת וְהַמִּשְׁפָּחָה
אֲשֶׁר־יִלְכְּדֶנָּה יְהוָֹה תִּקְרַב לַבָּתִּים
וְהַבַּיִת אֲשֶׁר יִלְכְּדֶנּוּ יְהוָֹה יִקְרַב
לַגְּבָרִים׃ טו וְהָיָה הַנִּלְכָּד בַּחֵרֶם יִשָּׂרֵף
בָּאֵשׁ אֹתוֹ וְאֶת־כָּל־אֲשֶׁר־לוֹ כִּי עָבַר
אֶת־בְּרִית יְהוָֹה וְכִי־עָשָׂה נְבָלָה

תרגום

לִמְחָר אֲרֵי כִדְנַן אֲמַר יְיָ אֱלָהָא דְיִשְׂרָאֵל. חֶרְמָא בֵינָךְ יִשְׂרָאֵל לָא תִכּוּל לְמֵיקַם קֳדָם בַּעֲלֵי דְבָבָךְ עַד דְתַעְדוּן חֶרְמָא מִבֵּינֵיכוֹן׃ יד וְתִתְקַרְבוּן בְּצַפְרָא לְשִׁבְטֵיכוֹן וִיהֵי שִׁבְטָא דְיִתְאַחַד מִן קֳדָם יְיָ יִקְרַב לְזַרְעָן וְזַרְעִיתָא דְיִתְאַחַד מִן קֳדָם יְיָ תִּקְרַב לְבָתִּין וּבֵיתָא דְיִתְאַחַד מִן קֳדָם יְיָ יִתְקָרַב לְגַבְרַיָא׃ טו וִיהֵי דְיִתְאַחַד בְּחֶרְמָא יִתּוֹקַד בְּנוּרָא יָתֵיהּ וְכָל דִי לֵיהּ אֲרֵי עֲבַר עַל קְיָמָא דַיְיָ וַאֲרֵי עֲבַד דְלָא כָשַׁר בישראל

ת״א עשה נבלה . סנהדרין מ״ד :

רד״ק

(יד) אשר ילכדנה ה'. אמרו כי העבירים לפני הארון והנלכד הוא שהיה הארון קולטו שלא היה יכול לזוז משם ועוד אמרו כי העמיד כל השבטים לפני האורים והתומים ואבני החושן היו כתובים בו שמות השבטים ומי שאבנו כהה הוא הנלכד וכהה אבנו של יהודה ולדעת המשפחות והגברים עשו בקלפי על פי הגורל : יקרב למשפחות . פי' לגברים ראשי משפחות : תקרב לבתי' . לראשי בתי המשפחה : יקרב לגברי'. לאנשי הבית : (טו) ישרף באש אותו ואת כל אשר לו . לפי

רש״י

(יד) לבתים · יש במשפחה אחת הרבה בתי אבות · לגברים · לראשי גולגולת כל אנשי הבית יבאו לגורל : (טו) (תוס') ישרף באש · האהל והמטלטלין: אתו ואת כל אשר לו · כדין המפורש למטה אותו והבהמה בסקילה והזקף שהוא על באש מוכיח שהוא נפרד מאותו שכן מצינו מקראות שהטעם מחלקן כמו אחרי דרך מבוא השמש שאחרי מופלג מדרך על ידי הטעם וכן פתרונו הנלכד בחרם ישרף באש הראוי לישרף כמו שמפרש למטה : אותו ואת כל אשר לו · כדין האמור למטה וזה מקרא קצר ודומה לו כנ

רלב״ג

לא היו צריכין לזה אבל יתבאר להם האיש בעצמו שעשה זה . והנה יפול ספק מה בענין הגורל איך יתכן שנאמר בו כי מה' כל משפטו והנה ענין משפטו הוא בקרי אלא שהיתר זה הספק לא יקשה עם מה שהשרשנו וביארנו בספר מ"י כי בעניים אשר בקרי סדור והגבלה ואולם בזה המקום לא יהיה זה הספק רושם כי כבר היתה הטלתו ע"י נביא לפני ה' כמו שזכרנו ועם כל זה הנה ראוי שנשתדל בהיתרו מלד שאר הגורלות: (טו) והנה היתה מלות השם ית' שהנלכד בחרם ישרף באש כי הוא ברור אלל השם יתברך שלא יפול הגורל כי אם על החוטא ועם כל זה מלינו שהתחכם יהושע אל שיודה עכן זה קודם שפטו אותו בזה המשפט ואי אפשר שנאמר שכבר עשה זה יהושע כדי שיוכל לשפטו בדין ומפני שלא היו שם עדים רלה שתהיה שם הודאת פיו וזה לשתי סבות הא' שמה שהגיע ידיעתו בזה האופן מהשם ית' הוא ממה שלא אפשר שיפול בענינו ספק ולא מחלוקת והשנית כי אין להודאת פיו מבא בזה המשפט כלל כמו שהושרש בפ' משפטים ולזה ידמה שכבר היה זה הענין באופן שזכרוהו רבותינו ז"ל רולה

מצודת ציון

מלחמ' (יואל ד'):(טו) נבלה. דבר מגונה כמו נבלה ידבר (ישעי' לב)

מצודת דוד

הרעה הזאת : (יד) ונקרבתם . מול הארון : לשבטיכם . כל שבט לבד : ילכדנו ה'. להיות נלכד לפני הארון לבל יוכלו לזוז ממקומו לפי שעה : יקרב למשפחות . אחר יזוזו ממק״ם יקרבו שוב למשפחות : לבתים . כי המשפחה תחלק עוד לבתי אבות : לגברים לאנשים יחידים : (טו) הנלכד בחרם . הנלכד לפני הארון בעבור שמעל בחרם :

## Commentary Digest

*he and all that he has — "according to the law specified below: He and the cattle by lapidation. The accent zakef which appears over the word:* באש (with fire) *indicates that it is separate from* אותו (he); *for we find verses which the accent divides, such as:* אחרי דרך מבוא השמש, *"far past* (the Jordan), *the way of the going down of the sun,"*[5] *in which* אחרי (far past) *is separated from* דרך (the way) *by the accent. And thus is its interpretation: And he that is taken with the accursed thing — shall be burned with fire that which is fit to be burned, as is explained below. He*

God of Israel, There is an accursed thing in your midst, O Israel; you will not be able to stand before your enemies, until you remove the accursed thing from among you. 14. In
the morning, therefore, you shall be brought near according to your tribes; and it shall be, that the tribe which the Lord takes shall come near by families; and the family which the Lord takes shall come near by households; and the household which the Lord takes shall come near man by man. 15. And
it shall be, he that is taken with the accursed thing shall be burned with fire, he and all that he has; because he has transgressed the covenant of the Lord, because he has wrought an infamous deed

### Commentary Digest

it further. According to derash, "וגם" (and also) is repeated five times, to teach us that by this act of taking from the sacred, they had transgressed the Five Books of Moses, i.e. had completely broken the law.[1] — K

12. *because they have become accursed* — D explains this passage as meaning that they have become accomplices to Achan, who transgressed the ban against the doomed things, by not warning him of his wrongdoing and its consequences.

*destroy the consecrated thing* — i.e. the one who *transgressed* the ban. — D. Also, in v. 13, "the accursed thing" alludes to Achan, who *took* the accursed thing.

14. *be brought near* — to the Ark. — D See below v. 16.

*which the Lord takes* — or indicates. This indication was by the stone of that tribe in the "hoshen" becoming pale,[2] and also by the Holy Ark exerting a magnetic force that caused the tribe to be temporarily rooted to their spots. The latter was also the indication for the family, for the household, and for the particular man.[3] According to the first explanation, the family, household, and individual, were determined by lot. — K According to some authorities, the entire procedure was done by lot.[4] See below v. 17.

*by households* — "*One family contained many households.*" — R

*man by man* — "*by heads; all the men of the household were to come to the casting of lots.*" — R

15. (Supplement) *shall be burned with fire* — "*The tent and the movable property.*"

בְּיִשְׂרָאֵל׃ טז וַיַּשְׁכֵּם יְהוֹשֻׁעַ בַּבֹּקֶר
וַיַּקְרֵב אֶת־יִשְׂרָאֵל לִשְׁבָטָיו וַיִּלָּכֵד
שֵׁבֶט יְהוּדָה׃ יז וַיַּקְרֵב אֶת־מִשְׁפַּחַת
יְהוּדָה וַיִּלְכֹּד אֵת מִשְׁפַּחַת הַזַּרְחִי
וַיַּקְרֵב אֶת־מִשְׁפַּחַת הַזַּרְחִי לַגְּבָרִים
וַיִּלָּכֵד זַבְדִּי׃ יח וַיַּקְרֵב אֶת־בֵּיתוֹ לַגְּבָרִים
וַיִּלָּכֵד עָכָן בֶּן־כַּרְמִי בֶן־זַבְדִּי בֶן־זֶרַח
לְמַטֵּה יְהוּדָה׃ יט וַיֹּאמֶר יְהוֹשֻׁעַ אֶל־עָכָן
בְּנִי שִׂים־נָא כָבוֹד לַיהוָה אֱלֹהֵי יִשְׂרָאֵל

בְּיִשְׂרָאֵל׃ טז וְאַקְדֵּים יְהוֹשֻׁעַ בְּצַפְרָא וְקָרֵיב יָת יִשְׂרָאֵל לְשִׁבְטוֹהִי וְאִתְאֲחֵד שִׁבְטָא דְבֵית יְהוּדָה׃ יז וְקָרֵיב יָת זַרְעֵית יְהוּדָה וַאֲחַד יָת זַרְעֵית זֶרַח וְקָרֵיב יָת זַרְעֵית זֶרַח לְגֻבְרַיָּא וְאִתְאֲחֵד זַבְדִּי׃ יח וְקָרֵיב יָת בֵּיתֵיהּ לְגֻבְרַיָּא וְאִתְאֲחֵד עָכָן בַּר כַּרְמִי בַּר זַבְדִּי בַּר זֶרַח לְשִׁבְטָא דִיהוּדָה׃ יט וַאֲמַר יְהוֹשֻׁעַ לְעָכָן בְּרִי שַׁוִּי כְעַן יְקָרָא קֳדָם יְיָ אֱלָהָא דְיִשְׂרָאֵל וְהַב קדמוהי

ת״א עכן. סנהדרין מד:

**רש״י**

מכה יכוסי ויגע באליר ולא פירש מה יהיה לו ובדברי הימים פירש יהיה לראש אף כאן לא פי' מה יהיה באותו וכל אחר לו ולמטה פי': (טז) ויקרב את ישראל. לפני הכהן מקום שהשבטים כתובים ומסר לו הקב"ה סימן שהשבט שחטא אבנו כהה וכהת' אבנו של יהודה: (יז) ויקרב את משפחת יהודה. לגורל אחד קרב ראשי המשפחות אדם אחד מכל המשפח' והטילו גורל על מי יפול ואח"כ על כל בתי אבות של אותה משפח' ובא אדם אחד מכל בית אב לגורל ואחר כך באו כל אנשי אותה הבית: (יט) שים נא כבוד. התחיל להוציא לעז על הגורל אמר לו בגורל אתה בא עלי אתה ואלעזר הכהן גדולי הדור אתם הטל הגורל על שניכם ויפול על האחד אמר לו שים נא כבוד בבקש' ממך אל תוציא לעז

**רד״ק**

שעבר בחרם יחרם כל רכושו ובניו ובנותיו הקטנים שהם בכלל ממונו ואצל העונש ואם ביניהם היו גדולים הם בני עונש לפי שראו ושתקו ועברו בחרם ואשה לא היתה לו ואם היתה לו לא ידעה דבר כי העלים ממנה שהרי הטמין אות' תחת הקרקע ומה שאמר ישרף באש כמו שנשרפה העיר שהיתה חרם כן ישרף העובר על החרם וכל אשר לו שהוא חרם: (יז) ויקרב את משפח' יהודה. הקריב שבט יהודה לראשי משפחות וזכר משפחה במקום שבט וקצר למשפחות הכל לקצר כי כן דרך המקרא: וילכד את משפחת הזרחי. זה לבדו וילכד מן הקל בענין זה ושאר וילכד מן נפעל ופי' וילכד הארון לבדו: לגברים. לאנשי ראשי בתי המשפחה: וילכד זבדי. שהיה ראש בית אב ויקרב אנשי הבית וילכד עכן: (יט) בני שים נא כבוד לה'. בקש ממנו שיתודה על עונו לשני דברים האחד לכפרת עונו שתהא מיתתו כפרתו בהודאת עונו ומכאן למדנו שכל המומתין מתודין ולמדנו כי כופר עונו מדכתיב יעכרך ה' ביום הזה ביום הזה נעכר ולא לעולם הבא והשני כדי שיודו בני ישראל בגורל

ותן

אי בקליש' הארון ויאמרו כי אמת הוא וכן אמרו רז"ל שאמ' עכן ליהושע בגורל אתה בא עלי אתה ואלעזר הכהן שני גדולי

**רלב״ג**

לומר שבכלל היה עכן ומשפחתו מוציאין לעז על הגורל כשהיו אומרים שאם יפילו הגורל על שני אנשים לדיקים הנה יפול בלי ספק על אחד מהם עם היותו בלתי חוטא בזה ולזה זה התרעומ' והמחלוקת שהיה אפשר שיתחדש מזה התחכם יהושע להשתדל

**מצודת דוד**

(יז) משפחת יהודה. גם השבט נקרא משפחה: לגברים. איש איש ראש לבית אב: וילכד זבדי. הוא היה ראש לבית אב: (יח) לגברים. לאנשים יחידים: (יט) כבוד לה'. כי כאשר יראו שבדין נלכדת יהיה כבוד לה':

## Commentary Digest

established). *He said: By casting lots are you coming upon me (to establish my guilt)? If a lot were cast between you and Eleazar the High Priest, the two greats of the generation, it would fall on one (of you).*

*Said he to him: "I ask you not to find fault with the method of casting lots, through which method the land is destined to be divided."* — R [4] By admission of his sin and thereby to the efficacy of the lots cast, Achan would be assured of absolvement of his sin. In fact, it is from this passage that the rule is established that all criminals condemned to death are bidden to admit their guilt before execution. — K[4]

in Israel. 16. And Joshua rose up early in the morning and
brought Israel near by their tribes; and the tribe of Judah
was taken. 17. And he brought near the family of Judah;
and He took the family of the Zarhites; and he brought the
family of the Zarhites near man by man; and Zabdi was taken.
18. And he brought his household near man by man; and
Achan, the son of Carmi, the son of Zabdi, the son of Zerah,
of the tribe of Judah, was taken. 19. And Joshua said to
Achan, My son, give, I pray you, glory to the Lord, God of
Israel,

## Commentary Digest

*and all that he has — according to the law explained below. This is a brief verse, and similar to it: "whosoever smites the Jebusites and gets up to the tower."[1] He does not explain what will be done to him. In (I) Chronicles, however, he explains: 'shall be chief.'[2] Here also, he did not specify what would be done to 'him and all that he has,' and below he specifies."* Supplement to R.[2]* The power of a ruler to pronounce a curse and punish its violators by death, is based on Lev. XXVII:29: None devoted, that may be devoted by man, shall be ransomed; he shall surely be put to death.[3]

16. *and brought Israel near — "before the 'hoshen,' the place where the* (names of) *the tribes were inscribed.[3]* And the Holy One, Blessed be He, gave him a sign that the tribe which sinned — his stone would fade; and Judah's stone faded."* — R[3]**

17. *the family of Judah* — i.e. the tribe of Judah, also known as a family. — D

*and he brought near the family of Judah — "to a casting of lots. He brought near the heads of the families, one man from each family, and they cast lots on whom it would fall, and afterwards on each household, i.e. one man of each household came to the lot casting, and afterwards all the men of that household came."[3]*** — R[4]

*and He took* — i.e. the Almighty indicated by lot, or the Holy Ark by itself. See above v. 14.

*and Zabdi was taken* — as he was the head of the household. — D

19. *give, I pray you, glory — "He began to criticize the method of casting lots* (by which his guilt had been

וְתֶן־ל֣וֹ תוֹדָ֑ה וְהַגֶּד־נָ֥א לִי֙ מֶ֣ה עָשִׂ֔יתָ אַל־
תְּכַחֵ֖ד מִמֶּֽנִּי׃ כ וַיַּ֧עַן עָכָ֛ן אֶת־יְהוֹשֻׁ֖עַ
וַיֹּאמַ֑ר אָמְנָ֗ה אָנֹכִ֤י חָטָ֙אתִי֙ לַיהוָה֙
אֱלֹהֵ֣י יִשְׂרָאֵ֔ל וְכָזֹ֥את וְכָזֹ֖את עָשִֽׂיתִי׃
כא וָאֵרֶא בַשָּׁלָל אַדֶּרֶת שִׁנְעָר אַחַת
טוֹבָה וּמָאתַיִם שְׁקָלִים כֶּסֶף וּלְשׁוֹן זָהָב
אֶחָד חֲמִשִּׁים שְׁקָלִים מִשְׁקָלוֹ וָאֶחְמְדֵם

וארא קרי

קֳדָמוֹהִי הוֹדָאָה וְחַוֵּי
כְּעַן לִי מָה עֲבַדְתָּא לָא
תְכַסֵּי מִינִּי׃ כ וַאֲתֵיב
עָכָן יָת יְהוֹשֻׁעַ וַאֲמַר
בְּקוּשְׁטָא אֲנָא חָבִית
קֳדָם יְיָ אֱלָהָא דְיִשְׂרָאֵל
וּכְדֵין וּכְדֵין עֲבָדִית׃
כא וַחֲזֵית בְּבִזְתָא אִצְטְלֵי
בַּבְלִי חַד שַׁפִּיר וּמָאתַן
סִלְעִין דִּכְסַף וְלִישָׁנָא
דְדַהֲבָא חַד חַמְשִׁין
סִלְעִין מַתְקְלֵיהּ

ת״א ותן לו תודה. סנהדרין מג: ויען עכן סנהדרין מג. עקידה שער מו: וכזאת וכזאת. סנהדרין מג: ואראה בשלל. סנהדרין מד עקידה שער מו:

## רד״ק

הדור אם אני מפיל עליכם על אחד מכם הוא נופל אמר לו יהושע לעכן בבקשה ממך אל תוציא לעז על הגורלות כי עתידה ארץ ישראל ליחלק בגורל: (כ) וכזאת וכזאת עשיתי. פירושו לפניו וארא בשלל ורז״ל דרשו כי מעל עכן בשלש׳ חרמים שנים בימי משה ואחד בימי יהושע שנא׳ כזאת וכזאת עשיתי והתודה עתה על שלשתן ויש אומר׳ בארבעה שלשה בימי משה חרמו של כנעני מלך ערד וחרמו של סיחון ועוג וחרמו של מדין. בכנעני שכתוב בו והחרמתי את עריהם. ובמדין שנתנו הזהב קדש לה׳. בסיחון ועוג אף על פי שכתוב בו בזונו לנו אי אפשר שלא הקדישו מן השלל לה׳ ואמרו מפני מה לא נענש בימי משה על שעבר בימי משה מהם אמרו שלא ענש על הנסתרות עד שעברו ישראל את הירדן פירוש לא ענש בגלוי שנאמר הנסתרות לה׳ אלהינו ומהם אמרו כי לא ענש על הנסתרות לעולם שנאמר עד עולם ועכשיו שענש על הנסתרות בגלוי לפי שלא היו נסתרות שהרי היו יודעים בו בניו ובנותיו: (כא) אדרת שנער. בגד חשוב שנעשה בבבל הנקר׳ שנער ובבראשית רבה

## רש״י

על הגורלות שבו עתידה הארץ ליחלק: (כ) ויען עכן. ראה בני יהודה נאספים למלחמה אמר מוטב שאמות אני לבדי ואל יהרגו כמה אלפים מישראל: וכזאת וכזאת עשיתי. גם בחרמים אחרים בימי משה שנא׳ והחרמתי את עריהם: (כא) וארא בשלל. התבוננתי במה שכתוב בתורה (דברים כ) ואכלת וגו׳: אדרת שנער. תרגומו אצטלא (דמילתא) בבלי שכל מלך שלא קנה לו פלטרין בארץ ישראל לא נתקררה דעתו במלכותו שנ׳ ואתן לך ארץ חמדת נחלת צבי צבאות גוים והיה למלך בבל פלטרין ביריחו וכשהי׳ בא לכאן לובש אותם:

## מנחת שי

ספרים חסר וא״ו: (כא) ואראה בשלל. ואראה ק׳ וכן הוא למערבאי והוא חד מן כ׳ מלין דכתיבין ה״א בסוף תיבותא ולא קרייא בסימן במסרה רבתא (מערכת אות הא׳) ואפשר לומר שהה״א רומזת למה שארז״ל שמעל עכן בחמשה חרמים ד׳ בימי משה וא׳ בימי יהושע ואמרו ג״כ שעבר על חמשה חומשי תורה שנאמר

## רלב״ג

שיספר עכן זה וכאשר הודה זה הענין ספר בכבר שלא יהושע מלאכים וירוצו האהלה ויורה מה שזכר שכבר שלאם שם במרוצה כי יהושע היה ירא שימהרו אנשי משפחתו להוציא משם זה לכסות.

## מצודת ציון

(יט): תודה. הודאה: תכחד. ענינו העלמה כמו ולא כחדו (איוב טו): (כ) אמנה. באמת: (כא) אדרת. טלית חשובה והוא

## מצודת דוד

ותן לו תודה. תן הודאה שאמת הדבר שמעל בחרם: מה עשית. ר״ל מה הם הדברים אשר לקחת מן החרם: (כ) וכזאת וכזאת עשיתי. הה״ל שאמר עשיתי עוד לדומה לזה במלחמ׳ הכנעני ובמלחמת מדין כי גם במלחמ׳ הכנעני נאמ׳ והחרמתי את עריהם (במ׳ כ״א) ובמדין ג״כ נתנו הזהב קדש לה׳: (כא) והנם. האדר׳ ולשון הזהב: תחתיה. תחת האדרת:

## Commentary Digest

*palace in the Land of Israel, experienced no satisfaction from his reign, as it is stated: "And I give you a coveted land, an inheritance desired by hosts of nations."*[6] *And the king of Babylonia had a palace in Jericho, and when he would come here he would wear them* (sic)." — R[7] The Midrash expresses itself even more emphatically, that any king who did not possess a palace in the land of Israel, was not considered a king. The Holy Land was considered so desirable that owning a palace there was a status

symbol. Achan rationalized his act by relating the origin of this garment. It was not a Canaanite garment; it belonged to a foreigner. I had no idea that it was included in the ban. — M

In view of the wealth of knowledge inherent in the word 'shinar,' it is unnecessary to refute the critics who amend the text to read אדרת שער, a mantle of hair.[8]

*goodly* — I could not resist the temptation. — M

*two hundred shekels of silver etc.* — things that could not be com-

and make confession to Him; and tell me now what you
have done; do not hide anything from me. 20. And Achan
answered Joshua, and said, Indeed I have sinned against the
Lord God of Israel, and thus have I done: 21. When I saw
among the spoils a goodly Babylonish garment, and two
hundred shekels of silver, and a wedge of gold of fifty shekels
weight, then I coveted them,

## Commentary Digest

*what you have done* — i.e. what you have taken from the devoted thing. — D

20. *And Achan answered* — "*He saw the children of Judah* (his tribe) *assembling for war* (in loyalty for one of their own); *and said* (to himself): *It is better that I alone die rather than many thousands of Israel be killed.*" — R[1] The choice of the word אנכי instead of אני (I) or simply חטאתי (I have sinned), lends emphasis. I alone have sinned etc. Why then should thousands be slain in battle? It is from this word that the rabbis deduce that Achan gave himself up to save Israel from an ensuing civil war.

*and thus and thus have I done* — Verse 21 explains this passage by telling us what Achan did. — K. The Talmud, however, accepts this verse literally, thus: —

*and thus and thus have I done* — "*also with other devoted things during Moses' time, as it is stated: 'and I will devote their cities.'*[2]" — R, K, and Y[3] In addition to violating the curse which Moses had pronounced on the spoils of the Canaanite king of Arad as mentioned by R, Achan also took of the spoils of Midian which were **sanctified for the sanctuary.[4] We suppose that after the conquest of Sihon and Og too, the Israelites sanctified** a portion of the spoils Of these spoils too, Achan had his share. Punishment for communal responsibility, however, was not meted out to the Jewish people until they had crossed the Jordan and accepted the covenant. — K and A[3]

21. *When I saw among the spoils* — 'I saw' can be interpreted figuratively, as: "*I reflected upon that which is written in the Torah: "And you shall* ***eat up the spoils of your enemies.***"[5]" — R and Y[1] Achan was critical of Moses' and Joshua's enactment of חרמים. He considered this passage a commandment and was overzealous in fulfilling it.

*a Babylonish garment* — a garment made in Shinar or Babylonia, as in Gen. XI. — K "*As the Targum renders: a Babylonish garment, for any sovereign who had not acquired a*

ויקחם והנם טמנים בארץ בתוך
האהלי והכסף תחתיה: כב וישלח
יהושע מלאכים וירצו האהלה והנה
טמונה באהלו והכסף תחתיה:
כג ויקחום מתוך האהל ויבאום אל-
יהושע ואל כל-בני ישראל ויצקם לפני
יהוה: כד ויקח יהושע את-עכן בן-זרח
ואת-הכסף ואת-האדרת ואת-לשון
הזהב ואת-בניו ואת-בנתיו ואת-
שורו ואת-חמרו ואת-צאנו ואת-אהלו

ואת

ורנגתינון ונסבתנון
והא אנון טמירין בארעא
בגו משכני וכספא
תחותא: כב ושלח יהושע
אזגדין ורהטו למשכנא
והא טמירין במשכניה
וכספא תחותא:
כג ונסיבונון מגו משכנא
ואיתיאונון לות יהושע
ולות כל בני ישראל
ואתיכונון קדם יי:
כד ודבר יהושע ית עכן
בר זרח וית כספא וית
אצטלא וית לישנא
דדהבא ודבר ית בנוהי
וית בנתיה וית תוריה
וית חמריה וית עניה
וית משכניה וית כל

ת"א ויליקס. סנהדרין מד: ואת האדרת. סנהדרין מד:

### רש"י

(כב) וירצו האהלה: שלא יקדימו שבט יהודה ויטלוה משם להכחיש את הגורל: (כג). ויציקם. ואתיכון ורבותי' אמרו בא והטבען לפני המקום אמר לפניו רבש"ע על אלו יפלו רובן של סנהדרין: (כד) ואת בניו וגו' וכל ישראל.

### רד"ק

אדרת שנער רבי חנינא בר רבי יצחק אומר פרפרא בבלאת ועוד בדברי רבותינו ז"ל רב אמר איצטילא דמילתא ושמואל אמר כרבלא דצריפאה: האהלי. בשתי ידיעות כמו והחצי הערכך והדומים לו. תחתיה. תחת האדרת: (כב) וירוצו האהלה. טעם וירוצו לשמחה שנגלה עון החרם על מי היה וישראל נקיים ורבי' שלמה כתב טעם וירוצו שלא יקדימו שבט יהודה ויטלום משם כדי להכחיש הגורל: טמונה. האדרת: (כג) ויציקם לפני ה'. ויעמידום לפני ה' כדי שיראו אותם כל ישראל וידעו כח החרם. ויזהרו מן החמדה ומן החרם ורז"ל אמרו ויציקם בא יהושע וחבטן בקרקע לפני המקום אמר רבונו של עולם על אלו תפול רובה של סנהדרין: (כד) את עכן בן זרח. סמך אותו לאבי אביו לקצר כי זרח היה ראש משפחה: לשון הזהב. ר"ל שבט זהב שדומה ללשון: ויעלו אותם עמק עכור. היה לו לומר ויורידו אבל נראה כי היה הר בין המחנה ובין

### רלב"ג

קלון עכן: (כג) וילקס לפני ה'. פירשו בו ויעמידום מענין מלוקי ארן והפסר עוד שיהיה מענין יליקה והרלון בזה שלשון הזהב היה טמון תוך האדרת והכסף היה תחתיה והיו בו מאתים שקלי' וכשהביאו זה אל יהושע ויבראל הנה פשט אותם שם כדי שיראה לעין שהיו שם אלה הדברי' שהודה עכן: (כד) ויקח יהושע את עכן. הנה יספק מספק למה נענשו בניו ובנותיו והם לא חטאו בזה וידמה אם כשנאמר שכבר היו קטנים והיו בזה במלכת קנינו

### מנחת שי

ה"פ גם כדאיתא בסנהדרין פרק נגמר הדין. ובמדרש תנחומא וארא בשלל ראיתי מה שכתוב בתורה ואכלת את שלל אויביך וגו' עיין כלי יקר: (כד) ואת לשון הזהב ואת בניו ואת בנתיו. שלשת הווי"ן בגעיא בס"ס ובדפוס ישן:

### מצודת דוד

(כב) וירצו. לבל יקחום קרובי עכן לכסות על קלונו: (כג) ויצקם. ר"ל פזרם לפני הארון למען יראו הכל אמתת הדבר: (כד) עמו.

### מצודת ציון

מלשון אדיר: שנער. עשו בשנער והוא בבל: ולשון. ר"ל ארוכס ומבוכה כלשון: (כג) ויציקם. מלשון יליקה ושפיכה:

## Commentary Digest

*and his ox and his ass* — "to destroy them, as it was said: And it shall be, he that is taken with the accursed thing shall be burned with fire, he and all that he has."[7] — R

render them as plural, there is no evidence to that effect. We have, therefore, followed the Targum in our translation.

*and his flock* — Heb. צאנו, a term including sheep and goats.

and took them; and, behold, they are hidden in the earth in
the midst of my tent, and the silver under it. 22. And Joshua
sent messengers and they ran to the tent and behold, it was
hidden in his tent, and the silver under it. 23. And they
took them from the midst of the tent, and brought them to
Joshua, and to all the children of Israel, and laid them out
before the Lord. 24. And Joshua, and all Israel with him,
took Achan the son of Zerah, and the silver, and the garment,
and the wedge of gold, and his sons, and his daughters, and
his ox, and his ass, and his flock, and his tent,

## Commentary Digest

pletely destroyed. — I, therefore, thought that they were not included in the ban. — M

*a wedge of gold* — lit. a tongue of gold, i.e. a bar of gold, shaped like a tongue. — K

*under it* — i.e. under the garment. — K

22. *and they ran to the tent* — "*lest the tribe of Judah arrive first and take it from there to cast a doubt on the efficacy of the lots.* — R[1] K explains that they ran for joy, since the guilty party was found out, and Israel would return to its previous state of divine favor.

23. *and laid them out* — lit. and poured them. They scattered them before the Holy Ark, so that everyone might come and inspect the articles individually. — D. K explains ויצקם like ויציגום (and they set them up), similar to: And they set up (ויצקו) the ark of God.[2] J renders: "*And they melted them. And our Rabbis state: "He threw them down before the Omnipresent. He said before Him, Lord of the Universe, "For these* (insignificant articles) *shall the majority of the Sanhedrin fall?*" "[3] — R The defective spelling of ויצקם indicates the singular: i.e. Joshua alone threw these articles before the Lord, and angrily complained to God of His harsh judgment upon His people.[4]

24. — *and his sons, and his daughters* — Perhaps because they were minors, they were punished along with Achan. — G[5] and K. R explains the passage to mean that his family and all Israel were to be present at the execution, "*to witness his chastisement, and so that they be deterred from doing as He* (had done)." — R[6]

*and his ox and his ass* — These nouns appear in the singular form. Accordingly, J renders them in the singular. Although many translators

ואת־כל־אשר־לו וכל־ישראל עמו
ויעלו אתם עמק עכור: כה ויאמר יהושע
מה עכרתנו יעכרך יהוה ביום הזה
וירגמו אתו כל־ישראל אבן וישרפו
אתם באש ויסקלו אתם באבנים:
כו ויקימו עליו גל־אבנים גדול עד היום
הזה וישב יהוה מחרון אפו על־כן קרא
שם המקום ההוא עמק עכור עד היום
הזה: ח א ויאמר יהוה אל־יהושע אל־
תירא ואל־תחת קח עמך את כל־עם

דיליה וכל ישראל עמיה
ואסיקו יתהון למישר
עכור: כה ואמר יהושע
מה עכרתנא יעכרינך יי
ביומא הדין ורגמו יתיה
כל ישראל באבניא
ואוקידו יתהון בנורא
בתר דרגימו יתהון
באבניא: כו ואקימו
עלוהי דגור אבנין רב
עד יומא הדין ותב יי
מתקוף רוגזיה על כן
קרא שמא דאתרא
ההוא מישר עכור עד
יומא הדין: א ואמר יי
ליהושע לא תדחל ולא
תתבר דבר עמך ית כל
עמא עבדי קרבא וקום

ת״א וכל ישראל עמו. סנהדרין מ״ד. מה: עכרתנו. סנהדרין מג מד: וישרפו אותם. סנהדרין מד:

קמץ בז״ק.

**רד״ק**

חצפק ואמר יעלו כנגד ההר ועל דרך הזה וירד הסלע: (כה) וירגמו. ואח״כ אמר וישרפו ואח״כ ויסקלו וכתב אדני אבי ז״ל כי דינם היה בשריפה כמו שכתוב ישרף באש אותו ואת כל אשר לו ופי׳ וירגמו אותו כשהיו מוליכין אותו לשריפה היו רוגמין ומשליכין עליו אבנים מרוב כעסם עליו וכשהיו בעמק עכור שרפו אותו ואת כל אשר לו ואחר כן ויסקלו אותו באבנים כסוס באבנים והם שרופים ואחר כן הקימו עליו גל אבנים גדול להיות לאות. ורז״ל פירשו וירגמו אותו אבן הוא לבדו וישרפו אותם באש בממונו הכתוב מדבר שכך נאמר לו מפי הגבורה הנלכד בחרם ישרף באש אותו ואת כל אשר לו אם כן מה תלמוד לומר וירגמו אותו לפי שבשבת גנב

**רש״י**

לראות ברדויו ויוסרו מלעשות כמוהו: **ואת שורו ואת חמורו** · לאבדם כמה שנא׳ והיה כל הנלכד בחרם ישרף באש אותו וגו׳: (כה) **וירגמו אתו וגו׳** · שחלל את השבת: **וישרפו אותם** · האהל והמטלטלין: **ויסקלו אותם** · השור והבהמה:

**מנחת שי**

(כה) מה עכרתנו: עיין מ״ש בפרשת נלבים על מה חרי:

**רלב״ג**

שלוה השם שיאבדו או שנאמר שלא הובאו שם בניו ובנותיו להמיתם אבל לראות המשפט כדי שיוסרו שכמו זה הפועל המגונה לא יעשו וממה שיורה על זה שכבר אמר אחר זה: (כה) וירגמו אותו כל ישראל אבן. ויקימו עליו גל אבנים גדול להורות שלא מת שם אדם זולתו ומ״ש וישרפו אותם באש ויסקלו אותם באבנים שב אל הבעלי חיים שהם שורו וחמורו ולאנו וספר שנשרפים באש אחר שסקלו אותם באבנים ולא כלל יחד סקילת הבעלי חיים עם סקילת עכן שהוא מבואר שלא יוכללו יחד בזה הענין האדם והבעלי חיים: (א) והנה זכר. שאחר זה שבה ההשגחה האלהית על ישראל ולוה השם יתברך שיעשו מלחמה בתחבולות עם אנשי

**מצודת ציון**

(כה) וירגמו. ענין השלכת אבנים: (כו) גל. גבוה תל:

**מצודת דוד**

הלכו עם יהושע: ויעלו. אם כי הלכו לעמק אמר ויעלו. כי טרם בואם אל העמק עלו דרך הר אל העמק הנקרא עמק עכור ע״ש המאורע: (כה) **מה עכרתנו**. ר״ל מה מאוד עכרתנו ולזה יעכרך ה׳: **וישרפו אותם**. האדרת הלשון והאהל וגו׳: **ויסקלו אותם**. בניו ובנותיו ושורו וגו׳. (ויתכן לפי שבניו ובנותיו ידעו מזה כמ״ש רז״ל (סנהדרין מ״ד) ולא גלו הדבר לכן נסקלו גם הם אולם רז״ל לא אמרו כן): (כו) **עליו**. על קברו: **עד היום הזה**. ר״ל עד עולם עומד הוא בגדלו: **על כן וגו׳ עד היום הזה**. ר״ל עדיין שמו עליו: ח (א) אל תירא. לפי שכבר נפלו בזה המקום היה ירא לגשת עוד לזה אמר לו אל תירא: כל עם. לזה לעשות כל

## Commentary Digest

led to the execution spot outside the camp. Hence, the expression וירגמו in contrast with ויסקלו of the latter passage, which means that after they had burned Achan and his property, they covered them with stones.

26. *And they raised over him a great heap of stones* — over Achan alone as a memorial of this incident. — K

*was called* — lit. he called.

*the Valley of Achor* — i.e. troubling.

*to this day* — i.e. forever.[4]

CHAPTER 8

1. *Fear not and be not dismayed* — Joshua was fearful of approaching

and all that he had; and they brought them up to the Valley
of Achor. 25. And Joshua said, Why have you troubled us?
The Lord shall trouble you this day. And all Israel stoned
him with stones, and burned them with fire, [after] they
[had] stoned them with stones. 26. And they raised over
him a great heap of stones to this day. So the Lord turned
from the fierceness of His anger. Therefore, the name of that
place was called, The Valley of Achor, to this day.

8

1. And the Lord said to Joshua, Fear not, and be not
dismayed; take all the people of war with you

## Commentary Digest

*and they brought them up to the Valley of Achor* — The road to the valley led through a hill, therefore, "they brought them *up*." — K and D

25. *this day* — This is an indication of the assurance of Achan to a share in the world to come (עולם הבא). "This day" excludes the time from this day onward. Thus, from this day onward, Achan would not be troubled, but would experience the pleasures of Paradise with the righteous. Like Achan, all who were condemned to death by the Sanhedrin, were instructed to confess before their execution, and were assured a share in the hereafter.[1]

*And all Israel stoned him with stones, and burned them with fire, (after) they (had) stoned them with stones* — This is J's paraphrase of the passage to eliminate the confusion of the repeated stonings and burning. Both Achan and his livestock were stoned, after which they were burned. Whether the inanimate objects were burnt is not mentioned in this verse. The Scripture repeats the stoning to differentiate between the stoning of the sinner himself and his property. — G. R, following the Talmud and Midrash, explains thus: —

*and they stoned him etc.* — "*for he had violated the Sabbath* (by taking the articles from Jericho on the day it had fallen, which was the Sabbath) — $R^2$

***and burned them*** — "*the tent and the movable property.*" — $R^3$

*and stoned them* — "*the ox and the* (other) *animals.*" — $R^3$ K explains the first stoning mentioned as a spontaneous outburst of anger by the people against Achan as he was being

המלחמה וקום עלה העי ראה | נתתי
בידך את־מלך העי ואת־עמו ואת־
עירו ואת־ארצו: ב ועשית לעי ולמלכה
כאשר עשית ליריחו ולמלכה רק־
שללה ובהמתה תבזו לכם שים־
לך ארב לעיר מאחריה: ג ויקם יהושע
וכל־עם המלחמה לעלות העי ויבחר
יהושע שלשים אלף איש גבורי החיל
וישלחם לילה: ד ויצו אתם לאמר ראו
אתם ארבים לעיר מאחרי העיר אל־
תרחיקו מן־העיר מאד והייתם כלכם
נכנים: ה ואני וכל־העם אשר אתי
נקרב אל־העיר והיה כי־יצאו
לקראתנו כאשר בראשנה ונסנו

**תרגום**

סק לעי חזי דמסרית
בידך ית מלכא דעי
וית עמיה ית קרתיה
וית ארעיה: ב ותעביד
לעי ולמלכה כמא
דעבדת ליריחו ולמלכה
לחוד עדאה ובעירה
תבזון לכון אתקן לך
כמנא לקרתא
מאחורהא: ג וקם יהושע
וכל עמא עבדי קרבא
למיסק לעי ובחר יהושע
תלתין אלפין גברא
גברי חילא ושלחינון
בליליא: ד ופקיד יתהון
למימר חזו דאתון כמנין
לקרתא מאחורי קרתא
לא תרחיקון מן קרתא
לחדא ותהון כולכון
מתקנין: ה ואנא וכל
עמא דעמי נתקרב
לקרתא ויהי ארי יפקון
לקדמותנא כד בקדמיתא
ונפוק קדמיהון:
ויפקון

ת״א לעי ולמלכה. סנהדרין מד:

**רש״י**

ח (ב) רק וגו׳ תבוזו לכם. ואל תחרימו השלל עוד: לפניהם

**רד״ק**

והוציא מיריחו והטמין באהלו ונסקל על חלול שבת ונשרף על שמעל בחרם ובנין שבשבת נלכדה יריחו שנאמר ויהי ביום השביעי וקבלו רז״ל שביעי לימי השבוע כמו שכתבנו: (ב) כאשר עשית ליריחו ולמלכה. כי הכל הרגו לפי הרב: תבזו

**רלב״ג**

העי לפי שהכל היה אפשר להחרימם בזה האופן בזולת עשיית מופת אחר כי הם יסכימו לצאת מהעיר לרדוף אחרי בני ישראל לפי שבפעם הראשונה נלחמו והנה הש״י לא יעשה מופת ללא צורך:

**מצודת דוד**

הסכנו׳ והתחבולו׳ האלו להטעו׳ העובדי כוכבים ומזלות למען יחשבו שכל נלחמם הוא בעבור רוב העם והתחבולות ולא יד ה׳ עשתה זאת ועי״ז יאספו כולם יחד להיו׳ גם המה עם רב ולהמתיק עלה והתחבולו׳ ברב יועצי׳ ובזה יהיה טובה לישראל כי את כולם יכו כאחד מבלי יצטרך ללכת מעיר לעיר להכות בה:(ב) מאחריה. לא מן העבר אשר תבואו אליה:(ד) נכונים. ללכת מהר בעת המצטרך:(ה) ונסנו. בכדי להטעות:

**מצודת ציון**

ח (ב) אורב. יושב במסתור המארב: (ה) ונסנו. מלשון

## Commentary Digest

too will be involved in the conquest, not only the Almighty, it is not necessary to place a ban on the city. — M

*behind it* — from the side opposite you. — D

4. *and all of you be ready* — for a forced march at the proper time. — D

5. *that we will flee before them* — i.e. we will intentionally retreat, for

and arise, go up to Ai. See, I have given into your hand the
king of Ai, and his people, and his city, and his land.
2. And you shall do to Ai and its king, as you did to Jericho
and its king; only its spoil and its cattle you shall take as
spoils to yourselves. Set yourself ambush for the city behind it.
3. And Joshua arose, and all the people of war, to go up
against Ai; and Joshua chose thirty thousand mighty men of
valor, and sent them away by night. 4. And he commanded
them, saying, Behold you shall lie in ambush against the city,
behind the city; do not go very far from the city, and all
of you be ready. 5. And I, and all the people that are with
me, will draw near to the city; and it shall be when they
come out against us, as at first, that we will flee before them.

## Commentary Digest

once again the city of Ai, the place that had caused such havoc to the Jewish people. Therefore, the Eternal reassures him that he is no longer to fear. — D and A. In the words of the Talmud, "It is not the 'arod'[1] who kills but it is the sin that kills."[2] Others interpret: Do not fear since I command you to take all the men of war. — P My purpose is that the victory shall be attributed to the entire army, not only to two or three thousand men. — A

2. *And you shall do to Ai — as you did to Jericho* — Although Ai was a small town,[3] the spies were mistaken in assuming that it could be conquered with ease, for it was highly fortified. For this reason, Joshua dispatched 30,000 men for an ambush, plus another 5,000 men for a second ambush, while the entire army was deployed in front of the city. This resulted in a complete annihilation of the city, to take revenge for the loss and humiliation suffered by the Jewish army previously. — A There was also the strategic reason of deterring the other kings of Canaan from helping Ai.

*only — you shall take as spoils to yourselves — "do not cause the spoils to be "cherem" (doomed) anymore* (as you did in Jericho)." — R

*Set yourself ambush* — Since you

לפניהם : ו ויצאו אחרינו עד התיקנו
אותם מן העיר כי יאמרו נסים לפנינו
כאשר בראשנה ונסנו לפניהם : ז ואתם
תקמו מהאורב והורשתם את העיר
ונתנה יהוה אלהיכם בידכם : ח והיה
כתפשכם את העיר תציתו את העיר
באש כדבר יהוה תעשו ראו צויתי
אתכם : ט וישלחם יהושע וילכו אל
המארב וישבו בין בית אל ובין העי
מים לעי וילן יהושע בלילה ההוא
בתוך העם : י וישכם יהושע בבקר

**תרגום**

ו וְיִפְּקוּן בַּתְרָנָא עַד דְנִגְגוֹד יַתְהוֹן מִן קַרְתָּא אֲרֵי יֵימְרוּן תְּבִירִין קֳדָמָנָא כִּדְבְקַדְמֵיתָא וְנִפּוֹק קֳדָמֵיהוֹן : ז וְאַתּוּן תְּקוּמוּן מִכְּמָנָא וְתִתָרְכוּן יַת קַרְתָּא וְיִמְסְרִנַהּ יְיָ אֱלָהֲכוֹן בִּידְכוֹן : ח וִיהֵי כְּמֵיחַדְכוֹן יַת קַרְתָּא תַּדְלְקוּן יַת קַרְתָּא בְּנוּרָא כְּפִתְגָמָא דַיְיָ תַּעַבְדוּן חֲזוֹ דְפַקֵדִית יַתְכוֹן : ט וּשְׁלַחִינוּן יְהוֹשֻׁעַ וַאֲזַלוּ לִכְמָנָא וִיתִבוּ בֵּין בֵּית אֵל וּבֵין עַי מִמַעְרַב לְעָי וּבָת יְהוֹשֻׁעַ בְּלֵילְיָא הַהוּא בְּגוֹ עַמָּא : י וְאַקְדֵים יְהוֹשֻׁעַ בְּצַפְרָא וּמְנָא יַת עַמָּא וּסְלִיק הוּא וְסָבֵי יִשְׂרָאֵל

**רד"ק**

לכם . כלומר זאת לא תהיה חרם כמו יריחו אבל תבזו אותה לכם לכל צרכיכם שלא יבא ממנ' אוצר ה' : (ו) התיקנו . שרשו נתק ר"ל עד שננתק אותם מן העיר ברדפם אחרינו : (ז) ואתם תקומו מהאורב . שם כמו והמארב וכמוהו שם בזה המשקל מלרע ואת היותר החרמנו . ויעזהו שורק : והורשתם את העיר . את יושבי העיר תגרשום ותכלום : (ח) כתפשכם . מקור בכ"ף : כדבר ה' תעשו . שהרי אמר לו כאשר עשית ליריחו ויריחו שרפו באש : ראו צויתי אתכם . כלומר שתהיו זריזים :
(ט) וילן יהושע בלילה ההוא בתוך העם . באמצע המחנה לן בלילה ההוא כדי לזרזם כלם להשכים בבקר ולערוך המלחמה :

**רש"י**

(ו) התיקנו אותם · לשון תיק שמוציאים מתיק העיר דיספורי"ר בלע"ז (מלה נוספת בלשון דעפורע"ר בל"א הערויסציהען וגם תיק נקרא בל"ל פורהה בל"א הייגע סייד) ויש לפותרו לשון נתיקה כמו התיקם כצאן לטבחה : (ז) והורשתם · ותתרכון : (ט) מים לעי · שהעי מקדם לבית אל ובית אל מים לעי : וילן יהושע וגו' בתוך העם ·

**מנחת שי**

ח (ט) וילכו אל המארב · בקצת ס"ס האל"ף בשוא לבדו וכן (בתילים י' וד"ה ב' י"ג) :

**מצודת ציון**

כיסם ובריח : (ו) הו קנו . ענין העתקה והסרה : (ז) והורשתם . ענין גרושין : (ח) ת. יתו . תבעירו כמו וילת אש בציון (איכה ד') : (ט) מים . ממערב :

**מצודת דוד**

(ו) ויצאו . ואז יצאו לרדוף אחרינו : עד התיקנו . ר"ל הכניס תועיל עד אשר נעתק אותם מן העיר לרדוף אחרינו כי יאמרו שבאמת בעבור הפחד נסים הם כאשר במלחמה הראשונה : ונסנו . ונוסיף לנוס עוד להרחיקם מן העיר : (ז) מהאורב . מהמקום שתהיו אורבים : את העיר . את הנשארים בעיר : (ח) כדבר ה' . שלוה לשרפה כמ"ש למעלה ועשית לה כאשר עשית ליריחו : ראו צויתי .

## Commentary Digest

10. *and counted the people* — J. Reviewed and inspected. — K, Z, and D

*and he — went up* — "*as the Omnipresent had said to him: "If he crosses before them, they will cross, and if not, they will not cross.""* — R[3] Thereby, Joshua rectifies the mistake he made of not accompanying the army to battle. Moreover, Joshua and the elders went before the army to encourage them in their battle against the feared inhabitants of Ai. — A

11. *and all the people — went up and drew near.* — The soldiers, of their own accord, drew near to the city, even without the explicit instructions and moral support of Joshua. — A

6. And they will come out after us until we have drawn them
from the city; for they will say, They flee before us, as at first.
And we will flee before them. 7. And you shall rise up from
the ambush, and drive out (those remaining in) the city;
and the Lord your God will deliver it into your hand.
8. And it shall be, when you have seized the city, that you
shall set the city on fire; according to the word of the Lord
shall you do. See, I have commanded you. 9. And Joshua
sent them; and they went to the place of ambush, and stayed
between Beth-el and Ai, on the west side of Ai; and Joshua
lodged that night among the people. 10. And Joshua rose
up early in the morning,

## Commentary Digest

the purpose of ambush described in the following verses. — D

6. *we have drawn them out* — Heb. התיקנו *"an expression of* תיק, *a sheath, i.e. until we have taken them out of the sheath* (the protection afforded them by the fortifications of) *the city. Defourrer in Fr.* (to unsheathe, from fourreau, a sheath). *We may also interpret it as an expression of* נתיקה, *drawing out, as: Draw them out like flocks to the slaughter."*[1] — R The 'dagesh forte' in the 'tav' denotes the defective 'nun.' This opinion is shared by K.

7. *and drive out* — (R after J) all the inhabitants of the city, the soldiers having already left in pursuit of the Israelite forces fleeing before them. — K The word והורשתם, whose root ירש in the 'kal' conjugation denotes inheritance and possession, in the 'hiphil' conjugation denotes driving out and destroying.

8. *according to the word of the Lord shall you do* — The commandment was to do to Ai as had been done to Jericho which had been destroyed by fire. — K

*See, I have commanded you* — Therefore, hasten to do my bidding. — K and D

9. *on the west side of Ai* — *"for Ai was on the east side of Beth-el and Beth-el was on the west side of Ai."* — R[2]

*and Joshua lodged* — among the people — *"to be ready early in the morning."* — R To alert them all to rise up early in the morning and set the stage for the battle. — K

ויפקד את־העם ויעל הוא וזקני ישראל
לפני העם העי: יא וכל־העם המלחמה
אשר אתו עלו ויגשו ויבאו נגד העיר
ויחנו מצפון לעי והגי בינו ובין העי:
יב ויקח כחמשת אלפים איש וישם
אותם ארב בין בית־אל ובין העי מים
לעיר: יג וישימו העם את־כל־המחנה
אשר מצפון לעיר ואת־עקבו מים לעיר
וילך יהושע בלילה ההוא בתוך העמק:
יד ויהי כראות מלך־העי וימהרו

בינו קרי לעי קרי

## תרגום

ישראל קדם עמא לעי: יא וכל עמא עבדי קרבא דעמיה סליקו ואתקרבו ואתו לקבל קרתא ושרו מצפונא לעי וחילתא בינוהי ובין עי: יב ודבר כחמשא אלפין גברא ושוי יתהון כמנא בין בית אל ובין עי ממערב לעי: יג ושויאו עמא ית כל משריתא דמצפונא לקרתא וית כמניה מערב לקרתא ואזל יהושע בליליא ההוא בגו מישרא: יד והוה כד חזא מלכא דעי ואוחיאו ואקדימו ונפקו

ת״א בתוך העמק. ערובין סג מגלה ג סנהדרין מד:

## רש״י

להיות נכון בהסכמת הבקר: (י) ויעל הוא · כמו שאמר לו המקום אם הוא עובר לפניהם עוברין ואם לאו אין עוברין: (יב) ויקח כחמשת אלפים איש · אורב אחר אורב אחד קרוב לעיר מחברו: (יג) וישימו העם · שימה זו לשון הזמנה סמוך להומה להלחם כמו שנאמר בבן הדד במלכים שימו על העיר וישימו: ואת עקבו. ואת ארבו כמו ויעקבני: וילך יהושע בלילה ההוא בתוך העמק·

## רד״ק

(י) ויפקד. השגיח בהם ונתן עינו עליהם איך הם מוכנים למלחמ': (יא) וכל העם המלחמ'. חסר הנסמך ומשפט העם עם המלחמה כמו הארון הברית: (יב) ויקח כחמשת אלפים איש. שיהיו גם כן אורב אולי שם אות' סמוך לעי יותר מן הראשונים. (יג) וישימו. האורב והמחנה שמו עצמם. ויקרבו לעיר יותר ממה שהיו וכן אומר במלחמת בן הדד על שומרון ויאמר שימו וישימו על העיר: ואת עקבו. כתרגומו וית כמניה כלומר מארבו מן ויעקבני כי המארב הוא ערמ': וילך יהושע בלילה ההיא בתוך העמק. כלומר הלך הוא ואחרי' עמו בתוך העמק שהמחנה

## רלב״ג

(יג) וילך יהושע בלילה ההוא בתוך העמק. אמשוב זה שמחשבתו והשתדלותו לא היתה בלילה ההוא כי אם בסידור העם בדבר המלחמה הזאת וכדי שיבטח לבם יותר ולא ירך לבבם על מה שהיו נגפים בראשונה עלה יהושע וזקני ישראל לפני העם ולזה היה יהושע והזקנים במקום היותר מסוכן וזכר עם זה לזאת הסבה בעינו לפי מה שאחשוב שכבר לן יהושע בלילה ההוא בתוך העמק כי העמק הוא המקום היותר שפל והוא היותר מסוכן שבמקומות בדבר המלחמה והנה לקח יהושע מהשלשים אלף שבחר חמשה אלפים איש היה אורב בין ישראל ובין העי מים לעיר והנה הם היו במקום קרוב למקום יהושע עד שיתכן בהם שיראו כשיטה יהושע את ידו בכידון והוא הרומח אשר בו הנס והיו הנשארים קרובים להם באופן שנתקבלו כולם בעת ההיא ויבואו אל העיר וילכדוה: (יד) והנה זכר וכבר ילאו הכני׳ העיר לקראת ישראל למלחמה למועד לפני הערבה אמר למועד להורות בבכמו העת שהיום בילאו

## מנחת שי

(יא) והגי בינו. בינו קרי ומה שנמסר במקרא גדולה וג' חסר' בליש׳א מקומו הראוי לו הוא על מלת והגי שהם ג' חסר' אל״ף וסימנהון בסוף וזאת הברכה במ״ג: (יב) ויקח כחמשת אלפים איש וישם אותם. בספרים מדויקיים כתיבת יד ודפוסים ראשונים מלת אותם מלא וא״ו וכן ראוי על פי המסורת שהזכרתי למעלה בסימן ז׳: בין בית אל ובין העי מים לעיר. חלוקים הספרים והמסורות במקצת ספרים כתיב לעיר וקרי לעי וכן כתב בעל כלי יקר ובמקצתם כתיב וקרי לעיר וחלוקים גם כן בפסוק ויזעקו כל העם אשר בעיר שבסמוך ובספר אחר יען זה האחרון כתיב וקרי בעי. ויונתן תרגם הראשון ממערב לעי והאחרון בקרתא בעי דומה שהראשון כתוב וקרי לעי והאחרון כתיב בעיר וקרי בעי ותרגם הקרי והכתיב. ורד״ק כתב אשר בעיר כן כתיב וקרי בעי ועל הראשון לא כתב מאומה ובמסרה גדולה נמסר עי ב׳ כתיב עיר וסימנהון ויקח כחמשת אלפים: ויזעקו כל העם. מסורת אחריתי וישלחם יהושע לעי. וכל העם המלחמה לעי. ויקח כחמשת אלפים לעיר. וישימו את העם לעיר. ובחילופים

## מצודת דוד

ר״ל הזהרו ואל תמרו פי: (י) ויפקד. השגיח בהם אם המה מוכנים למלחמה: (יב) וישם אותם אורב. שם עוד אורב אחד יותר קרוב אל העיר: (יג) וישימו העם. העם עצמם הזמינו למלחמה את המחנה וגו' וגם הזמינו את עקבו והוא האורב: בתוך העמק.

## מצודת ציון

(י) ויפקד. ענין השגחה: (יא) והגי. והעמק: (יג) וישימו. ענין הזמנה למלחמה כמו שימו אל העיר (מ״א כ): עקבו. תרגמו מארבו והוא מלשון ויעקבני זה פעמים (בראשית כ״ז) שהוא ענין ערמה:

## Commentary Digest

Joshua and others went through the camp which was camped in the valley, to ascertain that the sentinels were awake, lest they be taken by surprise.

The rabbis interpret עמק here in the sense of עמק, depth of profundity. *"Our Rabbis said that he lodged in the depth of the Law."* — R[2] Joshua delved into the very depths of an involved, intricate problem of Jewish law, fulfilling the instruction given him as the spiritual leader of Israel and the disciple of Moses: "And you shall meditate therein day and

and counted the people, and he and the elders of Israel ent
up before the people to Ai. 11. And all the people of war
that were with him, went up, and drew near, and came before
the city, and camped on the north side of Ai; and the valley
was between him and Ai. 12. And he took about five thousand
men, and set them to lie in ambush between Beth-el and Ai,
on the west side of Ai. 13. And the people set all the host
that was on the north of the city, and their liers in wait on
the west of the city. And Joshua went that night into the
midst of the valley. 14. And it was when the king of Ai
saw, they hastened

**Commentary Digest**

12. *And he took about five thousand men* — *"one ambush, following the other ambush, closer to the city than its fellow."* — R A suggests that the second ambush was stationed closer to the city to wage battle with the inhabitants should they emerge unexpectedly. He also suggests that the first group of thirty thousand men was sent in secret under cover of darkness. Since the people were unaware of its existence, they set up the second ambush, independent of the first. According to this interpretation, we must render: And it (meaning the people) took about five thousand men, etc.

13. *And the people set* — *"This setting is an expression of preparation near the wall, to wage war, as it is stated concerning the son of Hadad in (I) Kings* (XX:12): *"Set upon the city." And they set."* — R. K renders: And all the people with all the camp set (themselves); i.e. they drew nearer to the city. According to A, this reflects on the courage and morale of the forces deployed, doing so of their own accord, since Joshua was with the first group.

*and their liers in wait* — Heb. עקבו *"their liers in wait, like: 'For he has tricked me* (ויעקבני).'"[1] — R Lying in wait implies cunning and trickery. — K and Z

* *And Joshua went that night into the midst of the valley* — Joshua placed himself in the most forward and unprotected spot of the entire front, in order to raise the morale of the troops. — G According to K,

וישכימו ויצאו אנשי־העיר לקראת־
ישראל למלחמה הוא וכל־עמו למועד
לפני הערבה והוא לא ידע כי־ארב לו
מאחרי העיר: טו ויגעו יהושע וכל־
ישראל לפניהם וינסו דרך המדבר:
טז ויזעקו כל־העם אשר בעיר לרדף
אחריהם וירדפו אחרי יהושע וינתקו
מן־העיר: יז ולא־נשאר איש בעי ובית
אל אשר לא־יצאו אחרי ישראל ויעזבו
את־העיר פתוחה וירדפו אחרי ישראל:

בעי קרי

ונפקו אנשי קרתא
לקדמות ישראל לאנחא
קרבא הוא וכל עמיה
לזמנא דמתקן ליה
לקדם מישרא ואינון לא
ידעין ארי כמנא להון
מאחורי קרתא:
טו ואתברו יהושע וכל
ישראל קדמיהון ואפכו
לאורח מדברא:
טז ואתכנישו כל עמא
די בקרתא בעי למרדף
בתריהון ורדפו בתר
יהושע ואתנגידו מן
קרתא: יז ולא אשתאר
אנש בעי ובית אל דלא
נפקו בתר ישראל
ושבקו ית קרתא כד
פתיחא ורדפו בתר
ישראל

## רד"ק

שם לראות שומרי המחנה אם הם ערים או ישנים פן יצאו אנשי העי פתאום עליהם והכום: (יד) למועד. כתרגומו לזמנא דמתקן ליה כלומ' שהכין המלך ואמר בשעה פלונית נהיה מוכנים כלנו לצאת למלחמה: לפני הערבה. לפני המישור אשר היה את פני העיר: (טו) וינגעו. הראו עצמם נגועים ונסים

## רש"י

אמרו רבותינו שלן בעומקה של הלכה: (יד) למועד. לזמן היום שנועדו יחד מאתמול באותה שעה נלא שהיו מנחשים ומעוננים: (טו) וינגעו. לשון נגע ואתברו. הראו עצמן

לפניהם וגם הם היו נגועים כי אי אפש' שהיו נסים לפניהם שלא היו נגועים בהם ואלו לא היו נגועים אלא מראים עצמם נגועים לכך היה אומר ויתנגעו מבנין התפעל בי כן המשפט: דרך המדבר. מקום מרעה הבהמות יקרא מדבר בין סמוך לעיר ובין רחוק מן העיר לפי' אמר ורעו כבשים כדברם כעד' בתוך הדברו והוא מתרגם וינהגו ודבר לפי שהרועה נוהג שם המקנה: (טז) ויזעקו. נתקבצו לרדוף אחריהם ולפי שהקבוץ ואסיפת העם הוא על ידי זעקה לפי' נאמר בזה הלשון: אשר בעיר. כן כתיב וקרי בעי והכתוב מורה אשר בעי וגבולה וכן כתיב ולא נשאר איש בעיר לרדוף אחריהם והקרי מורה שנזעקו כל הנשערים

## מנחת שי

שבין בני ארץ ישראל ובין בני בבל כתוב למערבאי ב' פסוק לעיר כתוב וקרי. למדינחאי לעיר כתיב לעי ק' ע"כ. ולא איתברר מהתם הי ניהו: (טז) ויזעקו כל העם אשר בעיר בעי קרי כן כתב רד"ק ובעל כלי יקר ועי' מ"ש לעיל בסמוך: (יז) בעי ובית אל. חד מן דסבירין וכבית וסימן נמסר (פרשת וארא ומלכים ב'

## רלב"ג

לקראתם בפעם הראשונה ילאו עתה כי זה ממה שיחזק לב אנשי ישבי העי ויחשובו שכמו שנלחו אז ינלחו עתה ואמר לפני הערבה כי במקום ההוא לפי מה שאחשוב היו מנלחים בפעם הראשונה או אומר לפני הערבה כי מהמקום ההוא יתכן שלא היו יכולין לראות האורב אשר מאחרי העיר וזאת התחבולה הנכונה ללחום בקלות כי בראותם עשן העיר עולה השמימה אשר שם טפם ונשיהם לא נשאר להם כח ולא רלון האומד והשיעור להלחם עם ישראל באופן ראוי וזה מבואר מאד:

## מצודת ציון

(יד) למועד. לזמן כמו למועד אשוב אליך (שם י"ח): ר"ל מוכים ונחלשים:

## מצודת דוד

להתקרב אל העיר: (יד) למועד. לזמן שילאו במלחמה הראשונה: (טו) וינגעו. הראו עלמם כאלו היו מנוגעים (טז) ויזעקו. נתקבלו מזעקת המאסף:

## Commentary Digest

*and they left the city open, and pursued Israel* — The only ones left in Ai were the women and children. They thought that since they were putting the enemy to flight, there was no danger to their wives and children, and, therefore, left the gates of the city open. — M. L.

Others say that quite the contrary, the pursuers wished to leave the city open as a refuge, lest the enemy turn on their pursuers and pursue them. — M. L.

and rose up early, and the men of the city went out against
Israel to battle, he had all his people, at a time appointed,
before the plain; but he did not know that there was an
ambush against him behind the city. 15. And Joshua and all
Israel pretended to be beaten before them, and fled by way of
the desert. 16. And all the people that were in Ai were called
together to pursue them; and they pursued Joshua, and were
drawn away from the city. 17. And there was not a man left
in Ai or Beth-el, that did not go out after Israel; and they left
the city open, and pursued Israel.

## Commentary Digest

night,"[1] and for which omission he had been admonished previously by the archangel Michael.[2]

14. *at a time appointed* — *"at the time of day which they had planned* (or *been advised) on the preceding day, "at that time we will go out," for they were soothsayers and diviners."* — R They were, therefore, told by their seers that that day was auspicious for the Jewish forces fleeing before them. This caused them to leave the city in pursuit of the Jewish forces. It may mean simply at the time the king ordered them to leave the city. — K G and D explain that they went out against Israel at the same time of day that they had attacked them the first time. This made them confident that they would defeat Israel as they had done previously. — G

*before the plain* — where they had previously defeated the Jewish forces. They were, however, unaware of Joshua's elaborate preparations this time. — G

15. *pretended to be beaten* — Heb. וינגעו, *"an expression of a plague* (*or beating*). (J renders) *and — were broken. They showed themselves as though they were beaten before them."* — R, K, and D

— *the desert* — K translates it as pasture.

16. *were called together* — or assembled. — K and D

17. *And there was not a man left in Ai or Beth-el* — In v. 16, the word has the 'kethib' of בעיר (in the city), implying that no one was left in Ai or its environs, which included Beth-el. — K

יח וַיֹּאמֶר יְהוָה אֶל־יְהוֹשֻׁעַ נְטֵה בַּכִּידוֹן
אֲשֶׁר־בְּיָדְךָ אֶל־הָעַי כִּי בְיָדְךָ אֶתְּנֶנָּה
וַיֵּט יְהוֹשֻׁעַ בַּכִּידוֹן אֲשֶׁר־בְּיָדוֹ אֶל־
הָעִיר׃ יט וְהָאוֹרֵב קָם מְהֵרָה מִמְּקוֹמוֹ
וַיָּרוּצוּ כִּנְטוֹת יָדוֹ וַיָּבֹאוּ הָעִיר וַיִּלְכְּדוּהָ
וַיְמַהֲרוּ וַיַּצִּיתוּ אֶת־הָעִיר בָּאֵשׁ׃ כ וַיִּפְנוּ
אַנְשֵׁי הָעַי אַחֲרֵיהֶם וַיִּרְאוּ וְהִנֵּה עָלָה
עֲשַׁן הָעִיר הַשָּׁמַיְמָה וְלֹא־הָיָה בָהֶם
יָדַיִם לָנוּס הֵנָּה וָהֵנָּה וְהָעָם הַנָּס הַמִּדְבָּר
נֶהְפַּךְ אֶל־הָרוֹדֵף׃ כא וִיהוֹשֻׁעַ וְכָל־
יִשְׂרָאֵל רָאוּ כִּי־לָכַד הָאֹרֵב אֶת־הָעִיר
וְכִי עָלָה עֲשַׁן הָעִיר וַיָּשֻׁבוּ וַיַּכּוּ אֶת־
אַנְשֵׁי הָעָי׃ כב וְאֵלֶּה יָצְאוּ מִן־הָעִיר
לִקְרָאתָם

**תרגום**

יִשְׂרָאֵל׃ יח וַאֲמַר יְיָ
לִיהוֹשֻׁעַ אֲרֵים בְּרוּמְחָא
דִי בִידָךְ עַל עַי אֲרֵי
בִּידָךְ אֲמַסְרִינַהּ וַאֲרֵים
יְהוֹשֻׁעַ בְּרוּמְחָא דְבִידֵיהּ
עַל קַרְתָּא׃ יט וְכַמְנָא
קָם בִּפְרִיעַ מֵאַתְרֵיהּ
וּרְהַטוּ כַּדְאָרֵים יְדֵיהּ
וְעָלוּ לְקַרְתָּא וְכַבְשׁוּהָ
וְאוֹחִיאוּ וְאַדְלִיקוּ יַת
קַרְתָּא בְּנוּרָא׃
כ וְאִתְפְּנִיאוּ אֲנָשֵׁי עַי
לַאֲחוֹרֵיהוֹן נַחֲזוֹ
וְהָא סְלֵיק תְּנָנָא
דְקַרְתָּא לְצֵית שְׁמַיָּא
וְלָא הֲוָה בְהוֹן חֵילָא
לְמֵעֲרַק לְכָא וּלְכָא
וְעַמָּא דְאַפֵּיךְ לְמַדְבְּרָא
אִתְחֲזַר עַל רָדְפָא׃
כא וִיהוֹשֻׁעַ וְכָל יִשְׂרָאֵל
חֲזוֹ אֲרֵי כְבַשׁ כְּמָנָא יַת
קַרְתָּא וַאֲרֵי סְלֵיק תְּנָנָא
דְקַרְתָּא וְתָבוּ וּמְחוֹ יַת
אֲנָשֵׁי עַי׃ כב וְאִלֵּין נְפַקוּ
מִן קַרְתָּא לְקֳדָמוּתְהוֹן
והוו

**רש"י**

(יח) נטה בכידון. היא היה סימן לאורב לצאת מן המארב בראותו הכידון נטוי על העיר כידון ספידור בלע"ז והוא (עשפארא). (בל"א אין גראסעס שווערד): (כ) ידים. כח: והעם הנס המדבר. ישראל שנסו אל המדבר כמו שאמור למעלה נהפך להלחם אל הרודף: (כב) ואלה יצאו מן העיר. האורב שהצית

**רד"ק**

בעי ובבית אל: (יח) בכידון. כתרגומו ברומחא: (כ) ידים. מקום כמו רועות על ידיהם או כח כתרגומו חילא: אל הרודף. ישראל שהיו נסים אל המדבר נהפך אל אנשי העי שהיו רודפים אותם: (כד) בשדה. במדבר השדה כולל מקום זרע העבוד ומקום מרעה הבהמות גם כן לפיכך פי' במדבר אשר רודפים בו:

**מנחת שי**

כ') במסרה גדולה: (כא) את אנשי העי. במקרא גדולה נכתב על זה מלאנו בספר ישן העיר עד כאן. ובכל ספרים שלפני כתיב וקרי ... יא לאיתי מ

**מצודת דוד**

(יח) נטה בכידון. לעשות סימן להאורב לבא אל העיר: (כ) אל הרודף. הם אנשי העי שהיו מתחלה רודפים לישראל: (כב) ואלה.

**מצודת ציון**

(יח) בכידון. ברומח: (כ) ידים. מקום כמו יד אבשלום (ש"ב י"ח): (כב) בתוך. באמצע כמו והעיר בתוך (במדבר ל"ה):

## Commentary Digest

and had no power to flee — A, K and Z render: place. I.e. they had no place to flee.

*and the people that fled to the desert* — "*The Israelites who fled to the desert, as it is stated above, turned back to fight upon the pursuers.*" — R

22. *And the others came out of the city* — "*the ambush who had set fire to the city.*" — R After burning the city, they came out to hem in the enemies from both sides.

18. And the Lord said to Joshua, Stretch out the spear that is
in your hand, toward Ai; for I will give it into your hand. And
Joshua stretched out the spear that was in his hand, toward
the city. 19. And the ambush arose quickly out of their place,
and they ran as soon as he had stretched out his hand; and
they entered into the city, and took it, and hastened and set
the city on fire. 20. And the men of Ai looked behind them,
and saw, and behold, the smoke of the city ascended up to
heaven, and they had no power to flee this way or that way;
and the people that fled to the desert, turned back upon the
pursuers. 21. And Joshua and all Israel saw that the ambush
had taken the city, and that the smoke of the city ascended.
Then they turned back and slew the men of Ai. 22. And the
others came out of the city

## Commentary Digest

18. *Stretch out the spear* — *"This was the signal for the group lying in ambush to emerge from the ambush when they would see the spear stretched out toward the city."**

The small ambush of five thousand men, since they were nearer, saw the signal of the outstretched spear, and notified the larger ambush of thirty thousand men. The large ambush set fire to Ai and the smaller one attacked the smaller city of Beth-el. — M. L.

Some say that at the very moment that Joshua stretched out the spear, a divine spirit of might descended upon him. Through Joshua's renewed strength, the two ambushes likewise gained strength, and like lions, attacked both cities. — M. L.

19. *And the ambush arose quickly out of their place* — i.e. each of the two groups who lay in ambush, and "they *both* ran etc. and entered into the city." — A

20. *power* — J and R. lit. hands, hands being the symbol of strength or power. When they saw the city going up in smoke with their families and belongings, they became disheartened

* *espada in Spanish, a sword.* — R

לִקְרָאתָם וַיִּהְיוּ לְיִשְׂרָאֵל בַּתָּוֶךְ אֵלֶּה
מִזֶּה וְאֵלֶּה מִזֶּה וַיַּכּוּ אוֹתָם עַד־בִּלְתִּי
הִשְׁאִיר־לָהֶם שָׂרִיד וּפָלִיט׃ כג וְאֶת־מֶלֶךְ
הָעַי תָּפְשׂוּ חָי וַיַּקְרִבוּ אֹתוֹ אֶל־יְהוֹשֻׁעַ׃
כד וַיְהִי כְּכַלּוֹת יִשְׂרָאֵל לַהֲרֹג אֶת־כָּל־
יֹשְׁבֵי הָעַי בַּשָּׂדֶה בַּמִּדְבָּר אֲשֶׁר רְדָפוּם
בּוֹ וַיִּפְּלוּ כֻלָּם לְפִי־חֶרֶב עַד־תֻּמָּם *
וַיָּשֻׁבוּ כָל־יִשְׂרָאֵל הָעַי וַיַּכּוּ אֹתָהּ לְפִי־
חָרֶב׃ כה וַיְהִי כָל־הַנֹּפְלִים בַּיּוֹם הַהוּא
מֵאִישׁ וְעַד־אִשָּׁה שְׁנֵים עָשָׂר אֶלֶף כֹּל
אַנְשֵׁי הָעָי׃ כו וִיהוֹשֻׁעַ לֹא־הֵשִׁיב יָדוֹ
אֲשֶׁר נָטָה בַּכִּידוֹן עַד אֲשֶׁר הֶחֱרִים אֵת
כָּל־יֹשְׁבֵי הָעָי׃ כז רַק הַבְּהֵמָה וּשְׁלַל

וַהֲווֹ לְיִשְׂרָאֵל בִּמְצִיעָא
אִלֵּין מִכָּא וְאִלֵּין מִכָּא
וּמְחוֹ יַתְהוֹן עַד דְּלָא
אִשְׁתְּאַר לְהוֹן שְׁאָר
וּמְשֵׁיזֵיב׃ כג וְיָת מַלְכָּא
דְעַי אַחֲדוּ כַּד חַי וְקָרִיבוּ
יָתֵיהּ לְוָת יְהוֹשֻׁעַ׃
כד וַהֲוָה כַּד שֵׁיצִיאוּ יִשְׂרָאֵל
לְקַטָּלָא יַת כָּל יָתְבֵי עַי
בְּחַקְלָא בְּמַדְבְּרָא דִּי
רְדַפוּנוּן בֵּיהּ וְאִתְקְטָלוּ
כּוּלְּהוֹן לְפִתְגַם דְּחָרֶב
עַד דִּשְׁלִימוּ וְתָבוּ כָּל
יִשְׂרָאֵל לְעַי וּמְחוֹ יָתַהּ
לְפִתְגַם דְּחָרֶב׃ כה וַהֲווֹ
כָּל דְּאִתְקְטָלוּ בְּיוֹמָא
הַהוּא מִגְּבַר וְעַד אִתְּתָא
תְּרֵי עֲשַׂר אַלְפִין כָּל
אֱנָשֵׁי עָי׃ כו וִיהוֹשֻׁעַ לָא
אָתֵיב יְדֵיהּ דַּאֲרִים
בְּרוּמְחָא עַד דְּגַמַּר יַת
כָּל יָתְבֵי עָי׃ כז לְחוֹד
בְּעִירָא וַעֲדֵי קַרְתָּא
הַהִיא׃

פסקא באמצע פסוק

**מנחת שי**

מחלוקת: (כב) עד בלתי השאיר לו שריד ופליט. במקצת ספרים כ״י ודפוסים אחרונים כתיב להם וכן תרגם יונתן. ובס״א כ״י כתיב לו וק׳ להם. אבל בס״ם מדוייקים כ״י ודפוסים קדמונים כתוב לו ואין כאן קרי וכתיב כלל. וכן הוא במסורת כתיב גם בעל כלי יקר טרח לפרש מלת לו בלשון יחיד הגם דבאומרו ויכו אותם מורה הפך: (כד) ויהי ככלות ישראל וגו׳ עד תמם וישבו כל ישראל וגו׳. במקרא גדולה יש פיסקא באמצעות פסוק ולא ראיתי באחד ספרים גם התכם

**העיר**

**מצודת ציון**

**שריד**. ביור ושארית כמו שרידי חרב (ירמיה ל״א): **ופליט**. גם

**מצודת דוד**

אנשי האורב: (כד) **ויכו אותה**. הנשים והטף:

## Commentary Digest

from Jericho. He commanded them to destroy the city to commemorate the divine assistance which had been given them. Through this, they would be reminded that because of their sins they had been defeated, and through their repentance they were victorious. Thus, they would be scrupulous in their observance of the law. He did not ban its rebuilding, however, because it was not very suitable for rebuilding.

On the other hand, since the city was taken also through their own strategy and heroism, and to prevent a

against them, so that they were in the midst of Israel, some
on this side, and some on that side; and they smote them, so
that they let none of them remain or escape. 23. And the
king of Ai they seized alive, and brought him to Joshua.
24. And it was when Israel made an end of slaying all the
inhabitants of Ai in the field, in the desert where they chased
them, and when they had all fallen by the edge of the sword
until they were consumed, that all the Israelites returned to
Ai and smote it with the edge of the sword. 25. And so it
was, that all that fell that day, both of men and women,
were twelve thousand, all the people of Ai. 26. And Joshua
did not draw back his hand that he had stretched out
with the spear, until he had completely destroyed all the
inhabitants of Ai. 27. Only the cattle and the spoils of

## Commentary Digest

23. *And the king of Ai they seized alive* — for there was none to protect him. — P This illustrates the magnitude of the victory over Ai. They had destroyed the entire city and captured the king. — A

24. *and smote it* — the women and children therein. — D, who had not been consumed by the fire. — A

26. *And Joshua did not draw back his hand* — from fighting and slaying the inhabitants of Ai. He had actively participated in the entire campaign from beginning to end. — A See above v. 10.

*until he had completely destroyed all the inhabitants of Ai* — in conformance with the Pentateuchal precept concerning the nations of Canaan: You shall not spare a soul. You shall completely destroy them, etc.[1] He destroyed the city completely to deter other Canaanitish kings from resisting the Israelites when they would hear that Ai had been leveled to the ground.

Since this victory had been accomplished by a combination of divine assistance and human strategy and heroism, Joshua treated Ai differently

העיר ההיא בזזו להם ישראל כדבר
יהוה אשר צוה את־יהושע: כח וישרף
יהושע את־העי וישימה תל־עולם
שממה עד היום הזה: כט ואת־מלך העי
תלה על־העץ עד־עת הערב וכבוא
השמש צוה יהושע וירידו את־נבלתו
מן־העץ וישליכו אותה אל־פתח שער
העיר ויקימו עליו גל־אבנים גדול עד
היום

ההיא בזו להון ישראל
כפתגמא דיי דפקיד ית
יהושע: כח ואוקיד
יהושע ית עי ושויה
תל חריב לעלם לצדו
עד יומא הדין: כט וית
מלכא דעי צלב על
צליבא עד עידן רמשא
וכמיעל שמשא פקד
יהושע ואחיתו ית
נבלתיה מן צליבא ורמו
יתיה במעלנא תרע
קרתא ואקימו עלוהי
דגור אבנין רב עד יומא
הדין

## רד"ק

(כט) וכבא השמש. כמו שכתוב לא תלין נבלתו על העץ ועל כל הנתלה בארץ ישראל מצות הכתוב:

## רלב"ג

(כט) והנה נתלה מלך העי ולא הלינו נבלתו על העץ כמו שהזהירה התורה גם בהרוגי בית דין שלא לטמא האויר והקימו עליו גל של אבנים בפתח שער העיר כדי שיתפרסם זה לבאר מלכי הע"ג ויראו מהלחם עם ישראל:

ואולם התועלות הנמשכות מזה הספור הם י"ד:

התועלת הראשון הוא במצות והוא מה שזכר מענין המילה ומזה המקום למדנו במי שאיחר עשיית מצוה מהראוי שיקיימנה תכף בימצא מקום שיוכל לקיימה ולזה תמצא שתכף במצאו ישראל מקום הפנאי שיחנו בו עד שתחיה מכתם צוו בעשיית המילה ואולם אחר עבור אבל משה נתבאר' להם כי תוך שלשה ימים יסעו לעבר הירדן כמו שנזכר במה שקדם ומזה המקום יתבאר שמי שלא מל בשמיני לאיזה סבה שתהיה הנה אין ראוי לו שימתין עליה אחרי מצאו מקום לעשייתה: הב' הוא במדות והוא שראוי כשיביאנו הענין לעשות פעולה מצערת הנה ראוי שיעשה אותה באופן אשר יגיע בו לו צער יותר מעט מצער ולזה באה המצוה ליהושע שיעשה חרבות צורים וימול בהם בני ישראל: הג' הוא במצות והוא כשימשך מעשיית המילה סכנה לתינוק ראוי שתמנע ממנו ולזה ספר שכבר נמנעו מלימול במדבר בשנת לכתם במדבר ארבעים שנה ועל פי ה' יחנו ועל פי ה' יסעו ולזה לא היו יודעים מתי יבא להם הצווי ליסע כי בהעלות הענן יצטרכו ללכת כי ע"פ ה' יסעו ולזה יתכן שאם היו מלים אולי יבא להם הצווי ליסע קודם חיות מכת המילה ותהיה בזה סכנה לתינוק ולמולים ולזאת הסבה זכר גם בזה המקום שכבר ישבו בני ישראל תחתם עד חיותם: הד' והוא בעיון תועלת המצות הוא ללמדנו שים למצות המילה רושם בהתמד' ההשגחה בישראל עד שהיו נכנסים לירושת הארץ ולזה זכר שהקדים מצות המילה קודם שישתדלו בענין המלחמ' ולזה ג"כ אמר היום גלותי את חרפת מצרים לפי הביאור האחרון שזכרנו בו וכבר הארכנו המאמר איך יגיע זה התועלת מזאת המצוה בביאורנו לדברי התורה: הה' הוא במצות והוא להוסיף ביאור על מה שנאמר בתורה בהנפת העומר שהוא ממחרת השבת שלא רצה בו שבת בראשית כמו שהיו אומ' הצדוקים: הו' הוא בעיון והוא שהש"י לא יעשה מופת ללא צורך ולזה אמר שתכף כשיוכלו לאכול מעבור הארץ שבת המן: הז' הוא בעיון והוא שהנביא ראוי שיכין עצמו לנבואה שיצטרך אליה והוא בששים מחשבתו שם ולזה זכר שכבר היה יהושע ביריחו כשהגיע לו הנבואה ההיא ר"ל שכבר שוטטה מחשבתו שם כי הוא לא היה עדין ביריחו: הח' והוא בעיון להודיע כי בהתערב ענין ההשגות הדמיונות יקרה במקצת דברים המגיעים במראה הנבואה שיהיו לפי הדמיונות אשר שוטטה מחשבתו בהם וזה מבוא גדול לעמוד על הרבה מהדברים בא הספור בהם בענייני הנבואות ולזה זכר בזה המקום כי יהושע היה מדמה תחלה בזה האיש שיהיה מאנשי המלחמה אשר לו או אשר כנגדו: הט' הוא להיישיר ישראל כשיאמינו בשם ית' ויראו ממנו כי זה כלו מגיע אותם אל הצלחתם הנפשיי' עם שבזה יתיישרו בזאת ההצלחה אשר השתדלו' בה עתה: הי' הוא במדות והוא שאין ראוי שיקפח שכר כל בריה אך ראוי שישולם גמול על כל מעשה טוב ולזה תמצא שצוה יהושע להחיות רחב וכל אשר אתה בבית ונתן הסבה בזה כי ההחבאה את המלאכים אשר שלח יהושע ולא נתן הסבה בזה שבועת המרגלים לה כי לא נקשרו ישראל בזה מפני שבועת' לה כי לא היה להם רשות על זה מישראל ולא היו ראשי העם שיקשרו העם בשבועתם וכן סיפר בסוף הענין כי רחב וכל אשר אתה בבית החיה יהושע ותשב בקרב ישראל כי החביאה המלאכים אשר שלח ואחר שכבר היתה הסכמתו להחיות רחב וכל אשר אתה בבית בעבור הטוב שגמלה למרגלים הנה הסכים יהושע שיעשה זה ע"י המרגלים כדי שיקיימו שבועתם לה: הי"א הוא במדות והוא שהוא ראוי לכל כלל מתאחד למנוע קצת האנשים לקצת מחטוא לשי"ת כי כבר יענשו הכלל בחטא היחיד הלא תראה כי עכן מעל בחרם ועל כל העדה היה קצף ולזאת הסבה צותה התורה הוכח תוכיח את עמיתך: הי"ב הוא במדות והוא שאין ראוי למושל שיעשה בכחו מה שאפשר שתפול בו טענה שלא יעשה בצדק ואע"פ שצווה בזה מפי הגבורה אך ראוי שיתחכם להסיר הטענה ההיא באופן שלא תתחדש בזה מריבה וקטטה כי אולי יגיע מזה הפסד רב ובזה יתקיים מה שבאתהו המצוה עליו מאת השם ולזה תמצא שכבר התחכם יהושע שיודה עכן חטאו לסלק מעליו הטענה והמחלוקת ואעפ"י שכבר היה אפשר לו להשלים

## מצודת ציון

הוא ענין בהירות כמו להשאיר לנו פליטה (עזרא ט'): (כח) תל. מלשון תילין ודגורין להיות כן עד עולם לבלי אפשר להפנות והוא ענין גוזמא והפלגה: (כט) נבלתו. אף גוף אדם המת נקרא נבלה:

that city, Israel took for a prey to themselves, according to
the word of the Lord which He had commanded Joshua.
28. And Joshua burnt Ai, and made it a heap forever, a
desolation to this day. 29. And the king of Ai he hanged
on a gallows until evening, and as the sun set, Joshua
commanded, and they took his carcass down from the gallows,
and they threw it at the entrance of the gate of the city, and
raised upon it a great heap of stones to this day.

## Commentary Digest

recurrence of the Achan episode, Joshua sanctioned acquisition of the spoils. — A

27. *had commanded Joshua* — See above v. 2 and v. 26.

After the Achan episode, the Jews were very reluctant to derive any benefit from the spoils of Ai. They were ready to make everything *cherem* were it not for the divine command to Joshua. Everything they took from the spoils was with the intention to fulfill a divine decree. — K. Y.

28. *And Joshua burnt Ai* — Joshua himself completed the burning of the city and hanged the king of Ai while the people were plundering the spoils for themselves. He followed the precedent of his master Moses, who busied himself with Joseph's remains while the people were gathering the spoils of Egypt. — K. Y.

*a heap forever* — I.e. it was left as a heap of debris and ashes, so large that it would be impossible to clear away. This is written as an exaggeration. — D

29. *And the king of Ai he hanged* — to inspire courage in Israel and fear in the remaining nations of Canaan. — A

*on a gallows* — a pole inserted into the earth, not a growing tree. — J See San. 46a.

*and as the sun set, Joshua commanded, and they took his carcass down* — as it is written: "Do not leave his carcass overnight on the gallows, but bury him on the same day."[1] This applies to anyone, Jew or non-Jew, who is hanged in Eretz Israel. — K See II Sam. XXI.*G and A write that this was done in order not to contaminate and defile the land and the air, as the verse mentioned concludes, "And do not defile your land." So, too, in Ezek., XXXIX:12 — "And the house of Israel shall bury them (the armies of Gog) in order to purify the land."

*at the entrance of the gate of the city, and raised upon it a great heap of stones* — as a sign that the king of the city lies buried there, to serve as a deterrent to the other kings of Canaan. — A and G

*See also K 10:27.

הַיּ֥וֹם הַזֶּֽה׃ ל אָ֣ז יִבְנֶ֤ה יְהוֹשֻׁ֙עַ֙ מִזְבֵּ֔חַ
לַיהוָ֖ה אֱלֹהֵ֣י יִשְׂרָאֵ֑ל בְּהַ֖ר עֵיבָֽל׃
לא כַּאֲשֶׁ֣ר צִוָּ֣ה מֹשֶׁ֣ה עֶבֶד־יְ֠הוָה אֶת־
בְּנֵ֨י יִשְׂרָאֵ֜ל כַּכָּת֗וּב בְּסֵ֙פֶר֙ תּוֹרַ֣ת מֹשֶׁ֔ה
מִזְבַּח֙ אֲבָנִ֣ים שְׁלֵמ֔וֹת אֲשֶׁ֛ר לֹא־הֵנִ֥יף
עֲלֵיהֶ֖ן בַּרְזֶ֑ל וַיַּעֲל֨וּ עָלָ֤יו עֹלוֹת֙ לַיהוָ֔ה
וַיִּזְבְּח֖וּ שְׁלָמִֽים׃ לב וַיִּכְתָּב־שָׁ֖ם עַל־
הָאֲבָנִ֑ים אֵ֗ת מִשְׁנֵה֙ תּוֹרַ֣ת מֹשֶׁ֔ה אֲשֶׁ֣ר

הָדֵין׃ ל בְּכֵן בְּנָא יְהוֹשֻׁעַ מַדְבְּחָא קֳדָם יְיָ אֱלָהָא דְיִשְׂרָאֵל בְּטוּרָא דְעֵיבָל׃ לא כְּמָא דְפַקִּיד מֹשֶׁה עַבְדָּא דַיְיָ יָת בְּנֵי יִשְׂרָאֵל כְּמָא דִכְתִיב בְּסִפַר אוֹרַיְתָא דְמֹשֶׁה מַדְבַּח אַבְנִין שַׁלְמִין דְלָא אֲרֵים עֲלֵיהוֹן בַּרְזְלָא וְאַסִּיקוּ עֲלוֹהִי עֲלָוָן קֳדָם יְיָ וְנַכִיסוּ נִכְסַת קוּדְשִׁין׃ לב וּכְתַב תַּמָּן עַל אַבְנַיָּא יָת פַּתְשֶׁגֶן אוֹרַיְתָא

ת"א אז יבנה. שבת נו סנהדרין מד:

רד"ק

(ל) אז יבנה. אז כשעברו ישראל את הירדן ואין מוקדם ומאוחר בתורה כי כן כתיב בספר תורת משה והיה ביום אשר תעברו את הירדן וגו' והקמות לך אבנים גדולות ושדת אותם בשיד ובנית שם מזבח וגו' ואז היתרו הבכות כל זמן שהיו בגלגל וכן אמרו רבותינו ז"ל בו ביום עברו את הירדן ובאו להר גריזים ולהר עיבל והביאו את האבנים ושדום בשיד וכתבו עליהם את כל דברי התורה ובנו מזבח והעלו עולות ושלמים ואכלו ושתו ושמחו וברכו וקללו וקפלו את האבנים ולני אמרו אין הבמה נתרת אלא על ידי נביא שנאמר אז יבנה יהושע ומלת יבנה עתיד במקום עבר ויבא זה עם קשר מלת אז בהרבה מקומות כמו אז ישיר משה אז ישיר ישראל אז יבדיל משה אז ידבר יהושע אז יבנה שלמה אז תבאנה אז יקהל שלמה: (לב) את משנה תורת משה. כן ושנתם לבניך אף על פי שאינו משרשו ופירושו לשון התורה ופירושה על דרך כלל וכתב רבינו סעדיה ז"ל כי כתבו בהם

רש"י

את העיר: (ל) אז יבנה וגו'. פרשה זו כתובה ע"ד מוקדם ומאוחר שמיום שעברו את הירדן עשה כן: (לב) ויכתב שם על האבנים. כן הנה האבנים האמורים למעלה לאחר מעשה וזה קיפלו הסיד מעליהם והביאום הגלגל:

רלב"ג

מלות הש"י בזולת הודאת פיו כי לא היה יכולת לאחד מבני ישראל למרות את פי הנביא כמו שאמרו אליו כל איש אשר ימרה את פיך וגו' ולזאת הסבה לוה יהושע ג"כ למלאכיו שירולו לאוהל עכן כדי שימלאו מה שהודה ואז יתפרסם זה לישראל ולזאת הסבה הליקום ופזרום לפני ה' כדי שיתפרסם לכלם שכבר היה מבואר במה שהביאו מלאכי יהושע אותם הדברים שהודה עכן: הי"ג והוא במדות והוא שראוי לכל משתדל בעשיית פועל מה שלא יקצר מהמלאכת הסבות המביאות התכלית אשר יכוין ומלהשכית כל הסבות המונעות' התכלית ההוא ולזאת הסבה תמלא שסודר ענין יהושע במלחמה עם יושבי העי בכל אלו התחבולות הנפלאות' וזה שכבר היו ישראל הנראים למלך העי בעמק ולזה יבטחו יושבי העי לצאת עליהם למלחמה כי הם היו בחולשה בתכלית לפי המקום ההוא שהיו בו ר"ל מפני היותם בעמק עם שכבר חזק לבם עוד מפני היות זה כמו המועד והמקום שהיו ישראל נגפים לפני יושבי העי בפעם הראשונה וחזק לבם גם כן לרדוף כלם אחריהם באופן שהניחו העיר פתוחה כי הם ראו אותם כלם נסים דרך המדבר והם לא ידעו שיהיה קלת החיל מאחריהם ובזה נשלם להם בקלות הכנס האורב בעיר והצית העיר באש והוא הקל מאד בענין המלחמה כי בראותם עשן העיר נבהלו מפני מות טפם ונשיהם ואבוד קניניהם וסגר זה להם דלתי ההשתדלות בענין מלחמה' שיתנהגו בה באופן ראוי ולזה מתו כולם בקלות ולזאת הסבה בעינה תלו מלך העי והקימו עליו גל אבנים גדול לידע הנשארים: הי"ד והוא בדעות הוא שהש"י לא ישנה טבע המציאות ומנהגו לעשות מופת אם לא יביאו לזה הכרח מה ולזה תמצא כי מפני שהיה אפשר הכרתת יושבי העי בקלות בכמו אלו התחבולות מגד מה שקרה במלחמה הראשונה שהיו ישראל נגפים לפניהם הנה לא הסכים הש"י שיעשה זה בדרך מופת: (ל) אז יבנה יהושע מזבח לה'. עד והארון שקטה ממלחמה. זכר שכבר בנה יהושע מזבח לה' אלהי ישראל בהר עיבל: (לא) כאשר לוה משה וגו'. אבנים שלמות אשר לא הניף עליהם ברזל. כמו שלותה התורה וזה ממה שיורה שמה שאמר בתורה ואם מזבח אבנים תעשה לי היא מלוה לא רשות עם שכבר באה המלוה בבניית המזבח בהר עיבל וזכר שכתב שם על אבני המזבח פתשגן תורת משה אשר כתבה לפני בני ישראל והנה כבר נתבאר בתורה שכבר שדו אותם בסיד כדי שיכתבו שם כתב מבואר ואחשוב שמה שנכתב שם הוא זאת הברכה והקללה אשר קראו בזה המקום כתוב בתורת משה וזהו מ"ש שכבר קרא שם את כל דברי התורה הברכה והקללה וזה לאות שמה שנכתב שם לא היה בו זולת זה ואם אי אפשר אלא שיורה שנכתב שם כל התורה הנה אין זה זר מאוד כל שכן אם היה המזבח גדול וגבוה ובכלל הנה אם היה כגודל מזבח בית שני לפי מה שספרו ממנו רבותינו ז"ל היה מכיל זה בכתיבה בינונית. והנה זה הוא הנראה בעיני ר"ל שמה שנכתב שם כלל התורה ואי אפשר שנאמר שיהיה משנה תורת משה רמז לעשרת

מצודת ציון

(לב) משנה. מלשון שנים:

מצודת דוד

(לב) משנה תורת משה. כפל אלא הדברים קרוי משנה תורה

## Commentary Digest

accept the Torah, but did not, their doom was sealed. Rabbi Simeon says: They first whitewashed the stones with lime, and then wrote the words thereupon. The words were inscribed in all seventy languages, to facilitate their comprehension by all the surrounding peoples. — K[5] Although R states that the *Israelites* peeled off the stones, it is unlikely that they peeled off the

30. Then Joshua built an altar to the Lord God of Israel
on Mount Ebal. 31. As Moses, the servant of the Lord,
commanded the children of Israel, as it is written in the book
of the law of Moses, an altar of whole stones, upon which
no (man) has lifted up any iron. And they offered upon it
burnt-offerings to the Lord and sacrificed peace-offerings.
32. And he wrote there upon the stones a copy of the law
of Moses, which

## Commentary Digest

30. *Then Joshua etc.* — *"This section is written in the manner of 'earlier' and 'later' (events combined), for on the day they crossed the Jordan he did so."* — R R and K reiterate the maxim: There is no 'earlier' and 'later' (no chronological order) in events or laws of the Scripture.[1] We explain "Then" as the day of the crossing of the Jordan, for so was the Biblical command: "And it shall be on the day that you will cross the Jordan ... you shall erect large stones ... and you shall build there an altar."[2] A explains the building of the altar at this point as an expression of national pride and thanks for the great victory over Ai after the initial defeat. Moreover, since the initial defeat was a clear illustration of divine retribution, Joshua saw it fit to remind the people of the blessings and curses enumerated in Deut. Thus, he maintains that the chapter was written in chronological order, explaining thus: Then, after the Ai episode, Joshua built an altar, etc.

Since the Tabernacle was in Gilgal, the altar on Mt. Ebal constituted a במה or 'high place.' This was permissible only by the sanction of a prophet, as in this case, by the command of Moses, executed through Joshua.[3]

31. *as it is written in the book of the Law of Moses* — Deut. XXVII:5.

32. *And he wrote there on the stones* — *"They are the aforementioned stones.. After this event* (of building the altar) *they peeled the lime off them and brought them to Gilgal."* — R

The Rabbis of the Talmud differ as to the procedure of writing the Torah on the stones. Rabbi Judah says that they wrote the words directly on the stones and subsequently whitewashed them with lime over the script. The Lord gave the heathens the power of extra-sensory perception, whereupon they sent their clerks who peeled off the lime and copied the inscription. Since they had the opportunity to

כְּתַב לִפְנֵי בְּנֵי יִשְׂרָאֵל: לג וְכָל־יִשְׂרָאֵל
וּזְקֵנָיו וְשֹׁטְרִים ׀ וְשֹׁפְטָיו עֹמְדִים מִזֶּה ׀
וּמִזֶּה ׀ לָאָרוֹן נֶגֶד הַכֹּהֲנִים הַלְוִיִּם נֹשְׂאֵי ׀
אֲרוֹן בְּרִית־יְהוָה כַּגֵּר כָּאֶזְרָח חֶצְיוֹ אֶל־
מוּל הַר־גְּרִזִים וְהַחֶצְיוֹ אֶל־מוּל הַר־עֵיבָל
כַּאֲשֶׁר צִוָּה מֹשֶׁה עֶבֶד־יְהוָה לְבָרֵךְ
אֶת־הָעָם יִשְׂרָאֵל בָּרִאשֹׁנָה: לד וְאַחֲרֵי־

דְמֹשֶׁה דִכְתַב קֳדָם בְּנֵי
יִשְׂרָאֵל: לג וְכָל יִשְׂרָאֵל
וְסָבוֹהִי וְסָרְכוֹהִי וְדַיָּנוֹהִי
קָיְמִין מִכָּא וּמִכָּא
לַאֲרוֹנָא קֳדָם כַּהֲנַיָא
לֵוָאֵי נָטְלֵי אֲרוֹנָא
דִקְיָמָא דַיְיָ כְּגִיּוֹרָא
כְּיַצִּיבָא פַּלְגֵיהוֹן לָקֳבֵל
טוּרָא דִגְרִיזִין וּפַלְגֵיהוֹן
לָקֳבֵל טוּרָא דְעֵיבָל כְּמָא
דְפַקִּיד מֹשֶׁה עַבְדָא
דַיְיָ לְבָרָכָא יָת עַמָּא
יִשְׂרָאֵל בְּקַדְמֵיתָא:
לד וּבָתַר כֵּן קְרָא יָת כָּל

כן

פתגמי ת״א ובוטריס ובופטיו. סוטה לב: נגד הכהנים. (סוטה כה) : והתליו · סוטה לו :

רש״י

(לג) לברך את העם ישראל בראשונה · להקדים ברכות לקללות ברוך האיש אשר לא יעשה פסל ומסכה :

רד״ק

מספר המצות כמו שהן כתובות בהלכות ובאזהרות ויפה אמר כי לא יתכן שכתבו בהן כל התורה רק הצורך דרך כלל ונחלקו רבותינו ז״ל מהם אמרו על גבי האבנים כתבוה ואחר כך שדו אות׳ בשיד ומהם אמרו מתחלה שדו את האבנים וכתבו התורה על גבי השיד ואמרו כי בשבעים לשון כתבו אותם דברי התורה כמו שנאמר בתורה באר היטב כדי שיבינו אותם כל עם ולשון שיראו אותם: (לג) חציו. ו׳ שבטים עלו להר גריזים שמעון ולוי ויהודה ויששכר ויוסף ובנימין וששה להר עיבל ראובן גד ואשר וזבולון דן ונפתלי והכהנים והלוים והארון עומדים למטה הכהנים מקיפים את הארון והלוים מקיפים את הכהנים וישראל מזה ומזה הפכו הלוים פניהם כלפי הר גריזים ופתחו בברכה שנאמר לברך את העם ישראל בראשונה וכך הוא מפורש בתורה את הברכה על הר גריזים ואת הקללה על הר עיבל והיה אם שמוע תחלה ואחר כן והיה אם לא תשמע ופתחו ואמרו ברוך האיש אשר לא יעשה פסל ומסכה וגו׳ ואלו ואלו עונין אמן הפכו פניהם כלפי הר עיבל ופתחו בקללה ארור האיש אשר יעשה פסל וגו׳ ואלו ואלו עונין אמן עד שגומרין כסדר הזה ברכות וקללות כך סדרו רבותינו זכרם לברכה והקשו ואמרו איך אנו אומרים כי הלוים היו למטה והלא לוי למעלה שהרי היה הוא אחד מן הששה שבטים שהיו בהר גריזים ופירושו כי זקני כהונה ולויה למטה והשאר למעלה ומהם אמרו כל הראוי לשירות למטה והשאר למעלה: והחציו. כמו האהלי הערכך והדומים להם שבאו בשתי ידיעות ורבותינו ז״ל דרשו בו כי בא הה״א למעט כי מעטים היו במספר החצי של הר עיבל מהחצי של הר גריזים ואף על פי שלוי למטה מפני שהיה יוסף עמהם שנאמר בהם ואנכי עם רב וגו׳ ומה שאמר אל מול הר גריזים אל מול הר עיבל שלא עמדו על ההר אלא בשיפוע ההר ובהר גריזים ובהר עיבל יש מחלוקת בדברי רבותינו ז״ל הלא המה בעבר הירדן ואילך דברי רבי יהודה אחרי דרך מבוא השמש מקום שהחמה זורחת אצל אלוני מורה ונאמר להלן ויעבור אברם בארץ עד מקום שכם עד אלון מורה מה אלון מורה האמור להלן שכם אף אלון מורה האמור כאן שכם וזהו הר גריזים והר עיבל שבין הכותיים ר׳ אליעזר אומר לא זה הוא הר גריזים והר עיבל שבין הכותיים הלא המה בעבר הירדן סמוך לירדן דרך מבוא השמש מקום שהחמה שוקעת בארץ הכנעני והלא אינה אלא ארץ חוי היושב בערבה והלא בין הרים וגבעות הן יושבין מול הגלגל·והלא לא ראו את הגלגל ובירוש׳ לדברי רבי אליעזר מהו הר גריזים והר עיבל ב׳ גבשושיות עשו לאחד קראו הר גריזים ולאחד קראו הר עיבל: (לד) ואחרי כן. הברכה

רלב״ג

הדברות עד שנאמר שלא כתב שם כי אם עשרת הדברים וזה שהוא זכר שכבר כתבם משה לפני בני ישראל ומה שכתב שם משה לפני בני ישראל היה כלל התורה לא עשר הדברים לבד וקצת המפרשים אמרו שכבר כתב שם רמזים קלרים מתרי״ג מלות כמו הענין באזהרו׳ הנה נהגו לקראם בחג השבועות שיש בהם רמזים קלרים מתרי״ג מלות וזה רחוק בעיני שכבר נזכר בתורה וכתבת על האבנים את כל דברי התורה הזאת באר היטב וזה מורה שמה שנכתב בתורה היה מבואר באופן שלם. והנה זכר שעשו שם כמו שלוה משה

מצודת דוד

כי בו נאמר שנית מה שנאמר באריכות הספרים שלפניה : (לג) נגד הכהנים הלוים. הכהנים בני לוי אשר עמדו עם הארון באמצע ואמרו הברכה והקללה: חציו. ששה שבטים: לברך וגו׳ בראשונה. בתחילה פתחו ואמרו ברוך האיש אשר לא

מצודת ציון

(לג) כאזרח. זה ישראל גמור מלידה: מול. נגד:

## Commentary Digest

"Amen." The blessings and curses were pronounced alternately, first a blessing and then a curse. The difficulty presented by the dual position of the Levites, both on Mt. Gerizim and in the valley between the mountain, is solved by the Rabbis of the Talmud. Rabbi Eliezer ben Jacob says: The elders among the priests and Levites stood below, while the others stood on Mt. Gerizim. Rabbi Josiah says: Those fit for Levitical service stood below, while the others stood above on the mountain.[7]

The location of these two mountains is likewise discussed in the Talmud. Rabbi Judah holds that they are mountains commonly known by

he wrote in the presence of the children of Israel. 33. And all Israel, and their elders and officers and their judges, stood on this side of the Ark and on that side, before the priests the Levites, the bearers of the Ark of the covenant of the Lord, the stranger as well as the native born, half of them over against Mount Gerizim and half of them over against Mount Ebal, as Moses the servant of the Lord had commanded, to bless the people of Israel first.

## Commentary Digest

lime upon which the commandments were inscribed. It is more likely that they peeled off the lime which served as cement between the stones.[1]

*a copy of the Law of Moses* — The commentators express various opinions in interpreting this passage. According to SG, the gist of all the 613 mitzvoth was recorded. Others say that this refers to the Decalogue which serves as the basis of all the commandments.[2] — A Others explain this as the Book of Deut., which is a repetition of the Law and is known as Mishneh Torah. — D after commentators quoted by A. N[3] quotes ספר תאגי (the Book of Crowns) as stating that the entire Pentateuch was copied on the stones, with all the crowns on the letters as they are written in the Torah scrolls. He conjectures that either the stones were gigantic or that the script fitted on them miraculously.

33. *half of them* — Six tribes ascended Mt. Gerizim: Simeon, Levi, Judah, Issachar, Joseph, and Benjamin. The other six tribes ascended Mt. Ebal: Reuben, Gad, Asher, Zebulun, Dan, and Naftali. The priests, the Levites, and the Ark, stood below, the priests encircling the Ark, and the Levites encircling the priests, and all Israel standing on the mountains on either side. — K

*over against Mount Gerizim* — on the slope of the mountain, to reconcile this passage with Deut. XXVII:12 — K, A.

*to bless the people of Israel first* — *"to pronounce the blessings before the curses: Blessed be the man who will not make a graven or molten image."* — R[4] The Levites turned their faces toward Mt. Gerizim and commenced with the blessings: Blessed be the man etc. All the curses enumerated in the chapter were first pronounced conversely as blessings.[5] After each blessing, all the people replied, "Amen." Subsequently, the Levites turned their faces toward Mt. Ebal and pronounced the curses as enumerated in the Scriptures.[6] Again, all the people replied,

כן קרא את־כל־דברי התורה הברכה
והקללה ככל־הכתוב בספר התורה:
לה לא־היה דבר מכל אשר־צוה משה
אשר לא־קרא יהושע נגד כל־קהל
ישראל והנשים והטף והגר ההלך
בקרבם: ט א ויהי כשמע כל־המלכים
אשר בעבר הירדן בהר ובשפלה ובכל
חוף הים הגדול אל־מול הלבנון החתי
והאמרי הכנעני הפרזי החוי והיבוסי:

פתגמי אוריתא ברכן
ולוטין ככל דכתיב
בספרא דאוריתא:
לה לא הוה פתגמא מכל
די פקיד משה דלא קרא
יהושע קדם כל קהלא
דישראל ונשיא וטפלא
וגיוריא דאזלין ביניהון:
א והוה כד שמעו כל
מלכיא די בעברא
דירדנא בטורא
ובשפלתא ובכל ספר
ימא רבא די לקביל
ליבנן חתאי ואמוראי
כנענאי פריזאי חואי
ויבוסאי

רד"ק

והקללה. הוא שאמרו ברוך האיש ארור האיש או פי׳ והיה אם שמוע תשמע יהי׳ אם לא תשמע: (לה) לא הי׳ דבר. נרא׳ מהפסוק כי אחר שקראו הלוים הברכה והקללה פתח יהושע וקרא באזניהם כל המצות מצות עשה ומצות לא תעשה: והגר ההולך בקרבם. כמו שכתוב בתורה בפרשת הקהל וגרך אשר בשעריך: ואמר ההולך שהיו מתגיירין מן האומות בכל מסעיהם מפני

מנחת שי

ומלתו כתב במקרת שלו לריך עיון אם יש כאן פיסקא: (לה) והנשים והטף. במקצת ספרים הטי"ת בקמץ:

רלב"ג

מענין הברכה והקללה לא נפל דבר ממה שנזכר מזה בפרש׳ כי תבא: (א) עוד זכר כי כאשר שמעו כל המלכים אשר בעבר הירדן מה שעשה יהושע וישראל לירחו ולעי התחכמו ולקחו עלה בזה להתחבר יחד כדי שיעזרו קצתם לקצתם ולא יוכלו אחד אחד כמו שהגיע

מצודת ציון

ט (א) ובשפלה. בעמק: חוף. שפת:

מצודת דוד

יעשה פסל וגו׳ ואחר זה אמרו ארור האיש וגו׳ וכן כל הארורים: (לד) קרא. יהושע היה הקורא כמ"ש במקרא שלאחריו: את כל דברי התורה. וחוזר ומפרש שקרא הברכה והקללה ככל הכתוב בתורה והם פרשת והיה אם שמוע תשמע וגו׳ והיה אם לא תשמע וגו׳ האמורות בסדר כי תבא והדומים להם: (לה) לא היה דבר. מן הברכה והקללה: אשר צוה. ר"ל האמור בתורה: ט (א) כשמוע. אשר כבשו את העי ברוב עם ובתחבולה:

## Commentary Digest

### CHAPTER 9

1. *the Hittite, etc.* — all the six nations of Canaan, the Girgashite having exacuated and left for Africa.[2]

*heard* — that the Israelites had conquered Ai through stealth and strategy, (not through a miracle as they had taken Jericho), they gathered together to war with Joshua. They thought that by force of numbers, they would be victorious. — D and M This explanation is similar to G's who explains that they realized that Israel was stronger than any one of them, since they had already defeated the mighty walled city of Jericho and also defeated Ai. Their only hope, therefore, lay in banding together in an alliance. Alshich explains that this verse corresponds with V:1: And it came to pass, when all the kings of the Amorites ... heard that the Lord had dried up the waters of the Jordan ... that their heart melted, nor was there spirit in them anymore, because of the children of Israel. At this time, Joshua sent three epistles to all the nations of Canaan, which stated: Those who wish to evacuate may evacuate; those who wish to make

34. And afterward he read all the words of the law, the blessing and the curse, according to all that is written in the book of the Torah. 35. There was not a word of all that Moses commanded, which Joshua did not read before all the congregation of Israel, with the women, and the little ones, and the strangers that walked among them.

## 9

1. And it was when all the kings that were on this side of the Jordan, in the hill-country, and in the valley, and on all of the shore of the great sea opposite Lebanon, the Hittite, the Amorite, the Canaanite, the Perizzite, the Hivite, and the Jebusite, heard (of this),

### Commentary Digest

these names, those inhabited by the Samaritans. Rabbi Eliezer objects to this opinion, since these mountains do not meet the specifications enumerated in Deut. XI:30. He, therefore, introduces the novel idea that these were two hillocks formed by the Israelites for this occasion, within sight of Gilgal. — K[1]

34. *he read* — i.e. Joshua himself read the Torah, as below v. 35. — D

*the blessing and the curse* — previously recited by the Levites, or perhaps the following chapter, which embodies the covenant entered into in the plains of Moab. This chapter prophesies the Roman conquest of the Holy Land and the subsequent diaspora. - K, D and A

35. *There was not a word of all that Moses commanded* — of the blessings and curses that Joshua did not read. He continued to read from Deut. XXIX:9 to the end of XXX. — A and D. K explains that Joshua read in detail all the two hundred forty-eight positive commandments and the three hundred sixty-five negative commandments, after the Levites had completed their readings.

*and the strangers that "walked" among them* — Heb. ההולך, connoting constant entering of strangers into the fold of Judaism. These were the thinking individuals among the nations, who realized what miracles were unfolding before their very eyes, and joined the ranks of the Jewish nation. — K

ב וַיִּתְקַבְּצוּ יַחְדָּו לְהִלָּחֵם עִם־יְהוֹשֻׁעַ וְעִם־יִשְׂרָאֵל פֶּה אֶחָד׃ ג וְיֹשְׁבֵי גִבְעוֹן שָׁמְעוּ אֵת אֲשֶׁר עָשָׂה יְהוֹשֻׁעַ לִירִיחוֹ וְלָעָי׃ ד וַיַּעֲשׂוּ גַם־הֵמָּה בְּעָרְמָה וַיֵּלְכוּ וַיִּצְטַיָּרוּ וַיִּקְחוּ שַׂקִּים בָּלִים לַחֲמוֹרֵיהֶם וְנֹאדוֹת יַיִן בָּלִים וּמְבֻקָּעִים וּמְצֹרָרִים׃

יְבוּסָאֵי׃ ב וְאִתְכְּנָשׁוּ כַּחֲדָא לְאַגָּחָא קְרָבָא עִם יְהוֹשֻׁעַ וְעִם יִשְׂרָאֵל סִיעָא חֲדָא׃ ג וְיָתְבֵי גִבְעוֹן שְׁמַעוּ יַת דִּי עֲבַד יְהוֹשֻׁעַ לִירִיחוֹ וְלָעָי׃ ד וַעֲבַדוּ אַף אִינוּן בְּחוּכְמָא וַאֲזַלוּ וְנַסִיבוּ שַׂקִּין בָּלָן לַחֲמָרֵיהוֹן וְזִיקִין דַּחֲמַר בָּלָן וּמְבַזְעִין וּמְצָרְרִין׃

ומסנן ונעלות

### רש"י

ט (ד) ויעשו גם המה בערמה. כמו שעשו בני יעקב בערמה בחמור אבי שכם שהיה חוי ויושבי גבעון מן החוי היו כמ"ש בענין: ויצטירו. עשו עצמן כהולכים בשליחות מל' וציר בגוים שולח. וכל תיבה שתחלת יסודה לצ"י כשהי' מתפעלת בלשון מתפעל או נתפעל באה טי"ת בתוכה והולקת את אותיות ברבי התיבה כמו מה נצטדק מגזר' צדק שהומר נצטדק וכן גיטמיה ילטבע מגזר' לבע: שקים בלים. שיהיו נראים כבאים מארץ רחוקה: ומצררים. לשון

### רד"ק

הנפלאות אשר היו שומעים ורואים: (ב) פה אחד. בהסכמ' אחת ועצה אחת ועל הדרך הזה ת"י סיעה חדא ולא פירש הקבוץ הזה עד שספר מעשה יושבי גבעון כי בעבורם התקבצו כמו שמספר למטה: (ד) גם המה. דרשו בו לרבות על בני יעקב שבאו להם במרמה כמו שאומר במרמה וידברו והם היו החוי ויש לפרש גם לרבות על בני יריחו ועי כי הם עשו עם בני ישראל להשמר מהם כמו שאמר ויריחו סוגרת ומסוגרת או להלחם עמהם כמו עי והם עשו גם הם כן אבל בערמה באו אליהם להשלים עמהם. ויש לפרש עוד גם לרבות על ערמת ישראל לפי מחשבת החוי כי הם חשבו כי בערמה הכו ישראל יריחו ועי ששלחו להם להשלים כדי שלא ישמרו מהם ואחר כך הכום והם באו להם בערמה אף על פי שהם בעצמם ידעו כי סופם לגלות להם ערמתם חשבו אחרי שיכרתו לנו ברית לא יעברו על בריתם אף על פי שיתגלה להם הערמה אחר כן: ויצטירו. עשו עצמם צירים ומלאכים באים מארץ רחוקה ומן

### רלב"ג

הגלות ליריחו ולעי מפני היותם יחידים והנה זאת היתה העלה שלקחו בזה אלו המלכים והתחכמו בה: (ד) וזכר עם זה ביושבי גבעון שגם הם עשו בערמה לקחת עלה בלא יגיעם נזק מפני בני ישראל וזה אמרו גם הם כי הראשונים עשו מה שעשו לקחת על זה עלה בלא יהרימום ישראל והלו לקחו עלה אחרת והערימו בזה האופן שזכר: ויצטירו. הוא מענין ציר נאמן לשולחיו והטעם

### מנחת שי

ט (ד) וילכו ויצטירו. כתיב והתרגום בדלי"ת וכבר תפס עליו רד"ק:

### מצודת דוד

(ב) ויתקבצו. להיות גם הם עם רב ויועלים הרבה להתחכם במלחמה עמהם: (ג) ליריחו ולעי. ר"ל בשמעו שני דברים הפכים כי יריחו כבשו בנס והעי בתחבולות ובחרב עם ולזה סבינו הדבר בערמה עבור להטעותם כאמור למטלה: (ד) ויעשו גם המה בערמה. כמו שעשו ישראל: ויצטירו. עשו עצמם כשלוחים באים מארץ מרחק כי שם ציר הונח על השלוח למרחוק וכמ"ש ותשלחי ציריך עד מרחוק (ישעיה נ"ז): בלים להטעות את ישראל לחשוב שבאו מדרך מרחק הדרך בלו: ומצררים. מקושרים סביבות הבקיעים:

### מצודת ציון

(ב) פה אחד. ר"ל בעצה אחת: (ד) ויצטירו. עשו עצמם כשלוחים כמו ציר אמונים (משלי י"ג): בלים. מורקבים: ונאדות. הם כלי היין: ומבקעים. מלשון בקיעה: ומצררים. מקושרים כמו לצור כספו (בראשית מ"ב):

## Commentary Digest

in order to throw them off guard, and thereby defeat them. They, likewise, acted with wile to trick the Israelites into accepting them as allies. D explains that just as the Israelites had acted with wile in their campaign against Ai, so the Gibeonites acted with wile to trick the Israelites. R, and K, quoting unknown Midrashic sources, explain thus: *"Just as Jacob's* ***sons dealt cunningly with Hamor the*** *father of Shechem who was a Hivite;*[1] *and the inhabitants of Gibeon were also from the Hivites, as it is stated in this episode."* — R In Deut. XXIX:10, R and Y explain that Canaanites came in Moses' time and tried to trick him by disguising. Now, the Gibeonites *also* acted with wile...[2]

**and disguised themselves as ambassadors.** Heb. ויצטירו. *"They made themselves like message carriers, from the expression of:* "(וציר) *And a messenger was sent among the nations."*[3] *Now, every word, the beginning of whose root is 'zade,' when it is used as reflexive in the form of* מתפעל *or* נתפעל, *a 'teth' comes in the middle*

2. That they gathered together to war with Joshua and with Israel, with a single accord. 3. And the inhabitants of Gibeon heard what Joshua had done to Jericho and to Ai. 4. And they also acted with wile, and they went, and disguised as ambassadors, and they took worn sacks for their donkeys, and wine bottles, rotten, split, and tied together.

## Commentary Digest

peace may make peace; those who wish to wage war, shall wage war. As mentioned above, the Girgashites evacuated and fled to Africa. The Gibeonites made peace, as below. The thirty-one kings waged war and fell. The Scripture relates here that when the kings of Canaan heard of the miraculous drying up of the Jordan, they sought to conceal their feelings of fright. They, therefore, assembled, and united to form one mighty army to wage war against Joshua's forces. They hoped to strike fear in the hearts of Joshua's soldiers.

A explains that the kings heard of Joshua's building an altar and inscribing the Torah on its stones. Since the Torah can be referred to as the Jewish constitution, it was as though Joshua was establishing his law on foreign soil. He was playing the role of the conqueror planting his flag on conquered territory. He, therefore, posed a threat to all the kings of Canaan. They, accordingly, formed a united front to oppose him.

2. *with a single accord* — lit. one mouth. They all concurred to oppose Joshua, not to follow the example of the Girgashites, nor to make peace like the Gibeonites. — Alshich

3. *And the inhabitants of Gibeon* —independent of their king, who was in conference with the other kings of Canaan. — A

*had done to Jericho and to Ai* — I.e. the Jews had conquered Jericho in a completely miraculous fashion by having the walls sink into the ground. **On the other hand, they had conquered Ai by a clever military strategem. Thus, the Gibeonites realized that the Jews were able warriors in the natural sense, and were also aided by supernatural means. — D**

4. *And they also acted with wile* — "Also" here refers to the course of action taken by the other nations of Canaan in face of the common danger of Israel, that of banding together to fight. It also refers to Jericho's course of action, that of locking and bolting the gates, and Ai's course of action, that of military offensive. Gibeon, on the other hand, decided to join with Israel rather than try to beat them. — K and G K further suggests that the Gibeonites thought that the Israelites had sent messages of peace to Jericho and Ai

ה וּנְעָלוֹת בָּלוֹת וּמְטֻלָּאוֹת בְּרַגְלֵיהֶם
וּשְׂלָמוֹת בָּלוֹת עֲלֵיהֶם וְכֹל לֶחֶם צֵידָם
יָבֵשׁ הָיָה נִקֻּדִים: ו וַיֵּלְכוּ אֶל־יְהוֹשֻׁעַ
אֶל־הַמַּחֲנֶה הַגִּלְגָּל וַיֹּאמְרוּ אֵלָיו וְאֶל־
אִישׁ יִשְׂרָאֵל מֵאֶרֶץ רְחוֹקָה בָּאנוּ וְעַתָּה
כִּרְתוּ־לָנוּ בְרִית: ז וַיֹּאמְרוּ אִישׁ־יִשְׂרָאֵל
אֶל־הַחִוִּי אוּלַי בְּקִרְבִּי אַתָּה יוֹשֵׁב וְאֵיךְ

ויאמר ק׳

### תרגום

ה וּמְסָנֵי בְּלָן וּמְרַקְעִין
בְּרַגְלֵיהוֹן וּכְסוּתָא בְּלָיָא
עֲלֵיהוֹן וְכֹל לְחֵם
זְוָדֵיהוֹן יְבֵשׁ הֲוָה כְּסָנִין:
ו וַאֲזַלוּ לְוַת יְהוֹשֻׁעַ
לְמַשְׁרִיתָא לְגִלְגָּלָא
וַאֲמַרוּ לֵיהּ וּלְאֱנָשׁ
יִשְׂרָאֵל מֵאַרְעָא רְחִיקָא
אֲתֵינָא וּכְעַן גְּזָרוּ לָנָא
קְיָם: ז וַאֲמַרוּ אֱנָשׁ
יִשְׂרָאֵל לְחִוָּאָה דִּלְמָא
בֵּינָנָא אַתּוּן יָתְבִין
ואיכדין

ת״א מארץ רחוקה. גיטין מו:

### רש״י

(ה) נקדים. מבוקעים לשון הרמי גיריה דהיטי דמגרי זיקי: הרש״ך בלע״ז [הרסענז פרברהגנט] לשון מוקד וכן תרגומו יונתן כסנין: (ז) אולי בקרבי אתה יושב. שמא מיושבי

### רד״ק

התיבה שתירגם אותו יונתן כמו בדלת איזדודו מן צדה שתרגמו זוודי׳: (ה) נקדים. ת״ת כסנין ודברי רבותינו ז״ל פת הבאה בכסנין והוא פת עושים אותו כענין יבשין וכוססין אותו בבית המשתה ועוד מפרשים אותו מענין נקוד וטלוא כלומר מעופש היה והלח׳ המעופש הוא נקודים כי יש בלחם המעופש אדום וירוק ושחור נקודים נקודים: (ז) ויאמרו. כן כתיב וקרי ויאמר והכתיב על הפרט והקרי על הכלל כמ״ש איש ישראל: אל החוי מבני חוי היו גבעון והערים הסמוכות להם שהיו בזאת העצה. ובדרש מה הוא החוי וכי חוים היו אלא שעשו מעשה חויא פי׳ נחש כלו׳ שרמו את ישראל כמו הנחש שרמה את חוה: אולי בקרבי אתה יושב. שאם היו יודעין שהם מארץ כנען היו אסורים לכרות להם ברית שנא׳ לא תכרת להם ברית ולא תחנם והברית הוא שיהיו בשלום עמם ולא יהיו עבדים להם ומקבלים מצותם וזה אסר׳ התורה ואף על פי שכולם אם היו משלימים היו מקבלים אותם כמו שכתוב לא היתה עיר אשר השלימה אל בני ישראל בלתי החוי יושבי גבעון וגו׳ מכלל שאם השלימו היו מקבלים אותם כן הוא אבל בתנאי שיכריתו ע״ג מארצם ושיקבלו עליהם שבע מצות שהוזהר בהם אדם הראשון כמו שאמר הכתוב פן יחטיאו אותך לי משמע כל זמן שהם בחטא ואינם מקיימים שבע מצות שחייבים בהם בני נח אסור להניחם לשבת בארץ אבל מצוה להחרימם ושלא להיות מהם נשמה ואם היו משלי מים

### מנחת שי

(ז) ויאמרו איש ישראל. ויאמר קרי והוא חד מן מלין דכתיבין וא״ו בסוף תיבותא ולא קריי׳ וסימן (במלכים א׳ י״ב) במ״ג: אכרות לך. בס״ס אל״ף במאריך וכל הספרים כתיב בוא״ו וקרי בקמץ חטיף והוא חד מן תיבותא דיתירות וא״ו והטפין קמלין וסימן נמסר במסרה רבתא מערכת אות הוא״ו ודין כמי הוא חד מן ב׳ מלאים וא״ו וחברו וברית עולם אכרות להם (ישעיה ס״ט)

### רלב״ג

בהם הראו עצמם כאילו הם שלוחים באים ממרחק: (ה) נקדים. הוא הפת היבש שמתפרך מצד יבשו לפירורין דקים: (ו) מארץ רחוקה באנו. יתכן שנתפרסם להם מה שצותה התורה לישראל שלא יחיו כל נשמה מהעירים הקרובות אליה׳ אם לא יסכימו להשלים עמהם וכבר שלח אליהם יהושע בכללות ר״ל לאלו המקומות הקרובי׳ וקרא להם לשלום ולא השלימו ולזה היה מחויב שלא יחיה מהם כל נשמה כמו שנזכר בפרשת שופטים ואמנם אמר לו שכבר שלח יהושע לקרוא לשלום לכל מקומות הגוים האלה כי היה מחוייב להם לקרוא לשלום אל כל עיר ועיר קודם שיבאו להלחם כמו

### מצודת ציון

(ה) ונעלות. מנעלים שברגליהם: ומטלאת. ענין חלוף בגוונים כמו במות טלאות (יחזקאל ט״ז): צידם. מזונם: נקדים. מנומר בחברבורות כמו נקודים וברודים (בראשית ל״א):

### מצודת דוד

(ה) ומטלאת. כי בעת התייבשן המנעלים יתחלפו בכמה גוונים: נקדים. כי בהתייבש הלחם יתעפש ובו נקודים לבנים וירוקים ושחורים: (ו) מארץ רחוקה. לא מארץ כנען אשר הוזהרתם שלא תחיה כל נשמה ולזה כרתו לנו ברית להחיותינו: (ז) בקרבי. בקרב הארץ הניתן לי והוא ארץ כנען:

## Commentary Digest

for peaceful acceptance of Israel's claim to Canaan, and they had not accepted (choosing rather to go to war); and Gibeon, not being aware of Israel's law, thought that no one of Canaan would ever be accepted.[7] Rabad, in his glosses, however, maintains that Joshua only offered the choice of peace before crossing the Jordan. The covenant exacted through Gibeon's wiles, was, therefore, not legally binding on Israel. It was only upheld in order not to cause חלול השם i.e. the dishonor of Israel. K explains that the Gibeonites heard of Joshua's offer of peace to Jericho and Ai, after which he destroyed them. They, therefore, had no confidence in his peace offers. A explains that they were averse to accepting Joshua's peace terms which included acceptance of the Noachite laws and a state of servitude.

5. And worn, patched shoes on their feet, and worn garments upon them, and all the bread of their provisions was dry and mouldy. 6. And they went to Joshua to the camp at Gilgal, and said to him and to the men of Israel: "We have come from a distant land, and now make a covenant with us."
7. And each of the men of Israel said to the Hivites: "Perhaps you dwell in my midst, and how

## Commentary Digest

*thereof, and separates the root letters of the word, like:* [1]מה נצטדק *'How will we justify ourselves?' from the root* צדק, *(that he says* נצטדק*),*[2] *and so:* גשמה יצטבע *'his body will be bathed,'*[3] *from* צבע." — R It would appear that J had the reading ויצטידו, interpreting it in the sense of צדה — food — And they provided themselves with food. — K See R, v. 12.

***wine bottles, rotten — so that they should appear like people coming from a distant land.* — R**

*and tied up* — Heb. ומצררים — Z, D, and K in Shoroshim. R, however, explains this as: *"a synonym for* מבקעים, *split. This is an Aramaic expression, as:* ציריא דחיטי, *'the splits of the wheat kernels,*[4] דמיצרי זיקי, *'which split the sacks.'"*[5] — R

5. *and patched* — Heb. ומטלאת. — K in Shoroshim. Z and D explain: spotted with mould.

*and all the bread...was dry and mouldy* — lit. speckled (with mould). — K, Z, and D. G renders: crumbling. R explains: *"arsin in French, an expression of* מוקד, *burned (or toasted), and so did J render* כסנין." — R

**Hardtack, common provision for sailors, and others who travel long distances, since it resists spoilage. It is nibbled** on, not eaten in any large quantity at once. Thus, it is called 'כסנין,' from the word כוסס, to nibble. — K

6. *We have come from a distant land* — and are not included in your law, which states: You shall not spare any soul.[6] — G and D

*and now make a covenant with us* — Maimonides states: Joshua sent three proclamations to the inhabitants and kings of Canaan before entering. The first of these stated that anyone who wished to leave might leave. The second stated that anyone desirous of making peace with Israel, (i.e. accepting the seven Noachite laws and living in peace with Israel) would be accepted in a peaceful fashion. The third proclamation warned of Joshua's intention of warring with the remaining nations of Canaan. If so, why did the inhabitants of Gibeon resort to wiles (to create the impression that they came from a distant land)? Because Joshua had originally sent to all the inhabitants of Canaan asking

אכרות־לך ברית: ח ויאמרו אל־יהושע
עבדיך אנחנו ויאמר אליהם יהושע מי
אתם ומאין תבאו: ט ויאמרו אליו
מארץ רחוקה מאד באו עבדיך לשם
יהוה אלהיך כי־שמענו שמעו ואת כל־
אשר עשה במצרים: י ואת ׀ כל־אשר
עשה לשני מלכי האמרי אשר בעבר
הירדן לסיחון מלך חשבון ולעוג מלך־
הבשן אשר בעשתרות: יא ויאמרו אלינו

ואיכדין נגזר לכון קים:
ח ואמרו ליהושע עבדך
אנחנא ואמר להון
יהושע מן אתון ומנן
אתיתון: ט ואמרו ליה
מארע רחיקא לחדא
אתו עבדך לשמא דיי
אלהך ארי שמענא ית
שמע גבורתיה וית כל
דעבד במצרים: י וית
כל דעבד לתרין מלכי
אמוראי די בעברא
דירדנא לסיחון מלכא
דחשבון ולעוג מלכא
דמתנן דבעשתרות:
יא ואמרו לנא סבנא וכל
יתבי ארענא למימר
סבו

יתיר ו׳

## רד"ק

ועוקרים ע"ג ומקבלים שבע מצות צריך עוד שיהיו למס ויהיו עובדים לישראל ונכבשים תחת ידיהם כמו שהוא אומר יהיו לך למס ועבדוך וכן אמר בשלמה מלך ישראל כל העם הנותר כן האמורי החתי והפרזי החוי והיבוסי ויעלם שלמה למס עובד עד היום הזה אם כן מה בין שאר אומות לשבעה עממים יש ביניהם זה הדבר כי שאר האומות אם היו עושין מלחמה ולא רצו להשלים היו הורגים כל זכר בהם והנשים והטף היו בוזזים להם ומחיים אותם לעבדים אבל בשבע אומות אם לא רצו להשלים היה מצוה שלא לחיות מהם כל נשמה שנאמר רק מהעמים לא תחיה כל נשמה ולכל האומות קוראים להם שלום תחלה שנ׳ וקראת אליה לשלום ואפי׳ שבע אומות בכלל חוץ מעמון ומואב שנאמר לא תדרוש שלומם וטובת׳ א"כ אחר שהשלימו יושבי גבעון למה היו הורגים אותם בני ישראל לולי השבועה לפי שהטעו אותם וכרתו להם ברית בטעות והיה בדין להרגם אם לא היה בדבר חלול השם מפני השבועה כי אף על פי שהיתה השבועה בטעות אם לא יקיימוה היה בדבר חלול השם כי רבים ישמעו בשבועה ולא ישמעו בטעות ובעת השבועה לא הזכירו תנאי בשבועה ולפי שהטעו אותם הקשו בעבודתם ולא הניחום שיהיו למס עובד בלבד אלא שיהיו חוטבי עצים ושואבי מים לעדה. ויש מרבותינו ז"ל שאמרו כי נדר או שבועה שנעשה ברבים אין לו היתר ולמדו זה הדבר מדבר הגבעונים שלא הכום בעבור שנשבעו להם והחולקים עליהם

זקיניני

אמרו כי בדבר הגבעונים לא חלה השבועה עליהם כלל שהרי מוטעים היו ומה שלא הרגום מפני קידוש השם שיאמרו העולם כמה חמורה עליהם שבועת ה׳ כי אפילו נעשית בטעות לא יעברו עליה והפוסקי׳ מוכיחים כדברי מי שאמר כי מפני שנעשית השבועה ברבים אין לו היתר שהרי אמרו הנשיאים ולא יהיה עלינו קצף על השבועה ואם לא היה בדבר אלא מפני קדוש השם מה קצף היה בזה ואמרו רבותי׳ ז"ל כי שלשה כתבים שלח יהושע בכניסתן לארץ שלח להם מי שרוצה להשלים יבא וישלים וחזר ושלח להם מי שרוצה לעשות מלחמה יעשה מלחמה וחזר ושלח להם מי שרוצה לפנות יפנה מי שהאמין בהקב"ה וחרד לדבריו הלך לו לאפריקי ואמר בדרש כי הכנעני הוא שפנה מפני זה זכה להקרא לארץ ישראל ארץ כנען על שמו וזכה לארץ טובה שהיא אפריקי ויש אומרים כי הפריזי פנה לפניהם והלך לו אם כן למה הוצרכו יושבי גבעון להערים וקבלו השלום לפי שיהושע שלח בכלל לכלם ויושבי גבעון חשבו הלא גם כן שלח ליריחו ולעי להשלים והנה הכה אותם אולי לא יקיים הבטחתו ליושבי הארץ הזאת ובמרמת הוא שולח להם להשלים כדי שלא ישמרו מהם לפיכך עשו גם המה בערמה ואמרו כי מארץ רחוקה הם כדי שיכרתו להם ברית: (ח) ויאמרו אל יהושע וגו׳. מארץ רחוקה מאד. כי שמענו שמעו ואת כל אשר עשה במצרים ואת כל אשר עשה לשני מלכי האמורי וגו׳. זכרו מצרים וסיחון ועוג ולא זכרו

## רלב"ג

כנזכר בפרשה וכבר זכר במקומות שכבר פשה יהושע ככל אשר ציה ה׳ את משה ולזה יקויים שנודה שכבר שלח זה יהושע לאלו

## מנחת שי

רק הוא בחולם: (י) בעשתרות. בספרים כ״י מדוייקים ודפוסים ישנים מלא וכן במסורת כל נביאים וכתובים מלא בר מן חד ויסירו בני ישראל (שמואל א׳ ז׳): (יא) ויאמרו אלינו זקינינו. הזי״ן בגעיא בספרים כ״י מדוייקים ודפוסים ישנים:

זבפ״א כ״י קדמון אלף דחסר וכן אמרו בב״ר פ׳ מ״ט אמר ר׳ יוחנן כל צדיקים שנאמרו בסדום צדקים כתיב דהא אינם אלא צדיקים ניבל״ם פי׳ גרועים בפירות

## מצודת דוד

(ח) עבדים אנחנו. כאומר אין לנו פסק עם כל העם הזה כי הלא לא נכולם נהיה עבדים כ״א לך לבדך כאומר ואדוני הלא ישכיל לדעת שאין אנו מארץ כנען: מי אתם. מאיזה עם: ומאין. מאיזה מדינה: (ט) רחוקה מאד. ולא יהיה א״כ ניכר לך לא העם ולא המדינה: לשם ה׳. בעבור פרסום שם ה׳: (יא) עבדיכם אנחנו. להעלות את העם: כרתו לנו ברית

can I make a covenant with you?" 8. And they said to Joshua: "We are your servants." And Joshua said to them, "Who are you and from where do you come?" 9. And they said to him, "From a very distant land have your servants come, because of the Name of the Lord your God, for we have heard of His fame, and all that He did in Egypt. 10. And all that He did to the two kings of the Amorites, that were on the other side of the Jordan, to Sihon king of Heshbon, and to Og king of Bashan, who was in Ashtaroth.

## Commentary Digest

8. *And they said to Joshua* — Seeing that the men of Israel were suspicious of them, they went to Joshua himself. — A

*"We are your servants."* — We wish to have no dealings with your entire people; we are servants to you alone. — A and D

*"Who are you and from where do you come?"* — Why do you wish to be my servants, unless you are Canaanites and are trying to save yourselves? — Alshich

9. *because of the Name of the Lord your God* — We wish to be your servants in order to serve the Lord *your* God. — Alshich

*and all that He did in Egypt...*

10. *And all that He did to the two kings of the Amorites...* — They carefully avoided any mention of the recent happenings, of the miraculous crossing of the Jordan and the campaigns of Jericho and Ai, in order to create the impression that they had come from a very distant country, and had not yet heard of these events. — K and A

Alternatively, take provision in your hand as a present for the Jews who will come forth to greet you. Scripture says, *Take in your hand;* not, *Take for yourself.* Hence we derive that the Gibeonites were advised to take provisions as presents for the Jews. — K. Y.

11. *"Take provision in your hand for the journey, and go toward them* — Our elders advised us thus: You are traveling a long way through strange territory. Nobody knows you, and nobody will sell you provisions. Therefore, take for yourselves provisions for the entire journey until you go towards them.

זְקֵינֵינוּ וְכָל־יֹשְׁבֵי אַרְצֵנוּ לֵאמֹר קְחוּ
בְיֶדְכֶם צֵידָה לַדָּרֶךְ וּלְכוּ לִקְרָאתָם
וַאֲמַרְתֶּם אֲלֵיהֶם עַבְדֵיכֶם אֲנַחְנוּ וְעַתָּה
כִּרְתוּ־לָנוּ בְרִית׃ יב זֶה ׀ לַחְמֵנוּ חָם
הִצְטַיַּדְנוּ אֹתוֹ מִבָּתֵּינוּ בְּיוֹם צֵאתֵנוּ
לָלֶכֶת אֲלֵיכֶם וְעַתָּה הִנֵּה יָבֵשׁ וְהָיָה
נִקֻּדִים׃ יג וְאֵלֶּה נֹאדוֹת הַיַּיִן אֲשֶׁר מִלֵּאנוּ
חֲדָשִׁים וְהִנֵּה הִתְבַּקָּעוּ וְאֵלֶּה
שַׂלְמוֹתֵינוּ וּנְעָלֵינוּ בָּלוּ מֵרֹב הַדֶּרֶךְ
מְאֹד׃ יד וַיִּקְחוּ הָאֲנָשִׁים מִצֵּידָם וְאֶת־
פִּי יְהוָה לֹא שָׁאָלוּ׃ טו וַיַּעַשׂ לָהֶם יְהוֹשֻׁעַ
שָׁלוֹם וַיִּכְרֹת לָהֶם בְּרִית לְחַיּוֹתָם

סָבֵי בְּיֶדְכוֹן זְוָדִין לְאוֹרְחָא וְאֱזִילוּ לְקַדָמוּתְהוֹן וְתֵימְרוּן לְהוֹן עַבְדֵיכוֹן אֲנַחְנָא וּכְעַן גְּזוֹרוּ לָנָא קְיָם׃ יב דֵין לַחְמָנָא כַּד חֲמִים אִזְדְּוַדְנָא יָתֵיהּ מִבָּתָּנָא בְּיוֹם מִפְּקָנָא לְמֵיתֵי לְוָתְכוֹן וּכְעַן הָא יָבֵישׁ וַהֲוָה כִסְנִין׃ יג וְאִלֵּין זִיקִין דַּחֲמַר דִּי מְלֵינָא כַּד חַדְתִּין וְהָא אִתְבְּזָעוּ וְאִלֵּין תּוּתְבָנָא וּמְסָנָנָא בְּלִיאוּ מִסְּגֵי אוֹרְחָא לַחֲדָא׃ יד וְקַבִּילוּ גַּבְרַיָּא לְפִתְגָמֵיהוֹן וְאוּלְפַן מִן קֳדָם יְיָ לָא תְּבָעוּ׃ טו וַעֲבַד לְהוֹן יְהוֹשֻׁעַ שְׁלָם וּגְזַר לְהוֹן קְיָם לְקַיָּמוּתְהוֹן וְקַיִּימוּ לְהוֹן רַבְרְבֵי

**רד"ק**

הירדן לפי שהיה דבר מצרים וסיחון ועוג מימים קדמונים ודבר הירדן היה מזמן קרוב כלומר הראו ליהושע שלא שמעו דבר הירדן כל כך היא רחוקה ארצם: (יא) זקינינו. נכתב ביו"ד המשך בין הקו"ף והנו"ן שלא כמנהג ובדרש א"ר יוחנן זקינינו כתיב זקני אשמאי היו: (יב) הצטדנו אותו. לשון ספוק מזון מן צדה לדרך ופי' לקחנו אותו מבתינו להצטיר בו הדרך: (יד) ויקחו. יש מפרשים אותו כמו למדו מן לקח טוב כלומר למדו והבינו מצידם שהיה יבש כי אמת אמרו. ויש לפרש ויקחו

**רש"י**

הארץ אתם: (יב) הצטידנו. ל' צידה כשהוצאנוה לצידה לדרך: (יד) ויקחו האנשים מצידם. קבלו דבריהם שאלום בפיהם לשון ואשר לא צדה:

**מנחת שי**

שלא נגמרו ונוטרים ברות אך לא היו לדיקים לגמרי ורש"י גרים נכלים בכ"ף כמו ויתנכלו ר"ל לדיקים ראתים היא דעתיה דר' יוחנן דאמר ר"י ואמרו אליו זקננו ופל יושבי ארלנו זקננו כתי' זקני אשמאי היינו סבי דבהתא פי' זקני בושה ע"כ. ומערוך ערך זקן זקננו כתוב זקני אשמאי סבין דקלון ובספרים ראיתי חילופים אחרים ובא' מהם נכתב לית אלא דאלא וכ"כ רד"ק במכלל דף ק"ד.

**רלב"ג**

המקומות קודם שיספים להצאם עמהם כמו שכתבו רבותינו ז"ל ולזה הערימו כשאמרו שהם באו מארץ רחוקה ועשו עצמם עבדים לישראל והיה מחוייב לפי משפטי התורה שיקבלום בברית ויהיו להם למס ועבדום: (טו) ויעש להם יהושע שלום ויכרות להם ברית לחיותם ונשבעו להם לחיותם ונשבעו להם נשיאי העדה והנה היתה סבת טעות ישראל ונופלם בזה הענין כי לא שאלו את פי ה' עם היות אלעזר הכהן שהיה אלעזר ומוה שהיה כבר נביא ואלעזר הכהן שהיה אללו אורים ותומים

**מצודת ציון**

(יב) הצטידנו. מלשון צידה ומזון:

**מצודת דוד**

להחיותינו: (יב) זה לחמנו. אשר תראו בידינו הנה בהיותו עדיין חם לקחנו אותו לצידה לדרך: הנה יבש. בעבור זמן הרב מגודל מרחק הדרך: (יג) חדשים. בעת מלואם היו חדשים: (יד) ויקחו. ר"ל לקחו מופת ולאיה מיובש לידם והאמינו להם.

## Commentary Digest

Lord, through the "Urim v'Tumim" worn by Eleazar the high Priest. Since the Torah commanded: "And before Eleazar the priest shall he stand, who shall enquire for him by the judgment of the Urim before the Lord,"[2] Joshua should have consulted him. — G

15. *And Joshua made peace with them, and made a covenant with them* — i.e. a treaty as between two equals, in contrast to the law requiring any peace with the seven nations of Canaan to include a condition of servitude.[3]

*to let them live* — i.e. not a full-

11. And our elders and all the inhabitants of our country spoke to us saying, 'Take provision in your hand for the journey, and go towards them, and say to them, 'We are your servants; and now make a covenant with us.'
12. This our bread we took hot for our provision out of our houses on the day we set out to go to you; but now, behold, it is dry, and has become mouldy.
13. And these wine-skins which we filled, were new; and, behold they are split. And these our garments and our shoes are worn because of the very long journey."
14. And the men took of their provision, and did not ask counsel of the mouth of the Lord.
15. And Joshua made peace with them, and made a covenant with them to let them live;

## Commentary Digest

12. *we took . . . for our provision* — Heb. הצטידנו, *"an expression of* צידה, *provisions, i.e. when we took it out for provisions for the journey."* — R, K, and Z

14. *And the men took of their provision* — It may be understood that they learned or deduced from their provision that they told the truth. It may also be understood literally, that they partook of their provisions as a token of entering into a treaty with them. — K R explains this figuratively: *"They accepted their words, for they captured them with their mouths* (מצידם meaning from their hunting or capturing) *an expression of: "and he who did not* (צדה) *hunt,"*[1] — R. A suggests that the men accepted part of the provisions as a bribe to make a treaty with them. They, therefore, did not ask counsel of the mouth of the Lord. — Alshich explains that only the bread showed signs of age, but the other provisions were fresh and well preserved. Since the men of Israel took of the provisions, they should have noticed this contrast and inconsistency, and asked counsel of the Lord. The Scripture criticizes them by stating: And the men took of their provisions, yet, nevertheless, they did not ask the counsel of the mouth of the Lord.

*and did not ask counsel of the mouth of the Lord* — They made the mistake of not asking counsel of the

וַיִּשָּׁבְעוּ לָהֶם נְשִׂיאֵי הָעֵדָה: טז וַיְהִי
מִקְצֵה שְׁלֹשֶׁת יָמִים אַחֲרֵי אֲשֶׁר־כָּרְתוּ
לָהֶם בְּרִית וַיִּשְׁמְעוּ כִּי־קְרֹבִים הֵם אֵלָיו
וּבְקִרְבּוֹ הֵם יֹשְׁבִים: יז וַיִּסְעוּ בְנֵי־יִשְׂרָאֵל
וַיָּבֹאוּ אֶל־עָרֵיהֶם בַּיּוֹם הַשְּׁלִישִׁי
וְעָרֵיהֶם גִּבְעוֹן וְהַכְּפִירָה וּבְאֵרוֹת
וְקִרְיַת יְעָרִים: יח וְלֹא הִכּוּם בְּנֵי יִשְׂרָאֵל
כִּי־נִשְׁבְּעוּ לָהֶם נְשִׂיאֵי הָעֵדָה בַּיהוָה
אֱלֹהֵי יִשְׂרָאֵל וַיִּלֹּנוּ כָל־הָעֵדָה עַל־
הַנְּשִׂיאִים: יט וַיֹּאמְרוּ כָל־הַנְּשִׂיאִים אֶל־
כָּל־הָעֵדָה אֲנַחְנוּ נִשְׁבַּעְנוּ לָהֶם בַּיהוָה
אֱלֹהֵי יִשְׂרָאֵל וְעַתָּה לֹא נוּכַל לִנְגֹּעַ
בָּהֶם: כ זֹאת נַעֲשֶׂה לָהֶם וְהַחֲיֵה
אוֹתָם וְלֹא־יִהְיֶה עָלֵינוּ קֶצֶף עַל־הַשְּׁבוּעָה

בְּרַבְרְבֵי כְּנִשְׁתָּא: טז וַהֲוָה מִסוֹף תְּלָתָא יוֹמִין בָּתַר דִּגְזָרוּ לְהוֹן קְיָם וּשְׁמָעוּ אֲרֵי קְרִיבִין אִינוּן לֵיהּ וּבֵינֵיהוֹן אִינוּן יָתְבִין: יז וּנְטָלוּ בְּנֵי יִשְׂרָאֵל וַאֲתוֹ לְקִרְוֵיהוֹן בְּיוֹמָא תְּלִיתָאָה וְקִרְוֵיהוֹן גִּבְעוֹן וּכְפִירָה וּבְאֵרוֹת וְקִרְיַת יְעָרִים: יח וְלָא מְחוֹנוּן בְּנֵי יִשְׂרָאֵל אֲרֵי קַיִּימוּ לְהוֹן רַבְרְבֵי כְּנִשְׁתָּא בְּמֵימְרָא דַּיְיָ אֱלָהָא דְיִשְׂרָאֵל וְאִתְרָעֲמוּ כָּל כְּנִשְׁתָּא עַל רַבְרְבַיָּא: יט וַאֲמַרוּ כָּל רַבְרְבַיָּא לְכָל כְּנִשְׁתָּא אֲנַחְנָא קַיֵּימְנָא לְהוֹן בְּמֵימְרָא דַּיְיָ אֱלָהָא דְיִשְׂרָאֵל וּכְעַן לָא נִכּוֹל לְאַנְזָקָא בְּהוֹן: כ דָּא נַעֲבֵיד לְהוֹן וּנְקַיֵּים יַתְהוֹן וְלָא יְהֵי עֲלָנָא רְגָזָא עַל קְיָמָא דִי
קיימנא

**ת״א** ולא הכום. כתובות עה גטין מו. הדורים אתם (קדושין סה):

## רד״ק

כמשמעו שלקחו מצידם ואכלו ממנו בברית כדי שיבטחו בהם ויונתן תרגם וקבילו גבריא לפתגמיהון: (כ) והחיה אותם

## אשר

## רלב״ג

כמו שאמרה התורה ולפני אלעזר הכהן יעמוד ושאל לו במשפט האורים והנה זאת השבועה אף ע״פ שהיתה בטעות לא הסכימו לעבור עליה כי יהיה בזה חלול השם אלא הע״ג ויאבדו שאין יראת ה׳ ביבראל והנה הנשיאים החיום באופן הראוי אילו היו מבלי[illegible] עמהם תחלה כי התורה אמרה והיה כל העם הנמצא בה יהיו לך למס ועבדוך אלא שבכבר הכבידו ענין עבדות הזה וזה שבכבר היה אפשר לפי משפטי התורה אלו היו ההקים שיעשו מס

## מנחת שי

ובס׳ זקינו נכתב בי׳ המסר בין הקו״ף והנו״ן בלא כמנהג, ובדפוס א״ד יוהנן זקננו כתיב זקני [illegible] היו על״ל. והמדפיס לא ידע לזהור ועשה מלת זקנינו במהדפס מלה דמלא וצריך להיות חסר דהסר: (טז) כי קרבים. חסר וא״ו כי לא

## מצודת דוד

או לקחו מצידם ואכלו לקיים ברית ואהבה: (כ) זאת. ר״ל הדבר

## מצודת ציון

(יח) וילנו. מלשון תלונה ותערומות:

## Commentary Digest

19. *"We have sworn to them by the Lord, the G-d of Israel* — We, the princes, have sworn. If you had sworn, since you are not empowered to make a treaty with them, your oath would not be binding, but since we the princes have sworn, we must abide by our oath. Moreover, since we swore *to them,* it is an oath made for the benefit of someone else and according to his understanding. Therefore, our mistake does not invalidate the oath. Moreover, we swore by the name of God and according to His knowledge. It is, therefore, binding under all circumstances. — M. L.

and the princes of the congregation swore to them. 16. And it was at the end of three days after they had made a covenant with them, that they heard that they were their neighbors, and that they dwelt among them. 17. And the children of Israel journeyed, and came to their cities on the third day. And their cities were Gibeon, and Chephirah, and Beeroth, and Kiriath-jearim. 18. And the children of Israel did not smite them, because the princes of the congregation had sworn to them by the Lord, the G-d of Israel. And all the congregation complained against the princes. 19. And all the princes said to all the congregation, "We have sworn to them by the Lord, the God of Israel; now, therefore, we may not touch them. 20. This we will do to them, and let them live; and there will be no wrath upon us, because of the oath

## Commentary Digest

fledged covenant covering all contingencies, but only an agreement not to kill them in conformity with the general rule of the seven nations. — A

*and the princes of the congregation swore to them* — The princes of the tribes, without consulting Joshua or their own tribesmen, swore to uphold the covenant. — A

17. *And their cities were Gibeon and Chephirah and Beeroth and Kiriath-jearim* — The first three mentioned were later in the territory of Benjamin, north of Jerusalem.[1] Kiriath-jearim was on the boundary of Judah and Benjamin.[2]

18. *And the children of Israel did not smite them, because the princes ... had sworn to them* — The covenant made by Joshua, being executed under the mistaken impression of Gibeon being a distant nation, had no legality. However, the abrogation of an oath is of such extreme gravity that, even if such oath was entered into by mistake, it must be abided by. Otherwise, non-Jews would be led to believe that the Jewish people are careless with their word, even though it is incorporated into a solemn oath.[3]

אשר־נשבענו להם׃ כא ויאמרו אליהם
הנשיאים יחיו ויהיו חטבי עצים ושאבי־
מים לכל־העדה כאשר דברו להם
הנשיאים׃ כב ויקרא להם יהושע וידבר
אליהם לאמר למה רמיתם אתנו
לאמר רחוקים אנחנו מכם מאד ואתם
בקרבנו ישבים׃ כג ועתה ארורים אתם
ולא־יכרת מכם עבד וחטבי עצים
ושאבי־מים לבית אלהי׃ כד ויענו את־
יהושע ויאמרו כי הגד הגד לעבדיך
את אשר צוה יהוה אלהיך את־משה
עבדו לתת לכם את־כל־הארץ
ולהשמיד את־כל־ישבי הארץ מפניכם

**תרגום**

קימנא להון׃ כא ואמרו להון רברביא ייחון ויהוו מלקטי אעין ומלן מיא לכל כנשתא כמא דמלילו להון רברביא׃ כב וקרא להון יהושע ומליל עמהון למימר למא שקרתון בנא למימר רחיקין אנחנא מנכון לחדא ואתון ביננא יתבין׃ כג וכען ליטין אתון ולא יפסקון מנכון עבדין ומלקטי אעין ומלן מיא לבית מקדשא דאלהי׃ כד ואתיבו ית יהושע ואמרו ארי חואה אתחוא לעבדך ית דפקיד יי אלהך ית משה עבדיה למתן לכון ית כל ארעא ולשיצאה ית כל יתבי ארעא מן קדמיכון ודחילנא לחדא לנפשתנא מן קדמיכון ועבדנא ית פתגמא

**רד"ק**

מקור׃ (כא) יחיו ויהיו חוטבי עצים ושואבי מים לכל העדה. זה מקרא קצר כי הנשיאים אמרו יחיו ויהיו חוטבי עצים ושואבי מים והמקרא אחז דרך קצרה ואמר ויהיו בפתח הויו לשון עבר יהיו כאשר דברו להם הנשיאים וזה מעיד כי כן אמר להם הנשיאים ומה שאמרו הם לכל העדה ויהושע אמר להם לבית אלהי הא כיצד כל זמן שהיו העדה במחנה עד שלא נחלקה הארץ היו הוטבי עצים ושואבי מים לעדה אבל לאחר שנחלקה הארץ והיו ישראל בעירו ובנחלתו נשארו הם הוטבי עצים ושואבי מים לבית אלהים בגלגל ובשילה ובנוב ובגבעון ובית עולמים כמו שאמר אל המקום אשר יבחר ואמרו

**מנחת שי**

נמנה במסורת עם המלאים׃ (כא) יחיו ויהיו. מטעים ביה דסבירין בוא״ו תחת הו״ו והוא בפתח׳ מסורת פרשה תרומה ועיין בפירוש רד״ק׃ ויהיו חטבי עצים. בלא מאריך בתי״ת׃ כאשר דברו להם. כתיב במקרא גדולה שמלא בס״א יען מוגה אליהם ובכל ספרים שלפני כתוב להם ולא ראיתי בו מחלוקת׃ (כב) למה רמיתם. דגש ומלעיל באין הטרחא עושה מלרע׃ אנחנו. החית בוא״ו לבדו׃ (כג) עבד וחטבי עצים. בלא מאריך בתי״ת׃ (כד) הגד הגד. שתי הגימלי״ן

**רלב"ג**

מה לישראל ויפטרו מעבדות אחר אלא שיעמדו ביניהם שפלים כעבדים אבל אם העמיסו עליהם שיעבדום בגופם באלו העבודות הנכבדו׳ ר״ל שיהיו חוטבי עצים ושואבי מים לכל העדה וזה היה אפשר עם קיום תנאיהם כי הם עבו עצמם עבדים לישראל ועם כל זה ראו להרחות להם לכבוד השם שלא עשקו מהם הקם הראוי

**מצודת ציון**

(כא) חוטבי. ענין כריתה וחתוך וכן לחטוב עצים (דברים י״ט)׃

**מצודת דוד**

הזאת להחיות אותם בע״כ נעשה להם בלא יקצוף ה׳ על בטול השבועה׃ (כא) ויאמרו אליהם הנשיאים יחיו. ר״ל הנה בעבור השבועה לא תגידו לא יחיו וכאומר אך נתבונן מה נעשה עמהם בגמול הרמאות׃ ויהיו וגו׳. ר״ל הגמול היה שהיו חוטבי כו׳ כאשר גזרו הנשיאים כי כל העדה שמעו להם׃ (כג) ועתה. ר״ל עתה בעת המלחמה תהיו ארורים להיות עבדים לכל העדה

## Commentary Digest

are not of the children of Israel." According to R[3], a marital ban was placed upon Gibeon. Rabbeinu Tam maintains that the ban upon Gibeon and all of the seven nations is of Biblical origin.[4]

which we swore to them." 21. And the princes said to them,
"Let them live..." So they became hewers of wood and
drawers of water to all the congregation, as the princes had
spoken to them. 22. And Joshua called for them, and he
spoke to them, saying, "Why have you deceived us, saying,
'We are very far from you,' when you dwell among us?
23. And now you are cursed, and there shall never fail to be
slaves from you, and hewers of wood and drawers of water
for the house of my God." 24. And they answered Joshua,
and said, "Because it was certainly told to your servants how the Lord your God commanded His servant Moses to give you all the land, and to destroy all the inhabitants of the land from before you;

## Commentary Digest

21. *as the princes had spoken to them* — i.e. this action was taken upon the advice of the princes, although no specific mention is made of this advice. It is implied by the words: "So they became..." that the princes had advised this action. — K

22. *And Joshua called for them, and he spoke to them* — Joshua, in this moment of anger at the trickery of Gibeon, did not punish them until he had first spoken to them. In this, he followed the example of the Almighty, who first chastised Aaron and Miriam for speaking against Moses, and then departed in anger.[1]

23. *Now you are cursed* — Joshua adopted the extreme of cursing the Gibeonites, because they had taken the course of the accursed serpent, (חוי meaning snake), tricking Israel even as the snake had deceived Eve.[1]* — K

*hewers of wood and drawers of water for the house of my God* — The status of the Gibeonites is thus one of slaves. Joshua, however, only imposed upon them the onus of slaves while the temple was standing. King David[2] decreed that they should be barred for all time from joining the Jewish people: "And the Gibeonites

ונירא מאד לנפשתינו מפניכם ונעשה
את־הדבר הזה : כה ועתה הננו בידך
כטוב וכישר בעיניך לעשות לנו עשה :
כו ויעש להם כן ויצל אותם מיד בני־
ישראל ולא הרגום : כז ויתנם יהושע
ביום ההוא חטבי עצים ושאבי־מים
לעדה ולמזבח יהוה עד־היום הזה אל־
המקום אשר יבחר : י א ויהי כשמע
אדני־צדק מלך ירושלם כי־לכד
יהושע את־העי ויחרימה כאשר עשה

תרגום

פתגמא הדין : כה וכען
הא אנחנא מסירין בידך
כמא דתקין וכמא
דכשר בעינך למעבד
לנא עבד : כו ועבד להון
כן ושזיב יתהון מיד בני
ישראל ולא קטלונון :
כז ומנינון יהושע ביומא
ההוא לקטי אעין ומלן
מיא לכנשתא ולמדבחא
דיי עד יומא הדין
לאתרא די יתרעי :
י א והוה כד שמע אדני
צדק מלכא דירושלם
ארי כבש יהושע ית עי
וגמרה כמא דעבד
ליריחו

ה״א ויתנם יהושע . יבמות עט. (קדושין כה) :

רד״ק

רבותינו ז״ל כי כיון שנתנם יהושע חוטבי עצים ושואבי מים גזר עליהם שלא יבאו בקהל כלומר שלא יתחתנו ישראל בהם והלה אסורן בזמן שבית המקדש קיים שהרי אמר לבית אלהי משמע כל זמן שהיו חוטבי עצים ושואבי מים לבית אלהי וזהו כל זמן שבית המקדש קיים בא דוד וגזר עליהם לעולם וכן כתיב בספר עזרא ומן הנתינים שנתן דוד והשרים לעבודת הלוים : (כד) ונעשה את הדבר הזה . בצרי שלא כמנהג וכבר כתבנו הדומים להם בספר מכלל : (כה) ועתה הננו בידך . קל ובשו״א הנו״ן הראשונה : (א) אדני צדק . כל מלכי ישראל היו נקראים בזמן ההוא מלכי צדק או אדני צדק כמו שנאמר ומלכי צדק

רלב״ג

להם מפני בואם עמהם בברית כי כבר רמו אותם באמרם שהיו מארץ רחוקה והם מפני זה בלתי מבועדים להם לעשות חסד להם אחר זולתי מה שיוכרתו בו מלך בבועתם להם . ולפי שהשבועה והברית היה לחיותם ושיהיו הם עבדים לישראל הנה כבר קיימו הנשיאים עמהם בזה האופן . והנה הוסיף יהושע על עבודתם שהסכימו עליו הנשיאים שיהיו חוטבי עצים ושואבי מים לבית ה׳ ולזה היו חוטבי עצים ושואבי מים לכל העדה ולמזבח ה׳ : (א) אדוני צדק מלך ירושלם . מצאנו שמו בתורה מלכי צדק וידמה שכל מלכי ירושלם היה שמם מלכי צדק או אדוני צדק כי הכל ענין אחד כמו שהיה שם מלכי מצרים פרעה והנה זכר כי ה׳ מלכי האמורי הם וכל מחניהם חנו על גבעון וילחמו עליה וכאשר שלחו אנשי גבעון ליהושע שיעזרם כי ראוי לאדון שיציל עבדיו מיד הנלחמים עליהם וידמה שבאל יהושע את פי ה׳ על זה ועלה מן הגלגל הוא וכל עם המלחמה עמו וכל גבורי החיל וכאשר אמר הש״י אל יהושע קודם זה שאלו את פיו על דבר זאת המלחמה שלא יירא מהמלכים האלה וממחניהם כי בידו יתנם והוא מיהר לבא עליהם כל הלילה ויהומם ה׳ לפני ישר׳ ויכם ישראל מכה גדולה בגבעון וירדפם דרך מעלה בית חורון וגו׳ ויהי בנוסם מפני בני ישראל נלחם ה׳ גם מן השמים

מנחת שי

דגושות : ונעשה . בצירי שלא כמנהג : (כה) הנני בידך . קל ובשו״א הנו״ן הראשונה ובמסורת ד׳ וסימן הננו בידך הננו עלמך (שמואל ב׳ ריש סימן ה׳) הננו אתנו לך (ירמיה ג׳) הננו לפניך באשמתינו (עזרא סוף סימן ט׳) : (כז) חטבי . אין טעם בחי״ת רק בבי״ת : ושאבי מים . הטעם בשי״ן כחבריו דלעיל ולא בבי״ת :

י (א) ויהי כשמע . פליגי בה ספרי התיק הוא הרפה . ועיין מ״ש (בשופטים

מצודת דוד

אבל לבית ה׳ תהיו לעולם עבדים ולא יכרת הדבר : (כו) ויעש להם כן . כמ״ש הוא להיות עבדים לכל העדה בעת המלחמה ולבית ה׳ לעולם : ולא הרגום . כאשר חשבו בתחלה : (כז) לעדה ולמזבח וגו׳ עד היום הזה . ר״ל לעדה בעת המלחמה ולמזבח ה׳ עד היום הזה : אל המקום . במקום שיעמוד המזבח שמה יעבדו אם בשילה וכו׳ אם בירושלים : י (א) ויהיו בקרבם . התחברו עמהם

מצודת ציון

י (א) אדני צדק . כך שמו :

## Commentary Digest

mately found for the sanctuary. Gibeon was to continue their servitude not only at Gilgal, where the altar was now standing, but also in the place where the altar would stand hence.[2]

CHAPTER 10

1. *Adonizedek, king of Jerusalem* — All kings of Jerusalem were known by the name "Zedek" (righteousness) as we find: "And Malchizedek, king

and we were very afraid for our lives because of you, and
have done this thing. 25. And now, behold, we are in your
hand. As it seems good and right to you to do to us, do."
26. And he did so to them, and he delivered them from the
hand of the children of Israel, and they did not slay them.
27. And Joshua made them that day hewers of wood and
drawers of water for the congregation, and for the altar of
the Lord, to this day, in the place which He would choose.

## 10

1. And it came to pass, when Adonizedek, king of Jerusalem,
heard that Joshua had taken Ai, and had completely destroyed
it; as he had done

### Commentary Digest

24. *and we were very afraid* — Although their real reason was that they desired to make a treaty and be saved from slavery, they told Joshua that they tricked him to save their lives. They thought this excuse would be more impressive. — A

25. *As it seems good and right* — i.e. a combination of good, which implies kindness and clemency, and right, which implies justice. — A

26. *And he did so to them* — as they had beseeched him, a verdict of clemency and justice combined, as follows:

*and he delivered them* — This was his clemency. Since the entire peace treaty was made under false premises, he was permitted to kill them. Thus, sparing their lives was leniency.

27. *And Joshua made them... hewers of wood etc.* — This was justice. — A

*for the congregation* — As long as the Israelites were still in a military camp, prior to the division of the land, when the Israelites settled each in his own city, the Gibeonites were to be slaves of the congregation. After the division of the land, when each tribe settled in its own territory, they were to remain slaves of the sanctuary.[1] — K This was more lenient than the decision of the princes, who made them slaves of the entire congregation. — A

*for the altar...in the place which He would choose* — Joshua and Israel knew that a permanent place (Shiloh and later Jerusalem) would be ulti-

לִירִיחוֹ וּלְמַלְכָּהּ כֵּן־עָשָׂה לָעַי וּלְמַלְכָּהּ
וְכִי הִשְׁלִימוּ יֹשְׁבֵי גִבְעוֹן אֶת־יִשְׂרָאֵל
וַיִּהְיוּ בְּקִרְבָּם׃ ב וַיִּירְאוּ מְאֹד כִּי עִיר
גְּדוֹלָה גִּבְעוֹן כְּאַחַת עָרֵי הַמַּמְלָכָה
וְכִי הִיא גְדוֹלָה מִן־הָעַי וְכָל־אֲנָשֶׁיהָ
גִּבֹּרִים׃ ג וַיִּשְׁלַח אֲדֹנִי־צֶדֶק מֶלֶךְ־
יְרוּשָׁלִַם אֶל־הוֹהָם מֶלֶךְ־חֶבְרוֹן וְאֶל־
פִּרְאָם מֶלֶךְ־יַרְמוּת וְאֶל־יָפִיעַ מֶלֶךְ־
לָכִישׁ וְאֶל־דְּבִיר מֶלֶךְ־עֶגְלוֹן לֵאמֹר׃
ד עֲלוּ־אֵלַי וְעִזְרֻנִי וְנַכֶּה אֶת־גִּבְעוֹן כִּי־
הִשְׁלִימָה אֶת־יְהוֹשֻׁעַ וְאֶת־בְּנֵי יִשְׂרָאֵל׃
ה וַיֵּאָסְפוּ וַיַּעֲלוּ חֲמֵשֶׁת ׀ מַלְכֵי הָאֱמֹרִי
מֶלֶךְ יְרוּשָׁלִַם מֶלֶךְ־חֶבְרוֹן מֶלֶךְ־יַרְמוּת
מֶלֶךְ־לָכִישׁ מֶלֶךְ־עֶגְלוֹן הֵם וְכָל־
מַחֲנֵיהֶם וַיַּחֲנוּ עַל־גִּבְעוֹן וַיִּלָּחֲמוּ עָלֶיהָ׃
ו וַיִּשְׁלְחוּ אַנְשֵׁי גִבְעוֹן אֶל־יְהוֹשֻׁעַ אֶל־

**תרגום**

לִירִיחוֹ וּלְמַלְכַּהּ כֵּן עֲבַד לְעַי וּלְמַלְכַּהּ וַאֲרֵי אַשְׁלִימוּ יָתְבֵי גִבְעוֹן עִם יִשְׂרָאֵל וַהֲווֹ בֵּינֵיהוֹן׃ ב וּדְחִילוּ לַחֲדָא אֲרֵי קַרְתָּא רַבְּתָא גִּבְעוֹן כַּחֲדָא מִקִּרְוֵי מַלְכְוָתָא וַאֲרֵי הִיא רַבָּא מִן עַי וְכָל גַּבְרָהָא גִּבָּרִין׃ ג וּשְׁלַח אֲדֹנִי צֶדֶק מַלְכָּא דִירוּשְׁלֵם לְוָת הוֹהָם מַלְכָּא דְחֶבְרוֹן וּלְוָת פִּרְאָם מַלְכָּא דְיַרְמוּת וּלְוָת יָפִיעַ מַלְכָּא דְלָכִישׁ וּלְוָת דְּבִיר מַלְכָּא דְעֶגְלוֹן לְמֵימַר׃ ד סַקוּ לְוָתִי וְסַעֲדוּנִי וְנִמְחֵי יָת יָתְבֵי גִבְעוֹן אֲרֵי אַשְׁלֵמַת עִם יְהוֹשֻׁעַ וְעִם בְּנֵי יִשְׂרָאֵל׃ ה וְאִתְכְּנִשׁוּ וּסְלִיקוּ חַמְשָׁא מַלְכֵי אֱמוֹרָאָה מַלְכָּא דִירוּשְׁלֵם מַלְכָּא דְחֶבְרוֹן מַלְכָּא דְיַרְמוּת מַלְכָּא דְלָכִישׁ מַלְכָּא דְעֶגְלוֹן אִנּוּן וְכָל מַשִׁרְיָתְהוֹן וּשְׁרוֹ עַל גִּבְעוֹן וַאֲגִיחוּ קְרָבָא עֲלַהּ׃ ו וּשְׁלַחוּ אֱנָשֵׁי גִבְעוֹן לְוָת יְהוֹשֻׁעַ לְמַשְׁרִיתָא

**מנחת שי** **המחנה**

י׳) ובדוכתי אחריני: (ג) מלך ירושלם. בספרים כ״י ובדפוס יש הין כתיב מלא וכן חבריו שבענין. וכל ירושלם שבמקרא חסר יו״ד אחר למ״ד חוץ מחמשה הכתובים במסורת ירמיה סימן כ״ו וד״ה ב׳ ריש סימן כ״ה ואף הותם הכתובים בלא יו״ד היו״ד נקראת אף על פי שאינה כתובה כמ״ש במכלל דף ק״י וכמ״ש בירמיה ח״ב [illegible] וכן הוא בגבולות [illegible] סב [illegible] הוא בלא [illegible] ירושלם. וכתב בעל יפה תואר בס פר׳ [illegible]

**מצודת דוד**

עם ישראל: (ב) כי עיר גדולה. ועכ״ז לא עלרו כח להלחם והמסו כוס לב אנשי המלחמה: (ד) כי השלימה. והרעו לעבות כי הביאו מורך בלב כל: (ו) אל תרף ידיך. לעזוב אותנו בידם: (ט) כל הלילה. למען לא ירגישו ויבא פתאום:

## Commentary Digest

Israel of any major city as a military center and settlement. Since Jericho and Ai had been completely destroyed, Gibeon would serve the Israelites and their families and belongings, as a rallying point. — A

to Jericho and her king, so had he done to Ai and her king;
and that the inhabitants of Gibeon had made peace with
Israel, and were among them; 2. That they feared greatly,
because Gibeon was a great city, as one of the royal cities,
and because it was greater than Ai, and all her men were
mighty. 3. And Adonizedek, king of Jerusalem, sent to
Hoham, king of Hebron, and to Piram, king of Jarmuth, and
Japhia, king of Lachish, and to Debir, king of Eglon, saying,
4. "Come up to me and help me, and we will smite Gibeon,
for it has made peace with Joshua and with the children of
Israel." 5. And the five kings of the Amorites, the king of
Jerusalem, the king of Hebron, the king of Jarmuth, the king
of Lachish, the king of Eglon, gathered together and went up,
they and all their camps, and encamped on Gibeon, and made
war against it. 6. And the men of Gibeon sent to Joshua to

## Commentary Digest

of Salem," the name by which Jerusalem was known at that time. This was a fitting name for Jerusalem, the center of justice and righteousness. — K[1]

2. *because Gibeon was a great city — ...and all her men were mighty* — and the fact that they had seen fit to make peace with Israel, rather than risk war, caused a serious loss of morale on the part of the troops of the other kings. — D

4. *for it (Gibeon) had made peace with Joshua and with the children of Israel* — and through this tactic has caused weakness to strike at the heart of all the inhabitants of Canaan, and they should be punished accordingly. — D The clarion call for a campaign against Gibeon was of a two-fold purpose: first, to punish Gibeon for having committed the cowardly and dastardly act of making peace with the enemy; and secondly, to deprive

הַמַּחֲנֶה הַגִּלְגָּלָה לֵאמֹר אַל־תֶּרֶף יָדֶיךָ
מֵעֲבָדֶיךָ עֲלֵה אֵלֵינוּ מְהֵרָה וְהוֹשִׁיעָה
לָּנוּ וְעָזְרֵנוּ כִּי נִקְבְּצוּ אֵלֵינוּ כָּל־מַלְכֵי
הָאֱמֹרִי יֹשְׁבֵי הָהָר׃ ז וַיַּעַל יְהוֹשֻׁעַ מִן־
הַגִּלְגָּל הוּא וְכָל־עַם הַמִּלְחָמָה עִמּוֹ וְכֹל
גִּבּוֹרֵי הֶחָיִל׃ ח וַיֹּאמֶר יְהוָה אֶל־יְהוֹשֻׁעַ
אַל־תִּירָא מֵהֶם כִּי בְיָדְךָ נְתַתִּים לֹא־
יַעֲמֹד אִישׁ מֵהֶם בְּפָנֶיךָ׃ ט וַיָּבֹא אֲלֵיהֶם
יְהוֹשֻׁעַ פִּתְאֹם כָּל־הַלַּיְלָה עָלָה מִן־
הַגִּלְגָּל׃ י וַיְהֻמֵּם יְהוָה לִפְנֵי יִשְׂרָאֵל
וַיַּכֵּם מַכָּה־גְדוֹלָה בְּגִבְעוֹן וַיִּרְדְּפֵם דֶּרֶךְ
מַעֲלֵה בֵית־חוֹרֹן וַיַּכֵּם עַד־עֲזֵקָה וְעַד־
מַקֵּדָה׃ יא וַיְהִי בְּנֻסָם מִפְּנֵי יִשְׂרָאֵל
הֵם בְּמוֹרַד בֵּית־חוֹרֹן וַיהוָה הִשְׁלִיךְ

לְמַשְׁרִיתָא לְגִלְגְּלָא
לְמֵימַר לָא תְרַשֵּׁל יְדָךְ
מֵעַבְדָךְ סַק לְוָתַנָא
בִּפְרִיעַ וּפְרוֹק לָנָא
וְסַעֲדְנָא אֲרֵי אִתְכְּנַשׁוּ
עֲלָנָא כָּל מַלְכֵי אֱמוֹרָאָה
יָתְבֵי טוּרָא׃ ז וּסְלֵיק
יְהוֹשֻׁעַ מִן גִלְגְּלָא הוּא
וְכָל עַמָּא עָבְדֵי קְרָבָא
עִמֵּיהּ וְכָל גִּבָּרֵי חֵילָא׃
ח וַאֲמַר יְיָ לִיהוֹשֻׁעַ לָא
תִדְחַל מִנְהוֹן אֲרֵי בִידָךְ
מְסַרְתִּינוּן לָא יִתְעַתַּד
אֱנָשׁ מִנְהוֹן קֳדָמָךְ׃
ט וַאֲתָא לְוָתְהוֹן יְהוֹשֻׁעַ
בִּתְכֵּיף כָּל לֵילְיָא סְלֵיק
מִן גִלְגְּלָא׃ י וְתַבְרִינוּן
יְיָ קֳדָם יִשְׂרָאֵל וּמְחָנוּן
מְחָתָא רַבָּא בְּגִבְעוֹן
וּרְדָפוּנוּן בְּאוֹרַח מַסְקָנָא
דְּבֵית חוֹרוֹן וּמְחָנוּן עַד
עֲזֵקָה וְעַד מַקֵּדָה׃
יא וַהֲוָה בְּמִפְּכֵיהוֹן מִן
קֳדָם יִשְׂרָאֵל אִנּוּן
בְּמַחְתָּנָא דְּבֵית חוֹרוֹן
וּמִן קֳדָם יְיָ אִתְרְמִיאָה
עֲלֵיהוֹן

ת״א ויהי בנוסם. ברכות נד ע״ב כס:

מנחת שי

יתיר י׳ — עליהם

דקרינן ירושלים הוא חסר יו״ד לפלא ו כמ״ש התוספת בפ״ב דתענית (דף ט״ו בד״ה הר) וירו במקום יהלה כי הוא״ו כאל״ף ה״א בגימטריא: (ח) כי בידך נתתים. בדפוסים אחרונים כתוב בידך ונמסר עליו יתיר יו״ד ואין כן בספרים כ״י גם לא בדפוסים ראשונים:

מצודת דוד

(י) דרך מעלה. בדרך העולה לבית חורון: עד עזקה. כי ברחו דרך בה ורדפום והכום בדרך עד עזקה וכו׳: (יא) הם במורד. כשהם ירדו במורד ההר: אבנים. אבני ברד: עד עזקה. בכל הדרך אשר נסו ממורד בית חורון עד בואם לעזקה נפלו עליהם אבני הברד: רבים. מרובים במספר:

מצודת ציון

(ו) תרף. מלשון רפיון: (ט) פתאום. ענין מהירות מבלי הרגשה מקודם: (י) ויהומם. מלשון מהומה ובלבול:

## Commentary Digest

seen him leave Gilgal. — D He accomplished this by forced marches.

10. *And the Lord confused them before Israel*—Every place the Scripture mentions confusion, it fails to explain how the confusion came about. Scripture explains in one place, whence we learn the character of confusion in all other places. This is explained in the Baraitha entitled the *Thirty-two methods by which the Aggadah is expounded.* "Something that is hidden in one place and explained in another, how is that? And as Samuel was offering up the burnt-offering, the Philistines drew near for war against Israel, and the Lord thundered with a loud noise on that day, and confused them (I Sam. 7:10). Here we learn that confusion is through noise, and from here we learn what confusion is in all places where it is not explained. — J. K.

the camp to Gilgal, saying, "Do not slack your hands from your servants; come up to us quickly, and save us, and help us, for all the kings of the Amorites that dwell in the mountains are gathered together against us." 7. So Joshua ascended from Gilgal, he, and all the people of war with him, and all the mighty men of valor. 8. And the Lord said to Joshua, "Do not fear them, for I have delivered them into your hand; not a man of them shall stand before you." 9. And Joshua came to them suddenly; he had gone up from Gilgal all night. 10. And the Lord confused them before Israel, and slew them with a great slaughter at Gibeon, and they chased them by the way that goes up to Beth-horon, and smote them to Azekah, and to Makkedah. 11. And it was as they fled from before Israel, and were in the descent of Beth-horon, that the Lord cast down

**Commentary Digest**

6. *"Do not slack your hands from your servants ... save us and help us* — although we have tricked you. Since now we are your servants, it is proper for you to protect us. "Save us" (הושיעה) and "help us" (עזרנו). If you are not prepared to be of total assistance to us (ישועה), at least render us partial aid (עזרה). — M

7-8. *So Joshua ascended from Gilgal... And the Lord said to Joshua, "Do not fear them ..."* — Joshua was not fully convinced of the wisdom of committing the Jewish armies in defense of a segment of the local population, who had so shamelessly defrauded the Israelites. But the Lord commanded him to go to war in defense of even the lowliest citizen, for, if distinctions were to be drawn as to for whom it is worthy of committing the armies to go to war, the most dire consequences would ultimately be realized.[1] This rule became a cardinal principle of Jewish law, and was carried out by King David in defense of the rights of the Gibeonites.[2]

9. *he had gone up from Gilgal all night* — i.e. he came upon them suddenly because he had gone up from Gilgal all night, and no one had

עֲלֵיהֶם אֲבָנִים גְּדֹלוֹת מִן־הַשָּׁמַיִם עַד־
עֲזֵקָה וַיָּמֻתוּ רַבִּים אֲשֶׁר־מֵתוּ בְּאַבְנֵי
הַבָּרָד מֵאֲשֶׁר הָרְגוּ בְּנֵי יִשְׂרָאֵל בֶּחָרֶב׃
יב אָז יְדַבֵּר יְהוֹשֻׁעַ לַיהוָה בְּיוֹם תֵּת יְהוָה
אֶת־הָאֱמֹרִי לִפְנֵי בְּנֵי יִשְׂרָאֵל וַיֹּאמֶר ׀
לְעֵינֵי יִשְׂרָאֵל שֶׁמֶשׁ בְּגִבְעוֹן דּוֹם וְיָרֵחַ

עֲלֵיהוֹן אַבְנִין רַבְרְבָן מִן שְׁמַיָּא עַד דַּאֲתוֹ לַעֲזֵקָה וּמִיתוּ סַגִּיאִין דְּמִיתוּ בְּאַבְנֵי בַרְדָּא מִדְּקַטִּילוּ בְּנֵי יִשְׂרָאֵל בְּחַרְבָּא׃ יב בְּכֵן שַׁבַּח יְהוֹשֻׁעַ קֳדָם יְיָ בְּיוֹמָא דִמְסַר יְיָ יָת אֱמוֹרָאָה קֳדָם בְּנֵי יִשְׂרָאֵל נַאֲמַר לְעֵינֵי יִשְׂרָאֵל שִׁמְשָׁא בְּגִבְעוֹן אוריך

ת״א אז ידבר יהושע. עקידה שער יג: ביום תת. תענית כח ע״ב כה:

רד״ק

מלך שלם הוא ירושלם כמו שכתוב ויהי בשלם סכו ונראו כן בעבור ירושלם שהוא מקום צדק: (יב) אז ידבר יהושע. ת״י בכן שבח יהושע ויתכן כי אחר התפלה היתה השירה והשירה לא הזכיר או השירה היא וידום השמש והתפלה היא ויאמר לעיני ישראל שמש בגבעון דום וכן זוכר אותה בדרש זו השירה במנין עשר שירות ולשון ידבר מורה על שירה לא על תפלה כמו וידבר דוד לה׳ את דברי השירה. ויאמר בתפלתו לעיני ישראל שמש בגבעון דום כלומר הפלא הזה יראה היום לעיני ישראל או לעיני ישראל דבק עם ויאמר כלומר התפלה הזאת אמרה בקול לפני ישראל ופי׳ דום המתן כמו דמו עד הגיענו אליכם כלומר שיעמוד גלגל השמש במקומו ולא ירוץ כמשפטו: וירח בעמק אילון. ולירח אמר גם כן שיעמוד בעמק

בעמק רש״י

י (יב) אז ידבר. אמר שירה תחת השמש לפי שאמר לשמש דום. דום מלומר שירה וכל זמן שהוא דומם עומד ואינו מהלך שבכל עת הילוכו הוא אומר שירה ופשוטו של מקרא דום ל׳ המתנה כמו אם כה יאמר אלינו דומו וכן

רלב״ג

ושמית מהם באבני הברד יותר ממאשר הרגו בני ישראל בחרב: (יב) אז ידבר יהושע לה׳. בזאת הפר׳ יש ספקות רבות ראוי לעיין בהם האחד הוא באם היה בהשמש עמד ובטל מהתנועה הכללית לו הנה היה זה המופת יותר נפלא לאין שיעור מהמופתים שנעשו ע״י משה וזה כי המופתים ההם היו בשנוי טבע הנמצאות אלו השפלות והוא יותר נפלא לאין שיעור מה שיתחדש בי אלו הנמצאות הנכבדות לגמות את הפקידים מבלוע על הנמצאות השפלות אלו לבמות ענין סדורם כי בהם נעלמם מחסרון הסדר וישוער מה שלא יעלם ובכלל הנה זה ממה שאין צריך ביאור למי שעיין באלו העמוקות וכבר ביארנו זה באופן שלם בו׳ מספר מלחמות ה׳ ואם היה הענין כן הנה זה סותר מה שאמרה התורה שלא קם נביא עוד בישראל כמשה לכל האותות והמופתים אשר עשה משה לעיני כל ישראל ואם אמרנו שבכבר נעשה כמו זה המופת ע״י משה ואם לא נזכר בתורה כמו שאמרו קצת רז״ל הנה נבאר זה הספק בעינו כי כבר היה בזה לו יהושע בגדול במופתים הנעשים על יד משה רבינו עליו השלום עם שאם היה הענין כן היה ראוי שלא תשתוק התורה מלספר זה המופת הנפלא כי הנחנו כלאה מכונת התורה לפרסם ענין המופתים והנפלאות כי זה ממה שיבוא להאמין בשם יתברך כמו שנזכר בתורה הענין המופתים שנעשו לפרעה אמר ולמען תספר באזני בנך וגו׳ וידעתם כי אני ה׳ ועוד כי כבר ידאה משפטי אלו הדברים שלא נתבטל השמש מתנועתו ולא הירח וזה יתבאר מפנים מהם מה שאמר ולא אץ לבוא כ״ל שלא מהר לבוא וזה לא יבלול ממנו התנועה אבל יבלול ממנו מהירות התנועה והמאמר שזה דרכו יחייב לו התנועה בכמו אלו המאמרים הבלתים אבר ידובר בהם בדברים מדרך מה הוא ומתם מה שאמר שמש בגבעון דום וירח בעמק אילון ולא אמר שמש דום וירח אבל לקח להם מקום רחב היו נראים אז אל המקום ההוא והוא מבואר שמי שיבלול התנועה מהמקום הרחב לא יבלול התנועה במוחלט כי כבר אפשר שיתנועע במקום רחב ההוא וכבר יחייב זה המאמר בכמו המאמרים הבלתים לשמש ולירח התנועה והמבל במי שיאמר שפלוני עמד באהלו כך וכך ימים הנה לא יתקיים מזה אלא שלא יצא מאהלו אבל שבכבר יתנועע באהלו הו לא יהיה זה המאמר מדרך מה הוא כי יחייב למי שיבלול ממנו התנועה שיאמר שלא יתנועע לא שלא יצא מאהלו וזה מבואר למי שעיין בסדרים

מצודת ציון

(יב) תת. מלשון נתינה: דום. המתן כמו דומו עד הגיענו אליהם (ש״א י״ד):

מצודת דוד

(יב) לה׳. בשם ה׳ ובצליחותו: ויאמר. הוא הדבור האמור למעלה ועל שהפסיק בדברים אמר שוב ויאמר: שמש בגבעון דום. כי בעת ההיא עמד השמש נוכח גבעון וחשש פן ישקע בעונתו ולא יוכלו לרדוף אחרי האויב באישון הלילה ולזה אמר להשמש שלא ילך מהלכו וימתין עוד נוכח גבעון במקום שהוא עומד: וירח

## Commentary Digest

did not the sun, the moon, and the stars bow down before my grandfather Joseph? Are you not, therefore, my slave, bidden to do my command?" The allegorical meaning here is clear: Man is the crown of the entire creation, and all that was created before, even the celestial bodies, is subservient to the ideal man, personified by Joseph.

*in the sight of Israel* — See N, end of Deut. and Akedah, ch. 13.

great stones from heaven upon them to Azekah, and they died. There were more who died with the hailstones than whom the children of Israel slew with the sword.
12. Then Joshua spoke to the Lord on the day when the Lord delivered up the Amorites before the children of Israel, and he said in the sight of Israel, "Sun, stand still upon Gibeon, and Moon

## Commentary Digest

11. *that the Lord cast down great stones from heaven...There were more who died from the hailstones* — These stones had been suspended in the air since the days of Moses, who caused hailstones to fall upon Egypt.[1] Upon the cessation of the plague of hail, the falling hailstones were suspended in the air. Only now, since Joshua was a fitting successor to Moses, did they fall from heaven.[2] This miracle is considered of such importance that anyone who views these rocks is required to recite the special blessing: "Who performed miracles for our ancestors in this place.[2]

12. *Then Joshua spoke* — or praised. — J. Although the text of the praise is absent from the text, the Scripture informs us that Joshua, nevertheless, praised the Almighty after his prayer to Him. It is also possible that the words: "Sun, stand still upon Gibeon, etc." comprise the prayer, while the entire v. 13 comprises the song of praise recited by Joshua to the Almighty. This latter theory is supported by the Mechilta,[3] which lists this among the ten songs mentioned in the Scriptures. — K Similarly, R explains: *"He recited a song instead of the sun, since he bade the sun, 'Be silent.' I.e. be silent* (by refraining) *from reciting* (your) *song. And as long as it is silent, it stands still and does not continue on its orbit, for all the time of its revolution it recites* (its) *song.*[4] *The simple explanation of the verse is, however,* (דום) *is an expression of waiting, like: 'if they say thus to us, 'wait!''* (דומו),[5] *and so, 'wait* (דום) *for the Lord.'"*[6] — R According to Maimonides, who believed the heavenly bodies to be alive, and praise the Almighty in a marvelous manner, this Midrash may be interpreted literally. Otherwise, it may be explained that the angels who guide the sun,[7] recite their song of praise to the Almighty.

In the Midrash,[4] the dialogue between Joshua and the sun is graphically portrayed. The sun maintained that it was older than Man, having been created on the fourth day, while Adam was created on the sixth day. Thereupon, Joshua responded, "But

אוֹרִיךְ וְסִיהֲרָא בְּמֵישַׁר אַיָּלוֹן: יג וְאוֹרִיךְ שִׁמְשָׁא וְסִיהֲרָא קָם עַד דְּאִתְפְּרַע עַמָּא יִשְׂרָאֵל מִבַּעֲלֵי דְבָבֵיהוֹן הֲלָא הִיא כְתִיבָא עַל סִפְרָא דְאוֹרַיְתָא וְקָם שִׁמְשָׁא בְּפַלְגוּת שְׁמַיָּא וְלָא דְחַק

בְּעֵמֶק אַיָּלוֹן: יג וַיִּדֹּם הַשֶּׁמֶשׁ וְיָרֵחַ עָמָד עַד־יִקֹּם גּוֹי אֹיְבָיו הֲלֹא־הִיא כְתוּבָה עַל־סֵפֶר הַיָּשָׁר וַיַּעֲמֹד הַשֶּׁמֶשׁ בַּחֲצִי הַשָּׁמַיִם וְלֹא־אָץ לָבוֹא כְּיוֹם תָּמִים:

ת״א וידם השמש. ברכות ס תענית כ עקידה מד גב : עד יקם . ע״ג כה : ויעמד השמש . ע״ג ע״ה :

כולו קבין

## רש״י

דום לה׳: וירח בעמק אילון. אותו שעה היה הירח עומד כנגד עמק אילון והוא רחוק מגבעון שהרי גבעון בגבול בנימין ואילון בגבול דן: (יג) הלא היא כתובה. דבר זה נכתב בתורה שאמר לו יעקב ליוסף זרעו של אפרים יהיה מלא הגוים וגו׳ אימתי כיום שעמדה חמה ליהושע נתמלא כל

## רד״ק

אילון ואף על פי שגבעון היה בגבול בנימן ואילון בגבול דן ידמה כי רדפו אותם והכום מגבעון עד אילון ובגבעון היה חצי היום כשהתפלל שיעמוד השמש והאל שמע בקולו כמו שאמר ויעמוד השמש בחצי השמים ועמד עד שיעור שבין עמידתו ומרוצתו היה כיום תמים והוא היום הארוך שבשנה והוא יום תקופת תמוז וכשבא השמש היו בעמק אילון והאיר הירח והיה הירח אז בן הדומה בתחלת החדש או בשלישיתו והתפלל עליו שיעמוד הירח להאיר להם עד שתכלה נקמתם באויביהם וכן היה כמו שאמר וירח עמד עד יקום גוי אויביו וזאת הפליאה כתובה על ספר הישר והוא ספר תורת משה והוא מה שאמר הקב״ה יתברך נגד כל עמך אעשה נפלאות וגו׳ כמו שפירש א״א ז״ל כי שתי אותות אמר לו בפסוק ההוא קריעת פני משה והוא מה שאמר כי נורא הוא אשר אני עושה עמך ועמידת השמש ליהושע והוא מה שאמר נגד כל עמך אעשה נפלאות ונתן לו אות קרוב להאמי׳ באות רחוק ובדרש שלשים ושש שעות עמדו השמש והירח כיצד המלחמה היתה בערב שבת ונתיירא יהושע שלא יחללו ישראל את השבת ופשט ידיו למעלה שיעמוד השמש ביום הששי כשיעור יום שבת והירח כשיעור ליל שבת ומוצאי שבת והם שלשים ושש שעות: (יג) עד יקם גוי אויביו.

## רלב״ג

הסגולות אשר למלאכת המופתים ומהם מה שאמר ולא היה כיום ההוא לפניו ואחריו לשמוע ה׳ בקול איש כי ה׳ נלחם לישראל הורה בזה כי זה המופת הוא בענין המלחמה בעצמותה ואם היה זה המופת בעמידה מהתנועה לא היה לו רושם בענין המלחמה כלל ומהם כי יתבאר מדבריו כי הש״י לא יעשה מופתים כי אם ללורך או לקנות דעות אמיתיות ולא נזכר בכאן רושם בזה המופת באחד מאלו הגדדים ומהם שכבר התבאר בספר מלחמות ה׳ כי המופת לא יהיה על יד נביא באלו הנמצאות העליונים ר״ל הגרמים השמימיים ולזה הוא מבואר שלא היה זה המופת בזה הענין אבל יתבאר בתחלת המחשבה שהיה בו המופת בזה הספר׳ ואם יספק עלינו מספק על מה שהבארנו בזה ויאמר שכבר נראה שיעשה המופת ע״י נביא בשנוי סדר תנועת הסדר והוא מה שאמר ישעיה לחזקיה כשאמר מה אות כי ירפא ה׳ לי ועליתי ביום השלישי בית ה׳ ויעידהו הלך הצל י׳ מעלות אם ישוב הצל אחורנית י׳ מעלות והוא מבואר שתנועת הצל לא תהיה כי אם בתנועת השמש ולזה יתחייב מזה שנוי סדר תנועת השמש נאמר לו כי כשעיינו היטב במאמרים שבאו בזה המקום יתחייב שלא היה זה המופת בהשתנות סדר תנועת השמש הנה איך יתכן כשאמר בזה יהיה נקל הנה איך שיפתה זה הסידור הוא ענין נפלא מאוד ולזה ראוי שנבאר הדברים ההם ויתבאר מזה מה היה ענין המופת ההוא ונאמר כי ידמה לפי הנראה לנו שכבר שם ישעיה בזה הבחירה בזה המופת לחזקיה ואמר בזה האות יהיה באחד מב׳ דרכים האחד שילך הצל י׳ מעלות יותר על מה שהלך בזולת זמן או שישוב הצל אחורנית י׳ מעלות והוא מבואר שאם היה זה המופת היה בענין המלחמה כמו שזכרנו ולזה הוא מבואר בזה המופת היה בזולת שנוי סדר תנועת השמש וזה יהיה לפי מה שאומר והוא שכבר יתבאר בחוש שכאשר יהיו עננים תחת השמש באופן שירשם בהם צל נגלות ויראו הנה הם יראו שיהיה השמש בזולת מקום שהוא עם שכבר יראה אז נטיית צל השמש שיעור רב במעט זמן למזרח או למערב לצפון או לדרום לפי מצב העננים ההם ואל תנועתם וזה ממה שאין בו ספק כי תמיד יראה זה מן האופן בזה האופן ולפי שכבר ראה חזקיה אז מהעננים ומצד תנועתם שנקל לצל לנטות עשר מעלות יותר על מה שהלך שאל שיהיה הענין בהפך מה שהיה נראה שהיה נכון אז מצד תנועת העננים ההם ולזה שאל שישוב אחורנית הצל עשר מעלות והנה בספר ישעיה אמר ותשב השמש עשר מעלות במעלות אשר ירדה ר״ל לפי החוש אבל מופתי היה בצל כמו שנזכר בו אמר הנני משיב את צל המעלות ובכאן הותר זה הספק ואם ילוה אחד על כל פנים שיהיו אלו המופתים בשנוי סדר תנועת השמש לא אקפיד עליו בזה ומי יתן וכל הטועים לא יטעו יותר מזה השעור כי זה מגדיל לפי מחשבתו עולם הש״י ויכלתו ואחר שנתיישב זה הנה נשוב לבאר דברי זאת הפרשה ואומר שמאמר יהושע היה בטרם שיסור השמש מהיות על גבעון והירח מהיות על עמק אילון תשלם נקמת גוי אויביו אבל קצר הכתוב בזה ויורה על זה מה שאמר אחריו וידום השמש וירח עמד עד יקום גוי אויביו והרצון בזה שכבר דמם השמש בגבעון וירח בעמק אילון עד שנשלמה זאת המלחמה מהנקמה וזה היה ענין נפלא כי לא די שיעד שינקמו ישראל מהקמים עליהם אבל יעד עם זה שזאת הנקמה תשלם בזמן קצר כזה ולזה אמר ולא היה כיום ההוא לפניו ואחריו לשמוע ה׳ בקול איש כי ה׳ נלחם לישראל ולזה היו יכולים להשלים הנקמה בזה הזמן הקצר כי יד הש״י לא תקצר ואמר לשמוע ה׳ וגו׳ לפי שלא יעדו הש״י שתשלם זו הנקמה בזה הזמן קצר אבל הש״י שמע לקולו על דרך מקים דבר עבדו ועצת מלאכיו ישלים: (יג) והנה ספר הישר המחובר שהיה נקרא כך ואבד עם הגלות וכבר רבו בו הפירושים לרבותינו ז״ל ולאוי

## מצודת דוד

בעמק אילון. כי אז כבר עלתה הירח ועמדה נוכח עמק אילון ואמר לה שגם היא תמתין במקומה ולא תלך מהלכה ואולי חשש שאם תלך הירח מהלכה תבוא נוכח השמש במקום עמידתו ותאפיל אור השמש: (יג) וידם השמש. ר״ל כן היה שעמדו השמש וירח במקומם: עד יקום. עד אשר השלימו ישראל להתנקם מאויביו: הלא היא. הדבר הזה הלא כתובה להבטחה בספר הישר והיא התורה כשאמר בה על אפרים וזרעו יהיה מלא הגוים (בראשית מ״ח) והוא היום הזה שעמדו השמש והירח ליהושע הבא מזרעו ונתמלא כל העולם שמעו: ויעמוד השמש. עכביו מפרש המקום שעמד בה: בחצי השמים. ר״ל לפי הנראה בהאופן ההוא: ולא אץ לבוא. לא היה ממהר לשקוע כדרכו מעולם למהר לבית שקיעתו ללכת בהתמדה מבלי עמידה: כיום תמים. ר״ל נתעכב לעמוד במקום א׳ כשיעור יום שלם שהוא כ״ד שעות:

## מצודת ציון

(יג) איביו. מאויביו: אץ. ענין מהירות כמו ואץ ברגלים (משלי יט): לבוא. לשקוע כמו כי בא השמש (בראשית כ״ח):

in the valley of Ajalon." 13. And the sun stood still, and the moon stayed, until the people had avenged themselves upon their enemies. Is this not written in the book of Jashar? (which is the Torah)? So the sun stood still in the midst of the heaven, and it did not hasten to go down exactly a whole day.

## Commentary Digest

*and moon in the valley of Ajalon* — "*At that time, the moon was standing opposite the valley of Ajalon, which is far from Gibeon, for Gibeon is within the borders of Benjamin*[1] (in the south), *and Ajalon is within the borders of Dan*[2] (in the north)." — R Joshua asked that the sun remain suspended over Gibeon and the moon over the valley of Ajalon. According to the Midrash,[3] the battle took place on Friday, and Joshua asked that the day be lengthened so that there would be no need to desecrate the approaching Sabbath. — K A explains the passage as indicating the extent of the battle: from Gibeon, where the main battle was fought, to the valley of Ajalon, where the Israelites pursued the enemy.

13. *Is it not written* (*already*) *in the book of Jashar?* — "*This matter is written in the Torah* (i.e. the Pentateuch) *that Jacob said to Joseph, "His seed* (*of Ephraim*) *will fill the nations.*"[4] *When? On the day that the sun stood still for Joshua, the entire world was filled with Joshua's fame, and the sun stood still in the midst of the heaven, and it did not hasten to go down exactly a whole day.*" — R[5] 'The book of Jashar' refers to one book — The Torah-Pentateuch, the book of the 'yesharim' — the upright, the patriarchs, Abraham, Isaac, and Jacob, who are referred to as upright.[6] Moreover, the central theme of the Torah is: "And you shall do what is upright and good."[7]

*So the sun stood still in the midst of the heaven, and it did not hasten to go down exactly a whole day* — Twice the sun stopped, once at noon and once shortly before its setting.[8] According to one opinion in the Talmud, each time, it stood still for twenty-four hours, making a total of forty-eight hours. See also A and R. Hisdai Crescas in the "Ohr Hashem."

יד ולא היה כיום ההוא לפניו ואחריו
לשמע יהוה בקול איש כי יהוה נלחם
לישראל: טו וישב יהושע וכל־ישראל
עמו אל־המחנה הגלגלה: טז וינסו
חמשת המלכים האלה ויחבאו
במערה במקדה: יז ויגד ליהושע לאמר
נמצאו חמשת המלכים נחבאים

תרגום

למיעל כיום שלים: יד ולא הוה כיומא ההוא קדמוהי ובתרוהי דאתקבלת קדם יי צלות אנש ארי במימריה יי מגיח קרבא לישראל: טו ותב יהושע וכל ישראל עמיה למשריתא לגלגלא: טז ואפכו חמשא מלכיא האלין ואטמרו במערתא במקדה: יז ואתחוא ליהושע למימר אשתכחו חמשא מלכיא

ת"א לשמוע ה'. שם על עקדה שער ג פב:

רד"ק

כמו מאויביו וכן השמרו לכם עלות בהר: (יד) ולא היה כיום ההוא. ואף על פי שהיה שוב השמש אחורנית לחזקיהו האות ההוא היה לאות ולמופת ונתנו השם בעבור שיאמין חזקיהו שיחיה מחליו והוא כאחד מן המופתים שנעשו על ידי משה אבל דרך תפלה שיתפלל אדם על שנוי הטבע ונעתר הבורא לאותה תפלה אם לא יהיה לתת בו אות ומופת לא היה ולא יהיה וזהו שאמר לשמוע בקול איש כי ה' נלחם לישראל: (יז) נחבאים. בשוא הבי"ת: במערה במקדה. במערה שהיתה בגבול מקדה:

רש"י

העולם שמעו של יהושע ויעמד השמש בחצי השמים ולא אץ לבוא כיום תמים:

מנחת שי

(טו) אל המחנה הגלגלה. הה"א בחטף פתח:

רלב"ג

שתדע כי השמש יחדש היום ולזה נאמר שהיום ירד מאד כשקרב השמש לערב כי אז יחלש אור השמש ומה שהיה בו אור השמש יותר חזק הוא בעת היותו בחצי השמים הנה זה מבואר בנפשו מן הקום וזה יתבאר גם כן ממה שאמר והנה לצדיקים כאור נוגה הולך ואור עד נכון היום רלה לומר שאורו יוסף עד נכון היום כן אנה לצדיקים מתיבר תמיד אל תוספת השלמות והוא מבואר שבעת היות השמש בחצי השמים לא תוכל בו ירידה כי אם בעת ארוך וזה מבואר מאד למי שעיין בחכמת התכונה עיון מעט וזה יתבאר גם כן מאד כלי המבט כמו האצטורלאביי ורביע העיגול כי אז לא תוכל לשמש ירידה באלו הכלים כמו אלי שעה ולזה אמר שכבר עמד השמש אז בחצי השמים כי כן היה מחויב כי הם היו אצל גבעון והיו רואים השמש על גבעון ולא מהר השמש לרדת כמו שדרך היום התמים שלא ימהר השמש לרדת בו ואחשב שאורך עיר גבעון היה ממזרח למערב וזאת התנועה לא תוכל מאד לשמש אצל חצי היום למיעוט שיעור ירידתו הנה זכר שמאד הנטייה הנראית לו מאד הירידה לא ילא שלא יראה כנגד גבעון אף על פי שהיתה רחבה לך כי לא מיהר לבוא כמשפט ענין השמש אצל סמיכות היום. וכאשר נכלם ביאור דברי זאת הפרשה והותרו הספקות הנופלות בה: (טו) וזכר אחר זה חזירת יהושע בענין זאת המלחמה למהר להחריס אלו הגוים ובכבר הגיע לישראל מעולם הצלחה שכלם שבו בשלום לא הוכה אחד מהם ולא השתדלו האויבים להכות אחד

מצודת ציון

מלשון חס ובלם: (טז) ויחבאו. נסתרו והוא מלשון מחבואה:

מצודת דוד

(יד) כיום ההוא. להיות בו פלא כזה לשמוע וכו' כאשר שמע בקול יהושע להעמיד השמש והירח: כי ה'. הפלא הזה נעשה בעבור שה' נלחם לישראל ובעבורם עשה: (טו) וישב יהושע. אחר כל המעשים האמורים במקראות שלאחריו:

## Commentary Digest

have been a military blunder on Joshua's part to return to Gilgal and then to begin the pursuit and the follow-up of the victory at Gibeon. This explains why this verse is repeated at the end of the chapter. — A M comments, "And Joshua *thought to* return — to Gilgal," but was detained by the discovery of the kings.

*saying* — I.e. he was advised *to announce* that the five kings were found and to offer a bounty to the valiant soldier who would enter the cave and vanquish them. Joshua, however, rejected this counsel. He felt that this was not the time to fight with the five kings. The main objective was to pursue the enemy and liquidate them. — K. Y.

14. And there was no day like that before it or after it, that
the Lord hearkened to the voice of a man, for the Lord
fought for Israel. 15. And Joshua returned, and all Israel
with him, to the camp to Gilgal. 16. And these five kings
fled, and hid themselves in a cave at Makkedah. 17. And
Joshua was told, saying, The five kings have been found hidden

## Commentary Digest

14. *And there was no day like that before it or after it* — Our sages tell us that similar events took place in Moses' time, when the sun stood still for him during the war with Sihon, and in the days of the Second Temple, when the sun stood still for the famed benefactor of the Jews, Nakdimon ben Gurion. These, however, were not accompanied by hailstones, nor did they last as long as that of Joshua.[1] Azulai suggests another difference, viz. that a human being ventured to recite the sun's song in its stead. His interpretation of the passage will be presented below.

*for the Lord fought for Israel* — I.e. although the Pentateuch concludes with the statement, "And there rose not up another prophet in Israel like unto Moses," it does not contradict this passage, that Joshua's miracle was superior to that of his master, for Joshua was locked in combat, and "the Lord fought for Israel." It was not in Joshua's merit alone that this event took place, but also in the merit of the entire people of Israel. Azulai explains the verse thus: *And there was no day like that before it or after it* — that the sun was stopped for such a length of time.

*that the Lord hearkened to the voice of a man* — who recited a song of praise instead of the sun.

*for the Lord fought for Israel* — by raining down hailstones on the enemy.

15. *And Joshua returned, and all Israel with him, to the camp to Gilgal* — after the incidents related in the following verses. — D

16. *And these five kings fled* — These five kings were united in battle, and were united in their defeat. They fled together and hid together as one unit. This is apparent from the word חמשת instead of חמשה, denoting a unit of five. — K. Y.

17. *And Joshua was told* — All these verses serve as an elaboration of the passage; "until the people had avenged themselves upon their enemies."[2] All this time, the sun and moon remained standing. Thus, the entire account until verse 13, inclusive, is the general narrative, while the account from v. 16 to the conclusion of the chapter, is the detailed repetition of the same. It would certainly

| | |
|---|---|
| במערה במקדה: יח ויאמר יהושע גלו | טמירין במערתא במקדה: יח ואמר |
| אבנים גדלות אל־פי המערה והפקידו | יהושע קריבו אבנין רברבין קדם פומא |
| עליה אנשים לשמרם: יט ואתם אל־ | דמערתא ומנו עלה גברין למטרהון: |
| תעמדו רדפו אחרי איביכם וזנבתם | יט ואתון לא תקומון רדופו בתר בעלי |
| אותם אל־תתנום לבוא אל־עריהם | דבביכון ותדבקון יתהון לא תשבקונון למיעל |
| כי נתנם יהוה אלהיכם בידכם: כ ויהי | לקרויהון ארי מסרינון יי אלהכון בידיכון: כ והוה |
| ככלות יהושע ובני ישראל להכתם | כד שיצי יהושע ובני ישראל למקטלהון |
| מכה גדלה־מאד עד־תמם והשרידים | מחתא רבתא לחדא עד דשלימו ומשיזביא |
| שרדו מהם ויבאו אל־ערי המבצר: | אשתזיבו מנהון ועלו לקרוין כריכן: כא ותבו |
| כא וישבו כל־העם אל־המחנה אל־ | כל עמא למשריתא לות יהושע למקדה |
| יהושע מקדה בשלום לא־חרץ לבני | בשלם לא הוה נזקא לבני ישראל למדחק |
| ישראל לאיש את־לשנו: כב ויאמר | גבר ית נפשיה: כב ואמר יהושע פתחו ית פומא |

**רש"י**

(יח) גלו. גלגלו אבנים על פי המערה: (כא) לא חרץ לבני ישראל. הרי זה מקרא קצר לא חרץ ההורג לאיש מבני ישראל את לשונו: חרץ. לשון דבור הלשון וכן לא יחרץ כלב לשונו. וכן אז תחרץ דדוד תקרא תצעק קול תשואות המלחמה:

**רד"ק יהושע**

(יט) וזנבתם. תכריתו זנבם והוא סוף המחנה: (כ) ויבאו. וי"ו ויבואו כפ"א רפה בלשון ישמעאל וענין הפסוק כן והשרידים אשר שרדו מהם באו אל ערי המבצר: (כא) מקדה בשלום. למעלה אמר וישב יהושע וכל ישראל עמו אל המחנה הגלגלה תהלה אחרי כלות המלחמה שבו הגלגלה וכאשר אמר ליהושע כי המלכים נחבאים במערה במקדה בא לו למקדה עד קצה המחנה וצוה ממה שאומר שצוה ואחר שזנבו אותם שבו מקדה וצוה להמית את המלכים: לאיש את לשונו. ת"י לא הוה נזקא לבני ישראל למדחק גבר ית נפשיה וכן תרגם אנקלוס לא יחרץ כלב לשונו לא ינזק כלבא בלישניה אבל י"ת לשונו נפשיה. והמפרשים פירשו כי למ"ד לאיש נוספת ופירשו איש מהם לא חרץ לבני ישראל את לשונו ולמ"ד זו כלמ"ד הרגו

**מצודת דוד**

(יח) גלו אבנים. לבל יצאו משם וינוסו: (יט) וזנבתם אותם. הכו ההולכים בסוף המחנה: (כ) עד תמם. כי הנשארים היו מעט מן המעט וכאלו תמו כולם: והשרידים שרדו. הנשארים אשר נשארו מהם באו אל ערי המבצר:

**מצודת ציון**

(יח) גלו. גלגלו: והפקידו. מלשון פקיד וממונה: (יט) וזנבתם. מלשון זנב ור"ל סוף המחנה כזנב הזה שהוא סוף הגוף:(כ)והשרידים שרדו. הנשארים נשארו כמו פליט ושריד (איכה ב׳): (כא) חרץ.

(כא) לא חרץ וגו׳ לאיש. ר"ל אפילו לאיש אחד בהיותו יחידי לא חרץ עליו מי לשונו לדבר מאומה רע כי נפל פחדם על כל:

## Commentary Digest

managed to enter the fortified cities. Alternatively, And the rest; i.e. those who were destined to remain alive, remained of them, no others; and they entered the fortified cities. — K. Y.

21. *none whetted his tongue against any of the children of Israel* — *"This is a short verse* (the subject being absent in the original, meaning), *No whetter whetted his tongue to any of the children of Israel."* — R. I. e. none shouted even at an individual soldier. The fighting spirit of the Canaanites was completely broken. — D

*whetted* — Heb. חרץ, *"an expres-*

in a cave at Makkedah. 18. And Joshua said, "Roll great stones to the mouth of the cave, and appoint men by it to guard them. 19. And don't you stay; pursue your enemies, and smite the hindmost of them. Do not let them enter their cities, for the Lord your God has delivered them into your hand." 20. And it was when Joshua and the children of Israel had made an end of slaying them with a very great slaughter until they were consumed, that the rest which remained of them entered the fortified cities. 21. And all the people returned to the camp to Joshua to Makkedah in peace; none whetted his tongue against any of the children of Israel.

## Commentary Digest

18. *Roll* — Heb. (גלו) — *"roll (גלגלו) great stones onto the mouth of the cave."* — R and Z This is the more familiar form in rabbinic literature. Roll great stones, etc. — lest the kings emerge suddenly and escape. — D Find huge stones that cannot be readily lifted, and roll them onto the mouth of the cave. — K. Y. Scripture relates here the intense and energetic manner in which Joshua pursued the war, not relenting for one moment in the chase, in order to effect a complete victory over the enemy and his leaders. — G

19. *and smite the hindmost of them* — or attack them in the rear "וזנבתם" The root is "זנב," meaning "tail" or hindmost part of the camp. — K, D, and Z. Since their leaders are imprisoned in the cave, the entire army is considered as a *tail.* — K. Y.

*Do not let them enter their cities* — therefore, afford protection to the fugitives, and the task of the Israelites would be made increasingly difficult. In this , the Israelites were successful. See v. 20: "And the children of Israel had made an end of slaying them with a very great slaughter . . . that the rest (i.e. a small remnant) entered the fortified cities.

20. *that the rest which remained of them entered the fortified cities* — K Lit. *And the rest remained of them, and they entered* . . . This may be rendered thus: And the rest remained because of them; i.e. because of the children of Israel, who were slothful in pursuing the battle, and therefore, they

יְהוֹשֻׁעַ פִּתְחוּ אֶת־פִּי הַמְּעָרָה וְהוֹצִיאוּ
אֵלַי אֶת־חֲמֵשֶׁת הַמְּלָכִים הָאֵלֶּה מִן־
הַמְּעָרָה׃ כג וַיַּעֲשׂוּ כֵן וַיּוֹצִיאוּ אֵלָיו אֶת־
חֲמֵשֶׁת הַמְּלָכִים הָאֵלֶּה מִן־הַמְּעָרָה
אֵת ׀ מֶלֶךְ יְרוּשָׁלַםִ אֶת־מֶלֶךְ חֶבְרוֹן
אֶת־מֶלֶךְ יַרְמוּת אֶת־מֶלֶךְ לָכִישׁ אֶת־
מֶלֶךְ עֶגְלוֹן׃ כד וַיְהִי כְּהוֹצִיאָם אֶת־
הַמְּלָכִים הָאֵלֶּה אֶל־יְהוֹשֻׁעַ וַיִּקְרָא
יְהוֹשֻׁעַ אֶל־כָּל־אִישׁ יִשְׂרָאֵל וַיֹּאמֶר אֶל־
קְצִינֵי אַנְשֵׁי הַמִּלְחָמָה הֶהָלְכוּא אִתּוֹ
קִרְבוּ שִׂימוּ אֶת־רַגְלֵיכֶם עַל־צַוְּארֵי
הַמְּלָכִים הָאֵלֶּה וַיִּקְרְבוּ וַיָּשִׂימוּ אֶת־
רַגְלֵיהֶם עַל־צַוְּארֵיהֶם׃ כה וַיֹּאמֶר אֲלֵיהֶם
יְהוֹשֻׁעַ אַל־תִּירְאוּ וְאַל־תֵּחָתּוּ חִזְקוּ
וְאִמְצוּ כִּי כָכָה יַעֲשֶׂה יְהוָה לְכָל־

**תרגום**

דִמְעַרְתָּא וְאַפִּיקוּ לְוָתִי
יַת חַמְשָׁא מַלְכַיָא הָאִלֵין
מִן מְעַרְתָּא׃ כג וַעֲבַדוּ
כֵן וְאַפִּיקוּ לְוָתֵיהּ יַת
חַמְשָׁא מַלְכַיָא הָאִלֵין
מִן מְעַרְתָּא יַת מַלְכָּא
דִירוּשְׁלֵם יַת מַלְכָּא
דְחֶבְרוֹן יַת מַלְכָּא
דְיַרְמוּת יַת מַלְכָּא
דְלָכִישׁ יַת מַלְכָּא
דְעֶגְלוֹן׃ כד וַהֲוָה כַּד
אַפִּיקוּ יַת מַלְכַיָא הָאִלֵין
לְוַת יְהוֹשֻׁעַ וּקְרָא יְהוֹשֻׁעַ
לְכָל אֱנָשׁ יִשְׂרָאֵל וַאֲמַר
לְשִׁלְטוֹנֵי גִבְרֵי מְגִיחֵי
קְרָבָא דַאֲזַלוּ עִמֵיהּ קְרַבוּ
שַׁווּ יַת רִגְלֵיכוֹן עַל
צַוְרֵי מַלְכַיָא הָאִלֵין
וּקְרִיבוּ וְשַׁוִיאוּ יַת
רִגְלֵיהוֹן עַל צַוְרֵיהוֹן׃
כה וַאֲמַר לְהוֹן יְהוֹשֻׁעַ
לָא תִדְחֲלוּן וְלָא
תִתַּבְּרוּן תְּקִיפוּ וְעַלִימוּ
אֲרֵי כְּדֵין יַעֲבֵד יְיָ לְכָל
בַּעֲלֵי דְבָבֵיכוֹן דְאַתּוּן
מְגִיחִין קְרָבָא בְּהוֹן׃
ומחנון

**רד"ק**

לאבנר. והשלישי לאבשלום והדומים להם שכתבנו בספר מכלל בחלק הדקדוק ממנו ואפשר לפרש למ"ד לאיש משמשת ופי' לאיש מבני ישראל כלומר אין צריך לומר לבני ישראל לרבים אוביכם מהם שלא חרץ איש מהגוים האלה את לשונו כי אפילו לאיש אחד מבני ישראל לא חרץ איש מהגוי' את לשונו: (כד) ההלכוא. באל"ף נח נוסף עם הוי"ו וכן ולא אבוא שמוע וכן כל הוא

**מנחת שי**

(כג) ויעשו כן ויוציאו אליו. כתוב הספרים מלא וא"ו ול"ע ממה שאכתוב בד"ה ב' סי' א': (כד) ויהי כהוציאם. במקצת דפוסים יש מאריך בה' אבל בספרים כ"י ודפוסים ישנים הוא געיא בכ"ף: ההלכוא. חד מן מלין דכתיבין אל"ף בסוף

**רלב"ג**

מהם כי נפל פחדם עליהם וזהו אמרו על לך המשל לא חרץ לבני ישראל לאיש את לשונו: (כד) וצוה יהושע לקציני אנשי המלחמה שהלכו אתו שישימו רגליהם על צוארי מלכים האלה למען יירא שנשארים מלהלחם בישראל ולזאת הסבה תלם על חמשה עלים והשיבום במערה ושמו אבנים גדולות על פי המערה עם שזם

**מצודת ציון**

ענין תנועה כמו אז תחרץ (ש"ב ה'): (כד) קציני. ענין שררה כמו קצין תהיה לנו (ישעיה ג'):

## Commentary Digest

five gallows and threw their corpses into the cave wherein they had hidden previously. — G This act was the fulfillment of the final verse of Moses' blessing to the children of Israel prior to his demise: And you shall tread upon their high places.[1] This alludes to the highest officials, or sovereigns of the Canaanites.[2]

25. *Fear not...for thus shall the Lord do* — An additional purpose of this act was to encourage the Israelites to continue to wage war against the seven nations of Canaan.

22. And Joshua said, Open the mouth of the cave, and bring out those five kings to me from the cave. 23. And they did so, and they brought forth those five kings to him from the cave: the king of Jerusalem, the king of Hebron, the king of Jarmuth, the king of Lachish, and the king of Eglon. 24. And it was when they brought out those kings to Joshua, that Joshua called for all the men of Israel, and said to the chiefs of the men of war that went with him, Come near, put your feet upon the necks of these kings. And they came near, and put their feet upon their necks. 25. And Joshua said to them, Fear not, nor be dismayed, be strong and of good courage, for thus shall the Lord do to all

## Commentary Digest

*sion meaning speech of the tongue, and so: "— no dog whetted* (יחרץ) *its tongue."*[1] *And so: "Then shall you shout* (תחרין)*,"*[2] *stated concerning David. You shall call out, you shall shout a battle cry."* — R

24. *And it was when they brought out these kings to Joshua* — These words are apparently superfluous after the preceding verse. Scripture narrates to us that although it would have been normal for the five kings to remain in the cave and wait for the Israelites to come in and kill them, they so disheartened that they immediately surrendered, and walked out into the hands of their enemies. Upon seeing this, Joshua called all the men of Israel to witness the utter submission of these kings to Israel, and to see the chiefs place their feet upon their necks. — K. Y.

*that Joshua called for all the men of Israel* — to witness this scene of utter subjugation of the five kings.

*put your feet upon the necks of these kings* — to strike fear into the hearts of the remaining Canaanites, so that they refrain from waging war with the Israelites. For this very reason, Joshua later hanged them on

כו וּמְחָנוּן יְהוֹשֻׁעַ בָּתַר
כֵּן וְקַטְלִינוּן וּצְלַבִינוּן
עַל חַמְשָׁא צְלִיבִין וַהֲווֹ
צְלִיבִין עַל צְלִיבַיָא עַד
רַמְשָׁא: כז וַהֲוָה לְעִידָן
מֵיעַל שִׁמְשָׁא פַּקֵּיד
יְהוֹשֻׁעַ וְאַחֵיתוּנוּן מֵעַל
צְלִיבַיָא וּרְמוֹנוּן
לִמְעַרְתָּא דְאִטְּמָרוּ תַמָּן
וְשַׁוִּיאוּ אַבְנִין רַבְרְבָן עַל
פּוּמָא דִמְעַרְתָּא עַד כְּדַן
יוֹמָא הָדֵין: כח וְיַת
מַקֵּדָה כְּבַשׁ יְהוֹשֻׁעַ
בְּיוֹמָא הַהוּא וּמְחָא
לְפִתְגַם דְּחָרֶב וְיַת
מַלְכָּא גְּמַר יַתְהוֹן וְיַת
כָּל נַפְשָׁתָא דִי בַהּ לָא
אַשְׁאַר מְשֵׁיזֵיב וַעֲבַד
לְמַלְכָּא דְמַקֵּדָה כְּמָא
דַעֲבַד לְמַלְכָּא דִירִיחוֹ:
כט וַעֲבַר יְהוֹשֻׁעַ וְכָל
יִשְׂרָאֵל עִמֵּיהּ מִמַּקֵּדָה
לְלִבְנָה וַאֲגִיחַ קְרָבָא עִם
לבנה

אֹיְבֵיכֶם אֲשֶׁר אַתֶּם נִלְחָמִים אוֹתָם:
כו וַיַּכֵּם יְהוֹשֻׁעַ אַחֲרֵי־כֵן וַיְמִיתֵם וַיִּתְלֵם
עַל חֲמִשָּׁה עֵצִים וַיִּהְיוּ תְּלוּיִם עַל־
הָעֵצִים עַד־הָעָרֶב: כז וַיְהִי לְעֵת | בּוֹא
הַשֶּׁמֶשׁ צִוָּה יְהוֹשֻׁעַ וַיֹּרִידוּם מֵעַל
הָעֵצִים וַיַּשְׁלִכֻם אֶל־הַמְּעָרָה אֲשֶׁר
נֶחְבְּאוּ־שָׁם וַיָּשִׂמוּ אֲבָנִים גְּדֹלוֹת עַל־פִּי
הַמְּעָרָה עַד־עֶצֶם הַיּוֹם הַזֶּה: כח וְאֶת־
מַקֵּדָה לָכַד יְהוֹשֻׁעַ בַּיּוֹם הַהוּא וַיַּכֶּהָ
לְפִי־חֶרֶב וְאֶת־מַלְכָּהּ הֶחֱרִם אוֹתָם
וְאֶת־כָּל־הַנֶּפֶשׁ אֲשֶׁר־בָּהּ לֹא הִשְׁאִיר
שָׂרִיד וַיַּעַשׂ לְמֶלֶךְ מַקֵּדָה כַּאֲשֶׁר עָשָׂה
לְמֶלֶךְ יְרִיחוֹ: כט וַיַּעֲבֹר יְהוֹשֻׁעַ וְכָל־
יִשְׂרָאֵל עִמּוֹ מִמַּקֵּדָה לִבְנָה וַיִּלָּחֶם עִם־

לבנה

### רד"ק

שבמקרא וה"א ההלכיא במקום אשר כמו ה"א ההקדיש שמואל והדומים לא כי לא תבוא ה"א הידיעה על העוברים: (כז) ויהי לעת בא השמש. מפני טומאת הארץ היו הנתלים נקברים אף על פי שאינם מבני ישראל כמו שאומר ולא תטמא את אדמתך כי המת שאינו נקבר הוא טומאת הארץ לפיכך צוה כן יהושע לעשות למלך העי ולחמשת המלכים האלה וכן לעתיד בגוג ומגוג אמר וקברים בית ישראל למען טהר את הארץ: (כח) כאשר עשה למלך יריחו. להודיע כי לא תפשוהו חי ותלוהו אחר כן

### רלב"ג

היה מזכיר לישראל ענין המופת שנעשה בזאת המלחמה: (כח) עוד זכר שכבר לכד יהושע מקדה ולבנה ולכיש ועגלון וחברון ודביר

### מנחת שי

תיבותא ולא קריי' וסימן נמסר בריש ס' (לך לך ובדניאל ג') במ"ג. (ועיין רד"ק): (כח) ואת מלכה החרם. באל"ף מאריך בה"א ומלת מלכה בטעם סגול ומלת החרם בגלגל: החרם אותם. בדפוס בומבורגי קע"ח נכתב בגליון אותה וכן בתרגום שם גמיר יתה גם בספרים כתוב אותה. ובספרים אחרים מדוייקים כתוב אותם ותרגום שלהם יתהון וכן הוא במאיר נתיב וכן פירוש בעל כלי יקר:

### מצודת דוד

(כז) עד עצם וכו'. ר"ל והמה מונחים שם עד עלם וכו' ר"ל עד עולם:

## Commentary Digest

had fled from the battle and took refuge in Makkedah. — K. Y. Moreover, it was miraculous that the inhabitants of Makkedah remained in the city and did not flee. — M. L.

*and he did to the king of Makkedah as he had done to the king of Jericho* — i.e. killing him immediately during the course of battle, not as they had

your enemies against whom you fight. 26. And afterward
Joshua smote them, and slew them, and hanged them on
five poles; and they were hanging upon the poles until the
evening. 27. And it was at the time of the setting of the
sun, that Joshua commanded, and they took them down off
the poles, and cast them into the cave wherein they had been
hidden, and laid great stones on the mouth of the cave until
this very day. 28. And on that day, Joshua took Makkedah
and smote it with the edge of the sword, and its king he
utterly destroyed, them and all the souls that were therein; he
let none remain; and he did to the king of Makkedah as he
had done to the king of Jericho. 29. And Joshua passed on
from Makkedah, and all Israel with him, to Libnah; and he
fought against Libnah.

## Commentary Digest

26. *And afterwards Joshua smote them, and slew them* — I.e. after a time, Joshua smote them and then slew them. These tactics were part of the effort to encourage the Israelites to continue their war against the Canaanites. — K.Y.

27. *And it was at the time of the setting of the sun, that Joshua commanded* — See above, VIII:29, and Commentary Digest ibid.

*and laid great stones on the mouth of the cave until this very day.* — This was to be a perpetual memorial of the miracles the Lord had wrought for them in that cave. — M. L.

28. *And on that day, Joshua took Makkedah* — Although it was a fortified city, the Jews overwhelmed its surviving garrison on that day in the flush of victory. From there they continued on to Libnah,[1] Lachish,[2] and the other cities enumerated, not pausing during the campaign, until its completion. See below, v. 42: "And all these kings and their lands did Joshua take *at one time,* for the God of Israel fought for Israel." The entire southern sector of Eretz Israel was now in their hands.

*them and all the souls that were therein* — This includes refugees who

לבנה: ל ויתן יהוה גם־אותה ביד
ישראל ואת־מלכה ויכה לפי־חרב
ואת־כל־הנפש אשר־בה לא־השאיר
בה שריד ויעש למלכה כאשר עשה
למלך יריחו: לא ויעבר יהושע וכל־
ישראל עמו מלבנה לכישה ויחן עליה
וילחם בה: לב ויתן יהוה את־לכיש ביד
ישראל וילכדה ביום השני ויכה לפי־
חרב ואת־כל־הנפש אשר־בה ככל
אשר־עשה ללבנה: לג אז עלה הרם
מלך גזר לעזר את־לכיש ויכהו יהושע
ואת־עמו עד־בלתי השאיר־לו שריד:
לד ויעבר יהושע וכל־ישראל עמו
מלכיש עגלנה ויחנו עליה וילחמו
עליה: לה וילכדוה ביום ההוא ויכוה

לבנה: ל ומסר יי אף יתה בידא דישראל וית מלכה ומחה לפתגם דחרב וית כל נפשתא די בה לא אשאר בה משיזיב ועבד למלכא כמא דעבד למלכה דיריחו: לא ועבר יהושע וכל ישראל עמיה מלבנה ללכיש ושרא עלה ואגיח קרבא בה: לב ומסר יי ית לכיש בידא דישראל וכבשה ביומא תנינא ומחה לפתגם דחרב וית כל נפשתא דבה בכל דעבד ללבנה: לג בכן סליק הורם מלכא דגזר למסעד ית לכיש ומחהי יהושע וית עמיה עד דלא אשתאר ליה משיזיב: לד ועבר יהושע וכל ישראל עמיה מלכיש לעגלון ושרו עלה ואגיחו קרבא עלה: לה וכבשוה ביומא ההוא ומחוהא לפתגם דחרב

לפי

רד"ק

כמו שעשו למלך העי ולחמשת המלכים אלא הרגוהו בכלל ההרוגים כמו שאמר ויכהו לפי חרב ואת מלכה : (לג) ביום

מנחת שי

(לג) לעזר את לכיש . בעין בס"ה לבדו בכמה ספרים כ"י ודפוסים ישנים : (לה) החרים . באה מארק בה"א וכן ואת כל הנשמה החרים בסמוך (פ' מ') :

רלב"ג

באופן בהכס יהושע מקדש ברנע עד עזה ואת כל ארץ גשן עד גבעון בזמן קצר מדובק באין הפסק וזהו אמרו ואת כל המלכים האלה ואת ארצם לכד יהושע פעם אחת ואחר כך יהושע וכל ישראל המחנה הגלגל כי שם היה המחנה כמו שזכרנו :

## Commentary Digest

one of the five kings captured in the cave, and since no new king had been appointed in the interim, no king is mentioned here. — K.Y.

*on the second day* — of the siege. — K Alternatively, this may refer to the second day of the week. Since the long day was Friday, they camped until after the Sabbath, and resumed the battle on Sunday. On Monday, they captured the city. — K. Y.

30. And the Lord delivered it also, and its king, into the
hand of Israel; and he smote it with the edge of the sword,
and all the souls that were therein; he let none remain in it;
and he did to its king as he had done to the king of Jericho.
31. And Joshua passed on from Libnah, and all Israel with
him, to Lachish, and encamped against it, and fought against
it. 32. And the Lord delivered Lachish into the hand of
Israel; and he took it on the second day, and smote it with the
edge of the sword, and all the souls that were in it, according
to all that he had done to Libnah. 33. Then Horam king
of Gezer came up to help Lachish; and Joshua smote him
and his people until he left him none remaining. 34. And
from Lachish Joshua passed on to Eglon, and all Israel with
him; and they encamped against it, and fought against it.
35. And they took it on that day, and smote it

## Commentary Digest

done to the king of Ai, whom they first captured, and then put to death. — K

29. *And Joshua passed on from Makkedah . . . to Libnah and he fought against Libnah.* — This battle took place on the same day as the battle against the five kings. — M. L.

30. *And the Lord delivered it also* I.e. the Lord delivered Libnah into their hands on the same day that the sun and the moon stood still. — K. Y.

31. *And encamped against it* — They did not enter into battle immediately because they were fatigued from the battle of the five kings. Moreover, Lachish was stronger than Libnah. They, therefore, commenced the attack on the morrow. — K. Y.

32. *And the Lord delivered Lachish into the hand of Israel* — Since this conquest was not accomplished on the day of the miracles, the word *also* is missing. Since the king of Lachish was

לְפִי־חֶרֶב וְאֵת כָּל־הַנֶּפֶשׁ אֲשֶׁר־בָּהּ
בַּיּוֹם הַהוּא הֶחֱרִים כְּכֹל אֲשֶׁר־עָשָׂה
לְלָכִישׁ׃ לו וַיַּעַל יְהוֹשֻׁעַ וְכָל־יִשְׂרָאֵל עִמּוֹ
מֵעֶגְלוֹנָה חֶבְרוֹנָה וַיִּלָּחֲמוּ עָלֶיהָ׃
לז וַיִּלְכְּדוּהָ וַיַּכּוּהָ לְפִי־חֶרֶב וְאֶת־מַלְכָּהּ
וְאֶת־כָּל־עָרֶיהָ וְאֶת־כָּל־הַנֶּפֶשׁ אֲשֶׁר־
בָּהּ לֹא־הִשְׁאִיר שָׂרִיד כְּכֹל אֲשֶׁר־
עָשָׂה לְעֶגְלוֹן וַיַּחֲרֵם אוֹתָהּ וְאֶת־כָּל־
הַנֶּפֶשׁ אֲשֶׁר־בָּהּ׃ לח וַיָּשָׁב יְהוֹשֻׁעַ וְכָל־
יִשְׂרָאֵל עִמּוֹ דְּבִרָה וַיִּלָּחֶם עָלֶיהָ׃
לט וַיִּלְכְּדָהּ וְאֶת־מַלְכָּהּ וְאֶת־כָּל־עָרֶיהָ
וַיַּכּוּם לְפִי־חֶרֶב וַיַּחֲרִימוּ אֶת־כָּל־נֶפֶשׁ
אֲשֶׁר־בָּהּ לֹא הִשְׁאִיר שָׂרִיד כַּאֲשֶׁר
עָשָׂה לְחֶבְרוֹן כֵּן־עָשָׂה לִדְבִרָה וּלְמַלְכָּהּ

דְּחָרֶב וְיָת כָּל נַפְשָׁתָא
דְּבַהּ בְּיוֹמָא הַהוּא גְּמַר
כְּכֹל דַּעֲבַד לְלָכִישׁ׃
לו וּסְלִיק יְהוֹשֻׁעַ וְכָל
יִשְׂרָאֵל עִמֵּיהּ מֵעֶגְלוֹן
לְחֶבְרוֹן וַאֲגִיחוּ קְרָבָא
עֲלַהּ׃ לז וּכְבָשׁוּהָא
וּמְחוּהָא לְפִתְגָם דְּחָרֶב
וְיָת מַלְכַּהּ וְיָת כָּל
קִרְוָהָא וְיָת כָּל נַפְשָׁתָא
דְּבַהּ לָא אַשְׁאַר מְשֵׁיזֵיב
כְּכֹל דַּעֲבַד לְעֶגְלוֹן וְגַמַּר
יָתַהּ וְיָת כָּל נַפְשָׁתָא
דְּבַהּ׃ לח וְתָב יְהוֹשֻׁעַ
וְכָל יִשְׂרָאֵל עִמֵּיהּ לִדְבִיר
וַאֲגִיחַ קְרָבָא עֲלַהּ׃
לט וּכְבָשַׁהּ וְיָת מַלְכַּהּ
וְיָת כָּל קִרְוָהָא וּמְחוֹנוּן
לְפִתְגָם דְּחָרֶב וְגַמִּירוּ יָת
כָּל נַפְשָׁתָא דִי בַהּ לָא
אַשְׁאַר מְשֵׁיזֵיב כְּמָא
דַּעֲבַד לְחֶבְרוֹן כֵּן עֲבַד
לִדְבִיר וּלְמַלְכַּהּ וּכְמָא
דעבד

רד"ק

השני. ביום השני לחנייתם עליה: (לז) ואת מלכה. והנה היה מלך חברון מחמשת המלכים שתלו אלא ידמה שהמליכו אחר כן מלך בחברון: ואת כל עריה. ואת כל הערים ואנשי הערים אשר על גבולה הקרואי' על שמה: (לח) וישב יהושע. נראה כי כשעלה מעגלון לחברון עבר על דביר ולא נלחם עליה כי ראה להלחם בחברון ואחר שלכד חברון שב לדביר ונלחם עליה:

וכאשר

מצודת דוד

(לז) ואת מלכה. יתכן שהמליכו עליהם מלך אחר כי למעלה נאמר שיהושע המית מלך חברון: ואת כל עריה. הערים הסמוכים לה:

## Commentary Digest

*and all its cities* — its entire metropolitan area. — K and D

38. *And Joshua returned . . . to Debir . . . and he took it* — See below XV:-15-17, Jud. I:12-13, where Othniel is credited with its capture, singlehanded. Abarbanel explains that Othniel led the attack upon Debir, while M maintains that Othniel captured the suburbs, while Joshua captured the city proper. The rabbinic interpretation is cited by R, below XV:15.

39. *As he had done to Hebron* — i.e. to the second king of Hebron. See above v. 37, Commentary Digest.

with the edge of the sword, and all the souls that were in it
he completely destroyed that day, according to all that he had
done to Lachish. 36. And Joshua went up from Eglon, and
all Israel with him, to Hebron; and they fought against it.
37. And they took it, and smote it with the edge of the
sword and its king and all its cities, and all the souls that
were in it; and he left none remaining, according to all that
he had done to Eglon, but destroyed it completely and all the
souls that were in it. 38. And Joshua returned, and all Israel
with him, to Debir; and he fought against it. 39. And he
took it and its king, and all the cities thereof; and they smote
them with the edge of the sword, and completely destroyed
all the souls that were in it; he left none remaining. As he had
done to Hebron, so he did to Debir and to its king,

## Commentary Digest

33. *Then Horam king of Gezer came up to help Lachish* — The meaning of *then* is not clear. He obviously could not come to help them after they had been destroyed. Perhaps he came while they were engaged in battle, and instead of affording assistance to Lachish, he and his army were destroyed. (Perhaps he came while they were engaged in battle, and instead of affording assistance to Lachish, he and his army were destroyed) with them. Alternatively, he may have heard while the battle was in progress, but arrived after the city had capitulated, and met his end by the hand of the Israelites. — K'li Y'kar

37. *And they took it* — See below XIV:6-15, where it would appear that Hebron was captured at the very end of the military campaign, and Commentary Digest ibid.

*and smote it with the edge of the sword, and its king* — Although the king of Hebron is already mentioned as having been captured[1] and put to death,[2] it is possible that Hebron had immediately appointed a new king, who was now put to death by the edge of the sword. — K and D

This king, however, was not the equal of his predecessor, and was therefore not listed in Ch. 12 among the thirty-one kings that Joshua vanquished. — K. Y.

וְכַאֲשֶׁר עָשָׂה לְלִבְנָה וּלְמַלְכָּהּ׃ מ וַיַּכֶּה
יְהוֹשֻׁעַ אֶת־כָּל־הָאָרֶץ הָהָר וְהַנֶּגֶב
וְהַשְּׁפֵלָה וְהָאֲשֵׁדוֹת וְאֵת כָּל־מַלְכֵיהֶם
לֹא הִשְׁאִיר שָׂרִיד וְאֵת כָּל־הַנְּשָׁמָה
הֶחֱרִים כַּאֲשֶׁר צִוָּה יְהוָה אֱלֹהֵי יִשְׂרָאֵל׃
מא וַיַּכֵּם יְהוֹשֻׁעַ מִקָּדֵשׁ בַּרְנֵעַ וְעַד־עַזָּה
וְאֵת כָּל־אֶרֶץ גֹּשֶׁן וְעַד־גִּבְעוֹן׃ מב וְאֵת
כָּל־הַמְּלָכִים הָאֵלֶּה וְאֶת־אַרְצָם לָכַד
יְהוֹשֻׁעַ פַּעַם אֶחָת כִּי יְהוָה אֱלֹהֵי יִשְׂרָאֵל
נִלְחָם לְיִשְׂרָאֵל׃ מג וַיָּשָׁב יְהוֹשֻׁעַ וְכָל־
יִשְׂרָאֵל עִמּוֹ אֶל־הַמַּחֲנֶה הַגִּלְגָּלָה׃
יא א וַיְהִי כִּשְׁמֹעַ יָבִין מֶלֶךְ־חָצוֹר וַיִּשְׁלַח
אֶל־יוֹבָב מֶלֶךְ מָדוֹן וְאֶל־מֶלֶךְ שִׁמְרוֹן

**תרגום**

בְּעֲבַד לְלִבְנָה וּלְמַלְכַּהּ׃
מ וּמְחָא יְהוֹשֻׁעַ יָת כָּל אַרְעָא טוּרָא וְדָרוֹמָא וּשְׁפֵלְתָּא וּמַשְׁפַּךְ מְרַמָתָא וְיָת כָּל מַלְכֵיהוֹן לָא אַשְׁאַר מְשֵׁזִיב וְיָת כָּל נִשְׁמָא גַמַר כְּמָא דְפַקֵד יְיָ אֱלָהָא דְיִשְׂרָאֵל׃
מא וּמְחָנוּן יְהוֹשֻׁעַ מֵרְקַם גֵיאָה וְעַד עַזָה וְיָת כָּל אֲרַע גוֹשֶׁן וְעַד גִבְעוֹן׃
מב וְיָת כָּל מַלְכַיָא הָאִילֵין וְיָת אַרְעֲהוֹן כְּבַשׁ יְהוֹשֻׁעַ בְּזִמְנָא חֲדָא אֲרֵי יְיָ אֱלָהָא דְיִשְׂרָאֵל בְּמֵימְרֵיהּ אֲגִיחַ קְרָבָא לְיִשְׂרָאֵל׃
מג וְתָב יְהוֹשֻׁעַ וְכָל יִשְׂרָאֵל עִמֵיהּ לְמַשְׁרִיתָא לְגִלְגָלָא׃
א וַהֲוָה כַּד שְׁמַע יָבִין מַלְכָּא דְחָצוֹר וּשְׁלַח לְוַת יוֹבָב מַלְכָּא דְמָדוֹן וּלְוַת מַלְכָּא דְשִׁמְרוֹן וּלְוַת מלכא׃

**רד"ק**

(מ) והנגב. כתרגומו ודרומא: והאשדות. כמו אשדות הפסגה כתרגום משפך מרמתא והוא מדרון ההר או הפסגה נקרא כן לפי שהמים היורדים על ההר נשפכים מן ההר דרך מדרון: (מא) ארץ גושן. אין זה של מצרים: (מב) פעם אחת. כלומר שלא הוצרך לצור על עיר ולא האריכו ימי המלחמה אלא

**רש"י**

(מ) והאשדות. מקום שמי הגבעות שופכים: (מא) מקדש ברנע ועד עזה. מלד דרומית של א"י הוא מן המזרח למערב ולא הספיק לכבוש כל המילר ונשאר מעזה עד הים הוא שאמר למטה זאת הארץ הנשארת העזתי והאשדודי וגו':

**רלב"ג**

(א) עוד זכר שכאשר שמע זה יבין מלך חלור שלח אל יובב מלך מדון ואל מלך שומרון ולמלכים רבים זולתם להתקבץ יחד ולהלחם עם ישראל כדי שלא יפלו בידם אחד אחד כמו שעשו שאר המלכים ובאו עם רב כחול אשר על שפת הים להלחם עם ישראל:

**מצודת ציון**

(מ) והנגב. מקום נגוב ויבש כי חרבו פני האדמה (בראשית ח') תרגומו נגבו וכן אלן הנגב נתתני (לקמן ט"ו): והשפלה. העמק: והאשדות. מדרון ההרים שהמים נשפכים ויורדים שם וכן אשדות הפסגה (דברים ג') כי שופך דם. (בראשית ט') תרגומו דישוד דמא:

**מצודת דוד**

(מב) פעם אחת. לפי שהשי"ת לכד בפעם א' לזה אמר שכל אלו לכד בפעם אחת: (מג) וישב יהושע. היא השבה עלמה האמורה למעל':

## Commentary Digest

### CHAPTER 11

1. In this chapter is described the northern campaign, against the forces led by the king of Hazor.

*And it was, when Jabin king of Hazor heard*—that the kings fell one by one, he sent to Jobab king of Madon . . . to unite against Israel. — G Alternatively, when Jabin king of Hazor heard that Joshua had returned Gilgal to rest after the southern campaign, he assumed that the Israelites were not in a position to fight at that time. He, therefore, decided to organize all the kings of the north to attack them. — K. Y. Moreover, when they heard that Joshua had destroyed all the southern kings, he called to his allies to gather and avenge their deaths. — M. L.

as he had done also to Libnah and to her king. 40. And
Joshua smote all the country (of) the hills and of the south,
and of the valley, and of the falls, and all their kings. He
left none remaining, but destroyed every soul, as the Lord
God of Israel had commanded. 41. And Joshua smote them
from Kadesh-barnea to Gaza, and all the land of Goshen to
Gibeon. 42. And all these kings and their land did Joshua
take at one time, because the Lord God of Israel fought for
Israel. 43. And Joshua returned, and all Israel with him, to
the camp, to Gilgal.

11

1. And it was, when Jabin king of Hazor heard, he sent to
Jobab king of Madon, and to the king of Shimron,

**Commentary Digest**

*as he had done also to Libnah and to her king.* — The Scripture mentions specifically Libnah, to remove all doubt as to which of the two kings of Hebron the previous reference is made.

40. *and of the south* — K after J.

*and the falls* — *the place where the water of the hills pours down.* — R

Z renders: the desert.

41. *from Kadesh-barnea to Gaza* — "*This is from the south side of Eretz Israel*[1] *from east to west. He was, however, unable to conquer the entire boundary, thus there remained from Gaza to the* (Mediterranean) *Sea. This is what the Scripture states below:*[2] *This is the land that yet remained...*[3]*the Gazathites, and the Ashdodites, etc.*" — R

*and all the land of Goshen* — This is not the Goshen of Egypt. — K. It is rather in the section of Judah in the South.[4]

*to Gibeon* — in the section of Benjamin, north of Jerusalem. — M[5]

42. *And all these kings and their land did Joshua take at one time* — i.e. the southern campaign was a "blitzkrieg," completed in an astoundingly short time, Joshua and his forces harassing the fleeing Canaanites relentlessly. The Northern campaign, described in the subsequent chapter, was to take an immeasurably longer time.

מלכא דאכשף: ב ולות
מלכיא דמצפונא
בטורא ובמישרא דרום
גינוסר ובשפלתא
ובפלכי דור מערבא:
ג כנענאה ממדינחא
וממערבא ואמוראה
וחתאה ופריזאה
ויבוסאה בטורא וחואה
בשפולי חרמון בארע
מצפיא: ד ונפקו אינון
וכל משריתהון עמהון
עם סגי כחלא דעל כיף
ימא לסגי וסוסון
ורתיכון סגי לחדא:
ה ואזדמנו כל מלכיא
האילין ואתו ושרו כחדא
על מי מרום לאגחא
קרבא עם ישראל:
ו ואמר יי ליהושע לא
תדחל מן קדמיהון ארי
מחר

ואל־מלך אכשף: ב ואל־המלכים אשר
מצפון בהר ובערבה נגב כנרות
ובשפלה ובנפות דור מים: ג הכנעני
ממזרח ומים והאמרי והחתי והפרזי
והיבוסי בהר והחוי תחת חרמון בארץ
המצפה: ד ויצאו הם וכל־מחניהם עמם
עם־רב כחול אשר על־שפת־הים לרב
וסוס ורכב רב־מאד: ה ויועדו כל
המלכים האלה ויבאו ויחנו יחדו אל־מי
מרום להלחם עם־ישראל: ו ויאמר
יהוה אל־יהושע אל־תירא מפניהם
כי

**רש"י**

**יא (ב) נגב כנרות.** דרום גינוסר: **ובנפות דור.** פלכי דור קונטדו"ש בלע"ז (בל"א לאנד שאפט געגענד): **מים.** מערבה:

**רד"ק** הר' בקמץ

בפעם אחת לכדום כולם זאת אחרי זאת בלא הפסק: **(ב) אשר מצפון:** בשו"א ועיקרו בקמץ כי איננו סמוך ויתכן **לפרשו** סמוך לבית בהר ובערבה כאילו אמר מצפון ההר כי כן דרך הלשון לסמוך על אות השמוש כמו השוכני באהלים וזולתו **כמו שכתבנו** בספר מכלל: נגב כנרות. לדרום כנרת וכנרות קבוץ כנרת וזה תרגום גינוסר והיא ארץ שמנה מאד **ורבותינו ז"ל** הפליגו בספור שבח פירותיהם והקבוץ ר"ל שהיו מקומות נחלקים וכלם היו שמנים: ובנפות דור. האחד ממנו נפה **והסמוך** לנפת דור וענינם מחוז מחוזים וכת"י פילכי: (ג) והחוי תחת חרמון. פירוש החוי שהיה יושב תחת חרמון ואמר תחת כי חרמון היה הר כמו שכתוב עד הר חרמון ופי' בארץ המצפה כי חרמון זה בארץ המצפה או פירושו כי כל **המלכים נועדו בארץ המצפה** להלחם עם יהושע ואפשר שזה המקום הוא המצפה שהיו מתקבצים שם **ישראל תמיד ולפי שהיתה שם תשועה גדולה** היו נועדים שם כי במלחמה האחרת שעשה יהושע עם חמש' המלכים **אף על פי שהיתה תשועה גדולה לא היו אלא** חמשת מלכים ואלו היו מלכים רבים ואפשר כי בנה שם יהושע מזבח מפני התשועה הגדולה שהיתה **שם ומפני זה היו ישראל** נקבצים שם בעת שהיו צריכים למלחמה או לדבר גדול וכן מצאנו ביפתח לפני ה' במצפה וכן **בדבר פלגש בגבעה אל**

**רלב"ג**

**(ו)** ויעד הש"י ליהושע שלא יירא מהם ומהמונם כי כעת מחר יתנם הש"י חללים לפני ישר'. וצוה לעקור סוסיהם ולשרוף מרכבותיהם שלא יקחום ישראל ויבטחו בם מענין המלחמות ושלא יאמרו שכחם **ועוצם** ידם עשה להם את החיל הזה ולא יסיח מבטחם בש"י ויתבהל

**מנחת שי**

**יא (ג) ואל** המלכים. הוא"ו בגעיא בספרים כ"י ודפוס ישן: **נגב כנרות.** בספרים כ"י מדוייקים הכ"ף במאריך והנו"ן בשוא לבדו ורפה וכ"כ במכלל דף ר"כ כל כנרות בשוא בלא סמיכות והוא קל והכ"ף **מעמדת בגעיא** עכ"ל ור' אליה המדקדק כתב ובמדויקים הנו"ן בחטף פתח ועיין ג"כ **(במלכים** א' ט"ו):

**מצודת דוד**

**יא (ג) תחת חרמון.** תחת הר חרמון: **בארץ המצפה.** הר חרמון היה בארץ המצפה:

**מצודת ציון**

**יא (ב) ובערב'.** כמישור: **נגב כנרות.** לדרום כנרות והיא שם מקום: **ובנפות דור.** מחוזות וגלילות של דור כמו יפה נוף (תהלים מ"ח): **(ה) ויועדו.** מלשון וועד ואסיפה:

## Commentary Digest

nized a tremendous army, well equipped with horses and chariots. — A.

6. *"Be not afraid of them* — Joshua was afraid of these kings for three reasons: (1) Perhaps the Israelites did not merit God's aid against such overwhelming odds; (2) perhaps the great miracles that had been wrought on their behalf had decreased the merits they had; (3) perhaps someone had committed a sin, as in the case of Achan, and therefore, they were not worthy of a victory over the numerous armies of their foes. — M. L.

and to the king of Achshaph. 2. And to the kings that were
on the north of the mountains, and of the plains south of
Chinnaroth, and in the valley, and in the regions of Dor on
the west. 3. (To) the Canaanite on the east and on the west,
and (to) the Amorite, and the Hittite, and the Perizzite, and
the Jebusite in the mountains, and (to) the Hivite under
Hermon in the land of Mizpah. 4. And they went out, they
and all their hosts with them, many people, as the sand that
is upon the seashore in multitude, with many horses and
chariots. 5. And all these kings met together, they came and
camped together at the waters of Merom, to fight with Israel.
6. And the Lord said to Joshua, "Be not afraid of them,

## Commentary Digest

2. *on the north of the mountains* — or, on the north, on the mountains and in the plains. — K

*south of Chinnaroth* — *"south of Ginosar."* — R and K after J. This is the region around Tiberias on the Sea of Galilee. Its fruits are famed for their extreme sweetness.[1]

*and in the region of Dor* — *"the provinces of Dor, Contree in French."* — R after J

*on the west.* — R after J.

3. *and (to) the Hivite under Hermon in the land of Mizpah* — Mt. Hermon and the neighboring hill in the northern part of Upper Gallilee command a view of the entire surrounding region, thus the name "Mizpah," meaning lookout. K maintains that, after this mightiest of all Joshua's wars, against the northern alliance, an altar and a house of prayer and assembly was built in commemoration of the successful waging of this war. References to this gathering place are found in Jud. XI:11, and in I Sam. VII:5, X:17.

4. *And they went out, they and all their hosts with them, many people . . . with many horses and chariots.* — They thought that the five kings were vanquished because of their insufficient numbers and their lack of horses and chariots. They, therefore, orga-

כִּי מָחָר כָּעֵת הַזֹּאת אָנֹכִי נֹתֵן אֶת־כֻּלָּם
חֲלָלִים לִפְנֵי יִשְׂרָאֵל אֶת־סוּסֵיהֶם
תְּעַקֵּר וְאֶת־מַרְכְּבֹתֵיהֶם תִּשְׂרֹף בָּאֵשׁ׃
ז וַיָּבֹא יְהוֹשֻׁעַ וְכָל־עַם הַמִּלְחָמָה עִמּוֹ
עֲלֵיהֶם עַל־מֵי מֵרוֹם פִּתְאֹם וַיִּפְּלוּ בָּהֶם׃
ח וַיִּתְּנֵם יְהוָה בְּיַד־יִשְׂרָאֵל וַיַּכּוּם וַיִּרְדְּפוּם
עַד־צִידוֹן רַבָּה וְעַד מִשְׂרְפוֹת מַיִם
וְעַד־בִּקְעַת מִצְפֶּה מִזְרָחָה וַיַּכֻּם עַד
בִּלְתִּי הִשְׁאִיר־לָהֶם שָׂרִיד׃ ט וַיַּעַשׂ
לָהֶם יְהוֹשֻׁעַ כַּאֲשֶׁר אָמַר־לוֹ יְהוָה
אֶת־סוּסֵיהֶם עִקֵּר וְאֶת־מַרְכְּבֹתֵיהֶם
שָׂרַף בָּאֵשׁ׃ י וַיָּשָׁב יְהוֹשֻׁעַ בָּעֵת הַהִיא

**תרגום**

מְחַר כְּעִידָנָא הָדֵין אֲנָא מְסַר יָת כּוּלְהוֹן קְטִילִין קֳדָם יִשְׂרָאֵל יָת סוּסָוָתְהוֹן תְּעַקַּר וְיָת רְתִיכֵיהוֹן תּוֹקֵד בְּנוּרָא׃ ז וַאֲתָא יְהוֹשֻׁעַ וְכָל עַמָּא עָבְדֵי קְרָבָא עִמֵּיהּ עֲלֵיהוֹן וְאִינוּן שְׁרַן עַל מֵי מֵרוֹם בִּתְכֵיף וּנְפַלוּ בְהוֹן׃ ח וּמְסָרִינוּן יְיָ בִּידָא דְיִשְׂרָאֵל וּמְחוֹנוּן וּרְדָפוּנוּן עַד צִידוֹן רַבְּתָא וְעַד חֲרִיצֵי יַמָּא וְעַד בִּקְעַת מִצְפַּיָא מַדִינְחָא וּמְחוֹנוּן עַד דְּלָא אִישְׁתְּאַר לְהוֹן מְשֵׁיזִיב׃ ט וַעֲבַד לְהוֹן יְהוֹשֻׁעַ כְּמָא דַאֲמַר לֵיהּ יְיָ יָת סוּסָוָתְהוֹן עַקַּר וְיָת רְתִיכֵיהוֹן אוֹקֵד בְּנוּרָא׃ י וְתָב יְהוֹשֻׁעַ בְּעִדָּנָא הַהִיא

וכבש

ת"א סוסיהם תעקר. ע"ג י"ג:

**רש"י**

(ח) משרפות מים · תרגם יונתן חריצי ימא בעוטין חרילין ומי הים יולאין לתוכן ונשרפין מחום השמש ונעשים מלח:

**רד"ק**

ה' המצפה וכן אמר שמואל במלחמ' פלשתים קבצו אלי כל ישראל המצפ' וכן כשהמליך שאול ויצעק שמואל את העם אל ה' המצפה נראה מכל אלה הפסוקי' כי מזבח היה שם ובית מקודש לתפלה ולקבוץ ישראל באותן הימים: (ח) צידון רבה. רבת עם ידמה שהיתה צידון אחרת קטנה ממנה: משרפות מים. ת"י חריצי ימא והם המלחיות שעושין עליהם מים מלוחים ומושכין חריצין ונשרפין לשמש ונעשים מלח: (ט) את סוסיהם עקר. להודיע כי מה שאמר לו השם את סוסיהם תעקר דרך מצוה אמר לו. ויש לשאול מה טעם אמר לו מצוה זאת במלחמה זו מה שלא צוה לו במלחמה אחרת ויש לפרש כי במלחמות האחרות לא היו בהם סוס ורכב כי אם בלכידת העיירות היו המלחמות גם חמשת המלכים על גבעון באו ללכדה ולא היו צריכין לסוס ורכב אבל זו המלחמה היתה מערכה שערכו מלחמה עם רב להלחם עם ישראל והיו צריכים לסוסים ולרכב והיו עמהם לרוב כמה שכתוב וראית סוס ורכב עם רב ממך ולא תמצא שאמר כן במלחמות אחרות וצוה הקב"ה לאבד הסוסים והרכב שהיו הגוים נלחמים בהם ובטחו ברכבם כי רב ולא ידעו כי שקר הסוס לתשועה וישראל בלא רכב וסוס נצחום והפילום חללים כי לה' התשועה לפיכך לא רצה האל ית' שיבוזו

**רלב"ג**

להם כי הוא מגלה הגוים האלה ולא הם: (י) וזכר אחר זה בכלל לכד יהושע את חצור והכה כי ממלך חצור היתה התחלת

**מצודת ציון**

(ו) תעקר. תסיר העיקר כמו וכל תבואתי תשרש (איוב ל"א)

**מצודת דוד**

(ח) משרפות מים. הבריכות במי הים נקווים בהם והחמה

## Commentary Digest

ceived a report of the details of the battles, and be alerted. — K. Y.

*and smote its king with the sword* — Joshua slew the king of Hazor alone, not among the people of the city who fell in battle. This was to avenge himself and his people of Jabin who initiated the campaign against them, and led *all these kingdoms* into battle. Alternatively, this king was not Jabin, but a regent appointed in his stead when he left the city to engage in battle. The Scripture tells us that Hazor had a new king, *for Hazor was formerly the head of all these kingdoms.* I.e. since Hazor was such an important city, it would not allow its king to leave without appointing another one in his stead. — K.Y.

for tomorrow at this time, I will deliver them up all slain
before Israel. You shall cripple their horses, and burn their
chariots with fire." 7. And Joshua, and all the people of
war with him, came upon them by the waters of Merom
suddenly; and they fell upon them. 8. And the Lord delivered
them into the hand of Israel, and they smote them, and
chased them to great Zidon, and to Misrephoth-maim, and
to the valley of Mizpeh eastward; and they smote them until
they left them none remaining. 9. And Joshua did to them
as the Lord had bidden him; he crippled their horses, and
burnt their chariots with fire. 10. And Joshua turned back
at that time,

### Commentary Digest

6. *cripple their horses* — Heb. תעקר, cause the hoofs to be removed from below the knees so that the horses can no longer be used in battle.[1] Although this would seem wanton destruction and unnecessary pain for a living creature, it is permissible as an instrument of battle. The Israelites were taught through this tactic in order not to depend on their own strength in any future war, — G, K Other animals and spoils of war, useful for peaceful purposes, could be taken by the troops as booty, but not those specifically used for war. The Torah[2] forbids a king to amass three things: Horses, wives, and silver and gold. The last mentioned, refers only to the levying of heavy taxes on the populace for the purpose of enriching the royal coffers, but not to spoils of war, which are permitted in any amount.[3] Horses, however, since they are used specifically for war, are not permitted in any manner, and must be destroyed in the manner prescribed.

8. *great Zidon* — to distinguish it from the lesser Zidon. — K

*Misrephoth-maim* — "*J renders: Ditches of the sea, for they would make ditches, into which the sea water would flow and burn up* (evaporate) *from the heat of the sun, and become salt.*" — R

9. *And Joshua did to them as the Lord had bidden him* — Joshua did to the kings all that the Lord had bidden him, while they were still alive. He allowed them to witness the futility of their armaments and their military equipment. — K. Y.

10. *And Joshua turned back at that time* — I.e. Joshua hastened at that time to take Hazor before they re-

וַיִּלְכֹּד אֶת־חָצוֹר וְאֶת־מַלְכָּהּ הִכָּה בֶחָרֶב כִּי־חָצוֹר לְפָנִים הִיא רֹאשׁ כָּל־הַמַּמְלָכוֹת הָאֵלֶּה׃ יא וַיַּכּוּ אֶת־כָּל־הַנֶּפֶשׁ אֲשֶׁר־בָּהּ לְפִי־חֶרֶב הַחֲרֵם לֹא נוֹתַר כָּל־נְשָׁמָה וְאֶת־חָצוֹר שָׂרַף בָּאֵשׁ׃ יב וְאֶת־כָּל־עָרֵי הַמְּלָכִים הָאֵלֶּה וְאֶת־כָּל־מַלְכֵיהֶם לָכַד יְהוֹשֻׁעַ וַיַּכֵּם לְפִי־חֶרֶב הֶחֱרִים אוֹתָם כַּאֲשֶׁר צִוָּה מֹשֶׁה עֶבֶד יְהוָה׃ יג רַק כָּל־הֶעָרִים הָעֹמְדוֹת עַל־תִּלָּם לֹא־שְׂרָפָם יִשְׂרָאֵל זוּלָתִי אֶת־חָצוֹר לְבַדָּהּ שָׂרַף יְהוֹשֻׁעַ׃ יד וְכֹל שְׁלַל הֶעָרִים הָאֵלֶּה וְהַבְּהֵמָה

וּכְבַשׁ יָת חָצוֹר וְיָת מַלְכַּהּ קְטַל בְּחַרְבָּא אֲרֵי חָצוֹר מִלְקַדְמִין הִיא רֵישׁ כָּל מַלְכְּוָתָא הָאִלֵּין׃ יא וּמְחוֹ יָת כָּל נַפְשָׁתָא דִּי בַהּ לְפִתְגָּם דְּחָרֶב גְּמִירָא לָא אִשְׁתְּאַר כָּל נִשְׁמָא וְיָת חָצוֹר אוֹקֵד בְּנוּרָא׃ יב וְיָת כָּל קִרְוֵי מַלְכַיָּא הָאִלֵּין וְיָת כָּל מַלְכֵּיהוֹן כְּבַשׁ יְהוֹשֻׁעַ וּמְחָנוּן לְפִתְגָּם דְּחָרֶב גַּמַּר יָתְהוֹן כְּמָא דְּפַקֵּיד מֹשֶׁה עַבְדָּא דַיְיָ׃ יג לְחוֹד כָּל קִרְוַיָּא דְּקַיְמִין עַל תּוּקְפֵיהוֹן לָא אוֹקְדִינוּן יִשְׂרָאֵל אֱלָהֵין יָת חָצוֹר בִּלְחוֹדַהּ אוֹקֵיד יְהוֹשֻׁעַ׃ יד וְכָל עֲדֵי קִרְוַיָּא הָאִלֵּין וּבְעִירָא בַּזּוּ לְהוֹן בְּנֵי יִשְׂרָאֵל לְחוֹד יָת כָּל אנשא

ת״א זוה משה. יבמות לו סנהדרין מד (פלה טו שקלים מב):

**רש״י**

(יג) העמדות על תלם. שלא נהרסה חומתם כמו ירידו שנפל' חומת' וכן העי שנאמר בה וישימה תל עולם שממה: זולתי את חצור לבדה. במסורת שרפה משה לוה ומסר לו כן בבראשית רבה בויצלה יעקב:

**רד״ק** **בזוז**

ישראל להם הסוסים והמרכבות כדי שלא יבטחו בהם גם הם ויחשבו בלבם כי עם הסוסים יעשו המלחמות לפיכך צוה יהושע לעקר הסוסים ולשרוף המרכבות ולא צוה להמית הסוסים כי לא היה דבר שאסור בהנאה ושאר הבהמות שהיה בהם כמו רכב חמור רכב גמל לא צוה לעקור אלא שיקחום לצרכם אבל הסוסים שאינם אלא למלחמה אותם צוה לעקור כדי שלא יקחום ויבטחו בהם ולא אמר להרגם דרך השחתה כי אסור להשחית הנבראים אם לא לצורך או לאסור בהנאה והעיקור הוא לנשר פרסות הבהמה מן הארכובה ולמטה ולא תמות הבהמה בזה הדבר אלא שלא תוכל ללכת ואם תמצא מרעה במקומה תחיה: (יג) על תלם. ת״י תקפיהון כלומר שהיו עומדות בחזקתם שלא הפילו חומותיהם בלכדם אותם ולא שרפם זולתי חצור לפי שהיתה ראש הממלכות ויפחדו הנשארים ובדרש כי משה מסר לו שישרוף חצור ועל פיו עשה יהושע ששרף חצור וכן אמרו ר׳

**רלב״ג**

זאת המלחמה והנה כל העם אשר בה לא השאיר כל נשמה ואת כל ערי המלכים האלה ואת כל מלכיהם כלם לכד יהושע ויכה האדם

**מנחת שי**

(יב) ואת כל ערי. הוא״ו בגעיא בס״ס: המלכים האלה. בספרים כ״י מדוייקים הלמד במאריך וכן הוא לב״א: ואת כל מלכיהם. הוא״ו בגעיא בס״ס:

**מצודת דוד**

סורפקן ונעשים מלח: (י) כי חצור וגו׳. ולזה פתח בה תחלה: (יג) על תלם. ר״ל בגבהם שלא נפלו חומותיהם בעת הכבוש:

**מצודת ציון**

ומשפטו תסיר הסובב ממקומו ור״ל שיכרות הרגלים שהם העיקר והיסוד לבהמה: (י) לפנים. בימים הקדמונים: (יג) תלם.

## Commentary Digest

all those cities that remained in their places and did not wage war with the Jews, Israel did not burn, save Hazor only, which was the place the foes assembled to wage war against Israel. — Maharzav.

The Midrash continues: R. Eleazar said: Because of a tradition he burnt it. The Holy One Blessed be He said to Moses, and Moses said to Joshua. The Midrash explains the change in the wording: *did Joshua burn,* rather than *did Israel burn,* as in the earlier part of the verse. Israel was reluctant to burn Hazor. Only Joshua, in observing the tradition from Moses, with which he was charged, burnt it — Maharzav and K. Y. K. and A see it as a deterrent to any future coalition against Israel. Since Hazor was the leader of this coalition, it was singled out for total destruction. Az. suggests that refugees from all the allied cities were hidden in Hazor. Therefore, it was burned.

and took Hazor, and smote its king with the sword, for Hazor
was formerly the head of all these kingdoms. 11. And they
smote all the souls that were therein with the edge of the
sword, utterly destroying them; there was not a soul left.
And he burnt Hazor with fire. 12. And all the cities of
these kings, and all their kings, Joshua took, and smote them
with the edge of the sword, and he utterly destroyed them,
as Moses the servant of the Lord had commanded. 13. But
all the cities that stood in their strength, Israel burned
none of them, save Hazor only, did Joshua burn. 14. And all
the spoil of these ctites, and the cattle,

**Commentary Digest**

11. *And they smote all the souls* — Heb. הנפש, i.e. the living beings, meaning the animals.

*there was not a soul left* — Heb. נשמה, i.e. a human being. Jewish thought differentiates between the soul of a human being and that of an animal.[1] This difference finds expression in the two Hebrew words: נפש, נשמה.

13. *that stood in their strength* — J. *"whose walls were not destroyed, like Jericho, whose walls fell, and so Ai, concerning which it is stated:[2] "And made it a heap forever, a desolation.""* — R and K. D and Z renders: that stood at their height, explaining in like manner.

*save Hazor only* — *"because of a tradition he burned it. Moses commanded and transmitted it to him.* — *In G.R., in the portion entitled: And Jacob sent."*[3] — R. The Midrash reads as follows: Said R. Samuel, In three places the gentiles assembled to wage war against Jacob's children; but the Holy One Blessed be He did not allow them to do so: (1) In the time of Jacob, *And a fear inspired by God was on the cities that were around them;* (2) in the days of Jonathan, *And became a trembling inspired by God;* (3) in the days of Joshua, they attempted to pursue but the Holy One Blessed be He did not allow them. Now, where did they gather? To Hazor, as it is written: *But all the cities that stood on their hill, Israel burned none of them, save Hazor only, did Joshua burn.* Rabbi Samuel takes this verse to mean that

בָּזְזוּ לָהֶם בְּנֵי יִשְׂרָאֵל רַק אֶת־כָּל־
הָאָדָם הִכּוּ לְפִי־חֶרֶב עַד־הִשְׁמִדָם
אוֹתָם לֹא הִשְׁאִירוּ כָּל־נְשָׁמָה: טו כַּאֲשֶׁר
צִוָּה יְהוָה אֶת־מֹשֶׁה עַבְדּוֹ כֵּן־צִוָּה
מֹשֶׁה אֶת־יְהוֹשֻׁעַ וְכֵן עָשָׂה יְהוֹשֻׁעַ לֹא־
הֵסִיר דָּבָר מִכֹּל אֲשֶׁר־צִוָּה יְהוָה אֶת־
מֹשֶׁה: טז וַיִּקַּח יְהוֹשֻׁעַ אֶת־כָּל־הָאָרֶץ
הַזֹּאת הָהָר וְאֶת־כָּל־הַנֶּגֶב וְאֵת כָּל־
אֶרֶץ הַגֹּשֶׁן וְאֶת־הַשְּׁפֵלָה וְאֶת־הָעֲרָבָה
וְאֶת־הַר יִשְׂרָאֵל וּשְׁפֵלָתֹה: יז מִן־הָהָר
הֶחָלָק הָעוֹלֶה שֵׂעִיר וְעַד־בַּעַל גָּד
בְּבִקְעַת הַלְּבָנוֹן תַּחַת הַר־חֶרְמוֹן וְאֵת

אֱנָשָׁא מְחוֹ לְפִתְגָם
דְּחָרֶב עַד דִּי שֵׁיצִיאוּ
יַתְהוֹן לָא אַשְׁאָרוּ כָּל
נִשְׁמָא: טו כְּמָא דְּפַקִּיד
יְיָ יַת מֹשֶׁה עַבְדֵּיהּ כֵּן
פַּקֵּד מֹשֶׁה יַת יְהוֹשֻׁעַ
וְכֵן עֲבַד יְהוֹשֻׁעַ לָא
בַטֵּיל פִּתְגָמָא מִכָּל
דְּפַקִּיד יְיָ יַת מֹשֶׁה:
טז וְאַחְסֵין יְהוֹשֻׁעַ יַת כָּל
אַרְעָא הָדָא טוּרָא וְיַת
כָּל דָּרוֹמָא וְיַת כָּל
אַרְעָא דְגוֹשֶׁן וְיַת
שְׁפֶלְתָּא וְיַת מֵישְׁרָא
וְיַת טוּרָא דְיִשְׂרָאֵל
וּשְׁפֶלְתֵיהּ: יז מִן טוּרָא
פְּלִיגָא דְּסָלִיק לְשֵׂעִיר
וְעַד מֵישַׁר גָּד בְּבִקְעַת
לִבְנָן שְׁפוֹלֵי טוּרָא
דְחֶרְמוֹן וְיַת כָּל מַלְכֵיהוֹן
כְּבַשׁ וּמְחָנוּן וְקַטְלִינוּן:
יומן

ושפלתו קרי

**רד"ק**

אליעזר אומר במסרה שרפה הקב"ה אמר למשה ומשה אמר ליהושע ועוד אמרו בקשו לרדוף ולא הניחם הקב"ה והיכן נתכנסו בחצור לפיכך שרפה וזה אחד משלשה מקומות שנתכנסו אומות העולם לעשות מלחמה עם בני יעקב ולא הניחם הקב"ה: (טז) ארץ הגשן. אין זה גושן של מצרים ובדרש אומר כי היה גשן של ארץ מצרים והוא נבלעת בתוך ערי ישראל כמו שאמר ויעל לקראת אביו גושנה מלמד שהיא בעליה כלפי ארץ ישראל ובזכות שהלך יהודה בשליחות אביו להורות לפניו זכה שיהיה לחלקו ארץ גשן שהיא טובה: ואת הר ישראל ושפלתה. ה"א במקום וי"ו כה"א אהלה ופירושו הר יעקב אבינו ששכן שם והוא נקרא על שמו: (יז) מן ההר החלק. ת"י טורא פליגא כלומר שהיה נחלק חציו הנה וחציו

כל

**רש"י**

(יז) ההר החלק. טורא שעיע מחליק ההר החלק עד בעל גד מצר המזרחי ולא הספיק לכבוש בחייו את כל המצר עד הצפון. תוספתא: בעל גד מישר גד:

**מנחת שי**

(טז) ושפלתה. ושפלתו קרי:

**רלב"ג**

אשר בהם לפי חרב עד השמידם אותם לא השאירו כל נשמה:

**מצודת ציון**

מל' הר וגובה: (יז) בעל. תרגומו מישר:

**מצודת דוד**

(טז) ואת הר ישראל. אשר ישב בו ישראל אבינו ונקרא על שמו: (יז) ההר החלק. בסיס נחלק לבנים אחת הנה ואחת הנה: העולה. אשר עולה עד בשעיר:

## Commentary Digest

17. *From the smooth mount* — "טורא שעיע"[4] *smooth. The smooth mount to Baal-Gad on the eastern border, and he was unable to conquer the entire border to the north, during his lifetime."* — Addendum to R. This mountain was devoid of any vegetation, hence it was called: "the smooth

the children of Israel took for a prey to themselves; but every man they smote with the edge of the sword, until they destroyed them, they did not leave over a soul. 15. As the Lord commanded Moses His servant, so did Moses command Joshua, and so did Joshua; he left nothing undone of all that the Lord commanded Moses. 16. And Joshua took all this land: the hills, and all the south country, and all the land of Goshen, and the valley, and the plain, and the mountain of Israel, and its valley: 17. From the divided smooth mount that goes up to Seir, to Baal-gad in the valley of Lebanon under mount Hermon; and

## Commentary Digest

15. *As the Lord commanded Moses ... so did Joshua* — Scripture records here that this seeming cruelty on Joshua's part was actually the fulfillment of a divine command. Compassion here would have been out of place. Compare the Biblical promise after the annihilation of עיר הנדחת (a completely idolatrous community)[1]: "And He will give you mercy and will have mercy upon you." He who attempts to be more compassionate than his Creator, will eventually bring evil upon himself and his posterity. Our sages stated very appropriately:[2] "He who is compassionate to the cruel will eventually be cruel to the compassionate. Doeg the Edomite who advised Saul to spare Agag, king of Amalek, later slew Nob the priestly city." Similarly, Saul, who was a party to sparing Agag, later pursued David in a deadly chase. Furthermore, Saul's compassion resulted in the rise of Haman, a descendant of Agag, who threatened the very existence of the Jewish people.

16. *and all the land of Goshen* — According to the Midrash,[3] this is identified with the land of Goshen, which was settled by the Jews upon entering Egypt, and was in the northeast corner of that country, adjacent to the Holy Land. This was within the territory of Judah, appropriately, as a reward for his seeking it out as a settling place for his aged father Jacob, upon his arrival in Egypt. — K. P rejects the literal interpretation of this Midrash, explaining that since Judah sought out Goshen of Egypt to settle his father's household, his tribe was rewarded with Goshen of the Holy Land, a choice territory—bearing the same name.

כָּל־מַלְכֵיהֶם לָכַד וַיַּכֵּם וַיְמִיתֵם: יח יָמִים
רַבִּים עָשָׂה יְהוֹשֻׁעַ אֶת־כָּל־הַמְּלָכִים
הָאֵלֶּה מִלְחָמָה: יט לֹא־הָיְתָה עִיר
אֲשֶׁר הִשְׁלִימָה אֶל־בְּנֵי יִשְׂרָאֵל בִּלְתִּי
הַחִוִּי יֹשְׁבֵי גִבְעוֹן אֶת־הַכֹּל לָקְחוּ
בַמִּלְחָמָה: כ כִּי מֵאֵת יְהוָה ׀ הָיְתָה
לְחַזֵּק אֶת־לִבָּם לִקְרַאת הַמִּלְחָמָה
אֶת־יִשְׂרָאֵל לְמַעַן הַחֲרִימָם לְבִלְתִּי
הֱיוֹת לָהֶם תְּחִנָּה כִּי לְמַעַן הַשְׁמִידָם

**תרגום**

יח יומין סגיאין עבד
יהושע ית כל מלכיא
האלין קרבא: יט לא
הות קרתא דאשלימת
עם בני ישראל אלהן
חואה יתבי גבעון ית
כולא נסיבו בקרבא:
כ ארי מן קדם יי הות
לתקפא ית לבהון
לסדרא קרבא עם ישראל
בדיל לגמרותהון בדיל
דלא למהוי להון רחמין
ארי בדיל לשציותהון
כמא דפקד יי ית משה:

ואתא

**תולדות אהרן** כי מאת ה'. עקדה שער לו:

**רש"י**

(יח) **ימים רבים עשה יהושע**. בגנותו ספר הכתוב שהיה מתכוין לדחות את כבוש הארץ כדי להאריך ימיו לפי שנאמר ואתה תנחילנה אותם. במדרש תנחומא:

**רד"ק**

כאשר הנה וי"מ כמו אנכי איש חלק כלומר שלא חיו בה אילנות: בעל גד. כתרגומו מישר גד: (יח) ימים רבים. ולמעלה אמר לכד יהושע פעם אחת ר"ל כי כל המלכים ההם שזכר לכד בפעם אחת בלי הפסק קודם ששבו אל חמחנה הגלגלה ואחר כך עשה מלחמה ימים רבים עם שאר מלכי הארץ עד שלקח הכל ויש בו דרש שנענש יהושע על שנתעצל במלחמת המלכים כמו שנאמר ימים רבים שהרי א"ל הקב"ה כאשר הייתי עם משה אהיה עמך ולמה חסרו משנותיו י' שנים אלא אמר יהושע אם אני מנחיל הארץ במהרה לישראל ועושה להם המלחמות מיד אמות אמר הקב"ה לא כך עשה משה רבך כשאמרתי לו נקום נקמת בני ישראל מאת המדינים אחר תאסף אל עמך מיד וידבר משה אל העם החלצו ואתה עלה בלבך כך הנני מחסר משנותיך אמר דוד עליו השלום רבות מחשבות בלב איש ועצת ה' הוא תקום: (כ) לחזק את לבם. זה היה לשתי סבות האחת שהיה זה עונש עונם כמו בפרעה ויחזק ה' את לב פרעה והשנית כמו שאומר הטעם כי למען השמידם כאשר צוה ה' את משה כמו שכתוב כי

**רלב"ג**

(יח) וזכר כי ימים רבים עשה יהושע מלחמה את כל המלכים האלה וזה לאות שכבר נתעלל יהושע בענין זאת המלחמה ובראשונה היה משתדל בזריזות ולזה אמרו רז"ל שכבר עשה זה כדי להאריך חייו כי כבר ייעדו השם כי הוא ינחיל לישראל את הארץ: וזכר שלא היתה עיר אשר השלימה את בני ישראל בלתי החוי יושבי גבעון שהשלימו עמהם בערמה כמו שזכר וזה מורה כי אפילו משבעה עממים אם השלימו עם ישראל היה מחוייב להם שלא יהרגום אבל יקבלו על עצמם להיות להם למס ועבדום ולזה הוא מבואר כי מ"ש בפ' שופטים כי תקרב אל עיר להלחם עליה לתפשה הוא כלל לכל עיר היה או מאחיה משבעה עממין או מזולתם ואולם ההבדל בזה בין שבעה עממין ובין זולתם הוא שאם לא ישלימו והיו משבעה עממין יתחייב להם שלא יחיו כל נשמה ואם יהיו מזולתם יחיו להם הנשים

**מצודת דוד**

(כ) **לבלתי היות להם תחנה**. מן בני ישראל: **כי למען**

**מצודת ציון**

(כ) **תחנה**. חנינה ורחמים:

all their kings he took, and smote them, and put them to
death. 18. Joshua made war a long time with all these kings.
19. There was not a city that made peace with the children
of Israel, save the Hivites, the inhabitants of Gibeon; they
took all in battle. 20. For it was from the Lord to harden
their hearts, (that they should come) against Israel in battle,
that they might destroy them completely, and that they might
have no favor, that they might destroy them

## Commentary Digest

mount." J renders: From the divided mount. It sloped evenly in both directions, one slope toward Eretz Israel and one toward Seir. — K

*Baal-gad — "the plain of Gad."* — R, K, and Z from J

In Chapter X:41, the southern boundary is described; here the eastern boundary.

18. *Joshua made war a long time with all these kings* — in contrast with the kings of the southern sector of Eretz Israel, whom he conquered "at one time."[1] — K *"This sentence is a rebuke to Joshua, for he intended to delay the conquest of the Land in order to lengthen his lifespan, for it was stated: [2]"And you shall cause them to inherit it.""* — Mid. T.[3] — R The Rabbis contrast Joshua to his master Moses, who executed his communal duties even at the expense of his very life. When the Almighty enjoined him: "Take revenge for the children of Israel from the Midianites; thereafter you will be gathered to your people,"[4] he performed his duty immediately, although he might have delayed this war, and thereby have lengthened his lifespan. Joshua, on the contrary, sought to lengthen his lifespan by extending the period of the wars, and not devoting his full energy to their immediate and successful conclusion. For this, his lifespan, which should have equalled Moses' one hundred and twenty years, was shortened to one hundred and ten years. — K[4*]

20. *to harden their hearts* — I.e. they were unable to make peace with Israel, God having deprived them of the power of choice, just as He had done to Pharaoh in the days of Moses. ("And the Lord strengthened the heart of Pharaoh."[4**]) The Jews were

כַּאֲשֶׁר צִוָּה יְהוָה אֶת־מֹשֶׁה׃ כא וַיָּבֹא
יְהוֹשֻׁעַ בָּעֵת הַהִיא וַיַּכְרֵת אֶת־הָעֲנָקִים
מִן־הָהָר מִן־חֶבְרוֹן מִן־דְּבִר מִן־עֲנָב
וּמִכֹּל הַר יְהוּדָה וּמִכֹּל הַר יִשְׂרָאֵל עִם־
עָרֵיהֶם הֶחֱרִימָם יְהוֹשֻׁעַ׃ כב לֹא־נוֹתַר
עֲנָקִים בְּאֶרֶץ בְּנֵי יִשְׂרָאֵל רַק בְּעַזָּה בְּגַת
וּבְאַשְׁדּוֹד נִשְׁאָרוּ׃ כג וַיִּקַּח יְהוֹשֻׁעַ אֶת־

**תרגום**

כא וַאֲתָא יְהוֹשֻׁעַ בְּעִדָּנָא
הַהִיא וְשֵׁיצֵי יָת גִּבָּרַיָּא
מִן טוּרָא מִן חֶבְרוֹן מִן
דְּבִיר מִן עֲנָב וּמִכֹּל
טוּרָא דִיהוּדָה וּמִכֹּל
טוּרָא דְיִשְׂרָאֵל עִם
קִרְוֵיהוֹן גַּמְרִינוּן יְהוֹשֻׁעַ׃
כב לָא אִשְׁתְּאַר גִּבָּרַיָּא
בַּאֲרַע בְּנֵי יִשְׂרָאֵל לְחוֹד
בְּעַזָּה בְּגַת וּבְאַשְׁדּוֹד
אִשְׁתְּאָרוּ׃ כג וּנְסֵיב
יְהוֹשֻׁעַ יָת כָּל אַרְעָא
כְּכֹל דִּי מַלֵּיל יְיָ עִם
משה

## רד"ק

אתן בידכם את כל יושבי הארץ וגו׳. ואמר פן יחטיאו אותך לי: להם תחנה. כמו חנינה ורחמנות: (כא) ויכרת את הענק׳. ולמעלה הוא אומר כי כלב הורישם כלב עשה במצות יהושע שנתן לו את ההר ועוד יראה בספ׳ שופטים כי אחרי מות יהושע הורישום בני יהודה והאמת כי בחיי יהושע הורישו ישראל חברון והענקים אשר בהר חברון הכל הכריתו ומה שאמר כי כלב הורישם לפי שנתן לו יהושע חברון על פי ה׳ נקראת המלחמה על שמו ועל שם שבטו שהוא שבט יהודה והם השתדלו יותר במלחמה ההיא ופי׳ וילך יהודה אל הכנעני היושב בחברון שנאמר בספר שופטים וכבר הלך אבל ספר אותו שם עם מה שכבשו אחרי מות יהושע וכן וילחמו בני יהודה בירושלם פירושו וכבר נלחמו כי מלך ירושלם הוא

כל

בחשבון ל״א מלכים שהכה יהושע ובני ישראל: הר יהודה. נקרא כן ע״ש סופו כי קודם שלקחו אותו לא היה נקרא כן: הר ישראל. כמו שפירשנו למעלה: (כב) רק בעזה. ומה שאמר בספר שופטים וילכד יהודה עזה ואת גבולה וגו׳ אחרי מות יהושע היה זה אבל בחיי יהושע הם הכריתו הענקים מן חברון ומן אלה המקומות שזכר ונשארו בעזה ובשאר ערי פלשתים עד שלכדם אחר כן יהודה: (כג) והארץ שקטה ממלחמה. שלא התעוררו עוד הכנענים להאסף ולהלחם עם ישראל כי ראו כי נפלו לפניהם בכל המלחמות וגם ישראל עמדו באותה הארץ שכבשו ולא התעוררו לכבוש עוד וכשזקן יהושע אמר לו האל יתברך שיזרז ישראל לכבוש הארץ הנשא׳ ואמר ליהושע שיחלק אותה בחייו והתחיל בשני השבטים

## רלב"ג

והסוף:(כא) עוד זכר שכבר הכרי׳ יהושע הענקי׳ וכו׳ והנה נזכר במה שיבא כי כלב בן יפונה הכרית הענקי׳ מחברון ועתניאל בן קנז לכד דביר וזה בלתי סותר למה שכתבנו כי הכל היה מייחס ליהושע כי הוא היה הראש המנהיג אותם בזה: (כג) והנה נזכר אחר זה כי כבר נשאר הרבה עדין מן הארץ לרשתה אלא שעכ״ז כבר חלקה להם יהושע בנחלה לישראל לשבטיהם כמו שזכר אחר זה. וזכר עם זה שהארץ שקטה ממלחמה כי לא היו נלחמים עם ישראל ולא ישראל עמם ואע״פ שכבר נשאר הרבה מן הארץ לרשתה:

ואולם התועלות המגיעים מזה הספור הם אלו:

התועלת הראשון במדות והוא מה שזכר מענין המזבח הר עיבל ומה שנלוה בזה ממה שנצטוו לעשות

שם כמו שזכר בפרשת כי תבא והנה התועלת בזו המצוה היא להוסיף אזהרה לישראל בענין שמירת התורה ולזה נכתבה שם ובאה שם הברכה למול הר גריזים למי שיקימה והקללה למול הר עיבל למי שיסור ממנה כי בזה היכרה אל בתדבק בשלמות ההשגחה האלהית בית׳ ויהיו מפני זה יותר ראוים לירושת הארץ: והשני במדות והוא שראוי לאדם להתישב בדברים שיעשה אותם שלא למהר בעשייתם בזולת עצה ואע״פ שכבר יראה בתחלת המחשבה בהענין ההוא ראוי שיעשה הנה תראה מה שקרה לישראל

עם יושבי גבעון מפני שמהרו לכרות להם ברית טרם שאלו את פי ה׳ כי כבר השיגה להם הטעה אחר זה כי זה ממה שהביאם לעבור באופן מה ממה שצוה בתורה שלא להיות כל נשמה מהערים הקרובות אם לא מהערים הרחוקות אבל לא מערי הגוים האלה ר״ל מז׳ עממין: השלישי והוא במצות והוא כי השבועה אבל לפי הדין היתה שבועה כגון זאת לפי שהיתה שבועה בטעות עם שכבר היתה באופן מה לעבור על דברי תורה ראוי שתקויים עם מי שהיגו מהכבי אומותינו כדי שלא יהיה בם חלול השם ואולם הכבידו ענין עבודתם כמו שזכרנו לתת להם גמול מה על מרמתם: הרביעי והוא במדות והוא שראוי לאדון להשגיח על עבדיו ולהצילם מיד הקמים עליהם הלא תראה איך התנהג יהושע עם אנשי גבעון ואע״י שכבר רמו אותו לעזור להם כנגד ה׳ המלכים הרמים עליהם: החמישי הוא לפרסם ענין הנפלאות בעשה אז השם לישראל בזאת המלחמה עד שכבר המית מהם באבני הברד יותר ממה שהרגו ישראל בחרב ובתוך הזמן הקלר שהגביל יהושע כשלמה נקמת גוי אויביו להורות כי ה׳ נלחם לישראל ולפרסם זה המופת והפלאות זכרו לוה שישימו ה׳ המלכים תוך המערה ולשום אבנים גדולות על פי המערה להעיר כי לנהן ענין המלחמה הזאת לא רצו להמתין שיוליאו המלכים האלה משם אבל שמו הא

## מצודת ציון

(כא) הענקים. בני אדם גבהי הקומה:

## מצודת דוד

השמידם. כי חיזק לבבם למען השמידם: (כא) מן חברון. אף כי כלב הוריש הענקים מחברון ייחס הדבר אל יהושע לפי שבימיו הוריש וכל נצחון המלחמה יחשב אל המושל על הצבא:

as the Lord had commanded Moses. 21. And at that time,
Joshua came and cut off the 'Anakim from the mountains,
from Hebron, from Debir, from 'Anab, and from all the
mountains of Judah, and from all the mountains of Israel;
Joshua destroyed them completely with their cities. 22. There
was no 'Anakim left in the land of the children of Israel;
only in Gaza, in Gath, and in Ashdod, they remained.
23. And Joshua took

## Commentary Digest

left no alternative but to war against them, for coexistence with them was forbidden, as the Scripture states: "They shall not dwell in your land, lest, they cause you to sin."[1]

21. *the 'Anakim* — giants, men of enormous height.

*from Hebron, from Debir* — Although Caleb led the drive against Hebron,[1]* and Othniel conquered Debir,[2] these campaigns were under the overall leadership of Joshua. — K

G[3] maintains that the Debir mentioned in Judges, is distinct from this one.

*the mountains of Judah* — the mountains which were later known by this name. — K

22. *only in Gaza* — which was conquered by the tribe of Judah after Joshua's death.[4] — K

כל־הארץ ככל אשר דבר יהוה אל־
משה ויתנה יהושע לנחלה לישראל
כמחלקתם לשבטיהם והארץ שקטה
ממלחמה: יב א ואלה | מלכי הארץ
אשר הכו בני־ישראל וירשו את־
ארצם בעבר הירדן מזרחה השמש
מנחל ארנון עד־הר חרמון וכל־הערבה
מזרחה: ב סיחון מלך האמרי הישב
בחשבון משל מערוער אשר על־שפת־
נחל ארנון ותוך הנחל וחצי הגלעד
ועד יבק הנחל גבול בני עמון:
ג והערבה עד־ים כנרות מזרחה ועד

**תרגום**

משה ויהבה יהושע
לאחסנא לישראל
כפלגותיהון לשבטיהון
וארעא שדוכת
מלמעבד קרבא:
א ואלין מלכי ארעא
דמחו בני ישראל וירתו
ית ארעהון בעברא
דירדנא מדנח שמשא
מנחלא דארנון עד
טורא דחרמון וכל
מישרא מדינחא:
ב סיחון מלכא אמוראה
דיתיב בחשבון שליט
מערוער דעל כיף נחלא
דארנון וגו נחלא ופלגות
ארע גלעד ועד יובקא
נחלא תחומא דבני
עמון: ג ומישרא עד ים
גינוסר מדינחא ועד ימא
דמישרא ימא דמלחא
מדינחא

**רש"י**

יב (א) אשר הכו בני ישראל. בימי משה: (ב) ועד יבק הנחל. שהם גבול ארץ בני עמון סוף מצר ארץ בני עמון ומשם והלאה היו בני עמון מושלים:

**רד"ק**

ים שהם יהודה ויוסף כי נאמר לו ברוח הקדש שאלו ינחלו תחלה כי הם ראשי ישראל ואלה יעמדו על גבולי ארץ ישראל יהודה מדרום ויוסף מצפון והשבעה שבטים ביניהם וכיון שעלה גורל לאלו השבטים השנים וכבשו הגבולים חשבו כי כל הארץ נכבשת כי המערב הים הגדול גבולו והמזרח הירדן וים כנרת לפיכך נתעצלו לכבוש שבעה שבטים עד שבאו לשילה כי לא היו חוששין כיון שהיו הגבולים בידם והכנענים הנשארים היו ביניהם וכל ישראל היו להם ערים הרבה לשבת בארץ הנכבש' וכאשר באו לשילה אחר י"ד שנה משבאו לגלגל אמר להם יהושע שיכתבו הערים שבין יהודה ויוסף ויעשו מהם שבעה חלקים ואחר כך יטילו גורל ביניהן על פי הקלפי ועל פי ה' לז' השבטים:

**רלב"ג**

על פי המערה אבנים גדולות ונשארו שם אנשי' לשמרם בדרך שלא יאחרו ענין המלחמה הזאת וימהרו לרדוף אחר הנשארים קודם שיבואו אל עריהם בדרך שתבלם הנקמה תוך העת שהגביל יהושע: הששי והוא במדות שראוי לאדם בהיותו ביום טובה שישמח בו ר"ל שבאשר יראה היותו מצליח במה שעשה ראוי שימהר ויחיש מעשיו ולא ימתין לעשות מה שיוכל לעשות ביום אחד למחרת היום ההוא כי לא ידע מה ילד יום ולזה תמצא שספר איך עלה הענין ליהושע בהשתדלותו בזריזות בענין המלחמה עד שבכבר זכר שבפעם אחת נלח יהושע מלכים רבים ואת ארצם והם עשרים מלכים שנזכרו בענין הלא קודם מלך חצור ואחר זה כשהתרשל בזה לא נלח בימים רבים כי אם י"א מלכים שתמצא ממלך חצור עד סוף זכר המלכים ההם ולו השתדל בזה יהושע בזריזות אולי היה מכלה כל הגוים האלה אשר הוא בכוף הענין לישראל לפח ולמוקש: (א) ואלה מלכי הארץ עד סוף הספר. זכר התלה מה שנעשה ע"י

**מנחת שי**

יב (א) וירשו. חסר יו"ד ע"פ המסורת והרד"ק במכלול עיין מ"ש (במלכים ב' י"ז): (ג) עד ים כנרות. עיין מ"ש לעיל סימן י"א:

**מצודת דוד**

(כג) במחלקתם. כפי המחלוקת האמורה למטה: לשבטיהם. לכל שבט ושבט חלק לבד: יב (ב) יבק הנחל. שם מקום סמוך להנחל והיה מגבול בני עמון: (ג) והערבה. גם היא היתה ממשלת סיחון:

**מצודת ציון**

(כג) שקטה. נחה כמו הארץ יראה ושקטה (תהלים ע"ו):

## Commentary Digest

Holy Land. See Deut. III:13: "To all of the Bashan, to that will be called "land of Rephaim," and R ad loc.

2. *Sihon king of the Amorites etc.* — The details of these conquests are related in Num. XXI:21-35, Deut. II:31-III:17.

*and the middle of the river* — I.e. 'Aroer was in the midst of the river. It was situated on an island in the middle of the River Arnon. — K. Y.

*and to the river Jabbok* — "For there was the border of the land of

the whole land, according to all that the Lord had spoken to Moses; and Joshua gave it for an inheritance to Israel according to their divisions by their tribes. And the land rested from war.

## 12

1. And these are the kings of the land, whom the children
of Israel smote, and possessed their land on the other side
of the Jordan toward the rising of the sun, from the river
Arnon to Mt. Hermon, and all the plain on the east:
2. Sihon king of the Amorites, who dwelt in Heshbon, and
ruled from 'Aroer, which is on the bank of the river Arnon,
and the middle of the river, and over half Gilead, and to the
river Jabbok, which is the border of the children of 'Ammon;
3. And the plain to the sea of Chinneroth on the east, and to

**Commentary Digest**

23. *according to their divisions by their tribes* — as is explained in the following chapters. — D

*And the land rested from war* — i.e. there was a sort of "peaceful coexistence" between Israel and the Canaanites, the former discontinuing their conquest of the remaining territory and leaving entire regions to the Canaanites, and the latter not assembling again to attempt to drive out the invading Israelites. See below XIII:1: "And Joshua was old, advanced in years...and there remains yet very much land to possess." — K

CHAPTER 12

1. *And these are the kings of the land whom the children of Israel smote* — *"in the times of Moses."* — R In verses 1-6, a summary is given of the war fought by Moses on the eastern bank of the Jordan, and the victory over Sihon and 'Og and the division of their land to the tribes of Reuben, Gad, and half of Manesseh From verse 7 onward, a recount is given of Joshua's battles against thirty-one kings. Equal importance is given to both conquests, for all of this is included in the boundaries of the

יָם הָעֲרָבָה יָם־הַמֶּלַח מִזְרָחָה דֶּרֶךְ
בֵּית הַיְשִׁמוֹת וּמִתֵּימָן תַּחַת אַשְׁדּוֹת
הַפִּסְגָּה: ד וּגְבוּל עוֹג מֶלֶךְ הַבָּשָׁן מִיֶּתֶר
הָרְפָאִים הַיּוֹשֵׁב בְּעַשְׁתָּרוֹת וּבְאֶדְרֶעִי:
ה וּמֹשֵׁל בְּהַר חֶרְמוֹן וּבְסַלְכָה וּבְכָל־
הַבָּשָׁן עַד־גְּבוּל הַגְּשׁוּרִי וְהַמַּעֲכָתִי וַחֲצִי
הַגִּלְעָד גְּבוּל סִיחוֹן מֶלֶךְ־חֶשְׁבּוֹן: ו מֹשֶׁה
עֶבֶד־יְהוָה וּבְנֵי יִשְׂרָאֵל הִכּוּם וַיִּתְּנָהּ
מֹשֶׁה עֶבֶד־יְהוָה יְרֻשָּׁה לָרֻאוּבֵנִי וְלַגָּדִי
וְלַחֲצִי שֵׁבֶט הַמְנַשֶּׁה: ז וְאֵלֶּה מַלְכֵי
הָאָרֶץ אֲשֶׁר הִכָּה יְהוֹשֻׁעַ וּבְנֵי יִשְׂרָאֵל
בעבר

**תרגום**

מַדִינְחָא אוֹרַח בֵּית
יְשִׁמוֹת וּמִדָרוֹמָא תְּחוֹת
מַשְׁפַּךְ מְרָמְתָא:
ד וּתְחוּם עוֹג מַלְכָּא
דְמַתְנָן מִשְּׁאַר גִּבָּרַיָא
דְיָתֵיב בְּעַשְׁתָּרוֹת
וּבְאֶדְרֶעִי: ה וְשַׁלִּיט
בְּטוּרָא דְחֶרְמוֹן וּבְסַלְכָה
וּבְכָל מַתְנָן עַד תְּחוּם
גְשׁוּרָאָה וְאַפְקִירוֹס
וּפַלְגוּת אֲרַע דְגִלְעָד
תְּחוּם סִיחוֹן מַלְכָּא
דְחֶשְׁבּוֹן: ו מֹשֶׁה עַבְדָא
דַיְיָ וּבְנֵי יִשְׂרָאֵל מְחוֹנוּן
וִיהָבַהּ מֹשֶׁה עַבְדָא דַיְיָ
יְרוּתָא לְשִׁבְטָא דְרְאוּבֵן
וּלְשִׁבְטָא דְגָד וּלְפַלְגוּת
שִׁבְטָא דִמְנַשֶּׁה: ז וְאִלֵּין
מַלְכֵי אַרְעָא דִי מְחָא
יְהוֹשֻׁעַ וּבְנֵי יִשְׂרָאֵל
בעברא

**רש"י**

(ה) וחצי הגלעד גבול סיחון. שם היה מיצר ממשלת סיחון כמ"ש למעלה שחצי הגלעד היה שלו וזה חצי השני של עוג:

**מנחת שי**

הישימות. יש מחלוקת בספרים ובמסורת ד' וסימניהון ויחנו על הירדן מבית (פרשת מסעי). והערבה עד ים הכלח. ובית פעור ואשדות סי' י"ג דסיפרא. הבני פתח את כתף מואב (יחזקאל כ"ה). סימן אורייתא הישמת כתיב. יהושע הישמות כתי' יחזקאל הישימות. כן מצאתי במסרה כ"י והובאה ג"כ במ"ג (פרשת מסעי) וביחזקאל סימן הנזכר ומ"ש שם ד' כתובין כן נראה שצריך למחוק דנוסחאות כ"י אינו והפשר לומר על צד הדוחק ד' כתובין כן בתי"ו לבסוף והם ד' האמורים א' של תורה וג' של נביאים והלא כאחריני דכתיבין הישימן במ"ן ועיין מ"ש (בפרשת מסעי): (ו) לראובני. הרי"ש במאריך ונקודתה שורק והאל"ף נתה כמ"ש פעמים רבות: ולחצי שבט הַמְנַשֶּׁה כל המנשה רפי: מלכי כנען ובני המן ארית ע"ג ארית ולבנה ע"ג לבנה כדאיתא בשילהי פ"ק דמגילה ונמ"ש בשירת הים ושירת האזינו ובירושלמי פ' בני העיר רבי זעירא ורבי ירמיה בשם רב שירת הים ושירת דבורה נכתבים ארית ע"ג לבינה ולבינה ע"ג ארית עשרת בני המן ומלכי כנען נכתבים ארית ע"ג ארית ולבינה ע"ג לבינה דכל בליין דכן לא קאים מאי כדון למצוה או לעיכוב א"ר יוסי בר"ח בר אחוי דרב הושעיה נחיר את כד הוינן קיימין קמי תנותה דרבי הושעיה חביבך עבר ר' בא בר זבדא ואהלון ליה ואמר בשם רב לעיכוב ע"כ. ועיין בהלכות סופרים שהביא בעל הלכות גדולות:

**רלב"ג**

משה מזאת המלחמה ואמר בזה תחלה אשר הכו בני ישראל והנה ראוי שייחס זה למשה עמהם כי על ידו נעשה ולזה זכר בסוף כי משה עבד ה' ובני ישראל עשו זה והנה לא הזכיר בזה תחילה שם משה להורות כי משה אעפ"י שגדלה מעלתו מאד הנה היה נלוחו אלה המלכים בזכות ישראל מצד ברית השם יתעלה כרות עם אבותיהם כמו שנזכר בתורה. ואחר זה זכר מלכי הארץ אשר הכה יהושע ובני ישראל בעבר הירדן ימה ושכבר נתנה יהושע לשבטי ישר' ירושה כמחלקות' לפי האופן הנזכר בתורה:

**מצודת ציון**

יב (ד) הרפאים. הענקים על שמרפים ידי רואיהם כי יפחדו מהם:

**מצודת דוד**

ומתימן. ומפאת הדרום משל תחת אשדות הפסגה: (ד) וגבול עוג וגו'. רלה לומר גם גבול עוג ירשו: (ה) גבול סיחון. אצל גבול סיחון כי חצי הגלעד השנית של סיחון היתה:

## Commentary Digest

children of Israel smote these two mighty kings and took their land, nevertheless . . . *and Moses the servant of the Lord gave it for an inheritance to the Reubenites* . . . I.e. this highly valued land he gave without hesitation to the two and a half tribes. This illustrates Moses' integrity. — K. Y.

He distributed it as a slave distributes his master's property, without any selfish interests in mind. Moreover, since Moses distributed it as an agent of the Lord, the division was final and uncontestable. — M. L.

the sea of the plain, the salt sea on the east, the way to
Beth-hajeshimoth, and from the south, under the falls of
Pisgah; 4. And the border of 'Og, king of Bashan, of the
remnant of the giants, who dwelt at Ashtaroth and at Edrei.
5. And reigned in Mt. Hermon, and in Salcah, and in all
Bashan, to the border of the Geshurites and the Maachathites,
and half Gilead, the border of Sihon, king of Heshbon.
6. Moses the servant of the Lord, and the children of Israel
smote them; and Moses the servant of the Lord gave it for
an inheritance to the Reubenites, and the Gadites, and the
half tribe of Manasseh. 7. And these are the kings of the
land whom Joshua and the children of Israel smote

## Commentary Digest

*the children of 'Ammon, the edge of the territory of the land of the children of 'Ammon, and from there on, the children of 'Ammon were ruling."* — R

*which is the border of the children of 'Ammon* — Scripture is illustrating the strength of Sihon's borders: On one side he ruled from 'Aroer, which was surrounded on all sides by water; on one side he was bounded by the kingdom of 'Og; on the other side he was bounded by the kingdom of the children of 'Ammon, which the children of Israel were admonished: Harass them not nor contend with them (Deut. 2:19) — K. Y.

Although 'Og was a remnant of the giants, nevertheless, the Israelites vanquished him and conquered his land. — M. L.

*who dwelt at Ashtaroth and at Edrei* — Although he dwelt in a stronghold, surrounded by mountains and boulders, they, nevertheless, vanquished him. — M. L.

3. *Pisgah* — a lofty mountain peak.

4. *And the border of 'Og* — i.e. they also possessed the land of 'Og. — D

*giants* — Heb. **רפאים**, related to **רפה**, (weak). Those who saw them became weak from fright. — Z

5. *and half Gilead, the border of Sihon* — "*There was the border of Sihon's realm, as it was stated above* (2) *that half of Gilead was his, and this second half was 'Og's.*" — R

6. *Moses the servant of the Lord, and the children of Israel smote them* — I.e. although Moses and all the

בְּעֵבֶר הַיַּרְדֵּן יָמָּה מִבַּעַל גָּד בְּבִקְעַת
הַלְּבָנוֹן וְעַד־הָהָר הֶחָלָק הָעֹלֶה
שֵׂעִירָה וַיִּתְּנָהּ יְהוֹשֻׁעַ לְשִׁבְטֵי יִשְׂרָאֵל
יְרֻשָּׁה כְּמַחְלְקֹתָם: ח בָּהָר וּבַשְּׁפֵלָה
וּבָעֲרָבָה וּבָאֲשֵׁדוֹת וּבַמִּדְבָּר וּבַנֶּגֶב
הַחִתִּי הָאֱמֹרִי וְהַכְּנַעֲנִי הַפְּרִזִּי הַחִוִּי
וְהַיְבוּסִי: ט מֶלֶךְ יְרִיחוֹ אֶחָד מֶלֶךְ הָעַי
אֲשֶׁר־מִצַּד בֵּית־אֵל אֶחָד: י מֶלֶךְ
יְרוּשָׁלַםִ אֶחָד מֶלֶךְ חֶבְרוֹן אֶחָד: יא מֶלֶךְ
יַרְמוּת אֶחָד מֶלֶךְ לָכִישׁ אֶחָד: יב מֶלֶךְ
עֶגְלוֹן אֶחָד מֶלֶךְ גֶּזֶר אֶחָד: יג מֶלֶךְ דְּבִר
אֶחָד מֶלֶךְ גֶּדֶר אֶחָד: יד מֶלֶךְ חָרְמָה
אֶחָד מֶלֶךְ עֲרָד אֶחָד: טו מֶלֶךְ לִבְנָה
אֶחָד מֶלֶךְ עֲדֻלָּם אֶחָד: טז מֶלֶךְ מַקֵּדָה

בְּעִבְרָא דְיַרְדְּנָא מֵעַרְבָא
מִמֵּישַׁר גָּד בְּבִקְעַת
לִבְנָן וְעַד טוּרָא פָּלְגָא
דְּסָלִיק לְשֵׂעִיר וַהֲבַהּ
יְהוֹשֻׁעַ לְשִׁבְטַיָּא יִשְׂרָאֵל
יָרוּתָא כְּפַלְגוּתְהוֹן
ח בְּטוּרָא וּבִשְׁפֶלְתָּא
וּבְמֵישְׁרָא וּבְמַשְׁפַּךְ
מַרְמָתָא וּבְמַדְבְּרָא
וּבִדְרוֹמָא חִתָּאֵי
וֶאֱמוֹרָאֵי וּכְנַעֲנָאֵי
וּפְרִזָאֵי וְחִוָּאֵי וִיבוּסָאֵי:
ט מַלְכָּא דִירִיחוֹ חַד
מַלְכָּא דְעַי דְּבִסְטַר בֵּית
אֵל חַד: י מַלְכָּא
דִירוּשְׁלֵם חַד מַלְכָּא
דְחֶבְרוֹן חַד: יא מַלְכָּא
דְיַרְמוּת חַד מַלְכָּא
דְלָכִישׁ חַד: יב מַלְכָּא
דְעֶגְלוֹן חַד מַלְכָּא דְגֶזֶר
חַד: יג מַלְכָּא דִרְבִיר חַד
מַלְכָּא דְגֶדֶר חַד:
יד מַלְכָּא דְחָרְמָה חַד
מַלְכָּא דַעֲרָד חַד:
טו מַלְכָּא דְלִבְנָא חַד
מַלְכָּא דַעֲדֻלָּם חַד:
טז מַלְכָּא דְמַקֵּדָה חַד
מַלְכָּא

רד״ק
אחר
(ט) מלך יריחו אחד . כל אלה שלשים ואחד מלכים שזוכר לא היה מלך על עיר אחת לבדה אלא כל עיר ועיר שזוכר
היתה ראש ממלכתו ר״ית מושל על עיירות וכפרים אחרים :

מצודת דוד
(ט) מלך יריחו אחד . מוסב על המקרא שלפני פניו זאלה מלכי הארץ וגו' מלך יריחו וגו' :

## Commentary Digest

was sufficiently powerful to have captured seventy sovereign rulers, still did not merit being included among the thirty-one kings of Canaan.[2] Although **Joshua** had not yet conquered all the regions mentioned, their kings had already committed their forces in the war, and had been captured and slain.

9. — 24. — *one...one...one* — This is an allusion to the viceroy of each king. Hence, the total of all the potentates overcome by Joshua, was sixty-two.[1]

13. *the king of Geder, one* — A city near the coast, not far from Gaza. Its conquest was not mentioned because there was nothing unusual about it. — D. S.

14. *The king of Hormah, one* — a city in the south, not far from the Dead Sea. Its conquest, too, was not mentioned previously. — D. S.

*the king of 'Arad, one;* — a city in the south, near Hormah. Its king had attacked the Jews after Aaron's death (Num. 21:1). — D. S.

on this side of the Jordan on the west, from Baal-gad in the
valley of Lebanon, to the smooth divided mountain that goes up to
Seir; and Joshua gave it to the tribes of Israel for an inheritance,
according to their divisions; 8. In the mountains and valleys and
in the plains and in the falls, and in the wilderness, and in the south
country: the Hittites, the Amorites, and the Canaanites, the
Perizites, the Hivites, and the Jebusites: 9. The king of Jericho,
one; the king of Ai, which is next to Beth-el, one; 10. The king of
Jerusalem, one; the king of Hebron, one; 11. The king of Jarmuth,
one; the king of Lachish, one; 12. the king of 'Eglon, one; the king
of Gezer, one; 13. The king of Debir, one; the king of Geder, one;
14. The king of Hormah, one; the king of 'Arad, one; 15. The king
of Libnah, one; the king of 'Adulam, one; 16. The king of
Makkedah,

## Commentary Digest

7. *And these are the kings of the land whom Joshua and the children of Israel smote* — Although their conquests were many, there was still much of the land remaining to be conquered. — D. S.

8. *the Hittites* — Scripture begins listing the six nations from the north. —D. M.

9. *The king of Jericho, one;* — This follows v. 7: And these are the kings of the country which Joshua and the children of Israel smote. ... — D Each of these thirty-one kings mentioned was sovereign ruler, not only of the capital city listed, but also of the entire surrounding area. — K These kings were primarily rulers of states outside the borders of the Holy Land. Possession of territory in this land, however, was a status symbol, qualifying them for the upper echelon of royalty.[1] An idea of the power and wealth of each of these kings can be had from the following verse in Jud. I:6-7: "And Adoni-Bezek fled, and they pursued him and caught him... And Adoni-Bezek said, "Three score and ten kings... gathered food under my table." Adoni-Bezek, then, who

אֶחָ֑ד מֶ֥לֶךְ בֵּֽית־אֵ֖ל אֶחָֽד׃ יז מֶ֤לֶךְ תַּפּ֙וּחַ֙
אֶחָ֔ד מֶ֥לֶךְ חֵ֖פֶר אֶחָֽד׃ יח מֶ֤לֶךְ אֲפֵק֙ אֶחָ֔ד
מֶ֥לֶךְ לַשָּׁר֖וֹן אֶחָֽד׃ יט מֶ֤לֶךְ מָדוֹן֙ אֶחָ֔ד
מֶ֥לֶךְ חָצ֖וֹר אֶחָֽד׃ כ מֶ֨לֶךְ שִׁמְר֤וֹן מְראוֹן֙
אֶחָ֔ד מֶ֥לֶךְ אַכְשָׁ֖ף אֶחָֽד׃ כא מֶ֤לֶךְ תַּעְנַךְ֙
אֶחָ֔ד מֶ֥לֶךְ מְגִדּ֖וֹ אֶחָֽד׃ כב מֶ֤לֶךְ קֶ֙דֶשׁ֙
אֶחָ֔ד מֶֽלֶךְ־יָקְנְעָ֥ם לַכַּרְמֶ֖ל אֶחָֽד׃ כג מֶ֥לֶךְ
דּ֛וֹר לְנָפַ֥ת דּ֖וֹר אֶחָ֑ד מֶֽלֶךְ־גּוֹיִ֥ם לְגִלְגָּ֖ל
אֶחָֽד׃ כד מֶ֥לֶךְ תִּרְצָ֖ה אֶחָ֑ד כָּל־מְלָכִ֖ים
שְׁלֹשִׁ֥ים וְאֶחָֽד׃ יג א וִֽיהוֹשֻׁ֣עַ זָקֵ֔ן בָּ֖א
בַּיָּמִ֑ים וַיֹּ֨אמֶר יְהוָ֜ה אֵלָ֗יו אַתָּ֤ה זָקַ֙נְתָּה֙
בָּ֣אתָ בַיָּמִ֔ים וְהָאָ֛רֶץ נִשְׁאֲרָ֥ה הַרְבֵּֽה־

לא קרי א׳

מַלְכָּא דְבֵית אֵל חַד׃
יז מַלְכָּא דְתַפּוּחַ חַד
מַלְכָּא דְחֵפֶר חַד׃
יח מַלְכָּא דַאֲפֵק חַד
מַלְכָּא דְלַשָּׁרוֹן חַד׃
יט מַלְכָּא דְמָדוֹן חַד
מַלְכָּא דְחָצוֹר חַד׃
כ מַלְכָּא דְשִׁמְרוֹן מְרָאוֹן
חַד מַלְכָּא דְאַכְשָׁף חַד׃
כא מַלְכָּא דְתַעְנַךְ חַד
מַלְכָּא דִמְגִדּוֹ חַד׃
כב מַלְכָּא דְקֶדֶשׁ חַד
מַלְכָּא דְיָקְנְעָם לְכַרְמְלָא
חַד׃ כג מַלְכָּא דְדוֹר
לְפַלְכֵי דוֹר חַד מַלְכָּא
דְעַמְמִין לְגִלְגְּלָא חַד׃
כד מַלְכָּא דְתִרְצָה חַד
כָּל מַלְכַיָּא תְּלָתִין וְחַד׃
א וִיהוֹשֻׁעַ סִיב עָל בְּיוֹמִין
וַאֲמַר יְיָ לֵיהּ אַתְּ סְבַתָּא
עָלְתָא בְּיוֹמִין וְאַרְעָא
אִשְׁתְּאָרַת סַגִּיאָה
לחדא

### רש״י

(כג) לנפת דור · לפלכי דור : יג (א) והארץ נשארה הרבה מאד · ממה שאמרתי לאברהם נשארה לרשתה שלא נכבשה :

### מנחת שי

(כ) מלך שמרון מראון. חד מן מ״ח מלין דכתבין אל״ף באמצעות תיבותא ולא קריא : (כא) מלך תענך . במקצת ספרים כתיבת יך ובדפוסים ישנים העין בשו״א לבדו והעי״ן בפתח וכן ביהושע י״ז וב״ה ובשופטים כ״ה ובימ׳ ה׳ ומלכים א׳ ד׳) : יג (א) אתה זקנתה . ב׳ חד מלא וחד חסר וסימני אתה זקנתה באת בימים אתה זקנת ובניך לא הלכו בדרכיך (שמואל א ח) דיהושע מלא

### רלב״ג

(א) והנה זכר כי יהושע היה זקן בא בימים והארץ נשארה הרבה מאד לרשתה ולא יתכן לו מלד זקנותו להשלים המלחמה עם מלכים הנשארים וצוה מאת הש״י שיפילה לישראל בנחלה כאילו כבשוה כלם ר״ל לט׳ השבטים וחצי שבט מנשה כי הב׳ שבטים וחצי לקחו חלקם מעבר לירדן והולם לשבט הלוי לא נתן נחלה כמו שנאמר בתורה והולם נתנו ללוים בארץ ערים לשבת ומגרשיהם למקניהם וקנינם כמו שלוה הש״י את משה בתורה :

### מצודת ציון

(כג) לנפת דור . כמהו דור: גוים . מקום נקבצו שמה מכמה עו״ג וכן הדעל מלך גוים (בראשית י״ד) :

### מצודת דוד

(כב) מלך יקנעם לכרמל. יקנעם שם עיר המלוכה והיתה סמוכה לעיר כרמל והליה תתבד וכן מלך דור וגו׳ וכן מלך גוים וגו׳ : יג (א) זקן בא בימים . זקן יאמר לשון בני אדם המוחש הנראה באדם מלובן השער והקמטת הפנים ולפעמים מקדים לבא בלא עת ולזה פירש ואמר בא בימים כאומר הנה בא בזמנו לפי הימים : הרבה

## Commentary Digest

Contemporary exegetes, however, explain that this king ruled over the entire Sharon, on the coast of the Mediterranean between Dor and the Yarkon. — D. S.

15. *'Adulam* — in the south near Jarmuth. — D. S.

CHAPTER 13

1. *old, advanced in years.* — He appeared old, and was, indeed, advanced in years. — D. Joshua, at the time of Israel's entry into the Holy Land, was eighty-two.[1]

*there remains yet very much land* — *"of that which I promised to Abraham[2] remains to be possessed, for it has not been conquered."* — R. Only most of the southern and eastern boundaries were defined, and the backbone of Canaan's nations had been broken. Beyond that, much remained to be possessed, which would be impossible during Joshua's lifetime. — D

one; the king of Bethel, one; 17. The king of Tappuah,
one; the king of Hepher, one; 18. The king of Aphek, one;
the king of Lasharon, one; 19. The king of Madon, one;
the king of Hazor, one; 20. The king of Shimron-meron,
one; the king of Achshaph, one; 21. The king of Ta'nach,
one; the king of Megiddo, one; 22. The king of Kedesh,
one; the king of Jokne'am of Carmel, one; 23. The king of
Dor of the regions of Dor, one; the king of the nations of
Gilgal, one; 24. The king of Tirzah, one; all the kings
thirty-one.

## 13

1. Now Joshua was old, advanced in years; and the Lord said to him, "You are old and advanced in years, and there remains yet very much land

### Commentary Digest

17. *Tappuah* — in the center of the land, between Shiloh and Shechem. — D. S. It later was given to Ephraim, although it was within the boundary of Manasseh. The surrounding land, however, was given to Manasseh (17:8).

*Hepher* — We find a city called Gath-hepher in the inheritance of Zebulun (19:13). We find also a city called Hapharaim in the inheritance of Issachar (19:19). Hepher may be identical with one of these cities. The archaeologists, however, claim that it is identical with Tel Avshar, north of Kitutz Meazarot, in the valley known as Emek Hepher. — D. M.

18. *Aphek* — Neither the battle with Aphek nor the location of Aphek is described in Scripture. The general opinion of the archaeologists is that Aphek is near Sharon, near the Mediterranean. It is known as Tel Aphek, near the source of the Yarkon (presently called Rosh Ha'ayin). It is approximately 5 kilometers northeast of Petach Tikvah. It is possible, however, that this is the city of Aphek in the north of the land in the territory of Asher (19:30), or Aphekah near the Amorite border in Lebanon (13:4). — D. M.

*Lasharon* — According to Jonathan, the name of the city was Lasharon.

מְאֹד לְרִשְׁתָּהּ: ב זֹאת הָאָרֶץ הַנִּשְׁאֶרֶת
כָּל־גְּלִילוֹת הַפְּלִשְׁתִּים וְכָל־הַגְּשׁוּרִי:
ג מִן־הַשִּׁיחוֹר אֲשֶׁר עַל־פְּנֵי מִצְרַיִם וְעַד
גְּבוּל עֶקְרוֹן צָפוֹנָה לַכְּנַעֲנִי תֵּחָשֵׁב
חֲמֵשֶׁת ׀ סַרְנֵי פְלִשְׁתִּים הָעַזָּתִי
וְהָאַשְׁדּוֹדִי הָאֶשְׁקְלוֹנִי הַגִּתִּי וְהָעֶקְרוֹנִי
וְהָעַוִּים: ד מִתֵּימָן כָּל־אֶרֶץ הַכְּנַעֲנִי
וּמְעָרָה אֲשֶׁר לַצִּידֹנִים עַד־אֲפֵקָה עַד

תרגום

לְחָדָא לְמֵירְתַהּ: ב דָּא
אַרְעָא דְּאִשְׁתְּאָרַת כָּל
תְּחוּמֵי פְּלִשְׁתָּאֵי וְכָל
גְּשׁוּרָאֵי: ג מִן שִׁיחוֹר דִּי
עַל אַפֵּי מִצְרַיִם וְעַד
תְּחוּם עֶקְרוֹן צִפּוּנָא עַל
אַרְעָא כְנַעֲנָאֵי תִּתְמְנֵי
חַמְשָׁא טוּרָנֵי פְלִשְׁתָּאֵי
עַזָּתָאֵי וְאַשְׁדּוֹדָאֵי
אַשְׁקְלוֹנָאֵי גִּתָּאֵי
וְעֶקְרוֹנָאֵי וְעַוָּאֵי:
ד מִדָּרוֹמָא כָּל אַרְעָא
כְנַעֲנָאֵי וּמְעַרְתָּא דִּי
לְצִידוֹנָאָה עַד אֲפֵק עַד
תחום

ת״א חמשת סרני פלשתים. חולין ס:

רש״י

כגב׳: (ב) גלילות. הספר מרקא״ש בלע״ז (מרקא״ש בל״א גרענלען גרענץ לאנדשאפט): (ג) מן השיחור. הוא נילוס הוא נהר מצרים הוא סמוך לתחום מקצוע דרומית מערבית של ארץ ישראל כמו שאמר בואלה מסעי ולמדנו כאן שלא כיבש יהושע בחייו כל מצר הדרומי אלא ממדבר צין הוא ההר החלק העולה שעירה עד הנילוס הוא התחום עזה האמור למעל׳ מקדש ברנע עד עזה: ועד גבול עקרון צפונה. העקרוני יושב על הים ומתפשט לצד הצפון יותר מן האחרים: לכנעני תחשב. מארץ הכנעני שנתתי לאברהם הוא: חמשת סרני פלשתים וגו׳. הוא סוף גמר המצר עד הים הגדול שבמערב: העזתי והאשדודי וגו׳. ששה סרנים הוא מונה ומתחלה קראן חמשת אר״י אידוניקו שלהם ה׳ החשובים חמשה היו שהעוים אינו מונה מן הסרנים החשובים ועוד יש לפרש חמשת סרני פלשתים העזתי והאשדודי והאשקלוני והגתי והעקרוני הם חמשה ועוד נשאר לכבוש ארץ העוים שאינם מן הפלשתים: (ד) מתימן כל ארץ הכנעני. פסוק ראשון מונה מצד הדרומי ומן המזרח למערב וזה מונה את רוחב אותו המקצוע הנותר לכבש כמה הוא מן הדרום לצפון: מתימן כל ארץ הכנעני. מתימן זו ומעזה לצידונים עד אפיקה עד האמורי:

רד״ק גבול

(ב) גלילות. כמו גבול או כמו מחוז וכן גליל הגוים: (ג) מן השיחור. הוא נילוס נחל מצרים והוא למקצוע דרומית מערבית של ארץ ישראל שלא כבש יהושע כל מצר הדרומית אלא ממדבר צין הוא הר החלק העולה שעירה עד הנילוס הוא התום עזה האמור למעלה מקדש ברנע עד עזה: חמשת סרני פלשתים. הוא גמר המצר עד הים הגדול שבמערב וסרנים ענינם שרים: חמשת סרני. והעוים שזוכר בסוף הפסוק אינו ממנינם. ובדברי רבותינו ז״ל ששה סרנים הוא מונה ומתחלה קראם חמשה אמר ר׳ יוחנן אידונריקי שלהם חמשה פי׳ אידונריקי החשובים שבהם היו חמשה והעוים אינו מן הסרנים החשובים ועוד בדבריהם עוים מתימן באו וסמכו ענינו לפסוק הבא אחריו: (ד) מתימן. ולפי פשט הפ׳ מתימן פי׳ מדרום

מצודת דוד

מאד. ולא תוכל לכבוש הכל בחייך: (ג) לכנעני תחשב. והלא ארץ הכנעני נתתי לישראל: והעוים. המה לא מפלשתים:

מצודת ציון

יג (ב) גלילות. מחוזות: (ג) השיחור. שם הנהר: סרני. ענין שררה:

## Commentary Digest

4. *From the south, all the land of the Canaanites* — *"The preceding verse describes* (the region) *from the south side from east to west, and this verse describes the width of that region, which remained to conquer, how much it was from south to north."* (Thus we explain) — *From the south* — *"From the south, i.e. Mearah that belongs to the Sidonians, to Aphek, to the Amorites."*—R

Others explain thus: From the south, all the land of the Canaanites, to the north, Mearah that belongs to the Sidonians, to Aphek. From east to west, the areas extended as far as the border of the Amorites. — M.

to be possessed. 2. This is the land that yet remains: all the borders of the Philistines, and all of the Geshurites. 3. From the Shihor, which is before Egypt, to the borders of Ekron northward, which is counted to the Canaanites: the five lords of the Philistines: the Gazathites, and the Ashdodites, the Ashkelonites, the Gittites, and the 'Ekronites; also the 'Avim.
4. From the south, all the land of the Canaanites, and Mearah that belongs to the Sidonians, to Aphek, to

## Commentary Digest

2. *borders* — Heb. גלילות.*— R K and Z explain it as 'regions.'

3. *From the Shihor* — *"i.e. the Nile synonymous with the brook of Egypt. It adjoins the southwestern border of Eretz Israel, as is stated in* "ואלה *מסעי."*[1] *We learn here that in Joshua's lifetime, he did not conquer the entire southern border, except from the desert of Zin (which is the divided smooth mount that goes up to Seir)*[2] *to the Nile. This is the boundary of Gaza which is stated above: "From Kadesh-Barnea to Gaza."* "[3] — R and K. According to "Kaftor Vo-ferah" Chapter XI, this refers to Wadi-el-Arish.

*to the border of Ekron northward* — *"The 'Ekronites dwell by the sea and spread out farther northward than the others."* — R

*which is counted to the Canaanites* — *"i.e. It is a part of the land of Canaan which I gave to Abraham."* — R and D

*the five lords of the Philistines* — *"This is the end of the border to the Mediterranean Sea which is in the west."* — R and K

*the Gazathites, and the Ashdodites, etc.* — *"He enumerates six, yet in the beginning he calls them five. Said Rabbi Johanan:* (He counts) *their prominent ones. The prominent ones were five, for he does not count the 'Avim among the prominent lords.*[1] *We may also explain thus: The five lords of the Philistines: The Gazathites, and the Ashdodites, and the Ashkelonites, and the Gittites, and the 'Ekronites, these are the five. And there also remained to conquer, the land of the 'Avim who are not of the Philistines."* — R Others explain that the 'Avim were descended from Teman the son of Eliphaz the son of Esau. They abandoned their people and joined the Philistines in order to learn and practice their religion.[2] Still others explain the words: "and the 'Avim" as connected to the following verse, thus explaining: "And the 'Avim from the south," not from the Philistines.[3]

---

* *marche in O. F.*

גבול האמרי: ה והארץ הגבלי וכל־
הלבנון מזרח השמש מבעל גד תחת
הר־חרמון עד לבוא חמת: ו כל־ישבי
ההר מן־הלבנון עד־משרפת מים כל־
צידנים אנכי אורישם מפני בני ישראל
רק הפלה לישראל בנחלה כאשר
צויתיך: ז ועתה חלק את־הארץ הזאת
בנחלה לתשעת השבטים וחצי
השבט המנשה: ח עמו הראובני והגדי
לקחו נחלתם אשר נתן להם משה
בעבר הירדן מזרחה כאשר נתן להם
משה עבד יהוה: ט מערוער אשר על־

**תרגום**

תחום אמוראה:
ה וארעא גבלי וכל לבנן
מדנח שמשא ממישר
גד שפולי טורא דחרמון
עד מעלנא דחמת:
ו כל יתבי טורא מן לבנן
עד חרצי ימא כל
צידונאי במימרי
אתרכינון מן קדם בני
ישראל לחוד פליגהא
לישראל באחסנא כמא
דפקידתך: ז וכען פליג
ית ארעא הדא באחסנא
לתשעה שבטין ופלגות
שבטא דמנשה: ח עמיה
שבטא דראובן ושבטא
גד קבילו אחסנתהון
דיהב להון משה בעברא
דירדנא מדינחא כמא
דיהב להון משה עבדא
דיי: ט מערוער דעל כיף
נחלא

**רד"ק**

כלומר מצד דרום נשארה כל ארץ הכנעני: (ה) והארץ הגבלי. חסר הנסמך ומשפטו הארץ ארץ הגבלי וכן הארון הברית: (ח) עמו הראובני והגדי. עם חצי שבט מנשה האחד ואמר עמו ואף על פי שלא זכרו לפי שזכר החצי האחר אמר עמו כאילו זכרו:

**רש"י**

(ה) והארץ הגבלי וכל הלבנון מזרח השמש · ובמלר מזרחי נשאר לכבוש במקלוע הצפון כל הלבנון מבעל גד עד סוף המלר וברוחב מן המזרח למערב עד לבא חמת זהו כל מלר הצפוני שלבא חמת במקלוע צפונית מערבית בחלה מסעי: (ו) אנכי אורישם · אחרי מותך: הפלה לישראל בנחלה · ויכבוש לאחר זמן כל שבט ושבט מה שנפל בגורלו: (ח) עמו הראובני והגדי · עם חצי הראשון של מנשה הראובני והגדי לקחו נחלתם: (ט) מערוער אשר על שפת וגו' · מונה והולך כל ארץ עבר הירדן ואח"כ מפרש גבול כל שבט ושבט ויתן משה למטה פלוני ופלוני:

**מנחת שי**

דבמואל חסר. ועיין מסורת הברית הגדול סימן תתקנ"ב: (ו) אנכי אורישם. בספרים כתיבת יד מדוייקים ובדפוסים ישנים ביו"ד: (ח) הראובני. עיין לעיל סימן י"ב: כאשר נתן להם משה עבד ה'. י' דמטעין דסבירין אשר בקריאה. מסורת יונה סימן א':

**מצודת דוד**

(ו) אנכי אורישם. אחרי מותך אני אגרשם לפניהם: הפילה. הפל הגורל ביניהם על מה שכבר כבשו ועל מה שלא כבשו עדיין וכל שבט יכבוש את חלקו: כאשר צויתיך. כמ"ש ולו את יהושע וגו' הוא ינחיל (דברים ג'): (ז) ועתה חלק. ר"ל בתחלה חלק הארץ לתשעה חלקים ומחלה כמנין השבטים הנוחלים ואחר זה הטל הגורל לדעת איזה חלק למי: (ח) עמו. ר"ל לפי שעם חצי השני משבט מנשה לקחו הראובני והגדי חלק נחלתם (ועם שלא הוזכר למעלה החצי השני משבט מנשה על"ז אמר עמו הואיל והזכיר חצי האחד): כאשר נתן להם משה. מוסב על לקחו נחלתם ור"ל מאז כאשר נתן להם משה הנחלה ההיא לקחו אותה ונתרצו בה וא"כ הדבר קיים ואין לתת להם עוד בהעבר הזה.

## Commentary Digest

their inheritance, they accepted it as binding. Hence, they have no more claim to the territory west of the Jordan. — D

9. *From 'Aroer — "He goes on to describe the entire land on the other*

the border of the Amorites. 5. And the land of the Giblites, and all the Lebanon, toward the sunrising, from Baal-gad under Mount Hermon to the entering into Hamath. 6. All the inhabitants of the hill country from Lebanon to Misrephoth-maim, and all the Sidonians, I will drive them out from before the children of Israel; only divide it by lot to the Israelites for an inheritance, as I have commanded you. 7. And now, divide this land for an inheritance to the nine tribes, and the half tribe of Manasseh. 8. With him, the Reubenites and the Gadites have received their inheritance, which Moses gave them, beyond the Jordan eastward, even as Moses the servant of the Lord gave them. 9. From 'Aroer, that is upon

## Commentary Digest

5. *And the land of the Giblites, and all the Lebanon, toward the sunrising* — *"And on the eastern border, there remained to conquer in the northern end, all the Lebanon, from Baal-Gad to the end of the border, and in the width from east to west, to the entering ino Hamath. This is the entire northern boundary, for the entering into Hamath is at the northwestern corner, in "אלה מסעי."" — R*

6. *I will drive them out — "after your death."* — R

*only divide it by lot to the Israelites as an inheritance — "and subsequently, each tribe will conquer that which fell into its lot."* — R It was no longer necessary to have the entire nation in arms, for each tribe was now strong enough to deal with the enemy within its borders. — A According to Maimonides, the division was necessary to give subsequent conquests communal status (כבוש רבים).[1]

7. ***And now, divide this land*** — I.e. at first, divide the land into nine and a half parts, according to the number of tribes that will inherit this land, and then, distribute the parts by casting lots . — D

8. *With him — i.e. "with the first half tribe of Manasseh, the Reubenites and Gadites received their inheritance."* — R

*even as Moses — gave them* — An alternate rendering is: when Moses — gave them, i.e. when Moses gave them

שְׂפַת־נַחַל אַרְנוֹן וְהָעִיר אֲשֶׁר בְּתוֹךְ־
הַנַּחַל וְכָל־הַמִּישֹׁר מֵידְבָא עַד־דִּיבוֹן׃
י וְכֹל עָרֵי סִיחוֹן מֶלֶךְ הָאֱמֹרִי אֲשֶׁר מָלַךְ
בְּחֶשְׁבּוֹן עַד־גְּבוּל בְּנֵי עַמּוֹן׃ יא וְהַגִּלְעָד
וּגְבוּל הַגְּשׁוּרִי וְהַמַּעֲכָתִי וְכֹל הַר חֶרְמוֹן
וְכָל־הַבָּשָׁן עַד־סַלְכָה׃ יב כָּל־מַמְלְכוּת
עוֹג בַּבָּשָׁן אֲשֶׁר־מָלַךְ בְּעַשְׁתָּרוֹת
וּבְאֶדְרֶעִי הוּא נִשְׁאַר מִיֶּתֶר הָרְפָאִים
וַיַּכֵּם מֹשֶׁה וַיֹּרִשֵׁם׃ יג וְלֹא הוֹרִישׁוּ בְּנֵי
יִשְׂרָאֵל אֶת־הַגְּשׁוּרִי וְאֶת־הַמַּעֲכָתִי
וַיֵּשֶׁב גְּשׁוּר וּמַעֲכָת בְּקֶרֶב יִשְׂרָאֵל עַד
הַיּוֹם הַזֶּה׃ יד רַק לְשֵׁבֶט הַלֵּוִי לֹא נָתַן
נַחֲלָה אִשֵּׁי יְהוָה אֱלֹהֵי יִשְׂרָאֵל הוּא
נַחֲלָתוֹ כַּאֲשֶׁר דִּבֶּר־לוֹ׃ טו וַיִּתֵּן

משה

נַחְלָא דְאַרְנוֹן וְקַרְתָּא דִי
בְגוֹ נַחְלָא וְכָל מֵישַׁר
מֵידְבָא עַד דִּיבוֹן׃ י וְכָל
קִרְוֵי סִיחוֹן מַלְכָּא
דֶאֱמוֹרָאָה דִי מְלַךְ
בְּחֶשְׁבּוֹן עַד תְּחוּם בְּנֵי
עַמּוֹן׃ יא וְאַרְעָא גִלְעָד
וּתְחוּם גְּשׁוּרָאָה
וְאַפִּיקִירוֹס וְכָל טוּרָא
דְחֶרְמוֹן וְכָל מַתְנַן עַד
סַלְכָה׃ יב כָּל מַלְכוּת
עוֹג בְּמַתְנַן דִי מְלַךְ
בְּעַשְׁתָּרוֹת וּבְאֶדְרֶעִי
וְהוּא אִשְׁתְּאַר מִשְּׁאָר
גִּבָּרַיָא וּמְחָנוּן מֹשֶׁה
וְתָרְכִינוּן׃ יג וְלָא תָרִיכוּ
בְּנֵי יִשְׂרָאֵל יָת גְּשׁוּרָאָה
וְיָת אַפִּיקִירוֹס וִיתֵיב
גְּשׁוּרָאָה וְאַפִּיקִירוֹס בְּגוֹ
יִשְׂרָאֵל עַד יוֹמָא הָדֵין׃
יד לְחוּד לְשִׁבְטָא דְלֵוִי
לָא יְהַב אַחְסָנָא קוּרְבָּנַיָא
דַיְיָ אֱלָהָא דְיִשְׂרָאֵל
אִינוּן אַחְסַנְתֵּיהּ כְּמָא
דְמַלֵּיל לֵיהּ׃ טו וִיהַב

משה

רש״י

(יב) מיתר הרפאים · שהרג כדרלעומר והמלכים אשר אתו כמו שנא׳ ויכו את רפאים בעשתרות קרנים:

מצודת דוד

(יד) אשי ה׳ . קדשי המזבח הניתן לאחר שקרבו מתיריו על האש: לו . למסה: (טו) למשפחותם . ר״ל לא נתן משה להם ביחד לשבט עלמם יחלקו ביניהם רק הוא בעצמו חלק לכל משפחה חלקה:

מצודת ציון

(ט) המישור . מקום ישר ושוה: (יב) וירשם . גרשם:

## Commentary Digest

14. *Only to the tribe of Levi he gave no inheritance* — Although the forty-eight cities given to the tribe of Levi[3] are a full inheritance, going beyond the mere right of residence,[4] yet they were awarded to them after all the tribes had been granted their portions, and after the Tabernacle had been established in Shiloh, after the fourteen years of conquest and division. This showed that the Levites received their part from the Eternal Himself, not by force of arms. — A[4]

*the sacrifices of the Lord G-d of Israel* made by fire — I.e. the remainder of the sacrifices, after the fat has been burned on the altar. — D These gifts due the priests of the tribe of Levi are enumerated in Num. 18:9-111. They include the מנחה — the meal-offering, the חטאת — the sin-offering, and the אשם — the guilt-offering. These are known as קדשי קדשים — the most holy sacrifices. In addition to this, they receive the breast and the thigh of the שלמים — the peace-offering, which is a sacrifice of lesser holiness.

the bank of the river Arnon, and the city that is in the midst
of the river, and all the plain of Medba to Dibon; 10. And
all the cities of Sihon king of the Amorites, who reigned in
Heshbon, to the border of the children of 'Ammon; 11. And
Gilead, and the border of the Geshurites and the Maachathites,
and all Mount Hermon, and all Bashan to Salcah; 12. All
the kingdom of Og in Bashan, who reigned in Ashtaroth and
Edrei, who remained of the remnant of the giants — these did
Moses smite, and cast them out. 13. Nevertheless, the children
of Israel did not expel the Geshurites or the Maachathites;
but the Geshurites and Maachathites dwell among the Israelites
until this day. 14. Only to the tribe of Levi he gave no
inheritance; the *sacrifices* of the Lord God of Israel made by
fire are his inheritance, as He said to him. 15. And Moses

gave

**Commentary Digest**

*side of the Jordan, after which he explains the boundary of each tribe. — And Moses gave to such and such a tribe etc."* — R

12. *who remained of the remnant of the giants (Rephaim)* — *"whom Chedorlaomer and the kings who were with him had slain, as it is stated: "And they smote the Rephaim in Ashteroth-Karnaim.""*[1] — R Sihon and Og were powerful kings, and were the only beings to survive the flood besides Noah and those with him in the ark.[2]

13. *Nevertheless, the children of Israel did not expel the Geshurites or the Maachathites* — I.e. it was the fault of the children of Israel that the Geshurites and the Maachathites were not expelled, not that of Moses. — K. Y.

*but the Geshurites and Maachathites dwell among the Israelites* — As punishment for the Israelites' negligence, the Geshurites and Maachathites united as one nation, as is alluded to by the singular form of וישב, — K. Y.

*among the Israelites* — Lit. in the midst of Israel. I.e. they remained in the midst of Israel, not near the border. Thus, they posed a greater threat to the Israelites' security. — K. Y.

מֹשֶׁה לְמַטֵּה בְנֵי־רְאוּבֵן לְמִשְׁפְּחוֹתָם׃
טז וַיְהִי לָהֶם הַגְּבוּל מֵעֲרוֹעֵר אֲשֶׁר עַל־
שְׂפַת־נַחַל אַרְנוֹן וְהָעִיר אֲשֶׁר בְּתוֹךְ־
הַנַּחַל וְכָל־הַמִּישֹׁר עַל־מֵידְבָא׃ יז חֶשְׁבּוֹן
וְכָל־עָרֶיהָ אֲשֶׁר בַּמִּישׁוֹר דִּיבוֹן וּבָמוֹת
בַּעַל וּבֵית בַּעַל מְעוֹן׃ יח וְיַהְצָה וּקְדֵמֹת
וּמֵפָעַת׃ יט וְקִרְיָתַיִם וְשִׂבְמָה וְצֶרֶת
הַשַּׁחַר בְּהַר הָעֵמֶק׃ כ וּבֵית פְּעוֹר
וְאַשְׁדּוֹת הַפִּסְגָּה וּבֵית הַיְשִׁמוֹת׃ כא וְכֹל
עָרֵי הַמִּישֹׁר וְכָל־מַמְלְכוּת סִיחוֹן מֶלֶךְ
הָאֱמֹרִי אֲשֶׁר מָלַךְ בְּחֶשְׁבּוֹן אֲשֶׁר הִכָּה
מֹשֶׁה אֹתוֹ וְאֶת־נְשִׂיאֵי מִדְיָן אֶת־אֱוִי
וְאֶת־רֶקֶם וְאֶת־צוּר וְאֶת־חוּר וְאֶת־רֶבַע
נְסִיכֵי סִיחוֹן יֹשְׁבֵי הָאָרֶץ׃ כב וְאֶת־בִּלְעָם בֶּן־בְּעוֹר

מֹשֶׁה לְשִׁבְטָא דִבְנֵי רְאוּבֵן לְזַרְעֲיָתְהוֹן׃ טז וַהֲוָה לְהוֹן תְּחוּמָא מֵעֲרוֹעֵר דִּי עַל כֵּיף נַחֲלָא דְאַרְנוֹן וְקַרְתָּא דִי בְגוֹ נַחֲלָא וְכָל מֵישְׁרָא עַד מֵידְבָא׃ יז חֶשְׁבּוֹן וְכָל קִרְוָהָא דִי בְמֵישְׁרָא דִיבוֹן וּבָמוֹת בַּעַל וּבֵית בַּעַל מְעוֹן׃ יח וְיַהְצָה וּקְדֵמוֹת וּמֵפָעַת׃ יט וְקִרְיָתַיִם וְשִׂבְמָה וְצֶרֶת הַשַּׁחַר בְּטוּרָא דְמֵישְׁרָא׃ כ וּבֵית פְּעוֹר וּמַשְׁפַּךְ מְרָמָתָא וּבֵית יְשִׁמוֹת׃ כא וְכָל קִרְוֵי מֵישְׁרָא וְכָל מַלְכְוַת סִיחוֹן מַלְכָּא דֶאֱמוֹרָאָה דִמְלַךְ בְּחֶשְׁבּוֹן דִּמְחָא מֹשֶׁה יָתֵיהּ וְיָת רַבְרְבֵי מִדְיָן יָת אֱוִי וְיָת רֶקֶם וְיָת צוּר וְיָת חוּר וְיָת רֶבַע רַבְרְבֵי סִיחוֹן יָתְבֵי אַרְעָא׃ כב וְיָת בִּלְעָם בר

ת״א בלעם בן בעור. סנהדרין קו:

רד״ק

(יט) בהר העמק. כתרגומו בטורא דמישרא: (כא) נסיכי סיחון יושבי הארץ. אלה חמשת מלכי מדין היו נסיכי סיחון בעוד שהיו סיחון והאמרי יושבי הארץ קודם שלכדום ישראל היו אלה נשיאי הארץ נסיכי סיחון כי תחת ממשלת סיחון

רש״י

(יט) בהר העמק. בטורא דמשרא:

הקוסם

מנחת שי

(טז) על מידבא. חד מן ט׳ דסבירין עד וקריין על וסימן נמסר במ״ג (פרשת ויחי) ולפיכך תרגום יונתן עד מידבא ועיין מ״ש (בנחמיה סי׳ י״ג): (יח) ויהצה. הס״א בצוא לבדו בספרים מדוייקים. ומקלתם היו״ד בקמץ:

מצודת ציון

(כא) נסיכי. ענין שררה:

מצודת דוד

(יט) בהר העמק. בהר שעמד בתוך העמק: (כא) יושבי הארץ.

## Commentary Digest

punishment for their straying after the daughters of Moab, and worshipping the idol Baal-peor. Zur was the most important of the kings of Midian. However, since he led his daughter Cozbi into harlotry in order to mislead the Israelites, he is counted third. See Rashi Num. 25:15. Targum Jonathan ben Uziel identifies him with Balak, king of Moab (*Ibid.* 16).

*dukes (vassals) of Sihon* — Midian was one of the countries subservient to the rule of Sihon. — K Before Sihon's

to the tribe of the children of Reuben *inheritance* according
to their families. 16. And their border was from 'Aroer, that
is on the bank of the river Arnon, and the city that is in the
midst of the river, and all the plain by Medba; 17. Heshbon,
and all her cities that are in the plain; Dibon, and Bamoth-
baal, and Beth-baal-meon. 18. And Jahaza, and Kedemoth,
and Mephaath. 19. And Kirjathaim, and Sibmah, and Zereth-
hashahar in the mount of the valley. 20. And Beth-peor, and
Ashdoth-pisgah, and Beth-jeshimoth. 21. And all the cities of
the plain, and all the kingdom of Sihon king of the Amorites,
who reigned in Heshbon, whom Moses smote; and the princes
of Midian: Evi, and Rekem, and Zur, and Hur, and Reba,
dukes of Sihon, inhabitants of the land. 22. And Balaam
the son of Beor,

**Commentary Digest**

17. *Heshbon, and all her cities* — Heshbon was the capital city of Sihon, he having captured it from Moab,[1] and was surrounded by other lesser cities and suburbs.

*Dibon, and Bamoth-baal, and Beth-baal-meon* — Although Dibon was built by the Gadites, it was given to the Reubenites. See Num XXXII:34-38, also R and N ad loc. who debate which were the original and which were the final names of Nebo and Baal-meon.

19. *the mount of the valley* — R and K from J. It is difficult to see what J adds to the understanding of the passage. Perhaps, J, who renders 'emek' as 'meshra' which is synonymous to 'mishor' or plain, wishes to convey the idea that this was not necessarily a valley, but a plain with a mountain in the middle. If we render 'emek' as valley, we encounter a difficulty, for a mountain cannot be in the middle of a valley, since the valley is formed by the space between two mountains.

20. *And Beth-peor* — the shrine of the idol, Baal-peor.[2]

*Ashdoth-pisgah* — the waterfall from the mountain peak. — J

21. *and the princes of Midian* — not 'with the princes of Midian.' — Sihon and Og were defeated and slain long before the war with Midian.[3]

*and Zur* — the father of Cozbi, the Midianitess who was slain with Zimri in Shittim, when the Israelites were stricken with a plague as a

הַקּוֹסֵם הָרְגוּ בְנֵי־יִשְׂרָאֵל בַּחֶרֶב אֶל־
חַלְלֵיהֶם: כג וַיְהִי גְּבוּל בְּנֵי רְאוּבֵן הַיַּרְדֵּן
וּגְבוּל זֹאת נַחֲלַת בְּנֵי־רְאוּבֵן
לְמִשְׁפְּחוֹתָם הֶעָרִים וְחַצְרֵיהֶן: כד וַיִּתֵּן
מֹשֶׁה לְמַטֵּה־גָד לִבְנֵי־גָד לְמִשְׁפְּחֹתָם:
כה וַיְהִי לָהֶם הַגְּבוּל יַעְזֵר וְכָל־עָרֵי
הַגִּלְעָד וַחֲצִי אֶרֶץ בְּנֵי עַמּוֹן עַד־עֲרוֹעֵר
אֲשֶׁר עַל־פְּנֵי רַבָּה: כו וּמֵחֶשְׁבּוֹן עַד־
רָמַת הַמִּצְפֶּה וּבְטֹנִים וּמִמַּחֲנַיִם עַד־
גְּבוּל לִדְבִר: כז וּבָעֵמֶק בֵּית הָרָם וּבֵית

בַּר בְּעוֹר קַסָּמָא קְטָלוּ בְּנֵי יִשְׂרָאֵל בְּחַרְבָּא עַל קְטִילֵיהוֹן: כג וַהֲוָה תְּחוּם בְּנֵי רְאוּבֵן יַרְדְּנָא וּתְחוּמֵיהּ דָּא אַחְסָנַת בְּנֵי רְאוּבֵן לְזַרְעִיתְהוֹן קִרְוַיָּא וּפַצְחֵיהֶן: כד וִיהַב מֹשֶׁה לְשִׁבְטָא דְגָד לִבְנֵי גָד לְזַרְעִיתְהוֹן: כה וַהֲוָה לְהוֹן תְּחוּמָא יַעְזֵר וְכָל קִרְוֵי גִלְעָד וּפַלְגוּת אַרְעָא בְּנֵי עַמּוֹן עַד עֲרוֹעֵר דִּי עַל אַפֵּי רַבָּה: כו וּמֵחֶשְׁבּוֹן עַד רָמַת מִצְפַּיָּא וּבְטוֹנִים וּמִמַּחֲנַיִם עַד תְּחוּם לִדְבִיר: כז וּבְמֵישְׁרָא בֵּית הָרָם וּבֵית נִמְרָה וְסָכּוֹת וְצִפּוּנָא שְׁאָר מלכות

רש"י | הצי הספר | רד"ק | נמ"ה

(כה) וחצי ארץ בני עמון · חלי מה שכבשו מארץ בני היה מדין בימים ההם: (כב) הקוסם. להודיע כי לא נביא היה אלא קוסם ונבואתו היתה לשעה או לכבוד ישראל בא אליו מלאך ה׳ לדבר הנבואות ההם. ויש לשאול איך מצאו בלעם שם והלא כתיב וילך וישב למקומו אלא שחזר שם לבקש שכרו על העצה שנתן להם למואב ולמדין להוציא בנותיהם היפות ויזנו ישראל עמהם ויהיה קצף ה׳ בהם וזהו שאמר לכה איעצך כמו שכתוב בדבר בלעם וכשראה שנתקיימה עצתו הלך למואב ולמדין לבקש שכרו מהם: אל חלליהם. עם חלליה׳ וכמוהו רבים ובתורה כתיב על חלליהם והוא גם כן כמו עם כמו ויבאו האנשים על הנשים עם הנשים ואחרים זולתו. ויש בו דרש שהיו מלכי מדין עושים כשפים עם בלעם ופורחין באויר כיון שהראה להם פנחס את הציץ נפלו על חלליהם ועוד אמרו על חלליהם שעשו לו ארבע מיתות ב"ד ועוד אמרו כי פנחס הרגו: (כג) הירדן וגבול. כתרגומו ירדנא

מנחת שי

(כג) ויהי גבול בני ראובן וגו׳ למשפחותם חד מן ח׳ מלאים כמ"ש בפרשת נשא יזהו בתראה דראובן: (כד) ויתן משה למטה גד וגו׳ למשפחתם חסר וכן וזאת נחלת בני גד למשפחתם שבסמוך והם קדמאה ובתראה דגד כמו שכתבתי (בפרשת נשא): (כו) ומחשבון עד רמת. חצי הספר ובמקרא גדולה לעיל בסוף מלכי כנען כתוב בגליון חצי הספר ואין שם מקומו רק כאן קודם פסוק ומחשבון. וכן כתב במקרא גדולה עלמה בסוף יהושע. וכן ראיתי בספרים כ"י שכתוב כאן חצי הספר בפסוקים וסך כולם שם מאות וחמשים ושנה ומחציתם שלש מאות ועשרים ושמנה. וזהו ראיה גדולה שצריך להכיר בני הפסוקים הנמלאים במקצת ספרים

מצודת דוד

מתושבי ארץ סיחון: (כב) אל חלליהם. עם שאר החללים ודומה להם ולא היה יכול להציל עצמו בקסמיו: (כג) וגבול. ר"ל גם גבול הירדן והם הערים הסמוכים לירדן גם המה לגבול ראובן יחשבו: למשפחותם. הנחלק לכל משפחה חלק לבד:

מצודת ציון

(כג) וחצריהן. עיירו׳ פרוזות מבלי חומה העומדי׳ סביב עיר חומה:

## Commentary Digest

slew him. — (K),[8] completing the zealotry he had begun at Shittim by the slaying of Zimri and Cozbi.[9]

*together with those that were slain by them* — lit. to those that were slain by them. The Rabbis tell us that by dint of his sorcery, Balaam enabled the kings of Midian to fly; and he too flew with them. When Phinehas showed them the holy golden plate which he wore on his forehead, engraved with the words, קדש לה׳ "Holy to the Lord," they all fell upon the slain ones, and were immediately slain by the Israelites. — K[10]

23. *and its border* — i.e. the cities bordering on the Jordan. — K and D

25. *and half the land of the children of 'Ammon*—"*half of what they conquered of the land of the children of 'Ammon and* (sic) *from Sihon.*" — R Perhaps this should read: Half of what they conquered of the land of the children of 'Ammon from Sihon. The

the soothsayer, did the children of Israel slay with the sword,
together with those that were slain by them. 23. And the
border of the children of Reuben was the Jordan and its
border. This was the inheritance of the children of Reuben
according to their families, the cities and their villages.
24. And Moses gave to the tribe of Gad, to the children of
Gad according to their families. 25. And their border was
Jazer, and all the cities of Gilead, and half the land of the
children of 'Ammon, to 'Aroer that is before Rabbah. 26. And
from Heshbon to Ramath-mizpeh, and Betonim; and from
Mahanaim to the border of Debir; 27. And in the valley,
Beth-haram, and Beth-

## Commentary Digest

conquest of Midian, and after Sihon's death, they were known as 'kings of Midian.' —N[1]

22. *Balaam the son of Beor the soothsayer did the children of Israel slay* — "soothsayer" — as opposed to "prophet." Although he prophesied at the time of Balak,[1*] he reached this pinnacle as a godly gift only temporarily, in honor of Israel, for the majority of his prophecies were directed toward Israel. — K The Talmud,[2] however, states that Balaam's prophecy was mainly to the Gentiles. The Talmud likewise states that Balaam was originally a prophet. but after he sought to curse Israel, he lost the gift of prophecy and resorted to soothsaying.[3]

*did the children of Israel slay* — Balaam had gone to Midian to collect his reward for his advice to entice the Israelites at Shittim,[4] and was put to the sword in the battle against Midian, because he attempted to dishearten the Jewish troops who had gone to attack Midian. He said to them, "If, when you were 600,000 strong, you were unable to best Moab and Midian, how will you accomplish this objective with only 12,000 men?[5] Balaam was rewarded like the proverbial camel who came asking for horns and whose ears were cut off instead.[3]

*with the sword* — Since Balaam had usurped the power of the mouth, the prerogative and ancient weapon of Israel, who conquered through prayer, so now Phinehas, who led the attack against Midian, slew Balaam with the traditional weapon of Esau: "And by your sword shall you live."[6] — R[7] Phinehas was the one who personally

נִמְרָה וְסֻכּוֹת וְצָפוֹן יֶתֶר מַמְלְכוּת סִיחוֹן
מֶלֶךְ חֶשְׁבּוֹן הַיַּרְדֵּן וּגְבֻל עַד־קְצֵה יָם־
כִּנֶּרֶת עֵבֶר הַיַּרְדֵּן מִזְרָחָה׃ כח זֹאת
נַחֲלַת בְּנֵי־גָד לְמִשְׁפְּחֹתָם הֶעָרִים
וְחַצְרֵיהֶם׃ כט וַיִּתֵּן מֹשֶׁה לַחֲצִי שֵׁבֶט
מְנַשֶּׁה וַיְהִי לַחֲצִי מַטֵּה בְנֵי־מְנַשֶּׁה
לְמִשְׁפְּחוֹתָם׃ ל וַיְהִי גְבוּלָם מִמַּחֲנַיִם כָּל־
הַבָּשָׁן כָּל־מַמְלְכוּת ׀ עוֹג מֶלֶךְ־הַבָּשָׁן
וְכָל־חַוֹּת יָאִיר אֲשֶׁר בַּבָּשָׁן שִׁשִּׁים עִיר׃
לא וַחֲצִי הַגִּלְעָד וְעַשְׁתָּרוֹת וְאֶדְרֶעִי עָרֵי
מַמְלְכוּת עוֹג בַּבָּשָׁן לִבְנֵי מָכִיר בֶּן
מְנַשֶּׁה לַחֲצִי בְנֵי־מָכִיר לְמִשְׁפְּחוֹתָם׃
לב אֵלֶּה אֲשֶׁר־נִחַל מֹשֶׁה בְּעַרְבוֹת
מוֹאָב מֵעֵבֶר לְיַרְדֵּן יְרִיחוֹ מִזְרָחָה׃ לג וּלְשֵׁבֶט הַלֵּוִי

**תרגום**

מַלְכוּת סִיחוֹן מַלְכָּא דְחֶשְׁבּוֹן יַרְדְּנָא וּתְחוּמֵיהּ עַד סְיָפֵי יַם גִּינוֹסַר עִבְרָא דְיַרְדְּנָא מַדִּינְחָא׃ כח דָא אַחֲסָנַת בְּנֵי גָד לְזַרְעֲיָתְהוֹן קִרְוַיָּא וּפַצְחֵיהֶן׃ כט וִיהַב מֹשֶׁה לְפַלְגוּת שִׁבְטָא דִמְנַשֶּׁה וַהֲוָה לְפַלְגוּת שִׁבְטָא דִבְנֵי מְנַשֶּׁה לְזַרְעֲיָתְהוֹן׃ ל וַהֲוָה תְּחוּמֵיהוֹן מִמַּחֲנַיִם כָּל מַתְנָן כָּל מַלְכוּתֵיהּ דְעוֹג מַלְכָּא דְמַתְנָן וְכָל כַּפְרָנֵי יָאִיר דִּבְמַתְנָן שִׁתִּין קִרְוִין׃ לא וּפַלְגוּת אַרְעָא דְגִלְעָד וְעַשְׁתָּרוֹת וְאֶדְרֶעִי קִרְוַיָּא מַלְכוּתֵיהּ דְעוֹג בְּמַתְנָן לִבְנֵי מָכִיר בַּר מְנַשֶּׁה לְפַלְגוּת בְּנֵי מָכִיר לְזַרְעֲיָתְהוֹן׃ לב אִלֵּין דִּי אַחְסִין מֹשֶׁה בְּמֵישְׁרַיָּא דְמוֹאָב מֵעִבְרָא לְיַרְדְּנָא דִירִיחוֹ מַדִּינְחָא׃ לג וּלְשִׁבְטָא דְלֵוִי לָא יְהַב

**רש"י** לא

עמון ומסיחון: (כז) הירדן וגבול ירדנה ותחומיה הערים שעל שפתו: (כח) הערים וחצריהם. הערים המוקפות חומה: וחצריהם. ערי הפרזו בלא חומה:

**רד"ק**

ותחומיה כלומר הערים הסמוכות אליו: (לא) לחצי בני מכיר. כי החצי האחר והם בני גלעד ששה בתי אבות לקחו נחלתם בארץ כנען:

**מנחת שי**

בסימן כ"א שם דבלתו הכי אין החשבון מכוון: (כט) ויתן משה לחצי שבט מנשה וגו' למשפחותם. מלא וכן וחצי הגלעד וגו' למשפחותם שבסמוך והם קדמאה ובתראה דמנשה. כמ"ש (בפרשת נח): (ל) ויהי גבולם ממחנים וגו' כתוב במקרא גדולה זה לשונו. ובספר ישן מלאתי ויהי כל גבולם ממחנים כל הבשן וכל ממלכות עוג מלך הבשן וכל חות יאיר ומונה מבחוץ כך עכ"ל. ולא ראיתי כזה בשום ספר: כָּל־הַבָּשָׁן כָּל־מַמְלְכוּת. כס"ה כי כל הבשן כל ממלכות במתג. וכו' הראשון בלבד ויש החזון ועיין מ"ש (בפרשה ראה על כל הבכור) מתוק

**מצודת ציון**

(ל) חות יאיר תרגומו כפרני יאיר:

**מצודת דוד**

(לא) לבני מכיר. חצי הגלעד וכו' נתן לבני מכיר לא לכולם כ"א לחצי בני מכיר: (לב) אלה אשר נחל. אלה הנחלות אשר הנחילם משה: (לג) ה' אלהי וגו'. ר"ל מותר אשי ה' היא נחלתם:

## Commentary Digest

for their progenitor Manasseh who caused the tribes to rend their clothes when he overtook them and accused them of stealing Joseph's silver cup (G. R. 84:20) — Porath Yosef

31. *to one half of the children of Machir* — for the other half, the children of Gilead, six families, took their inheritance in the land of Canaan. — K

nimrah, and Succoth, and Zaphon, the rest of the kingdom of Sihon king of Heshbon, Jordan and its border, to the edge of the Sea of Chinnereth on the eastern side of the Jordan.
28. This is the inheritance of the children of Gad, according
to their families, the cities and their villages. 29. And Moses
gave *inheritance* to the half tribe of Manasseh; and this was for the half tribe of the children of Manasseh according to
their families. 30. And their border was from Mahanaim, all
Bashan, all the kingdom of Og king of Bashan, and all the villages of Jair, which are in Bashan, threescore cities;
31. And half Gilead, and Ashtaroth, and Edrei, cities of the kingdom of Og in Bashan, were for the children of Machir the son of Manasseh, to one half the children of Machir
according to their families. 32. These are the tribes which
Moses caused to inherit in the plains of Moab, on the other
side of the Jordan eastward, facing Jericho. 33. But to the
tribe of Levi

**Commentary Digest**

Israelites did not wage war against Ammon, in accordance with the divine decree: "Harass them not, nor contend with them."[1] This was verified by Moses himself: "Only to the land of the children of Ammon did you not come near."[2] Likewise, Jephthah, in his reply to the king of Ammon, explains that Israel did not wage war with 'Ammon, but with Sihon, and conquered the land which he had taken from 'Ammon.[3]

27. *Jordan and its border* — J. lit. Jordan and border, i.e. *"the cities which are on its bank."* — R

28. *the cities and their villages* — *"the walled cities."* — R These served as fortified centers.

*and their villages* — *"open cities without walls."* — R These were the suburbs, surrounding the cities.

29. *And this was for the half tribe of the children of Manasseh* — This entire clause seems superfluous. We do not find this expression used in reference to the inheritance of any other tribe. It was written here to indicate that it was divinely predestined that the tribe of Manasseh be split into two parts as a punishment

| | |
|---|---|
| לֹא־נָתַן מֹשֶׁה נַחֲלָה יְהוָה אֱלֹהֵי | משה אַחסָנָא מְתַּן |
| יִשְׂרָאֵל הוּא נַחֲלָתָם כַּאֲשֶׁר דִּבֶּר לָהֶם׃ | דִיהַב לְהוֹן יְיָ אֱלָהָא |
| יד א וְאֵלֶּה אֲשֶׁר־נָחֲלוּ בְנֵי־יִשְׂרָאֵל | דְיִשְׂרָאֵל אִינוּן |
| בְּאֶרֶץ כְּנָעַן אֲשֶׁר נִחֲלוּ אוֹתָם אֶלְעָזָר | אַחסַנְתְּהוֹן כְּמָא דְמַלֵיל |
| הַכֹּהֵן וִיהוֹשֻׁעַ בִּן־נוּן וְרָאשֵׁי אֲבוֹת | לְהוֹן׃ א וְאִלֵין דְאַחְסִינוּ |
| הַמַּטּוֹת לִבְנֵי יִשְׂרָאֵל׃ ב בְּגוֹרַל נַחֲלָתָם | בְּנֵי יִשְׂרָאֵל בְּאַרְעָא |
| כַּאֲשֶׁר צִוָּה יְהוָה בְּיַד־מֹשֶׁה לְתִשְׁעַת | דִכְנַעַן דְאַחְסִינוּ יָתְהוֹן |
| הַמַּטּוֹת וַחֲצִי הַמַּטֶּה׃ ג כִּי־נָתַן מֹשֶׁה | אֶלְעָזָר כַּהֲנָא וִיהוֹשֻׁעַ |
| נַחֲלַת שְׁנֵי הַמַּטּוֹת וַחֲצִי הַמַּטֶּה מֵעֵבֶר | בַּר נוּן וְרֵישֵׁי אֲבָהַת |
| לַיַּרְדֵּן וְלַלְוִיִּם לֹא־נָתַן נַחֲלָה בְּתוֹכָם׃ | שִׁבְטַיָא לִבְנֵי יִשְׂרָאֵל׃ |
| ד כִּי־הָיוּ בְנֵי־יוֹסֵף שְׁנֵי מַטּוֹת מְנַשֶּׁה | ב בְּעַדְבָא אִתְפְּלֵגַת |
| וְאֶפְרָיִם וְלֹא־נָתְנוּ חֵלֶק לַלְוִיִּם בָּאָרֶץ | לְהוֹן אַחסַנְתְּהוֹן כְּמָא |
| | דְפַקֵיד יְיָ בִּידָא דְמֹשֶׁה |
| | לְתִשְׁעַת שִׁבְטִין וּפַלְגוּת |
| | שִׁבְטָא׃ ג אֲרֵי יְהַב מֹשֶׁה |
| | אַחסָנַת תְּרֵין שִׁבְטִין |
| | וּפַלְגוּת שִׁבְטָא מֵעִיבְרָא |
| | לְיַרְדְנָא וּלְלֵוָאֵי לָא יְהַב |
| | אַחסָנָא בֵּינֵיהוֹן׃ ד אֲרֵי |
| | הֲווֹ בְנֵי יוֹסֵף תְּרֵין שִׁבְטִין |
| | מְנַשֶּׁה וְאֶפְרַיִם וְלָא יְהַבוּ |
| | חוּלָק לְלֵוָאֵי בְּאַרְעָא |
| | אֱלָהֵן קִרְוִין לְמִתַּב |
| | ורוחיהון |

רש"י
יד (א) אשר נחלו אותם · אשר הנחילו אותם: (ד) כי היו בני יוסף שני מטות · תחת שבט לוי:

רד"ק
(ד) כי היו בני יוסף. אם תאמר לשבט לוי לא נתן נחלה היאך היו תשעה מטות וחצי המטה ושני מטות וחצי מעבר הירדן הנה י"ב ואם לוי אינו נמנה היאך היו י"ב לפי' אמר כי היו בני יוסף שני מטות והנה הם שנים עשר מטות: למקניהם ולקניינם. כתרגומו לבעיריהון ולגיתיהון ר"ל הבהמות הגסות ובהמות

מנחת שי
יד (ב) בגורל נחלתם כאשר צוה. י' דמטעים דסבירין אשר בקריאה מסורת יונה א':

מצודת דוד
יד (א) ואלה. ר"ל אלה הערים האמורים בסוף הענין: (ב) בגורל נחלתם. בגורל חלק להם נחלתם: (ג) כי נתן משה. יאמר מדוע חלק יהושע נחלה לתשעת המטות וחצי ואמר עם כי משה נתן לבני המטות וחצי וללוים לא נתן נחלה כי אין לתת להם כאשר לוה ה' ולא נשארו א"כ רק לוים לנחלה כ"א שמונת המטות וחצי עכ"ז הוכרח יהושע לחלק נחלה לתשעת המטות וחצי: (ד) כי היו. ר"ל לפי שבני יוסף נחלקו לשתי מטות והיו א"כ תשעה וחצי לבד הלוים אבל ללוים לא נתנו נחלה

מצודת ציון
יד (א) המטות. השבטים:

## Commentary Digest

J paraphrases: By lot was their inheritance distributed to them. This verse alludes to the Talmudic maxim that only the children of Israel received their inheritance by lot, but Joshua and Caleb received theirs by direct divine command (B.B. 122a) — Porath Yosef.

4. *For the children of Joseph were*

Moses gave no inheritance. The Lord God of Israel was their
inheritance, as he spoke to them.

14

1. And these are *the cities* which the children of Israel
inherited in the land of Canaan, which Eleazar the priest, and
Joshua the son of Nun, and the heads of the tribes of the
children of Israel, distributed for inheritance to them. 2. By
lot was their inheritance, as the Lord commanded through
Moses, for the nine tribes and for the half tribe. 3. For
Moses had given the inheritance of two tribes and a half tribe
on the other side of the Jordan, but to the Levites he gave
no inheritance among them. 4. For the children of Joseph
were two tribes, Manasseh and Ephraim, but they gave no
part to the Levites, in the land,

**Commentary Digest**

33. *But to the tribe of Levi, Moses gave no inheritance* — This is repeated[1] to emphasize that the part given to Reuben and Gad was an integral part of the Land of Israel, promised to Abraham, although it was east of the Jordan, and was not "a land of flowing with milk and honey."[2] Therefore, Levi was not given any part beyond the cities, for dwelling therein. Should, however, any land be annexed to Eretz Israel beyond the prescribed borders, the Levites are entitled to a share.[3]

*The Lord God of Israel was their inheritance* — J paraphrases — The presents which the Lord God of Israel gave them, are their inheritance.

CHAPTER 14

1. *And these are (the cities)* — paraphrased by D.

*distributed for inheritance to them* — lit. *"caused to inherit."* — R The 'pi'el' is used here instead of the 'hiph'iel.' The term נחלו, usually connotes inheritance from father to son. It is used here to indicate the power of the court: הפקר בית דין הפקר, i.e. whichever portion was indicated by Joshua and the elders, became binding as an inheritance.[4]

2. *By lot was their inheritance* —

כִּי אִם־עָרִים לָשֶׁבֶת וּמִגְרְשֵׁיהֶם
לְמִקְנֵיהֶם וּלְקִנְיָנָם: ה כַּאֲשֶׁר צִוָּה יְהוָה
אֶת־מֹשֶׁה כֵּן עָשׂוּ בְּנֵי יִשְׂרָאֵל וַיַּחְלְקוּ
אֶת־הָאָרֶץ: ו וַיִּגְּשׁוּ בְנֵי־יְהוּדָה אֶל־
יְהוֹשֻׁעַ בַּגִּלְגָּל וַיֹּאמֶר אֵלָיו כָּלֵב בֶּן־
יְפֻנֶּה הַקְּנִזִּי אַתָּה יָדַעְתָּ אֶת־הַדָּבָר
אֲשֶׁר־דִּבֶּר יְהוָה אֶל־מֹשֶׁה אִישׁ
הָאֱלֹהִים עַל אֹדוֹתַי וְעַל אֹדוֹתֶיךָ בְּקָדֵשׁ
בַּרְנֵעַ: ז בֶּן־אַרְבָּעִים שָׁנָה אָנֹכִי בִּשְׁלֹחַ
מֹשֶׁה עֶבֶד־יְהוָה אֹתִי מִקָּדֵשׁ בַּרְנֵעַ
לְרַגֵּל אֶת־הָאָרֶץ וָאָשֵׁב אֹתוֹ דָּבָר

**תרגום**

וּרְוָחֵיהוֹן לְבְעִירְהוֹן וּלְגֵיתֵיהוֹן: ה כְּמָא דְפַקֵּד יְיָ יָת מֹשֶׁה כֵּן עֲבַדוּ בְּנֵי יִשְׂרָאֵל וּפַלִּיגוּ יָת אַרְעָא: ו וּקְרִיבוּ בְנֵי יְהוּדָה לְוָת יְהוֹשֻׁעַ בְּגִלְגְּלָא נַאֲמַר לֵיהּ כָּלֵב בַּר יְפֻנֶּה קְנִיזָאָה אַתְּ יְדַעְתָּא יָת פִּתְגָמָא דְמַלֵּיל יְיָ עִם מֹשֶׁה נְבִיָּא דַיְיָ עַל עֵסֶק דִּילִי וְעַל עֵסֶק דִּילָךְ בִּרְקַם גֵּיאָה: ז בַּר אַרְבְּעִין שְׁנִין אֲנָא כַּד שְׁלַח מֹשֶׁה עַבְדָּא דַיְיָ יָתִי מֵרְקַם גֵּיאָה לְאַלָּלָא יָת אַרְעָא וַאֲתֵיבִית יָתֵיהּ פִּתְגָמָא כְּמָא דַהֲוָה עִם לִבִּי:

ואחי

ת"א כאשר ליה ה'. עקדה שער נד: בן ארבעים שנה. סנהדרין סט זבחים קיח ערכין יג:

**רד"ק**

דקות: (ז) כאשר עם לבבי. נראה כי כאשר היה עמהם עד שבאו אל המחנה היה מסכים עמהם בדברי' כדי שלא יהרגוהו וכאשר בא אל המחנה השיב דבר אמת כאשר עם לבבו וזהו שאמר כאשר עם לבבי ולא כאשר עם פי ובדרך הדרש לפי שהתחיל לדבר כדבריהם כשאמר ויהס כלב התחיל ואמר וכי זו בלבד עשה לנו בן עמרם והם חשבו כי מסייע היה להם ושתקו:

**רש"י**

(ז) כאשר עם לבבי. ולא כאשר עם פי שהמרגלים היו בעלה אחת וירא כלב לומר להם שלא יאמר כמותם וכשבא הכחישם וזהו שנא' שם עקב היתה רוח אחרת עמו שהיה

**רלב"ג**

(ו) והנה זכר שכבר נגשו בני יהודה אל יהושע בגלגל כי היה המשכן שם אז ולזה היה שם יהושע והנה באו לשם עם כלב לכבודו כי נשיא היה עליהם ויורה על זה כי הוא לבדו דבר עם יהושע ולמדנו ממאמרו זה ארבעים וחמש שנה מאז דבר ה' את הדבר הזה אל משה כי שבעה שנים היה זמן כבוש הארץ כמו שזכרו רבותי' ז"ל וזה כי בשנה השנית לצאת בני ישראל מארץ מצרים נסעו ישראל כמו שנזכר בפרשת במדבר סיני ואחר מיניס שלח משה המרגלים ולפי שמעת היות משה לפני פרע' עד יום מותו היו ארבעים שנה כי הוא היה בן פ' בעמדו לפני פרע' הנה כבארו מעת בא המרגלים עד יום מותו ל"ה ויותר על זה מה שנשאר

**מצודת ציון**

(ד) ומגרשיהם. הם הבנינים הסמוכים להעיר מחוץ לחומה וכאלו נגרשו ממנה: למקניהם. הם בהמות גסות: ולקנינם. הם בהמות דקות: (ו) אדותי. תרגומו עסק דילי וכן על כל

**מצודת דוד**

לא משה ולא יהושע: לשבת. ר"ל לבד לדור בהם ולא להיות שלהם לגמרי: (ה) כאשר צוה ה'. שלא לתת נחלה ללוים: ויחלקו. ביניהם חלקו ולא נתנו ממנה ללוים: (ו) ויגשו בני יהודה. לעזור לכלב בשאלת בקשתו: על אדותי וגו'. שנהיה ונבוא אל הארץ ולא נמות במדבר: (ז) עם לבבי. כי בפיו היה בעלה אחת עם יתר המרגלים כי פחד מהם ובבואו לפני משה

## Commentary Digest

*not say the same as they. But, when he came, he contradicted them. That is what is stated there: "Because there was another spirit with him,"*[3] *for he said to them one version with his mouth, while he had another version in his heart."* — R[4] and K. A

save cities to dwell in, and the open land about them, for their cattle and for their flocks. 5. As the Lord commanded Moses, so the children of Israel did, and they divided the land. 6. Then the children of Judah came to Joshua in Gilgal; and Caleb the son of Jephunneh the Kenizzite said to him, "You know the thing that the Lord spoke to Moses the man of God concerning me and concerning you in Kadesh-barnea. 7. I was forty years old when Moses the servant of the Lord, sent me from Kadesh-barnea to spy out the land; and I brought him back word

## Commentary Digest

*two tribes* — *"instead of the tribe of Levi."* — R Hence, there were nine and a half tribes in the land of Canaan, even though the tribe of Levi was excluded.

*save cities to dwell in and the open land around them* — See Num. XXXV:2-8. The Talmud[1] discusses at length the plan for these cities. According to R, there was a park of one thousand cubits completely surrounding the city, surrounded in turn by a strip one thousand cubits wide for planting and grazing. Rambam[2] maintains that the outer strip was two thousand cubits wide.

5. *As the Lord commanded Moses* — not to give any land to the tribe of Levi. — D *so the children of Israel did* — I.e. they had no selfish intentions in depriving the Levites of a share in the land. They did this solely to fulfill the Almighty's command. — P. Y.

This took place before the land was divided by lot among the tribes. This episode is recorded to inform us of Caleb's right to the city of Hebron, which he received. — D. S.

*and they divided the land* — among themselves. — D

6. *Then the children of Judah came to Joshua* — to support Caleb their chief in his claim on Hebron. — D and A

*concerning me and concerning you* — that we live to enter the land of Canaan, as opposed to the rest of the generation who died in the desert. — A and D

7. *I was forty years old* — and was in the age group of those who were condemned to die. — A

*as it was in my heart* — *"and not as it was in my mouth, for the spies were of one counsel, and Caleb was afraid to say to them that he would*

כַּאֲשֶׁר עִם־לְבָבִי׃ ח וְאַחַי אֲשֶׁר עָלוּ עִמִּי
הִמְסִיו אֶת־לֵב הָעָם וְאָנֹכִי מִלֵּאתִי
אַחֲרֵי יְהוָה אֱלֹהָי׃ ט וַיִּשָּׁבַע מֹשֶׁה בַּיּוֹם
הַהוּא לֵאמֹר אִם־לֹא הָאָרֶץ אֲשֶׁר
דָּרְכָה רַגְלְךָ בָּהּ לְךָ תִהְיֶה לְנַחֲלָה
וּלְבָנֶיךָ עַד־עוֹלָם כִּי מִלֵּאתָ אַחֲרֵי יְהוָה
אֱלֹהָי׃ י וְעַתָּה הִנֵּה הֶחֱיָה יְהוָה אוֹתִי
כַּאֲשֶׁר דִּבֵּר זֶה אַרְבָּעִים וְחָמֵשׁ שָׁנָה
מֵאָז דִּבֶּר יְהוָה אֶת־הַדָּבָר הַזֶּה אֶל־
מֹשֶׁה אֲשֶׁר־הָלַךְ יִשְׂרָאֵל בַּמִּדְבָּר

ח וְאַחַי דִסְלִיקוּ עִמִּי
תְּבָרוּ יָת לִבָּא דְעַמָּא
וַאֲנָא אַשְׁלֵמִית בָּתַר
דַחֲלְתָא דַיְיָ אֱלָהִי׃
ט וְקַיֵּים מֹשֶׁה בְּיוֹמָא
הַהוּא לְמֵימַר אִם לָא
אַרְעָא דִי דְרַכַת פַּרְסַת
רַגְלָךְ בַּהּ דִילָךְ תְּהֵי
לְאַחְסָנָא וְלִבְנָךְ עַד
עָלְמָא אֲרֵי אַשְׁלֵימְתָּא
בָּתַר דַחֲלְתָא דַיְיָ אֱלָהִי׃
י וּכְעַן הָא קַיֵּים יְיָ יָתִי
כְּמָא דִי מַלֵּיל דְנַן
אַרְבְּעִין וְחַמֵשׁ שְׁנִין
מֵעִידָן דְמַלֵּיל יְיָ יָת
פִּתְגָמָא הָדֵין עִם מֹשֶׁה
דַאֲזַל יִשְׂרָאֵל בְּמַדְבְּרָא
וכען

## רש"י

אומר להם אחד בפה ואחד בלב: (י) זה ארבעים וחמש שנה. למדנו שמהו בכיבוש הארץ שבע שנים שהרי בשנה השנית שלח משה המרגלים נשארו שלשים ושמונה שהלכו במדבר ושבע שכבשו הרי ארבעים וחמש:

## רד"ק

(ח) המסיו. נכתב ביו"ד שהוא במקום למ"ד הפועל והיה משפטו המסיו בשורק הוי"ו על דרך נטיו רגלי והדומים לו ובאה היו"ד נחה והוי"ו נעה שלא כמנהג וי"ו הרבים בלשון הקדש אבל בלשון ארמי ובא כמו כן אשתיו חמרא ורבי אחי רבי משה ז"ל כתבו בשקל הפעיל והוי"ו מקום למ"ד הפעל אמר כי כל אחד מאחי אשר עלו עמי המסו את לב העם: (ט) אשר דרכה רגלך בה. זו היא חברון שנאמר ויבא עד חברון ולא אמר ויבואו לפי שהמרגלים האחרים היו יראים לבא שם מפני הענקים כמו שאמר ושם אחימן וגו' כלומר אף על פי שהיו שם אלה הענקים הגדולים בא שם כלב לפי' אמר לו משה שתהיה לו חברון לנחלה ואם לא נזכר זה בספר התורה ידוע כי אמת היה אחר שאמר כלב ויהושע הודה לו וכן כתוב בשופטים ויתנו לכלב את חברון כאשר דבר משה: (י) החיה ה' אותי כאשר דבר. והביאותיו אל הארץ אשר בא שמה: זה ארבעים וחמשה. כי דבר המרגלים היה בשנה השנית לצאתם ממצרים והנה נשארו להם במדבר שלשים ושמנה שנה ושבע שכבשו הנה ארבעים וחמש ומזה ראו רז"ל כי בז' שנים כבשו הארץ וז' שחלקו ראו מפסוק בי"ד שנה אחר אשר הכתה העיר

ועתה

## רלב"ג

מהשנה השנית ולזה ראוי שיובן שמה שאמר בתורה שיעמדו מ' שנה על חטא המרגלים יתם' מלת עד והוא ל"ט שנה ולזה הו' מבואר שמעת מיתת משה רבינו ע"ה עד שאמר כלב זה המאמר היו ה' שנים וחלק מהשנה השביעית ולפי שלא נשלם זה הכבוש עד אחר זה וזה כי אחר שכבש כלב את חברון זכר שהארץ שקטה ממלחמה הנה זה מבואר שכבר יתכן שיהיו ימי הכבוש שבע שנים וכבר זכרו רבותינו ז"ל שימי החלוקה היו ג"כ שבע שנים ולא ידעתי לזה סמך שלם וידמה שכבר קבלו זה בקבלה:

## מנחת שי

(ח) המסיו היו"ד נחה והוא"ו נעה שלא כמנהג שהיה משפטו בשורק הוא"ו ע"ד נטיו רגלי והדומים לו וכתב רבי יהודה שבא ע"ד לשון ארמי אשתיו חמרא וס' דניאל ה' ודומיהם עי' בפירש רד"ק ובמכלל ד' קס"ה ובשרשים: ערש מסה וס' הרכבה אות ה' ומ"ש (בדניאל ב'): (י) אותי כאשר דבר. בדפוס ישן ובמקצת ספרים כ"י מדוייקים הבי"ת בצירי ובא' מהם נמסר עליו לית וכל ההגה וסוף פסוק דכותה. וכדברים האלה כתב המכלל דף ע"ד וכאשר יצא דבר באתנח וסוף פ' הוא בצירי וכן בא בסגולה שהיא אחר זרקא בצירי ועתה הנה החיה ה' אותי כאשר דִּבֵּר והמסורת עליו לית כותיה צירי וכל אתנח וסוף פסוק צירי כותיה: (חמש ושמנים. אמר המגיה נפלאתי מאד על המדפיסים שהדפיסו מלא

## מצודת דוד

כאשר אותם: (ח) ואחי. המרגלים כולם המסו לב העם: מלאתי. השלמתי להחזיק דבר ה': (ט) אם לא. הוא ענין לשון שבועה כאלו אמר אם לא יהיה הדבר הזה אזי יהיה עונשו כך וכך וגזם ולא אמר וכן אם לא על פניך יברכך (איוב א'): אשר דרכה רגלך בה. זה חברון שנאמר ויבא עד חברון (במדבר י"ג) וכלב לבד בא להברון: (י) אשר הלך וגו'. במשך השנים האלו:

## מצודת ציון

אודות (ירמיה ג'): (ח) המסיו. מלשון המסה: מלאתי. ענין השלמה וגמר: (ט) דרכה. לעדה והוא מלשון דרך:

as it was in my heart. 8. And my brothers that went up
with me, made the heart of the people melt; but I fulfilled the
will of the Lord my God. 9. And Moses swore on that day,
saying, 'Surely the land upon which your foot has trodden
shall be your inheritance, and your children's forever, because
you have fulfilled the will of the Lord my God.' 10. And
now, behold, the Lord has kept me alive, as He spoke, these
forty-five years, from the time the Lord spoke this word to
Moses, while Israel walked in the wilderness;

**Commentary Digest**

and M explain thus: In my heart I knew that Moses was right, albeit my eyes beheld, as did the other spies the great giants and other difficulties in store for the conquerors of the land.

8. *And my brothers* — i.e. my fellow spies. — D and K

9. *upon which your foot has trodden* — the city of Hebron, where Caleb went alone to prostrate himself on the graves of the Patriarchs, and pray for divine protection from the plot of the spies. The Bible tells us: And they went up in the south and *he* came to Hebron, i.e. Caleb alone.[1] — The other spies feared the notorious giants who dwelt there. — A

10. *the Lord has kept me alive* — Just as He kept His promise to keep me alive, so will he keep His promise to give me the city of Hebron. — A

*these forty-fiive years* — "*We learn that the conquest of the land took seven years, for in the second year, Moses sent the spies. There remain thirty-eight years, during which the Israelites walked through the wilderness, and seven in which they conquered* (the land), *making a total of forty-five years.*" — R The subsequent division of the land also took seven years. — K[2]

ועתה הנה אנכי היום בן־חמש
ושמונים שנה׃ יא עודני היום חזק כאשר
ביום שלח אותי משה ככחי אז וככחי
עתה למלחמה ולצאת ולבוא׃ יב ועתה
תנה־לי את־ההר הזה אשר־דבר
יהוה ביום ההוא כי־אתה שמעת ביום
ההוא כי־ענקים שם וערים גדלות
בצרות אולי יהוה אותי והורשתים
כאשר דבר יהוה׃ יג ויברכהו יהושע
ויתן את־חברון לכלב בן־יפנה לנחלה׃
יד על־כן היתה־חברון לכלב בן־יפנה
הקנזי לנחלה עד היום הזה יען אשר

**תרגום**

וכען הא אנא יומא דין
בר תמנן וחמש שנין׃
יא עד כען אנא יומא דין
תקיף כדביומא דשלח
יתי משה כחילי כבכן
וכן חילי דכען לאגחא
קרבא ולמפק ולמיעל׃
יב וכען הב לי ית טורא
הדין דמליל יי ביומא
ההוא ארי את שמעתא
ביומא ההוא ארי גברין
תמן וקרוין רברבן כריכן
מאים יהא מימרא דיי
בסעדי ואירתינון כמא
דמליל יי׃ יג וברכיה
יהושע ויהב ית חברון
לכלב בר יפנה
לאחסנא׃ יד על כן הות
חברון לכלב בר יפנה
קנזאה לאחסנא עד
יומא הדין חלף דאשלם
בתר דחלתא דיי אלהא
דישראל

ת״א אנכי היום. סנהדרין סט זבחים קיט ערכין יג:

כ׳ רבתי · מלא

## רד״ק

כי ישראל לא מנו ליובלות ושמטו׳ אלא אחר שחלקו והפסוק אומר כי ארבע עשרה שנה אחר החרבן היה תחלת יובל כמו שאומר בראש השנה בעשור לחדש ואיזו היא שנה שראש השנה שלה בעשור לחדש הוי אומר זו שנת יובל צא והשוב משנכנסו ישראל לארץ אי אתה מוצא ארבע עשרה שנה אחר חרבן תחלת יובל אם לא תוציא י״ד שנה משנכנסו עד שמנו והם שבע שחלקו: מאז דבר ה׳. כי במצות האל אמר משה לכלב שתהיה לו חברון לנחלה: אשר הלך ישראל במדבר. טעמו לזה מ׳ וחמש שנה שזכר כלומר זה הזמן הארוך מן הדבר אשר דבר ה׳ עד היום לפי שהלך ישראל במדבר ל״ח שנה בעון המרגלים. וי״ת דאזל עם ישראל במדברא פי׳ טעם אשר הלך עם משה: (יא) וככחי עתה. באו שני כפי״ן הדמיון זה אחר זה כמי כעם ככהן כעבד כאדניו כאילו אמר העם ככהן והכהן כעם וכן כחי עתה ככחי אז וכחי אז ככחי עתה הכל בשוה: (יב) ה׳ אותי. כמו עמי וכן ואדברה אותך והדומים להם: (יג) ויתן את חברון לכלב. פי׳ שדה העיר וחצריה כי

## מנחת שי

וחסר ושמונים ו׳ מלאים וסימן נמסר בסדר בראשית ע״כ. והלא שם ובשופטים ד׳ ובמסרה רבתא נמסרו וה״ו מלאים והיו זה עמה׳ דה״כ פמו להו וכוו שבעה ע״כ): (יא) ככחי אז. במקצת דפוסים כ״ף ראשונה רבתי מה שאין כן בדפוסים ישנים ובספרים כ״י גם לא ראיתיה גדולה בשום נוסח מאלפה בינה דאותיות רבתות:

## מצודת ציון

(יב) בצורות. חזקות וסוא מל׳ צור: אותי. עמי אף כי הוא כמו״ס וכן ואדברה אותך: (יחזקאל ב׳): והורשתים. וגרשתים: (יד) יען. בעבור:

## מצודת דוד

(יא) עודני היום חזק. לפי שבא לשאול את חברון חשש פן ישיב יהושע לאמר הלא זקנת ואתה כמך ואיך תכבוש את חברון לזה אמר עודני חזק כמאז: ככחי אז. כמו הכח שהיה בי אז כזה הכח בי היום הן להלחם בעלמי הן לצאת ולבוא לפני העם להורותם תכסיסי המלחמה: (יב) ההר הזה. זה חברון: ביום ההוא. אשר הלכנו לתור את הארץ: כי ענקים שם. ומי יעלה כח להלחם בם: אולי ה׳ אותי. אולי יהיה ה׳ עמי לכבשם ולגרשם כאשר דבר לתת לי: (יג) ויברכהו. בילאה בהלחמו בם: את חברון. שדה העיר וחצריה אבל העיר עלמה היתה עיר מקלט והיא ומגרשיה היו לכהנים כמ״ש למטה: (יד) על כן. ר״ל לא באה לו בחלקו

and now, behold, I am this day eighty-five years old. 11. I am
still as strong this day as I was on the day that Moses sent
me; as my strength was then, even so is my strength now, for
war, both to go out, and to come in. 12. And now, give me
this mountain, of which the Lord spoke on that day, for
you heard on that day how the 'Anakim were there, and that
the cities were big and fortified. It may be that the Lord will
be with me, and I shall drive them out, as the Lord spoke."
13. And Joshua blessed him, and gave Hebron to Caleb the
son of Jephunneh for an inheritance. 14. Hebron, therefore,
became the inheritance of Caleb the son of Jephunneh the
Kenizzite to this day, because

## Commentary Digest

11. *I am still as strong* — Lest you fear that I will be unable to conquer the city because of my advanced age and the strength of the giants who dwell there, I inform you that I am still as strong as I was on the day that Moses sent me. — A and D

12. *this mountain* — i.e. Hebron. — D

*on that day* — when we went out to spy the land. — D

*how the 'Anakim were there* — and lest you ask, "Who has the power to wage war against them?" —

*It may be that the Lord will be with me, etc.* — D

13. *And Joshua blessed him* — that he succeed in his battle against the inhabitants of Hebron. — D

*and gave Hebron to Caleb the son of Jephunneh* — i.e. the villages surrounding Hebron. The city itself belonged to the priests and was a refuge city.[1] —

מְלֵּא אַחֲרֵי יְהוָה אֱלֹהֵי יִשְׂרָאֵל: טו וְשֵׁם
חֶבְרוֹן לְפָנִים קִרְיַת אַרְבַּע הָאָדָם
הַגָּדוֹל בָּעֲנָקִים הוּא וְהָאָרֶץ שָׁקְטָה
מִמִּלְחָמָה: טו א וַיְהִי הַגּוֹרָל לְמַטֵּה בְּנֵי
יְהוּדָה לְמִשְׁפְּחֹתָם אֶל־גְּבוּל אֱדוֹם
מִדְבַּר־צִן נֶגְבָּה מִקְצֵה תֵימָן: ב וַיְהִי
לָהֶם גְּבוּל נֶגֶב מִקְצֵה יָם הַמֶּלַח מִן־

דִּיִשְׂרָאֵל: טו וְשׁוּם חֶבְרוֹן מִלְּקַדְמִין קִרְיַת אַרְבַּע אֱנָשׁ רַב בְּגִבָּרַיָּא הוּא וְאַרְעָא שְׁדוּכַת מִלְּמֶעְבַּד קְרָבָא: א וַהֲוָה עַדְבָא לְשִׁבְטָא דִבְנֵי יְהוּדָה לְזַרְעֲיָתְהוֹן עַל תְּחוּם אֱדוֹם מַדְבְּרָא דְצִין דָרוֹמָא מִסְיָפֵי דָרוֹמָא: ב וַהֲוָה לְהוֹן תְּחוּם דָרוֹמָא מִסְיָפֵי יַמָּא דְמִלְחָא מִן כֵּיפָא דְמִתְפְּנֵי לְדָרוֹמָא: ונפק

רש״י

(טו) האדם הגדול בענקים הוא. אביהם של אחימן ששי ותלמי ארבע היה שמו. ד״א ע״ש האב וג׳ הבנים שכן קורא אותם ילידי הענק: והארץ שקטה ממלחמה. מוסב לענין הראשון לאחר שבע שכבשו סביבותיהם נכנעו האמוריים ולא נאספו עוד למלחמה עליהם לכך התחילו לעסוק בחילוק הארץ. ומדרש אגדה האדם הגדול בענקים הוא אברהם אבינו הוא שגרם להם שהארץ שקטה ממלחמה ארבעים שנה שנתעכבו במדבר בשכר שכבדו את הזקן בקרית ארבע שאמרו לו נשיא אלהים אתה בתוכנו:

טו (א) אל גבול אדום. סמוך למיצר אדום: נגבה. בתחום מיצר דרומי של ארץ ישראל: מקצה תימן. בסוף כל המיצר: (ב) ויהי להם גבול. מיצר דרומי של יהודה: מקצה ים המלח. הוא מקצוע דרומית מזרחית

רד״ק

העיר עצמה היתה מקלט כמו שאמר בספר ערי המקלט כי חברון ומגרשיה היו לכהנים: (טו) קרית ארבע. ארבע הוא שם הענק והוא האדם הגדול בענקים: שקטה ממלחמה. כי התעצלו בני ישראל להוריש הנשארים: (א) נגבה. בקצה תימן מדבר צין היה לצד דרום ולא כל דרום הגבול אלא מקצה דרומו: מן הלשון. לשון הים וי״ת כיפא דמיתפני לדרומא ר״ל

הלשן

מצודת דוד

וגורלו בתוך בני משפחתו ובעבור זה בא לחלקו חוזר ומפרש יען אשר מלא וגו׳: (טו) קרית ארבע. קרית איש שהיה שמו ארבע והוא היה אדם הגדול בענקים ור״ל גם למול ענקים היה נחשב לגדול וגובה הקומה: והארץ שקטה ממלחמה. כאילו אמר הנה הדבר הזה עם שנכתב פה אחר כל המלחמות מ״מ נהיה הדבר בזמן המלחמה ולאחר זה שקטה הארץ ממלחמה: טו (א) למשפחותם. מה שחלקו למשפחותם בי יתכן שחלקו לכל משפחה ומשפחה חלק לבד ולא היו מעורבבים אלה באלה: אל גבול אדום. לנחול אצל גבול אדום שעמדה בדרומה של ארץ ישראל: מדבר צין נגבה. ר״ל מדבר צין היתה מיצר הדרומי של יהודה וחוזר ומפרש מקצה תימן ור״ל לא שהיתה מדבר צין כל אורך מיצר הדרומי אלא מקצה תימן היתה וממנה היה מתחיל מיצר הדרומי: (ב) גבול נגב. מיצר הדרומי ממזרח בלפי המערב: מקצה ים המלח. אשר עמד במזרחו של ארץ ישראל ומשם התחיל

מצודת ציון

(טו) קרית. מלשון קריה ועיר: טו (א) גבול. מיצר וסוף:

## Commentary Digest

Edom touched the southwestern tip of Eretz Israel, where the boundary of Judah began, stretching in a line from east to west to the Mediterranean. — E. G.

*southward* — *"at the southern boundary of Eretz Israel."* — R I.e. the wilderness of Zin follows the border of Judah on the south, lying to the west of Edom. — E. G.

*at the uttermost part of the south* — *"at the end of the entire boundary."* — R The word for "south" here is "Taiman." The land of Edom was subdivided to the various families and tribes of the Edomites. Taiman, being the oldest of these tribes,[4] took the land adjacent to Eretz Israel. The word "taiman" thus became synonymous with south because the southern tip of Eretz Israel touches Taiman. — E. G.

2. *And their south border was* — i.e. *"the southern border of Judah."* — R

*from the edge of the Salt Sea* — *"that is the southeastern corner of Eretz Israel, in* אלה מסעי. — R[5]

he fulfilled the will of the Lord God of Israel. 15. And the
name of Hebron before was Kirjath-arba (the city of Arba);
*Arba* was the greatest man among the 'Anakim. And the land
had rest from war.

15

1. And the lot for the tribe of the children of Judah according
to their families, was to the border of Edom, to the wilderness
of Zin southward at the uttermost part of the south. 2. And
their south border was from the edge of the salt sea, from

## Commentary Digest

15. *Arba was the greatest man among the Anakim — "Arba was the name of the father of Ahiman, Sheshai, and Talmai. Another explanation is:* (It was called Kirjath-arba, the city of four) *because of the father and the three sons, for the scripture calls them the children of 'Anak."* — R[1]

*And the land had rest from war — "This refers back to the previous topic, i.e. after the seven years during which they conquered their surroundings, the Amorites were humbled, and no longer gathered to wage war upon them. Therefore, they began to engage in the division of the land. The Midrash Aggadah states that the greatest man among the 'Anakim was our father Abraham who was instrumental for them that the land rested from war the forty years that they tarried in the wilderness, as a reward for that which they honored the patriarch in Kirjath-arba, for they said to him. 'A Godly prince are you in our midst.'"*[2] — R[3]

CHAPTER 15

1. *The children of Judah* — In this chapter, the beginning of the actual division of the land is described. First, the tribes of Judah and of Joseph were apportioned, Judah in the south, and Joseph in the north. Judah occupied the entire southern boundary from east to west, so that the very word "Judah" became synonymous with South ("Negev"). Joseph occupied the major part of the North, known as Galillee ("Gallil"). So we read in Ch. 18:5: Judah shall remain in his border on the South, and the house of Joseph shall remain in their border on the North.

*according to their families* — The division of the land was according to the tribes and further subdivided among the families. — D

*to the border of Edom — "Adjacent to the border of Edom."* — R The northwestern corner of the land of

הַלָּשֹׁן הַפֹּנֶה נֶגְבָּה : ג וְיָצָא אֶל־מִנֶּגֶב
לְמַעֲלֵה עַקְרַבִּים וְעָבַר צִנָה וְעָלָה מִנֶּגֶב
לְקָדֵשׁ בַּרְנֵעַ וְעָבַר חֶצְרוֹן וְעָלָה אַדָּרָה
וְנָסַב הַקַּרְקָעָה : ד וְעָבַר עַצְמוֹנָה וְיָצָא
נַחַל מִצְרַיִם והיה תֹּצְאוֹת הַגְּבוּל יָמָּה
זֶה־יִהְיֶה לָכֶם גְּבוּל נֶגֶב : ה וּגְבוּל קֵדְמָה

והיו קרי

**תרגום**

ג וְנָפֵק לְמַדְרוֹמָא לְמַסְקָנָא דְעַקְרַבִּין וַעֲבַר לְצִין וּסְלֵיק מִדָּרוֹמָא לְרְקָם גֵּיאָה וַעֲבַר לְחֶצְרוֹן וּסְלֵיק לְאַדָּר וּמִסְתְּחַר לְקַרְקָעָה : ד וַעֲבַר לְעַצְמוֹן וְנָפֵק לְנַחְלָא דְמִצְרַיִם וַהֲווּ מַפְקָנוֹהִי דִתְחוּמָא לְמַעַרְבָא דֵין יְהֵא לְכוֹן תְּחוּם דָּרוֹמָא : ה וּתְחוּם קִידוּמָא

**רד"ק**

לשון סלע : (ג) אל מנגב . אל המקום שהיה מנגב למעלה עקרבים : (ד) זה יהיה לכם גבול נגב . היה לו לומר להם שהרי כל הפרשה ספור דברים הוא ויתכן פירושו כי כן יהיה הגבול להם כמו שנאמר בתורה הזה יהיה לכם גבול נגב :

**רש"י**

ים. של ארץ ישראל באלה מסעי : מן הלשון. של ים: (ג) ויצא אל מנגב למעלה עקרבים. ואינו אומר ויצא ונסב ותאר אלא במקום שהוא של גבול בולט אל החוץ או כונס לצד פנים שאינו הולך מכוון וכאן הוא בולט אל החוץ ובא מנגב למעלה עקרבים בדרום של מעלה עקרבים נמצא שמעלה עקרבים לפנים מן החוט ועבר ובא לו אל המערב : צנה. לצין וכל תיבה שצריכ' למ"ד בתחלת' הטיל לה ה"א בסופה : ועלה. כל מה שהוא עולה מן המזרח לצד ירושלים הוא עולה ומירושלים והלא' הוא יורד כאן למדנו שירושלים גבוהה מכל ארץ ישראל וירושלים אינה נזכרת במיצר זה שבמיצר לפונית של יהוד' היתה כמו שאמור בענין : ועלה מנגב לקדש ברנע. החוט הולך לדרומ' של קדש ברנע נמצאת קדש לפנים מן החוט : ועבר חצרון. לצד המערב הוא מוכ' והולך עד והיו תוצאותיו הימה : (ד) תוצאות. סופי של מיצר אל הים הגדול שהיא מיצר מערבי לכל א"י נמצא גבול יהוד' מחזיק כל ארכה של א"י מן המזרח למערב ועומד בדרומ' של א"י : (ה) וגבול קדמה. חוט המתוח למיצר מזרחי של יהוד' : ים המלח. שהוא מקצוע דרומית מזרחית

**מנחת שי**

טו (ד) והיה תוצאות. והיו ק' והוא חד מן ז' מלין בחד לישן דכתיבין ה"א בסוף תיבותא וקריין ו' וסימן ונסב לכם דמסעי . ועבר עצמונה דהכא . ויהי להם הגבול . ועבר הגבול . ותאר הגבול . תלתיהון בסיפרא סימן י"ח לאן אבדות (ירמיה נ') ועשיתי אותם לגוי אחד (יחזקאל ל"ז) ובמסורת הדפוס נמסר זה הסימן כאן ובפרשת מסעי במלות שונות והכונה א' ידפרשה מסעי חסר אותו דירמיה ודיחזקאל ומ"ש בס ו' ל"ל ז' :

**מצודת ציון**

(ב) הלשון. כאשר הים המשוך כלשון : (ה) לפאת. לצד ורוח :

**מצודת דוד**

מדבר צין : מן הלשון. של הים ההוא : (ג) ויצא. הגבול ההוא יצא כלפי חוץ להתרחב יותר ובא אל המקום שהיתה מנגב למעלה עקרבים א"כ היתה מעלה עקרבים לפנים מן הגבול וליהודה תחשב (כ"מ שנאמר ויצא ר"ל חוט המיצר יצא כלפי חוץ ונתרחב הנחלה שם וברוחב היא הנכה מבס והלאה וכ"מ שנאמר ונסב או ותאר ר"ל חוט המיצר סיבב רק המקום ההוא ואח"ז הזר חוט המיצר לרוחב הראשון או כשכלה הפאה האחת ומסבב לפאה אחרת וכ"מ שנא' תוצאות או ר"ל שם כלה הגבול לגמרי או ר"ל שם כלה ויצא רוחב הראשון כי משם והלאה נתקלר הנחלה וכאשר יראה בצורה) : ועבר צנה . משם עבר הגבול לצין כי הה"א בסופה עומדת במקום למ"ד בתחלה (כ"מ שנא' ועבר ר"ל המקום ישר ושוה וכ"מ שנא' ועלה ר"ל שעלה במעלה הר וכ"מ שנאמר וירד ר"ל שירד במורד הר) : מנגב לקדש ברנע. והיתה א"כ מנחלת בני יהודה : (ד) תוצאות הגבול. סוף הגבול כלה אל הים הגדול נמצא שהחזיק גבול יהודה כל אורך ארץ ישראל מן המזרח למערב : זה יהיה לכם. ר"ל זה הגבול יהיה לכל ישראל גבול הנגב מן המזרח למערב כאמור : (ה) וגבול קדמה. מדרום כלפי הצפון : ים המלח. כל אורך הים היה הגבול וברוחב כל נחלתו :

## Commentary Digest

opinion among the commentators as to whether this refers to the Nile or to the Wadi-El-Arish.[5]

*the goings out* — *"the end of the border is at the Great* (Mediterranean) *Sea, which is the western border of all Eretz Israel. Hence, the boundary of Judah occupies the entire length of Eretz Israel from east to west, and is situated in the south of Eretz Israel."* — R

5. *and the east border* — *"the line which is drawn along the east border of Judah."* — R

*the Salt Sea* — *"which is the south-eastern corner of the land, in "Eileh Massei."* — R

the bay that faces southward. 3. And it went out to the south side of Maaleh-Acrabbim, and passed along to Zin, and ascended on the south side of Kadesh-barnea, and passed along to Hezron, and went up to Adar, and circled to Karkaa. 4. From there it passed toward Azmon, and went to the river of Egypt; and the goings out of the boundary were at the sea. This shall be your southern boundary. 5. And the east border

## Commentary Digest

*the bay* — lit. the tongue, i.e. the tongue *"of the sea."* — R The extremity of the sea shaped like a tongue. — Z

*that faces southward* — The southernmost point of the Dead Sea, where the Sea narrows to the "Tongue," or gulf, is the southernmost point of Judah.

3. *And it went out to the south side of Maaleh-Acrabbim* (Scorpion Pass) — *"The Scripture uses the terms:* ויצא, *and it went out,* ותאר, *and it circled,* ונסב, *and it circled, only where the line of the boundary bulges outward, or is indented, and does not follow a straight course. Here, it bulges outward, and comes* מנגב למעלה עקרבים, *to the south of Maaleh-Acrabim. Hence, Maaleh-Acrabbim is within the line, and it passed it and continued westward."* — R

*to Zin* — Heb. צנה, *"same as* לצין, *Every word which needs a 'lamed' prefixed to it, may instead have a 'he' suffixed to it."*[1] — R. E. G. exlpains that the city was named Zinnah. It was the oasis of the desert of Zin, so called because of its peculiar palms, known as ציני הר הברזל.[2]

*and ascended* — *"As long as it ascends from the east toward Jerusalem, it ascends, and from Jerusalem and further, it descends. Hence, we learn that Jerusalem is the highest point in all Eretz Israel.*[3] *Jerusalem is not mentioned in this boundary, for it was in the northern border of Judah, as is mentioned in this chapter."*[4] — R

*and ascended on the south side of Kadesh-Barnea* — *"The line goes to the south of Kadesh-Barnea. Hence, Kadesh is within the line."* — R

*and it passed along to Hezron* — *He continues to count westward until: and its goings out* (sic) *were at the sea."* — R

*and circled to Karkaa* — J. E. G. boundary formed a semi-circle around the city of Karkaa and returned to its straight line.

4. *the river of Egypt* — We have already mentioned the difference of

ים המלח עד קצה הירדן וגבול לפאת צפונה מלשון הים מקצה הירדן: ו ועלה הגבול בית חגלה ועבר מצפון לבית הערבה ועלה הגבול אבן בהן בן ראובן: ז ועלה הגבול דברה מעמק עכור וצפונה פנה אל הגלגל אשר נכח למעלה אדמים אשר מנגב לנחל

**תרגום**

קידומא ימא דמלחא עד סיפי ירדנא ותחומא לרוח צפונא מכיף ימא מסיפי ירדנא: ו וסליק תחומא לבית חגלה ועבר מצפונא לבית מישרא וסליק תחומא לאבן בוהן בר ראובן: ז וסליק תחומא לדביר ממישר עכור וצפונא מתפני לגלגלא דלקביל מסקנא דאדמים דמדרום לנחלא ועבר תחומא

**רש"י**

לארץ כאלה מסעי: עד קצה הירדן· רחבו של גבול יהודה אינו אלא כנגד ים המלח עד מקום שהירדן נופל בים המלח שהירדן אף הוא במיצר מזרח של ארץ כנען כמו שנא' באלה מסעי במיצר מזרחי וירד הגבול הירדנ' והיו תוצאותיו ים המלח שהוא במקצוע: וגבול לפאת צפונה. הוא מיצר המתוח למיצר לפון מן המזרח למערב מלשון לים המלח ממקום שהירדן נופל בו שאמרנו שמשם כלה רוחב גבול מיצר המזרחי ועלה לצד המערב בית הגלה ועבר החוט מלפון לבית הערב' בדרום' של א"י בית הערב' נמצא בית הערב' בתוך גבול יהוד' לפנים מן החוט: (ו) ועלה הגבול אבן בהן· כל מה שהולך עד ירושלים הוא עולה: (ז) ועלה הגבול דבירה מעמק עכור· שהיה עמק עכור בין אבן בהן לדביר: וצפונה פונה אל הגלגל· וכשהגיע כנגד הגלגל מרחיב הגבול ויוצא חוט המיצר לצד הצפון אל הגלגל אשר הוא נוכח מעלה אדומים אשר המעל' בדרום הנחל כמוצא הנחל חוץ מן החוט שלא בגבול יהודה: מנגב לנחל. עמק ומדרון היה בלא מים:

**רד"ק**

(ו) אבן בהן בן ראובן. אדון המקום היה שמו בוהן בן ראובן וכן תרגם יונתן בר ראובן ושם המקום אבן אולי היתה שם אבן גדולה לסימן לגבול המקום: (ז) אל הגלגל אשר נכח למעלה אדמים. נקרא המקום גלגל ונקרא גלילות לענין ידוע אצלם ואדומים גם כן שם מקום נקרא כך לענין ידוע אצלם וכת"י למסקנא דאדמים: אל עין רוגל. ת"י לעין קצרא וקצרא בדברי רז"ל הוא כובס הבגדים ות"י שדה כבוס חקל משטא קצריא ונקרא הכובס רוגל לפי שמשפשף הבגדי' ברגליו

**מנחת שי**

(ו) אבן בהן בס"א לא בתי"ת וכן דלקמן סימן י"ח ע"ש:

**מצודת דוד**

עד קצה הירדן. קלהו הדרומי הנופל בים (אולם משם הלך הירדן בפאת הדרומי כלפי המערב וכבא בים הגדול כן אמרז"ל (בכורות נ"ה) וכזה ניחא מ"ש ויסע לוט מקדם (בראשית י"ג) כי פנה למערב לככר הירדן שכלפי המערב וניחא מ"ש ויבאו כו' בעבר הירדן (שם נ') ור"ל בעבר הירדן שכלפי המערב כי לא היה לורך להם ללכת בדרך עבר הירדן המזרחי): וגבול לפאת צפונה. מן המזרח כלפי המערב: מלשון הים. הפונה לפונה והוא מקלה הירדן הפונה לדרום: (ו) בית חגלה. ר"ל מלפונה כמוזכר בגבולי בנימין: מצפון וגו'. א"כ בית הערבה היתה לפנים מן המילר וליהודה תחשב (ואף כי בית הערבה נמנה היא בנחלת בנימין ל"ל שניים היו בשם אחד והיה לאחת שם גווי להבדיל ביניהן ולא הוזכר במקרא וכ"כ ל"ל בכ"מ שנזכר פעמים ושלש שם מקום אחד הן בנחלת שבט אחד הן בנחלת שני שבטים): (ז) מעמק עכור. כי מאבן בהן בן ראובן בא הגבול לעמק עכור עם שלא נזכר ומעלמו יוכן: וצפונה פונה. כשבא הגבול מול הגלגל היה חוט המילר מרחיב ויולא לצד לפון אל הגלגל אשר היא נוכח מעלה אדומים אשר המעלה הסיא עומדת בדרום הנחל והגבול הלך מהגלגל

**מצודת ציון**

(ו) אבן בוהן. הוא שם מקום: בן ראובן. עיר איש ששמו ראובן וכן מבין סימון (ירמיה מ"ח): (ז) נוכח. נגד:

## Commentary Digest

*"This was a steep canyon without water."* — R The southern slope of this canyon led to Adummim, as R explained in the previous paragraph. For this reason, R explains נחל as "valley," rather than "river." See also Deut. XXI:4, and Rambam, Laws of Homicide, Ch. 9: also comments of Tos. Yomtov to Sotah, ch. 9, Mishnah 5; and Sinai, Tammuz 5724 (July '64) and comment of Taz to Orach Chaim, ch. 688.

was the Salt Sea, even to the end of the Jordan. And their border in the north quarter was from the bay of the sea at the uttermost part of the Jordan.
6. And the border went up to Beth-hoglah, and passed along by the north of Beth-arabah; and the border went up to Eben of Bohan the son of Reuben.
7. And the border went up toward Debir from the Valley of Achor, and so northward, facing Gilgal, that is before the ascent to Adummim, which is on the south side of the valley,

## Commentary Digest

*even to the end of the Jordan* — *"The breadth of the boundary of Judah is only opposite the Dead Sea, up to the place where the Jordan empties into the Dead Sea, for the Jordan too is in the eastern border of the land of Canaan, as it is stated in "Eileh Mass'ei," concerning the eastern border; and the border descended to the Jordan, and its goings out were the Salt Sea,[1] which is at the corner."* — R

*And their border in the north quarter* — *"The borderline which is drawn along the northern border from east to west, is from the gulf of the Dead Sea, from the place where the Jordan empties into it, as we have stated that the eastern border ends there; and it went up westward to Beth-Hoglah, and the line passed on the north of Beth-Arabah in the south of Eretz Israel. Beth-Arabah* (sic) *hence, Beth-Arabah is in the boundary of Judah, within the line."* — R

6. *and the border went up to Eben of Bohan* — *"As long as the border goes toward Jerusalem, it goes up."* — R[2] The place was named "Eben," and it was owned by one Bohan the son of Reuben (not of the tribe of Reuben). Perhaps there was a stone of sufficient size and importance to serve as a landmark, hence the name "Eben," meaning "stone." — K

7. *And the border went up toward Debir from the Valley of Achor* — *"for the Valley of Achor was between Eben of Bohan and Debir."* — R The Valley of Achor ran in a north and south direction from a spot near Jericho, on the northern part of Benjamin, traversing all of Benjamin until it reached the border of Judah.[3] — E. G.

*and so northward, facing Gilgal* — *"And when the border reached opposite Gilgal, the border widens and the borderline goes out toward the north to Gilgal which is opposite the ascent to Adummim, the ascent being south of the valley. Hence, the valley is outside the line, not in the boundary of Judah."* — R

*on the south side of the valley* —

וְעָבַר הַגְּבוּל אֶל־מֵי עֵין־שֶׁמֶשׁ וְהָיוּ תֹצְאֹתָיו אֶל־עֵין רֹגֵל: ח וְעָלָה הַגְּבוּל גֵּי בֶן־הִנֹּם אֶל־כֶּתֶף הַיְבוּסִי מִנֶּגֶב הִיא יְרוּשָׁלָ͏ִם וְעָלָה הַגְּבוּל אֶל־רֹאשׁ הָהָר אֲשֶׁר עַל־פְּנֵי גֵי־הִנֹּם יָמָּה אֲשֶׁר בִּקְצֵה עֵמֶק־רְפָאִים צָפוֹנָה: ט וְתָאַר הַגְּבוּל מֵרֹאשׁ הָהָר אֶל־מַעְיַן מֵי נֶפְתּוֹחַ וְיָצָא

## תרגום

תְּחוּמָא לְמֵי עֵין שִׁמְשָׁא וַהֲוָן מַפְקָנוֹהִי לְעֵין קַצְרָא: ח וְסָלֵיק תְּחוּמָא לְחֵילַת בַּר הִנֹּם דִּלְעֵיבַר יְבוּס מִדָּרוֹמָא הִיא יְרוּשְׁלֵם וְסָלֵק תְּחוּמָא לְרֵישׁ טוּרָא דְּעַל אַפֵּי חֵילַת הִנֹּם מַעַרְבָא דִּבְסְיָפֵי מֵישַׁר גִּבָּרַיָא צִפּוּנָא: ט וְיִסְחַר תְּחוּמָא מֵרֵישׁ טוּרָא לְמַבּוּעֵי מֵי נֶפְתּוֹחַ וְנָפֵק לְקִרְוֵי טוּרָא

ת״א ותאר הגבול. זבחים נז

## רד״ק

בעת שמכבסם: (ח) גי בן הנם. ת״י חילת בר הנם והיה הגיא הזה סמוך לירושלם והוא המקום אשר טמא יאשיהו מפני הגלולים שהיו בו ושם אדוני המקום מקדם בן הנום והנום. ומה שנאמר ועלה הגבול והמקום היה גי אינו אומר ועלה כנגד הגיא אלא אל המקום שהיה בו הגיא בכל אלה הגבולים הוא אומר ועלה כי ירושלם גבוה מכל הארצות: עמק רפאים. ת״י מישר גבריא והוא שנאמר עליו כמלקט שבלים בעמק רפאים והיה המקום ההוא מאז מקום הגבורים הענקים: (ט) ותאר הגבול. כל ותאר ת״י יסחר כמו ובמחוגה יתארהו שהוא ענין סבוב. מעין מי נפתוח. הוא הנקרא בדברי רז״ל עין עיטם:

## רש״י

אל עין רגל. מעיין הכובסים תרגם יונתן עין קצרה וקורא את הכובס רוגל על שם שבועט את בגדי הצמר ברגליו (פולוש בלע״ז): (ח) ועלה וגו' גי בן הנם. עודנו עולה מעט עד עין עיטם ומשם והלאה הוא יורד וזהו שאמרו רבותינו ז״ל בשחיט' קדשי' סבור למבנייהו בעין עיטם שהוא גבוה מירושלים מעט: אל כתף היבוסי. נמצאת ירושלים חוץ מן החוט ואינה בגבול יהוד' אלא בגבול בנימין שהוא בצפונו של יהודה: (ט) ותאר. לשון ונסב בעוגל כמו ובמחוגה יתארהו ויונתן תרגם את כולם ויסחר:

## רלב״ג

(ח) ועלה הגבול גי בן הנם אל כתף היבוסי מנגב היא ירושלם. ידמה מזה המקום שירושלם לא נתחלקה לשבטים ואולם מה שאמר אחר זה ואת היבוסי יושבי ירושלם לא יכלו בני יהודה להורישם וישב היבוסי את בני יהודה בירושלם יורה שירושלם היתה מנחלת בני יהודה כי לא אמר לא יכלו בני ישראל להורישם אך אמר לא יכלו בני יהודה להורישם. וממה שאמר בנחלת בנימין במנין עריהם אשר נפלו להם בנחלה וצלע האלף והיבוסי היא ירושלם ידמה כי ירושלם היתה מנחלת בני בנימין ולזה נפלה המחלוקת אם נתחלקה ירושלם לשבטים אם לא. ובר יפול ספק במה שנזכר בכאן מנחלת בני יהודה שאחר כך נתנו קצת מעריהם למטה שמעון וזכר הספק בזה כי היה חלק בני יהודה רב מהם וינחלו בני שמעון בתוך נחלתם איך יתכן והנה היתה זאת החלוקה כלה בגורל על פי ה' האם נעלם ממנו דבר עד שיתן בתחלה לשבט יהודה יותר מהראוי ואחר כך כשראה שלא הספיק הוכרח לתת לשבט שמעון מנחלת בני יהודה הנה זה לא יתכן שידומ' בזה האופן והנכון כאמר בהיתר זה הספק כי תוך גבולות נחלת בני יהודה שהיו מכוונים מאת הש״י היו מן הערים יותר מן הראוי להם ולא נפלו כל הערים ההם לבני יהודה אך נמנו מפני היותם כלם בתוך גבולותיהם ואחר זה ביאר מה

## מצודת ציון

(ט) ותאר. ענין הקפה וסבוב כמו ובמחוגה יתארהו (ישעיה מ״ד):

## מצודת דוד

נכחו אל מעלה אדומים והנחל היה מן החוט המילר ולחוץ שלא בגבול יהודה: ועבר הגבול. ממעלה אדומים: והיו תוצאותיו וגו'. בצפון עין רוגל היה סוף הגבול בזה הרוחב ומשם והלאה נכנס חוט המילר לפנים ונתקלר הנחלה: (ח) ועלה הגבול. מעין רוגל נכנס הגבול לפנים לצד הדרום ועלה במעלה ההר לגי בן הנם אשר עמדה מצד ירושלים בדרומה (וירושלים עצמה היתה מנחלת בנימין אבל רצועה היתה יוצאת מנחלת יהודה ובאה בירושלי') ואמר ל' ועלה כי ירושלים היתה גבוה מכל א״י זולת עין עיטם: היא ירושלים. על היבוסי יאמר: ועלה הגבול אל ראש ההר. עודנו עולה עד מעין מי נפתוח והוא עין עיטם הנזכר בדרז״ל: ימה. ההר היה במערבה של גי בן הנם ובקצה הצפוני של עמק רפאים נמצא שעמק היה מגבול יהודה: (ט) ויצא אל ערי הר עפרון. ר״ל בעבר

and the border passed toward the waters of Enshemesh, and
the goings out thereof were at En-rogel.
8. And the border
went up by the valley of the son of Hinnom to the south
side of the Jebusite; the same is Jerusalem; and the border
went up to the top of the mountain that lies before the valley
of Hinnom westward, which is at the end of the valley of
the giants northward.
9. And the border circled from the top
of the mountain to the fountain of the water of Nephtoah,
and went out

## Commentary Digest

*at 'En-rogel* — *"the fountain of the launderers, according to J who renders:* עין קצרה*. The scripture calls the launderer* רוגל*, because he treads woolen clothing with his feet.* Heb. רגל." — R and K. The boundary went in a northwesterly direction from En-shemesh to 'En-rogel, from which point it continued in a due westerly course. — E. G.

The valley of the son of Hinnom is the narrow and deep valley that surrounds the Old City of Jerusalem on the west and the south. It was probably named after a Canaanite, similar to Eben of Bohan the son of Reuben. — D. M.

8. *And the border went up by the valley of the son of Hinnom* — *"It still goes up a little until 'En-'etam, and from there on it goes down. Now, this is what our Rabbis said in Zeb.*[1]*: 'They thought to build it* (the Temple) *in 'En-'etam, which is slightly higher than Jerusalem.'"* — R

*to the south side of the Jebusite: the same is Jerusalem* — כתף means the shoulder. Until this point the boundary has continuously sloped upward, so that Jerusalem, "the highest point in Israel"[1] is situated between the "shoulders of Benjamin."[2] The beauty of the geographical layout of the land of Israel is the subject of an interesting work, "The Concealed Biblical Maps" by Bezalel Ben-Har, Jerusalem 5721. Since the line passed on the south side of Jerusalem, *"Jerusalem is found to be outside the line, and not in the boundary of Judah, but in the boundary of Benjamin, which is north of Judah."* — R

9. *And* — *circled* — Heb. ותאר, *"an expression similar to* ונסב*, in a circle, like: "And with a compass he enrcircles it."*[3] Heb. יתארהו *J rendered them all* ויסחר*, and he encircled."* — R

*from the top of the mountain to the fountain of the water of Nephtoah* — The borderline continues to ascend to the fountain of the water of Nephtoah, also known as 'En-'etam, lying at the very top of the hill. This fount was twenty-three ells higher than the floor of the Temple court, and was the source of the High Priest's immersion water on Yom Kippur. — R,[4] K, and D

אל־ערי הר־עפרון ותאר הגבול בעלה
היא קרית יערים: י ונסב הגבול מבעלה
ימה אל־הר שעיר ועבר אל־כתף הר־
יערים מצפונה היא כסלון וירד בית־
שמש ועבר תמנה: יא ויצא הגבול אל־
כתף עקרון צפונה ותאר הגבול
שכרונה ועבר הר־הבעלה ויצא
יבנאל והיו תצאות הגבול ימה: יב וגבול
ים הימה הגדול וגבול זה גבול בני־
יהודה סביב למשפחתם: יג ולכלב בן
יפנה נתן חלק בתוך בני־יהודה אל־
פי יהוה ליהושע את־קרית ארבע אבי

**תרגום**

טורא דעפרון ויסחר
תחומא לבעלה היא
קרית יערים: י ומסתחר
תחומא מבעלה לימא
לטורא דשעיר ועבר
לעיבר טור יערים
מצפונא היא כסלון
ונחית לבית שמש ועבר
לתמנא: יא ונפק תחומא
לעבר עקרון לצפונא
ויסחר תחומא לשכרון
ועבר לטור בעלה ונפק
ליבנאל והוון מפקנוהי
דתחומא לימא:
יב ותחום מערבא ימא
רבא ותחומא דין תחום
בני יהודה סחור סחור
לזרעיתהון: יג ולכלב
בר יפונה יהב חולקא
בגו בני יהודה על
מימרא דיי ליהושע ית
קרית ארבע אבוהון
דגבריא

**ה"א** ולכלב. תמורה טז:

### רש"י

**ויצא אל וגו'** · ההיט יוצא לצד הצפון והגבול הרחיב עד ערי הר עפרון: **והאר הגבול בעלה** · אין זה לצד המערב אלא הבליט' לצד צפון: (י) **ונסב הגבול מבעלה ימה** · ועכשיו חוזר למגיננו הראשון מן המזרח למערב: **אל כתף וגו'** · שהיה הוט בצפונו של הר יערים נמצא הר יערים בתוך גבול יהודה לפנים מן החוט: (יא) **והיו תוצאות הגבול** · סוף המיצר: **ימה** · אל ים הגדול שהוא מיצר מערבי: (יג) **אל פי ה' ליהושע**. כמו שאמר הקב"ה

### רד"ק

(יב) הימה הגדול וגבול. וגבול יהודה למערב היה הים הגדול: וגבול ים. כלומר הים הגדול וגבולו היה גבול

### הענק

### רלב"ג

שהיה מאלו הערים לשבט שמעון ובזה נתקיים מה שאמר בתורה אחלקם ביעקב ואפיצם בישראל כמו שבארנו שם:

### מצודת דוד

הצפוני והיו משל יהודה: (י) ימה. כלפי המערב: מצפונה. נמצא הר יערים היא כסלון לפנים מן הגבול ומשל יהודה היתה: (יא) צפונה. והיה עקרון לפנים מן הגבול: תוצאות. סוף הגבול כלה אל הים הגדול: (יב) וגבול ים. גבול המערבי מן הצפון אל הדרום: הימה הגדול. הים הגדול היה לגבול: וגבול. ר"ל איי הים יחשבו גם הם לגבול יהודה ונחלתו היו: סביב למשפחותם. ר"ל המסבב נחלת כל משפחותם: (יג) אל פי ה'. ר"ל לא מעצמו נתנו יהושע לכלב כ"א ע"פ ה': אבי הענק. ר"ל ארבע היה אבי הענק ר"ל הגדול

## Commentary Digest

12. *And the west border* — i.e. from north to south. — D

*and the coast thereof* — This includes the islands of the sea. — D[1]

*round about, according to their families* — i.e. the boundary which encompasses the inheritance of all their families. — D

13. *according to the commandment of the Lord to Joshua* — lit. to the mouth of the Lord to Joshua, i.e. "*as the Most Holy, Blessed be He, said to Joshua.*" — R

to the cities of Mount Ephron; and the border circled to
Baalah, which is Kirjath-jearim. 10. And the border
compassed from Baalah westward to Mount Seir, and passed
along to the side of Mount Jearim, which is Chesalon, on the
north side, and went down to Beth-Shemesh, and passed on
to Timnah. 11. And the border went out to the side of
Ekron northward; and the border circled to Shicron, and
passed along to Mount Baalah, and went out to Jabneel; and
the goings out of the border were at the sea. 12. And the
west border was to the Great Sea, and the coast thereof, this
is the border of the children of Judah round about, according
to their families. 13. And to Caleb the son of Jephunneh
he gave a part among the children of Judah, according to
the commandment of the Lord to Joshua, even the city of
Arba the father of

**Commentary Digest**

*and it went out to etc.* — *"The line goes out to the north, and the boundary widens to the cities of Mount Ephron."* — R

*and the border circled to Baalah* — *"This is not to the west, but the bulge was to the north."* — R

*Kirjath-Jearim* — See I Sam. VII: 1, 2.

10. *And the border compassed from Baalah westward* — *"Now he returns to his previous enumeration* (of border cities) *from east to west."* — R

*to Mount Seir* — This mountain is distinct from Mount Seir of the land of Edom. It was so called because it was completely covered with brambles and reeds like a person covered with hair, Heb. שער. — E. G.

*to the side of Mount Jearim etc.* — *"for the borderline was north of Mt. Jearim. Hence, Mt. Jearim is within the boundary of Judah, within the borderline."* — R

11. *to the side of Ekron northward* — Hence, Ekron was within the boundary. — D

*and the goings out of the border* — *"the end of the boundary."* — R

*at the sea* — *"at the Great* (Med.) *Sea which is the western boundary."* — R

הָעֲנָק הִיא חֶבְרוֹן:
יד וַיֹּרֶשׁ מִשָּׁם כָּלֵב אֶת־שְׁלוֹשָׁה בְּנֵי הָעֲנָק אֶת־שֵׁשַׁי וְאֶת־אֲחִימַן וְאֶת־תַּלְמַי יְלִידֵי הָעֲנָק:
טו וַיַּעַל מִשָּׁם אֶל־יֹשְׁבֵי דְּבִר וְשֵׁם־דְּבִר לְפָנִים קִרְיַת־סֵפֶר:
טז וַיֹּאמֶר כָּלֵב אֲשֶׁר־יַכֶּה אֶת־קִרְיַת־סֵפֶר וּלְכָדָהּ וְנָתַתִּי לוֹ אֶת־עַכְסָה בִתִּי לְאִשָּׁה:
יז וַיִּלְכְּדָהּ עָתְנִיאֵל בֶּן־קְנַז אֲחִי כָלֵב וַיִּתֶּן־לוֹ אֶת־עַכְסָה בִתּוֹ לְאִשָּׁה:
יח וַיְהִי בְּבוֹאָהּ וַתְּסִיתֵהוּ לִשְׁאוֹל מֵאֵת־אָבִיהָ שָׂדֶה

**תרגום**

דְגִבָּרַיָא הִיא חֶבְרוֹן: יד וְתָרֵיךְ מִתַּמָן כָּלֵב יַת תְּלָתָא בְּנֵי גִבָּרַיָא יַת שֵׁשַׁי וְיַת אֲחִימָן וְיַת תַּלְמַי בְּנֵי גִבָּרַיָא: טו וּסְלֵיק מִתַּמָן לְוַת יָתְבֵי דְבִר וְשׁוּם דְּבִר מִלְקַדְמִין קִרְיַת אַרְכֵי: טז וַאֲמַר כָּלֵב דִּמְחֵי יַת קִרְיַת אַרְכֵי וְיִכְבְּשִׁנַּהּ וְאֶתֵּן לֵיהּ יַת עַכְסָה בְּרַתִּי לְאִתּוּ: יז וְכַבְשַׁהּ עָתְנִיאֵל בַּר קְנַז אֲחוּהִי דְכָלֵב וִיהַב לֵיהּ יַת עַכְסָה בְּרַתֵּיהּ לְאִתּוּ: יח וַהֲוָה בְּמֵיעֲלַהּ וְאַמְלְכַתֵּיהּ לְמִשְׁאַל מִן אֲבוּהָא חַקְלָא

ואהרכינת

ת״א עכסה. שם שם. וילכדה עתניאל. שם שם: ותסיתהו. שם:

**רד״ק**

יהודה לצד מערב וכת״י ותהומיה: (טו) ושם דביר לפנים קרית ספר. ארז״ל כי בלשון פרסי קוראין דביר לספר: (יז) עתניאל בן קנז אחי כלב. אמרו רז״ל כי אחיו מאמו הי׳ כי כלב בן יפונה היה ועתניאל בן קנז. ומה שאמר על כלב הקנזי ייחס אותו לבעל אמו ויתכן לפרש כי אחיו מאביו ומאמו היה והיה שם אביו כלב בן יפונה וקנז כי הרבה נמצאים שתי שמות לאדם אחד והנכון אצלי עוד כי קנז היה שם ראש המשפחה והתיחסו בני המשפחה אליו ובאמרו הקנזי או בן קנז הכל אחד כי רחוק הוא ליחס האדם לבעל אמו כי אפילו למשפחת האם לא מצאנו שיתיחס האדם כי אם לבית אבותיו מה שאמר כל אלה בני מכיר אבי גלעד והיה שגוב ויאיר בני בת מכיר בעבור הערי׳ שהיו ליאיר בארץ הגלעד אמר כן: (יח) ויהי בבואה. באות בית השמוש ופי׳ כבואה לבית בעלה: ותסיתהו. הסיתה בעלה לשאול מאת אביה שדה ולא רצה הוא לשאול וכשראתה כן ותצנח מעל החמור כלומר הפילה ותצנח

**רש״י**

ליהושע: (יד) ויורש משם כלב. לאחר מיתת יהושע כי עדיין בימי יהושע לא נלכדה חברון כמ״ש בספר שופטים ולא נכתבה כאן אלא מפני ההלוך׳: (טו) קרית ספר. רבותינו אמרו אלו הלכות שנשתכחו בימי אבלו של משה שהחזיר עתניאל בן קנז בפלפולו: (יז) אחי כלב. מאמו:

**מנחת שי**

(יז) ויתן לו את עכסה. התי״ו בסגול: (יח) ויהי בבואה. בבי״ת: מאת אביה. בס״ס ודפוסים ישנים יש מאריך כמ״ס:

**מצודת ציון**

(יח) ותצנח. ענין נפילה כמו ותצנה בארץ (שופטים ד׳) ור״ל

**מצודת דוד**

שבענקים: (יח) בבואה. בבית בעלה: ותסיתהו. הסיתה את בעלה

## Commentary Digest

18. *as she came* — into her husband's house. — K and D

*that she persuaded him* — her husband to permit her to ask her father for a field. — D K explains that she entreated her husband to ask her father for a field, but he refused. She, therefore, went by herself to ask her father, as the Scripture relates in the following verses.

the giants, which is Hebron. 14. And Caleb drove out
of there the three sons of the giant: Sheshai, and Ahiman,
and Talmai, the children of the giant. 15. And he went up
from there to the inhabitants of Debir; and the name of
Debir before was Kirjath-sepher. 16. And Caleb said, "He
who smites Kirjath-sepher and takes it, to him will I give
Achsah my daughter for a wife." 17. And Othniel the son
of Kenaz, the brother of Caleb, took it; and he gave him
Achsah his daughter for a wife. 18. And it came to pass, as
she came to him, that she persuaded him to ask of her father
a field;

## Commentary Digest

*the father of the giants* — i.e. the greatest of the giants, as above 14:15. According to R, above, he was the father of the three giants mentioned in the following verse.

14. *And Caleb drove out of there* — "*after Joshua's death, for during Joshua's lifetime Hebron was not yet taken, as it is stated in Jud.*[1] *It was only written here because of its relation to the division* (of the land)." — R

*the sons of the giant* — Arba, as above 14:15. J renders: the sons of the giants. It is unlikely that this is a proper name of a person, because of the definite article. Cf. Targum Onkelos, Num. XIII:33 and Deut. IX:2.

15. *Kirjath-sepher* — "*Our Rabbis said: These are the* (3,000) *laws which were forgotten during the mourning period for Moses, which Othniel the son of Kenaz reestablished through his great scholarship.*"[2] — R A states that the two words: יכה (smite) and ילכד (take) imply both physical conquest of the town and scholarly achievement.

16. *Achsah* — עכסה in Heb., derived from כעס, meaning anger. Her beauty was such that everyone who beheld her was apt immediately to quarrel with his own wife.[2]

17. *the brother of Caleb* — "*from his mother.*" — R Subsequently to the death of Caleb's father, Jephunneh, his mother married Kenaz, from whom she bore Othniel. Since Caleb was raised in the household of Kenaz, he is also known as the קנזי, the Kenizzite.[3] [4] K and A are of the opinion that the family name was Kenizzite after its progenitor, Kenaz. Thus, Caleb and Othniel were full brothers.

וַתִּצְנַח מֵעַל הַחֲמוֹר וַיֹּאמֶר־לָהּ כָּלֵב
מַה־לָּךְ: יט וַתֹּאמֶר תְּנָה־לִּי בְרָכָה כִּי
אֶרֶץ הַנֶּגֶב נְתַתָּנִי וְנָתַתָּה לִי גֻּלֹּת מָיִם
וַיִּתֶּן־לָהּ אֵת גֻּלֹּת עִלִּיּוֹת וְאֵת גֻּלֹּת
תַּחְתִּיּוֹת: כ זֹאת נַחֲלַת מַטֵּה בְנֵי־יְהוּדָה
לְמִשְׁפְּחֹתָם: כא וַיִּהְיוּ הֶעָרִים מִקְצֵה
לְמַטֵּה בְנֵי־יְהוּדָה אֶל־גְּבוּל אֱדוֹם
בַּנֶּגְבָּה קַבְצְאֵל וְעֵדֶר וְיָגוּר: כב וְקִינָה
וְדִימוֹנָה וְעַדְעָדָה: כג וְקֶדֶשׁ וְחָצוֹר
וְיִתְנָן: כד זִיף וָטֶלֶם וּבְעָלוֹת: כה וְחָצוֹר |
חֲדַתָּה וּקְרִיּוֹת חֶצְרוֹן הִיא חָצוֹר:

וְאִתְרְכִינַת מֵעַל חֲמָרָא
וַאֲמַר לַהּ כָּלֵב מַה לִיךְ:
יט וַאֲמַרַת הַב לִי
אַחְסַנְתָּא אֲרֵי לַאֲרַע
דָּרוֹמָא יְהַבְתַּנִי וְתִתֵּן לִי
אֲתַר בֵּית שַׁקְיָא דְמַיָא
וִיהַב לַהּ יַת בֵּית שַׁקְיָא
עִילָאֵה וְיַת בֵּית שַׁקְיָא
תַּחְתָּאָה: כ דָּא אַחְסָנַת
שִׁבְטָא דִבְנֵי יְהוּדָה
לְזַרְעֲיָתְהוֹן: כא וַהֲוָה
קִרְוַיָּא מִסְיָפֵי לְשִׁבְטָא
דִבְנֵי יְהוּדָה עַל תְּחוּם
אֱדוֹם בְּדָרוֹמָא קַבְצְאֵל
וְעֵדֶר וְיָגוּר: כב וְקִינָה
וְדִימוֹנָה וְעַדְעָדָה:
כג וְקֶדֶשׁ וְחָצוֹר וְיִתְנָן:
כד זִיף וָטֶלֶם וּבְעָלוֹת:
כה וְחָצוֹר חֲדַתָּה וּקְרִיּוֹת
חֶצְרוֹן הִיא חָצוֹר:

אמם

**ת״א** תנה לי ברכה. שם: וקינה ודימונה. גיטין ז: זיף וטלם. סוטה מה:

רש״י

(יח) **והצנח**. ואתרכינת הטתה עצמה ליפול לרגליו: (יט) **תנה לי ברכה**. פרנסה: **ארץ הנגב**. חרבה כמו חרבו פני האדמה ומתרגם נגיבו. שייק״א בלע״ז (ועשי״ג בל״א) דיר׳ (טראקן) בית מנוגב מכל טוב אדם שאין בו אלא תורה: **נתתני**. נתת לי כמו דברו לשלום דבר אליו בני יאמוני יאמו ממני ובשלם בשל להם: **גלת**. מעינות: (כא) **ויהיו הערים מקצה למטה בני יהודה**. בגבול מטה יהודה הוא שאמרו רבותינו לא מנה יהושע אלא עיירות העומדות על הגבולים:

רד״ק

אמם

עצמה מעל החמור שהיתה רוכבת עליו. ות״י ואתרכינת וכן תרגו׳ ותפל מעל הגמל: (יט) ברכה, ת״י אחסנתא ויתכן לפרש ברכה ממש שהיא תוספת טובה כלומר שיוסיף לו על מה שנתן לה כי ידמה שנתן לה ארץ צמאה ויבשה וזהו שאמרה ארץ הנגב נתתני תרגום חרבו המים נגיבו מיא ושאלה שיתן לה עוד השדה שהיו בו גלות המים להשקות ארץ הנגב שנתן לה ופי׳ נתתני נתת לי. ויש לפרש עוד ברכה כמו ברכת בצרי וי״ת ארץ הנגב ארי לארע דרומה יהבתני. ופי׳ גלות מים מעיינות כמו גל נעול או פירוש בריכות מים המכונסין וי״ת בית שקיא: (כא) ויהיו הערים מקצה למטה בני יהודה, פירוש כמו הפוך ויהי מקצה הערים למטה בני יהודה אל גבול אדום בנגבה ולפיכך נקדו בצרי לפי שהוא סמוך ובאמרו מקצה הוא שאמרו רז״ל לא מנה יהושע אלא הערים העומדות על הגבולים:

מצודת דוד

זפתה אותו לתת לה רשות שתשאל היא שדה מאביה: ותצנח מעל החמור. הפילה עצמה מעל החמור לנפול לארץ: מה לך. מה נחסר לך אשר תפילה לשאול עליו: (יט) כי ארץ הנגב נתתני. חלקת השדה אשר נתתי לי מאז היא ארץ נגובה מבלי מציאי מים: ונתת לי. לזה השאל אשר תתן לי חלקת שדה ובה מעין מים: את גלות. בתן לה שדה עם מעין ממעל ועם מעין מתחת: (כ) למשפחותם. הנחלק לכל משפחה לבד: (כא) מקצה. העומדים מקצה נחלת יהודה אצל גבול אדום בדרומה של יהודה: (כה) וחצור וגו׳. ארבע עיירות במקרא זה חצור א׳ חדתה ב׳ קריות

מצודת ציון

הפילה עצמה בכח וכאלו נפלה בארץ: (יט) ברכה. מתנה ומנחה כמו קח נא את ברכתי (בראשית ל״ג): הנגב. ענין יובש כמו כסופות בנגב (ישעיה כ״א): נתתני. נתת לי: גלות. מעין כמו גל נעול (ש״ה ד׳) ונקרא כן ע״ש סבובו וגלגלו: את. עם: עליות. מל׳ עליון:

## Commentary Digest

a husband for her, saying that he is arid, in the sense of being incapable of pursuing any occupation, being continually engrossed in study. The Talmud explains: You have given me springs of water, the Torah which is compared to water, but no sustenance. Caleb comforted his daughter, saying: "I have given you one who is steeped in the upper springs (of divine learn-

and she leaned off the donkey; and Caleb said to her, "What
is *wanting* to you?" 19. And she said, "Give me sustenance,
for you have given me an arid land; give me also springs of
water." And he gave her the upper springs and the nether
springs. 20. This is the inheritance of the tribe of the children
of Judah according to their families. 21. And the uttermost
cities of the tribe of the children of Judah toward the border
of Edom southward were Kabzeel, and Eder, and Jagur.
22. And Kinah, and Dimonah, and Adadah. 23. And Kedesh,
and Hazor, and Ithnan. 24. Ziph, and Telem, and Bealoth.
25. And Hazor, Hadattah, and Kerioth, and Hezron, which
is Hazor.

## Commentary Digest

*and she leaned* — ואתרכינת (J) *"She bent herself to fall at his feet."* — R A, K, and D explain that she actually threw herself off the donkey, to kiss her father's feet in her entreaty.

19. *sustenance* — R Heb. ברכה, usually translated "blessing." Blessing denotes increase and plenty.[1] She entreated him to increase his gift to her, and to give her a land from which she and her husband could sustain themselves. It may also be rendered like ברכה, a pool. J renders: an inheritance. — K D explains it like: Accept now my gift,[2] Heb. ברכתי. Thus, he renders: Give me a gift.

*an arid land* — Heb. נגב, *"like: "the face of the ground was dried,"[3] which Onkelos renders:* נגיבו. *Sec in French. I.e. a house which is arid* (devoid) *of all* earthly *good, a man who has nothing but Torah."* — R[4]

*you have given me* — *"i.e. you have given to me."* (The preposition is lacking in the Hebrew, thus appearing like a direct object. R continues to cite other examples of this structure. *"Like: "To speak to him peacefully*[5] (Heb. דברו," *"my children have gone forth from me,*[6] Heb. יצאוני"; *"he cooked for them the meat, Heb.* ובשלם."[7] — R

*springs* — R, K, and Z, as opposed to J, who renders: water holes, in which rain water has accumulated.

R, after the Talmud, interprets this entire episode figuratively. Achsah, not having any food, went to her father and brayed like a donkey. She complained to her father of his choice of

כו אֲמָם וּשְׁמַע וּמוֹלָדָה: כז וַחֲצַר גַּדָּה
וְחֶשְׁמוֹן וּבֵית פָּלֶט: כח וַחֲצַר שׁוּעָל וּבְאֵר
שֶׁבַע וּבִזְיוֹתְיָה: כט בַּעֲלָה וְעִיִּים וָעָצֶם:
ל וְאֶלְתּוֹלַד וּכְסִיל וְחָרְמָה: לא וְצִקְלַג
וּמַדְמַנָּה וְסַנְסַנָּה: לב וּלְבָאוֹת וְשִׁלְחִים
וְעַיִן וְרִמּוֹן כָּל־עָרִים עֶשְׂרִים וָתֵשַׁע
וְחַצְרֵיהֶן: לג בַּשְּׁפֵלָה אֶשְׁתָּאוֹל וְצָרְעָה
וְאַשְׁנָה: לד וְזָנוֹחַ וְעֵין גַּנִּים תַּפּוּחַ וְהָעֵינָם:
לה יַרְמוּת וַעֲדֻלָּם שׂוֹכֹה וַעֲזֵקָה:
לו וְשַׁעֲרַיִם וַעֲדִיתַיִם וְהַגְּדֵרָה וּגְדֵרֹתָיִם
עָרִים אַרְבַּע־עֶשְׂרֵה וְחַצְרֵיהֶן: לז צְנָן

כו אֲמָם וּשְׁמַע וּמוֹלָדָה: כז וַחֲצַר גַּדָּה וְחֶשְׁמוֹן וּבֵית פָּלֶט: כח וַחֲצַר שׁוּעָל וּבְאֵר שֶׁבַע וּבִזְיוֹתְהָא: כט בַּעֲלָה וְעִיִּים וְעָצֶם: ל וְאֶלְתּוֹלַד וּכְסִיל וְחָרְמָה: לא וְצִקְלַג וּמַדְמַנָּה וְסַנְסַנָּה: לב וּלְבָאוֹת וְשִׁלְחִים וְעַיִן וְרִמּוֹן כָּל קִרְוַיָּא עַשְׂרִין וּתְשַׁע וּפַצְחֵיהֶן: לג בִּשְׁפֶלְתָּא אֶשְׁתָּאוֹל וְצָרְעָה וְאַשְׁנָה: לד וְזָנוֹחַ וְעֵין גַּנִּים תַּפּוּחַ וְהָעֵינָם: לה יַרְמוּת וַעֲדֻלָּם שׂוֹכֹה וַעֲזֵקָה: לו וְשַׁעֲרַיִם וַעֲדִיתַיִם וְהַגְּדֵרָה וּגְדֵרוֹתַיִם קִרְוִין אַרְבַּע עַסְרֵי וּפַצְחֵיהֶן: לז צְנָן

ת"א ולקלג ומדמנה . גיטין ו : תפוח והעינם . סוטה י :

רד"ק

(לג) כל ערים עשרים ותשע . ובפרטם תמצא ל"ח והתשע היתרים היו לבני שמעון וספרם בנחלת בני יהודה בפרט לפי שהיי בנחלת בני יהודה כמו שאמר ויהי נחלתם בתוך נחלת בני יהודה ושם כתיב אלה הערים היתרים לשמעון באר שבע וחצר שועל בלה והיא בעלה שכתוב הנה ועצם ואלתולד ובתול זהו וכסיל שכתוב הנה וחרמה וצקלג ועין ורמון והנה הם עשר בזה המנין והם מנויות בנחלת בני שמעון ואין לנו נותרות אלא תשע אלא נאמר כי בלה אינו בעלה ובתול אינו כסיל אף על פי שהוא נראה כן ועוד יש ערים ספורות למטה שמעון בנחלת יהודה והם גם כן ספורות בנחלת בני שמעון והם עתר ועשן כמו שכתוב וצקלג שזכר הנה לבני יהודה חוכר אותה גם כן לבני שמעון ואנו רואים כי מיום שישב בה דוד היתה למלכי יהודה נאמר כי לקחוה בני ישראל בעת כבוש הארץ ונפלה לחלק שמעון ואחר כך לקחה מלך גת מהם עד שישב דוד בה על כן היתה למלכי יהודה מהיום ההוא והלאה: (לה) שוכה ועזקה. ועוד זוכר למטה שוכה וכן אשנה זוכר אותה בב' מקומות נקראים בשם אחד והיה לאחד מהם שם לווי להבדיל ביניהם ולא נזכר בכתוב : (לו) ערים ארבע עשרה . ובפרטן

רש"י

(לב) כל ערים עשרים ותשע . ובפרטן אתה מוצא שלשים ושמונה אלא אלה היתרות נטלו בני שמעון מהכל בני יהודה ונזכרות הם בנחלת שמעון באר שבע ומולד' וחצר שועל ועצם ואלתולד וחרמה וצקלג ועין ורמון הרי תשע היתרות המניות כאן : (לו) ערים ארבע עשרה . ובפרטן חמש עשרה אומר אני תפוח והעינם אחד הוא וזה

מנחת שי

(כח) ובזיותיה . חד מן מלין דסוף תיבותא יה ולא מפקי' ה' וסימן נזכר במ"ג סוף (פרשת בבלא) :

מצודת דוד

ג' חצרון היא חצור ד' ולא זהו חצור האמור בתחלת המקרא בנחלת בני שמעון והם באר שבע ומולדה חצר שועל ועצם
ולא זהו האמור במקרא שלפני פניו : (לג) עשרים ותשע . ואלתולד וחרמה וצקלג ועין ורמון : וחצריהן . ומגדל
וכפרטן תמצא ל"ח וזהו לפי שתשעה מהן לא נשארו לבני חצריהן : (לו) והגדרה וגדרתים . היא עיר אחת ונקראה
יהודה כי בני שמעון לקחום מהכל יהודה ונזכרות הנה בשתי השמות : (לז) צנן וגו' . גם אלו עמדו בשפלה אולם במחוז

26. Amam, and Shema, and Moladah. 27. And Hazar-gaddah,
and Heshmon, and Beth-pelet. 28. And Hazar-shual, and
Beer-sheba, and Bizjothjah. 29. Baalah, and Iim, and Ezem.
30. And Eltolad, and Chesil, and Hormah. 31. And Ziklag,
and Madmannah, and Sansannah. 32. And Lebaoth, and
Shilhim, and Ain, and Rimmon; all the cities are twenty-nine,
with their villages. 33. In the lowland, Eshtaol, and Zoreah,
and Ashnah. 34. And Zanoah, and En-gannim, Tappuah,
and Enam. 35. Jarmuth, and Adullam, Socoh, and Azekah.
36. And Sharaim, and Adithaim, and Gederah, and
Gederothaim; fourteen cities with their villages. 37. Zenan,

## Commentary Digest

ing and study) even as in the nether springs (of sustenance, which God will provide)." Caleb's vision came true, as Othniel was later the leader of the entire nation upon the demise of Joshua.[1]

Other commentators interpret this episode literally, that Achsah complained to her father Caleb about the arid land which he had given her. Some render, like R: You have given me an arid land. — K and Z. J renders: You have set me in the southland, explaining: נתתני, as the direct object.

21. *And the uttermost cities of the tribe of the children of Judah* — "*on the border of the tribe of Judah. That is what our Rabbis said: Joshua only enumerated the towns on the borders* (of every tribe)." — R[1*]

23, 25. *and Hazor, . . . And Hazor . . . and Hezron, which is Hazor* — There were three towns, all called Hazor (D), excluding Hazor of the north, which had been destroyed.[2]

32. *all the cities are twenty-nine* — "*When you count them, you find thirty-eight. These extra were taken by the children of Simeon from the territory of the children of Judah, and they are mentioned in the inheritance of Simeon: Beer-sheba, and Moladah, and Hazar-shual, and Ezem, and Eltolad, and Hormah, and Ziklag, and Ain, and Rimmon. These are the extra nine enumerated here.*"[3] — R, K, and D

*with their villages* — i.e. in addition to their villages. — D

36. *fourteen cities* — "*When you count them, you find fifteen. I say that Tappuah and Enam are one, and this*

וחדשה ומגדל־גד: לח ודלען והמצפה
ויקתאל: לט לכיש ובצקת ועגלון:
מ וכבון ולחמס וכתליש: מא וגדרות
בית־דגון ונעמה ומקדה ערים שש־
עשרה וחצריהן: מב לבנה ועתר ועשן:
מג ויפתח ואשנה ונציב: מד וקעילה
ואכזיב ומראשה ערים תשע וחצריהן:
מה עקרון ובנתיה וחצריה: מו מעקרון
וימה כל אשר־על־יד אשדוד וחצריהן:
מז אשדוד בנותיה וחצריה עזה בנותיה
וחצריה עד־נחל מצרים והים הגבול
וגבול: מח ובהר שמיר ויתיר ושוכה:
מט ודנה וקרית־סנה היא דבר: נ וענב

נחדשה ומגדל גד:
לח ודלען והמצפה
ויקתאל: לט לכיש
ובצקת ועגלון: מ וכבון
ולחמס וכתליש:
מא וגדרות בית דגון
ונעמה ומקדה קרוין
שית עסרי ופצחיהן:
מב לבנה ועתר ועשן
מג ויפתח ואשנה ונציב:
מד וקעילה ואכזיב
ומראשה קרוין תשע
ופצחיהן: מה עקרון
וכפרנהא ופצחהא:
מו מעקרון ומערבא כל
קרוניא דעל תחום
אשדוד ופצחיהן:
מז אשדוד כפרנהא
ופצחהא עזא כפרנהא
ופצחהא עד נחלא
דמצרים וימא רבה
ותחומיה: מח ובטורא
שמיר ויתיר ושוכה:
מט ודנה וקרית סנה היא
דביר: נ וענב ואשתמה
וענים

הגדול קרי ושוכ׳ קרי

רש״י

פירושו תפוח והעין שלו הוא עין תפוח האמור בנחלת מנשה אל יושבי עין תפוח: (מז) והים הגדול וגבול.

רד״ק

תמצא חמש עשרה ואפשר כי הגדרה וגדרתים עיר אחת: (מז) והים הגדול וגבול. כתיב הגבול כלומר כי הים היה גבולם וקרי הגדול:

מנחת שי

(לח) ויקתאל. לעולם כל קמץ על שני שואים יקרא חטוף ודומה לו ויקדעם האמור בסמוך ועוד כלל אחר כשיהיו שני שואים באמצע המלה ויהיה השוא השני תחת אות בג״ד כפ״ת הבנוית נעה ודגושה דגש קל כמו (כאשר יכתבו) ודומיהם ונמלאו אלו הבנים רפים יקתאל יקדעם ואולי מפני אחה״ע נרפו מכלל דף ק״ל. וכן יקתאל דמלכים ב׳ י״ד: (לט) ובצקת. הבי״ת בלא מאריך ולכן קריאתו בקמץ חטוף וכן בדפוס ישן הוא בחטף קמץ ממש כדרכו לעשות על החטפים קמצים: (מז) והים הגבול. הגדול קרי: (מח) ושוכה. בה״א ומה שכתוב במקצת ספרים ושוכו קרי הוא שלא לצורך:

מצודת דוד

אחרת ולזה מנה אלו לעצמן ואלו לעצמן וכ״כ נאמר בכ״מ שמנה אלו לבד ואלו לבד: (מא) וגדרות בית דגון. הן ב׳ עיירות האחת גדרות והשנית בית דגון: (מו) מעקרון וימה וגו׳. מעקרון ולצד המערב הים ליהודה כל הערים ההם אשר אצל מקום אשדוד וגם חצרי הערים ההם: (מז) עד נחל מצרים. שהיה בדרומה של יהודה: והים הגדול. ר״ל ועד הים הגדול שהיה במערבו: וגבול. גם גבול הים הם האיים אשר בים אף הם לנחלת יהודה יחשבו:

מצודת ציון

(מה) ובנותיה. הכפרים הסמוכים אליה: (מו) על יד. על מקום כמו יד אבשלום (ש״ב י״ח):

and Hadashah, and Migdal-gad, 38. And Dilean, and Mizpeh,
and Joktheel, 39. Lachish, and Bozkath, and Eglon, 40. And
Cabbon, and Lahmas, and Kithlish, 41. And Gederoth, Beth-
dagon, and Naamah, and Makkedah; sixteen cities with their
villages. 42. Libnah, and 'Ether, and 'Ashan, 43. And Iphtah,
and Ashnah, and Nezib, 44. And Keilah, and Achzib, and
Mareshah; nine cities with their villages. 45. 'Ekron, with
her towns and her villages, 46. From Ekron to the west, all
that were near Ashdod, with their villages, 47. Ashdod *with*
her towns and her villages, Gaza with her towns and her
villages, to the river of Egypt, and the Great Sea, and its
border. 48. And in the mountain, Shamir, and Jattir, and
Socoh, 49. And Dannah, and Kirjath-sannah, which is Debir,
50. And 'Anab,

### Commentary Digest

*is its explanation: Tappuah and its spring. That is 'En-tappuah which is mentioned in reference to the inheritance of Manasseh: 'to the inhabitants of 'En-tappuah.'"*[1] — R Perhaps R means to say that Just as the Tappuah of Manasseh had a spring called 'En-tappuah, so did the Tappuah of Judah have a spring called 'Enam. — P Others explain that Gederah and Gederothaim are one. — K and D

47. *and the Great (Med.) Sea* — The Kethib is הגבול, meaning the bordering sea, since the Mediterranean was the western border of Eretz Israel. — K

*and its border* — *"the islands in the sea* (adjacent to the coast),[2] *isles in old French."* — R

וְאֶשְׁתְּמֹה וְעָנִים׃ נא וְגֹשֶׁן וְחֹלֹן וְגִלֹה
עָרִים אַחַת־עֶשְׂרֵה וְחַצְרֵיהֶן׃ נב אֲרַב
וְדוּמָה וְאֶשְׁעָן׃ נג וְיָנִים וּבֵית־תַּפּוּחַ
וַאֲפֵקָה׃ נד וְחֻמְטָה וְקִרְיַת אַרְבַּע הִיא
חֶבְרוֹן וְצִיעֹר עָרִים תֵּשַׁע וְחַצְרֵיהֶן׃
נה מָעוֹן ׀ כַּרְמֶל וָזִיף וְיוּטָּה׃ נו וְיִזְרְעֶאל
וְיָקְדְעָם וְזָנוֹחַ׃ נז הַקַּיִן גִּבְעָה וְתִמְנָה
עָרִים עֶשֶׂר וְחַצְרֵיהֶן׃ נח חַלְחוּל בֵּית־צוּר
וּגְדוֹר׃ נט וּמַעֲרָת וּבֵית־עֲנוֹת וְאֶלְתְּקֹן
עָרִים שֵׁשׁ וְחַצְרֵיהֶן׃ ס קִרְיַת־בַּעַל הִיא
קִרְיַת יְעָרִים וְהָרַבָּה עָרִים שְׁתָּיִם
וְחַצְרֵיהֶן׃ סא בַּמִּדְבָּר בֵּית הָעֲרָבָה מִדִּין
וּסְכָכָה׃ סב וְהַנִּבְשָׁן וְעִיר־הַמֶּלַח וְעֵין גֶּדִי
עָרִים שֵׁשׁ וְחַצְרֵיהֶן׃ סג וְאֶת־הַיְבוּסִי

וינום קרי

וְעָנִים׃ נא וְגֹשֶׁן וְחֹלֹן
וְגִלֹה קִרְוִין חֲדָא עַסְרֵי
וּפַצְחֵיהֶן׃ נב אֲרַב
וְדוּמָה וְאֶשְׁעָן׃ נג וְיָנוּם
וּבֵית תַּפּוּחַ וַאֲפֵקָה׃
נד וְחֻמְטָה וְקִרְיַת אַרְבַּע
הִיא חֶבְרוֹן וְצִיעֹר קִרְוִין
תְּשַׁע וּפַצְחֵיהֶן׃ נה מָעוֹן
כַּרְמֶל וְזִיף וְיוּטָּה׃
נו וְיִזְרְעֶאל וְיָקְדְעָם
וְזָנוֹחַ׃ נז הַקַּיִן גִּבְעָה
וְתִמְנָה קִרְוִין עֲסַר
וּפַצְחֵיהֶן׃ נח חַלְחוּל בֵּית
צוּר וּגְדוֹר׃ נט וּמַעֲרָת
וּבֵית עֲנוֹת וְאֶלְתְּקֹן
קִרְוִין שִׁית וּפַצְחֵיהֶן׃
ס קִרְיַת בַּעַל הִיא קִרְיַת
יְעָרִים וְהָרַבָּה קִרְוִין
תַּרְתֵּין וּפַצְחֵיהֶן׃
סא בְּמַדְבְּרָא בֵּית מֵישְׁרָא
מִדִּין וּסְכָכָה׃ סב וְנִבְשָׁן
וְקִרְיַת מִלְחָא וְעֵין גֶּדִי
קִרְוִין שִׁית וּפַצְחֵיהֶן׃
סג וְיָת יְבוּסָאֵי יָתְבֵי
ירושלם

### מנחת שי

(נב) ארב ודומה. בכמה ספרים כ"י ורומה ברי"ש לא בדל"ת: ואשען. השי"ן בלא דגש: (נג) ויניס. במ"ס ובמקצת ספרים כתיב ויניס וקרי וינום ובמקצתם כתיב וקרי בוא"ו וכן בס"א כ"י נכתב בלד למערבאי וינום כתיב וקרי: *):(נו) ויקדעם. במקצת ספרים כ"י בדל"ת בחט"ף קמץ ועיין מ"ש לעיל על ויקתאל: (סג) לא יוכלו. יכלו קרי:

### מצודת דוד

(נה) וזיף. אין זה זיף האמור למעלה: (סג) היבוסי. שם האומה:

## Commentary Digest

mentioned in Gen. XXI:23: "And now swear to me here by God that you will not deal falsely with me, nor with my son nor even with my grandson...." The Jews were bound by this treaty and were unable to wage war against the Jebusites in Jerusalem. This state of affairs continued to the days of King David, when there no longer was living a grandson of Abimelech. Some say that the "blind and the lame" mentioned in 2 Sam. V:6, 7, 8, were images upon which the oath was inscribed.[2]

Rashi elaborates on this topic in II Samuel 5:6. See Commentary Digest.

A second view regarding the ancestry of the Jebusites is stated in P. E. Ch. 36. Here they are mentioned as being descended from the Hittites from whom Abraham purchased the Cave of Machpelah. Abraham entered into a covenant with them in exchange for the sale. Cf. R Deut. 12:17.

and Eshtemoh, and 'Anim, 51. And Goshen, and Holon, and
Giloh; eleven cities with their villages. 52. Arab, and Dumah,
and Eshean, 53. And Janum, and Beth-tappuah, and Aphekah,
54. And Humtah, and Kirjath-arba, which is Hebron, and
Zior; nine cities with their villages. 55. Maon, Carmel, and
Ziph, and Juttah, 56. And Jezreel, and Jokdeam, and Zanoah,
57. Cain, Gibeah, and Timnah; ten cities with their villages.
58. Halhul, Beth-zur, and Gedor, 59. And Maarath, and
Beth-anoth, and Eltekon; six cities with their villages.
60. Kirjath-baal, which is Kirjath-jearim, and Rabbah; two
cities with their villages. 61. In the wilderness, Beth-'arabah,
Middin, and Secacah. 62. And Nibshan, and the city of
Salt, and 'En-gedi; six cities with their villages. 63. As for
the Jebusites

**Commentary Digest**

51. *And Goshen* — This is not the Goshen mentioned above 10:41, 11:16. There the Scripture is dealing with a land near Egypt. The Goshen mentioned in this verse has not been identified — D. M.

52. *Arab* — Identified with A-Rabia, thirteen kilometers southwest of Hebron. — D. M.

53. *and Beth-tappuah* — Some identify this with Tappuah situated east of Juttah, and others identify it with Kefar Tappuah, situated five kilometers west of Hebron. — D. M.

55. *Ziph* — not the Ziph mentioned above.[1] — D

63. *the children of Judah could not drive them out* — "*We learned in Sifrei:*[1] *Rabbi Joshua the son of Korha says: They really could, but they were not permitted, because of the oath which Abraham had sworn to Abimelech. Now these Jebusites were not of the Jebusite nation, but the Tower of David which was in Jerusalem, was called Jebus, and the inhabitants of that section were of the Philistines. And when the children of Judah conquered Jerusalem, they did not drive out the inhabitants of that section.*" — R R refers to the treaty and oath

יוֹשְׁבֵי יְרוּשָׁלַםִ לֹא־יוּכְלוּ בְנֵי־יְהוּדָה לְהוֹרִישָׁם וַיֵּשֶׁב הַיְבוּסִי אֶת־בְּנֵי יְהוּדָה בִּירוּשָׁלַםִ עַד הַיּוֹם הַזֶּה׃
טז א וַיֵּצֵא הַגּוֹרָל לִבְנֵי יוֹסֵף מִיַּרְדֵּן יְרִיחוֹ לְמֵי יְרִיחוֹ מִזְרָחָה הַמִּדְבָּר עֹלֶה מִירִיחוֹ בָּהָר בֵּית־אֵל׃
ב וְיָצָא מִבֵּית־אֵל לוּזָה וְעָבַר אֶל־

יְרוּשְׁלֶם לָא יְכִילוּ בְּנֵי יְהוּדָה לְתָרָכוּתְהוֹן וִיתִיבוּ יְבוּסָאֵי עִם בְּנֵי יְהוּדָה בִּירוּשְׁלֶם עַד יוֹמָא הָדֵין׃ א וּנְפַק עַדְבָא לִבְנֵי יוֹסֵף מִיַּרְדְּנָא דִירִיחוֹ לְמַיָּא יְרִיחוֹ מַדִּינְחָא לְמַדְבְּרָא דְסָלִיק מִירִיחוֹ בְּטוּרָא לְבֵית אֵל׃ ב וּנְפַק מִבֵּית אֵל לְלוּז וַעֲבַר לִתְחוּם ארכי

### רש"י
יתיר ואו

ומין שבים שקורין אלבי"ש בלע"ז (בל"א איכזעלן): (סג) לא יכלו בני יהודה להורישם. שנינו בספרי ר' יהושע בן קרחה אומר יכולים היו אלא שלא היו רשאין מחמת השבועה שנשבע אברהם לאבימלך. ויבוסי זה לא ע"ש האומ' היה אלא מגדל דוד שהיה בירושלים ושמו יבוס ובני אותו מהוז מפלשתים היו וכשכבשו בני יהודה את ירושלים לא הוריש את בני אותו מחוז:
טז (א) ויצא הגורל לבני יוסף. במילר לפונה של גמר כיבושו של יהושע נפל להם הגורל כמו שאמר למטה ובני יוסף יעמדו על גבולם מצפון והרבה מן הארץ היה בין בני יהוד' ובין בני יוסף שנטלו שאר השבטי' אחריה' (ר"ל ביניה') כמו שמצינו בשבט בנימין ויצא גבול גורלם בין בני יהודה ובין בני יוסף: מירדן יריחו למי יריחו מזרחה. התחיל הגבול למזרח: המדבר עולה מיריחו. אל המדבר עולה

### רד"ק
גבול

(סג) לא יכלו בני יהודה להורישם. כתיב יוכלו כי אף בזמן העתיד לא יוכלו עד שיבא דוד וקרי יכלו כי לא יכלו אז להורישם בעת כבוש הארץ ויאמרו רז"ל יכולין היו אלא שלא היו רשאים מפני השבועה שנשבע אברהם לאבימלך והיבוסי הזה לא היה היבוסי משבעה גוים אלא אדם אחד שהיה שמו יבוס והיה מפלשתים מזרע אבימלך ונקרא המקום על שמו יבוס ואנשי המשפחה ההיא יושבי ירושלם היה שמם יבוסי מתיחסים אל יבוס וכן ארונה היבוסי שהיה מלך המקום ההוא ובמבצר המקום הזה הוא ציון שהיא בירושלם ועד דוד לא היה נכבש המקום הזה ולדעת רז"ל לא כבשוהו מפני השבועה ודוד הסיר העורים והפסחים שהיו צלמי נחשת והיה כתוב בהם דבר השבועה ואחר כך כבש המגדל ההוא ואחר כך קנה דוד או עיר היבוסי לישראל בממכר זהב בכתב לאחוזת עולם שנאמר ויתן דוד לארונה במקום וגו'. ועוד אמרו כי השבועה היתה לי ולניני ולנכדי וכשכבשו בני יהודה את ירושלם היה נכד אבימלך חי עדיין ולא יכלו לכבוש המצודה עדיין מפני השבועה ובימי דוד לא היה עוד הנכד חי ועוד נכתב כזה עוד בספר שמואל ולפי הפשט היה המבצר חזק ולא היה כח לבני יהודה להורישם אולי היתה סבה מאת ה' שלא תלכד המצודה ההיא עד מלוך דוד מלך ישראל כדי שתקרא על שמו לפי שהיה ראש ממלכת ישראל ומה שאמר עד היום הזה יהושע כתב כן כי הוא כתב ספרו לפי הקבלה ובימיו לא הורישם מירושלם ואף בימי דוד מצאנו שהיו שם: (ב) מבית אל לוזה. זה מקום היה שמו בית

### מצודת דוד

לא יכלו בני יהודה להורישם. כי גם להם חלק מה בירושלים עם בני בנימין כמ"ש רז"ל רצועה היתה יוצאת מחלקו של יהודה וכו': טז (א) לבני יוסף. הם מנשה ואפרים ונטלו סמוכים זה לזה אבל כל אחד נטל חלק לבד וגם נחלתם מלאו כל האורך של א"י ממזרח למערב וכמו נחלת יהודה: מירדן יריחו. מן הירדן שממול יריחו התחיל למשוך הגבול ובא אל מזרח מי יריחו והוא גבול הדרומי מן המזרח כלפי המערב: המדבר עולה מיריחו. ר"ל ממי יריחו עלה אל המדבר ובא בהר בית אל ולא זהו בית אל הקרויה לוז: (ב) לוזה.

## Commentary Digest

*to the wilderness that goes up from Jericho* — J Others render: *"To the wilderness, it (the border) goes up from Jericho and comes westward to Beth-el."* — R and D

2. *from Beth-el to Luz* — Luz was also known by the name Beth-el.[1] — K See also below XVIII:13 for a further explanation.

*Archi* — the name of a place. — J Hushai the Archite, mentioned in II Sam.[2] came from this place.[3]

the inhabitants of Jerusalem, the children of Judah could not drive them out; but the Jebusites dwelt with the children of Judah in Jerusalem to this day.

16

1. And the lot for the children of Joseph went out from the Jordan at Jericho, to the water of Jericho on the east, to the wilderness that goes up from Jericho on the mountain to Beth-el;
2. And it went out from Beth-el to Luz, and passed along to

## Commentary Digest

This passage can also be understood in its simple sense: Jerusalem was fortified to such an extent that it was impossible to take, commanding as it did, the entire surrounding terrain. A campaign against Jerusalem would have been too costly a venture. The children of Judah chose, therefore, the path of "peaceful coexistence," in the modern vernacular. It was only during the days of King David, when the Jewish armies, in the flush of victory over all their surrounding enemies, were able to achieve the conquest of the fortress. This feat, of course, made the city of Jerusalem eternally the city of David. — K Although the city of Jerusalem belonged to the tribe of Benjamin, Judah too had a share of the holy city, as our rabbis stated: A strip extended from Judah's territory and penetrated into Benjamin's territory, and there the altar was built. — D[3]

CHAPTER 16

1. *And the lot for the children of Joseph went out* — "*At the northern boundary of the end of Joshua's conquest, the lot fell for them, as he states below*[4]*: 'and the sons* (sic) *of Joseph shall remain in their border on the north.* (Should read: And the house of Joseph)' *Now much of the land was between the children of Judah and the children of Joseph, which the remaining tribes took after them,* (or between them), *as we find concerning the tribe of Benjamin: "and the border of their lot went out between the children of Judah and the children of Joseph."* "[5] — R Their boundary, just as that of Judah, occupied the entire width of Eretz Israel, from the Jordan on the East to the Mediterranean on the West, comprising the northern part of the land.

*from the Jordan at Jericho, to the water of Jericho on the east* — "*I.e. here the border started on the east.*" — R

גְּבוּל הָאַרְכִּי עֲטָרוֹת: ג וְיָרַד יָמָּה אֶל
גְּבוּל הַיַּפְלֵטִי עַד גְּבוּל בֵּית חוֹרֹן
תַּחְתּוֹן וְעַד גָּזֶר וְהָיוּ תֹצְאֹתָו יָמָּה:
ד וַיִּנְחֲלוּ בְנֵי יוֹסֵף מְנַשֶּׁה וְאֶפְרָיִם: ה וַיְהִי
גְּבוּל בְּנֵי אֶפְרַיִם לְמִשְׁפְּחֹתָם וַיְהִי גְּבוּל
נַחֲלָתָם מִזְרָחָה עַטְרוֹת אַדָּר עַד בֵּית
חוֹרֹן עֶלְיוֹן: ו וְיָצָא הַגְּבוּל הַיָּמָּה
הַמִּכְמְתָת מִצָּפוֹן וְנָסַב הַגְּבוּל מִזְרָחָה
תַּאֲנַת שִׁלֹה וְעָבַר אוֹתוֹ מִמִּזְרַח יָנוֹחָה:

תרגום

אַרְכִּי לַעֲטָרוֹת: ג וְנָחִית לְיַמָּא לִתְחוּם יַפְלִיט עַד תְּחוּם בֵּית חוֹרוֹן אַרְעָאָה וְעַד גֶּזֶר וִיהוֹן מַפְּקָנוּהִי לְיַמָּא: ד וְאַחְסִינוּ בְנֵי יוֹסֵף מְנַשֶּׁה וְאֶפְרָיִם: ה וַהֲוָה תְּחוּם בְּנֵי אֶפְרַיִם לְזַרְעֲיַתְהוֹן וַהֲוָה תְּחוּם אַחְסַנְתְּהוֹן מַדִּינְחָא עַטְרוֹת אַדָּר עַד בֵּית חוֹרוֹן עִילָאָה: ו וְנָפֵק תְּחוּמָא לְיַמָּא לְמִכְמְתָת מִצִּפּוּנָא וּמִסְתְּחַר תְּחוּמָא מִמַּדִּינְחָא לְתַאֲנַת שִׁלֹה וְעָבַר לֵיהּ ממדנח

תוצאתיו קרי

רד"ק

אל ואינו המקום שקרא יעקב אבינו בית אל כי אותו שמו לוז והנה הוא אומר שיצא הגבול מבית אל ללוז ומגבול בנימין היה לוז כמו שאומר בנחלת בנימין ועבר משם הגבול לוזה אל כתף

רש"י

הגבול מיריחו ובא לו לצד מערב לבית אל: (ה) **מזרחה עטרות אדר**. למזרח מתחיל מעטרות אדר ומשם רוחב תחומו עד בית חורון הרי רחבו: (ו) **ויצא הגבול הימה**. ארכו היתה לצד המערב אל המכמת' הולך החוט: **ונסב הגבול**. מתפשט רוחב התחו' לצד צפון והחוט יוצא בבליטתו במזרחה של תאנת שלה: **ועבר אותו**. ועבר הגבול את תאנת שילה ועבר החוט ממזרח של

מנחת שי

**טז** (ג) **גזר** והיו תצאתו. תיו ק' ובמקצת ספרים מלא וא"ו בתר תיו קמייתא המגס ע"פ המסורת דפרשת מסעי דהוי להיות חסר דנמסר שם כל תוריתא תוצאותיו כתיב. אל גבול היפלטי בהוא פסוק זה תצאתו כתיב אל ככף. בית חגלה סימן י"ח (יט) תוצאותיו כתיב ובהרא תצאתיו כתיב: גזר והיו תצאתו ימה. בס"א הימה ולא יתכן שבסימן כ"דנמסר כל הימה שבסיפרא ואין זה בתוכם והוי יודע דהתם במ"ג נמסר הימה ו' וטעות הוא וצריך להגיה ז' ולהוסיף וגבול ים והימה דלעיל בסימן ט"ו: (ה) עד בית חורן. במלה זו יש כל החלופים השייכים בחסר ויתיר במקצת ספרים חסר דחסר ומקצתם מלא דמלא וי"ס מלא

מצודת דוד

ר"ל מנגב לוז כמ"ש בגבול בנימין: (ג) **ימה**. לצד המערב: **עד גבול וגו'**. ר"ל מנגב לבית חורון תחתון: **תוצאותיו**. סוף הגבול כלה אל הים הגדול: (ד) **וינחלו**. בהגרלוה ההיא נחלו מנשה ואפרים: (ה) **למשפחותם**. להנחלה הנחלקת לכל משפחותם: **מזרחה**. גבול הרוחב הפונה למזרח היה מעטרות אדר שעמדה בלפונו של בנימין עד בית חורון עליון שעמדה בנחלת אפרים ולפי שמבית חורון עליון נתארך עוד הגבול כלפי מערב כמ"ש בענין א"כ גם שם היה גבול ברוחב לזה אמר מזרחה ר"ל גבול הרוחב הפונה למזרח ולא הגבול הפונה למערב: (ו) **ויצא הגבול הימה**. מבית חורון עליון יצא הגבול להתארך עוד כלפי המערב מלפון למכמתת שהיתה מנחלת מנשה: **ונסב הגבול**. להרוחב כלפי הצפון למזרחה של תאנת שלה ועבר את כל אורך תאנת שלה ולא עבר סמוך לה כ"א ממזרח של ינוחה אשר עמדה למזרחה של תאנת שלה ולא היה מנחלת אפרים לא תאנת שלה ולא ינוחה ומנחלת מנשה היו:

the border of Archi to 'Ataroth; 3. And it went down
westward to the border of Japhleti, to the border of lower
Beth-horon, and to Gezer; and its goings out were at the sea.
4. And the children of Joseph: Manasseh and Ephraim, took
their inheritance. 5. And the border of the children of
Ephraim according to their families was: the border of their
inheritance on the east side was 'Atroth-addar, to upper Beth-
horon; 6. And the border went out toward the west to
Michmetath on the northside; and the border turned about
eastward to Taanath-shiloh, and passed over it on the east of
Janoah;

## Commentary Digest

3. *Japhleti* — also the name of a place. — J This has no connection with Japhlet mentioned in I Chron.,[4] who was of the tribe of Asher.

*to the border of lower Beth-horon* — i.e. south of lower Beth-horon. — D

4. *And the children of Joseph . . . took their inheritance* — I.e. this strip was divided between the two tribes; Manasseh and Ephraim. — D

5. And the border of the children of Ephraim according to their families was — I.e. the first portion was allotted to Ephraim, in keeping with the blessing that Jacob pronounced on their progenitors, Ephraim and Manasseh: May G-d make you like Ephraim and Manasseh, in which he placed Ephraim before Manasseh. — K. Y., Az. *on the east side was 'Atroth-addar* — *"To the east it starts from 'Atroth-addar, and from there was the width of his boundary to Beth-horon; this is its width."* — R

6. *And the border went out toward the west* — *"Its length was to the west side, to Michmetath; the line went on the north of Michmetath."* — R

*and the border turned about* — *"The width of the boundary spread out toward the north, and the line went out with its bulge to the east of Taanath-shiloh."* — R

*and passed over it* — *"And the border passed Taanath-shiloh, and the line passed on the east of Janoah. All*

ז וְיָרַד מִיָּנוֹחָה עֲטָרוֹת וְנַעֲרָתָה וּפָגַע
בִּירִיחוֹ וְיָצָא הַיַּרְדֵּן: ח מִתַּפּוּחַ יֵלֵךְ
הַגְּבוּל יָמָּה נַחַל קָנָה וְהָיוּ תֹצְאֹתָיו
הַיָּמָּה זֹאת נַחֲלַת מַטֵּה בְנֵי־אֶפְרַיִם
לְמִשְׁפְּחֹתָם: ט וְהֶעָרִים הַמִּבְדָּלוֹת לִבְנֵי
אֶפְרַיִם בְּתוֹךְ נַחֲלַת בְּנֵי־מְנַשֶּׁה כָּל־
הֶעָרִים וְחַצְרֵיהֶן: י וְלֹא הוֹרִישׁוּ אֶת־
הַכְּנַעֲנִי הַיּוֹשֵׁב בְּגָזֶר וַיֵּשֶׁב הַכְּנַעֲנִי
בְּקֶרֶב אֶפְרַיִם עַד־הַיּוֹם הַזֶּה וַיְהִי לְמַס־
עֹבֵד: יז א וַיְהִי הַגּוֹרָל לְמַטֵּה מְנַשֶּׁה כִּי

תרגום

ממדנח לינוח: ז ונחית
מינוח לעטרות
ולנערתה ומערע ביריחו
ונפק לירדנא: ח מתפוח
אזיל תחומא לימא
לנחלא דקנה נהוון
מפקנוהי לימא דא
אחסנת שבטא דבני
אפרים לזרעיתהון:
ט וקרויא דמפרשן לבני
אפרים בגו אחסנת בני
מנשה כל קרויא
ופצחיהן: י ולא תריכו
ית כנענאי דיתיב בגזר
ויתיבו כנענאי בגו בית
אפרים עד יומא הדין
נהוו למסקי מסין פלחין:
א והוה עדבא לשבטא
דמנשה ארי הוא בוכרא
דיוסף

רש"י

ינוח כל זה בליטת הרוחב עד ויצא הירדן ושם עיר ושמה תפוח ומשם ויסב החוט למדת אורך הגבול ימה לנחל קנה: (ט) והערים המובדלות. וגם זה עוד מנחלת אפרים ערים היו להם מובדלות ומובלעות בתוך נחלת בני מנשה:

רד"ק

הוא לוזה נגבה הוא בית אל: (ט) המבדלות. בחירק המ"ם והוא תואר או החירק מקום שורק והוא פעול מבנין הפעיל ופי' הערים המבדלות לפי שאמר זאת נחלת מטה בני אפרים אמר ועוד היו להם ערים בתוך נחלת מטה בני מנשה מבדלות ונכרות וידועות להם כמו שכתב ומפרש אותם בספור נחלת בני מנשה: (א) כי הוא בכור יוסף. כלומר לפי שהיה הוא בכור יוסף ומכיר היה בכורו והיה איש מלחמה זה גרם לו שבאה לו הנחלה בארץ הגלעד כי בני גד ובני ראובן שאלו אותה הארץ מפני שהית

מנחת שי

וא"ו קדמאה וי"ס מלא וא"ו בתראה ועיין מסרה הכתובה במ"ג בסימן י"ח: (י) שלא. בכ"א:

מצודת דוד

(ז) וירד. כי שם כלה הרוחב וירד משם כלפי המזרח אל עטרות ופגע ביריחו. הגבול פגע ביריחו ר"ל במי יריחו ועבר דרך בה וכלה הגבול אל הירדן: (ח) מתפוח. היא עמדה אצל הירדן בגבול מנשה אבל היתה לאפרים כמ"ש בענין וממנה היה נמשך גבול כלפי המערב ובא אל נחל קנה מנגב וסופו כלה אל הים ובמקרא שלאחריו מפרש מה ענין הגבול הזה: זאת. ר"ל הגבול האמור במקראות שלפניו סביב נחלת מטה בני אפרי' הנחלק לכל משפחה ומשפח': (ט) והערים המבדלות. ר"ל הערים של בני אפרים אשר היו מובדלות ומופרשות מגבול נחלתו המה עמדו בתוך נחלת בני מנשה בהגבול האמור במקרא שלפניו: כל הערים. אשר עמדו באורך הגבול ההיא המה וחצריהן היו של בני אפרים: (י) ולא הורישו. חוזר על בני אפרים כי גזר היה מנחלתם מן הערים אשר עמדו בהגבול ההולך מתפוח אל הים: למס עובד. ר"ל לא מס ממון כ"א מס עבודה בגוף:
יז (א) כי הוא בכור. ר"ל אף שהוא הבכור והיה א"כ מהראוי לקחת גורלו ראשון מ"מ נתאחר מלקחת גורלו עד שלקח אפרים תחלה ואח"ז היה הגורל למטה מנשה וזה היה בעבור ברכת

7. And it went down from Janoah to 'Ataroth, and to Naarath,
and reached Jericho, and went out at the Jordan. 8. The
border went westward from Tappuah to the stream of Kanah;
and its goings out were at the sea. This is the inheritance of
the tribe of the children of Ephraim according to their families.
9. And the separated cities for the children of Ephraim among
the inheritance of the children of Manasseh, all the cities with
their villages. 10. And they did not drive out the Canaanites
that dwelt in Gezer; but the Canaanites dwelt among the
Ephraimites to this day, and they became servants under tribute.

17

1. And there was a lot for the tribe of Manasseh, for

## Commentary Digest

*this is the bulge of the width until 'And went out at the Jordan.' And there is a city named Tappuah, and from there the line turned about to the measure of the length of the border westward to the stream of Kanah."* — R

*Taanath-shiloh* — This was the farthest point from Shiloh, first religious center of permanence in Israel (for 369 years), where the sacrifices and "maaser shenie" (second tithe) were allowed to be eaten. In later years, when Shiloh had been divested of its sanctity, everyone who passed this point would sigh (תאנת-מתאנה) with pain upon this sorrowful reflection.[1]

9. *And the separated cities* – *"And this too is still of the inheritance of Ephraim: They had cities separated from their boundary, and enveloped by the inheritance of the children of Manasseh."* — R

Others explain that there were cities belonging to Ephraim that were enveloped by the border of Manasseh, yet they were conspicuously cities of Ephraim. — K

For this reason, the Scripture repeats: *all the cities and their villages,* to inform us that all these cities that appeared to belong to Ephraim, indeed belonged to Ephraim. — K. Y.

10. *servants under tribute* — For the Halachic ramifications of (tribute), see Rambam and Rabad, Laws of Kings, Ch. VI.

הוּא בְּכוֹר יוֹסֵף לְמָכִיר בְּכוֹר מְנַשֶּׁה
אֲבִי הַגִּלְעָד כִּי הוּא הָיָה אִישׁ מִלְחָמָה
וַיְהִי־לוֹ הַגִּלְעָד וְהַבָּשָׁן׃ ב וַיְהִי לִבְנֵי
מְנַשֶּׁה הַנּוֹתָרִים לְמִשְׁפְּחֹתָם לִבְנֵי
אֲבִיעֶזֶר וְלִבְנֵי־חֵלֶק וְלִבְנֵי אַשְׂרִיאֵל
וְלִבְנֵי־שֶׁכֶם וְלִבְנֵי־חֵפֶר וְלִבְנֵי שְׁמִידָע
אֵלֶּה בְּנֵי מְנַשֶּׁה בֶּן־יוֹסֵף הַזְּכָרִים
לְמִשְׁפְּחֹתָם׃ ג וְלִצְלָפְחָד בֶּן־חֵפֶר בֶּן
גִּלְעָד בֶּן־מָכִיר בֶּן־מְנַשֶּׁה לֹא־הָיוּ לוֹ
בָּנִים כִּי אִם־בָּנוֹת וְאֵלֶּה שְׁמוֹת בְּנֹתָיו
מַחְלָה וְנֹעָה חָגְלָה מִלְכָּה וְתִרְצָה׃
ד וַתִּקְרַבְנָה לִפְנֵי אֶלְעָזָר הַכֹּהֵן וְלִפְנֵי
יְהוֹשֻׁעַ בִּן־נוּן וְלִפְנֵי הַנְּשִׂיאִים לֵאמֹר

דְיוֹסֵף לְמָכִיר בּוּכְרָא
דִמְנַשֶּׁה אֲבוּהִי דְגִלְעָד
אֲרֵי הוּא הֲוָה גְבַר עָבֵיד
קְרָבִין וַהֲוָה לֵיהּ אַרְעָא
גִלְעָד וּמַתְנָן׃ ב וַהֲוָה
לִבְנֵי מְנַשֶּׁה דְאִשְׁתְּאָרוּ
לְזַרְעֲיַתְהוֹן וְלִבְנֵי
אֲבִיעֶזֶר וְלִבְנֵי חֵלֶק
וְלִבְנֵי אַשְׂרִיאֵל וְלִבְנֵי
שֶׁכֶם וְלִבְנֵי חֵפֶר וְלִבְנֵי
שְׁמִידָע אִילֵין בְּנֵי מְנַשֶּׁה
בַּר יוֹסֵף דְּכְרַיָּא
לְזַרְעֲיַתְהוֹן׃ ג וְלִצְלָפְחָד
בַּר חֵפֶר בַּר גִלְעָד בַּר
מָכִיר בַּר מְנַשֶּׁה לָא הֲווֹ
לֵיהּ בְּנִין אֱלָהֵן בְּנָן וְאִלֵּין
שְׁמָהַת בְּנָתֵיהּ מַחְלָה
וְנֹעָה חָגְלָה מִלְכָּה
וְתִרְצָה׃ ד וְקָרִיבָא
לָקֳדָם אֶלְעָזָר כַּהֲנָא
וְלָקֳדָם יְהוֹשֻׁעַ בַּר נוּן
וְלָקֳדָם רַבְרְבַיָּא לְמֵימַר

**רד"ק**

להם מקנה רב והיא היתה ארץ מקנה אבל חצי שבט מנשה לא היה לו אלא מפני גבורתו של מכיר שלכד הארץ וזו הברכה היתה לו מפני שהיה אביו בכור יוסף והוא היה בכור ג"כ ובעבורו רמז משה בברכתו בכור שורו הדר לו וקרני ראם קרניו

**רש"י**

יז (א) למכיר בכור מנשה. לפיכך נטל תחלה בימי

**מנחת שי**

יז (ד) ולפני הנשיאים. בספרים כ"י מדוייקים ובקצת דפוסים ישנים מלא דמלא ובדפוסים אחרונים הנשאים כתיב חסר י"ד קדמאה ומלא יו"ד תניינא ובמסורה סוף פרשה לך לך נמסר כל נשיאים וכתובים נשיאים כתיב בר מן ד' וכו' והויה דלא כמאן לכן נ"ל להגיה כל נשיאים וכתובים נשיאים כתיב מלא דמלא כמו שמצאתו זה בספרים המדוייקים וגם כל האחרים שבנשיאים וכתובים הם מלאים דמלאים וכל הספרים חוץ מהארבעה שאלתו מן הכלל.

**מצודת דוד**

יעקב שהקדימו בכל דבר: למכיר בכור מנשה. ר"ל אבל בבני מנשה בלא היתה סבה מה להקדים הצעיר להבכור לזה לקח הבכור תחלה: אבי הגלעד. ע"ש בנו גלעד היה נקרא. או ר"ל שר הגלעד ואמר ע"ש סופו: איש מלחמה. ובחר לשבת בעבר הירדן על הספר במקום סכנה להראות הע"ג את גבורתו ולזה היה לו הגלעד והבשן: (ב) ויהי. ר"ל ואמר זה היה הגורל לבני מנשה הנותרים לכל משפחם ומשפחה: הזכרים. לפי שאמר בענין שאף נקבות מבני מנשה לקחו נחלה לזה"א הזכרים שבמשפחותם:

## Commentary Digest

sidered as *the rest* — the inferior ones. Although the half-tribe that settled on the east of the Jordan were superior to their brethren in military prowess, spiritually, however, they were inferior to those who dwelt in the Holy Land proper. In v. 6, they are again referred to as *the rest.* — P. Y.

he was firstborn of Joseph; for Machir the firstborn of
Manasseh, the father of Gilead, because he was a man of war,
therefore, he had Gilead and Bashan. 2. There was also
a lot for the rest of the children of Manasseh according to
their families; for the children of Abiezer, and for the
children of Helek, and for the children of Asriel, and for the
children of Shechem, and for the children of Hepher, and
for the children of Shemida. These are the male children of
Manasseh the son of Joseph, by their families. 3. But
Zelophehad, the son of Hepher, the son of Gilead, the son of
Machir, the son of Manasseh, had no sons, but daughters;
and these are the names of his daughters: Mahlah, and Noah,
Hoglah, Milcah, and Tirzah. 4. And they came near before
Eleazar the priest, and before Joshua the son of Nun, and

## Commentary Digest

CHAPTER 17

1. *"for" he was the firstborn of Joseph* — Therefore, the lot was on his name, although it included Ephraim. — E.G.

כי can also be understood as "despite," for despite the fact that Manasseh was the firstborn, Ephraim was accorded his portion first, in conjunction with the blessing of Jacob in Gen. XLVIII:20. — A and D. K interprets this sentence in this manner: Although Manasseh did not have the flocks of sheep and herds of cattle that Gad and Reuben had, nevertheless, Machir, being the firstborn of Manasseh, himself the firstborn of Joseph, was a man of war, and conquered Gilead and Bashan on the eastern bank of the Jordan. This was implicit in Moses' blessing to the tribes of Joseph[1]: The firstborn... is glorious... he will gore even the ends of the earth. Similar to this is R's commentary, which reads thus: for Machir the firstborn of Manasseh — *"Therefore, he took first in Moses' days on the other side of the Jordan, and had Gilead and Bashan."* — R

*the father of Gilead* — Machir was known because of his son, Gilead. This may also be rendered: the **master of Gilead, since the land of Gilead was given to him.** — D

2. *for the rest of the children of Manasseh* — As compared to the other families of Manasseh, these are con-

יְהוָה צִוָּה אֶת־מֹשֶׁה לָתֶת־לָנוּ נַחֲלָה
בְּתוֹךְ אַחֵינוּ וַיִּתֵּן לָהֶם אֶל־פִּי יְהוָה
נַחֲלָה בְּתוֹךְ אֲחֵי אֲבִיהֶן: ה וַיִּפְּלוּ חַבְלֵי־
מְנַשֶּׁה עֲשָׂרָה לְבַד מֵאֶרֶץ הַגִּלְעָד
וְהַבָּשָׁן אֲשֶׁר מֵעֵבֶר לַיַּרְדֵּן: ו כִּי בְּנוֹת
מְנַשֶּׁה נָחֲלוּ נַחֲלָה בְּתוֹךְ בָּנָיו וְאֶרֶץ
הַגִּלְעָד הָיְתָה לִבְנֵי־מְנַשֶּׁה הַנּוֹתָרִים:
ז וַיְהִי גְבוּל־מְנַשֶּׁה מֵאָשֵׁר הַמִּכְמְתָת

יְיָ פַּקִּיד יַת מֹשֶׁה לְמִתַּן
לָנָא אַחְסָנָא בְּגוֹ אֲחָנָא
וִיהַב לְהוֹן עַל מֵימְרָא
דַּייָ אַחְסָנָא בְּגוֹ אֲחֵי
אֲבוּהֶן: ה וּנְפָלוּ עַדְבֵי
מְנַשֶּׁה עַסְרָא בַּר
מֵאַרְעָא דְגִלְעָד וּמַתְנַן
דְּמֵעִבְרָא לְיַרְדְּנָא:
ו אֲרֵי בְּנַת מְנַשֶּׁה
אַחְסִינוּ אַחְסָנָא בְּגוֹ
בְּנוֹהִי וְאַרְעָא גִלְעָד הֲוָת
לִבְנֵי מְנַשֶּׁה דְּאִשְׁתְּאָרוּ:
ז וַהֲוָה תְּחוּם מְנַשֶּׁה
מֵאָשֵׁר לְמִכְמְתָת דִּי עַל

ת״א חבלי מנשה. ב״ב קיח קיט (בס פז): אפי

### רש״י

מנשה בעבר הירדן ויהי לו הגלעד והבשן: (ה) ויפלו חבלי מנשה עשרה. ששה לששה בתי אבות המנויים למעלה וארבע לבנות צלפחד לא שתהא כל אחת בית אב לעצמ׳ אלא שנטלו ארבע׳ חלקים חלק של אביהם שהיה מיוצאי מצרים לפי מנין היוצאים ממצרים נתחלק׳ הארץ וחלקו עם אחיו בנכסי חפר אביו שהיה גם הוא מיוצאי מצרים ושהי׳ בכור ונטל שני חלקי׳. ועוד היה להם חלק אחי אביהם שמת במדבר בלא בנים ונטלו נחלה בחלקו כך אמרו רבותינו בבבא בתרא ולא הוזקק הכתוב להשמיענו מנין חלקי הבנות אלא ללמד שנטלו חלק בכורה ולהודיע שארץ ישראל חלק ירושה להם מוחזקת מאבותיהם שאילולי כן אין הבכור נוטל בראוי כבמוחזק: (ו) וארץ הגלעד. שבעבר הירדן היתה לבני מנשה

### רד״ק

בהם עמים ינגח יחדיו: (ה) ויפלו חבלי מנשה עשרה. בפתח החי״ת ומה שספר החבלים שנפלו למנשה להודיע חלקי בנות צלפחד כי הצי שבט מנשה הנותרים היו ששה בתי אבות אביעזר וחלק ואשריאל ושכם וחפר ושמידע ונטלו ששה חלקים ובנות צלפחד נטלו ד׳ חלקים חלק אביהם שהיה מיוצאי מצרים וליוצאי מצרים נתחלקה הארץ לדעת רבותי׳ ז״ל ואף על פי שיש ביניהם מחלוקת בדבר הרוב השוו בזה כי ליוצאי מצרים נתחלקה הארץ והנה בנות צלפחד נטלו חלק אביהם שהיה כיוצאי מצרים וחלקו עם אחיו בנכסי חפר שהיה גם הוא ביוצאי מצרים והלק בכורה שהיה צלפחד בכור והלק אחי אביהם אחר שהיה מיוצאי מצרים ומת במדבר בלא בנים וזכה צלפחד בירושתו עם אחיו: (ז) מאשר המכמתת. הגבול היה יוצא

### מנחת שי

תשכתכתי זה ראיתי אח״כ במסורת כ״י שכתוב בפירוש כל נביאים וכתובים כתיב נביאים: (ה) ויפלו חבלי מנשה. החי״ת בפתח והמסורת עליו לית דכוותיה

### מצודת דוד

(ד) אחינו. ר״ל אחי אבינו: אל פי ה׳. על פי ה׳ כמלותו: (ה) חבלי מנשה עשרה. בא״י עלמה לקחו עשרה מחוזות: (ו) כי בנות מנשה וגו׳. ר״ל לפי שבנות מנשה גם המה לקחו נחלה ובני מנשה הנותרים לקחו ארץ הגלעד לזה היה ראוי וכן שיקחו בא״י עלמה אלו העשרה מחוזות לא פחות ולא יותר כי החשבון הזה היה ראוי להם: (ז) ויהי גבול מנשה. הרוחב מלפון כלפי הדרום היה

### מצודת ציון

יז (ה) חבלי. המחוזות יקראו חבלים ע״ש כי בחבל יחולק נחלה:

## Commentary Digest

*who was also one of those who left Egypt; and* (3) *he was the firstborn, and received two portions; and* (4) *in addition, they had the share of their father's brother, who died in the wilderness without children, and they received inheritance in his share. Our Rabbis stated this in Baba Bathra.*[1] *It was not necessary for the scripture to relate to us the number of the daughters' shares, except to teach us that they received the firstborn share, and to inform us that Eretz Israel was an inherited share which belonged to them from the time of their forefathers, for otherwise, the firstborn does not receive an extra share of that which is fit to come into the father's possession, as he does in that which the father had already acquired."* — R

6. *and the rest...had the land of Gilead* — i.e. *"the rest of Manasseh's sons had the land of Gilead which was on the other side of the Jordan."* — R In view of the fact that Manasseh's daughters took inheritance with his sons, and the rest of his sons took

"The Lord commanded Moses to give us an inheritance among our brothers." According to the commandment of the Lord, he gave them an inheritance among the brothers of their father. 5. And there fell ten portions to Manasseh, besides the land of Gilead and Bashan, which is on the other side of the Jordan. 6. Because the daughters of Manasseh had an inheritance among his sons; and the rest of Manasseh's sons had the land of Gilead. 7. And the border of Manasseh was from Asher to Michmetath,

## Commentary Digest

4. *And they came near before Eleazar the priest, and before Joshua the son of Nun, and before the princes, saying* — It would have sufficed to say: *And they said before Eleazar the priest, and before Joshua the son of Nun . . . And they came near* is completely superfluous. Likewise, *saying* is unclear. It would have been clearer had Scripture stated: *And they said.* It can be explained thus: The daughters prepared their case before they came before Eleazar the priest, and before Joshua . . . *They came near . . . to say* I.e. they came near in order to state their case. — K. Y.

*commanded Moses* — Num. XXVII:7.

*among our brothers* — actually our father's brothers. — D

5. *portions* — Heb. חבלי, lit. "ropes," because land was measured in units of lengths of rope. — S. M.[1]

*And there fell ten portions to Manasseh* — "*I.e. six for the six fathers' houses enumerated above,*[2] *and four for the daughters of Zelophehad, not that each one should be considered an individual father's house,* (for they were five — Kara) *but they received four shares:* (1) *The share of their father who was one of those who left Egypt, and according to the number of those who left Egypt the land was apportioned;* (2) *and his share with his brothers in the property of Hepher,*

אֲשֶׁר עַל־פְּנֵי שְׁכֶם וְהָלַךְ הַגְּבוּל אֶל־הַיָּמִין אֶל־יֹשְׁבֵי עֵין תַּפּוּחַ׃ ח לִמְנַשֶּׁה הָיְתָה אֶרֶץ תַּפּוּחַ וְתַפּוּחַ אֶל־גְּבוּל מְנַשֶּׁה לִבְנֵי אֶפְרָיִם׃ ט וְיָרַד הַגְּבוּל נַחַל קָנָה נֶגְבָּה לַנַּחַל עָרִים הָאֵלֶּה לְאֶפְרַיִם בְּתוֹךְ עָרֵי מְנַשֶּׁה וּגְבוּל מְנַשֶּׁה מִצְּפוֹן לַנַּחַל וַיְהִי תֹצְאֹתָיו הַיָּמָּה׃ י נֶגְבָּה לְאֶפְרַיִם וְצָפוֹנָה לִמְנַשֶּׁה וַיְהִי הַיָּם גְּבוּלוֹ וּבְאָשֵׁר יִפְגְּעוּן מִצָּפוֹן וּבְיִשָּׂשכָר מִמִּזְרָח׃ יא וַיְהִי לִמְנַשֶּׁה בְּיִשָּׂשכָר וּבְאָשֵׁר בֵּית־שְׁאָן וּבְנוֹתֶיהָ וְיִבְלְעָם

**תרגום**

אַפֵּי שְׁכֶם וַאֲזַל תְּחוּמָא לְיָמִינָא לְיָתְבֵי עֵין תַּפּוּחַ׃ ח לִמְנַשֶּׁה הֲוַת אֲרַע תַּפּוּחַ וְתַפּוּחַ עַל תְּחוּם מְנַשֶּׁה לִבְנֵי אֶפְרָיִם׃ ט וְנָחִית תְּחוּמָא לְנַחְלָא דְקָנָה לְדָרוֹמָא לְנַחְלָא קִרְוַיָּא הָאִלֵּין לְאֶפְרַיִם בְּגוֹ קִרְוֵי מְנַשֶּׁה וּתְחוּם מְנַשֶּׁה מִצִּפּוּנָא לְנַחְלָא וַהֲוָן מַפְּקָנוֹהִי לְיַמָּא׃ י דָּרוֹמָא לְאֶפְרַיִם וְצִפּוּנָא לִמְנַשֶּׁה וַהֲוָה יַמָּא תְּחוּמֵיהּ וּבְאָשֵׁר מְעַרְעִין מִצִּפּוּנָא וּבְיִשָּׂשכָר מִמַּדִּינְחָא׃ יא וַהֲוָה לִמְנַשֶּׁה בְּיִשָּׂשכָר וּבְאָשֵׁר בֵּית שְׁאָן וְכַפְרָנָהָא וְיִבְלְעָם וְכַפְרָנָהָא וְיָת יָתְבֵי דֹאר וכפרנהא

**רש"י**

הנותרים: (ח) ארץ תפוח. הכפרים והחצרים ותפוח עצמו העיר היתה לבני אפרים: אל גבול מנשה. על מיצר מנשה לסוף גבולו: (ט) ערים האלה. מתפוח עד נחל קנה לאפרי' היו בתוך ערי מנשה: (י) נגבה לאפרים. אפרים נטל חלקו מדרום לצד הארץ שבין בני יהודה לשאר שבטים: וצפונה למנשה. מנשה נטל לצד צפון:

**מנחת שי**

וכל בחצל דכוותיה: (יא) בית שאן ובנותיה וגו'. רבים התלופים שנפלו בספרים בשאן ובנותיה שבפסוק זה ועל פי המסורה כולם שבפסוק מלאים וה"ו חוץ מן תענך ובנתיה שהוא חסר וכן במסורת כ"י ב' חסר בכיפלה עקרון תענך וכן מצאתי במסורת כ"י ז"ל ובנתיה ה' חסר בנביאים וסי' עקרון תענך דיהושע לעיל סימן ט"ו והכא תענך. יבלעם. דשופטים א'. ובנתיה באם תלתנה ירמיה ריש מ"ט. וכל אוריית' וכתובים דכוותה בר מן ו' וסימן מגדו. דור (ד"ה א ז) בית אל. יבנה (ד"ה ב'

**מצודת ציון**

(י) יפגעון. יפגשון:

**מצודת דוד**

מגבול בני אשר אשר נחלו מצפון מנשה עד מכמתת שעמדה מול מקצוע דרומית מערבית של נחלת אפרים לפני שכם שהיתה משל אפרים אשר עמדה במקצוע דרומית מערבית: והלך הגבול. מן המערב כלפי המזרח בצד הצפון: אל הימין. פונה היה באלכסון אל הדרום ובא אל יושבי עין תפוח: (ח) ארץ תפוח. המקומות אשר סביב תפוח אבל העיר תפוח עצמה עם שעמדה בגבול מנשה עכ"ז היתה לאפרים: (ט) וירד הגבול. ר"ל הגבול אשר ירד מתפוח לנחל קנה מדרום לנחל האמור למעלה הערים האלה אשר עמדו בהגבול ההוא המה היו לאפרים עם שעמדו בתוך ערי מנשה וכמו שכתוב למעלה: תוצאותיו. סוף גבול מנשה כלה אל הים: (י) נגבה לאפרים. בהרצועה שלקחו בני יוסף לקח אפרים בדרומה ומנשה בצפונה: גבולו. של מנשה: ובאשר. בגבול אשר: יפגעון. מנשה עם אשר בצפון מנשה: ממזרח. כי נחלת יששכר היתה אצל הירדן למזרחה של מנשה: (יא) ויהי למנשה וגו'. ערים היה לו

## Commentary Digest

southern part and Manasseh the northern part. — D

*his border* — i.e. Manasseh's. — D

*in Asher* — i.e. in Asher's border. — D

*and they met* — i.e. Manasseh and Asher in the north of Manasseh. — D

*and in Issachar on the east* — for Issachar's inheritance lay east of Manasseh, bordering on the Jordan. — D

11. *And Manasseh had in Issachar and in Asher* — I.e. Manasseh had cities within the neighboring territories of Issachar and Asher. — D

that is before Shechem; and the border went along on the
right to the inhabitants of En-tappuah. 8. The land of
Tappuah belonged to Manasseh, but Tappuah on the border
of Manasseh belonged to the children of Ephraim; 9. And
the border descended to the brook Kanah, southward of the
brook. These cities of Ephraim are among the cities of
Manasseh; the border of Manasseh was on the north side
of the river, and its outgoings were to the sea.
10. Southward it was Ephraim's and northward it was
Manasseh's, and the sea was his border; and they met in
Asher on the north, and in Issachar on the east. 11. And
Manasseh had in Issachar and in Asher: Beth-shean and her
towns, and Ibleam

## Commentary Digest

inheritance in the land of Gilead, these ten shares in Eretz Israel proper were exactly enough. — D

7. *And the border of Manasseh was from Asher* — on the north. — D

*to Michmetath* — on the south-west, which belonged to Ephraim. — D

*and the border went along* — from the west to the east, north of Ephraim. — D

*on the right* — It went diagonally southward and came to the inhabitants of 'En-tappuah. — D

8. *The land of Tappuah* — i.e. "*the villages and suburbs, but the city of Tappuah itself, belonged to the children of Ephraim.*" — R

*on the border of Manasseh* — "*on the boundary of Manasseh, at the end of his border.*" — R and D

9. *These cities* — "*from Tappuah to the brook of Kanah belonged to Ephraim among the cities of Manasseh.*" — R

10. *Southward it was Ephraim's* — "*Ephraim received his share from the south, toward the land between the children of Judah and the rest of the tribes.*" — R

*and northward it was Manasseh's* — "*Manasseh received the land to the north.*" — R I.e. of the strip appointed to Joseph, Ephraim was given the

ובנותיה ואת־ישבי דאר ובנותיה וישבי עין־דר ובנותיה וישבי תענך ובנתיה וישבי מגדו ובנותיה שלשת הנפת: יב ולא יכלו בני מנשה להוריש את־הערים האלה ויואל הכנעני לשבת בארץ הזאת: יג ויהי כי חזקו בני ישראל ויתנו את־הכנעני למס והורש לא הורישו: יד וידברו בני יוסף

וכפרנהא ויתבי עין דר וכפרנהא ויתבי תענך וכפרנהא ויתבי מגדו וכפרנהא תלתא פלכין: יב ולא יכילו בני מנשה לתרכא ית קרויא האלין ושרי כנענאה למתב בארעא הדא: יג והוה כד תקיפו בני ישראל ומניאו ית כנענאי למסקי מסין ותרכא לא תרכינון: יד ומלילו בני יוסף עם יהושע למימר מא דין יהבת לי אחסנא עדבא

ת"א וידברו בני יוסף . סוטה לו ב"ב קיח:

## רש"י

(יא) שלשת הנפת . תלתא פלכין ושלשת הנפות הנזכרים כאן של דור ושל עין דור היו כמו שאמור למעלה בספר זה מלך דור לנפות דור ובפסוק א' אומר לנפות דור מים וכאן כך הוא אומר ואת יושבי דור ובנותיה שלשת הנפת שהיו לה: (יב) ויואל. ואבה: (יד) וידברו בני יוסף . שבט מנשה: עד אשר

## רד"ק

מגבול אשר למכמתת שהוא שם מקום והוא הי' על פני שכם: (יד) וידברו בני יוסף . שבט בני מנשה אבל בני אפרים לא היה להם לצעוק כי יותר היו בצאתם ממצרים ממה שהיו בבואם לארץ אבל בני מנשה היה יותר מספרם כשנכנסו לארץ ממספרם כשיצאו ממצרים עשרים אלף וחמש מאות לפיכך צעקו לפי שאבותיה' שהיו מיוצאי מצרים היו מעטי' והיו הם עם רב ולא נטלו חלקם אלא כנגד אבותיהם שהיו יוצאי מצרים שנאמר לשמות מטות אבותם ינחלו . ומה שאמר לאלה תחלק הארץ איש לפי פקודיו להוציא את הטפלים שהיו אז פחותים מבני עשרים שלא נטלו חלק בארץ אלא לבני עשרים שנה נתחלקה ולחשבון יוצאי מצרים ולפחותים מבני עשרים לא נתחלקה אף על פי שהגיעו לכלל עשרים בשעת חילוק הארץ ומה שאומר גורל אחד וחבל אחד לפי שארץ ישראל נתחלקה לשבטים ועשו שנים עשר הלקים שוים מי שהיה עם רב בשבטו לא היה לו אלא כמו השבט האחר שהיו מעטים ומפני זה צעקו בני יוסף לפי שלא נתנו למנשה אלא כמו שבט אחר שהיה מעט ממנו ואף על פי שהיו עם רב וראיה עוד כי בני מנשה היו הצועקים ולא בני אפרים תשובתם ליהושע לא ימצא לנו ההר וגו' לאשר בבית שאן ובנותיה והוא היה למנשה ומה שנתחלקה הארץ על פי ה' ועל פי הגורל מפני החלק היפה והחלק הרע כי מי שבא לחלקו חלק היפה על פי הגורל היה לו ומי שבא לחלקו חלק

## רלב"ג

(יד) והנה זכר שנחלת בני יוסף באה יחד עד שבכר נכללה בגבולות אחרי' כמו שנזכר פה. וזכר אחר זה שבכר נתרעמו מזה ליהושע ואמרו לו מדוע נתת לנו נחלה גורל אחד וחבל אחד ואני עם רב עד אשר עד כה ברכני ה' ולכן יתכן שיתוסף זרע' מאד בזה האופן עד שלא תכילם הארץ שנפלה להם בנחלה והנה יתבאר אופנים מהמספר הנזכרי' בס' פינחס שבכר היו יותר ממטה ראובן ושמעון ובזה נתקי' מה שאמ' יעקב אפרי' ומנשה כראובן ושמעון יהיו לי כמו שביארנו במקומו. או ירלו בגורל אחד גורל מוגבל שלא יתכן להם להרחיבו כמה שעתיד והשיג

## מנחת שי

י"ג) שוכו . תמנה . (ד"ה ב כ"ח) אלה השמות הם מלאים ושאר הכתובים חסרים ועוד מלאתי לשון אחר בספרים מדוייקים כ"י ובנותיה ו' מלא בכתובים וסי' מגדו דור בית אל ישנה שוכו תמנה וכל נביאים דכותה במ"ה חסרים וסי' עקרון . תענך. דיהושע תענך . יבלעם . דשופטים . ובנתיה בלא תלתנה . וכל אוריתא דכותיהון ונמלאו שתי מסורות אלו שוות בכוונתן אלא במחלפות בגרסתן ומסור' הדפוס דסוף פרשת חקת לריכה תיקון : ואת ישבי דאר . בדפוס יש ובמקצת ספרים כ"י הוא"ו בגעיה : וישבי עין דר . ברוב הספרים חסר וא"ו ובדפוס יש כתב דאר באל"ף ולא יתכן כפי המסורת שנמסר לסימן . ד' כתיב אל"ף ואחד מהם הוא הראשון שבפסוק זה השני : תענך . בספרים כ"י מדוייקים העי"ן

## מצודת דוד

למנשה בתוך נחלת יששכר ואשר שהיו סמוכים אליו : שלשת הנפת.

## מצודת ציון

(יב) ויואל . ענין רצון כמו ולו הואלנו (לעיל ז') : (יג) והוריש.

and her towns, and the inhabitants of Dor and her towns, and
the inhabitants of 'En-dor and her towns, and the inhabitants
of Taanach and her towns, and the inhabitants of Megiddo
and her towns, the three regions. 12. And the children of
Manasseh could not drive out the inhabitants of these cities,
but the Canaanites were content to dwell in this land. 13. And
it came to pass, when the children of Israel became strong, that
they put the Canaanites to tribute, but did not drive them out.
14. And the children of Joseph spoke

## Commentary Digest

11. *the three regions* — "*three provinces* (J). *The three regions mentioned here were of Dor and 'En-dor, as aforementioned in this book*[1]*: "The king of Dor of the regions of Dor," and in another verse the Scripture states:*[2] *"and in the regions of Dor on the west." And here the Scripture states: The inhabitants of Dor and her towns,—which were the three regions that belonged to her."* — R

12. *were content* — Heb. ויואל — "*was willing.*" — R and Z. J, however, renders: And the Canaanites began to dwell in this land. Perhaps, he means that since the children of Manasseh were unable to drive them out, they acquired permanent status as inhabitants of the land, which they did not enjoy while they were in danger of expulsion.

13. *but did not drive them out* — Although the children of Israel became strong and were able to drive out the Canaanites, they, nevertheless, only put them to tribute, but did not drive them out. — K. Y.

the south, near Hormah. Its king had attacked the Jews after Aaron's death

14. *And the children of Joseph spoke* — i.e. "*The tribe of Manasseh.*" — R and K

אֶת־יְהוֹשֻׁעַ לֵאמֹר מַדּוּעַ נָתַתָּה לִּי נַחֲלָה גּוֹרָל אֶחָד וְחֶבֶל אֶחָד וַאֲנִי עַם־רָב עַד אֲשֶׁר־עַד־כֹּה בֵּרְכַנִי יְהוָה׃ טו וַיֹּאמֶר אֲלֵיהֶם יְהוֹשֻׁעַ אִם־עַם־רַב אַתָּה עֲלֵה לְךָ הַיַּעְרָה וּבֵרֵאתָ לְךָ שָׁם בְּאֶרֶץ הַפְּרִזִּי וְהָרְפָאִים כִּי־אָץ לְךָ הַר־אֶפְרָיִם׃

קמץ בז"ק

**תרגום**

עֲדָבָא חַד וְחוּלַק חַד וַאֲנָא עַם סַגִּי עַד דִּלְסַגִּי בָּרְכַנִי יְיָ׃ טו וַאֲמַר לְהוֹן יְהוֹשֻׁעַ אִם עַם סַגִּי אַתּוּן סַקוּ לְכוֹן לְחוּרְשָׁא וְתַתְקֵן לָךְ תַּמָּן אֲתַר בַּאֲרַע פְּרִזָּאֵי וְגִבָּרַיָּא אֲרֵי עָק לְכוֹן טוּרָא דְהַר אפרים

**תולדות אהרן**

אם עם רב אתה. סוטה לו ב"ב קיח:

**רד"ק**

רע על פי הגורל היה לו ואף על פי כן היו מעלין בכספים ומי שהיה לו חלק היפה היה מעלה בכספים למי שהיה לו חלק רע. ועי"ז הסדר היתה חלוקת הארץ אלעזר מלובש באורים ותומים ויהושע וכל ישראל עומדים לפניו וקלפי שבטים וקלפי תחומים מונחים לפניו והיה מכוין ברוח הקדש ואומר אם זבולין עולה התחום עכו עולה טרף בקלפי של שבטים ועלה בידו זבולין טרף בקלפי של התחומין ועלה בידו תחום עכו והיה מכוין ברוח הקדש עוד ואומר אם נפתלי עולה תחום גינוסר עולה טרף בקלפי של שבטים ועלה בידו נפתלי בקלפי של תחומין ועלה בידו תחום גינוסר וכן בכל שבט ושבט והשבט היה מחלק חלוקות לבתי אבות לפי יוצאי מצרים וזהו שאמר לרב תרבה נחלתו ולמעט תמעיט ומי שהיו רבים בתי אבות בצאתם ממצרים נטלו חלקים רבים ואע"פ שהיו עתה מעטים ומי שהיו מעטים בצאתם ממצרים נטלו חלקים מעטים ואע"פ שהיו עתה מרובים כמו בני יוסף ואף על פי שצעקו בני יוסף לא הועילה

**רש"י**

עד כה ברכני ה'. עד אשר ראית שנתרב' מניני ממנין ראשון למנין שני עשרים אלף וחמש מאות כמנין כ"ה בגמטריא במנין ראשון אתה מוצא במנשה בספר במדבר שנים ושלשים אלף ומאתים ובפנחס שנים וחמשים אלף ושבע מאות. דבר אחר עד אשר עד כה ברכה שנאמרה לאברהם כה יהיה זרעך נתקיים בי. ולפי פשוטו עד אשר עד כה. עד אשר כך כאשר אתה רואה: (טו) אם עם רב אתה. יש בך כח לכרות יערות ולפנותם כעין שקורין אישרטי"ר בלע"ז (ערשטער בל"א אויסשניידען) ושם תבנה ערים: ובראת. לשון כריתה כמו וברא אותהן בחרבותם אישרטרא"ש בלע"ז

**מנחת שי**

בפי"א נגדו וכן לעיל בסימן י"ב ולקמן בסי' כ"א: (טו) ויאמר אליהם יהושע. בספרים כ"י מלא יו"ד ובמקרא גדולה חסר. וכן במסרה גדולה נמסר ב' חסר ביהושע וסימן ויקרא יהושע בן נון אל סימן ו' ויאמר אלהם יהושע ע"כ. ולא ידעתי אם הוא זה או אחר דבסיפרא דהיכא אחריני: היערה. ברוב ספרים כ'

**רלב"ג**

להם יהושע מה שראוי שיתפייסו בו והוא שבתוך נחלתם בעצמה יתכן להם להרחיב גבולם וזה שבהר ההוא היה יער גדול ואם יכרתו העצים אשר בו יתכן להם לשבת בו: (טו) ועוד אמר להם שיפנו בארץ הפריזי

**מצודת ציון**

ענין גרושין: (יד) כה. ר"ל כמו שאתה רואה: (טו) ובראת. ענינו כריתה כמו וברא אותהן בחרבותם (יחזק' כ"ג): אץ. ענין מהירות כמו ולא אץ לבוא (לעיל י') ור"ל המקום צר וקטן ומהר

**מצודת דוד**

בשלש מחוזות עמדו השריס האלה: (יד) נתת לי. לכל בני יוסף למנשה ולאפרים: נחלה גורל אחד. ר"ל נחלה מועטת כאלו הוא גורל אחד ומחוז אחד: עם רב. ואין די לי בהנחלה הזאת: עד כה. עד אשר נתברכה כמו שאתה רואה: (טו) עלה לך היערה. ר"ל א"כ שאתה עם רב תוכל לעלות ביער של הפריזי והרפאים לכרות האילנות להיות לך מקום לשבת כי אלו היית מתי מספר לא היית יכול לעלות כח לכרות כ"כ אילני יער אבל הואיל ועם רב אתה יכול תוכל: כי אץ לך. אם דחוק וצר לך הר אפרים עם רוב גדלו:

## Commentary Digest

E.G. explains the operation of the lot as follows: The land was divided into equal portions, and a numerically larger tribe, such as Judah, was then given an additional strip of land from the adjacent portion of land. This accounts for the fact that the boundary was often very uneven. This explains also the plaint of the children of Joseph, who claimed an additional slice of land from their neighbors, because of their greater numbers. Joshua, however, responded that the adjacent forest and hill was potentially large enough to absorb all the additional population.[8]

15. *"If you are a numerous people — "you have strength to cut down forests and to clear them, similar to that which we call essarter in French, and there you shall build cities."* — R

*and cut down — "Heb.* ובראת, *an expression of cutting, like:*[9] *And they will cut them* (וברא אותהן) *with their swords, essarteras — in French."* — R

to Joshua, saying, "Why have you given me one lot and one portion for an inheritance, seeing I am a numerous people, forasmuch as the Lord has blessed me thus?" 15. And Joshua said to them, "If you are a numerous people, then go up to the forest, and cut down for yourself there in the land of the Perizzites and of the giants, if Mount Ephraim is too confined for you."

## Commentary Digest

*forasmuch as the Lord has blessed me thus?* — "*Forasmuch as you have seen that my number has increased from the first count to the second count by* 20,500, *signified by the numerical value of* כה. (25) *In the first count you find in Manasseh in the book of Numbers*[1] 32,200, *and in the Sidrah Pinchas,*[2] 52,700.[2]* *Another explanation is: forasmuch as the Lord has blessed me even until* כה, *the blessing which was bestowed on Abraham:*[3] "*So* (כה) *shall be your seed," was fulfilled in me. And according to peshat, forasmuch as the Lord has blessed me thus, as you see."* — R Only the tribe of Manasseh had grounds for such a complaint because of their sharp increase. The tribe of Ephraim, however, experienced a decrease from 40,500[4] to 32,500.[5]

Since the land was apportioned according to the number of adults above twenty years of age who left Egypt, the tribe of Manasseh would receive a proportionately small share. The division of the land was accomplished by Eleazar the High Priest, who was endowed with the power of רוח הקדש. He was adorned with the Urim and Tummim in the presence of Joshua and all Israel. He had two boxes lying before him: one containing lots bearing the names of the tribes, and the other containing lots bearing the names of the sections. He would announce through divine inspiration, "If the lot of Zebulun comes up, the boundary of Acre will come up with it." He would stir up the lots in both boxes, thrust one hand into the box of the tribes, and bring up Zebulun's lot. He would then thrust his other hand into the other box, and bring up the lot bearing the boundary of Acre. So would he go through all the tribes and all the sections of the land.[6] Joshua could not alter the divinely given share allotted to the children of Manasseh. He, therefore, advised both Ephraim and Manasseh to cooperate in developing the forest encompassed in their lot, and ultimately, by united effort, they would be successful in driving out the Canaanites completely, although they had iron chariots. — K[7]

טז וַיֹּאמְרוּ בְּנֵי יוֹסֵף לֹא־יִמָּצֵא לָנוּ הָהָר
וְרֶכֶב בַּרְזֶל בְּכָל־הַכְּנַעֲנִי הַיֹּשֵׁב בְּאֶרֶץ
הָעֵמֶק לַאֲשֶׁר בְּבֵית־שְׁאָן וּבְנוֹתֶיהָ
וְלַאֲשֶׁר בְּעֵמֶק יִזְרְעֶאל׃ יז וַיֹּאמֶר יְהוֹשֻׁעַ
אֶל־בֵּית יוֹסֵף לְאֶפְרַיִם וְלִמְנַשֶּׁה לֵאמֹר
עַם־רַב אַתָּה וְכֹחַ גָּדוֹל לָךְ לֹא־יִהְיֶה
לְךָ גּוֹרָל אֶחָד׃ יח כִּי הַר יִהְיֶה־לָּךְ כִּי

אֶפְרָיִם׃ טז נַאֲמַרוּ בְּנֵי יוֹסֵף לָא יַסְפֵּק לָנָא טוּרָא וּרְתִיכִין דְּפַרְזְלָא בְּכָל כְּנַעֲנָאֵי דְּיָתְבִין בְּאַרַע מֵישְׁרָא לְדִי בְּבֵית שְׁאָן וְכַפְרָנָהָא וּלְדִי בְּמֵישַׁר יִזְרְעֶאל׃ יז נַאֲמַר יְהוֹשֻׁעַ לְבֵית יוֹסֵף לְאֶפְרַיִם וְלִמְנַשֶּׁה לְמֵימַר עַם סַגִּי אַתּוּן וְחֵיל סַגִּי לְכוֹן לָא יְהֵי לְכוֹן עַדְבָא חַד׃ יח אֲרֵי טוּרָא יְהֵי לָךְ אֲרֵי חוּרְשָׁא הוּא ותתקניניה

### רש"י

(דיא זאלסט אויסגיידען) : איץ. דחוק ; (טז) לא ימצא לנו ההר. כי אך הוא לנו כאשר אמרת: לא ימצא. לא יספיק: ורכב ברזל. ומה שאתה אומר לעלות היער ולכבוש בארץ הפריזי והרפאים עם חזק הוא אותו כנעני ורכב ברזל לו. ואל תתמה אם קראו לפריזי ורפאים כנעני כי כולם בני כנען היו: (יח) כי הר יהיה לך. אותו שאמרתי לך עלה לך היערה: כי יער הוא ובראתו. כי יער הוא ואינו ראוי אלא לעם רב ויבראוהו ויפנוהו: ובראתו.

### רד"ק

להם צעקתם כי לא היה יכול יהושע להוסיף להם נחלתם אלא כמו שנתנה להם על פי ה' על פי הגורל אבל יהושע נתן להם עצה שיכרתו היער שהיה סמוך לחלק והוא היה ההר שהיה לאפרים ועמק ההר ההוא היה למנשה ואמר להם שהם יתפשטו בחלק אפרים ובארץ הפריזי והרפאים וזהו שאמר כי אין לך הר אפרים כלומר אם דחוק לך הר אפרים תוסיף לך עוד אחר שתכרות יער ההר תוסיף לך עוד בארץ הפריזי והרפאים

### רלב"ג

והרפאים הסמוכים להם וילחמו עמהם ויירשו ארצם אם לא יספיק להם הר אפרי' עם יערו וענו בני יוסף לא יספיק לנו ההר עם יערו ומה שאמרת לנו ללכת' עם הפריזי והרפאים הנה לא נוכל כי רכב ברזל בכל הכנעני היושב בארץ העמק לאשר בבית שאן ובנותיה ולאשר בעמק יזרעאל: (יז) והשיב להם יהושע הנה באמת עם רב אתה וכח גדול לך מלד הכבוי אשר אתה מתרבה תמיד ולזה הוא מבואר שמה בנתתי לך איננו גורל אחד מוגבל שלא יתכן הרחבתו: (יח) וזה כי הר יהיה לך תוכל להרחיב את גבולך בו כי יער הוא ובראתו וזה תמה שיתכן לך בקלות מלד היותך עם רב והיה לך עוד תולאות ההר ההוא ותרחיב גבולך מהלך ההוא כי תוריש את הכנעני מלד כחך הגדול והמלחמה עמו לא יתכן לזולתך משאר השבטים לפי שרכב ברזל לו והזק הוא אך אתה תגלהו כי עם גדול אתה וכח גדול לך:

### מנחת שי

ודפוסים ישנים העי"ן בשו"א לבדו : (טז) לא ימצא לנו. המסורת עליו לית ומלעיל:

### מצודת דוד

(טז) לא ימצא לנו ההר. אמת הדבר שאין מספיק לנו הר אפרים: ורכב ברזל. ר"ל ואם תשיב לומר הלא נחלתם גם העמק ועמו הלא יספיק ע"ז נשיב אמרים כי יושבי העמק חזקים ביותר ואנשי הרכב שמה בברזל וא"א לכבשם: לאשר בבית שאן וגו'. מפרש לומר שהם אשר בבית שאן וכו' הניתן לנחלת מנשה: בעמק יזרעאל. כי יזרעאל עצמה היתה מנחלת יששכר ולבד העמק היתה מנחלתם: (יז) עם רב אתה. ולזה יש לך כח גדול ללחם ולהרחיב את גבולך שלא יהיה לך נחלה מועטת כאלו הוא גורל אחד: (יח) כי הר יהיה לך. ר"ל היער אשר אמרתי העומד בהר הנה זה יהיה לך מבלי

### מצודת ציון

יעברו מן הקלה אל הקלה: (טז) ימצא. ענין די הספוק כמו ומצא להם (במדבר י"א):

drive out the Canaanite —

*because he has iron chariots — "and none of the other tribes is big enough to wage war with him."* — R

*for he is strong — "and you have the ability, and must drive him out. Our Rabbis explained:*[1] *Go up to the forest — Hide in the forests lest the evil eye have power over you."* — R K explains the dialogue between Joshua and the children of Joseph in the following manner. The mountain belonged to Ephraim, while the valley belonged to Manasseh. Joshua advised the tribe of Manasseh to occupy Mount Ephraim by clearing the forests and driving out the Perizzites and the Rephaim therefrom. The Ephraimites would surely agree to this plan, since their forests would be cleared, the land would be settled, and the enemies would be driven out. Upon this, the tribe of Manasseh rejoined, "The

16. And the children of Joseph said, "The hill is not enough
for us; and all the Canaanites that dwell in the land of the
valley have chariots of iron, they who are of Beth-shean and
her towns, and they who are of the Valley of Jezreel."
17. And Joshua spoke to the house of Joseph, to Ephraim and
to Manasseh, saying, "You are a numerous people, and have great
power; you shall not have one lot; 18. But the mountain
shall be yours, for

## Commentary Digest

*confined* — Heb. אץ. — R This term usually means to hurry. (See above X:13.) I.e. the hill is so narrow that one can hurry from one end to the other in a short time.

16. *The hill is not enough* — "For *it is too confined for us, as you said."* — R

*is not enough* — Heb. לא ימצא. — R and Z

*iron chariots* — *"and what you say, to go up to the forest and to conquer in the land of the Perizzites and the giants (Rephaim),* is no easy task, for *those Canaanites are a mighty nation and have iron chariots. Do not wonder if the Scripture calls the Perizzites and Rephaim Canaanites, for they were all children of Canaan."* — R[1]

17. *you shall not have one lot* — Since you have the power to clear the forest, your share will not be considered confined as one lot, since it is potentially as wide and roomy as two lots. — D

18. *But the mountain shall be yours* — *"the one concerning which I said to you, 'go up to the forest.'"* — R

*for it is a forest, and you shall cut it down* — *"for it is a forest, and it is only fit for a numerous people, who will cut it down and clear it."* — R

*and you shall cut it down* — *"for you are a great people."* — R

*and its outgoings shall be yours* — i.e. the border which goes out of this mountain, and further. — D

*for you shall drive out the Canaanite* — *"since you are a great people."* — R. D explains thus: Since you will occupy the mountain, you will easily be able to defeat those who dwell in the valley.

*though he has iron chariots* — Heb. כי, usually rendered, "because." The difficulty involved here is obvious. Therefore, we render: Though he has iron chariots, and though he is strong. — D. R, however, explains thus: You, the children of Joseph, must

יער הוא ובראתו והיה לך תצאתיו כי
תוריש את הכנעני כי רכב ברזל לו כי
חזק הוא: יח א ויקהלו כל עדת בני
ישראל שלה וישכינו שם את אהל
מועד והארץ נכבשה לפניהם: ב ויותרו
בבני ישראל אשר לא חלקו את

ותתקניניה ויהי לך מפקנוהי ארי תתרכון ית כנענאי ארי רתיכין דפרזלא ליה ארי תקיף אינון: א ואתכנשו כל כנשתא דבני ישראל לשלה ואשריאו תמן ית משכן זמנא וארעא אתכבישת קדמיהון: ב ואשתארו בבני ישראל דלא פליגו ית אחסנתהון

רד"ק

הסמוכים: (יח) ובראתו והיה לך. פי' תכרות יער הפריזי והרפאים ויהיה לך ההר ההוא ליישוב ותרחיב בו נחלתך ברצון בני אפרים כי הם יתרצו בזה כי טוב להם שיהיה יישוב משיהיה יער ועוד כדי שיורישו הפרזי והוא הכנעני שזכר כי כל שבעה אומות נקראים כנענים כי כלם היו בני כנען לפיכך אמר להם ולא יהיה לך גורל אחד כלומר שתוסיף גורלך בנחל' בני אפרי' והם אמרו לא ימצא לנו ההר אף על פי שנכרת היער ועוד אם תאמר שנוסף בערי הפרזי והרפאים רכב ברזל לכנעני היושב בעמק ההר ההוא ואנהנו יראים ממנו אמר להם יהושע לאפרים ולמנשה לאפרים אמר שיעזרו לבני מנשה ויתרצו בכרתם היער לטובתם ולמנשה אמר אחר שאתה עם רב כח גדול לך ויכול אתה להוריש את הכנעני יושב העמק וגם לא תורישנו יזיק לך כי רכב ברזל לו ולפיכך צריך שתתחזק עד שתורישנו: ובראתו. ענין כריתה וכן וברא אותהן בחרבותם וי"ת ותתקין לך תמן אתר דיש מפרשים ענין בחירה מענין ברו לכם איש: (א) ויקהלו כל עדת בני ישראל שילה וישכינו שם את אהל מועד. זה היה אחר י"ד שנה משבאו לארץ שבע שכבשו ושבע שחלקו וי"ד שנים אלו היה אוהל מועד בגלגל ואחר כך השכינוהו בשילה ואז באסרו הבמות כל זמן שהיה בשילה ואמרו רז"ל כי עשו בית של אבנים מלמטה והיריעות מלמעלה כמו שאמר דוד וארון אלהים יושב בתוך היריעה כלומר שעדיין לא היה אלא בתוך היריעה ועוד ראוי זה מן הכתוב שאמר ותביאהו בית ה' שילה אלמא בית הוה וכתיב משם ויטש משכן שילה אהל שיכן באדם אלמא אהל היה הא כיצד מלמד שלא היה שם תקרה אלא בית אבנים מלמטה ויריעות מלמעלה והיה שם בשילה שס"ט שנה עד שהגלו

רש"י

אתה שאתה עם רב: והיה לך תוצאותיו כי תוריש את הכנעני. על ידי שאתה עם רב: כי רכב ברזל לו. ואין אחד משאר השבטים כדי להלחם בו: כי חזק הוא. ואתה יש בך היכולת ותורישנו. ורבותינו פירשו עלה לך היער' החביאו עצמכם ביערות שלא תשלוט בכם עין הרע: יח (א) וישכינו שם את אהל מועד. עשו במדבר ולא היה שם תקרה אלא בית של אבנים מלמטן ויריעות מלמעלן כך שנינו בשחיטת קדשים: והארץ נכבשה לפניהם. משנקבע המשכן היתה הארץ נוחה

רלב"ג

(א) והנה זכר אחר זה שכבר נקהלו כל עדת בני ישראל שילה וישכינו שם את אוהל מועד ולקחוהו מהגלגל והנה זכר שהארץ אשר נכבשה היתה לפניהם והיו רואין אותה וחלקו אותה לשבטים הנזכרים שלאה נהלתם בכללה תוך המקום הנכבש ואולם השבטים הנשארים לא נתבררה נחלתם עדין בכללות ואף על פי שנתברר מה שיגיע לנחלתם מהארץ הנכבשת ולזה אמר בכבר נותרו בבני ישראל אשר לא חלקו

מצודת ציון

יח (ב) ויותרו. מל' נותר:

מצודת דוד

טורח רב כי יער הוא ולא ימלאו בה הרבה אנשים להלחם עמך: ובראתו. ואתה תכרות האילנות לשבת בה ובזה יהיה לך תוצאותיו ר"ל הגבול היוצא מההר ההוא ולהלאה בבני תוריש. בי במה שתשב בהר תוכל בקלות לירש את הכנעני היושב בעמק אשר בבית שאן וכו': כי רכב. אף שיש לו אנשי רכב כברזל ואף שהוא חזק כי היושב למעלה בהר מאד יתחזק על היושב מתחת בעמק: יח (א) והארץ נכבשה. מעת השכינו את אהל מועד בשלה שהיתה בנחלת בני יוסף עזרם ה' וכבשו הארץ מה שלא יכלו לכבוש מקודם כמ"ש למעלה: (ב) אשר לא חלקו. היות כי לא ידעו עדיין גבולת הארץ לחלקם בגורל:

## Commentary Digest

*curtains above. Thus we learned in Tract. Zeb.*"[2] — R Shiloh is referred to as "the house of the Lord,"[3] and also as "the tent,"[4] and "the tent of Joseph."[5] Hence, our rabbis deduce that it was a combination of a house and a tent.[5*] — K

The erection of Shiloh took place fourteen years after the Israelites entered the land. Previously, the Tabernacle had been in Gilgal. It stood in Shiloh for 369 years, until its destruction during the days of

it is a forest, and you shall cut it down; and its outgoings shall be yours, for you shall drive out the Canaanite, though he has iron chariots, and though he is strong.

18

1. And the entire congregation of the children of Israel assembled at Shiloh, and set up the tent of meeting there. And the land was subdued before them. 2. And there remained among the children of Israel seven tribes, who had not yet received their inheritance.

## Commentary Digest

hill is not enough for us; and all the Canaanites that dwell in the land of the valley have chariots of iron...." Therefore, the valley which is necessary for our population, is impregnable. Thereupon, Joshua requested of the children of Ephraim to join the children of Manasseh in their battle against the Canaanites. He enjoined them — ...you shall drive out the Canaanites, *because* he has iron chariots, and *because* he is strong — Therefore, his presence in the valley, represents a threat to your security in the hills.

Ramban, Num. 54, explains that the two tribes of Joseph were given one lot which was then divided into two, to be shared by Ephraim and Manasseh. Since Manasseh had increased considerably, this land did not suffice for them. Since the children of Manasseh could not drive out the Canaanites, they found their territory inadequate.

CHAPTER 18

1. *and set up the tent of meeting there* — *"which they had constructed in the wilderness. There was no ceiling, but a stone structure below, and*

נחלתם שבעה שבטים: ג ויאמר יהושע אל־בני ישראל עד־אנה אתם מתרפים לבוא לרשת את־הארץ אשר נתן לכם יהוה אלהי אבותיכם: ד הבו לכם שלשה אנשים לשבט ואשלחם ויקמו ויתהלכו בארץ ויכתבו אותה לפי נחלתם ויבאו אלי: ה והתחלקו אתה לשבעה חלקים יהודה יעמד על־גבלו

תרגום: אחסנתהון שבעה שבטין: ג ואמר יהושע לבני ישראל עד אימתי אתון מתרשלין למיעל למירת ית ארעא דיהב לכון יי אלהא דאבהתכון: ד הבו לכון תלתא גברין לשבטא ואשלחינון ויקומון ויהלכון בארעא ויכתבון יתה לפום אחסנתהון וייתון לותי: ה ויפלגון יתה לשבעה חולקין דבית יהודה יקומון על תחומיהון מדרומא ודבית

### רש"י

ליכנס לפניהם: (ב) שבעה שבטים. שכבר קבלו נחלתם ראובן וגד וחצי שבט מנשה בימי משה בעבר הירדן ובארץ כנען כבר נפל גורל ליהודה ואפרים ולחצי שבט מנשה הרי ה' שבטים: (ג) מתרפים. מתרשלין: (ד) לשבט. לכל שבט מן השבעה: לפי נחלתם. לשבעה חלקים ולא בשוה אלא לפי השבטים הראוין להלקם לרב לפי רובו ולמעט לפי מיעוטו כמה שנא' לרב תרבה נחלתו וגו': (ה) והתחלקו אותה לשבעה חלקים. איתה שנכבשה כבר והעתידה ליכבש: יהודה יעמוד על גבלו מנגב. א"י ששם נפל

### רד"ק

פלשתים את הארון ועליו נאמר ויטש משכן שילה אהל שיכן באדם: (ב) שבעה שבטים. כי ראובן וגד וחצי שבט מנשה לקחו נחלתם מעבר לירדן ובארץ כנען כבר נפל הגורל ליהודה ולאפרים ולחצי שבט מנשה כמו שפירש' למעלה למה קדמו הם בפסוק והארץ שקטה ממלחמת הראשון: (ה) והתחלקו אתה. פירוש והתחלקו בה פירוש בשבעה חלקים שיכתבו יהיו מתחלקים אותם שבעה שבטים באותה הארץ: יהודה יעמוד על גבולו. כמו שנפל גורלו לדרום ארץ ישראל וכן בית יוסף

### רלב"ג

את נחלתם שבעה שבטים וגו': (ד) לזה צוה יהושע שישלחו שלשה אנשים לשבט ויתהלכו בארץ ויכתבו אותה לפי נחלתם ויבאו אליו כדי להשוים להם הארץ בכללה וזה לאות שאחר שנתחלק' הארץ אשר כבשו יהושע ובני ישראל הוציאו אוהל מועד מהגלגל ולזה אמרו רז"ל שכבר עמד שם י"ד שנה שבע שכבשו ושבע שחלקו והנה יספק מספק איך צוה להם לכתוב את הארץ שבעה חלקים והנה לא היו השבטים

### מנחת שי

יח (ג) אבותיכם. במקצת ספרים מלא דמלא וכן במסורת יהושע כולם מלאים: (ד) ויתהלכו. אין ביו"ד מאריך: ויכתבו אותה. במקצת ספרים מלא וכן נכון על פי המסורת דפרשת בלק אבל והתחלקו אתה שבסמוך חסר כי הוא אחד מן החסרים: (ה) על גבולו מנגב. במקרא גדולה כתוב

### מצודת דוד

שבעה שבטים. כי לחמש' כבר חלקו כי משה חלק לב"ר ולב"ג ולחצי מנשה ויהושע חלק לבני יהודה ולבני אפרי' ולחצי מנשה: (ג) עד אנה וגו' אשר נתן וגו'. ר"ל הן ידעתי מחשבותיכם מה שאינכם שולחים לכתוב גבולות הארץ ולחלקה כי התחשבו אם כ"א יכיר חלקו פן יפרדו איש מאחיו ולא ילחם האחד בעבור החלק אחר ולז"א עד מתי יהיה לכם רפיון ידים הלא ה' הוא הנותן לכם את הארץ וא"כ אף בשלא יעזור האחד לחבירו תוכלו להם כי ה' ילחם לכם: (ד) לפי נחלתם. לפי מספר החלקים המצטרך להנחיל: (ה) לשבעה חלקים.

### מצודת ציון

(ג) עד אנה. עד מתי: מתרפים. מל' רפיון: (ד) הבו. תנו

3. And Joshua said, "How long are you slack to come in to
possess the land, which the Lord God of your forefathers has
given you? 4. Appoint for yourselves three men for each
tribe; and I will send them, and they shall arise, and go through
the land, and describe it according to their inheritance; and
they shall come to me. 5. And they shall divide it into
seven parts; Judah shall remain in his border

## Commentary Digest

Samuel. The last high priest to serve there was Eli.[1]

The halachic status of Shiloh is similar to Jerusalem of a later date, in that no במות (private altars) were allowed during its existence.[2]

*And the land was subdued before them* — *"since the Tabernacle was permanently established, the Land became much easier for them to conquer."* — R and D

2. *seven tribes* — *"for Reuben, Gad, and the half tribe of Manasseh had already received their inheritance in the days of Moses on the other side of the Jordan; and in the land of Canaan, the lot had already fallen for Judah, and Ephraim, and for the other half tribe of Manasseh. Thus, five tribes* were provided for." — R

3. *slack* — Heb. מתרפים. — R from J, Z

4. *for each tribe* — *"I.e. for each tribe of the seven."* — R

*according to their inheritance* — *"into seven parts, not equal ones, but in proportion to the size of the tribes, to the larger tribe according to its largeness, and to the smaller tribe according to its smallness, as is stated: "To the larger, you shall give a larger inheritance etc."*[3] — R

5. *And they shall divide it into seven parts* — *"both that which has already been conquered, and that which is yet to be conquered."* — R

*Judah shall remain in his border on the south* — *"of Eretz Israel, for there fell to his lot the entire southern boundary."* — R

מִנֶּגֶב וּבֵית יוֹסֵף יַעַמְדוּ עַל־גְּבוּלָם
מִצָּפוֹן׃ ו וְאַתֶּם תִּכְתְּבוּ אֶת־הָאָרֶץ
שִׁבְעָה חֲלָקִים וַהֲבֵאתֶם אֵלַי הֵנָּה
וְיָרִיתִי לָכֶם גּוֹרָל פֹּה לִפְנֵי יְהוָה אֱלֹהֵינוּ׃
ז כִּי אֵין־חֵלֶק לַלְוִיִּם בְּקִרְבְּכֶם כִּי־כְהֻנַּת
יְהוָה נַחֲלָתוֹ וְגָד וּרְאוּבֵן וַחֲצִי שֵׁבֶט
הַמְנַשֶּׁה לָקְחוּ נַחֲלָתָם מֵעֵבֶר לַיַּרְדֵּן
מִזְרָחָה אֲשֶׁר נָתַן לָהֶם מֹשֶׁה עֶבֶד יְהוָה׃
ח וַיָּקֻמוּ הָאֲנָשִׁים וַיֵּלֵכוּ וַיְצַו יְהוֹשֻׁעַ אֶת־
הַהֹלְכִים לִכְתֹּב אֶת־הָאָרֶץ לֵאמֹר לְכוּ

**תרגום**

וּדְבֵית יוֹסֵף יְקוּמוּן עַל תְּחוּמֵיהוֹן מִצִּפּוּנָא׃ ו וְאַתּוּן תִּכְתְּבוּן יַת אַרְעָא לְשִׁבְעָא חוּלָקִין וְתֵיתוּן לְוָתִי הָלְכָא וְאַרְמֵי לְכוֹן עַדְבָא הָלְכָא קֳדָם יְיָ אֱלָהָנָא׃ ז אֲרֵי לֵית חוּלָק לְלֵוָאֵי בֵּינֵיכוֹן אֱלָהֵן מַתְּנָן דִּיהַב לְהוֹן יְיָ אִינוּן אַחְסַנְתְּהוֹן וְגָד וּרְאוּבֵן וּפַלְגוּת שִׁבְטָא דִמְנַשֶּׁה קַבִּילוּ אַחְסַנְתְּהוֹן מֵעִבְרָא לְיַרְדְּנָא מַדִּינְחָא דִּיהַב לְהוֹן מֹשֶׁה עַבְדָּא דַיְיָ׃ ח וְקָמוּ גֻּבְרַיָּא וַאֲזַלוּ וּפַקֵּיד יְהוֹשֻׁעַ יַת דְּאָזְלוּ לְמִכְתַּב יַת אַרְעָא לְמֵימַר אֱזִילוּ וְהַלִּיכוּ בארעא

**רש״י**

לו גורל כל המילר הדרומי: ובית יוסף וגו׳ מצפון. לפוני למה שנכבש כבר ועוד יש הרבה לכבוש לד המילר מבעל גד עד לבא חמת שהוא אלל הר ההר במילר לפוני והשבעה שבטים יחלקו אותה שבין יהודה ליוסף ואותה העומדת ליכבש: (ו) ויריתי. והשלכתי כמו ירה בים:

**רד״ק**

יעמדו על גבולם כמו שנפל גורלם לארץ צפון של ארץ ישראל וביניהם יקחו נחלתם שבעה שבטים הנותרים בארץ הנכבשת ואשר עתידה להכבש: (ו) ואתם. אמר כנגד השלוחים לכתוב הארץ: ויריתי. והשלכתי: (ז) כי כהונת ה׳ נחלתו. כמו שאמר בכתוב אישי ה׳ ונחלתו יאכלון והם כהנת ה׳: (ח) ויקומו. וכאשר קמו האנשים ללכת הזהירם ואמר להם כך

**רלב״ג**

שוים והחזר׳ אותה להכרו׳ לרב נחלתו ולהמעיט למעט ואם אמרנו שהם היו יודעים מספר כל שבט ושבט אשר להם תחלק הארץ ולפי סיחם ההוא היו כותבים החלקים שהם לא יסיה כושם ליריית הגורל אחר זה כי לא יתכן שיגיע לשבט ההוא כי אם החלק אשר כתבו לו לפי סיחם והכוון בעיני שבשבעת החלקים היו שוים וירה הגורל אחר זה יהושע לפני ה׳ בשילה ומשם לקח כל אחד מהשבטים ההם חלקו לפי הראוי לו אם מעט הוסיפו לו החלק הראוי לו ואם היה יותר רב מהראוי לו פחתו לו:

**מנחת שי**

גבלו ונמסר עליו ה׳ חסרים ובכל ספרים כ״י מדוייקים ודפוסים ישנים מלא וה״ו וכן ראוי שלא נמנה זה במסורת עם ה׳ חסרים בליגנה וסימן נמסר במ״ג פרשת

**מצודת ציון**

הומנה כמו הכה נלכנה (בראשית י״א): (ט) הנה. להמקום הזה: ויריתי. והשלכתי כמו ירה בים (שמות ט״ו): פה. במקום הזה:

**מצודת דוד**

כי עוד לשבעה יחלקו כי יהודה יעמוד לנחול גבולו מנגב א״י ובית יוסף יעמדו לנחול גבולם מצפון ממה שכבר נכבש ונשארו עוד שבעה: (ו) ואתם. ר״ל השלוחים ההולכים במקום כולכם: (ז) כי אין חלק. יאמר עוד למה שבעה חלקים ואמר כי אין חלק ללוים וגד וראובן וחצי מנשה לקחו וכו׳ והלא ליהודה וליוסף חלק הו׳ ונשארו עוד שבעה: כהונת ה׳. הראוי להם לקחת חלף עבודת כהונתם: (ח) האנשים. השלוחים: ויצו יהושע. ר״ל

## Commentary Digest

eat the offerings of the Lord made by fire, and His inheritance. — K

Another parallel passage is found in Num 18:20, . . . *I am your share and your inheritance.* Onkelos renders: *The gifts that I have given you are your share and your inheritance.* Jonathan renders our verse with the identical words used by Onkelos: *The gifts that the Lord gave them are their inheritance.*

8. *And the men arose, and went; and Joshua charged* . . . — I.e. when they arose, to go, Joshua charged them. — K

on the south, and the house of Joseph shall remain in their border on the north. 6. You shall describe the land into seven parts, and bring it here to me, and I will cast lots for you here before the Lord your God. 7. For the Levites have no part among you, for the priesthood of the Lord is their inheritance; and Gad, and Reuben, and half the tribe of Manasseh, have taken their inheritance on the eastern side of the Jordan, which Moses the servant of the Lord gave them." 8. And the men arose, and went; and Joshua charged those that went to describe the land, saying, "Go

## Commentary Digest

*and the house of Joseph ... on the north* — "*I.e. the north of the already conquered land. There is, however, much more to conquer: The side of the boundary from Baal-gad to the coming to Hamath,*[1] *which is near Mount Hor, in the northern boundary, and the seven tribes shall divide that which is between Judah and Joseph, and also that which is yet to be conquered.*" — R

6. *and I will cast* — Heb. ויריתי, "*and I will cast* (or throw), *like: 'He cast into the sea.'*"[2] — R

7. *For the Levites have no part* — Therefore, there were only seven remaining tribes, otherwise there would be eight. — D

*for the priesthood of the Lord is their inheritance* — This passage is parallel to Deut. XVIII:1: They shall

והתהלכו בארץ וכתבו אותה ושובו
אלי ופה אשליך לכם גורל לפני יהוה
בשלה: ט וילכו האנשים ויעברו בארץ
ויכתבוה לערים לשבעה חלקים על־
ספר ויבאו אל־יהושע אל־המחנה
שלה: י וישלך להם יהושע גורל בשלה
לפני יהוה ויחלק־שם יהושע את־
הארץ לבני ישראל כמחלקתם: יא ויעל
גורל מטה בני־בנימן למשפחתם ויצא
גבול גורלם בין בני יהודה ובין בני
יוסף: יב ויהי להם הגבול לפאת צפונה
מן־הירדן ועלה הגבול אל־כתף יריחו
מצפון ועלה בהר ימה והיה תצאתיו
מדברה בית און: יג ועבר משם הגבול

תרגום

בארעא וכתובו יתה
ותובו לותי והכא ארמי
לכון עדבין קדם יי
בשלה: ט ואזלו גבריא
ועברו בארעא וכתבוה
לקרויא לשבעא חולקין
על ספרא ואתו לות
יהושע למשריתא
לשלה: י ורמא להון
יהושע עדבא בשלה
קדם יי ופליג תמן
יהושע ית ארעא לבני
ישראל כפלגותהון:
יא וסליק עדבא שבטא
דבני בנימן לזרעיתהון
ונפק תחום עדביהון
בין בני יהודה ובין בני
יוסף: יב נהוה להון
תחומא לרוח צפונא מן
ירדנא וסליק תחומא
לעיבר יריחו מצפונא
וסליק בטורא לימא
נהון מפקנוהי למדבר
בית און: יג ונעבר מתמן
תחומא ללוז דלעבר
דלוז

**ה"א** גורל לפני ה'. זבחים קיח (סנהדרין כג): ועלה הגבול. זבחים נד בכורות נה:

והיו קרי

**רש"י**

(יב) ויהי להם הגבול לפאת צפונה. ויהי מיצר גבול הצפוני שלהם הירדן שבמזרח מתחיל המיצר ועלה אל כתף יריחו מצפון ועלה משם אל המערב אל עבר יריחו ומושך החוט בצפונה של יריחו נמצאת יריחו לפנים מן החוט בחלק בנימין: מדברה בית און. למדבר של בית און: (יג) ועבר משם. לצד המערב: לוזה

**רד"ק**

וכך תעשו: (יב) מדברה בית און. סמוך לבית און לפיכך הבי"ת פתוחה ר"ל למדבר בית און:

**מנחת שי**

ריו שרה (פסוק י"ז): (ח) בשלה. בה"א וכן אל המחנה שלה שבסמוך וכתנם כתבו עליהם במקצת ספרים לו ק': (י) לבני ישראל כמחלקותם. במקצה גדולה וקסנה כתוב בגליון ס"א לפני ולא ראיתי כן בשום ספר: (יב) ימה והיה. והיו קרי ועיין לעיל סימן ט"ו: מדברה. במקצת ספרים הבי"ת בקמ"ץ אמנם כפי המסורת דישעיה ריש סימן ט"ז ראוי להיות בפתח וכן במכלל דף רכ"ה וכאו מדברה בית און. מדברה דמשק (מלכים א' י"ט) הבי"ת בפת"ח אע"פ שאתריהן

**מצודת דוד**

אז אוהם על זאת: (ט) לערים. לפי גודל הערים עיר גדולה מול שתי עיירות קטנות: (י) כמחלקותם. כפי החלוקה המפורשת במקראות שלפנינו: (יא) למשפחות. הנחלק לפי המשפחות: (יב) לפאת צפונה. מן המזרח כלפי המערב היה התחלת הגבול מן הירדן: מצפון. א"כ היתה יריחו לפנים מן הגבול ומשל בנימין היתה: בהר. הוא הר בית אל המוזכר בגבול בני יוסף. ימה. לצד המערב: תוצאתיו. סוף הגבול בזה הרוחב ומשם והלאה נכנס חוץ המיצר לפנים ונתקצר נחלתו: (יג) נגבה. א"כ לא היתה לוז

and walk through the land, and describe it, and return to me,
and I will cast lots for you here before the Lord in Shiloh."
9. And the men went and passed through the land, and
described it by cities into seven parts in a book, and they came
to Joshua to the camp at Shiloh. 10. And Joshua cast lots for
Shiloh before the Lord; and there Joshua divided the land
to the children of Israel according to their divisions. 11. And
the lot of the tribe of the children of Benjamin came up
according to their families; and the border of their lot went
out between the children of Judah and the children of Joseph.
12. And their border on the north side was from the Jordan; and
the border went up to the side of Jericho on the north, and
went up through the hill westward; and its goings out were
to the wilderness of Beth-aven. 13. And the border went
over from there

## Commentary Digest

9. *by cities* — according to the size of the cities, one large city as equal to two small ones. — D

10. *according to their divisions* — i.e. according to the division described in the following verses. — D

11. *according to their families* — i.e. divided according to their families. — D

12. *And their border on the north side was from the Jordan*—"*and their northern border was the Jordan, for the border started at the east, and went up to the side of Jericho on the north, i.e. it went up from there westward to the side of Jericho, and the line is drawn on the north of Jericho. Hence, Jericho is within the line, in Benjamin's part.*" — R

*its goings out* — i.e. the end of the border at this width. From here on, the line turns inward, and the territory becomes narrower. — D

*to the wilderness of Beth-aven* — Heb. מדברה בית און. — R[1]

13. *went over from there* — "*westward.*" — R

לוזה אל־כתף לוזה נגבה היא בית־אל
וירד הגבול עטרות אדר על־ההר
אשר מנגב לבית־חרון תחתון: יד ותאר
הגבול ונסב לפאת־ים נגבה מן־ההר
אשר על־פני בית־חרון נגבה והיה
תצאתיו אל־קרית־בעל היא קרית
יערים עיר בני יהודה זאת פאת־ים:

והיו קרי

**תרגום**

דלוז דרומא היא בית
אל ונחית תחומא
עטרות אדר על טורא
דמדרום לבית חורון
ארעאה: יד ותאר
תחומא ומסתחר לרוח
מערבא לדרומא מן
טורא די על אפי בית
חורון דרומא ונהוון
מפקנוהי על קרית בעל
היא קרית יערים קרתא
דבני יהודה דא רוח
מערבא

ת״א ויתאר הגבול. זבחים קיח בכורות נה:

**רש״י**

אל כתף לוזה נגבה היא בית אל. שקראה יעקב ולא זו היא בית אל שאצל העי שהרי אומר בגבול יוסף וילא מבית אל לוזה למדנו ששנים היו ולוז לא בחלק בנימין היתה שהרי הוט המיצר מלוז ולפנים הוא כמו שהוא אומר אל כתף לוזה נגבה. ההוט הולך בדרומה של לוז כמלאת לוז מן ההוט ולחוץ בנחל' בני יוסף ובית אל היתה בחלק בנימין כמ״ש למטה בענין: (יד) ותאר הגבול ונסב לפאת ים נגבה. בעטרות אדר כלה אורך הצפוני מן המזרח למערב ומשם נסב ההוט לגבול המערב של בנימין לילך נגבה מן הצפון לדרום הוט המערבי מן ההר אשר על פני בית חורון נגבה מן ההר אשר בדרום' של בית חורון משם היה מתחיל מקצוע מערבית לפוני' של בנימין ובא לו החוט מצפון לדרום: והיו תוצאותיו. מקצוע מערבית דרומית שלו אל קרית יערים של יהודה נמצא רוחב גבול בנימין נוטל כל רוחב הארץ שבין יהודה לאפרים גבול דרומי שלו עם גבול צפוני של יהודה ושם היתה ירושלים כמו שאמ' למטה בענין לפיכך הי' לשני השבטים חלק בה וגבול צפוני של בנימין ודרומי של אפרים נוגעין זה בזה ושם היתה שילה בחלק אפרים כמה שנאמר ויטש משכן שלו וגו' וימאס באהל יוסף ובשבט אפרים לא בחר ואף לבנימין היה בו חלק וכן שנינו בשחיטת קדשים בשלשה מקומות שרתה להם שכינה לישראל בשלה ונוב וגבעון ובית העולמים ובכולן לא שרתה אלא בחלקו של

**מנחת שי**

כה כאן לפי שהם סמוכים. והמסורה דמשק שקראה צ״ל מסכים למסורת שלנו. (וכ״ה במס״ק מלכים א׳ י״ט ט״ו): (יד) נגבה והיה. והיו קרי כתי׳

**מצודת ציון**

(יד) ותאר. וסבב:

**מצודת דוד**

מנחלת בנימין ומשל אפרים היתה: היא בית אל. כי יעקב קרא ללוז בית אל כמו שאמור בתורה ולא זה הוא בית אל שעמדה אצל העי אשר היתה מנחלת בנימין: על ההר אשר מנגב לבית חרון תחתון. ולא היתה א״כ מנחלתו ומשל אפרים היתה: (יד) ותאר הגבול. הגבול סיבב בפאת המערבי מן הצפון אל הדרום: מן ההר. הגבול נמשך מן ההר וכו' העומד בצפון והלך כלפי הדרום וכלה.

## Commentary Digest

*Hence, the width of Benjamin's boundary occupies the entire width of the land between Judah and Ephraim. His southern border coincides with Judah's northern border, where Jerusalem was situated, as it is stated further in this chapter*[4]*; therefore, both tribes had a share in it. Benjamin's northern border coincides with Ephraim's southern border, and there was Shiloh in Ephraim's territory, as it is said:*[5] *"And He despised the tent of Joseph, and the tribe of Ephraim He did not choose. Benjamin too, had a share in it, as we learned in Tractate Zeb.:*[6] *in three places did the Divine Presence rest in Israel: In Shiloh, and Nob* (and Gibeon, counted with Nob as one place), *and the Temple, and in all of them, it rested only in the part belonging to Benjamin."* — R Benjamin is the one son of Jacob who was born in the land of Israel and who did not bow before Esau.[1]

to Luz, to the side of Luz, which is Beth-el, southward; and the border descended to 'Atroth-adar, on the hill that lies on the south side of lower Beth-horon.
14. And the border was circled, and encompassed the west side southward, from the hill that lies before Beth-horon southward; and its goings out were at Kirjath-baal, which is Kirjath-jearim, a city of the children of Judah; this was the west side.

## Commentary Digest

*to Luz, to the side of Luz, which is Beth-el, southward* — "*the city which Jacob called Beth-el. This is not the city of Beth-el which is near Ai,*[1] *for the Scripture states regarding the border of Joseph:* [2]*'And it went out from Beth-el to Luz.' Hence, we deduce that there were two. Now, Luz was not in Benjamin's territory, for the borderline was on the inner side of Luz, as the Scripture statess "to the side of Luz...southward." The line goes south of Luz; hence, Luz is outside of the line, in the inheritance of the children of Joseph, while Beth-el is in the territory of Benjamin, as is stated below*[3] *in this chapter.*" — R

14. *And the border was circled, and encompassed the west side southward* — "*in 'Atroth-adar, the length of the northern boundary from east to west, ends; and from there, the line encompassed the western border of Benjamin to go southward, i.e. from north to south. The western borderline extended from the hill that lies before Beth-horon, southward, i.e. from the hill which lies south of Beth-horon, from there began the northwest corner of Benjamin, and the borderline went from north to south.*" — R

*and its goings out were* — "*i.e. his south-western corner, was at Kirjath-jearim which belonged to Judah.*

טו וּפְאַת־נֶגְבָּה מִקְצֵה קִרְיַת יְעָרִים וְיָצָא
הַגְּבוּל יָמָּה וְיָצָא אֶל־מַעְיַן מֵי נֶפְתּוֹחַ׃
טז וְיָרַד הַגְּבוּל אֶל־קְצֵה הָהָר אֲשֶׁר עַל־
פְּנֵי גֵּי בֶן־הִנֹּם אֲשֶׁר בְּעֵמֶק רְפָאִים
צָפוֹנָה וְיָרַד גֵּי הִנֹּם אֶל־כֶּתֶף הַיְבוּסִי
נֶגְבָּה וְיָרַד עֵין רֹגֵל׃ יז וְתָאַר מִצָּפוֹן וְיָצָא
עֵין שֶׁמֶשׁ וְיָצָא אֶל־גְּלִילוֹת אֲשֶׁר־נֹכַח
מַעֲלֵה אֲדֻמִּים וְיָרַד אֶבֶן בֹּהַן בֶּן־
רְאוּבֵן׃ יח וְעָבַר אֶל־כֶּתֶף מוּל־הָעֲרָבָה
צָפוֹנָה וְיָרַד הָעֲרָבָתָה׃ יט וְעָבַר הַגְּבוּל
אֶל

מַעַרְבָא׃ טו וְרוּחַ דָרוֹמָא
מִסְּיָפֵי קִרְיַת יְעָרִים וְנָפֵק
תְּחוּמָא לְיַמָּא וְנָפֵיק
לְמַבּוּעֵי מֵי נֶפְתּוֹחַ׃
טז וּנְחַת תְּחוּמָא לִסְטַר
טוּרָא דִי עַל אַפֵּי חֵילַת
בַּר הִנֹּם דִי בְּמֵישַׁר
גִּבָּרַיָא צִפּוּנָא וּנְחַית
לְחֵילַת בַּר הִנֹּם לְעִיבַר
יְבוּס דָרוֹמָא וּנְחַית לְעֵין
קַצְרָא׃ יז וְתָאַר מִצִּפּוּן
וְנָפַק לְעֵין שֶׁמֶשׁ וְנָפֵיק
לִגְלִילָא דִי לָקֳבֵיל
מַסְּקָנָא דַאֲדֻמִּים וּנְחַית
לְאֶבֶן בּוֹהַן בַּר רְאוּבֵן׃
יח וְעָבַר לְעִיבְרָא
דִלְקֳבֵיל מֵישְׁרָא צִפּוּנָא
וּנְחַית לְעַרְבְתָה׃
יט וְעָבַר תְּחוּמָא לְעִיבַר
בֵּית

רש"י

בנימין: זאת פאת ים. רוח מערבי מעטרות אדר עד קרית יערים: (טו) ופאת נגבה. ומיצר דרומי לבנימין והוא לצפוני של יהודה. וכל התחומין המנוין כאן נתנו בצפונו של יהודה וכל מקום שכתוב כאן וירד כתוב ביהודה ועלה לפי שכאן הוא מונה מן המערב למזרח ושם מונה מן המזרח למערב: ויצא הגבול ימה. אם יש אחד ולא ידעתי איזה

מנחת שי

שאמרתי לעיל בסי' ט"ו: (יז) אבן בהן. בה"א כדלעיל בסימן ט"ו ומה שכתוב עליו במ"ג יהודה ועלה אבן בהן. ר"פ פסוק דלעיל דהוא בגורל יהודה ועלה

מצודת דוד

הגבול בקרית בעל היא קרית יערים שהיא במיצר הצפוני של יהודה: (טו) ופאת נגבה. גבול הדרומי מן המערב כלפי המזרח היה מתחיל מקצה קרית יערים: ימה. אל הים ולא זהו ים הגדול העומד במערב והים הזה היה מצפון יהודה ושם כי לא הוזכר למעלה וכ"כ יצאה בהרבה מקומות שבאחד יזכיר ולא בשני עם בהיה גבולם זה אצל זה: (טז) וירד הגבול. כי מעין מי נפתוח שהיא עין עיטם היתה במקום הגבוה שבכל א"י לזה אמר וירד: אשר בעמק רפאים. ההר עומד בעמק רפאים בצפונה: אל כתף. אשר עומדת בכתף היבוסי מנגב א"כ היבוסי היא ירושלים עומדת בנחלת בנימין: (יז) ותאר מצפון. הגבול בא בפאת מערב והקיף את עין רוגל מצפונו והיתה א"כ משל יהודה: ויצא עין שמש. מן עין רוגל יצא לעין שמש: אל גלילות. היא גלגל האמור בגבול יהודה הצפוני ובשתי השמות נקראה ואצל גלגל יצא הגבול כלפי הדרום ונתרחב נחלת בנימין: (יח) ועבר. משם עבר מעבר המקום הנקרא מול הערבה בצד הצפוני ולא היתה א"כ מנחלת בנימין: הערבתה. הוא בית הערבה המוזכר בגבול יהודה והגבול היה מצפונו:

מצודת ציון

(יז) נכח. נגד: (יט) לשון. קצה הים הסמוך כלשון:

## Commentary Digest

*to the side of the Jebusite on the south* — i.e. which stood on the south side of the Jebusite, which is Jerusalem. Hence, Jerusalem is within the boundary of Benjamin. — D

17. *And it circled from the north* — The border came on the west side and encompassed En-rogel from the north. Hence, En-rogel belonged to Judah. — D

*to Geliloth* — Gilgal mentioned as being on the northern border of Judah.[2] — D

18. *to the side over against the Arabah* — or plain. — J Others render: to the side of Mul-haarabah. — D

*northward* — thus belonging to Judah. — D

*Arabah* — also known as Beth-arabah,[3] and belonging to Judah, since the border ran on its north. — D

15. And the south side was from the end of Kirjath-jearim, and
the border went out to a sea, and went out to the spring of the
waters of Nephtoah. 16. And the border went down to the
end of the mountain that lies before the valley of the son of
Hinnom, and which is in the valley of the giants (Rephaim)
on the north, and descended to the valley of Hinnom, to the
side of the Jebusite on the south, and descended to 'En-rogel.
17. And it circled from the north, and went out to 'En-shemesh,
and went out to Geliloth, which is over against the ascent of
Adumim, and descended to Eben of Bohan the son of Reuben.
18. And it passed along to the side over against the 'Arabah
northward, and it went down to the 'Arabah. 19. And the
border passed along

## Commentary Digest

*this was the west side* — *"the west side from Atroth-adar to Kirjath-jearim."* — R

Since Scripture traces the boundary on the northern side from the Jordan toward the west, then the western boundary toward the south, it continues to trace the southern boundary from west to east. — K. Y.

15. *And the south side* — *"and the southern boundary of Benjamin which is identical with the northern boundary of Judah. All the borders enumerated here, have been enumerated in reference to the north of Judah, and every place which is described here as going down, is described in reference to Judah as going up, because here he counts from west to east, and there he counts from east to west."* — R[1]*

Alternatively, we may render: *And the border went out to the west.* Although the border is being traced from west to east, the goings out of the border, i.e. the bulge was directed in the opposite direction. — K. Y.

*and the border went out to a sea* — Heb. ימה, — *"to a sea, and I do not know which sea this is."* — R This is not the Mediterranean Sea in the west, but rather an inland sea north of Judah. — D

*the spring of the waters of Nephtoah.* — The highest point in Eretz Israel.[1]** Hence, follows: —

16. *And the border went down.*

*which is in the valley of the giants on the north* — The mountain was situated at the northern of the valley of the giants. — D

אֶל־כֶּתֶף בֵּית־חָגְלָה צָפוֹנָה וְהָיָה
תֹּצְאוֹתָיו הַגְּבוּל אֶל־לְשׁוֹן יָם־הַמֶּלַח
צָפוֹנָה אֶל־קְצֵה הַיַּרְדֵּן נֶגְבָּה זֶה גְּבוּל
נֶגֶב׃ כ וְהַיַּרְדֵּן יִגְבֹּל־אֹתוֹ לִפְאַת־קֵדְמָה
זֹאת נַחֲלַת בְּנֵי בִנְיָמִן לִגְבוּלֹתֶיהָ סָבִיב
לְמִשְׁפְּחֹתָם׃ כא וְהָיוּ הֶעָרִים לְמַטֵּה בְּנֵי
בִנְיָמִן לְמִשְׁפְּחוֹתֵיהֶם יְרִיחוֹ וּבֵית־חָגְלָה
וְעֵמֶק קְצִיץ׃ כב וּבֵית הָעֲרָבָה וּצְמָרַיִם
וּבֵית־אֵל׃ כג וְהָעַוִּים וְהַפָּרָה וְעָפְרָה׃
כד וּכְפַר הָעַמֹּנִי וְהָעָפְנִי וָגָבַע עָרִים
שְׁתֵּים־עֶשְׂרֵה וְחַצְרֵיהֶן׃ כה גִּבְעוֹן
וְהָרָמָה וּבְאֵרוֹת׃ כו וְהַמִּצְפֶּה וְהַכְּפִירָה

**תרגום**

בֵּית חָגְלָה לְצִפּוּנָא וַהֲווֹן מַפְקָנוּהִי דִתְחוּמָא לְכֵיף יַמָּא דְמִלְחָא צִפּוּנָא לְסְיָפֵי יַרְדְּנָא דָרוֹמָא דֵין תְּחוּם דָרוֹמָא׃ כ וְיַרְדְּנָא תְּחוּמָא לֵיהּ לְרוּחַ קִידוּמָא דָא אַחְסָנַת בְּנֵי בִנְיָמִין לִתְחוּמָהָא סְחוֹר סְחוֹר לְזַרְעֲיָתְהוֹן׃ כא וַהֲוָה קִרְוַיָּא לְשִׁבְטָא דִבְנֵי בִנְיָמִין לְזַרְעֲיָתְהוֹן יְרִיחוֹ וּבֵית חָגְלָה וּמֵישַׁר קְצִיץ׃ כב וּבֵית מֵישְׁרָא וּצְמָרַיִם וּבֵית אֵל׃ כג וְהָעַוִּים וְהַפָּרָה וְעָפְרָה׃ כד וּכְפַר הָעַמּוֹנָה וְהָעָפְנִי וְגָבַע קִרְוִין תַּרְתָּא עַסְרֵי וּפַצְחֵיהֶן׃ כה גִּבְעוֹן וְרָמְתָא וּבְאֵרוֹת׃ כו וּמִצְפַּיָא וכפירה

ת"א [illegible]

**רש"י**

[illegible]

**מנחת שי**

[illegible]

**מצודת דוד**

[illegible]

## Commentary Digest

21. *And the Valley of Keziz* — I.e. a city in the Valley of Keziz. Its location is unknown. — D. M.

22. Zemaraim — It is theorized that Mt. Zemaraim that is in Mt. Ephraim (2 Chron. 13:4) was named after this city. The mountain is near Beth-el, but the location of the city is unknown. — D. M.

23. *'Avim* — Perhaps named for the tribe mentioned above 13:3, and in Deut. 2:23. See above Commentary Digest. The location of this city is unknown. — D. M.

to the side of Beth-hoglah northward; and the outgoings of
the border were at the bay of the Salt Sea to the north, at the
south end of the Jordan; this was the south border. 20 And
the Jordan borders it on the east side. This was the inheritance
of the children of Benjamin, by its borders round about,
according to their families. 21. And the cities of the tribe
of the children of Benjamin according to their families, were:
Jericho, and Beth-hoglah, and the Valley of Keziz. 22. And
Beth-arabah, and Zemaraim, and Beth-el. 23. And 'Avim,
and Parah, and 'Ophrah. 24. And Cephar-haamonah, and
'Ophni, and Geba; twelve cities with their villages. 25. Gibeon,
and Ramah, and Beeroth. 26. And Mizpeh, and Chephirah,

## Commentary Digest

19. *to the side of Beth-hoglah northward* — Hence, Beth-hoglah belongs to Judah, not to Benjamin. The Beth-hoglah mentioned in v. 21 is another city known by the same name. — D

*at the bay of the Salt Sea to the north* — "*to the north of the bay. Hence the entire bay is in Judah's territory.*" — R D renders: at the north bay of the Salt Sea.

*at the . . . end of the Jordan* — "*the place where the Jordan empties into the Dead Sea. This was described as the north-eastern corner of Judah, and here the Scripture describes it as the south-eastern corner of Benjamin.* — R and D

*this is the south border* — from west to east. — D

20. *And the Jordan borders it on the east side* — i.e. "*the Jordan was the eastern boundary of Benjamin, for the Jordan runs opposite the width of his entire boundary on the east.*" — R

וְהַמֹּצָה: כז וְרֶקֶם וְיִרְפְּאֵל וְתַרְאֲלָה:
כח וְצֵלַע הָאֶלֶף וְהַיְבוּסִי הִיא יְרוּשָׁלִַם
גִּבְעַת קִרְיַת עָרִים אַרְבַּע־עֶשְׂרֵה
וְחַצְרֵיהֶן זֹאת נַחֲלַת בְּנֵי־בִנְיָמִן
לְמִשְׁפְּחֹתָם: יט א וַיֵּצֵא הַגּוֹרָל הַשֵּׁנִי
לְשִׁמְעוֹן לְמַטֵּה בְנֵי־שִׁמְעוֹן לְמִשְׁפְּחוֹתָם
וַיְהִי נַחֲלָתָם בְּתוֹךְ נַחֲלַת בְּנֵי־יְהוּדָה:
ב וַיְהִי לָהֶם בְּנַחֲלָתָם בְּאֵר־שֶׁבַע וְשֶׁבַע
וּמוֹלָדָה: ג וַחֲצַר שׁוּעָל וּבָלָה וָעָצֶם:
ד וְאֶלְתּוֹלַד וּבְתוּל וְחָרְמָה: ה וְצִקְלַג
וּבֵית־הַמַּרְכָּבוֹת וַחֲצַר סוּסָה: ו וּבֵית

זְכַפִּירָה וְהַמֹּצָה: כז וְרֶקֶם
וְיִרְפְּאֵל וְתַרְאֲלָה:
כח וְצֵלַע אֶלֶף וִיבוּסָאֵי
הִיא יְרוּשְׁלֶם גִּבְעַת
קִרְיַת קִרְוִין אַרְבַּע עַסְרֵי
וּפַצְחֵיהֶן דָא אַחְסָנַת בְּנֵי
בִנְיָמִן לְזַרְעֲיָתְהוֹן:
א וּנְפַק עַדְבָא תִנְיָנָא
לְשִׁמְעוֹן לְשִׁבְטָא דִבְנֵי
שִׁמְעוֹן לְזַרְעֲיָתְהוֹן וַהֲוָה
אַחְסַנְתְּהוֹן בְּגוֹ אַחְסָנַת
בְּנֵי יְהוּדָה: ב וַהֲוָה לְהוֹן
בְּאַחְסַנְתְּהוֹן בְּאֵר שֶׁבַע
וְשֶׁבַע וּמוֹלָדָה: ג וַחֲצַר
שׁוּעָל וּבָלָה וְעֶצֶם:
ד וְאֶלְתּוֹלַד וּבְתוּל
וְחָרְמָה: ה וְצִקְלַג וּבֵית
הַמַּרְכָּבוֹת וַחֲצַר סוּסָה:
ו וּבֵית לְבָאוֹת וְשָׁרוּחֶן
קִרְוִין תְּלַת עַסְרֵי
וּפצחיהן

**רש"י**

רוחב כל גבולו למזרח: (כח) וצלע האלף והיבוסי היא ירושלים. כל אחת עיר לעצמה וכן גבעת קרית חמש עריס בפסוק זה:
יט (א) ויצא הגורל השני. שני לבנימין שגורל בנימין היה ראשון לשבעה השבטים שאמר יהושע לשלוחיו

**רד"ק**

(כח) וצלע האלף. הם שתי ערים וכן הוא אומר בארץ בנימין בצלע וכתיב וצלע אלף וכן גבעת קרית הם שתי ערים: והיבוסי היא ירושלם. ובגורל בני יהודה אמר ג"ב כי היבוסי היא ירושלם בחלק יהודה והנה אומר כי היא לבנימין כן הוא כי לכל אחד מהם היה לו חלק בה ואמרו רז"ל כי רצועה יוצאה מחלקו של יהודה לחלקו של בנימין ובה מזבח בנוי והיה בנימין הצדיק מצטער עליה לבלעה שנאמר חופף עליו כל היום ובין כתפיו שכן ויש אומרים המזבח היה בחלקו של בנימין שנא' ובין כתפיו שכן וי"א כי בין שניהם היה המזבח והנה יהודה היה עולה גי בן הנם כתף היבוסי והיה עולה אל ראש ההר אשר על פני גי בן הנם ימה אשר בקצה עמק רפאים ומראש ההר אל מעין מי נפתוח ואמרו כי הוא עין עיטם הנזכר בדברי רז"ל וחלק בנימין היה כנגדו חלק יהודה היה עולה אל ההר וחלק בנימין היה יורד אל קצה ההר אשר בגי בן הנם אשר בעמק רפאים והיה יורד אל כתף היבוסי היא ירושלם נמצא שבין שניהם היה הגבול הזה זה עולה וזה יורד: (ב) באר שבע ושבע. עיר אחת:

**מנחת שי**

(כח) וצלע האלף והיבוסי היא ירושלם. בס"א כ"י וְהַיְבוּסִי הִיא ירושלים. בסופר הִיא־ירושלם במאריך ובמקף: יט (א) בני שמעון למשפחותם. חד מן ח' מלאים וזהו קדמאה דשמעון כמ"ש בפרשת נשא: (ד) ואלתולד. ברוב הספרים מלא אחם: (ה) וצקלג. הלמ"ד בקמץ במקצת הספרים ומקצתן בפתח וי"ס בהגד"י במאריך:

**מצודת דוד**

(כח) וצלע האלף. חמשה עיירות במקרא זה צלע א' האלף ב' יבוסי ג' גבעת ד' קרית חמשה: יט (א) בתוך וגו'. היה מובלע בנחלת יהודה בתוך הגבול האמור למעלה: (ב) באר שבע ושבע. היא עיר אחת ובשמי

## Commentary Digest

*ate seven lots."* — R I.e. Benjamin, Simeon, Zebulun, Issachar, Asher, Naftali, and Dan.

*to Simeon, to the tribe of the children of Simeon* — The repetition indicates that the tribe of Simeon received two types of inheritance; one portion like all the other tribes, and one portion in the midst of Judah's territory. The first portion was that enclosed in Judah's territory, which had already fallen to Judah. Since it was not the normal type of inheritance, Simeon is not referred to the tribe of Simeon, but merely as Simeon. It was as though Judah had given it to them as charity.

The second portion was a normal inheritance like that of other tribes. Therefore, they are referred to as the tribe of the children of Simeon. — P. Y.

and Mozah. 27. And Rekem, and Irpeel, and Taralah.
28. And Zelah, Eleph, and the Jebusite, which is Jerusalem,
Gibeath, and Kirjath; fourteen cities with their villages. This
is the inheritance of the children of Benjamin according to
their families.

## 19

1. And the second lot came out to Simeon, to the tribe of
the children of Simeon according to their families; and their
inheritance was in the midst of the inheritance of the children
of Judah. 2. And they had in their inheritance, Beer-sheba,
and Sheba, and Moladah. 3. And Hazar-shual, and Balah,
and Ezem. 4. And Eltolad, and Bethul, and Hormah. 5. And
Ziklag, and Beth-hamarcaboth, and Hazar-susah.

### Commentary Digest

28. *And Zelah, Eleph, and the Jebusite, which is Jerusalem* — *"Each one is a separate city, and so are Gilbeath and Kirjath, totaling five cities in this verse."* — R, K, and D E.G., however, counts Zelah Eleph as one and Gibeath Kirjath as one. Although the total number of cities mentioned in verses 25-28, according to this count, adds up to only twelve, Scripture speaks of "Fourteen cities" because in addition to these twelve which were walled cities, and subject to special regulations,[1] there were two other large cities, not mentioned by name. This is a *general principle* to be kept in mind in dealing with *all* the boundaries listed.

CHAPTER 19

1. *And the second lot came out* — *"i.e. second to that of Benjamin, for Benjamin's lot was the first of the seven tribes whose messengers Joshua charged with: "And they shall divide it into seven parts,"*[2] *for Judah and Joseph had already received* their parts, *as it is stated there: "Judah shall remain in his border on the south." From here on, he proceeds to enumer-*

לְבָאוֹת וְשָׁרוּחֶן עָרִים שְׁלֹשׁ־עֶשְׂרֵה
וְחַצְרֵיהֶן: ז עַיִן רִמּוֹן וָעֶתֶר וְעָשָׁן עָרִים
אַרְבַּע וְחַצְרֵיהֶן: ח וְכָל־הַחֲצֵרִים אֲשֶׁר
סְבִיבוֹת הֶעָרִים הָאֵלֶּה עַד־בַּעֲלַת בְּאֵר
רָמַת נֶגֶב זֹאת נַחֲלַת מַטֵּה בְנֵי־שִׁמְעוֹן
לְמִשְׁפְּחֹתָם: ט מֵחֶבֶל בְּנֵי יְהוּדָה נַחֲלַת
בְּנֵי שִׁמְעוֹן כִּי־הָיָה חֵלֶק בְּנֵי־יְהוּדָה רַב
מֵהֶם וַיִּנְחֲלוּ בְנֵי־שִׁמְעוֹן בְּתוֹךְ נַחֲלָתָם:
י וַיַּעַל הַגּוֹרָל הַשְּׁלִישִׁי לִבְנֵי זְבוּלֻן
לְמִשְׁפְּחֹתָם וַיְהִי גְּבוּל נַחֲלָתָם עַד־
שָׂרִיד: יא וְעָלָה גְבוּלָם לַיָּמָּה וּמַרְעֲלָה
וּפָגַע בְּדַבָּשֶׁת וּפָגַע אֶל־הַנַּחַל אֲשֶׁר עַל־
פְּנֵי יָקְנְעָם: יב וְשָׁב מִשָּׂרִיד קֵדְמָה מִזְרַח

**תרגום**

וּפַצְחֵיהֶן: ז עֵין רִמּוֹן וְעֶתֶר וְעָשָׁן קִרְוִין אַרְבַּע וּפַצְחֵיהֶן: ח וְכָל פַּצְחַיָּא דִּי בִסְחָרָנוּת קִרְוַיָּא הָאִלֵּין עַד בַּעֲלַת בְּאֵר רָאמַת דָּרוֹמָא דָא אַחְסָנַת שִׁבְטָא דִבְנֵי שִׁמְעוֹן לְזַרְעֲיָתְהוֹן: ט מֵעֲדַב בְּנֵי יְהוּדָה אַחְסָנַת בְּנֵי שִׁמְעוֹן אֲרֵי הֲוָה חֵילָק בְּנֵי יְהוּדָה סַגִּי מִנְּהוֹן וְאַחְסִינוּ בְּנֵי שִׁמְעוֹן בְּגוֹ אַחְסַנְתְּהוֹן: י וּסְלֵיק עַדְבָא תְּלִיתָאָה לִבְנֵי זְבוּלֻן לְזַרְעֲיָתְהוֹן וַהֲוָה תְּחוּם אַחְסַנְתְּהוֹן עַד שָׂרִיד: יא וּסְלֵיק תְּחוּמְהוֹן לְיַמָּא וּמַרְעֲלָא וּמָעֲרַע בְּדַבָּשֶׁת וּמָעֲרַע בְּנַחְלָא דִּי עַל אַפֵּי יָקְנְעָם: יב וְתָב מִשָּׂרִיד לקידומא

**רד"ק**

(ט) רב מהם. היה חלקם יותר ממה שראוי להם כי כבשו הרבה מהארץ ובני שמעון עלו עמם להלחם כמו שכתוב בספר שופטים

**רש"י**

והתחלקו אותה לשבעה חלקים שכבר נטלו יהודה ויוסף כמו שנאמר שם יהודה יעמוד על גבולו מנגב וגו' מכאן ואילך מונה והולך שבעה גורלות: (ט) רב מהם. מן הראוי להם: (יב) כסלת תבור. אומר אני שהוא לשון כסלים פלנק"ש

**מנחת שי**

(ז) ושרוחן. בחי"ת לא בה"א והוא בסגול ברוב הספר ויש מהן בצירי: (ח) ראמת נגב. כן כתיב בכמה ספרים כ"י ודפוסים ישנים באל"ף ונמסר עליו

**מצודת ציון**

יט (ט) מחבל. ענין מחוז:

**מצודת דוד**

השמות נקראה: (ז) עין רמון. הם ב' עיירות האחת עין והשנית רימון: (ח) רמת נגב. מקום הרם והגבוה בפאת הדרום: (ט) מחבל. מהמחוז הניתן בתחלה לבני יהודה נתנו אח"ז לבני שמעון לנחלה: כי היה. כי הנחלה הניתן בתחלה לבני יהודה היתה מרובה מהראוי להם ולזה נחלו בני שמעון בתוכם: (י) עד שריד. העומדת בסוף גבול א"י במקצוע לפונית מערבית: (יא) ועלה גבולם. משריד בפאת המערבי מצפון לנגד הדרום: לימה. אל הים ומשם למעלה וכו': (יב) ושב משריד. ושב הגבול משריד

## Commentary Digest

10. *Sarid* — which is situated at the northwestern extremity of Eretz Israel. — D

11. *And the border went up* — from Sarid on the west, from north to south. — D

*to the sea* — J and D. E.G. renders: to Yamah. "Westward" would be incorrect, since we are tracing the border southward.

6. And Beth-lebaoth, and Sharuhen; thirteen cities and their
villages. 7. Ain, Rimmon, and Ether, and Ashan; four cities
and their villages; 8. And all the villages that were round
about these cities to Baalath-beer, Ramah of the South. This is
the inheritance of the children of Simeon according to their
families. 9. Out of the lot of the children of Judah was the
inheritance of the children of Simeon; for the portion of the
children of Judah was too much for them; therefore the
children of Simeon inherited in the midst of their inheritance.
10. And the third lot came up for the children of Zebulun
according to their families; and the border of their inheritance
was to Sarid. 11. And their border went up to the sea, and
Maralah, and reached to Dabbesheth, and reached the river
that is before Jokneam; 12. And turned from Sarid eastward
toward the sunrising

## Commentary Digest

2. *Beer-sheba, and Sheba* — counted as one city. — K Sheba is called Bizjothjah above[1] among the cities of Judah. — EG

*Balah* — called Baalah above.[2] — E.G.

4. *Bethul* — called Chesil above.[3] — E.G.

5. *Beth-hamarcaboth and Hazar-susah* — Madmannah and Sansannah mentioned above.[4] — E.G.

6. *Beth-lebaoth and Sharuhen-Lebaoth* and Shilhim above.[5] — E.G.

8. *Ramah of the South* — can be understood as: highest point of the South. — D

9. *too much for them lit. more than they* — "*more than was fit for them.*" — R They conquered much of their land with the aid of the tribe of Simeon, as in Judges.[6] Therefore, it was fitting that they receive their lot within Judah. — K E.G. explains thus: This was because of Jacob's curse[7]: I will divide them in Jacob and scatter them in Israel." Simeon was given his part within Judah's territory, while Levi was scattered in many cities throughout all of Israel.[8]

הַשֶּׁמֶשׁ עַל־גְּבוּל כִּסְלֹת תָּבֹר וְיָצָא אֶל־
הַדָּבְרַת וְעָלָה יָפִיעַ׃ יג וּמִשָּׁם עָבַר קֵדְמָה
מִזְרָחָה גִּתָּה חֵפֶר עִתָּה קָצִין וְיָצָא רִמּוֹן
הַמְּתֹאָר הַנֵּעָה׃ יד וְנָסַב אֹתוֹ הַגְּבוּל
מִצְּפוֹן חַנָּתֹן וְהָיוּ תֹּצְאֹתָיו גֵּי יִפְתַּח־אֵל׃
טו וְקַטָּת וְנַהֲלָל וְשִׁמְרוֹן וְיִדְאֲלָה וּבֵית
לָחֶם עָרִים שְׁתֵּים־עֶשְׂרֵה וְחַצְרֵיהֶן׃
טז זֹאת נַחֲלַת בְּנֵי־זְבוּלֻן לְמִשְׁפְּחוֹתָם

לְקִידוּמָא מַדְנַח שִׁמְשָׁא
עַל תְּחוּם כִּסְלוֹת
תָּבוֹר וְנָפֵיק לְדָבְרַת
וּסְלִיק לְיָפִיעַ׃
יג וּמִתַּמָּן עֲבַר לְקִידוּמָא
מַדִּינְחָא גִּתָּה חֵפֶר
עִתָּה קָצִין וְנָפֵיק לְרִמּוֹן
דִּמְתוּאַר וּמִתַּמָּן מִסְתְּחַר
לְנֵעָה׃ יד וּמִסְתְּחַר לֵיהּ
תְּחוּמָא מִצִּפּוּנָא לְחַנָּתוֹן
וַהֲווֹן מַפְקָנוֹהִי לְחֵילַת
יִפְתַּח אֵל׃ טו וְקַטָּת
וְנַהֲלָל וְשִׁמְרוֹן וְיִדְאֲלָה
וּבֵית לָחֶם קִרְוִין תַּרְתָּא
עַסְרֵי וּפַצְחֵיהֶן׃ טז דָּא
אַחְסָנַת בְּנֵי זְבוּלֻן

רש"י

בלע"ז (פלאנק בל"א זייטען דינוג) [כמו ויקרא ג' ד'] לא בגובהו ולא בשיפולו אלא בשיפועו וסמוך לאמצעו קרב לצד אחוריו ומלצד פניו כדרך שהכסלים עומדות בבהמה ובמקום שהוא אומר אזנות תבור סמוך לראשו הוא במקום האזנים: (יג) קדמה מזרחה גתה חפר. ממזרח לגת החפר שם עירו של יונה בן אמיתי: עתה קצין. שם העיר עתה קצין: המתואר הנעה. המוסב אל נעה כלומר משם תאר הגבול

רד"ק

ויאמר יהודה לשמעון אחיו וגו': (יג) גתה חפר. הוא גת החפר אשר משם היה יונה בן אמתי הנביא כמו שנאמר עליו אשר מגת החפר: המתואר. כתרגומו דמסתחר: (טו) ובית לחם. אינו בית לחם אשר ליהודה כי תמצא ערים נקראים

מנחת שי

לית כתיב אל"ף וכמ"ש בפתח לא בחולם וי"ם כתוב רמת בלא אל"ף: (יב) הדברת. בעקלת ספרים הדל"ת בלא מאריך וכן לקמן סימן כ"א: (יג) גתה חפר. לא מפיק עפ"א מסורת הגדול: (יד) והיו תוצאתיו. בס"א כ"י כתיב והיה וקרי והיו וטעות הוא שאין זה מן הכתובים בה"א וקרין בוא"ו. כמ"ש לעיל סימן ט"ו: יפתח אל. ב' בענין ותרין מלין ומקף ביניהון: (טו) וידאלה. בס"א כ"י ברים וכן במ"ג נכתב בלדו ס"א וירהלה ברים ע"כ. ובשאר הספרים בדל"ת: (טז) בני זבולן

מצודת דוד

ללכת ממערב כלפי המזרח בפאת הצפונה והלך על גבול כסלות תבור וכו': (יג) ומשם. ומן יפיע עבר כלפי הדרום במזרחו של גת החפר והיתה א"כ מנחלת זבלון: עתה קצין. ר"ל ממזרח גת החפר עבר לעתה קצין והוא שם מקום: המתאר הנעה. אשר היה מסבב את הנעה: (יד) ונסב אתו. הגבול הזה סיבב את רמון בצפונה של חנתון אשר עמדה בצפון רימון א"כ רימון וחנתון והנעה היו משל זבולון: והיו תוצאותיו. סוף הגבול של הרוחב כלה אל גי יפתח אל אשר עמדה בגבול צפוני של אשר: (טו) וקטת וגו'. ר"ל עם קטת וכו' היה שתים עשרה כי במקרא זה חשב ה' עיירות ושבעה מאותן שזכר בהגבול והנשארים היו לבני השבט

מצודת ציון

(יג) המתאר. המסבב:

## Commentary Digest

15. *Beth-lehem* — This town is distinct from the Beth-lehem of Judah. — K

*twelve cities* — the five enumerated in this verse, plus seven of the border cities. The rest belonged to the neighboring tribes. — D

M counts Sarid, Maralah, Jokneam, Japhia, Gath-hepher, 'Ittah-kazzin, and Rimmon, excluding Hannathon as being south of the southern border.

Rashi ms., Jerusalem 1974, reads as follows: *The Rabbi enumerated them to me thus: Maralah, Dabbesheth, Dabrath, Japhia, Gath-hepher, Ittah-kazzin, Rimmon, Kattath, Nahallal, Shimron, Idalah, and Beth-lehem.* We find a similar count in J.K., omitting Dabrath. It is obviously an error, since this leaves us but eleven cities instead of twelve.

on the border of Chisloth-tabor, and it went out to Dabrath,
and went to Japhia; 13. And from there it passed along
on the east of Gath-hepher, to Ittah-kazzin, and it went out
to Rimmon, and from there circled to Neah; 14. And the
border about it on the north side of Hannathon; and its
outgoings were in the valley of Jiphthah-el; 15. And Kattath,
and Nahallal, and Shimron, and Idalah, and Beth-lehem; twelve
cities with their villages. 16. This is the inheritance of the
children of Zebulun according to their families,

### Commentary Digest

12. *Chisloth-tabor* — "*I believe that this is an expression of "flanks"* (כסלים), *flancs in French* (as in Lev. III:4), *not at its peak, nor at its base, but on its slope near the middle, near the rear, but on the front side, as the flanks are situated in an animal.* (Thus, we render: The Flanks of Mt. Tabor.) *The place which the Scripture refers to as Aznoth-tabor, is near its peak, in the place of the ears* (אזנים)." — R

13. *And from there* — i.e. from Japhia. — D

*to 'Ittah-Kazzin* — "*The name of the city was Ittah-kazzin* (not 'Eth-kazzin)." — R

*and from there circled to Neah* — lit. "*which circles to Neah, i.e. from there the border circled to Neah. Thus J rendered: And it went out to Rimmon, and from there circled to Neah.*" — R

14. *And the border turned about it* — i.e. the border turned about Rimmon north of Hannathon, which was north of Rimmon. Hence, Neah, Rimmon, and Hannathon were all part of Zebulun. — D

*the valley of Jiphtah-el* — which was situated at the northern boundary of Asher.[2] — D

M counts Sarid, Maralah, Jokneam, Japhia, Gath-hepher, 'Ittah-kazzin, and Rimmon, excluding Hannathon as being south of the southern border.

הֶעָרִים הָאֵלֶּה וְחַצְרֵיהֶן׃ יז לְיִשָּׂשכָר
יָצָא הַגּוֹרָל הָרְבִיעִי לִבְנֵי יִשָּׂשכָר
לְמִשְׁפְּחוֹתָם׃ יח וַיְהִי גְּבוּלָם יִזְרְעֶאלָה
וְהַכְּסוּלֹת וְשׁוּנֵם׃ יט וַחֲפָרַיִם וְשִׁיאֹן
וַאֲנָחֲרַת׃ כ וְהָרַבִּית וְקִשְׁיוֹן וָאָבֶץ׃
כא וְרֶמֶת וְעֵין־גַּנִּים וְעֵין חַדָּה וּבֵית פַּצֵּץ׃
כב וּפָגַע הַגְּבוּל בְּתָבוֹר וְשַׁחֲצוּמָה וּבֵית
שֶׁמֶשׁ וְהָיוּ תֹּצְאוֹת גְּבוּלָם הַיַּרְדֵּן עָרִים
שֵׁשׁ־עֶשְׂרֵה וְחַצְרֵיהֶן׃ כג זֹאת נַחֲלַת
מַטֵּה בְנֵי־יִשָּׂשכָר לְמִשְׁפְּחֹתָם הֶעָרִים
וְחַצְרֵיהֶן׃ כד וַיֵּצֵא הַגּוֹרָל הַחֲמִישִׁי לְמַטֵּה
בְנֵי־אָשֵׁר לְמִשְׁפְּחוֹתָם׃ כה וַיְהִי
גְּבוּלָם חֶלְקַת וַחֲלִי וָבֶטֶן וְאַכְשָׁף׃ כו וְאַלַּמֶּלֶךְ

ושחצימה ק׳

**תרגום**

לזרעיתהון קרויא האלין ופצחיהן׃ יז ליששכר נפק עדבא רביעאה לבני יששכר לזרעיתהון׃ יח והוה תחומהון יזרעאל וכסלות ושונם׃ יט נחפרים ושיאון ואנחרת׃ כ והרביה וקשיון ואבץ׃ כא ורמת ועין גנים ועין חדה ובית פצץ׃ כב ומערע תחומא בתבור ושחצימה ובית שמש והוון מפקנוהי דתחומהון לירדנא קרוין שית עסרי ופצחיהן׃ כג דא אחסנת שבטא דבני יששכר לזרעיתהון קרויא ופצחיהן׃ כד ונפק עדבא חמישאה לשבטא דבני אשר לזרעיתהון׃ כה והוה תחומהון חלקת וחלי ובטן ואכשף׃ כו ואלמלך ועמעד ומשאל

**רד״ק**

בשם אחד בשני מקומות כמו שכתבנו וכן מצאנו בית לחם אשר ליהודה מבית לחם יהודה נראה כי אחד היה.

**מנחת שי**

למשפחותם. זהו בתראה דזוגין מן ח׳ מלאים שכתבתי בפרשת נשא: (יז) לבני יששכר למשפחותם. זהו קדמאה דיששכר מן ח׳ מלאים כמ״ש בפ׳ הנ״ל: (יח) ותפרים ושיאון. בס״ן ימנית ועיי׳ מ״ש בפרשת ואתחנן סי׳ ד׳: (כב) ושחצומה ושחצימה קרי: (כג) מטה בני יששכר למשפחתם. חסר חד בתראה דיששכר שלא נמנה עם המלאים בפרשת. נשא: (כד) בני אשר למשפחותם. חד מן ח׳ מלאים וזהו קדמאה דאשר כמ״ש בפ׳ הנ״ל:

**מצודת דוד**

שמלדו: (יח) ויהי גבולם. הגבול הלך ביזרעאל והיא היתה סמוכה לנחלת מנשה כי עמק יזרעאל היתה של מנשה כמו שכתוב למעלה: והכסלות. ומיזרעאל הלך לכסלות וכו׳: (כב) ובית שמש. לא זהו בית שמש הנזכר בנחלת נפתלי היושב בצפון יששכר ולא זהו שהיה בגבול יהודה: גבולם. על שני הגבולים יאמר על הצפוני ועל הדרומי שניהם כלו אל הירדן: (כה) ויהי גבולם.

## Commentary Digest

*their border* — Both borders: the northern and the southern ended at the Jordan. — D

25. *And their border was* — i.e. the western border from south to north. — D

these cities with their villages. 17. The fourth lot came out
to Issachar, for the children of Issachar according to their
families. 18. And their border was Jezreel, and Chesulloth,
and Shunem, 19. And Hapharaim, and Shion, and Anaharath.
20. And Rabbith, and Kishion, and Ebez, 21. And Remeth,
and En-gannim, and En-haddah, and Beth-pazzez; 22. And
the border met in Tabor, and Shahazimah, and Beth-shemesh;
and the outgoings of their border were at Jordan; sixteen
cities with their villages. 23. This is the inheritance of the
tribe of the children of Issachar according to their families,
the cities and their villages. 24. And the fifth lot went out for
the tribe of the children of Asher according to their families.
25. And their border was Helkath, and Hali, and Beten, and
Achshaph. 26. And Alammelech,

### Commentary Digest

18. *And their border was Jezreel* — neighboring on the territory of Manasseh, to whom the Valley of Jezreel belonged.[1] — D

*and Chesulloth* — and from Jezreel the border went to Chesulloth etc. — D

All these points form the border from the boundary of Zebulun to Mount Tabor. — E.G.

22. *And the border met in Tabor* — Thus Mt. Tabor belonged to three tribes: Mt. Tabor to Issachar, Chisloth-tabor, to Zebulun, and Aznoth-tabor to Naftali. — E.G.

*Shahazimah* — Perhaps this name originates from the word — *shahaz* — one of the names of the lion, as delineated in San. 88a. This was probably the habitat of lions, near the Jordan, as in Jer. 49:19, 50:44. — D. M.

*Beth-shemesh* — not to be confused with Beth-shemesh of Judah or Beth-shemesh of Naftali. — D

ועמעד ומשאל ופגע בכרמל הימה
ובשיחור לבנת: כז ושב מזרח השמש
בית דגן ופגע בזבלון ובגי יפתח־אל
צפונה בית העמק ונעיאל ויצא אל־
כבול משמאל: כח ועברן ורחב וחמון
וקנה עד צידון רבה: כט ושב הגבול
הרמה ועד־עיר מבצר־צר ושב הגבול
חסה ויהיו תצאתיו הימה מחבל
אכזיבה: ל ועמה ואפק ורחב ערים
עשרים ושתים וחצריהן: לא זאת נחלת
מטה בני־אשר למשפחתם הערים

ומשאל ומערע בכרמלא
לימא ובשיחור לבנת:
כז ותאב ממדנח שמשא
בית דגון ומערע בזבולן
ובחילת יפתח אל
לצפונא בית מישרא
ונעיאל ונפיק לכבול
משמאלא: כח ועברון
ורחב וחמון וקנה עד
צידון רבה: כט ותאב
תחומא לרמתא ועד
קרוין כריכן קרוי תוקפא
ותאב תחומא לחוסה
ויהון מפקנוהי לימא
מעבר אכזיב: ל ועמה
ואפק ורחוב קרוין תרתין
ועשרין ופצחיהן: לא דא
אחסנת שבטא דבני
אשר לזרעיתהון קרויא
האלין

תולדות אהרן
ועד עיר מבצר. מגלה ה מכות י׳:

רש״י
לנעה וכן תרגם יונתן ונפיק לרמון ומתמן מסתחר לנעה: (כט) מבצר צור. קרוין כריכן קרוי תוקפא: צר. לשון צור: מחבל אכזיבה. מעבר אכזיבה מגורל כזיב.

והיו קרי

רד״ק
(כט) עיר מבצר צר. מבצר שהיה בצור גבוה:

מנחת שי
(כז) בית דגן. הגימ״ל בחולם ונמסר עליו לית וחסר ובמקצת דפוסים הגימ״ל בקמץ וטעות הוא: ופגע בזבלון. במקצת ספרים מדוייקים חסר וא״ו קדמאה ומלא וא״ו בתראה וכן חברו דלקמן בפרשה ופגע בזבלון מנגב והם ע״פ המסורת ט׳ כתיב כן וסימן נמסר במ״ג פ׳ ויגש וכן מצאתים במסרה כ״י: (כט) ויהיו. והיו קרי: מחבל. במקצת ספרים החי״ת בסגול ומקצתן בצירי וכן מצאתי כתוב בגליון אחד מס״ם שכן הוא בהללי בצירי:

מצודת דוד
הגבול הלך בפאת המערב מדרום כלפי הצפון לחלקת וכו׳: (כו) ופגע. הגבול פגע בכרמל העומדת במערב: (כז) ושב. הגבול שב ממערב כלפי המזרח בפאת הצפוני והלך אל בית דגון: בזבולן. בגבול זבולן שהיה בצפונו ־ ובגי יפתח אל צפונה. מצפון לגי יפתח אל והיתה א״כ מנחלת אשר ולמעלה כלתה רוחב גבול זבולן כמ״ש למעלה: בית העמק. מגי יפתח אל בא הגבול לבית העמק וכו׳: משמאל. מצפון כבול והיתה א״כ משל אשר: (כח) ועברון. משמאל כבול בא לעברון: (כט) ושב הגבול. מצידון רבה חזר הגבול מצפון כלפי הדרום אל הרמה וכו׳: ושב הגבול חוסה. מעיר מבצר צור חזר הגבול ממזרח כלפי המערב אל חוסה: מחבל אכזיבה. כי מחוסה בא הגבול לחבל אכזיבה ומשם כלה הגבול אל הים הגדול: (ל) ועומה ואפק ורחוב. ר״ל עם שלשת הערים האלה אשר לא עמדו על הגבול היה לו ערים עשרים ושתים והם שלש אלו וי״ט מאלו שעמדו על

מצודת ציון
(כט) מבצר צר. מבצר סמוכי בצור:

## Commentary Digest

30. *'Ummah also, and Aphek, and Rehob* — I.e. including these three cities, which were not situated on the border, Asher's cities totaled twenty-two, the nineteen border cities enumerated above, and the three cities listed in this verse. — D

31. *This is the inheritance of the tribe of the children of Asher* — Asher indeed inherited extensive territory, thus fulfilling the blessing bestowed on them by Moses . . . *Iron and copper will be your lock . . .* (Deut. 33:25). His territory extended to the sea, as Scripture states in Judges 5:17: Asher dwelt by the coast of the seas and abided by its bays. They did not succeed, however, in driving out the Canaanites from a large portion of their inheritance. Asher did not drive out the inhabitants of Acco nor the inhabitants of Zidon, nor of Achlab nor Achzib, nor Helbah, nor Aphik, nor Rehob. (Jud. 1:31). — D. M.

and Amad, and Misheal; and it met in Carmel westward, and
in Shihor-libnath; 27. And it turned toward the sunrising to
Beth-dagon, and met in Zebulun, and in the valley of Jiphtah-el
toward the north side of Beth-emek, and Neiel, and it went
out to Babul on the left, 28. And Ebron, and Rehob, and
Hammon, and Kanah, to great Zidon; 29. And the border
turned to Ramah, and to the fortress city of the rock; and the
border turned to Hosah; and the outgoings thereof were to the
sea from the lot of Achzib. 30. Ummah also, and Aphek,
and Rehob; twenty-two cities with their villages. 31. This is
the inheritance of the tribe of the children of Asher according
to their families, these cities with their villages.

## Commentary Digest

26. *and it met in Carmel westward* — And the border met in Carmel which is situated in the west. — D E.G. and M render: in the sea of Carmel. This view is shared by J.

This sea adjoins the mountain range of Carmel, near the Valley of Zebulun. —D. M.

*Shihor-Libnath* — the river of Libnath — E. G.

27. *and met in Zebulun* — north of Asher. — D

*on the left* — i.e. on the north of Asher. — D and E.G.

28. *to great Zidon* — all these cities belonged to Asher, as is stated in Jud. I:31: Asher did not drive out the inhabitants of Acco nor the inhabitants of Zidon. This Zidon was at the north of Eretz Israel, not to be confused with the Sidon of Phonecia. — M

29. *And the border turned* — southward. — D

*to the fortress city of the rock* — a fortress built on a lofty rock. — K and Z. R quotes J, thus: *"fortified cities, strong cities."* — R

*rock* — Heb. צר, *"an expression of* צור, *a rock."* — R. This should not be rendered: the fortress city of Tyre, since it was not yet built. — M

*and the border turned to Hosah* — from the fortress city of the rock, from east to west to Hosah. — D

*from the lot of Achzib* — lit. *"from the rope of Achzib,*[1] *from the lot of Chezib."* — R From there, the border ended at the Mediterranean Sea. — D

האלה וחצריהן: לב לבני נפתלי יצא
הגורל הששי לבני נפתלי למשפחתם:
לג ויהי גבולם מחלף מאלון בצעננים
ואדמי הנקב ויבנאל עד־לקום ויהי
תצאתיו הירדן: לד ושב הגבול ימה
אזנות תבור ויצא משם חוקקה ופגע
בזבלן מנגב ובאשר פגע מים וביהודה
הירדן מזרח השמש: לה וערי מבצר
הצדים צר וחמת רקת וכנרת: לו ואדמה
והרמה וחצור: לז וקדש ואדרעי ועין
חצור: לח ויראון ומגדל־אל חרם ובית־
ענת ובית שמש ערים תשע־עשרה
וחצריהן: לט זאת נחלת מטה בני־נפתלי

**תרגום**

האלין ופצחיהן: לב לבני נפתלי נפק עדבא שתיתאה לבני נפתלי לזרעיתהון: לג והוה תחומהון מחלף מאלון בצעננים ואדמי הנקב ויבנאל עד לקום והוון מפקנוהי לירדנא: לד ותב תחומא לימא לאזנות תבור ונפק מתמן לחקקה ומערע בזבולן מדרומא ובאשר יערע ממערבא וביהודה ירדנא מדנח שמשא: לה וקרוין כריכן הצדים צר וחמת רקת וכנרת: לו ואדמה והרמה וחצור: לז וקדש ואדרעי ועין חצור: לח ויראון ומגדל אל חרם ובית ענת ובית שמש קרוין תשע עשרי ופצחיהן: לט דא אחסנת שבטא דבני נפתלי לזרעיתהון

**תולדת אהרן**

פתלף. (מגלה ט):

**רש"י**

(לה) וערי מבצר. הן לנפתלי הגדים לר:

**רד"ק**

(לד) אזנות תבור. ולמעלה בחלק זבולן אומר כסלות תבור ושני

**מנחת שי**

(לג) מאלון. בדפוסים אחרונים האל"ף בפתח ובכל ספרים כ"י קדמונים בצירי: לנגב' זו ובדפוס ישן האל"ף בקמץ ובשאר ספרים בפתח: חקקה. פליגי על (לד) אזנות. במקרא גדולה כתוב עליו ס"א מוגה אזנו פ"כ. ואין להשית אוזן קו"ף קדמאה אם דגש או רפי ובמקצת ספרים החי"ת בוא"ו שורק: ופגע בזבלן.

**מצודת דוד**

הגבול והנשארים היו לבני השבט אשר אצלו: (לב) לבני נפתלי למשפחותם. הנחלק לבני נפתלי לכל משפחה ומשפחה: (לג) ויהי גבולם. גבולם הלך בפאת הדרומי ממערב כלפי המזרח מחלף וכו': (לד) ושב הגבול ימה. חזר הגבול ממזרח כלפי המערב בפאת הצפוני ובא לאזנות תבור: מנגב. מנגב של זבולון והוא לסוגה של נפתלי: מים. ממערבה של נפתלי והוא מזרחה של אשר: וביהודה הירדן. ובגבול יהודה פגע בהירדן העומד במזרח כי גבול צפון יהודה כלה בקצה הירדן הדרומי ולנפתלי היה כל הירדן לנחלה א"כ פגע בגבול יהודה בסוף הירדן וה"ה שפגע בכל השבטים שהיה גבולם עד הירדן אבל בא לומר שאף שהיה נחלת יהודה בסוף הדרומי מ"מ פגע גם בו: (לה) וערי מבצר. ר"ל ואלה ערי מבצר של נפתלי הגדים וכו': (לח) תשע

## Commentary Digest

size, not big cities such as the fortress cities were. Near the fortress city of Kedesh, there was a smaller city, also known as Kedesh. This was dedicated as a refuge city for the unintentional murderers. — Makkoth 10a

38. *nineteen cities* — sixteen fortress cities, plus three border cities. The remaining border cities belonged to the neighboring tribes. — D

32. The sixth lot came out to the children of Naphtali, for the children of Naphtali according to their families. 33. And their border was from Heleph, from Elon-bezaanannim, and Adami, Nekeb, and Jabneel, to Lakum; and its outgoings were at the Jordan; 34. And the border turned westward to Aznoth-tabor, and went out from there to Hukkok, and met in Zebulun on the south, and met in Asher on the west, and in Judah at the Jordan toward the sunrising. 35. And the fortress cities are Ziddim, Zer, and Hammath, Rakkath, and Chinnereth. 36. And Adamah, and Haramah, and Hazor. 37. And Kedesh, and Edrei, and En-hazor. 38. And Iron, and Migdal-el, Horem, and Beth-'anath and Beth-shemesh; nineteen cities with their villages. 39. This is the inheritance of the tribe of the children of Naphtali

## Commentary Digest

33. *And their border* — on the south from west to east. — D

34. *And the border turned westward* — The northern border went from east to west. — D

*Aznoth-tabor* — identical with Chisloth-tabor in Zebulun's territory. — K[1]

*on the south* — of Zebulun, which is the north of Naphtali. — D

*on the west* — of Naphtali, which is the east of Asher. — D

*and in Judah at the Jordan* — Since Judah bordered on the southern end of the Jordan, and the entire Jordan belonged to Naphtali, Naphtali's border met Judah's at the Jordan. Actually, Naphtali's border met that of all the tribes that bordered on the Jordan. Judah is singled out to tell us that Naphtali's border met even Judah's which was the extreme south, and certainly all the other tribes north of it. — D

35. *And the fortress cities* — which *belonged to Naphtali were: Ziddim, Zer, etc."* — R and D

*Rakkath* — identical with the present city of Tiberias.[2]

37. *And Kedesh* — This city is not to be identified with the refuge city mentioned below (20:7). The refuge cities were to be cities of moderate

למשפחתם הערים וחצריהן: מ למטה
בני־דן למשפחתם יצא הגורל השביעי:
מא ויהי גבול נחלתם צרעה ואשתאול
ועיר שמש: מב ושעלבין ואילון ויתלה:
מג ואילון ותמנתה ועקרון: מד ואלתקה
וגבתון ובעלת: מה ויהד ובני־ברק וגת־
רמון: מו ומי הירקון והרקון עם־הגבול
מול יפו: מז ויצא גבול בני־דן מהם ויעלו
בני־דן וילחמו עם־לשם וילכדו אותה
ויכו אותה לפי־חרב וירשו אותה וישבו
בה ויקראו ללשם דן כשם דן אביהם:

לזרעיתהון קרויא
ופצחיהן: מ לשבטא
דבני דן לזרעיתהון
נפקא עדבא שביעאה:
מא נהוה תחום
אחסנתהון צרעה
ואשתאול וקרית שמשא:
מב ושעלבין ואילון
ויתלה: מג ואילון
ותמנתה ועקרון:
מד ואלתקה וגבתון
ובעלת: מה ויהד ובני
ברק וגת רמון: מו ומי
הירקון ורקון עם תחומא
די לקביל יפו: מז ונפק
תחום בני דן מנהון
וסליקו בני דן ואגיחו
קרבא עם לשם וכבשו
יתה ומחו יתה לפתגם
דחרב וירתו יתה ויתיבו
בה

ת״א ללשם דן. בכורות נה:

**רש״י**

(מא) צרעה ואשתאול. משל יהודה היה ונפל גורל בני דן סמוך להם: (מז) ויצא גבול בני דן מהם. כאן נטלו קלת ועוד נפל להם גורל במקום אחר רחוק מגבולם ושאר שבטים מפסיקין בנתים: וילחמו עם לשם. לאחר זמן בימי עתניאל בן קנז. ובימי פסל מיכה כמה שנאמר בספר שופטים: לשם. היא ליש האמורה בס׳ שופטים:

**רד״ק**

שמות היו לו לענין ידוע אצלם: (מד) וגבתון ובעלת. אינו בעלת הנזכר למעלה בנחלת בני יהודה כי אותו שמו בעלה בח״א וזה בעלת בת״ו ורז״ל אמרו כי שניהם אחד והקשו הפסוקים ותרצו בתים של יהודה ושדות של דן: (מז) ויצא גבול בני דן מהם.

**מנחת שי**

עיין מה שכתוב לעיל על ופגע בזבלון: (מז) וירשו. חד מן ד׳ חסרים ע״פ המסורת כמ״ש במלכים ב׳ י״ז וסיו״ד במאריך:

**מצודת דוד**

עשרת. ר״ל עם ערי המכלל היה לו תשע עשרה שהם עשר ערי מכלל ועוד שלוש מאלו שעמדו על הגבול והנשארים היו לבני השבט שאלו: (מא) צרעה ואשתאול. יתכן שאין אלו שהיו בגבול יהודה ונחלת דן היה במקלוע לפאת מערבית של יהודה: (מג) ועקרון. לא זהו שהיה בגבול יהודה: (מו) עם הגבול וגו׳. ר״ל הערים ההם היו מנחלת דן עם הגבול של מול יפו: (מז) ויצא גבול בני דן מהם. ר״ל גבול נחלת דן יצא בגורל פחות מהראוי להם ולא הספיק להם ולזה עלו לאח״ז להלחם בלשם והוא ליש האמורה בספר

**מצודת ציון**

(מז) וירשו. מלשון ירושה:

## Commentary Digest

*Leshem — "identical with Laish mentioned in the Book of Judges."*[5] — R, K, and D It is also identical with the cave of Pamias, on Banias, situated at the headwater of the Jordan.[6] K questions whether Leshem was included in Dan's lot. or whether they took on their own initiative. Its location at the northeastern extremity of Eretz leads us to believe that it may not have been a part of Eretz Israel proper, but annexed to it. Its very extremity is illustrated by the wellknown expression: "From Dan to Beer-sheba."[7]

according to their families, the cities and their villages.
40. And the seventh lot came out for the tribe of the children
of Dan according to their families. 41. And the bonder of their
inheritance was Zorah, and Eshtaol, and 'Ir-shemesh, 42. And
Shaalbin, and Ajalon, and Ithlah. 43. And Elon, and
Thimnathah, and 'Ekron, 44. And Eltekeh, and Gibbethon,
and Baalath, 45. And Jehud, and Bene-berak, and Gath-
rimmon, 46. And Me-Jarkon, and Rakkon, with the border
opposite Joppa. 47. And the border of the children of Dan
went out from them; and the children of Dan went up and
fought against Leshem, and took it, and smote it with the edge
of the sword, and possessed it, and dwelt in it, and called
Leshem, Dan, after the name of Dan their father.

## Commentary Digest

41. *Zorah, and Eshtaol* — *"They belonged to Judah, and the lot of the children of Dan fell adjacent to them."* — R[1] It is also possible that these were not the same cities mentioned above. — D

43. *and 'Ekron* — not to be confused with 'Ekron which belonged to Judah.[2] — D

44. *Baalath* — not Baalah which belonged to Judah. Our rabbis, however, consider them the identical city, and explain that the houses belonged to Judah, while the fields belonged to Dan.[3] — K

46. *with the border* — i.e. all these cities belonged to Dan with the border which was opposite Joppa. — D

47. *And the border of the children of Dan went out from them* — *"The children of Dan took part* (of their inheritance) *here, and they also received a lot elsewhere far from their border, with the other tribes intervening between them."* — R Thus, we explain: The remaining part of the border of the children of Dan was far away from them. D and K explain: The border of the children of Dan came out in a lot which was inadequate for them. They, therefore, needed additional land, which they acquired by waging war with Leshem.

*and fought against Leshem* — *"at a later time, in the days of Othniel the son of Kenaz and in the days of Micah's graven image, as is stated in the book of Judges."*[4] — R

מח זֹאת נַחֲלַת מַטֵּה בְנֵי־דָן לְמִשְׁפְּחֹתָם
הֶעָרִים הָאֵלֶּה וְחַצְרֵיהֶן: מט וַיְכַלּוּ לִנְחֹל
אֶת־הָאָרֶץ לִגְבוּלֹתֶיהָ וַיִּתְּנוּ בְנֵי־יִשְׂרָאֵל
נַחֲלָה לִיהוֹשֻׁעַ בִּן־נוּן בְּתוֹכָם: נ עַל־פִּי
יְהוָה נָתְנוּ לוֹ אֶת־הָעִיר אֲשֶׁר שָׁאָל
אֶת־תִּמְנַת־סֶרַח בְּהַר אֶפְרָיִם וַיִּבְנֶה
אֶת־הָעִיר וַיֵּשֶׁב בָּהּ: נא אֵלֶּה הַנְּחָלֹת
אֲשֶׁר נִחֲלוּ אֶלְעָזָר הַכֹּהֵן וִיהוֹשֻׁעַ בִּן־
נוּן וְרָאשֵׁי הָאָבוֹת לְמַטּוֹת בְּנֵי־יִשְׂרָאֵל
בְּגוֹרָל בְּשִׁלֹה לִפְנֵי יְהוָה פֶּתַח אֹהֶל
מוֹעֵד וַיְכַלּוּ מֵחַלֵּק אֶת־הָאָרֶץ: כ א וַיְדַבֵּר

**תרגום**

בַהּ וּקְרוֹ לְלֶשֶׁם דָן כְּשׁוּם
דָן אֲבוּהוֹן: מח דָא
אַחְסָנַת שִׁבְטָא דִבְנֵי דָן
לְזַרְעֲיָתְהוֹן קִרְוַיָא הָאִלֵין
וּפַצְחֵיהֶן: מט וְשֵׁיצִיאוּ
לְאַחְסָנָא יַת אַרְעָא
לִתְחוּמָהָא וִיהַבוּ בְנֵי
יִשְׂרָאֵל אַחְסָנָא לִיהוֹשֻׁעַ
בַּר נוּן בֵּינֵיהוֹן: נ עַל
מֵימְרָא דַיְיָ יְהַבוּ לֵיהּ יַת
קַרְתָּא דִי שְׁאֵל יַת תִּמְנַת
סֶרַח בְּטוּרָא דְאֶפְרַיִם
וּבְנָא יַת קַרְתָּא וִיתֵיב
בַהּ: נא אִילֵין אַחְסְנָתָא
דִי אַחְסִין אֶלְעָזָר כַּהֲנָא
וִיהוֹשֻׁעַ בַּר נוּן וְרֵישֵׁי
אֲבָהָתָא לְשִׁבְטַיָא דִבְנֵי
יִשְׂרָאֵל בְּעַדְבָא בְּשִׁלֹה
קֳדָם יְיָ בִּתְרַע מַשְׁכַּן
זִמְנָא וְשֵׁיצִיאוּ מִלְפַלָגָא
יַת אַרְעָא: א וּמַלֵיל יְיָ

ת״א תמנת סרח. ב״ב קכב: אלה הנחלות. יבמות פט גיטין לו: וידבר ה׳. מכות יא:

קמץ בז״ק

**רש״י**

(נא) אשר נחלו. הנחילו:

**רד״ק**

פחות כהם שלא הספיקה להם הארץ הנכבשת לחלקם והוצרכו ללכת אל לשם הוא ליש הנזכר בספר שופטים ולכבוש אותה ומגורלם היתה לשם אלא שלא היתה נכבשת עם שאר השבטים והם כבשוה לאחר זמן בימי פסל מיכה ויש לפרש כי לשם לא היתה מהארץ הנחלקת לשבעה חלקים ובני דן כל הגורל שנפל להם היה להם אלא שהם היו רבים ולא היה חלקם מספיק לבתי אבות שהיו בשבטים ויצאו לארץ רחוקה חוץ מחלקי השבטים וגלו אותה והיתה הארץ טובה והלכו להם שם ולכדוה והיא היתה סוף תחום ארץ ישראל שהיה להם בימים ההם כמו שאמר מדן ועד באר שבע ובדברי רז״ל אמר רבי יצחק לשם זו פמיים ותניא ירדן יוצא ממערת פמיים ואמרו אמר רבי יוחנן למה נקרא שמה ירדן שיורד מדן: (נא) וראשי האבות למטות. כמו אבות המטות כלומר ראשי בתי אבות לכל שבט ושבט ורז״ל סמכו בזה הפסוק להפקר

**מנחת שי**

כ (א) וידבר ה׳ אל יהושע לאמר. בכל ספר יהושע כתיב ויאמר ה׳ וכאן נא׳ וידבר. הדבור לשון עז הוא ובמכות פ׳ אלו הן הגולין

**רלב״ג**

(נ) ואחר זה זכר שבכבר נתנו ליהושע בן נון העיר אשר שאל והיה זה ע״פ ה׳ להעיד שלא היה מבואו פניה בענין ירושת הארץ:

**מצודת דוד**

פוספים והיתה מחוץ לגבול א״י ולא בגבולה (ובמקצוע לפוני׳ מזרחי׳ היתה מול נחלת נפתלי כי אמרו״ל ירדן נקרא ע״ש שיורד מדן והוא לשם והירדן הלא יתחיל במקצוע צפונית מזרחית וזב״ה מדן ועד באר שבע (ש״א ג׳) ורז״ל מקצה א״י עד קצהו באלכסון כי דן היה במקצוע צפונית מזרחית ובאר שבע היה במקצוע דרומית מערבית כי משל נחלת שמעון היתה שלקחו בהמקצוע ההיא): (מח) הערים האלה. האמורים למעלה: (מט) לנחול. להנחיל ע״י הגורל: לגבולותיה. לפי הגבולים האמורים למעלה: (נ) על פי ה׳. שאלו באורים ותומים וע״פ נתנו לו את העיר אשר שאל והיא תמנת סרח: (נא) נחלו. הנחילו לישראל בגורל: וראשי האבות למטות. ראשי בתי אבות של מטות בני ישראל: בגורל. חוזר לתחלת המקרא לומר אלה הנחלות אשר נחלו בגורל: ויכלו מחלק. השלימו מלוהת הארץ בגורל:

## Commentary Digest

*the tent of meeting* — The tent of meeting had been erected in Shiloh fourteen years after the Israelites had entered the land. See above 18:1.

48. This is the inheritance of the tribe of the children of Dan
according to their families, these cities with their villages.
49. And they made an end of dividing the land for inheritance
by its borders; the children of Israel gave an inheritance to
Joshua the son of Nun among them. 50. According to the
word of the Lord they gave him the city which he asked,
Timnath-serah in Mount Ephraim; and he built the city and
dwelt in it. 51. These are the inheritances, which Eleazar
the priest, and Joshua the son of Nun, and the heads of the
(houses of) the fathers of the tribes of the children of Israel,
divided for an inheritance by lot in Shiloh before the Lord, at
the entrance of the tent of meeting. And they made an end of
dividing the land.

## Commentary Digest

48. *these cities* — i.e. the aforementioned. — D

*by its borders* — i.e. by the aforementioned borders. — D

50. *According to the word of the Lord* — They consulted the Urim and Tummim. — D Joshua's portion was not chosen by lot.[1]

*Timnath-serah* — See infra XXIV:30, Commentary Digest. It is noteworthy that Joshua, the great leader, who brought Israel into the Holy Land, should request but a small town, whose land is not fit for cultivation, or whose fruits are inferior.

51. *and the heads of the (houses of) the fathers* — See above XIV:1, Commentary Digest.

*divided for an inheritance* — lit. *"caused to inherit."* — R R explains that the pi'el conjugation is used here instead of the hiph'il (causitive).

יְהוָה אֶל־יְהוֹשֻׁעַ לֵאמֹר׃ ב דַּבֵּר אֶל־בְּנֵי
יִשְׂרָאֵל לֵאמֹר תְּנוּ לָכֶם אֶת־עָרֵי הַמִּקְלָט
אֲשֶׁר־דִּבַּרְתִּי אֲלֵיכֶם בְּיַד־מֹשֶׁה׃ ג לָנוּס
שָׁמָּה רוֹצֵחַ מַכֵּה־נֶפֶשׁ בִּשְׁגָגָה בִּבְלִי־
דָעַת וְהָיוּ לָכֶם לְמִקְלָט מִגֹּאֵל הַדָּם׃
ד וְנָס אֶל־אַחַת ׀ מֵהֶעָרִים הָאֵלֶּה וְעָמַד
פֶּתַח שַׁעַר הָעִיר וְדִבֶּר בְּאָזְנֵי זִקְנֵי
הָעִיר־הַהִיא אֶת־דְּבָרָיו וְאָסְפוּ אֹתוֹ
הָעִירָה אֲלֵיהֶם וְנָתְנוּ־לוֹ מָקוֹם וְיָשַׁב
עִמָּם׃ ה וְכִי יִרְדֹּף גֹּאֵל הַדָּם אַחֲרָיו וְלֹא־
יַסְגִּרוּ אֶת־הָרֹצֵחַ בְּיָדוֹ כִּי בִבְלִי־דַעַת
הִכָּה אֶת־רֵעֵהוּ וְלֹא־שֹׂנֵא הוּא לוֹ

עִם יְהוֹשֻׁעַ לְמֵימָר׃
ב מַלֵּיל עִם בְּנֵי יִשְׂרָאֵל
לְמֵימַר הָבוּ לְכוֹן יַת קִרְוֵי
שֵׁיזָבוּתָא דְמַלֵּילִית
עִמְּכוֹן בִּידָא דְמֹשֶׁה׃
ג לְמֶעֱרוֹק לְתַמָּן קָטוֹלָא
דְיִקְטוֹל נַפְשָׁא בְּשָׁלוּ
בְּלָא מַדְּעֵיהּ וִיהוֹן לְכוֹן
לְשֵׁיזָבָא מִגָּאֵל דְּמָא׃
ד וְיֵעֱרוֹק לַחֲדָא מִקִּרְוַיָּא
הָאִלֵּין וִיקוּם בְּמַעֲלָנָא
דְתַרְעַ קַרְתָּא וִימַלֵּיל
קֳדָם סָבֵי קַרְתָּא הַהִיא
יַת פִּתְגָּמוֹהִי וִיכַנְשׁוּן
יָתֵיהּ לְקַרְתָּא לְוָתְהוֹן
וְיִתְּנוּן לֵיהּ אֲתַר וִיתֵיב
עִמְּהוֹן׃ ה וַאֲרֵי יִרְדּוֹף
גָּאֵל דְּמָא בָּתְרוֹהִי וְלָא
יִמְסְרוּן יַת קָטוֹלָא בִּידֵיהּ
אֲרֵי בְּלָא מַדְּעֵיהּ קְטַל
יַת חַבְרֵיהּ וְלָא סָנֵי הוּא
לֵיהּ מֵאִתְמָלֵי
ומדקדמוהי

ת"א דבר אל בני ישראל. מכות יא: זקני העיר. שם:

## רד"ק

בית דין שהיו בא"י הפקר ואמרו וכי מה ענין ראשים אצל אבות אלא לומר לך מה אבות מנחילין את בניהם כל מה שירצו אף ראשים מנחילין את העם כל מה שירצו: (ב) תנו לכם את ערי. אחר שנאמר ויכלו מחלק את הארץ צום על ערי המקלט שלא נצטוו בה על ידי משה גם כן אלא אחר ירושה וישיבה שנאמר כי יכרית ה' אלהיך וגו': (ד) ונתנו לו מקום. פירשו רז"ל שלא יהא שוכר בית כל ימי שבתו שם שנאמר ונתנו לו מקום:

## מנחת שי

א"ר אחא בר חנינא מפני מה נאמרה פ' רוצחים בל' עזה מפני שהם של תורה

## רלב"ג

(ב) ואחר זכר שכבר נתנו ערי מקלט מעבר לירדן כמו שבאה המלוה בזה בתורה ולא נצטרכנו לפרש בזה המקום דבר זו המלוה לפי שכבר פירשנו זה בבאורינו לדברי תורה ונתנו גם כן ללוים ערים לשבת ומגרשיהם לבהמתם כמו שנזכר בתורה וזה גם כן היה על פי השם יתברך ובזה נשלם ללוים מה שאמר אחלקם ביעקב וגו' כי היו מפוזרים בכל השבטים:

## מצודת דוד

ב (ב) לכם. להנאתכם: (ג) למקלט. לקלוט את הרוצח מיד גואל הדם לבל יהרגנו כאשר יחם לבבו: (ד) את דבריו. איך שגג בהריגה: ואספו אותו. עם שלא ידעו שהאמת אתו: (ה) גואל הדם. קרוב הנרצח הרוצה לנקום נקמתו: אחריו. אל עיר מקלטו: ולא יסגירו. ר"ל אנשי העיר יעזרו להרוצח ולא ימסרו אותו ביד גואל הדם: כי בבלי דעת. אם הרג בבלי דעת: ולא שונא. לומר

## מצודת ציון

ב (ב) המקלט. ע"ש שקולטת את הרוצחים שאין מדרך עיר אחרת להניח להרוצחים לדור בה: (ג) לנוס. ענין בריחה: בבלי דעת. בלא כוונה: מגואל. מלשון גאולה כי בהנקם נקמת הנרצח נגאולה תחשב לו: (ד) ואספו. ענין הכנסה כמו מאסף אותם (שופטים י"ט) (ה) יסגירו. ענין מסירה כמו להסגיר לאדום (עמוס א'):

## 20

1. And the Lord spoke to Joshua, saying, 2. "Speak to the
children of Israel, saying, 'Prepare for you cities of refuge,
of which I spoke to you through Moses: 3. To which a
slayer that kills any person unawares, unwittingly, shall flee
and they shall be for you as a refuge from the avenger of blood.
4. And he shall flee to one of those cities, and he shall stand
at the entrance of the gate of the city, and shall declare his
cause in the ears of the elders of that city, they shall take
him into the city to them, and give him a place, and he shall
dwell among them. 5. And if the avenger of blood pursue
him, they they shall not deliver the slayer into his hand,
because he smote his neighbor unwittingly, and did not hate
him

### Commentary Digest

2. *Prepare for you cities of refuge* — Now that the division of the Promised Land was complete, the Jews were commanded to set aside cities of refuge, as Moses had proclaimed in the Torah[1]: "When the Lord your God will cut off the nations ...and you will dwell in their cities and houses, three cities shall you set aside... — K

*for you* — i.e. for your benefit. — D

3. *as a refuge* — to take in the slayer and protect him from the nearest of kin of the slain, who would avenge the blood of his kinsman. — D

4. *his cause* — how he murdered unintentionally. — D

*they shall take him in* — although he has not yet proven his case. — D

*and given him a place* — i.e. rent free. Just as the Levites were given the right to live there, so also, the unwitting slayer had the right to live in these cities, and was therefore entitled to live there rent free. — K[2]

5. *because he smote his neighbor unwittingly* — i.e. if he smote his neighbor unwittingly. — D

*and did not hate him* — that we should believe that he killed him steathily. — D If the murderer was an enemy of the murdered, he is not afforded the benefit of refuge, unless it is certain that the act of murder could not have been intentional.[3]

מִתְּמ֖וֹל שִׁלְשׁ֑וֹם: ו וְיָשַׁ֣ב ׀ בָּעִ֣יר הַהִ֗יא
עַד־עָמְד֞וֹ לִפְנֵ֤י הָֽעֵדָה֙ לַמִּשְׁפָּ֔ט עַד־
מוֹת֙ הַכֹּהֵ֣ן הַגָּד֔וֹל אֲשֶׁ֥ר יִהְיֶ֖ה בַּיָּמִ֣ים
הָהֵ֑ם אָ֣ז ׀ יָשׁ֣וּב הָרוֹצֵ֗חַ וּבָ֤א אֶל־עִירוֹ֙
וְאֶל־בֵּית֔וֹ אֶל־הָעִ֖יר אֲשֶׁר־נָ֥ס מִשָּֽׁם:
ז וַיַּקְדִּ֜שׁוּ אֶת־קֶ֤דֶשׁ בַּגָּלִיל֙ בְּהַ֣ר נַפְתָּלִ֔י
וְאֶת־שְׁכֶ֖ם בְּהַ֣ר אֶפְרָ֑יִם וְאֶת־קִרְיַ֥ת
אַרְבַּ֛ע הִ֥יא חֶבְר֖וֹן בְּהַ֥ר יְהוּדָֽה: ח וּמֵעֵ֜בֶר
לְיַרְדֵּ֤ן יְרִיחוֹ֙ מִזְרָ֔חָה נָתְנ֞וּ אֶת־
בֶּ֧צֶר בַּמִּדְבָּ֛ר בַּמִּישֹׁ֖ר מִמַּטֵּ֣ה רְאוּבֵ֑ן
וְאֶת־רָאמֹ֤ת בַּגִּלְעָד֙ מִמַּטֵּה־גָ֔ד

ומִקַדְמוֹהִי י וִיתֵיב בְּקַרְתָּא הַהִיא עַד דִיקוּם קֳדָם כְּנִשְׁתָּא לְדִינָא עַד דִימוּת כַּהֲנָא רַבָּא דִי יְהֵי בְּיוֹמַיָא הָאִינוּן בְּכֵן יְתוּב קָטוֹלָא וְיֵיעוֹל לְקַרְתֵּיהּ וּלְבֵיתֵיהּ לְקַרְתָּא דִי עֲרַק מִתַּמָן: ז וְזַמִינוּ יַת קֶדֶשׁ בְּגָלִילָא בְּטוּרָא דְבֵית נַפְתָּלִי וְיַת שְׁכֶם בְּטוּרָא דְבֵית אֶפְרַיִם וְיַת קִרְיַת אַרְבַּע הִיא חֶבְרוֹן בְּטוּרָא דְבֵית יְהוּדָה: ח וּמֵעִיבְרָא לְיַרְדְנָא דִירִיחוֹ מַדִינְחָא יְהָבוּ יַת בֶּצֶר בְּמַדְבְּרָא בְּמֵישְׁרָא מִשִּׁבְטָא דִרְאוּבֵן וְיַת רָאמוֹת בְּגִלְעָד מִשִּׁבְטָא דְגָד וְיַת גולן

**רד"ק**

(ו) עד עמדו לפני העדה למשפט עד מות הכהן הגדול. הרוצח היה נס אל אחת הערים ובית דין שולחין אחריו ומביאין אותו לעומד למשפט אם נתחייב מיתה הורגין אותו אם נתחייב גלות משיבין אותו שם שנאמר וישב שם עד מות הכהן הגדול והמקרא קצר וטעם עד מות הכהן הגדול פירשוהו רז"ל רבי מאיר אומר רוצח מקצר ימיו של אדם וכהן גדול מאריך ואינו דין שיהא המקצר לפני המאריך ר' אומר הרוצח מטמא את הארץ ומסלק את השכינה וכהן גדול מטהר וגורם לשכינה שתשרה על אדם בארץ אינו

**רש"י**

כ (ו) עד עמדו וגו' למשפט. אם יפטר מגלות יפטר ואם יתחייב גלות יחזור לעיר מלקטו וישב שם עד מות הכהן הגדול: (ח) ומעבר לירדן יריחו מזרחה נתנו. בימי משה

**מנחת שי**

עיין ילקוט יהושע רמז ל' וכלי יקר: (ח) ואת גלון. גולן קרי:

**מצודת ציון**

שלשום. יום מהשלישי מהיום הזה: (ז) ויקדישו. ויזמינו כמו קדשו קהל (יואל ב'): בגליל. באחן הגליל והוא שם מדינה בא"י:

**מצודת דוד**

שהיה מעריש בדבר: (ו) למשפט. לדונו אם הוא חייב גלות וכאשר ילא חייב יחזור לעיר מקלטו וישב בה עד ימות הכהן הגדול: אז.

## Commentary Digest

double row running north and south, similar to two rows of vines in a vineyard.[4] Kedesh in Galillee, Shechem in Ephraim, and Hebron in Judah, represent one city for each of the three major provinces of Israel west of the Jordan.[5] They parallel the three cities of the eastern side of the Jordan.

from before. 6. And he shall dwell in that city until he stand before the tribunal for judgment, until the death of the High Priest that shall be in those days. Then shall the slayer return, and come to his own city, and to his own house, to the city from which he fled." 7. And they set apart Kedesh in Galilee Mount Naphtali, and Shechem in Mount Ephraim, and Kirjatharba, which is Hebron, in the mountain of Judah. 8. And on the other side of the Jordan at Jericho eastward, they had assigned Bezer in the wilderness upon the plain out of the tribe of Reuben, and Ramoth in Gilead out of the tribe of Gad,

## Commentary Digest

*from before* — lit. from yesterday and the day before yesterday. — Z

6. *until he stand before the tribunal for judgment* — *"If he be freed from exile, he is dismissed. If, however, he is sentenced to exile, he is remanded to his refuge city, where he must dwell until the death of the High Priest."* — R[1] Thus, the Scripture gives two instances of the termination of the murderer's stay in the refuge city: (1) In the case of his being exonerated, he must stay only "until he stand before the tribunal for judgment"; and (2) in the case of his being found guilty of unwitting murder, which could have been avoided, "until the death of the High Priest. — Azulai.

*until the death of the High Priest* — Rabbi Meir says: The murderer shortens man's life, while the High Priest lengthens it (through his prayer that no misfortunes occur). It is improper that he who shortens man's life shall be in the presence of him who lengthens it. Rabbi (Judah the Prince) says: The murderer defiles the land, and dismisses the Divine Presence, while the High Priest purifies the land and causes the Divine Presence to rest on the inhabitants of the land. — K[1] The Talmud[2] maintains that the High Priest is held morally responsible for any unintentional murder taking place, because of his failure to pray that such misfortunes ,be averted.

8. *And of the other side of the Jordan at Jericho eastward, they had assigned* — *"during Moses' time, as it is stated: Bezer in the wilderness etc."*[3] — R

The six cities of refuge, namely, the three already set aside by Moses on the eastern side of the Jordan, and the three now set aside by Joshua on the western side, were arranged in a

ואת־גולן בבשן ממטה מנשה: ט אלה
היו ערי המועדה לכל בני ישראל ולגר
הגר בתוכם לנוס שמה כל־מכה־נפש
בשגגה ולא ימות ביד גאל הדם עד־
עמדו לפני העדה: כא א ויגשו ראשי
אבות הלוים אל־אלעזר הכהן ואל־
יהושע בן־נון ואל־ראשי אבות המטות
לבני ישראל: ב וידברו אליהם בשלה
בארץ כנען לאמר יהוה צוה ביד־משה
לתת־לנו ערים לשבת ומגרשיהן
לבהמתנו: ג ויתנו בני־ישראל ללוים
מנחלתם אל־פי יהוה את־הערים
האלה ואת־מגרשיהן: ד ויצא הגורל

גוֹלָן בְּמַתְנַן מִשִּׁבְטָא
דִמְנַשֶּׁה: ט אִלֵּין הֲוָאָה
קִרְוַיָּא דִמְזַמְּנָן לְכָל בְּנֵי
יִשְׂרָאֵל וּלְגִיוֹרַיָּא דִּי
יִתְגַּיְּירוּן בֵּינֵיהוֹן לְמֶעֱרַק
לְתַמָּן כָּל דְּיִקְטוֹל נַפְשָׁא
בְּשָׁלוּ וְלָא יְמוּת בִּידָא
דְגָאִיל דְּמָא עַד דִּיקוּם
קֳדָם כְּנִשְׁתָּא: א וּקְרִיבוּ
רֵישֵׁי אֲבָהַת לֵיוָאֵי לְוָת
אֶלְעָזָר כַּהֲנָא וּלְוָת
יְהוֹשֻׁעַ בַּר נוּן וּלְוָת רֵישֵׁי
אֲבָהַת שִׁבְטַיָּא לִבְנֵי
יִשְׂרָאֵל: ב וּמַלִּילוּ עִמְּהוֹן
בְּשִׁלֹה בְּאַרְעָא דִכְנַעַן
לְמֵימַר יְיָ פַּקִּיד בְּיַד
מֹשֶׁה לְמִתַּן לָנָא קִרְוִין
לְמִתַּב וּרְוָחֵיהֶן
לִבְעִירָנָא: ג וִיהָבוּ בְּנֵי
יִשְׂרָאֵל לְלֵוָאֵי
מֵאַחְסַנְתְּהוֹן עַל מֵימְרָא
דַיְיָ יָת קִרְוַיָּא הָאִלֵּין וְיָת
רְוָחֵיהֶן: ד וּנְפַק עַדְבָא

לזרעית

רד"ק — גולן קרי — רש"י

(ט) המועדה. ההזמנה דין שיהיה זה אצל זה: (ט) ערי המועדה. שהיו נעדים שם כל סנהדרי את כלר במדבר וגו':

מנחת שי

כא (ד) למשפחות הקמצי. הקו"ף בגעיא ברוב הספרים:

מצודת דוד — מצודת ציון

(ט) עד עמדו. עד יעמוד למשפט לדונו אחרי מות הכהן הגדול: אם הוא חייב מיתה וכאשר יצא חייב אז ביד גואל הדם להמיתו: (ט) המועדה. מלשון ועד וקבוץ להתאסף כהן והכולאים כמו בהר מועד (ישעיה י"ד):

כא (ב) לתת לנו וגו'. ר"ל ולזאת תנו לנו: (ג) אל פי ה'. על פי מלותו: האלה. האמורות למטה. (ד) מן הלוים. שהיו מן

## Commentary Digest

murderer was warned, and the witnesses do possess all the proper qualifications, the court performs[2] the execution.

CHAPTER 21

2. *in Shiloh* — after the sanctuary had become established in a more or less permanent location, and they had become servants of the Lord in this permanent sanctuary. — Azulai

*in the land of Canaan* — after all the tribes had received their shares of the land. Only then, could the Levites demand their cities, a number of which were to be given by each tribe from its inheritance. — Azulai M claims that the dedication of the Levitic cities was contingent upon the setting aside of the six refuge cities.

He bases this conclusion on the Biblical precept: "And the cities which you shall give to the Levites, the six cities of refuge... and with them you shall give forty-two cities."[3] Hence, the forty-two were to be given in addition to the six. The Levites, therefore, waited until the six were set aside for their purpose.

*cities to dwell in* — A queries whether these cities were the property

and Golan in Bashan out of the tribe of Manasseh. 9. These
were the cities set apart for all the children of Israel and
for the stranger that sojourns among them, that whosoever
kills any person unawares might flee there, and not die by the
hand of the avenger of blood, until he stood before the tribunal.

## 21

1. And the heads of the fathers' [houses] of the Levites approached Eleazar the priest, and Joshua the son of Nun, and
the heads of the fathers' [houses] of the tribes of the
children of Israel; 2. And they spoke to them in Shiloh in
the land of Canaan, saying, "The Lord commanded through
Moses to give us cities to dwell in, and the open land
around them for our cattle." 3. And the children of Israel
gave to the Levites from their inheritance, according to the
commandment of the Lord, these cities and the open land
around them. 4. And the lot went out

### Commentary Digest

9. *set apart* — lit. the cities *"of setting apart, those set apart for this."* — R

*for all the children of Israel* — irrespective of their places of residence. Thus, a resident of the eastern side of the Jordan might flee to a refuge city on the west, and vice-versa. — Azulai

*and for the stranger that sojourns among them* — a non-Jew who has taken upon himself to observe the seven Noahidic commandments.[1]

*and not die by the hand of the avenger of blood* — even the intentional murderer —

*until he stood before the tribunal* — Only upon the verdict of guilty, delivered by the tribunal of twenty-three judges, would the murderer be exposed to the wrath of the avenger of blood. This verdict is delivered when the murder was committed because of the failure to take the proper precautions to avert it; also, if the murderer was not warned, or if the witnesses do not possess all the qualifications for acceptance. When the

למשפחת הקהתי ויהי לבני אהרן
הכהן מן־הלוים ממטה יהודה וממטה
השמעני וממטה בנימן בגורל ערים
שלש עשרה: ה ולבני קהת הנותרים
ממשפחת מטה־אפרים וממטה־דן
ומחצי מטה מנשה בגורל ערים עשר:
ו ולבני גרשון ממשפחת מטה־יששכר
וממטה־אשר וממטה נפתלי ומחצי
מטה מנשה בבשן בגורל ערים שלש
עשרה: ז לבני מררי למשפחתם ממטה
ראובן וממטה־גד וממטה זבולן ערים
שתים עשרה: ח ויתנו בני־ישראל

לזרעית קהת והוה לבני אהרן כהנא מן ליואי משבטא דיהודה ומשבטא דשמעון ומשבטא דבנימן בעדבא קרוין תלת עשרי: ה ולבני קהת דאשתארו מזרעית שבטא דאפרים ומשבטא דדן ומפלגות שבטא דמנשה בעדבא קרוין עשר: ו ולבני גרשון מזרעית שבטא דיששכר ומשבטא דאשר ומשבטא דנפתלי ומפלגות שבטא דמנשה במתנן בעדבא קרוין תלת עשרי: ז לבני מררי לזרעיתהון משבטא דראובן ומשבטא דגד ומשבטא דזבולן קרוין תרתי עשרי: ח ויהבו בני ישראל

**רש"י**

היעודות לכך: כא (ה) ולבני קהת הנותרים. הם בני משה ובני יצהר והברון ועוזיאל: ממשפחת מטה אפרים.

**רד"ק**

מכה נפש בשגגה והוא שם בשקל מוסדה מן מוסדות הצלעות: (ז) לבני מררי. בזה הפסוק אומר כי שתים עשרה ערים היו לבני מררי ממטה ראובן וממטה גד וממטה זבולון ולמטה בספור הערים לא כתוב אלא שמנה ערים ממטה זבולון ארבע ממטה גד ד' וממטה ראובן לא כתב ויש ספרים מוגה בהם

**מנחת שי**

(ה) ולבני קהת הקו"ף בגע"א: (ו) ולבני גרשון ממשפחות מטה יששכר. במ"ג חסר ומסור עליו ג' חסר בנביא ובמקצת ספרים כת"י מדוייקים

**מצודת דוד**

הלוים מבני לוי: ממטה יהודה. הגורל בא להם ממטה יהודה וכו': (ה) הנותרים. כי בני אהרן שהיו מבני קהת לקחו ממטה יהודה וכו' והנותרים מבני קהת שהם בני משה ובני יצהר והברון ועוזיאל לקחו ממטה אפרים וכו': (ו) בבשן. ר"ל החצי שלקחו נחלתם בעבר הירדן המזרחי בארץ הבשן: (ז) למשפחותם. שנחלק לשבת בהן משפחה משפחה לבד ופי' באחד וכמו כן בכולן:

## Commentary Digest

6. *in Bashan* — i.e. the half-tribe which took its inheritance on the eastern side of the Jordan, in the land of Bashan. — D

7. *twelve cities* — Below, in verses 34-38, the Scripture enumerates four cities from Gad and four cities from Zebulun. The first set of verses 36 and 37, was inserted from I Chron. VI:63-64, according to R. Hai Gaon. — K

— K A reason must be given for the omission of the Levitic cities donated by the tribe of Reuben. K. Y. suggests that since all the Levitic cities served as refuge cities, it was obvious that Reuben, who had exerted himself to save the life of his brother Joseph, would donate of his cities toward this end. It was therefore unnecessary to mention them.

Manasseh.[1]—K

for the families of the Kohathites; and the children of Aaron
the priest, who were of the Levites, had by lot, from the tribe
of Judaḥ, and from the tribe of Simeon, and from the tribe of
Benjamin, thirteen cities. 5. And the rest of the children of
Kohath had by lot ten cities from the families of the tribe of
Ephraim, and from the tribe of Dan, and from the half-tribe
of Manasseh. 6. And the children of Gershon had by lot from
the families of the tribe of Issachar, and from the tribe of
Asher, and from the tribe of Naphtali, and from the half-tribe
of Manasseh in Bashan, thirteen cities. 7. For the children of
Merari according to their families, there were twelve cities
from the tribe of Reuben and from the tribe of Gad, and from
the tribe of Zebulun. 8. And the children of Israel gave

## Commentary Digest

of the Levites, or whether the Levites were merely permitted to use cities which belonged to other tribes.

3. *these cities* — i.e. the following cities. — D

4. *And the lot went out for the families of the Kohathites; and the children of Aaron the priest* — The Scripture relates the wondrous phenomenon of the lots. They fell in order of the sanctity of the Levitic families: first, the lot of the priests; then the lot of the Kohathites the bearers of the Holy Ark; and then the lots of the children of Gershon and Merari. It was also fitting that the priests receive their share from the tribe of Judah, the kingly tribe, from the tribe of Simeon whose cities were surrounded by Judah's territory, and from the tribe of Benjamin, from which the first two kings of Israel were destined to emanate. — Azulai

5. *And the rest of the children of Kohath* — *"They are the children of Moses, and the children of Izhar, and Hebron, and Uzziel."* — R[1] and D

*from the families of the tribe of Ephraim* — *"These cities fell to them from the inheritance of the tribe of the children of Ephraim, for they received cities in the inheritance of each tribe, as it is stated:*[2] *'From the many you shall take many, and from the few you shall take few; each tribe according to its inheritance which they inherit, shall give of its cities to the Levites.'"* — R

לַלְוִיִּם אֶת־הֶעָרִים הָאֵלֶּה וְאֶת־
מִגְרְשֵׁיהֶן כַּאֲשֶׁר צִוָּה יְהוָה בְּיַד־מֹשֶׁה
בְּגוֹרָל׃ ט וַיִּתְּנוּ מִמַּטֵּה בְּנֵי יְהוּדָה
וּמִמַּטֵּה בְּנֵי שִׁמְעוֹן אֵת הֶעָרִים הָאֵלֶּה
אֲשֶׁר־יִקְרָא אֶתְהֶן בְּשֵׁם׃ י וַיְהִי לִבְנֵי
אַהֲרֹן מִמִּשְׁפְּחֹת הַקְּהָתִי מִבְּנֵי לֵוִי כִּי
לָהֶם הָיָה הַגּוֹרָל רִאישֹׁנָה׃ יא וַיִּתְּנוּ לָהֶם
אֶת־קִרְיַת אַרְבַּע אֲבִי הָעֲנוֹק הִיא
חֶבְרוֹן בְּהַר יְהוּדָה וְאֶת־מִגְרָשֶׁהָ
סְבִיבֹתֶיהָ׃ יב וְאֶת־שְׂדֵה הָעִיר וְאֶת־
חֲצֵרֶיהָ נָתְנוּ לְכָלֵב בֶּן־יְפֻנֶּה בַּאֲחֻזָּתוֹ׃

### תרגום

יִשְׂרָאֵל לְלֵוָאֵי יָת קִרְוַיָּא
הָאִלֵּין וְיָת רְוָחֵיהֶן כְּמָא
דְפַקֵּד יְיָ בִּידָא דְמֹשֶׁה
בְּעַדְבָא׃ ט וִיהָבוּ
מִשִּׁבְטָא דִבְנֵי יְהוּדָה
וּמִשִּׁבְטָא דִבְנֵי שִׁמְעוֹן
יָת קִרְוַיָּא הָאִלֵּין
דְאִתְפְּרַשָׁא בִּשְׁמָהָן׃
י וַהֲוָה לִבְנֵי אַהֲרֹן
מִזַּרְעֲיַת קְהָת מִבְּנֵי לֵוָאֵי
אֲרֵי לְהוֹן הֲוָה עַדְבָא
בְּקַדְמֵיתָא׃ יא וִיהָבוּ
לְהוֹן יָת קִרְיַת אַרְבַּע
אֲבוּהוֹן דְגִבָּרַיָּא הִיא
חֶבְרוֹן בְּטוּרָא דִיהוּדָה
וְיָת רְוָחָהָא סַחֲרָנָהָא׃
יב וְיָת חֲקַל קַרְתָּא וְיָת
פַּצְחָהָא יְהָבוּ לְכָלֵב בַּר
יְפֻנֶּה בְּאַחְסַנְתֵּיהּ׃
ולבני

ה"א ולת סדה העיר. כ"כ קנג מכות י':

### רש"י

ראשונה קרי

מנחלת שבט בני אפרים נפלו להם אלה הערים שבכל שבט ושבט נטלו כמה שנאמר מאת הרב תרבו ומאת המעט תמעיטו איש כפי נחלתו אשר ינחלו יתן מעריו ללוים: (ט) אשר יקרא אתהן בשם. לפי שלא הזכיר למעלה שמות הערים שנתנו להם ולמטה הוא מפרש את שמותם לכך אמר אשר יקרא אתהן בשם:

### רד"ק

וממטה ראובן את בצר ואת מגרשיה את יהצה ואת מגרשיה את קדמות ואת מגרשיה ואת מיפעת ואת מגרשיה ערים ארבע ולא ראיתי שני פסוקים אלו בשום ספר ישן מדוייק אלא מוגה במקצתם וראיתי כי נשאל רבינו האיי ז"ל בזאת השאלה והשיב אף על פי דהכא לא חשיב להו בדברי הימים חשיב להו נראה מהשובתו כי אינן כתובים בספריהם: (ט) אשר יקרא אתהן. מתחלה ספר מנין הערים ואח"כ ספר שמם ומניינם כמו שהיו קוראים אותו באותו הזמן ופי' אשר יקרא אשר יקרא הקורא כמו ויגד ליעקב והדומים לו: (י) כי להם היה הגורל ראשונה. נכתב באל"ף וביו"ד האל"ף שרש והיו"ד למשך וכן הראשון אדם תולד באל"ף וביו"ד: (יא) אבי הענק. שם כלל לענקים ופי' אבי גדול הענקים כמו שנאמר עליו האדם הגדול בענקים ואבי שם גדולה כמו אבי קרית יערים אבי דבר גדול דבר אליך הנביא והדומים להם:

### מנחת שי

אלה וא"ו ופסוק לבני גרשון ממשפחות הלוים דלקמן בפרשה חסר וכן נמסר ג' חסר בנביא ובמס"ג נמסר כאן וכן ג' חסר בנביא ולא יתכן דאם כן הוו לכו ד': (י) ויהי לבני אהרן ממשפחות. במקצת ספרים מלא וא"ו וכן נכון על פי המסורת שנמסר כאן במ"ג ג' חסר בנביאים ובלאחם כם בפרשה זו ואין זה מהם: הקהתי. במקצת ספרים הקוף בחטף קמץ: ראישנה. ראשונה ק' ונכתב בשני נחום האל"ף והיו"ד כמו כל הכאים (ישעיה ל'):

### מצודת דוד

בגורל. מי מהשבטים יתן למי מן הלוים: (ט) אשר יקרא. ר"ל אשר למטה בענין יפרש השמות: (י) ממשפחות. אשר היו ממשפחות הקהתי: כי להם וגו' ראשונה. ר"ל לפי שבא להם הגורל ראשונה לזה לקחו ראשונה ולא בעבור מעלת הכהונה: (יב) באחזתו. בחלק

## Commentary Digest

He did this to entreat them to pray for divine aid to resist the plot of the spies who slandered the Holy Land. Since he had gone to Hebron for divine assistance, he was granted the city of Hebron as his possession (Sotah 32b. See Rashi Num. 13:22).

to the Levites by lot these cities with the open land around
them, as the Lord had commanded through Moses. 9. And they
gave from the tribe of the children of Judah, and from the
tribe of the children of Simeon, these cities that will be mentioned by name. 10. And it was for the children of Aaron, of the
families of the Kohathites, of the children of Levi, for theirs
was the first lot. 11. And they gave them the city of Arba
father of the 'Anok (giants) which is Hebron in the hill-
country of Judah, and the open land around it. 12. And the
fields of the city, and its villages, they gave to Caleb the son
of Jephunneh in his possession.

## Commentary Digest

9. *these cities that will be mentioned by name* — *"Since above he did not mention the names of the cities which they gave them, and below he enumerates them, he, therefore, states: These cities that will be mentioned by name."* — R, K, and D

11. *father of the Anok (giants)* — or, the greatest of the giants, as above, XIV:15. — K

*in his possession* — i.e. as his inheritance. — D

12. *they gave to Caleb the son of Jephunneh* — This was in keeping with the divine promise of ". . . and to him I will give the land upon which he trod, and and to his children . . ." — Deut. 1:36. This refers to Hebron, where Caleb went to prostrate himself on the graves of the Patriarchs.

יג וְלִבְנֵ֣י ׀ אַהֲרֹ֣ן הַכֹּהֵ֗ן נָֽתְנוּ֙ אֶת־עִ֣יר
מִקְלַ֣ט הָרֹצֵ֔חַ אֶת־חֶבְר֖וֹן וְאֶת־מִגְרָשֶׁ֑הָ
וְאֶת־לִבְנָ֖ה וְאֶת־מִגְרָשֶֽׁהָ׃ יד וְאֶת־יַתִּר֙
וְאֶת־מִגְרָשֶׁ֔הָ וְאֶת־אֶשְׁתְּמֹ֖עַ וְאֶת־
מִגְרָשֶֽׁהָ׃ טו וְאֶת־חֹלֹן֙ וְאֶת־מִגְרָשֶׁ֔הָ וְאֶת־
דְּבִ֖ר וְאֶת־מִגְרָשֶֽׁהָ׃ טז וְאֶת־עַ֣יִן וְאֶת־
מִגְרָשֶׁ֗הָ וְאֶת־יֻטָּה֙ וְאֶת־מִגְרָשֶׁ֔הָ אֶת־
בֵּ֥ית שֶׁ֖מֶשׁ וְאֶת־מִגְרָשֶׁ֑הָ עָרִ֣ים תֵּ֔שַׁע
מֵאֵ֕ת שְׁנֵ֖י הַשְּׁבָטִ֥ים הָאֵֽלֶּה׃ יז וּמִמַּטֵּה֙
בִנְיָמִ֔ן אֶת־גִּבְע֖וֹן וְאֶת־מִגְרָשֶׁ֑הָ אֶת־
גֶּ֖בַע וְאֶת־מִגְרָשֶֽׁהָ׃ יח אֶת־עֲנָתוֹת֙ וְאֶת־
מִגְרָשֶׁ֔הָ וְאֶת־עַלְמ֖וֹן וְאֶת־מִגְרָשֶׁ֑הָ
עָרִ֖ים אַרְבַּֽע׃ יט כָּל־עָרֵ֥י בְנֵֽי־אַהֲרֹ֖ן
הַכֹּהֲנִ֑ים שְׁלֹשׁ־עֶשְׂרֵ֥ה עָרִ֖ים וּמִגְרְשֵׁיהֶֽן׃
כ וּלְמִשְׁפְּח֤וֹת בְּנֵֽי־קְהָת֙ הַלְוִיִּ֔ם

## תרגום

יג וְלִבְנֵי אַהֲרֹן כַּהֲנָא
יְהָבוּ יַת קִרְיַת שֵׁיזָבוּת
קָטוֹלָא יַת חֶבְרוֹן וְיַת
רְוָחְהָא וְיַת לִבְנָה וְיַת
רְוָחְהָא: יד וְיַת יַתִּר
וְיַת רְוָחְהָא וְיַת אֶשְׁתְּמֹעַ
וְיַת רְוָחְהָא: טו וְיַת חֹלֹן
וְיַת רְוָחְהָא וְיַת דְבִר וְיַת
רְוָחְהָא: טז וְיַת עַיִן וְיַת
רְוָחְהָא וְיַת יֻטָּה וְיַת
רְוָחְהָא יַת בֵּית שֶׁמֶשׁ
וְיַת רְוָחְהָא קִרְוִין תְּשַׁע
מִן תְּרֵין שִׁבְטַיָא הָאִלֵין:
יז וּמִשִּׁבְטָא דְבִנְיָמִן יַת
גִבְעוֹן וְיַת רְוָחְהָא יַת
גֶבַע וְיַת רְוָחְהָא: יח יַת
עֲנָתוֹת וְיַת רְוָחְהָא וְיַת
עַלְמוֹן וְיַת רְוָחְהָא קִרְוִין
אַרְבַּע: יט כָּל קִרְוֵי בְּנֵי
אַהֲרֹן כַּהֲנַיָא תְּלַת עַשְׂרֵי
קִרְוִין וּרְוָחֵיהֶן:
כ וּלְזַרְעִית בְּנֵי קְהָת לֵוָאֵי
דְאִשְׁתְּאָרוּ מִבְּנֵי קְהָת
וַהֲוָאָה קִרְוֵי עַדְבֵיהוֹן
מִשִּׁבְטָא דִבְנֵי אֶפְרָיִם:

ויהבו

## רש"י

(יח) ואת עלמון. ודברי הימים ואת עלמת הוא בחורים

## רד"ק

(יח) ואת עלמון. הוא עלמת הנזכר בספר דברי הימים והוא

## מנחת שי

(יג) את חברון ואת מגרשה ואת לבנה ואת מגרשה. כתב המגיה במ"ג כולם מלאתי גם אני בס"א כ"י אך ברוב הספרים כולם חסרים: (כ) ויהי ערי הספרים יו"ד ובס"א יבן ומדוייק כולם חסרים במ"ב חברון לבנה ע"כ. וכן גורלם. סימן יהושע ויהי ערי גורלם. (ד"ס. א' ו') ויהי ערי גבולם.

## מצודת דוד

נחלתו: (יג) ולבני וגו' נתנו. את כל מספר הערים האלה:

13. And to the children of Aaron the priest they gave the city
of refuge for the slayer, Hebron and the open land around it,
and Libnah and the open land around it, 14. And Jattir with
the open land around it, and Eshtemoa with the open land
around it, 15. And Holon with the open land around it, and
Debir with the open land around it, 16. And 'Ain with the
open land around it, and Juttah with the open land around it,
and Beth-shemesh with the open land around it, nine cities
from these two tribes. 17. And from the tribe of Benjamin,
Gibeon and the open land arount it, Geba with the open land
around it, 18. 'Anathoth with the open land around it, and
'Almon with the open land around it, four cities. 19. All the
cities of the children of Aaron, the priests, were thirteen cities
and the open land around them. 20. And to the families of
the children of Kohath, the Levites,

## Commentary Digest

18. *Anathoth* — This was a well-known priestly city all during the first commonwealth. This was the birthplace of the prophet Jeremiah. See Jer. 1:1. It was not mentioned above at the end of Ch. 18 among the cities of Benjamin because it was not a walled city. — D. M.

*And 'Almon — "and in Chron.[1]: "and 'Alemeth." That is Bahurim[2] which J renders:* עלמות." — R, K Both roots denote youth. — K

הַנּוֹתָרִים מִבְּנֵי קְהָת וַיְהִי עָרֵי גוֹרָלָם
מִמַּטֵּה אֶפְרָיִם׃ כא וַיִּתְּנוּ לָהֶם אֶת־עִיר
מִקְלַט הָרֹצֵחַ אֶת־שְׁכֶם וְאֶת־מִגְרָשֶׁהָ
בְּהַר אֶפְרָיִם וְאֶת־גֶּזֶר וְאֶת־מִגְרָשֶׁהָ׃
כב וְאֶת־קִבְצַיִם וְאֶת־מִגְרָשֶׁהָ וְאֶת־בֵּית
חוֹרֹן וְאֶת־מִגְרָשֶׁהָ עָרִים אַרְבַּע׃
כג וּמִמַּטֵּה־דָן אֶת־אֶלְתְּקֵא וְאֶת־
מִגְרָשֶׁהָ אֶת־גִּבְּתוֹן וְאֶת־מִגְרָשֶׁהָ׃
כד אֶת־אַיָּלוֹן וְאֶת־מִגְרָשֶׁהָ אֶת־גַּת־
רִמּוֹן וְאֶת־מִגְרָשֶׁהָ עָרִים אַרְבַּע׃
כה וּמִמַּחֲצִית מַטֵּה מְנַשֶּׁה אֶת־תַּעְנַךְ
וְאֶת־מִגְרָשֶׁהָ וְאֶת־גַּת־רִמּוֹן וְאֶת־
מִגְרָשֶׁהָ עָרִים שְׁתָּיִם׃ כו כָּל־עָרִים עֶשֶׂר
וּמִגְרְשֵׁיהֶן לְמִשְׁפְּחוֹת בְּנֵי־קְהָת הַנּוֹתָרִים׃
כז וְלִבְנֵי גֵרְשֹׁנִּי מִמִּשְׁפְּחֹת הַלְוִיִּם מֵחֲצִי מַטֵּה
מְנַשֶּׁה אֶת־עִיר מִקְלַט הָרֹצֵחַ אֶת־גלון בַּבָּשָׁן וְאֶת־



כא וִיהַבוּ לְהוֹן יַת קִרְיַת
שֵׁיזָבוּת קָטוֹלָא יַת שְׁכֶם
וְיַת רְוָחְהָא בְּטוּרָא דְבֵית
אֶפְרַיִם וְיַת גֶּזֶר וְיַת
רְוָחְהָא׃ כב וְיַת קִבְצַיִם
וְיַת רְוָחְהָא וְיַת בֵּית
חורון וְיַת רְוָחְהָא קִרְוִין
אַרְבַּע׃ כג וּמִשִּׁבְטָא דְדָן
יַת אֶלְתְּקֵא וְיַת רְוָחְהָא
יַת גִּבְּתוֹן וְיַת רְוָחְהָא׃
כד יַת אַיָּלוֹן וְיַת רְוָחְהָא
יַת גַּת רִמּוֹן וְיַת רְוָחְהָא
קִרְוִין אַרְבַּע׃ כה וּמִפַּלְגוּת
שִׁבְטָא דִמְנַשֶּׁה יַת תַּעְנָךְ
וְיַת רְוָחְהָא וְיַת גַּת רִמּוֹן
וְיַת רְוָחְהָא קִרְוִין תַּרְתֵּין׃
כו כָּל קִרְוִין עֲשַׂר
וּרְוָחֵיהוֹן לְזַרְעֲיַת בְּנֵי
קְהָת דְאִשְׁתָּאֲרוּ׃
כז וְלִבְנֵי גֵרְשׁוֹן מִזַּרְעֲיַת
לֵוָאֵי מִפַּלְגוּת שִׁבְטָא
דִמְנַשֶּׁה יַת קִרְיַת שֵׁיזָבוּת
קָטוֹלָא יַת גוֹלָן בְּמַתְנַן
וְיַת רְוָחְהָא וְיַת

בעשתרה

גולן קרי

רד"ק

בחורים הנזכר בספר שמואל והכל לשון אחד: (כד) את גת רמון וכן נזכר במחצית שבט מנשה דן ומחצית מטה מנשה כל

מנחת שי

(כו) למשפחות בני קהת הנותרים במקצת ספרים למשפחות מלא וכן נכון על פי המסורת כמ"ש למעלה: (כז) את גלון. גולן קרי

who remained of the children of Kohath, the cities of their
lot were from the tribe of Ephraim. 21. And they gave them
the city of refuge for the slayer, Shechem with the open land
around it in the hill-country of Ephraim, and Gezer with the
open land around it, 22. And Kibzaim with the open land
around it, and Beth-horon with the open land around it, four
cities. 23. And from the tribe of Dan, Elteke and the open land
around it, Gibbethon with the open land around it, 24. Ajalon
and the open land around, Gath-rimmon with the open land
around it, four cities. 25. And from the half-tribe of Manasseh,
Taanach and the open land around it and Gath-rimmon and the
open land around it, two cities. 26. All the cities and the open
land around them for the families of Kohath that remained,
were ten. 27. And to the children of Gershon, of the families
of the Levites, (was given) from the half-tribe of Manasseh,
the city of refuge for the slayer, Golan in Bashan and

**Commentary Digest**

24. *Gath-rimmon* — distinct from the city of the same name, given to the Levites by the half-tribe of Manasseh.[1] — K.

מגרשה ואת־בעשתרה ואת־מגרשה
ערים שתים: כח וממטה יששכר את־
קשיון ואת־מגרשה את־דברת ואת־
מגרשה: כט את־ירמות ואת־מגרשה
את־עין גנים ואת־מגרשה ערים ארבע:
ל וממטה אשר את־משאל ואת־
מגרשה את־עבדון ואת־מגרשה:
לא את־חלקת ואת־מגרשה ואת־רחב
ואת־מגרשה ערים ארבע: לב וממטה
נפתלי את־עיר | מקלט הרצח את־
קדש בגליל ואת־מגרשה ואת־חמת
דאר ואת־מגרשה ואת־קרתן ואת־
מגרשה ערים שלש: לג כל־ערי הגרשני
למשפחתם שלש־עשרה עיר
ומגרשיהן: לד ולמשפחות בני־מררי
הלוים הנותרים מאת מטה זבולן את־

**תרגום**

בעשתרה וית רוחהא
קרוין תרתין:
כח ומשבטא דיששכר
ית קשיון וית רוחהא ית
דברת וית רוחהא:
כט ית ירמות וית רוחהא
ית עין גנים וית רוחהא
קרוין ארבע: ל ומשבטא
דאשר ית משאל וית
רוחהא ית עבדון וית
רוחהא: לא ית חלקת וית
רוחהא וית רחוב וית
רוחהא קרוין ארבע:
לב ומשבטא דנפתלי ית
קרית שזבות קטולא ית
קדש בגליל וית רוחהא
וית חמות דאר וית
רוחהא וית קרתן וית
רוחהא קרוין תלת: לג כל
קרוי בני גרשון
לזרעיתהון תלת עסרי
קרוין ורוחיהן:
לד ולזרעית בני מררי
ליואי די אשתארו מן
שבטא

מנחת שי

(כח) את דברת. במקצת ספרים הדל"ת בלא מאריך כדלעיל סימן י"ט: (לד) את קרתה. במקצת דפוסים ישנים ואת קרתה ובשאר ספרים כתיב

the open land around it, and Beeshterah with the open land
around it, two cities. 28. And from the tribe of Issachar,
Kishion and the open land around it, and Dobrath and the
open land around it. 29. Jarmuth and the open land around
it, 'Ein-gannim and the open land around it, four cities.
30. And from the tribe of Asher, Mishal and the open land
around it, 'Abdon and the open land around it. 31. Helkath
and the open land around it, and Rehob with the open land
around it, four cities. 32. And from the tribe of Naphtali,
the city of refuge of the slayer, Kedesh in Galilee and the
open land around it, and Hamoth-dor with the open land
arround it, and Kartan with the open land around it, three
cities. 33. All the cities of the Gershonites according to their
families were thirteen cities with the open land around them.
34. And to the families of the children of Merari, the rest of

the Levites, (was given) from the tribe of Zebulun

יָקְנְעָם וְאֶת־מִגְרָשֶׁהָ אֶת־קַרְתָּה וְאֶת־
מִגְרָשֶׁהָ׃ לה אֶת־דִּמְנָה וְאֶת־מִגְרָשֶׁהָ
אֶת־נַהֲלָל וְאֶת־מִגְרָשֶׁהָ עָרִים אַרְבַּע׃
לו * (וּמִמַּטֵּה רְאוּבֵן אֶת־עִיר מִקְלַט
הָרֹצֵחַ אֶת־בֶּצֶר בַּמִּדְבָּר וְאֶת־
מִגְרָשֶׁהָ וְאֶת־יַהְצָה וְאֶת־מִגְרָשֶׁהָ׃
לז אֶת־קְדֵמוֹת וְאֶת־מִגְרָשֶׁהָ וְאֶת־
מֵיפַעַת וְאֶת־מִגְרָשֶׁהָ עָרִים אַרְבַּע)׃
לו וּמִמַּטֵּה־גָד אֶת־עִיר מִקְלַט הָרֹצֵחַ
אֶת־רָמֹת בַּגִּלְעָד וְאֶת־מִגְרָשֶׁהָ וְאֶת־
מַחֲנַיִם וְאֶת־מִגְרָשֶׁהָ׃ לז אֶת־חֶשְׁבּוֹן
וְאֶת־מִגְרָשֶׁהָ אֶת־יַעְזֵר וְאֶת־מִגְרָשֶׁהָ
כָּל־עָרִים אַרְבַּע׃ לח כָּל־הֶעָרִים לִבְנֵי
מְרָרִי לְמִשְׁפְּחֹתָם הַנּוֹתָרִים מִמִּשְׁפְּחוֹת
הַלְוִיִּם וַיְהִי גּוֹרָלָם עָרִים שְׁתֵּים עֶשְׂרֵה׃
לט כֹּל עָרֵי הַלְוִיִּם בְּתוֹךְ אֲחֻזַּת בְּנֵי־יִשְׂרָאֵל

שִׁבְטָא דִזְבוּלֻן יָת יָקְנְעָם
וְיָת רְוָחֲהָא יָת קַרְתָּה
וְיָת רְוָחֲהָא׃ לה יָת דִּמְנָה
וְיָת רְוָחֲהָא יָת נַהֲלָל וְיָת
רְוָחֲהָא קִרְוִין אַרְבַּע׃
לו (וּמִשִּׁבְטָא דִרְאוּבֵן יָת
קִרְיַת שֵׁיזָבוּת קָטוֹלָא יָת
בֶּצֶר בְּמַדְבְּרָא וְיָת
רְוָחֲהָא יָת יַהְצָה וְיָת
רְוָחֲהָא׃ לז יָת קְדֵמוֹת
וְיָת רְוָחֲהָא יָת מֵיפַעַת
וְיָת רְוָחֲהָא קִרְוִין אַרְבַּע)׃
לו וּמִשִּׁבְטָא דְגָד יָת
קִרְיַת שֵׁיזָבוּת קָטוֹלָא יָת
רָמוֹת בַּגִלְעָד וְיָת רְוָחֲהָא
וְיָת מַחֲנַיִם וְיָת רְוָחֲהָא׃
לז יָת חֶשְׁבּוֹן וְיָת רְוָחֲהָא
יָת יַעְזֵר וְיָת רְוָחֲהָא כָּל
קִרְוִין אַרְבַּע׃ לח כָּל
קִרְוַיָּא לִבְנֵי מְרָרִי
לְזַרְעִיתְהוֹן דִּי אִשְׁתְּאָרוּ
מִזַּרְעִית לֵיוָאֵי וַהֲוָה
עַדְבְהוֹן קִרְוִין תַּרְתֵּי
עַסְרֵי׃ לט כָּל קִרְוֵי לֵיוָאֵי
בְּגוֹ אַחֲסָנַת בְּנֵי יִשְׂרָאֵל
קרוין

מנחת שי

את בצר ואת יהצה וגו׳ וגם במסורת מנו זה עם כ״ח את הכתובים בענין: קודם וממטה גד יש ספרים שכתוב כאן שני פסוקים ואלו הן: (לו) וממטה ראובן. את בצר ואת מגרשה ואת יהצה ואת מגרשה: (לז) את קדמות ואת מגרשה ואת מיפעת (ס״א את) ואת מגרשה ערים ארבע: וכן ראיתי בדפוסים ישנים. ופסוקים אלו הם גם בד״ה א׳ ס״ג ס״ד: ובס״ס ישנים כ״י פסוק ראובן כתוב באופן אחר: (לו) וממטה ראובן את עיר מקלט הרצח את בצר במדבר ואת מגרשה את יהצה (ס״א ואת יהצה) ואת מגרשה: וכן נראה נכון לפרש ד׳ ערים אלו לפי הסכום שכתוב בפ׳ ערים שתים עשרה ורד״ק כתוב לעיל בפסוק לבני מררי ז״ל בזה הפסוק אומר כי שתים עשרה ערים היו לבני מררי ממטה ראובן וממטה גד ממטה זבולן ולמטה בספור הערים לא כתב אלא שמונה ערים ממטה זבולן ארבע ממטה גד ארבע וממטה ראובן לא כתב. וי״מ מוגה בהם וממטה ראובן את בצר ואת מגרשה את יהצה ואת מגרשה את קדמות ואת מגרשה ואת מיפעת ואת מגרשה ערים ארבע: ולא ראיתי שני פסוקים אלו בשום ספר ישן מדוייק אלא מוגה במקצתם וראיתי כי כשאל רבינו האיי ז״ל בזאת השאלה והשיב אע״פ דהכא לא חשיב להו בד״ה חשיב להו נראה מתשובתו כי אינם כתובים בספריהם עכ״ל ועמ״ש במ״ג בגליון ומ״ש למעלה בסי׳ י״ג בחשבון אלי הספר בפסוקים: וחילוף כזה מצאתי בנחמי׳ סי׳ ז׳ ע״ש:

*בקצת ספרים יש כאן ב׳ פסוקים וממטה ראובן וגו׳. וטעות הוא ואינם ראוים להיות וע״י בפירוש הרד״ק ובמסרה וכן נמצא בג׳ ספרים ישנים מדויקים כתיבת יד:

Jokneam and the open land around it, Kartah with the open land around it, 35. Dimnah with the open land around it, Nahalal and the open land around it; four cities. (36. And from the tribe of Reuben, the city of refuge for the slayer, Bezer in the wilderness with the open land around it, and Jahzah with the open land around it. 37. Kedemoth with the open land around it, and Mephaath with the open land around it; four cities.) 36. And from the tribe of Gad, the city of refuge for the slayer, Ramoth in Gilead with the open land around it, and Mahanaim with the open land around it. 37. Heshbon with the open land around it, Jazer with the open land around it; four cities in all. 38. All these cities were for the children of Merari according to their families, those who remained of the families of the Levites, and their lot was twelve cities. 39. All the cities of the Levites in the midst of the possession of the children of Israel,

### Commentary Digest

35. *Dimnah* — also known as Rimmono.[1]

*Nahalal* — also known as Tabor[1] — E.G.

36. *And from the tribe of Reuben* — In other versions, this verse appears: And from the tribe of Reuben, Bezer and the land around it, and Jahzah and the open land around it. We have already noted[2] that according to the greatest authorities, these two verses, 36, 37, are not a part of the original Masoretic text, but were inserted as marginal notes to complement the twelve cities, four of which are missing. These four are recorded in I Chron. VI:63, 64, where the wording differs slightly.

עָרִ֕ים אַרְבָּעִ֥ים וּשְׁמֹנֶ֖ה וּמִגְרְשֵׁיהֶֽן׃
מ תִּֽהְיֶ֙ינָה֙ הֶעָרִ֣ים הָאֵ֔לֶּה עִ֣יר עִ֔יר
וּמִגְרָשֶׁ֖יהָ סְבִיבֹתֶ֑יהָ כֵּ֖ן לְכָל־הֶעָרִ֥ים
הָאֵֽלֶּה׃ מא וַיִּתֵּ֤ן יְהוָה֙ לְיִשְׂרָאֵ֔ל אֶת־כָּל־
הָאָ֕רֶץ אֲשֶׁ֥ר נִשְׁבַּ֖ע לָתֵ֣ת לַאֲבוֹתָ֑ם
וַיִּרָשׁ֖וּהָ וַיֵּ֥שְׁבוּ בָֽהּ׃ מב וַיָּ֨נַח יְהוָ֤ה לָהֶם֙
מִסָּבִ֔יב כְּכֹ֥ל אֲשֶׁר־נִשְׁבַּ֖ע לַאֲבוֹתָ֑ם
וְלֹא־עָ֨מַד אִ֤ישׁ בִּפְנֵיהֶם֙ מִכָּל־אֹ֣יְבֵיהֶ֔ם
אֵ֚ת כָּל־אֹ֣יְבֵיהֶ֔ם נָתַ֥ן יְהוָ֖ה בְּיָדָֽם׃ מג לֹֽא־
נָפַ֣ל דָּבָ֗ר מִכֹּל֙ הַדָּבָ֣ר הַטּ֔וֹב אֲשֶׁר־דִּבֶּ֥ר
יְהוָ֖ה אֶל־בֵּ֣ית יִשְׂרָאֵ֑ל הַכֹּ֖ל בָּֽא׃ כב א אָ֚ז
יִקְרָ֣א יְהוֹשֻׁ֔עַ לָרֻֽאוּבֵנִ֖י וְלַגָּדִ֑י וְלַחֲצִ֖י
מַטֵּ֥ה מְנַשֶּֽׁה׃ ב וַיֹּ֣אמֶר אֲלֵיהֶ֗ם אַתֶּ֤ם

תרגום

קִרְוִין אַרְבְּעִין וּתְמָנֵי
וְרָוְחֵיהֶן׃ מ יֶהֶוְיָן קִרְוַיָא
הָאִלֵין קִרְוֵי קִרְוֵי וְרָוְחָהָא
סַחְרָנָהָא כֵּן לְכָל קִרְוַיָא
הָאִלֵין׃ מא וִיהַב יְיָ
לְיִשְׂרָאֵל יַת כָּל אַרְעָא דִי
קַיֵים לְמִתַּן לַאֲבָהַתְהוֹן
וְאַחְסִינוּהָ וִיתִיבוּ בַהּ׃
מב וְאָנִיחַ יְיָ לְהוֹן מִסְחוֹר
סְחוֹר כְּכֹל דְקַיֵים
לַאֲבָהַתְהוֹן וְלָא קָם אֱנָשׁ
מִן קֳדָמֵיהוֹן מִן כָּל בַּעֲלֵי
דְבָבֵיהוֹן יַת כָּל בַּעֲלֵי
דְבָבֵיהוֹן מְסַר יְיָ
בִּידֵיהוֹן׃ מג לָא בְטֵיל
פִּתְגָמָא מִכֹּל פִּתְגָמוֹהִי
תַקִינַיָא דִי מַלֵיל יְיָ עַל
בֵּית יִשְׂרָאֵל כּוּלְהוֹן
אִתְקַיָימוּ׃ א בְּכֵן קְרָא
יְהוֹשֻׁעַ לְשִׁבְטָא דִרְאוּבֵן
וּלְשִׁבְטָא דְגָד וּלְפַלְגוּת
שִׁבְטָא דִמְנַשֶׁה׃ ב וַאֲמַר
לְהוֹן אַתּוּן נְטַרְתּוּן יַת
כָּל

רש״י

שיונתן מתרגם אותם עלמות: (מ) ומגרשיה סביבותיה. אלפים אמה לכל רוח:

מנחת שי

כב (א) לראובני הרי״ש במאריך ונקודה שלא שורק והאל״ף נחה כס״ס

רלב״ג

(מג) ואח״ז זכר שלא נפל דבר מכל הדבר הטוב אשר דבר ה׳ אל בית ישראל הכל בא ואף על פי שכבר נשארו בהן עדין כמו שזכר במה שקדם הנה זה בלתי סותר מה שנזכר בזה המקום כי כל הגוים אשר נלחמו בהם נפלו בידם ואולם נשארו אלו בסבת עצלות יהושע וישראל לא בסבת העדר השגחת השם יתברך מהם: (א) ואחר זכר שכבר קרא יהושע לראובני ולגדי ולחצי שבט מנשה והזהירם.

מצודת דוד

(מ) תהינה. הלוים: עיר עיר. לכל עיר ועיר מגרשיה סבובותיה: (מב) וינח ה׳. נתן להם מנוחה מסביב ולא נתגרו בהם הכו״ג: ולא עמד. לא נתקיים: (מג) לא נפל דבר. לא נחסר שום דבר: כב (ב) אשר צוה. שתעברו חלוצים לפני בני ישראל למלחמה:

## Commentary Digest

conquer, this was because of neglect on the part of Joshua and Israel, not the Almighty's failure to fulfill His word. — G

CHAPTER 22

1. *Then Joshua called* — "Then" refers to the completion of the seven year period of conquest and the seven year period of division.

were forty-eight cities with the open land around them. 40. These
cities shall be (to the Levites) each city and its open land
around; thus shall it be for all these cities. 41. And the Lord
gave to Israel the entire land that He swore to give to their
fathers, and they inherited it and dwelled in it. 42. And the
Lord gave them rest from about, according to all that He swore
to their fathers; and no man of all their enemies stood before
them; the Lord delivered all their enemies into their hand.
43. Not a thing was lacking from all the good things that the
Lord spoke to the house of Israel; all came to pass.

## 22

1. Then Joshua called the Reubenites, and the Gadites, and
the half-tribe of Manasseh. 2. And he said to them, "You

### Commentary Digest

40. *and its open land around* — *"two thousand ells on each side."* — R[1]

41. *And the Lord gave to Israel*— I.e. the Lord had already delivered the entire land into the hands of Israel. Had they sought to fulfill the Lord's commandment, they could have easily conquered it. They were neglectful, however, and conquered only what they needed for dwelling. — K. Y. survived. — D Alternatively, no one of their enemies stood up to rebel against them after the war with the thirty-one kings. Those enemies who *did* resist them, viz. the thirty-one kings — *the Lord delivered all their enemies* into their hand. — K. Y.

42. *and no man... stood* — i.e. survived. — D

43. *was lacking* — lit. fell. — D

*Not a thing was lacking from all the good things* — Although certain parts of the country were still left to

שְׁמַרְתֶּם אֵת כָּל־אֲשֶׁר צִוָּה אֶתְכֶם
מֹשֶׁה עֶבֶד יְהוָה וַתִּשְׁמְעוּ בְקוֹלִי לְכֹל
אֲשֶׁר־צִוִּיתִי אֶתְכֶם׃ ג לֹא־עֲזַבְתֶּם אֶת־
אֲחֵיכֶם זֶה יָמִים רַבִּים עַד הַיּוֹם הַזֶּה
וּשְׁמַרְתֶּם אֶת־מִשְׁמֶרֶת מִצְוַת יְהוָה
אֱלֹהֵיכֶם׃ ד וְעַתָּה הֵנִיחַ יְהוָה אֱלֹהֵיכֶם
לַאֲחֵיכֶם כַּאֲשֶׁר דִּבֶּר לָהֶם וְעַתָּה פְּנוּ
וּלְכוּ לָכֶם לְאָהֳלֵיכֶם אֶל־אֶרֶץ אֲחֻזַּתְכֶם
אֲשֶׁר ׀ נָתַן לָכֶם מֹשֶׁה עֶבֶד יְהוָה בְּעֵבֶר

כל דפקיד יתכון משה
עבדא דיי וקבילתון
למימרי לכל די פקדית
יתכון: ג לא שבקתון ית
אחוכון דנן יומין סגיאין
עד יומא הדין ונטרתון
ית מטרת תפקידתא
ממרא דיי אלהכון:
ד וכען אניח יי אלהכון
לאחוכון כמא די מליל
להון וכען אתפניאו
ואיזילו לכון לקרויכון
לארעא אחסנתכון דיהב
לכון משה עבדא דיי
בעברא

**רלב"ג**

מאד לשמור התורה וברכם ושלחם לאהליהם בנכסי' רבים ומקנה רב ובזהב ובכסף ובנחשת וברזל ובשלמות הרבה כי חלקו שלל אויביהם עם אחיהם וכן היה ראוי כי כן חלקו כל ישראל שלל הערים אשר באו להם בנחלה כמו שנזכר בתורה:

**מנחת שי**

בפרשת פינחס: (ד) כאשר דבר להם. חד מן ס' לשון דסבירין לשון וסימנם במסורה בפרשת בהעלתך סימן י"א: ועתה פנו ולכו. במקצת

**מצודת דוד**

(ד) הניח. נתן להם מקום מנוחה: פנו ולכו. פנו מכאן ולכו

**מצודת ציון**

כב (ד) הניח. מל' ממחה:

## Commentary Digest

*these many days* — fourteen years, seven of conquest and seven of division. — M

4. *as He spoke to them* — Deut. III:20.

*to your tents* — i.e. to your families.[2]

*gave you* — See Num. XXXII

have kept all that Moses the servant of the Lord commanded
you, and have obeyed me in all that I commanded you
3. You have not left your brothers these many days to this
day, but have kept the charge of the commandment of the
Lord your God. 4. And now the Lord your God has given rest
to your brothers, as He spoke to them; and now turn and go
to your dwellings, to the land of your possession, which Moses
the servant of the Lord gave you on the other side

## Commentary Digest

After this period had elapsed, the Reubenites, the Gadites, and the half-tribe of Manasseh were free to return to their families on the eastern bank of the Jordan. Yet, they did not do so. Joshua understood that this was due to their humility and subordination to him. He, therefore, summoned them and acknowledged their admirable deeds. He then dismissed them. — P.Y.

2. *"You have kept all that Moses ... commanded you* — In addition to the condition you contracted, to remain with your brothers until after the conquest, you kept that which Moses commanded you, to remain until after the division of the land. — M[1]

*the charge of the commandments* — or the safeguard of the commandments. Joshua could not add any commandments, but could enact safeguards to Divine law. — M Alternatively, *"You have kept all that Moses . . . commanded you* — I.e. the command to remain until after the seven years of conquest — *and have obeyed me in all that I commanded you* — I.e. you refrained from battle during the conquest of Jericho, which was conquered miraculously by marching around the city walls and sounding the *shofaros.*

3. *You have not left your brothers these* many days — I.e. you have remained until after the division of the land. This was a safeguard of Moses' commandment to remain until after the conquest.

*to this day* — I.e. to this day when I have summoned you before me.

*and you will keep the safeguard of the commandment of the Lord your God* — I.e. I am confident that since you kept the safeguard of Moses' command, that you will always keep the safeguard of the Lord's commandments. — P. Y.

הירדן: ה רק שמרו מאד לעשות את־
המצוה ואת־התורה אשר צוה אתכם
משה עבד־יהוה לאהבה את־יהוה
אלהיכם וללכת בכל־דרכיו ולשמר
מצותיו ולדבקה־בו ולעבדו בכל־
לבבכם ובכל־נפשכם: ו ויברכם
יהושע וישלחם וילכו אל־אהליהם:
ז ולחצי | שבט המנשה נתן משה
בבשן ולחציו נתן יהושע עם־אחיהם
מעבר הירדן ימה וגם כי שלחם יהושע

בעבר קרי

בעברא דירדנא: ה לחוד אסתמרו לחדא למעבד ית תפקדתא וית אוריתא די פקיד יתכון משה עבדא דיי למרחם ית יי אלהכון ולמהך בכל אורחן דתקנן קדמוהי ולמטר פקודהי ולאתקרבא לדחלתיה ולמפלח קדמוהי בכל לבכון ובכל נפשכון:
ו ובריכינון יהושע ושלחינון ואזלו לקרויהון: ז ולפלגות שבטא דמנשה יהב משה במתנן ולפלגיהון יהב יהושע עם אחיהון בעברא דירדנא למערבא ואף ארי שלחינון

### רד"ק

אחד מהם היה לו עיר ששמה גת רמון: (ז) ולחצי שבט המנשה. ואף על פי שזכרו כשקרא להם יהושע חזר לתת טעם איך הי' חצי שבט עם בני גד ובני ראובן: וגם כי שלחם. יש אומרים לחצי שבט מנשה ואף על פי שהיו בכלל וישלחם והנכון כי על כלם אמר אף על פי שאמר ויברכם יהושע וישלחו חזר אחר כן וגם כי שלחם ויברכם להשלים הדבר שאמר להם כאשר שלחם שאמר להם בנכסים רבים שובו ובדרש לאחר שנטלו רשות נשתהו שני ימים וחזרו ונטלו רשות פעם שנייה

### רש"י

כב (ז) וגם כי שלחם יהושע. לחצי שבט המנשה כאשר

### מנחת שי

דפוסים ישנים פנו וסעו ובאלה ספרים ולכו וכן תרגום יונתן ואיזילו: (ו) ויברכם יהושע. הרי"ש בשו"א לבדו כמנהגנו: (ז) ולחצי שבט המנשה. הה"א במאריך כחבריו שבענין. מעבר הירדן. בעבר קרי וכן הוא ברוב הספרים במסורה רבתא מערכת אות הבי"ת מנו ו' מלין דכתיבין ב' וקרין מ"ם ובסוף כתיב

### מצודת דוד

ומ': (ה) רק שמרו מאד. אף אם תרחיקו ממשכן ה': (ז) ולחצי שבט המנשה. בזה יתן טעם למה היה רק חצי שבט

## Commentary Digest

person is dealing with his fellow-men, he must think about the Almighty. This is possible for pious people who serve as a dwelling for the divine presence, as the Khuzari explains. Thus, we explain the two verses in ch. XXIII thus: You shall not think of the deities of the nations of Canaan, to mention their names or worship them. You must think only of the Lord your God in all your activities, as you have done to this day. While you were in the wilderness, the divine presence was obvious through the falling of manna and the protection of the clouds of glory. From this day on, I charge you with this same "clinging" although the manna and the clouds of glory have long ceased to accompany you.

6. *and dismissed them*—or escorted them.[3]

7. *And also when Joshua sent them away — "i.e. the half-tribe of Manasseh, as he had sent away the children of Reuben and Gad."* — R K explains that this is a repetition of the preceding verse. The Scripture relates that when he sent them away and blessed them, he also gave them a share of the booty, as in verse 8. The Rabbis tell us that after having taken leave from Joshua, the two and

of the Jordan. 5. Only take diligent heed to do the commandment and the Torah, which Moses the servant of the Lord commanded you, to love the Lord your God, and to walk in all His ways, and to keep His commandments, and to cling to Him, and to serve Him with all your heart and with all your soul." 6. And Joshua blessed them, and dismissed them; and they went to their tents. 7. And to the half-tribe of Manasseh, Moses had given [inheritance] in Bashan, but to the other half Joshua gave among their brothers on this side of the Jordan westward. And also, when Joshua dismissed them

## Commentary Digest

5. *Only take diligent heed* — although you will be a great distance from the sanctuary of the Lord. — D

*which Moses ... commanded you, to love the Lord, etc.* — Joshua repeats almost verbatim the program of Moses in Deut. X:12, 13; VI:22. This is necessary in view of their distance from Shiloh, spiritual center of Israel, as we have already noted.

*to walk in all His ways* — He is merciful, and you shall be merciful; He performs acts of lovingkindness, and you shall perform acts of lovingkindness. — R[1] It is of paramount importance for the Jew to emulate the Almighty in developing his character traits. The Kabalist, Rabbi Moses Kordivoro, in his renowned work, Tomer Deborah, elucidates this point by illustrating how man can emulate his Maker even by practicing the Thirteen Divine Attributes.

*to cling to Him* — Is it possible to say this (in a physical sense)? Is He not a consuming fire? Rather, the Torah means to cling to Torah scholars and sages, and I consider it as though you had clung to Him. — R[1] E sees in "clinging to Him," an allusion to the Hereafter, i.e. love Him, walk in His ways, keep His commandments, so that your soul will cling to Him in the Hereafter. N, in view of Joshua's admonition in the following chapter[2]; explains this as a warning against idolatry. "... nor shall you make mention of their deities, nor cause to swear by them; and you shall not serve them nor bow to them; but cling to the Lord your G-d, as you have done to this day." He also suggests that the Scripture demands that one always remember the Lord and His love, never taking his thoughts off Him. Even when a

אֶל־אָהֳלֵיהֶם וַיְבָרְכֵם׃ ח וַיֹּאמֶר אֲלֵיהֶם
לֵאמֹר בִּנְכָסִים רַבִּים שׁוּבוּ אֶל־אָהֳלֵיכֶם
וּבְמִקְנֶה רַב־מְאֹד בְּכֶסֶף וּבְזָהָב
וּבִנְחֹשֶׁת וּבְבַרְזֶל וּבִשְׂלָמוֹת הַרְבֵּה
מְאֹד חִלְקוּ שְׁלַל־אֹיְבֵיכֶם עִם־אֲחֵיכֶם׃
ט וַיָּשֻׁבוּ וַיֵּלְכוּ בְּנֵי־רְאוּבֵן וּבְנֵי־גָד וַחֲצִי
שֵׁבֶט הַמְנַשֶּׁה מֵאֵת בְּנֵי יִשְׂרָאֵל מִשִּׁלֹה
אֲשֶׁר בְּאֶרֶץ־כְּנָעַן לָלֶכֶת אֶל־אֶרֶץ
הַגִּלְעָד אֶל־אֶרֶץ אֲחֻזָּתָם אֲשֶׁר נֹאחֲזוּ
בָהּ עַל־פִּי יְהוָה בְּיַד־מֹשֶׁה׃ י וַיָּבֹאוּ אֶל־

שַׁלְחִינוּן יְהוֹשֻׁעַ
לְקִרְוֵיהוֹן וּבָרְכִינוּן׃
ח וַאֲמַר לְהוֹן לְמֵימַר
בְּנִכְסִין סַגִּיאִין תּוּבוּ
לְקִרְוֵיכוֹן וּבִבְעִירָא סַגִּי
לַחֲדָא בְּכַסְפָּא וּבְדַהֲבָא
וּבִנְחָשָׁא וּבְפַרְזְלָא
וּבִלְבוּשִׁין סַגִּי לַחֲדָא
פְּלִיגוּ בִּזַּת בַּעֲלֵי
דְבָבֵיכוֹן עִם אֲחֵיכוֹן׃
ט וְתָבוּ וַאֲזַלוּ בְּנֵי רְאוּבֵן
וּבְנֵי גָד וּפַלְגוּת שִׁבְטָא
דִמְנַשֶּׁה מִלְּוַת בְּנֵי
יִשְׂרָאֵל מִשִּׁלֹה דִּי
בְּאַרְעָא דִכְנַעַן לְמֵיזַל
לְאַרְעָא דְגִלְעָד לְאַרְעָא
אחסנתהון

### רש"י

שלא את בני ראובן וגד: (ח) עם אחיכם. בני ראובן ובני גד. ויש פותרין עם אחיכם שנשארו לשמור את

### רד"ק

וזהו שאמר וגם כי שלחם יהושע וגו': (ח) חלקו שלל אויביכם עם אחיכם. אם אמר לחצי שבט מנשה יהיה פירוש עם אחיכם בני גד ובני ראובן ואם אמר לכלם יהיה פירוש עם השבטים אשר בארץ כנען כמו שאמר בנכסים רבים שובו שתחלקו עם אחיכם השבטים הבזה ומי שמפרש עם אחיכם האנשים

### רלב"ג

(י) עוד זכר שבשובם לנחלתם מעבר לירדן פנו אל הירדן מזבח גדול למראה וחשבו ישראל בעשו זה להקריב עליו ונקהלו שילה לעלות עליהם לצבא והיתה עלתם לשלוח להם תחלה פנחס בן אלעז' הכהן ועשרה נשיאים עמו מתשעת המטות וחצי המטה לדעת מה זה ועל מה זה ולהזהירם ולהוכיחם על זה כי כבר הזהרו בתורה מעשות במת ליבור זולתי משכן ה' וגם במה ליחיד נאסרה מעת בואו אל המנוחה ואל הנחלה והנה היה משכן שילה מנוחה כמו שנתבאר בסוף זבחים ובית עולמים היה נחלה ולפי זה הענין היה מגד בה' כי הכוונה בשלא יעבד הש"י כי אם במקום אחד הוא להורות על היותו אחד כמו שביארנו בביאורנו לדברי התורה וזה הפך מה בעשו ישראל כשנשקעו בע"ג עד שתמלא שכבר היו להם בתי עבודת אלילים בכל עריהם אמר הנביא מספר גוותן כי מספר עריך היו אלהין

### מצודת דוד

כמנהג עם ב"ר וב"ג: וגם כי שלחם. ר"ל וגם זאת דבר להם כאשר שלחם והוא הדבר הנאמר במקרא שלאחריו: (ח) אליהם. לב"ר ולב"ג ולחצי שבט מנשה: עם אחיכם. הם אשר נשארו בעבר

### מצודת ציון

(ח) בנכסים. זה הלשון ידוע בדרז"ל כלול בה זהב וכסף וכליט ומקנה ומ' וכן עושר ונכסים (קהלת ה'): ובשלמות. ובגדים ויתהפך משמלה שלמה כמו מכבש כשב:

## Commentary Digest

all the spoils remain on the west side of the Jordan with the half-tribe which resided there.

At this point, Joshua decided that the two and a half tribes, although they received no inheritance in the land on the west of the Jordan, yet they received their share of the spoils acquired in its conquest. — D. S.

9. *And the children of Reuben . . . returned* — I.e. they returned from Joshua's city, Timnath-serah where he had summoned them to appear before him. — M

*and departed from the children of Israel out of Shiloh* — Instead of heading directly eastward toward the Jordan, they first went northward to the tabernacle in Shiloh, to take leave of the Almighty, whose *Shechinah* dwelt in Shiloh, and to take leave of the children of Israel assembled there. This act proved that the suspicion cast upon them in the following verses was entirely unfounded — M

to their dwellings, he blessed them. 8. And he said to them, saying, "Return with much wealth to your dwellings, and with very much cattle, with silver, and with gold, and with copper, and with iron, and with very many garments; divide the spoil of your enemies with your brothers." 9. And the children of Reuben and the children of Gad and the half-tribe of Manasseh returned, and departed from the children of Israel out of Shiloh, which is in the land of Canaan, to go to the country of Gilead, to the land of their possession, of which they were possessed, according to the word of the Lord through Moses. 10. And they came to

## Commentary Digest

a half tribes tarried several days, following which they returned to Joshua to take leave a second time. Rabbi Judan explains that Reuben and Gad were Joshua's soldiers. First, he accompanied them to the Jordan, where they took his leave and received his blessing. When they were about to cross the Jordan, they noticed that their beloved leader was left almost without a cortege. Thereupon, they delayed their departure, and escorted Joshua back to his dwelling, upon which he blessed them more than he had done previously, and dismissed them to their dwellings and families. This small incident illustrates the intense love which existed between Joshua and the Israelites.

Whether Jordan is an integral part of Eretz Israel, in all its ramifications, is a problem dealt with at great length by Rabbi Chaim David Azulai, eighteenth century Sephardic luminary, in his "Birkai Joseph," comment on Orach Chaim ch. 489.

8. ***divide the spoil . . . with your brothers*** — *the children of Reuben and the children of Gad. Some interpret this to mean: With your brothers who remained to guard the cities with the women and children, and did not cross the Jordan with the advance guard. They too received a share of the spoils."* — R This was a tradition from the time of Abraham,[2] later formalized by David.[3] K rejects the idea that there were men who remained in Gilead to guard the cities. See above Commentary Digest, IV:-13. A explains: *with your brothers, the other half-tribe of Manasseh;* i.e. since they were actually one tribe, a second division was necessary, lest

גלילות הירדן אשר בארץ כנען ויבנו
בני־ראובן ובני־גד וחצי שבט המנשה
שם מזבח על־הירדן מזבח גדול
למראה: יא וישמעו בני־ישראל לאמר
הנה־בנו בני־ראובן ובני־גד וחצי שבט
המנשה את־המזבח אל־מול ארץ
כנען אל־גלילות הירדן אל־עבר בני
ישראל: יב וישמעו בני ישראל ויקהלו
כל־עדת בני־ישראל שלה לעלות
עליהם לצבא: יג וישלחו בני־ישראל
אל־בני־ראובן ואל־בני־גד ואל־חצי

**תרגום**

אַחְסַנְתְּהוֹן דְאַחְסִינוּ בַהּ עַל מֵימְרָא דַיְיָ בִּידָא דְמֹשֶׁה: י וַאֲתוֹ לִגְלִילֵי יַרְדְנָא דִי בְּאַרְעָא דִכְנַעַן וּבְנוֹ בְנֵי רְאוּבֵן וּבְנֵי גָד וּפַלְגוּת שִׁבְטָא דִמְנַשֶׁה תַּמָן מַדְבְּחָא עַל יַרְדְנָא מַדְבַּח רַב לְמֶחֱזֵי: יא וּשְׁמָעוּ בְנֵי יִשְׂרָאֵל לְמֵימַר הָא בְנוֹ בְנֵי רְאוּבֵן וּבְנֵי גָד וּפַלְגוּת שִׁבְטָא דִמְנַשֶׁה יָת מַדְבְּחָא לְקֳבֵיל אַרְעָא דִכְנַעַן בִּגְלִילֵי יַרְדְנָא דִלְעִבַר בְּנֵי יִשְׂרָאֵל: יב וּשְׁמָעוּ בְנֵי יִשְׂרָאֵל וְאִתְכְּנִישׁוּ כָּל כְּנִשְׁתָּא דִבְנֵי יִשְׂרָאֵל לְשִׁלֹה לְמִיסַק עֲלֵיהוֹן לְחֵילָא: יג וּשְׁלַחוּ בְנֵי יִשְׂרָאֵל לְוַת בְּנֵי רְאוּבֵן וּלְוַת בְּנֵי גָד וּלְוַת פַּלְגוּת שִׁבְטָא דמנשה

ת״א מזבח גדול: עקידה שער י׳:

**רש״י**

הטרים עם הנשים והטף ולא עברו את הירדן עם החלוצים גם הם נטלו חלק בבזה: (יב) לעלות עליהם לצבא. לפי

**רד״ק**

אשר הניחו בארץ הגלעד לשמור הערים אין לו טעם כי נשיהם וטפם הוא שהניחו: (יב) לעלות עליהם לצבא. כמו בצבא כמו וישבו אתו לארץ לפניכם לחרב הרגתי לפצעי ולפי שחשבו כי להעלות עליו עולה וזבח עשו אותו ולהיות להם מזבח לבדם מבלי שיבאו למזבח ה׳ לשילה או באשר יהיה שם ומשבאו לשילה נאסרו הבמות שכך שנינו עד שלא הוקם המשכן היו הבמות מותרות משהוקם המשכן נאסרו הבמות באו לגלגל הותרו הבמות באו לשילה נאסרו הבמות באו לנוב וגבעון הותרו הבמות באו לירושלם נאסרו הבמות ולא היה להם היתר

**רלב״ג**

יסודה הנה אמרו ישראל לעלות עליה׳ לצבא להוכיחם על זה ולבער הרע מקרבם כי זה מדרכי התורה כמו שנתבאר בתורה בעיר הנדחת ולזאת הסבה עלו ישראל לצבא על אחיהם על דבר פילגש בגבעה והסבה בזה שישמעו הנשארים וייראו ולא יוספו לעשות הרע הזה כי אולי ילמדו מזה הנשארים ויסתבכו כלם בזה הפועל המגונה הלא תראה כי ירבעם בן נבט התחיל במרד ונמשכו למריו כל מלכי ישראל הבאים אחריו ונשקעו בו גם כן בסוף הענין מלכי יהודה והיה זה סבת גלות ישראל מארצם ואבדן רבים מהם ולזאת הסבה אחשב שאמרו פנחס והנשיאי׳ לבני ראובן ולבני גד ולחצי שבט המנשה המעט לנו את עון פעור אשר לא הטהרנו ממנו עד היום הזה

**מצודת ציון**

(י) על. אצל: (יב) לצבא. כמו בצבא ובאה הלמ״ד במקום הבי״ת

**מצודת דוד**

הירדן לשמור הנשים והטף והרכוש: (י) אשר בארץ כנען. ר״ל בשפת עבר הירדן המערבי שהיא מארץ כנען: למראה. ר״ל להיות למראה עינים לא לעולה וזבח: (יב) לצבא. אם לא יתקנו את אשר עותו כי הם חשבו שעשאוהו לעולה וזבח: (יג) וישלחו. טרם עלו

## Commentary Digest

*to look upon* — only, not for sacrifice. — D

12. *to go up to war against them* — if they would not rectify their error, for they thought that it was made for sacrifices. — D *"For high places had been banned since the establishment of the tabernacle at Shiloh."* — R The sacrificial service was to be performed in one place only, in Shiloh, where the Tabernacle had been set up. This was to impress upon the people the oneness of God. When they violated this ban and built high places, they were gradually drawn into idolatry, until the prophet Jeremiah denounced them by saying,[1] "... for the number of your cities, were your gods, O Judah." Therefore, the reaction was swift to this seeming wrong, just as in the case of the concubine of Gibeah,[2] lest this transgression spread throughout all Israel. — G See Hosea X:9, where the

the regions of the Jordan, that are in the land of Canaan, and
the children of Reuben and the children of Gad and the
half-tribe of Manasseh built an altar there by the Jordan, a
great altar to look upon. 11. And the children of Israel heard
say, "Behold, the children of Reuben and the children of Gad,
and the half-tribe of Manasseh have built an altar over against
the land of Canaan, in the regions of the Jordan, at the side
of the children of Israel." 12. And when the children of
Israel heard of it, the whole congregation of the children of
Israel assembled at Shiloh, to go up to war against them. 13.
And the children of Israel sent to the children of Reuben, and
to the children of Gad, and to the half-

## Commentary Digest

Alternatively, the children of Reuben, Gad, and the half-tribe of Manasseh hesitated to leave the Holy Land proper to return to the land of Gilead on the eastern side of the Jordan. Once they felt the sanctity of the land, it attracted them. Thus, Scripture says, "And . . . returned and departed." After they started to return to their homes, they came back and departed again. For three reasons they found parting difficult. One reason was:

*from the children of Israel* — They hesitated to part from the vast majority of their brothers, the children of Israel. The second reason was:

*out of Shiloh* — They found it difficult to leave the sanctuary of the Lord in Shiloh. The third reason was:

*which is in the land of Canaan* — They came back to kiss the stones of the Holy Land. It was very dear to them and they hesitated to leave it.

*to go to the country of Gilead* — This anguish was caused by the prospect of going to another land, the country of Gilead.

*to the land of their possession* — Even though it was the land of their possession, which is always dear to a person.

*of which they were possessed* — They were forced to return to that land because they had taken possession of it.

*according to the word of the Lord through Moses.* — Especially since it had been decreed by the Lord through Moses, they had no choice but to return. — K. Y.

10. *that are in the land of Canaan* — on the west side of the Jordan. — D

שֵׁבֶט־מְנַשֶּׁה אֶל־אֶרֶץ הַגִּלְעָד אֶת־
פִּינְחָס בֶּן־אֶלְעָזָר הַכֹּהֵן׃ יד וַעֲשָׂרָה
נְשִׂאִים עִמּוֹ נָשִׂיא אֶחָד נָשִׂיא אֶחָד
לְבֵית אָב לְכֹל מַטּוֹת יִשְׂרָאֵל וְאִישׁ
רֹאשׁ בֵּית־אֲבוֹתָם הֵמָּה לְאַלְפֵי יִשְׂרָאֵל׃
טו וַיָּבֹאוּ אֶל־בְּנֵי־רְאוּבֵן וְאֶל־בְּנֵי־גָד
וְאֶל־חֲצִי שֵׁבֶט־מְנַשֶּׁה אֶל־אֶרֶץ הַגִּלְעָד
וַיְדַבְּרוּ אִתָּם לֵאמֹר׃ טז כֹּה אָמְרוּ כֹּל
עֲדַת יְהוָה מָה־הַמַּעַל הַזֶּה אֲשֶׁר
מְעַלְתֶּם בֵּאלֹהֵי יִשְׂרָאֵל לָשׁוּב הַיּוֹם
מֵאַחֲרֵי יְהוָה בִּבְנוֹתְכֶם לָכֶם מִזְבֵּחַ
לִמְרָדְכֶם הַיּוֹם בַּיהוָה׃ יז הַמְעַט־לָנוּ אֶת־
עֲוֺן פְּעוֹר אֲשֶׁר לֹא־הִטַּהַרְנוּ מִמֶּנּוּ עַד
הַיּוֹם הַזֶּה וַיְהִי הַנֶּגֶף בַּעֲדַת יְהוָה׃

דמנשה לארעא גלעד
ית פנחס בר אלעזר
כהנא: יד ועשרא רברבין
עמיה רבא חד רבא חד
לבית אבא לכל שבטיא
דישראל וגבר ריש בית
אבהתהון אינון לאלפיא
דישראל: טו ואתו לות
בני ראובן ולות בני גד
ולות פלגות שבטא
דמנשה לארעא דגלעד
ומלילו עמהון למימר:
טז כדין אמרו כל כנשתא
דיי מא שקרא הדין די
שקרתון במימרא
דאלהא ישראל למיתב
יומא דין מבתר פולחנא
דיי במבנכון לכון מדבחא
למרדכון יומא דין
במימרא דיי: יז הזעיר
לנא ית חובא דפעור
דלא אדכינא מניה עד
יומא הדין והות מחתא
בכנשתא דיי: יח ואתון

תתובון

ת"א המעט לנו. עקדה שער פה:

### רד"ק

עוד לפיכך חשבוהו להם לעון ולמרד בה': (יד) ואיש ראש בית אבותם. כל איש מאלה העשרה שהלכו עם פנחס כל אחד

### מנחת שי

יחד חילוף מ' כתיב וקרי ב' מעבר. ולחצי שבט המנשה נתן משה בבשן: אהליכם ... ידכם. הרי"ם בגו"ל: (יד) ועשרה נשאים. חסר יו"ד קדמאה ומלא יו"ד בתראה וכן מצאתי במסורת כ"י כל נשיאים וכתובים נשיאם כתיב בר מן ד' נשיאים כמו שנמסרו במקרא גדולה סוף פרשת לך לך וזה אחד מהם ורואיתי מסרה אחרת

### מצודת דוד

לכך שלחו להוכיחם כי אולי ישובו: (יד) ואיש. כל אחד מעשרה הנשיאים היה הראש לבית אבותם והמה היו הראשים לכל אלפי ישראל: (טז) מה המעל. ר"ל למה מעלתם בה': בבנותכם. במה שבניתם: למרדכם. לעשות בזה מרידה בה': (יז) המעט. ר"ל וכי העון שבידנו מאז האם קל הוא עון פעור. העון שעבדו לפעור: לא הטהרנו. ר"ל לא נתכפר מכל וכל:

### מצודת ציון

וכן לסניכם לחרב (ויקרא כ"ו) ומשפטיו לחרב: (טז) המעל. המעט

## Commentary Digest

Israel?' Do you mean it as an altar for worshipping pagan deities (which includes two evils)?

(1) *to turn away this day from following the Lord* — i.e. to cease worshipping God, and —

(2) *that you might rebel this day against the Lord* — i.e. to worship instead pagan deities. — A

17. *the iniquity of Peor* — Num. XXV

*and there was a plague in the congregation of the Lord* — in con-

tribe of Manasseh, into the land of Gilead, Phinehas the son of Eleazar the priest. 14. And with him ten princes, one prince of a father's house for each of the tribes of Israel; and they were each one the head of the house of their fathers, among the thousands of Israel. 15. And they came to the children of Reuben, and to the children of Gad, and to the half-tribe of Manasseh, to the land of Gilead, and they spoke with them, saying. 16. "Thus said the whole congregation of the Lord, 'What treachery is this that you have committed against the God of Israel, to turn away this day from following the Lord, in that you have built an altar that you might rebel this day against the Lord. 17. Is the iniquity of Peor too little for us, from which we have not been cleansed until this day, and there was a plague in the congregation of the Lord.

## Commentary Digest

prophet complains of the indifference and complacency of the people of his day, in comparison to the reaction at Gibeah.

13. *And the children of Israel sent* — to warn them, perhaps they would repent. — D

13.-14. *Phinehas ... the priest* —, *and with him ten princes* — There was a suspicion that Reuben and Gad wished to demonstrate with the building of this altar, both political and religious independence from Shiloh. Therefore, Phinehas was sent to plead the cause of a central altar, and the ten princes to ensure the political unity of Israel under Joshua. — A

15. *and they spoke with them, saying* — I.e. they spoke with them to hear what they would reply to the accusation. — P. Y.

Alternatively, the Israelites did not suspect their brethren of erecting an altar for idolatrous purposes. They suspected, however, that the existence of an altar other than the central altar in Shiloh would eventually lead to idolatry. — K. Y. See above v. 12.

16. *'What treachery is this* — The nine and a half tribes considered also the suspicion that the two and a half tribes had constructed this altar for idolatrous purposes They, therefore, asked, 'What treachery is this that you have committed against the God of

יח וְאַתֶּם֙ תָּשֻׁ֣בוּ הַיּ֔וֹם מֵאַחֲרֵ֖י יְהוָ֑ה וְהָיָ֗ה
אַתֶּ֞ם תִּמְרְד֤וּ הַיּוֹם֙ בַּֽיהוָ֔ה וּמָחָר֙ אֶל־
כָּל־עֲדַ֣ת יִשְׂרָאֵ֔ל יִקְצֹֽף׃ יט וְאַ֨ךְ אִם־
טְמֵאָ֜ה אֶ֣רֶץ אֲחֻזַּתְכֶ֗ם עִבְר֨וּ לָכֶ֜ם אֶל־
אֶ֨רֶץ אֲחֻזַּ֤ת יְהוָה֙ אֲשֶׁ֤ר שָֽׁכַן־שָׁם֙ מִשְׁכַּ֣ן
יְהוָ֔ה וְהֵאָחֲז֖וּ בְּתוֹכֵ֑נוּ וּבַיהוָ֣ה אַל־
תִּמְרֹ֗דוּ וְאֹתָ֙נוּ֙ אַל־תִּמְרֹ֔דוּ בִּבְנֹֽתְכֶ֤ם
לָכֶם֙ מִזְבֵּ֔חַ מִֽבַּלְעֲדֵ֔י מִזְבַּ֖ח יְהוָ֥ה אֱלֹהֵֽינוּ׃
כ הֲל֣וֹא ׀ עָכָ֣ן בֶּן־זֶ֗רַח מָ֤עַל מַ֙עַל֙ בַּחֵ֔רֶם
וְעַֽל־כָּל־עֲדַ֥ת יִשְׂרָאֵ֖ל הָ֣יָה קָ֑צֶף וְהוּא֙
אִ֣ישׁ אֶחָ֔ד לֹ֥א גָוַ֖ע בַּעֲוֺנֽוֹ׃ כא וַֽיַּעֲנוּ֙ בְּנֵֽי־רְאוּבֵ֣ן וּבְנֵי־גָ֔ד

תתובון יומא דין מבתר
פולחנא דיי ויהי אתון
תמרדון יומא דין
במימרא דיי ומחר על
כל כנשתא דישראל יהי
רוגזא: יט וברם אם
מסאבא ארע אחסנתכון
עברו לכון לארע
אחסנת עמא דיי די
שרא תמן משכנא דיי
ואחסינו בינגא ובמימרא
דיי לא תמרדון ובנא לא
תמרדון במבניכון לכון
מדבחא בר ממדבחא
דיי אלהנא: כ הלא עכן
בר זרח שקר שקרא
בחרמא ועל כל כנשתא
דישראל הוה רוגזא והוא
גברא חד לא מית
בחוביה: כא ואתיבו בני

ת"א לא גוע בעונו. עקדה שער פג:

## רד"ק

היה בשבטו ראש בית אבות והמה היו הראשים לאלפי ישראל: (יט) ואך אם טמאה. פיר' אם טמאה בעיניכם לפי שאין המשכן שם עברו לכם אל ארץ אחוזת ה': ואותנו אל תמרדו. כמו ובנו אל תמרדו. וכן והתחלקו אותה כמו בה: (כ) מעל מעל. הראשון פעל עבר חציו קמץ וחציו פתח והשניי שם כלו פתח ושניהם מלעיל הראשון מפני השני: לא גוע בעונו. לא גוע לבדו וכמוהו לא אחת ולא שתים לא פעם אחת לבדה ולא שתים לבדן:

## רש"י

שנאסרו הבמות משנקבע המשכן בשילה: (יט) אם טמאה ארץ אחוזתכם. שלא בחר הקב"ה להשרות בה שכינתו: ואותנו אל תמרודו. כמו ובנו אל תמרודו:

## מנחת שי

כ"י אומרת בר מן ד' נביאים וגירסא ראשונה נ"ל עיקר: (כ) מעל מעל. כתב רד"ק בשרשים מעל האחרון שהוא פתוח כולו ומלעיל הוא שם וגם הראשון הוא מלעיל מפני סמיכותו לשם שהוא מלעיל אבל הראשון הוא חציו קמץ וחציו פתח שהוא פעל עבר ור' יהודה כתב כי הראשון מלרע ולא מצאנוהו כן בספרים

## רלב"ג

ויהי הנגף וגו': (יח) ואתם תשובו היום מאחרי ה' והיה אם אתם תמרדו בה' היום ומחר אל כל עדת ישראל יקצוף. והנה אמרו זה כי אולי זה העון מושך לב קצת העם עד שכמעט לא הטהרו ממנו עדין כי קצתם למדו מזה ונסתבכו בחטא הסתבכות מה כי זה דרך המרי ועוד כי הנגף היה בעדת ה' בעבור חטא היחידים מצד התאחדות שהיו מתאחדים בו כלל העם יקרה עונש לכלל בעבור חטא היחיד כמו שביארנו הסבה בזה בעון עכן ולזה יקרא שישובו היום מאחרי ה' ומחר אל כל עדת ישראל יקצוף אם מפני ההתאחדות שיהיה סבה לסור השגחות השם יתברך מהם כמו שבארנו במה שקדם ויקרה מזה העונשים בכללם על חטא אלו השבטים אם תשני המשכם אל החטא ולמדם קצתם מקצתם ולזה אמרו אותנו אל תמרדו כי מרדם בה' יהיה מרד בחטא ויהיה מרד בהם כי יראתם פן יספו בעונם ומצד האחר היה מרד גם כן וזה כי הפרטים הם תחת הכלל שם היתה סנהדרי גדולה אשר כל השבטים היו תחתיהם ואם יפרדו

## מצודת ציון

ופשע: (יח) ומחר. יש מחר שהוא לאחר זמן רב וכן כי ישאלך בנך מחר (שמות י"ג): (יט) ואותנו. ענינו כמו ובנו: מבלעדי. ענינו כמו זולת וכן בלעדי רק אשר אכלו הנערים (בראשית י"ד):

## מצודת דוד

בעדת ה'. אף באלו שלא חטאו היה הנגף על שלא מיחו: (יח) אתם תמרדו. ואנו הלא נקיים אנחנו מזה העון: ומחר. ר"ל לאח"ז בעת התשלומין יקצוף ה' על כולם על שלא מיחו ונהיה כולם נלקים ע"י א"כ בע"כ צריכין אנו למחות בידכם: (יט) ואך אם טמאה. אם בעיניכם טמאה ארץ אחוזתכם לפי שאין המשכן שם ובעבור זה תחשבו לומר שאין השגחת המקום עליכם רק על ידי אמצעית אשר השורר ואליו תעשו המזבח לעולה וזבח: עברו לכם. הלא זאת עשו עברו הנה והאחזו נחלה בתוכנו: ובה' אל תמרודו. כי גם בדבר זה יחשב למורד בה': ואותנו אל תמרודו. כי הואיל ועל ידכם יצא הקצף על כולנו כאלו מרדתם בנו: בבנותכם. במה שבניתם: (כ) לא גוע בעונו. תחסר מלת לבד ור"ל אף שהיה רק איש אחד ואין בדבר חלול ה' מ"מ לא גוע הוא לבד כי הקצף היה על כולם:

18. And you will turn away this day from following the Lord?
And it will be, since you rebel today against the Lord, that
tomorrow He will be angry with the whole congregation of
Israel. 19. However, if the land of your possesion is unclean,
then pass you over to the land of the possession of the Lord,
in which the Lord's tabernacle dwells, and take possession
among us; but do not rebel against the Lord, nor rebel against
us, in your building an altar besides the altar of the Lord our
God. 20. Did not Achan the son of Zerah commit a trespass
in the devoted thing, and wrath fell on all the congregation
of Israel? And that man did not perish alone in his iniquity."
21. Then the children of Reuben and the children of Gad

**Commentary Digest**

formity with the principle of communal responsibility. — A

18. *tomorrow* — at the time of retribution, not necessarily the following day. — D and Z

*He will be angry with the whole congregation of Israel* — i.e. those who are capable of protesting. Moreover, the other tribes may be influenced to emulate you in your worship of idols. — G, A, and D.

19. *However* — if you had no idolatrous intentions, but intend to build a private altar to God. — A

*if the land of your possession is unclean* — i.e. not fit for building an altar, even the במה קטנה, or private altar, as distinct from במה גדולה, or communal altar. "*For the Holy One, Blessed be He, did not choose it to cause His presence to rest therein.*" — R Since the tabernacle was not built on the eastern side of the Jordan. — K

*but do not rebel against the Lord* — to build an altar outside of the central sanctuary of Shiloh, since this is forbidden.[1]

*nor rebel against us* — "*Heb.* ואותנו, *instead of* ובנו אל תמרדו." — R

I.e. if you meant to demonstrate political independence. — A

20. *did not perish alone* — i.e. he caused the loss of thirty-six men in the battle of Ai.[2]

וַחֲצִי שֵׁבֶט הַמְנַשֶּׁה וַיְדַבְּרוּ אֶת־רָאשֵׁי אַלְפֵי יִשְׂרָאֵל׃ כב אֵל ׀ אֱלֹהִים ׀ יְהוָה אֵל ׀ אֱלֹהִים ׀ יְהוָה הוּא יֹדֵעַ וְיִשְׂרָאֵל הוּא יֵדָע אִם־בְּמֶרֶד וְאִם־בְּמַעַל בַּיהוָה אַל־תּוֹשִׁיעֵנוּ הַיּוֹם הַזֶּה׃ כג לִבְנוֹת לָנוּ מִזְבֵּחַ לָשׁוּב מֵאַחֲרֵי יְהוָה וְאִם־לְהַעֲלוֹת עָלָיו עוֹלָה וּמִנְחָה וְאִם־לַעֲשׂוֹת עָלָיו זִבְחֵי שְׁלָמִים יְהוָה הוּא יְבַקֵּשׁ׃ כד וְאִם־לֹא מִדְּאָגָה מִדָּבָר עָשִׂינוּ אֶת־זֹאת לֵאמֹר מָחָר יֹאמְרוּ בְנֵיכֶם לְבָנֵינוּ לֵאמֹר מַה־

רְאוּבֵן וּבְנֵי גָד וּפַלְגוּת שִׁבְטָא דִמְנַשֶּׁה וּמַלִּילוּ עִם רֵישֵׁי אַלְפַיָּא דְיִשְׂרָאֵל׃ כב אֵל אֱלֹהִים יְיָ אֵל אֱלֹהִים יְיָ קֳדָמוֹהִי יְדִיעַ וְיִשְׂרָאֵל בְּסוֹפָא יְדַע אִם בְּמֶרְדָּא וְאִם בְּשִׁקְרָא שְׁקַרְנָא בְּמֵימְרָא דַיְיָ לָא תִּפְרְקִינָנָא יוֹמָא הָדֵין׃ כג לְמִבְנָא לָנָא מַדְבְּחָא לְמֵיתַב מִבָּתַר פּוּלְחָנָא דַיְיָ וְאִם לְאַסָּקָא עֲלוֹהִי עֲלָתָא וּמִנְחָתָא וְאִם לְמֶעְבַּד עֲלוֹהִי נִכְסַת קוּדְשִׁין יְיָ הוּא יִתְבַּע׃ כד וְאִם לָא מִיּוּצְפָּא מִפִּתְגָם עֲבַדְנָא יָת דָּא לְמֵימַר מְחַר יֵימְרוּן בְּנֵיכוֹן לִבְנָנָא לְמֵימַר לֵית

תו"א אל אלהים. (ברכות יב מגלה ל"א שקלים מב):

רש"י

(כב) אל אלהים ה'. אל כל האלהים הוא ה' היודע כי לא במרד וגו' והכפל לו' שני פעמים אלהים בעוה"ז ובעוה"ב: אל תושיענו. כלפי שכינה אמרו: (כג) הוא יבקש. יפרע ממנו: (כד) מדאגה מדבר. מהמת דאגת יראת דבר הרפה עשינו כמו שמפרש פן יאמרו בניכם מחר להרף את בנינו כשילכו להקריב במשכן שילה שמא יאמרו מה לכם ולה' והלא גבול נתן בינינו וביניכם את הירדן זו דאגנו ועשינו כל

רד"ק

(כב) אל אלהים. כמו מלך מלכים ואלהים הם המלאכים יהוא יתברך אל אלהים ואדוני האדנים ואמר שני פעמים לחזק הדבר ולהעמידו: הוא יודע. פי' הוא יודע הלבבות ויודע כוונתנו: וישראל הוא ידע. מכאן ואילך ידע ישראל כי כוונתנו לטובה לא במרד ולא במעל: אל תושיעני. כנגד השם יתברך: (כד) מדאגה מדבר. דאגתנו מזה הדבר מחר יאמרו בניכם

מנחת שי

במדוייקים: (כב) אל ׀ אלהים ׀ יהוה אל ׀ אלהים ׀ יהוה הוא ידע. פסיקתא טובא איכא הכא ודכותייהו טובא בקריא כמ"ש במזמור פ"ט והד טעמא לכולהו וכן בירושלמי פרק הרואה שלשתם שם אחד כן כאינש דאמר בסיליוס קיסר אגוסטוס ובב"ר פ"א גרסינן שלשתן שם אלהים כן וכו' ובזוהר פרש' אחרי מות דף ס"ה אל דא נהירו דחכמת' ואקרי חסד אלהים דא גבורה יהוה דא שלימו דכולא רחמי ועל דא דכר ויקרא ארץ וגו' עוד בזוהר ג' שמות אלו שלשתן יחד הם אחד והוא חותמו של הקב"ה והם נקראים אמת. וכן במדרש שוחר טוב מזמור נ' אל אלקים יי' אל אלקים יי' הוא ידע מה ראו בני גד ובני ראובן להזכיר שמות הללו שני פעמים אל אלקים יי' שבהם ברא את העולם שנאמר אל אלקים יי' דבר ויקרא ארץ. אל אלקים יי' שבהם נתנה תורה לישראל. כי אנכי יי' אלקיך אל קנא כנגד שלש מדות שבהם נברא בחכמה בתבונה ובדעת שנא' ה' בחכמה יסד ארץ. כונן שמים בתבונה. בדעתו תהומות נבקעו ע"כ. ותמה אני על שני גדולי הדור רש"י ורד"ק

מצודת דוד

(כב) אל אלהים ה'. ר"ל ה' שהוא אל על כל אלהים והם המלאכים הקרואים אלהים וכפלו דבריהם לחזק מאמרם: הוא יודע. מאז יודע הוא שלבבינו נאמן לפניו: וישראל הוא ידע. ר"ל וכשהאריך הזמן גם ישראל ידע ויכיר כי כנים אנחנו: אל תושיענו. הסבו פניהם כלפי מעלה ואמרו אם מעשה המזבח היה במרד ובמעל אזי אל תושיענו ביום הזה ולא תאריך אפך: (כג) לבנות. ר"ל אם הכוונה היתה לבנות לנו מזבח לשוב מה' וכו': ה' הוא יבקש. אם הכוונה היתה על זאת אזי יבקש ה' מאתנו וישלם גמול: (כד) ואם לא. מוסב למעלה לומר והם לא עשינו את זאת מהמת דאגה ופחד מדבר אחר אזי ה' הוא יבקש: לאמר. עתה מפרשים דבריהם ואומרים כי אמרנו פן לאחה"ז יאמרו בניכם וכו': מה לכם ולה'. כאלו יאמרו מה לכם לה' ומה לה' לכם ר"ל אין להם חלק בה' ולא ה'

## Commentary Digest

*or if to offer upon it burnt-offering* — I.e. if we intend to use it for sacrifices outside the Tabernacle of Shiloh. — P. Y.

*Himself require it* — "He will punish us." — R

24. *for fear of this thing* — "Because of* דאגת*, i.e. the fear of insulting words we have done this, as the*

and the half-tribe of Manasseh answered, and spoke to the heads of the thousands of Israel. 22. "God, God, the Lord, God, God, the Lord, He knows, and Israel, he shall know; if it be in rebellion, or if in transgression against the Lord, save us not this day. 23. If we have built us an altar to turn away from following the Lord, or if to offer upon it burnt-offering or meal-offering, or if to offer peace-offerings upon it, let the Lord Himself require it; 24. And if we have not rather done it for fear of this thing, saying, 'In time to come, your children might speak to our children, saying, 'What

## Commentary Digest

21. *and spoke to the heads of the thousands of Israel* — There is no need to answer Phinehas, who came to ask concerning the spiritual unity of Israel, for "God... knows," i.e. that there is no intent on our part to build an independent altar for sacrifices other than the one at Shiloh. — A

22. *"God, God, the Lord,* — Our rabbis explain that the children of Reuben, Gad, and the half-tribe of Manasseh referred to the Deity with three Names, the identical Names which are mentioned in reference to the creation of the world[1] and to the giving of the Torah.[2] Thus, they affirmed their belief in the One God who created the world and who revealed His Law to Israel. With this affirmation, they sought to refute the suspicions against them, both that of idolatry, since they believed that the Almighty Himself created the world, and also that of building an altar outside the tabernacle, since they believed firmly in the revelation of the Torah which forbids this. — According to Minhath Shai[3] Others explain *"God of all the divine creatures* (angels), *He is the Lord, who knows that not in rebellion nor in transgression etc. The repetition of the Name of God* (is for the purpose of proclaiming their belief in one God both) *in this world and in the world to come."* — R. K and D differ by explaining that the repetition is merely for emphasis.

*save us not* — *"They directed this statement toward the Divine Presence."* — R and K

23. *If we have built us an altar to turn away from following the Lord* — I.e. if we have built an altar for the purpose of worshipping pagan deities.

לכם וליהוה אלהי ישראל: כה וגבול נתן
יהוה בינינו וביניכם בני־ראובן ובני־גד
את־הירדן אין־לכם חלק ביהוה
והשביתו בניכם את־בנינו לבלתי ירא
את־יהוה: כו ונאמר נעשה־נא לנו
לבנות את־המזבח לא לעולה ולא
לזבח: כז כי עד הוא בינינו וביניכם ובין
דורותינו אחרינו לעבד את־עבדת
יהוה לפניו בעלותינו ובזבחינו
ובשלמינו ולא־יאמרו בניכם מחר
לבנינו אין־לכם חלק ביהוה: כח ונאמר
והיה כי־יאמרו אלינו ואל־דרתינו מחר
ואמרנו ראו את־תבנית מזבח יהוה

**תרגום**

לית לכון חולק במימרא דיי אלהא דישראל:
כה ותחומא יהב יי בינ̇נא וביניכון בני ראובן ובני גד ית ירדנא לית לכון חולק במימרא דיי ויבטלון בניכון ית בננא בדיל דלא למדחל מן קדם יי:
כו ואמרנא נעביד כען לנא למבני ית מדבחא לא לעלתא ולא לנכסת קודשיא:
כז ארי סהיד הוא בינ̇נא וביניכון ובין דרנא בתרנא למפלח ית פולחנא דיי קדמוהי בעלותנא ובדבחתנא ובנכסת קודשנא ולא ימרון בניכון לבננא מחר לית לכון חולק במימרא דיי:
כח ואמרנא ויהי ארי יימרון לנא ולדרנא מחר ונימר חזו ית דמות מדבחא דיי די עבדו

**רד"ק**

לבנינו: (כח) ואמרנו. כאילו אמר ואמרו בנינו כי האבות במקום הבנים והבנים במקום האבות כמו ואותנו הוציא משם:

**מנחת שי**

בהם עושים השכינה חול ח"ו ופירשו אל האלהים ואדני האדנים ועיין שערי אורה סוף ד' ל"ז בשם תמיבי וסוף דף מ"ח: (כה) וגבול נתן ה' בינינו. במקצת ספרים כ"י מדוייקים מלא יו"ד קדמאה וחסר יו"ד תניינא ונמסר עליו לית חסר

**רלב"ג**

מהם ימרדו בזה: (כה) והנה היתה תשובתם כי לא עשו זה לא לעולה ולא לזבח אך להיות להם לזכר כי הם מעם ה' ומאמרו ילאו והמעבר היה רק בינם ובין ארץ ישראל ולזאת הסבה קראו שם המזבח

**מצודת ציון**

(כה) והשביתו. ענין בטול ומניעה כמו שבת מגש (ישעיה י"ד):
(כח) תבנית. צורת:

**מצודת דוד**

בכם: (כה) והשביתו. ובזה ימנעו את בנינו מליראה את ה': (כו) ונאמר. ובעבור זה אמרנו נעשה את זאת לבנות מזבח אולם לא לעולה וזבח: (כז) כי עד הוא. כי רק להיות הוא עד בינינו שגם אנחנו נעבוד את ה' כי גם לנו חלק בו כי המזבח אשר בינינו דומה הוא למזבח ה' ולזה יהבב לעד: ולא יאמרו. ולא יוכלו עוד לומר כזאת: (כח) ונאמר. בהיות המזבח בנוי נאמר כאשר יאמרו בניכם כזאת או נשיב להם ראו תבנית המזבח העומד לעד

## Commentary Digest

Jordan separates them from having a share in the Lord. Since one tribe is divided on both sides of the Jordan this proves that they are in reality one nation, and have as much connection with the Tabernacle as their brethren on the west bank. — K. Y.

27. *But that it may be a witness* — that we worship the Lord on His altar, of which this is a model. — D

28. *we shall say* — i.e. our children, who will be in our stead, will say . . . — K

have you to do with the Lord God of Israel? 25. For the Lord has made the Jordan a border between us and you, you children of Reuben and children of Gad; you have no part in the Lord. 'So shall your children make our children cease from fearing the Lord. 26. Therefore, we said, "Let us now prepare to build an altar for ourselves, not for burnt-offering, nor for sacrifice. 27. But that it may be a witness between us and you, and between our generations after us, that we might do the service of the Lord before Him with our burnt offerings, and with our sacrifices, and with our peace offerings, that your children will not say to our children in time to come, 'You have no part in the Lord.' 28. Therefore, we said, 'It will be when we shall say, "Behold the replica of the altar of the Lord

### Commentary Digest

*Scripture explains: Lest in time to come, your children say, to insult our children when they go to sacrifice in the Tabernacle of Shiloh, lest they say, 'what have you to do with the Lord? Did he not place the Jordan between us and you as a border?' We feared this, and made* (the altar). *Every* דאגה *in the Scriptures is an expression of fear, e.g. "I fear the Jews* (דאג)"[1] *of Zedekiah."* — R

Alternatively, for fear of this very thing, viz. that our children be estranged from the worship of the Lord, we erected this altar. — K. Y.

25. *you children of Reuben and children of Gad* — The fact that the half-tribe of Manasseh is among them will be forgotten. Were they to remember this, they would have no basis for their supposition that the

אֲשֶׁר־עָשׂוּ אֲבוֹתֵינוּ לֹא לְעוֹלָה וְלֹא
לְזֶבַח כִּי־עֵד הוּא בֵּינֵינוּ וּבֵינֵיכֶם׃
כט חָלִילָה לָּנוּ מִמֶּנּוּ לִמְרֹד בַּיהוָה וְלָשׁוּב
הַיּוֹם מֵאַחֲרֵי יְהוָה לִבְנוֹת מִזְבֵּחַ לְעֹלָה
לְמִנְחָה וּלְזָבַח מִלְּבַד מִזְבַּח יְהוָה אֱלֹהֵינוּ
אֲשֶׁר לִפְנֵי מִשְׁכָּנוֹ׃ ל וַיִּשְׁמַע פִּינְחָס
הַכֹּהֵן וּנְשִׂיאֵי הָעֵדָה וְרָאשֵׁי אַלְפֵי יִשְׂרָאֵל
אֲשֶׁר אִתּוֹ אֶת־הַדְּבָרִים אֲשֶׁר דִּבְּרוּ
בְּנֵי־רְאוּבֵן וּבְנֵי־גָד וּבְנֵי מְנַשֶּׁה וַיִּיטַב
בְּעֵינֵיהֶם׃ לא וַיֹּאמֶר פִּינְחָס בֶּן־אֶלְעָזָר
הַכֹּהֵן אֶל־בְּנֵי־רְאוּבֵן וְאֶל־בְּנֵי־גָד וְאֶל־
בְּנֵי מְנַשֶּׁה הַיּוֹם יָדַעְנוּ כִּי־בְתוֹכֵנוּ יְהוָה
אֲשֶׁר לֹא־מְעַלְתֶּם בַּיהוָה הַמַּעַל הַזֶּה
אָז הִצַּלְתֶּם אֶת־בְּנֵי יִשְׂרָאֵל מִיַּד יְהוָה׃

עֲבַדוּ אֲבָהָתַנָא לָא לַעֲלָתָא וְלָא לְנִכְסַת קוּדְשַׁיָא אֲרֵי סָהִיד הוּא בֵּינָנָא וּבֵינֵיכוֹן׃ כט חַס לָנָא מִנָנָא מִלְמֶחְטֵי קֳדָמוֹהִי מִלְמִרַד בְּמֵימְרָא דַיְיָ וּלְמֵיתַב יוֹמָא דֵין מִבָּתַר פּוּלְחָנָא דַיְיָ לְמִבְנֵי מַדְבְּחָא לַעֲלָתָא לְמִנְחָתָא וּלְנִכְסַת קוּדְשַׁיָא בַּר מִמַּדְבְּחָא דַיְיָ אֱלָהָנָא דִי קֳדָם מַשְׁכְּנֵיהּ׃ ל וּשְׁמַע פִּינְחָס כַּהֲנָא וְרַבְרְבֵי כְנִשְׁתָּא וְרֵישֵׁי אַלְפַיָא דְיִשְׂרָאֵל דִי עִמֵּיהּ יַת פִּתְגָמַיָא דִי מַלִּילוּ בְּנֵי רְאוּבֵן וּבְנֵי גָד וּבְנֵי מְנַשֶּׁה וּשְׁפַר בְּעֵינֵיהוֹן׃ לא וַאֲמַר פִּינְחָס בַּר אֶלְעָזָר כַּהֲנָא לִבְנֵי רְאוּבֵן וְלִבְנֵי גָד וְלִבְנֵי מְנַשֶּׁה יוֹמָא דֵין יְדַעְנָא אֲרֵי בֵינָנָא שַׁרְיָא שְׁכִינְתָּא דַיְיָ דְּלָא שְׁקַרְתּוּן בְּמֵימְרָא דַיְיָ שִׁקְרָא הָדֵין בְּכֵן שֵׁיזֵבְתּוּן יַת בְּנֵי יִשְׂרָאֵל מִיַּד

ת"א וישמע פנחס . זבחים ק"ח :

### רש"י

דאגה שבמקרא לשון יראה הוא כמו אני דואג את היהודי' דלדקיהו:(כח)כי עד הוא.שלא סילקנו עצמנו מתורת מזבח:

### רד"ק

(כט) חליל' לנו ממנו . לפי שאמרו להם ואותנו אל תמרודו אמרו הם מחמת עצמנו היינו חדלים מלמרוד בה' הניחו המרד

### רלב"ג

כי עד הוא בינותינו בי ה' האלהים : (ל) וישר הדבר בעיני פנחס ובעיני הנשיאים וישבו מאתם אל בני ישראל וברכו בני ישר' את השם

### מנחת שי

וכן הוא בדפוסים ישנים :(ל) וייטב בעיניהם . כתיב במכלול דף קכ"ד וייטב בעיניהם בעיני גד ובני ראובן נעדרה היו"ד פ"א הפעל מהמכתב כמו ויגדו לשאול וישר הדבר

### מצודת דוד

כי הלא לא נעבד עליו עולה וזבח ואם לא להיות לעד על מה נבנה : (כט) חלילה לנו ממנו . המרד בה' הוא חולין לנו מלד עצמינו . מבלי דבר התוכחה : מלבד . להיות עוד אחד זולת המזבח אשר לפני משכן ה' : (לא) היום ידענו וגו' . כאת בלבבכם להזהר מבוא כדמים ולדבר תחלה פא"פ כי רואים אנו אשר לא מעלתם המעל הזה אשר חשבנו ואדרבה אז בבנין המזבח הצלתם את בני ישראל מיד מכות

### מצודת ציון

(כט) חלילה . היא מל' חולין וגנאי :

## Commentary Digest

*Then you have saved the children of Israel from the hand of the Lord* — i.e. by building this altar, you have prevented the children of Israel from causing your children to cease fearing the Lord. Had they done so, they would surely have been punished by the hand of the Lord. Thus, you have saved them from that punishment. — D

which our fathers made, not for burnt-offerings, nor for sacrifices, but it is a witness between us and you. 29. Far be it from us that we should rebel against the Lord, and turn away this day from following the Lord, to build an altar for burnt offerings, for meal-offerings, or for sacrifices, besides the altar of the Lord our God that is before His tabernacle." 30. And Phinehas the priest and the princes of the congregation and the heads of the thousands of Israel who were with him, heard the words that the children of Reuben and the children of Gad and the children of Manasseh spoke, and it pleased them.
31. And Phinehas the son of Eleazar the priest said to the children of Reuben and to the children of Gad and to the children of Manasseh, "Today we know that the Lord is in our midst, that you did not commit this treachery. Then you have saved the children of Israel from the hand of the Lord."

## Commentary Digest

*'Behold the replica of the altar . . . not for burnt offerings* — Why then was it built? —

*but it is a witness between us and you.* — D — *"that we have not withdrawn ourselves from the law of the altar."* — R I.e. this model altar is symbolic that we are affiliated with the altar in Shiloh.

29. *Far be it from us to rebel against the Lord* — As a reply to the admonition in v. 18, the children of Reuben and Gad and the half-tribe of Manasseh state that they have no thought of ever rebelling against the Lord, and that no admonition is necessary. — K

31. *"Today we know that the Lord is in our midst* — since He withheld us from bloodshed by giving us the idea to discuss the matter before attacking. — D

*that you did not commit this treachery* — for we see that the truth is that you did not commit this treachery. — D

לב וַיָּשָׁב פִּינְחָס בֶּן־אֶלְעָזָר הַכֹּהֵן | 
וְהַנְּשִׂיאִים מֵאֵת בְּנֵי־רְאוּבֵן וּמֵאֵת בְּנֵי־
גָד מֵאֶרֶץ הַגִּלְעָד אֶל־אֶרֶץ כְּנַעַן אֶל־בְּנֵי
יִשְׂרָאֵל וַיָּשִׁבוּ אוֹתָם דָּבָר׃ לג וַיִּיטַב
הַדָּבָר בְּעֵינֵי בְּנֵי יִשְׂרָאֵל וַיְבָרְכוּ אֱלֹהִים
בְּנֵי יִשְׂרָאֵל וְלֹא אָמְרוּ לַעֲלוֹת עֲלֵיהֶם
לַצָּבָא לְשַׁחֵת אֶת־הָאָרֶץ אֲשֶׁר בְּנֵי־
רְאוּבֵן וּבְנֵי־גָד יֹשְׁבִים בָּהּ׃ לד וַיִּקְרְאוּ
בְּנֵי־רְאוּבֵן וּבְנֵי־גָד לַמִּזְבֵּחַ כִּי־עֵד הוּא
בֵּינֹתֵינוּ כִּי יְהוָה הָאֱלֹהִים׃ כג א וַיְהִי
מִיָּמִים רַבִּים אַחֲרֵי אֲשֶׁר־הֵנִיחַ יְהוָה
לְיִשְׂרָאֵל מִכָּל־אֹיְבֵיהֶם מִסָּבִיב וִיהוֹשֻׁעַ
זָקֵן בָּא בַּיָּמִים׃ ב וַיִּקְרָא יְהוֹשֻׁעַ

**תרגום**

מִיַד מֵימְרָא דַיְיָ׃ לב וְתָב
פִּינְחָס בַּר אֶלְעָזָר כַּהֲנָא
וְרַבְרְבַיָא מִלְוָת בְּנֵי
רְאוּבֵן וּמִלְוָת בְּנֵי גָד
מֵאַרְעָא גִלְעָד לְאַרְעָא
דִכְנַעַן לְוָת בְּנֵי יִשְׂרָאֵל
וַאֲתִיבוּ יַתְהוֹן פִּתְגָמָא׃
לג וּשְׁפַר פִּתְגָמָא בְּעֵינֵי
בְּנֵי יִשְׂרָאֵל וְאוֹדִיאוּ קֳדָם
יְיָ בְּנֵי יִשְׂרָאֵל וְלָא אֲמַרוּ
לְמִיסַק עֲלֵיהוֹן לְחֵילָא
לְחַבָּלָא יַת אַרְעָא דִבְנֵי
רְאוּבֵן וּבְנֵי גָד יָתְבִין
בַּהּ׃ לד וּקְרוֹ בְנֵי רְאוּבֵן
וּבְנֵי גָד לְמַדְבְּחָא אֲרֵי
סָהִיד הוּא בֵּינָנָא אֲרֵי
יְיָ הוּא אֱלָהִים׃ א וַהֲוָה
לִזְמַן יוֹמִין סַגִיאִין בָּתַר
דְאָנִיחַ יְיָ לְיִשְׂרָאֵל מִכָּל
בַּעֲלֵי דְבָבֵיהוֹן מִסְחוֹר
סְחוֹר וִיהוֹשֻׁעַ סִיב עַל
בְּיוֹמִין׃ ב וּקְרָא יְהוֹשֻׁעַ
לכל

ת״א ולא אמרו לעלות. פקדה שער פ״ה:

**רד״ק**

שהינו מורדים בכם: (לד) ויקראו. פי׳ קראו למזבח עד כי עד הוא בינותינו וכן ת״י וקרו בני גד ובני ראובן סהיד למדבחא הרי זה מן המקראות הקצרים וצריך להוסיף בו תיבה אחת ויקראו בני ראובן ובני גד למזבח עד:

**רש״י**

(לג) ויברכו אלהים. והודיאו קדם ה׳ בני ישראל: (לד) ויקראו בני ראובן ובני גד למזבח כי עד הוא.

**מנחת שי**

בעיניו (שמואל א׳ י״ח) ודומים רבים שם גם המכלל יופי כתב בא ביו״ד האיתן לבד ונפלה היו״ד פ״א הפעל מהמכתב ובספרים שלנו בין בדפוסים ובין בכ״י בשני יודין: (לב) וישבו. במקצת ספרים כ״י ודפוסים ישנים חסר יו״ד וכן נכון על פי המסורת שנמסר (בפרשת שלח לך) וישיבו י׳ ז׳ חסרים וג׳ מנהון ותשיב ואזיל לכולהו ודין הוא חד מן החסרים: (לד) ויקרא בני ראובן ובני גד למזבח כי עד וגו׳. במקצת ספרי הדפוס אחר מלת למזבח עד קרי ולא כתיב וכן נראה מפירוש בעלי כלי יקר ולא נמצא כן בספרים כ״י וגם רש״י כתב הרי זה מן המקראות הקצרים וצריך להוסיף בו תיבה אחת ויקראו בני ראובן ובני גד למזבח עד וכן משמע מפירוש רד״ק. גם בתרגומים שלנו ליכא מלת סהיד ורד״ק כתב שתרגום יונתן וקרו בני גד ובני ראובן סהיד למדבחא וכו׳ ומכל מקום אף לפי דבריו אינו אלא כמפרש. וכן כתב בעל לב אהרן המפרשים אמרו שחסר מלת עד:

**רלב״ג**

הנכבד ששמר אותם מעלות לצבא: (ב) ואחר זה זכר שכבר קרא יהושע לכל ישראל רוצה לומר למנהיגים אותם כי הוא רחוק שידבר

**מצודת דוד**

ה׳ כי מעתה לא יחטאו להשבית את בניכם מליראה את ה׳ ולא יענשו מבא״כ אם הכביתו כי אז לא היו נצולים מעונש: (לב) דבר. תשובה על דברי הבליהות: (לג) ויברכו אלהים. על אשר נתן בלבם ישלוח להם טרם ילחמו: ולא אמרו. לא חשבו עוד להלחם בם כי קבלו דבריהם הנאמרים באמת: (לד) ויקראו וגו׳ למזבח. תחסר מלת עד ור״ל ויקראו וכו׳ למזבח עד כי עד הוא ביניהו ובין בני ישראל היושבים בעבר הירדן המערבי אשר ה׳ הוא האלהים וכמוהם כמונו מאמינים את זאת באמונה שלימה: כג (א) מימים רבים.

32. And Phinehas the son of Eleazar the priest, and the princes,
returned from the children of Reuben, and from the children
of Gad, from the land of Gilead, to the land of Canaan, to the
children of Israel, and they brought them back word. 33. And
the thing pleased the children of Israel; and the children of
Israel blessed God, and they did not intend to go up against
them in battle, to destroy the land in which the children of
Reuben and Gad dwelt. 34. And the children of Reuben and
the children of Gad called the altar: 'for it is a witness between
us that the Lord is God.'

23

1. And it was after many days, after the Lord had given rest
to Israel from all their enemies round about, and Joshua was
old and come along in years; 2. That Joshua called

### Commentary Digest

32. *and they brought them back word* — a report of the success of their mission. — D

33. *And the thing pleased the children of Israel* — i.e. they accepted the statement of the children of Gad, Reuben, and Manasseh.

*and the children of Israel blessed God* — *"And the children of Israel thanked God."* — R from J Lest we render: And God blessed the children of Israel, with "blessed" appearing in the plural form, R quotes J to emphasize that "the children of Israel" is the subject. R also wishes to indicate that blessing the Almighty is not to be understood in the same sense as blessing a mortal. It is to be understood in the sense of thanksgiving.[1] They thanked the Lord for inspiring them with the plan to approach their brethren before attacking them. — D

*and they did not intend* — any longer to go up against them in battle, because they accepted their statement as the truth. — D M rejects this interpretation as being too obvious. The Scripture need not tell us that after the children of Israel had accepted the statement of their brothers, that they no longer intended to attack them. He, therefore, explains the entire verse in a different light. One may think that there was strife

לְכָל־יִשְׂרָאֵל לִזְקֵנָיו וּלְרָאשָׁיו וּלְשֹׁפְטָיו
וּלְשֹׁטְרָיו וַיֹּאמֶר אֲלֵהֶם אֲנִי זָקַנְתִּי בָּאתִי
בַּיָּמִים׃ ג וְאַתֶּם רְאִיתֶם אֵת כָּל־אֲשֶׁר
עָשָׂה יְהוָה אֱלֹהֵיכֶם לְכָל־הַגּוֹיִם הָאֵלֶּה
מִפְּנֵיכֶם כִּי יְהוָה אֱלֹהֵיכֶם הוּא הַנִּלְחָם
לָכֶם׃ ד רְאוּ הִפַּלְתִּי לָכֶם אֶת־הַגּוֹיִם
הַנִּשְׁאָרִים הָאֵלֶּה בְּנַחֲלָה לְשִׁבְטֵיכֶם
מִן־הַיַּרְדֵּן וְכָל־הַגּוֹיִם אֲשֶׁר הִכְרַתִּי וְהַיָּם
הַגָּדוֹל מְבוֹא הַשָּׁמֶשׁ׃ ה וַיהוָה אֱלֹהֵיכֶם
הוּא יֶהְדֳּפֵם מִפְּנֵיכֶם וְהוֹרִישׁ אֹתָם
מִלִּפְנֵיכֶם וִירִשְׁתֶּם אֶת־אַרְצָם כַּאֲשֶׁר
דִּבֶּר יְהוָה אֱלֹהֵיכֶם לָכֶם׃ ו וַחֲזַקְתֶּם
מְאֹד לִשְׁמֹר וְלַעֲשׂוֹת אֵת כָּל־הַכָּתוּב

לכל ישראל לסבוהי
ולרישוהי ולדינוהי
ולסרכוהי ואמר להון
אנא סיבית עלית
ביומין׃ ג ואתון חזיתון
ית כל דעבד יי אלהכון
לכל עממיא האלין מן
קדמיכון ארי יי אלהכון
מימריה מגיח לכון׃
ד חזו די פליגית לכון ית
עממיא די אשתארו
האלין באחסנא
לשבטיכון מן ירדנא
וכל עממיא די שיציתי
וימא רבא מעלני
שמשא׃ ה ויי אלהכון
הוא יתבריניון מן
קדמיכון ויתרך יתהון
מן קדמיכון ותירתון ית
ארעהון כמא די מליל יי
אלהכון לכון׃ ו ותתקפון
לחדא למטר ולמעבד
ית כל דכתיב בספר
אוריתא

רש"י

**כג** (ד) ראו הפלתי לכם. בגורל לנחלה: הגוים הנשארים. ליכבש:

רד"ק

ארי סהיד הוא ביננא: (ד) והים הגדול. פי' ועד הים הגדול כמו שכתוב ועד הים הגדול מבוא השמש יהיה גבולכם: (ה) יהדפם. בקמץ חטף הדל"ת:

רלב"ג

**דבריו** עם כל ישראל והנה אלו המנהיגים זכר בהדרגה וזכר הזקנים תחלה והם הסנהדרין לפי מה שאחשוב כי שם היה קבוץ החכמים והם המנהיגים כל העם ואחר זכר ראשי העם והם הנשיאים שכל א' מהם ראש לשבט אחד ואחר זכר ראשי עיר ועיר והם השופטים והשוטרים והודיעם מה שנמשך להם מהטוב בלכתם אחר השם יתעלה ומה שנמשך להם מהרע בעזבם אותו ולזה הזהיר' מהתחתן בגוים הנשארים בזמן ההוא כדי שלא ילמדו ממעשיהם ויבואו לעבור ברית ה' ולעבוד אלהים אחרים והזהירם גם כן שלא יזכירו שם אלהיהם ולא יגרמו להשבע בהם ושלא יעבדום ושלא ישתחוו כמו שבאו האזהרות על כל זה בתורה להודיעם שאם יעבו זה יהיה סבה לאבדם

מנחת שי

**כג** (ג) **לכל** הגוים האלה מפניכם. כן כתיב מפניכם לא מלפניכם. **ורחים** לדבר ממסורת (פרשת עקב) מלפניכם ג' וסימן והוריש ה' את כל הגוים האלה דהתם. וה' אלהיכם הוא יהדפם. תנינא דפסוק ידוע תדעו כי לא יוסיף וגו' לקמן בפרשה ולא נזכר זה בתוכם. כך נ"ל להגיה מסרה זו **שיש**

מצודת דוד

**מסוף** ימים רבים:(ג) הגוים האלה. אשר כבר כבשתם: (ד) הפלתי וגו'. ר"ל הפלתי הגורל להם וכו': הנשארים. אשר עדיין לא כבשתם: בנחלה. להלקם בנחלה להשבטים: מן הירדן. היושבים מן הירדן והלאה כלפי המערב: וכל הגוים וגו'. גם הם חלקתים בגורל: והים. מוסב על מן הירדן לומר מן הירדן ועד הים הגדול העומד במבוא השמש: (ה) יהדפם. את הנשארים:

מצודת ציון

(ג) לכם. בשבילכם: (ד) מבוא. ענין שקיעה כמו כי **בא** השמש (בראשית כ"ח): (ה) יהדפם. ענין דחיפה והכאה **כמו** תדפנו רוח (תהלים א): והוריש. יגרש:

## Commentary Digest

sensed the importance of admonishing the leaders of the people separately, for the fate of the people ultimately rests on the competence and integrity of its leaders. — G

A explains that Joshua actually called together the entire nation, and standing before him were the leaders enumerated, who could bear witness to Joshua's age.

*their officers* — Heb. שוטרים. See Commentary Digest to I:10.

3. *for the Lord your God, it is He that has fought for you* — The generation of the conquest was witness to the incontrovertibly divine, miraculous

all of Israel, their elders, and their heads, and their judges,
and their officers, and he said to them, "I am old and come
along in years. 3. And you have seen all that the Lord your
God has done to all these nations before you; for the Lord
your God, it is He that has fought for you. 4. Behold, I have
allotted to you for an inheritance, to your tribes, these nations
that remain from the Jordan, with all the nations that I have
cut off, to the Great Sea toward the setting of the sun. 5. And
the Lord your God, He shall push them out from before
you, and drive them out from before you, and you will
inherit their land, as the Lord your God has spoken to you.
6. And you shall be very resolute to keep and do all that is
written

## Commentary Digest

and jealousy between the two segments of Israel, and that the altar was but an excuse for entering into a civil war. Therefore, the Scripture tells us that: "...the thing pleased the children of Israel." They were happy that bloodshed was unnecessary, "and the children of Israel blessed God" and thanked Him for this, for *'they had never intended* to go up against them in battle, to destroy the land in which the children of Reuben and Gad dwelt.' They had intended to cause them to repent had they erected the altar for sacrifice. They feared they would be forced to attack them, but they never wanted to do so.

34. *And the children of Reuben and the children of Gad called the altar —: 'for it is a witness...'* — *"This is one of the short verses. It requires the addition of one word: 'And the children of Reuben and the children of Gad called the altar 'Witness.'"* — R, K, and D K quotes J as paraphrasing: 'called the altar 'witness.' M renders: 'called the altar (a name fitting its purpose), for it is a witness...'

CHAPTER 23

1. *and Joshua was old* — See above XI:18 and Commentary Digest.

2. *And Josdua called all Israel* — namely, elders, and their heads, and judges, etc. He did not call the entire nation, but its leaders, who represented it. Joshua

בְּסֵפֶר תּוֹרַת מֹשֶׁה לְבִלְתִּי סוּר מִמֶּנּוּ
יָמִין וּשְׂמֹאול׃ ז לְבִלְתִּי־בוֹא בַּגּוֹיִם
הָאֵלֶּה הַנִּשְׁאָרִים הָאֵלֶּה אִתְּכֶם וּבְשֵׁם
אֱלֹהֵיהֶם לֹא־תַזְכִּירוּ וְלֹא תַשְׁבִּיעוּ וְלֹא
תַעַבְדוּם וְלֹא תִשְׁתַּחֲווּ לָהֶם׃ ח כִּי אִם־
בַּיהוָה אֱלֹהֵיכֶם תִּדְבָּקוּ כַּאֲשֶׁר עֲשִׂיתֶם
עַד הַיּוֹם הַזֶּה׃ ט וַיּוֹרֶשׁ יְהוָה מִפְּנֵיכֶם
גּוֹיִם גְּדֹלִים וַעֲצוּמִים וְאַתֶּם לֹא־עָמַד
אִישׁ בִּפְנֵיכֶם עַד הַיּוֹם הַזֶּה׃ י אִישׁ־
אֶחָד מִכֶּם יִרְדָּף־אָלֶף כִּי יְהוָה אֱלֹהֵיכֶם
הוּא הַנִּלְחָם לָכֶם כַּאֲשֶׁר דִּבֶּר לָכֶם׃
יא וְנִשְׁמַרְתֶּם מְאֹד לְנַפְשֹׁתֵיכֶם לְאַהֲבָה
אֶת־יְהוָה אֱלֹהֵיכֶם׃ יב כִּי אִם־שׁוֹב

תרגום

אוריתא דמשה בדיל דלא למסטי מינה לימינא ולשמאלא׃ ז בדיל דלא לאתערבא בעממיא האלין די אשתארו האלין עמכון ובשום טעותהון לא תדכרון ולא תקימון ולא תפלחונון ולא תסגדון להון׃ ח אלהין בדחלתא דיי אלהכון תדבקון כמא דעבדתון עד יומא הדין׃ ט ותריך יי מן קדמיכון עממין רברבין ותקיפין ואתון לא קם אנש קדמיכון עד יומא הדין׃ י גברא חד מנכון ירדוף אלפא ארי יי אלהכון מימריה מגיח לכון כמא די מליל לכון׃ יא ותסתמרון לחדא לנפשתיכון למרחם ית יי אלהכון׃ יב ארי אם מיתב תתובון ותדבקון בשאר

יתיר ו׳

רד״ק

(ז) ולא תשביעו. פי׳ איש את חברו׃ (י) ירדוף אלף. עתיד במקום עבר ורבי׳ כמוהו׃

מצודת דוד

(ו) ימין ושמאל. הוא ענין מליצה והושאל מההולך דרך ישר שאין להטות ממנו לא לימין ולא לשמאל׃ (ז) לבלתי בוא בגוים. שלא תבואו לכלל להיות כמוהם׃ ולא תשביעו. ר״ל את הזולת׃ (ט) ויורש. ובעבור זה גרש ה׳ וכו׳ ואתם. ר״ל ואתם הלא ראיתם אשר לא עמד וכו׳׃ (י) איש אחד. כי אחד מכם היה רודף אלף׃ (יא) לנפשותיכם. בעבור קיום

## Commentary Digest

*nor exact oaths* [*by their name*] — Do not exact an oath from a pagan, since he will swear by his deities. The rabbis interpret this as prohibiting the formation of a partnership with a pagan, since the situation may arise that he will be required to swear.[2]

From the first infraction of the Jewish faith, intermarriage, there will surely follow a succession of even more serious sins: First, to mention their deities; then, to cause to swear by them; then, to serve them, and finally, to worship them by prostrating oneself before them.[3]

8. *But cling to the Lord your God* — See above XXII:5.

10. *One man of you chased a thousand, for it is the Lord your God that fights for you* — This is indisputable proof of divine aid. King

in the book of the Torah of Moses, so that you do not turn
from it right or left. 7. So that you do not come among these
nations, that remain with you; nor shall you make mention of
the name of their deities, nor exact oaths [by their name] and
you shall not serve them, nor bow to them; 8. But cling to
the Lord your God, as you have done to this day. 9. And
the Lord has driven out from before you great and mighty
nations. As for you, no man has stood before you to this day.
10. One man of you pursued a thousand, for it is the Lord your
God Who wages war for you, as He has spoken to you.
11. Take good heed to yourselves, to love the Lord your God.
12. For if you turn

**Commentary Digest**

manner in which the nations of Canaan had been vanquished. It was their duty to transmit these facts to the coming generation, for the Lord would not repeat these miracles simply for the benefit of scoffers. (See the divinely inspired words of N, Ex. XIII:16, also Ps. LXXVIII and CV.)

4. *Behold, I have allotted to you* — "*By lot for an inheritance.*" — R

*these nations that remain* — "*to be vanquished.*" — R Joshua and his Court (of seventy elders) divided all of Eretz Israel to the various tribes, although some of it had not yet been conquered. This was done in order that that part that would subsequently be taken by each tribe would not be considered as an individual conquest (כבוש יחיד), but as an integral part of Eretz Israel.[1]

*to the Great Sea* — lit. and the Great Sea. — K and D

5. *And the Lord your God, He shall push them out from before you* — Although Joshua will be gone, the Eternal will continue to cause His Providence to be with Israel. See E.R. Ex. I:6: Although Joseph and his brothers died, the God of Israel did not die. And the children of Israel multiplied. The continuity of Jewish history, noted in Ch. I, is here again emphasized.

7. *So that you do not come among these nations* — i.e. intermarry with them. — M

*nor shall you make mention of the name of their deities* — See Ex. XXII:13.

תָשֻׁבוּ וּדְבַקְתֶּם בְּיֶתֶר הַגּוֹיִם הָאֵלֶּה
הַנִּשְׁאָרִים הָאֵלֶּה אִתְּכֶם וְהִתְחַתַּנְתֶּם
בָּהֶם וּבָאתֶם בָּהֶם וְהֵם בָּכֶם׃ יג יָדוֹעַ
תֵּדְעוּ כִּי לֹא יוֹסִיף יְהוָה אֱלֹהֵיכֶם
לְהוֹרִישׁ אֶת־הַגּוֹיִם הָאֵלֶּה מִלִּפְנֵיכֶם
וְהָיוּ לָכֶם לְפַח וּלְמוֹקֵשׁ וּלְשֹׁטֵט
בְּצִדֵּיכֶם וְלִצְנִנִים בְּעֵינֵיכֶם עַד־אֲבָדְכֶם
מֵעַל הָאֲדָמָה הַטּוֹבָה הַזֹּאת אֲשֶׁר נָתַן
לָכֶם יְהוָה אֱלֹהֵיכֶם׃ יד וְהִנֵּה אָנֹכִי הוֹלֵךְ
הַיּוֹם בְּדֶרֶךְ כָּל־הָאָרֶץ וִידַעְתֶּם בְּכָל־
לְבַבְכֶם וּבְכָל־נַפְשְׁכֶם כִּי לֹא־נָפַל דָּבָר
אֶחָד מִכֹּל ׀ הַדְּבָרִים הַטּוֹבִים אֲשֶׁר
דִּבֶּר יְהוָה אֱלֹהֵיכֶם עֲלֵיכֶם הַכֹּל בָּאוּ

בִּשְׁאָר עַמְמַיָא הָאִלֵין דִי
אִשְׁתְּאָרוּ הָאִלֵין עִמְכוֹן
וְתִתְחַתְּנוּן בְּהוֹן
וְתִתְעָרְבוּן בְּהוֹן וְאִינוּן
וְיִתְעָרְבוּן בְּכוֹן: יג מִדַע
תִּדְעוּן אֲרֵי לָא יוֹסִיף
מֵימְרָא דַיְיָ אֱלָהֲכוֹן
לְתָרָכָא יָת עַמְמַיָא
הָאִלֵין מִן קֳדָמֵיכוֹן וִיהוֹן
לְכוֹן לְתַבִּיר וּלְתַקְלָא
וּלְסִיעַן נַטְלָן זַיִן
לְקִבְלֵיכוֹן וּלְמַשִׁרְיָן
מַקְּפָנְכוֹן עַד דְתֵיבְדוּן
מֵעַל אַרְעָא טַבְתָא הָדָא
דִיהַב לְכוֹן יְיָ אֱלָהֲכוֹן:
יד וְהָא אֲנָא אָזֵיל יוֹמָא
דֵין בְּאוֹרַח כָּל אַרְעָא
וְתִדְעוּן בְּכָל לִבְּכוֹן
וּבְכָל נַפְשְׁכוֹן אֲרֵי לָא
בְטֵיל פִּתְגָמָא חָדָא מִכָּל
פִּתְגָמַיָא תַקִּינַיָא דִי מַלֵיל
יְיָ אֱלָהֲכוֹן עֲלֵיכוֹן כּוּלְהוֹן
אִתְקַיָמוּ לְכוֹן לָא בְטֵיל
מִנְכוֹן

### רש״י

(יג) ולשוטט בצדיכם. ישוטטו לבוז ולשלול סביבותיכם: ולצנינים. לשון מסוכות וכן ובצו עליך הצן כלנה זו המקפת את האדם מכל רוחות כמו שנא׳ כצנה רצון תעטרני תסובבנו כמו גשאול ואנשיו עוטרים אל דוד ואל אנשיו עוטרי׳ סובבים;

### רלב״ג

מעל האדמה הטובה אשר נתן להם ה׳ ולזה הותם לאהבה את ה׳ ולדבקה בו ושיחזקו מאד לשמור ולעשות ככל הכתוב ולבלתי סור ממנו ימין

### מצודת דוד

ושבותיכם: (יב) תשובו. מאחרי ה׳ ובאה׳ בהם לקחת מבנותיהם: (יג) והיו לכם. הע״ג האלה: ולשוטט. ר״ל יבאיבו לכם כמכת השוט וכקוץ המנקר העין: (יד) בדרך כל הארץ. בדרך אשר כל הבריות הולכים בם ור״ל הנה אמות ככל בני אדם ולא ארא׳ בכל אשר יקרא אתכם לאחר זמן: וידעתם וגו׳. ר״ל עתה דעו והבינו בכל לב ובכל נפש את הקורות כי הלא לא נפל דבר מהדברים הטובים אשר דבר ה׳:

### רד״ק

(יג) ולשוטט. כמו ולשוט מן שוט לסוס: (יד) וידעתם בכל לבבכם ובכל נפשכם. כלומר שימו לבבכם ודעתכם על כל הדברי׳ הטובים שבאו אליכם ולא יתכן להיותם מקרים אלא בכונת מכוין אשר יעד אתכם בכל הטוב הזה ולא נפל דבר אחד מכל דברו אשר דבר תוכלו להכיר כי מאתו בא לכם הכל:

### מנחת שי

בלבול בדפוס: (יד) מכל הדברים הטובים. במקצת דפוסים ישנים כתיב: מִכָּל־הדברים בקמץ ובמקף ובכל ספרים כ״י ובאחר דפוסים בהולם ובמפס

### מצודת ציון

(יב) והתחתנתם. מלשון חתון: (יג) לפח. לרשת: ולמוקש. למכשול: ולשוטט. ענין שב׳ כמו שוט לסוס (משלי כ״ו) ובכסלם למ״ד ספעל: ולצננים. ענין קוצים וכן וצנים בצדיכם (במדבר ל״ג):

away, and cling to he remnant of these nations, that remain with you; and intermarry with them and mingle with them and they with you; 13. Know of a certainty that the Lord your God will not drive these nations out from before you, anymore; and they will be a snare and an obstacle to you, and a goad in your sides and thorns in your eyes, until you perish from this good land, which the Lord your God has given you.
14. And, behold, this day I am going the way of all the earth; and you shall know with all your hearts and with all your souls, that not one thing of all the good things that the Lord your God has spoken concerning you has failed; all have happened

## Commentary Digest

David, who slew only eight hundred,[1] attributed the missing two hundred to his own imperfection, which caused divine aid to be diminished.[2]

Returning to v. 8, it is noteworthy that A explains this as a condition: For if you cling to the Lord your God as you have done to this day; and therefore, has the Lord driven out from before you..., then, one man *will* chase a thousand, etc.

13. *a goad* — or whip, as: A whip (שוט) for the horse.[3] — K and Z

*and thorns* — Z I.e. they will cause you pain like a goad and like thorns. — D R explains: לשוטט in your sides — *"They will go about* (ישוטטו) *to pillage and loot around you."* — R

ולצננים — *"an expression meaning camps. And similar to this: "and they shall come upon you with camps* (הצן)*,"[4] like a shield* (כצנה) *which encompasses a person from three sides, as it is stated: "as with a shield* (כצנה)*," "with favor* (תעטרנו) *you encompass him,"[5] similar to: "and Saul and his men were surrounding* (עוטרים) *David and his men."[6]* עוטרים *means surrounding* (or encompassing)." — R

14. *the way of all the earth* — the way all earthly creatures must go, i.e. I am going to die. — D

*and you shall know with all your hearts and with all your souls* — i.e. you shall take to heart and understand that not one of all the good things... has failed. — D Reflect upon all the wondrous things which the Lord promised you and how He fulfilled His promise completely. This

לָכֶם לֹא־נָפַל מִמֶּנּוּ דָּבָר אֶחָד׃ טו וְהָיָה
כַּאֲשֶׁר־בָּא עֲלֵיכֶם כָּל־הַדָּבָר הַטּוֹב
אֲשֶׁר דִּבֶּר יְהוָה אֱלֹהֵיכֶם אֲלֵיכֶם כֵּן
יָבִיא יְהוָה עֲלֵיכֶם אֵת כָּל־הַדָּבָר הָרָע
עַד־הַשְׁמִידוֹ אוֹתְכֶם מֵעַל הָאֲדָמָה
הַטּוֹבָה הַזֹּאת אֲשֶׁר נָתַן לָכֶם יְהוָה
אֱלֹהֵיכֶם׃ טז בְּעָבְרְכֶם אֶת־בְּרִית יְהוָה
אֱלֹהֵיכֶם אֲשֶׁר צִוָּה אֶתְכֶם וַהֲלַכְתֶּם
וַעֲבַדְתֶּם אֱלֹהִים אֲחֵרִים וְהִשְׁתַּחֲוִיתֶם
לָהֶם וְחָרָה אַף־יְהוָה בָּכֶם וַאֲבַדְתֶּם
מְהֵרָה מֵעַל הָאָרֶץ הַטּוֹבָה אֲשֶׁר נָתַן
לָכֶם׃ כד א וַיֶּאֱסֹף יְהוֹשֻׁעַ אֶת־כָּל־
שִׁבְטֵי יִשְׂרָאֵל שְׁכֶמָה וַיִּקְרָא לְזִקְנֵי

מִנְּכוֹן פִּתְגָמָא חֲדָא׃
טו וִיהֵי כְּמָא דְאִתְקַיָּמוּ
עֲלֵיכוֹן כָּל פִּתְגָמַיָּא
תַקִּנַיָּא דִי מַלִּיל יְיָ
אֱלָהֲכוֹן עֲלֵיכוֹן כֵּן יַיְתֵי
יְיָ עֲלֵיכוֹן יַת כָּל פִּתְגָמַיָּא
בִּישַׁיָּא עַד דִּישֵׁיצֵי יַתְכוֹן
מֵעַל אַרְעָא טַבְתָא הָדָא
דִי יְהַב לְכוֹן יְיָ אֱלָהֲכוֹן׃
טז בְּמֶעְבַּרְכוֹן יַת קְיָמָא
דַיְיָ אֱלָהֲכוֹן דְּפַקֵּד יַתְכוֹן
וְתֵהְכוּן וְתִפְלְחוּן לְטַעֲוַת
עַמְמַיָּא וְתִסְגְּדוּן לְהוֹן
וְיִתְקִיף רוּגְזָא דַיְיָ בְּכוֹן
וְתֵיבְדוּן בִּפְרִיעַ מֵעַל
אַרְעָא טַבְתָא דִי יְהַב
לְכוֹן׃ א וּכְנַשׁ יְהוֹשֻׁעַ יַת
כָּל שִׁבְטַיָּא דְיִשְׂרָאֵל
לִשְׁכֶם וּקְרָא לְסָבֵי
יִשְׂרָאֵל

תולדות אהרן

ויאסוף יהושע. הוריות יח:

רד"ק

(טו) עד השמידו אותכם. בחולם האל"ף וכן ובראו אותהן ישפטו אותהם: (א) ויאסוף יהושע. פעם אחרת כי הנה כתב למעלה ויקרא יהושע לכל ישראל אלא אסף אותם פעם אחרת והוכיחם פעם ושתים כדי שיהיו נזהרים לשמור התורה: ויתיצבו לפני האלהים. נראה שהביאו ארון האלהים שם כדי לכרות הברית לפני הארון כמו שאמר ויכתוב יהושע בספר תורת אלהים נראה כי שם היה הארון שבו ספר התורה ואספם יהושע שכם ולא שילה שהיה הארון שם אולי על פי הדבור עשה זה שיכרתו הברית בשכם כי בו נתעכב אברהם אבינו תחלה כשנכנס לארץ כמו שכתוב ויעבור אברם בארץ עד מקום שכם ועוד כי שם נעשה נס גדול ליעקב אבינו ושיזכרו אותו וידבקו בה' לבדו ועוד כי תחלת הנחלה אשר היה ליעקב בארץ ישראל בשכם היה שקנה חלקת השדה מיד בני חמור אבי שכם ושם אמר להם יהושע הסירו אלהי הנכר אשר בקרבכם

מנחת שי

גלגל ולגרמיה: (טו) והיה כאשר בא וגו' אשר דבר ה' אלהיכם. בספר אחר כ"י כתוב עליכם וכן תרגום יונתן עליכון וגם במקצת ספרים יש הערה מחילוף זה אולם בשאר ספרים כתוב אליכם: עד השמידו אותכם. אין דומה לו בכל המקרא רצונו לומר לזה הפתוח הה"א כמשפט והמסורת עליו לית דכותיה וכן כתב החכם רבינו יונה בספר הרקמה:

רלב"ג

ושמאל והנה קרא ימין ההוספ' על דברי תורה וקרא שמאל הגרעון ממנה כי בזה יהיה נוטה מדרכי התורה: (א) ועוד זכר אח"ז שכבר אסף יהושע כל שבטי ישראל שכמה והביאם שם בברית ה' כשקיימו וקבלו עליהם שנית לעבוד את ה' והנה עשה זה יהושע להוסיף להם אזהרה שלא יעבדו אלהים אחרים כי נגלה לו מצד הנבואה כי סופם לנקות בזה והנה יוסיף זה להם החזקה מהמשך אחר העון הזה כי הם בעצמם קבלו עליהם זה לפני האלהים ולולי זה לא היה צריך לזה

מצודת דוד

(טו) והיה וגו'. וכמו שהיה כל דבר הטוב כן יהיה כל דבר הרע: (טז) בעברכם. כאשר תעברו את ברית ה' וכו': כד (א) לזקני ישראל וגו'. שיעמדו שם במקום כולם: לפני האלהים. לפני הארון אשר הביאו לשכם לכרות לפניו

to you, not one word of it has failed. 15. And it shall be,
that as all the good things that the Lord your God has spoken
to you have come to pass, so shall the Lord bring upon you
all the evil things, until He has destroyed you from this good
land, that the Lord your God has given you. 16. When you
transgress the covenant of the Lord your God, that He has
commanded you, and you will go and serve strange gods and
you will bow to them; then the wrath of the Lord will burn
against you, and you will perish quickly from upon the good
land that He has given you."

## 24

1. And Joshua gathered all the tribes of Israel to Shechem, and
he called the elders of

### Commentary Digest

is irrefutable proof of the existence of the Almighty and His Providence. — K

*not one word of it has failed* — The repetition implies that all God's wonders came about in the proper time, without delay. — T

15. *has spoken to you* — Other versions read: has spoken concerning you. — Minhath Shai from J and other editions of the text.

*so shall the Lord bring upon you all the evil things, until He has destroyed you...* — The Eternal, in His infinite mercy, will not drive you out upon the first transgression, but only after a series of other calamaties has not caused you to return from your evil ways. A detailed account of the progressive hardships visited upon Israel was already enumerated by Moses.[1]

16. *When you transgress the covenant* — The land of Israel was never an unconditional and irrevocable gift to Israel. It was only given on the conditions enumerated by Moses and Joshua, i.e. the observance of the Law. — Rashba[2]

CHAPTER 24

1. *And Joshua gathered all the tribes* — to admonish them a second time to keep the commandments of the Torah. — K It had been revealed to Joshua by prophecy that the Jews would be tempted to worship idols, and be punished for it. He, there-

ישראל ולראשיו ולשפטיו ולשטריו
ויתיצבו לפני האלהים: ב ויאמר יהושע
אל-כל-העם כה-אמר יהוה אלהי
ישראל בעבר הנהר ישבו אבותיכם
מעולם תרח אבי אברהם ואבי נחור
ויעבדו אלהים אחרים: ג ואקח את-
אביכם את-אברהם מעבר הנהר
ואולך אותו בכל-ארץ כנען וארב את-
זרעו ואתן-לו את-יצחק: ד ואתן ליצחק
את-יעקב ואת-עשו ואתן לעשו את-
הר שעיר לרשת אותו ויעקב ובניו

וארבה קרי

ישראל ולרישוהי ולדינוהי ולסרכוהי
ואתעתדו קדם יי: ב ואמר
יהושע לכל עמא כדנן
אמר יי אלהא דישראל
בעבר פרת יתבו
אבהתכון מעלמא תרח
אבוהי דאברהם ואבוהי
דנחור ופלחו לטעות
עממיא: ג ודברית ית
אבוכון ית אברהם
מעבר פרת ואובלית
יתיה בכל ארעא דכנען
ואסגיתי ית בנוהי
ויהבית ליה ית יצחק:
ד ויהבית ליצחק ית
יעקב וית עשו ויהבית
לעשו ית טורא דשעיר
למירת יתיה ויעקב
ובנוהי

ת"א בעבר נהרא. זוהר המזיר (פסחים לו): ואקח. כם סם: ויעקב ובניו. עקדה שער פט:

### רש"י

כד (ג) וארבה את זרעו. חסר ה"א כמה מריבות ונסיונות עשיתי עמו עד שלא נתתי לו זרע:

### רד"ק

כמו שאמר יעקב לבניו בשכם הסירו את אלהי הנכר אשר בתוככם: (ג) וארב. כתיב בלא ה"א וקרי וארבה בה"א ושניהם שוים בדרך הדקדוק ויש בו דרש כי הכתיב הוא לשון ריב ומסה כלומר הרבה נסיונות נסיתיו ועמד בכלם: ואתן לו את יצחק. ולא זכר את ישמעאל כי בן אמה היה ועוד שאמר לו גרש

### מנחת שי

כד (ג) וארב. וארבה קרי והוא חד מן כ"ט מלין דחסרין ה' בסוף תיבותא וקריין וסימן במסרה רבתא. ובירושלמי דפסחים פ' אלו עוברין אמר ר' אחא וארב כתיב כמה ריבים עשיתי עמו עד שלא נתתי לו את יצחק. ד"א נעשיתי

### רלב"ג

כי כמה שנקברו ישראל בעממי׳ הר סיני נקברו אלו הבאים אחריהם: (ב) והנה זכר להם זה הענין מה שאמר שהפליא חסדו השם יתעלה לנו והוא כי מתחלה היו כל אבותינו עובדי ע"ג והיה מושב׳ בעבר הנהר והש"י לקח משם אברהם אבינו והביאו לארץ כנען להיות הארץ ההיא נחלת כדי שיהיה זרעו יותר שלם: (ג) והנה זכר כי הוליך אותו בכל ארץ כנען כי במקומות רבים מהנה היו ובכלם באה אליו הנבואה להורות על שלמות הארץ ההיא למי שהיה מוכן אל השלמות: (ד) והנה זכר שנתן לו את יצחק ולא הזכיר שאר הבנים כי ביצחק לבדו יקרא לו זרע והוא ביצחק זכר שנתן לו את יעקב ואת עשו ולא נמנע מלהזכיר עשו לפי שהיה לו צורך להזכיר כי נתן לו את הר שעיר לירושה ונמנעו ישראל מלהלחם עמם עליה כמו שנזכר בתורה והוא מבני אברהם לא היה אחד שהזכרתו בתורה מלהלחם עמם: וזכר שיעקב ובניו ירדו מצרים והוציאם משם הש"י ע"י משה ואהרן

### מצודת דוד

הברית וכמ"ש בסוף הענין: (ב) בעבר הנהר וגו׳. הזכיר החסדים שעשה עמהם ואמר הלא מעולם ישבו אבותיכם בעבר הנהר ומאד נשתקעו באמונות כוזבות כאנשי הארץ ההיא: תרח אבי וגו׳. ר"ל הלא תרח היה אבי אברהם ואבי נחור ושניהם האב ונחור בנו עבדו ע"ג: (ג) ואקח. בחסדי נטיתי לבו מדרך אביו ואחיו ולקח אותו מביניהם שלא יהי׳ נמשך אחר דעתם הכוזב: ואולך אותו וגו׳. על כי הוא ארץ קדושה ורלוי להשראת שכינה: וארבה. ר"ל אף שהרביתי זרעו מישמעאל כמ"ש וגם את בן האמה וגו׳ כי זרעך הוא (בראשית כא) והוא הלא רק עליו שאל כמ"ש לו ישמעאל יחי׳ לפניך (שם יז) מ"מ עוד נתתי לו את יצחק כאשר הבטחתיו: (ד) את יעקב ואת עשו. כי לטובה יחשב ליעקב שהיה עם עשו בכרס אחד כי הוא שאב כל הזוהמא ויעקב יצא נקי: ואתן לעשו וגו׳. ר"ל מיד נתתי לו חלקו ושלא ישתעבד במצרים להיות נחשב מזרע יצחק להתקיים בו כי גר יהיה זרעך וכו׳ ודור רביעי ישובו הנה (שם טו): ויעקב וגו׳. להיות הם נחשבים לזרע ועליהם יאמר כי גר יהי׳ זרעך ובהם יתקיים ודור

## Commentary Digest

This is to avoid ascribing any divinity to pagan deities.

Joshua recounts here all the favors vouchsafed by the Almighty to the Jewish people. He starts with the surprise favor the Lord bestowed upon the patriarch Abraham, of leading him to truth in spite of his idolatrous background. These verses serve as one of the central themes for the Jew's recounting of the favors of the Almighty on the Seder night.[7]

Israel, and their heads, and their judges, and their
officers; and they presented themselves before God. 2. And
Joshua said to the whole nation, "Thus said the Lord God of
Israel, 'Your fathers dwelt on the other side of the river from
earliest time, Terah, the father of Abraham, and the father of
Nahor; and they served other gods. 3. And I took your father
Abraham from the other side of the river, and led him
throughout all the land of Canaan, and multiplied his seed,
and gave him Isaac. 4. And I gave to Isaac Jacob and Esau;
and I gave to Esau Mount Seir to inherit it; and Jacob and
his children

## Commentary Digest

fore, admonished them a second time against idolatry. — G A explains that Joshua had received no response to his first call. He, therefore, called a second convocation to which he put an ultimatum and received a satisfactory answer.

*to Shechem* — Although the spiritual center was at Shiloh, Joshua chose Shechem as the meeting place for eradicating idol worship in all its forms from Israel. He followed the precedent of the patriarch Jacob, who admonished his household at Shechem, "Remove the strange gods which are among you,"[1] the exact language employed by Joshua.[2] At this very spot, Jacob and his family escaped miraculously from the Hivvites and their allies who were determined to annihilate them.[3] Perhaps the remembrance of this miracle would influence them to cleave to the Almighty, and reject idol worship. Furthermore, this was the first point where Abraham had rested upon entering the Promised Land,[4] and the first plot of ground owned by Jacob.[5] It was, therefore, the fitting site for the covenant between Israel and the Almighty. — K

*before God* — The Holy Ark had been brought from Shiloh to Shechem, upon divine command, for this momentous occasion. — K, A, and D.

2. *on the other side of the river* — Euphrates.

*and they* — Terah and his son Nahor served other gods. — D

*other gods* — J renders: idols of the nations, following the Mechilta, quoted by R[6]: They are not really gods, but others (other nations) have made them for gods over themselves.

יֵרְדוּ מִצְרָיִם: ה וָאֶשְׁלַח אֶת־מֹשֶׁה וְאֶת־
אַהֲרֹן וָאֶגֹּף אֶת־מִצְרַיִם כַּאֲשֶׁר עָשִׂיתִי
בְּקִרְבּוֹ וְאַחַר הוֹצֵאתִי אֶתְכֶם: ו וָאוֹצִיא
אֶת־אֲבוֹתֵיכֶם מִמִּצְרַיִם וַתָּבֹאוּ הַיָּמָּה
וַיִּרְדְּפוּ מִצְרַיִם אַחֲרֵי אֲבוֹתֵיכֶם בְּרֶכֶב
וּבְפָרָשִׁים יַם־סוּף: ז וַיִּצְעֲקוּ אֶל־יְהוָה
וַיָּשֶׂם מַאֲפֵל בֵּינֵיכֶם וּבֵין הַמִּצְרִים
וַיָּבֵא עָלָיו אֶת־הַיָּם וַיְכַסֵּהוּ וַתִּרְאֶינָה
עֵינֵיכֶם אֵת אֲשֶׁר־עָשִׂיתִי בְּמִצְרָיִם
וַתֵּשְׁבוּ בַמִּדְבָּר יָמִים רַבִּים: ח וָאָבִיאָה
אֶתְכֶם אֶל־אֶרֶץ הָאֱמֹרִי הַיּוֹשֵׁב בְּעֵבֶר

**תרגום**

וּבְנוֹהִי נְחַתוּ לְמִצְרָיִם: ה וְשַׁלְחִית יַת מֹשֶׁה וְיַת אַהֲרֹן וּמְחִית יַת מִצְרָאֵי כְּמָא דַעֲבְדִית בֵּינֵיהוֹן וּבָתַר כֵּן אַפֵּקִית יַתְכוֹן: ו וְאַפֵּקִית יַת אֲבָהָתְכוֹן מִמִּצְרַיִם וַאֲתֵיתוּן לְיַמָּא וּרְדָפוּ מִצְרָאֵי בָּתַר אֲבָהָתְכוֹן בִּרְתִיכִין וּבְפָרָשִׁין לְיַמָּא דְסוּף: ז וּצְעִיקוּ קֳדָם יְיָ וְשַׁוִּי קַבְלָא בֵּינֵיכוֹן וּבֵין מִצְרָאֵי וְאַיְתֵי עֲלוֹהִי יַת יַמָּא וַחֲפָנוּן נַחְנָאָה עֵינֵיכוֹן יַת דִּי עֲבָדִית בְּמִצְרַיִם וִיתֵיבְתּוּן בְּמַדְבְּרָא יוֹמִין סַגִּיאִין: ח וְאַעֲלֵית יַתְכוֹן לַאֲרַע אֱמוֹרָאָה דְיָתֵיב בְּעִבְרָא דְיַרְדְּנָא וְאַגִּיחוּ קְרָבָא עמכון

**רד"ק**

את האמה הזאת ואת בנה: (ה) כאשר עשיתי בקרבו. הנגף שנגפתי אותם לא היה בפעם אחד אלא במכות רבות כאשר עשיתי המכות בקרבו: (ו) ותבאו הימה. כנגד אותם זקנים שעברו ים סוף וכן ותראנה עיניכם כנגד אותם זקנים שהיו עדיין בחיים: (ז) ויבא עליו את הים. על פרעה ואע"פ שלא זכרו הרי זכר מצרים או אמר עליו דרך כלל על מצרים ובדרש על כל יחיד ויחיד שבהם אמר שאם היה במצרים אחד שלא היה רוצה להכנס לים היה הגל מורדו לים: (ח) ואביאה. כתיב בה"א וקרי בלא ה"א והענין אחד:

**יתיר ה'**

**רש"י**

(ז) ויבא עליו את הים. על כל יחיד ויחיד שבהם שאם היה היחיד בורח שלא ליכנס בים גל של ים רודף אחריו

**מנחת שי**

לו אורב אין חטא מיתן ליה והין זכה מיתן ליה עיין יפה מראה שם: (ח) ואביאה. כתיב בה"א וקרי בלא ה"א והוא חד מן כ' מלין דכתיבין ה' בסוף תיבותא ולא

**רלב"ג**

כאשר הרבה להכות את מצרים ואחר זה רבו עליהם ורדפו אחריהם המצרים בחיל גדול וברכב ובפרשים והשיגו אותם חונים על הים עד שלא יכלו לברוח מהם והפליא השם ית' חסדו עמהם ושם ענן חושך מאוד בין ישראל ובין מצרים וסבב שטבעו המצרים בים באופן שנזכר בתורה והנה עיני קצת הדור ההוא ראו' בזמן ההוא אלו האותות והמופתים אשר עשה הש"י במצרים ואחר זה ישבו במדבר ימים רבים בסבת המרגלים ואחר זה הביא אותם אל ארץ האמרי היושב בעבר הירדן והוא ארץ סיחון ועוג שני מלכי האמרי ויירשו ישראל ארצם מלך העזר האלהי לא בחרבם ולא בקשתם ואחר זה השתדל בלק בן צפור נלחם בישראל כשקרא לבלעם בן בעור לקלל אותם ולא אבה הש"י לשמוע אל בלעם ויברך ברוך אותם והצילם השם ית' ממנו כמו שנזכר בתורה. ואח"ז עברתם את הירדן ובאת' אל יריחו וילחמו אותם ואח"ז נלחמו בהם בעלי יריחו והם מלכי האמרי והפרזי והכנעני והחתי והגרגשי החוי והיבוסי שנלחמו עם ישראל כמו שנזכר

**מצודת ציון**

(ה) ואנוף. ענין הכאה כמו ונגפו אשה הרה (שמות כ"א): (ז) מאפל. מלשון אופל וחושך:

**מצודת דוד**

רביעי ישובו הנה: (ה) ואנוף. ע"י משה ואהרן: כאשר עשיתי. ר"ל כאשר ידוע לכם מה עשיתי בקרבו: (ז) וישם מאפל. כמ"ש ויהי הענן והחשך (שמות י"ד): ויבא וגו'. ובזה הביא עליו את הים כ"א לא היה האופל היה א"כ רואה אשר ישראל הולכים בים ביבשה ולא היה א"כ רודף אחריהם בראות הנס ההוא ולא היה

## Commentary Digest

dence and faith, through the medium of the ten plagues visited upon Pharaoh and the Egyptians. — A The phrase "went down" (ירדו) as opposed to "were brought down" (הורד), emphasizes also the favor shown to Jacob by allowing him to go down of his own free will, as the father of the beloved sovereign, Joseph, rather than being forced to go down, to fulfill the prophecy to Abraham: "...your seed will be strangers ..."[5]* — Maharal

6. *and you came to the sea* — The second person employed here and in subsequent passages implies that there

went down into Egypt. 5. And I sent Moses and Aaron, and
I plagued the Egyptians, according to that which I did in their
midst; and afterward I brought you out. 6. And I brought
your fathers out of Egypt, and you came to the sea; and the
Egyptians pursued your fathers with chariots and horsemen to
the Red Sea. 7. And they cried to the Lord, and He put
darkness between you and the Egyptians, and brought the
sea upon him, and it covered him. And your eyes have seen
what I have done in Egypt. And you sojourned in the wilderness
many days. 8. And I brought you to the land of the Amorites,
who dwelt on the other side of

## Commentary Digest

3. *and led him throughout all the land of Canaan* — The Almighty began the spiritual betterment of Abraham by leading him into the Holy Land, which, from the creation, is suited to higher spiritual advancement and perfection. — D

*and multiplied his seed* — Heb. וָאַרְבֶּה. — "*defective* הא (וארב) (from the root ריב, to quarrel) *How many quarrels and tests did I cause him to endure before I gave him seed.*" — R[1] I tested him with many tests and he passed them all. — K Reference is made here to the ten tests with which the Almighty tested Abraham. See Aboth, ch. 5, Mishnah 3, Blackman.

4. *And I gave to Isaac Jacob and Esau* — Ishmael is not mentioned in the geneological development of Israel, since he was the son of Hagar the handmaid. Therefore, he is legally not considered a son of Abraham. On the other hand, Esau, Jacob's twin brother, was born of Rebecca the matriarch. Hence, the goodness of the Almighty in separating him from Jacob is of great import. — K D explains the phrase: "And I multiplied his seed" as a reference to Ishmael, as it is stated:[2] "And also the son of the maidservant will I make to a nation, for he is your seed." The following phrase, "and gave him Isaac," is to be understood as a special favor granted Abraham, who was content with Ishmael: "Would that Ishmael live before You."[3] Maharal[4] takes this phrase to include also the sons of Keturah.[5]

*and Jacob and his children went down into Egypt* — in order to be taught there the principles of Provi-

הַיַּרְדֵּן וַיִּלָּחֲמוּ אִתְּכֶם וָאֶתֵּן אוֹתָם בְּיֶדְכֶם
וַתִּירְשׁוּ אֶת־אַרְצָם וָאַשְׁמִידֵם מִפְּנֵיכֶם:
ט וַיָּקָם בָּלָק בֶּן־צִפּוֹר מֶלֶךְ מוֹאָב וַיִּלָּחֶם
בְּיִשְׂרָאֵל וַיִּשְׁלַח וַיִּקְרָא לְבִלְעָם בֶּן־
בְּעוֹר לְקַלֵּל אֶתְכֶם: י וְלֹא אָבִיתִי לִשְׁמֹעַ
לְבִלְעָם וַיְבָרֶךְ בָּרוֹךְ אֶתְכֶם וָאַצִּל
אֶתְכֶם מִיָּדוֹ: יא וַתַּעַבְרוּ אֶת־הַיַּרְדֵּן
וַתָּבֹאוּ אֶל־יְרִיחוֹ וַיִּלָּחֲמוּ בָכֶם בַּעֲלֵי־
יְרִיחוֹ הָאֱמֹרִי וְהַפְּרִזִּי וְהַכְּנַעֲנִי וְהַחִתִּי
וְהַגִּרְגָּשִׁי הַחִוִּי וְהַיְבוּסִי וָאֶתֵּן אוֹתָם
בְּיֶדְכֶם: יב וָאֶשְׁלַח לִפְנֵיכֶם אֶת־הַצִּרְעָה
וַתְּגָרֶשׁ אוֹתָם מִפְּנֵיכֶם שְׁנֵי מַלְכֵי

עִמְּכוֹן וּמְסָרִית יַתְהוֹן
בִּידְכוֹן וִירִיתְתּוּן יַת
אַרְעֲהוֹן וְשֵׁיצִיתִינוּן מִן
קֳדָמֵיכוֹן: ט וְקָם בָּלָק
בַּר צִפּוֹר מַלְכָּא דְמוֹאָב
וַאֲגִיחַ קְרָבָא בְּיִשְׂרָאֵל
וּשְׁלַח וּקְרָא לְבִלְעָם בַּר
בְּעוֹר לְמֵילַט יַתְכוֹן:
י וְלָא אֲבֵיתִי לְקַבָּלָא מִן
בִּלְעָם וּבָרִיךְ בִּרְכָא
יַתְכוֹן וְשֵׁיזְבוּת יַתְכוֹן מִן
יְדֵיהּ: יא וַעֲבַרְתּוּן יַת
יַרְדְּנָא וַאֲתֵיתוּן לִירִיחוֹ
וַאֲגִיחוּ קְרָבָא בְּכוֹן יָתְבֵי
יְרִיחוֹ אֱמוֹרָאֵי וּפְרִזָאֵי
וּכְנַעֲנָאֵי וְחִתָּאֵי
וְגִרְגָּשָׁאֵי חִוָּאֵי וִיבוּסָאֵי
וּמְסָרִית יַתְהוֹן בִּידְכוֹן:
יב וּשְׁלָחִית קֳדָמֵיכוֹן יַת
עַרְעִיתָא וְתָרְכִית יַתְהוֹן
מִן

### רש"י

וקולטו: (יא) וילחמו בכם בעלי יריחו האמורי והפרזי וגו'. כל ז' האומות נזכרין כאן לפי שיריחו עומדות על הספר והיתה נגרה ומנעולה של ארץ ישראל

### רד"ק

(ט) וילחם בישראל. והנה לא ראינו בתורה שנלחם בלק עם ישראל גם יפתח אמר אם נלחם בנו אלא פירושו זו המלחמה עשה ששלח לבלעם לקלל אתכם והראה מתוך מעשיו כי אילו היה יכול להלחם אתכם היה נלחם כמו שכתוב אולי אוכל נכה בו המחשבה חשבה הכתוב למעשה: (יא) בעלי יריחו. והנה לא ראינו שנלחמו בעלי יריחו בהם אבל הכתוב אומר ויריחו סוגרת ומסוגרת מפני בני ישראל אולי יצאו מיריחו מגדולי העיר אל מלכי כנען להזהירם ובין כך נלכדה יריחו והם היו עם המלכי' שנתקבצו אחר כן להלחם עם יהושע פה אחד ואם נאמר כי משבעה גוים שזכר הנה נתקבצו ליריחו לפי שהיתה עומדת על הספר היא מנעולה של ארץ ישראל ונתקבצו שם להלחם עם ישראל הנה לא ספר הכתוב מלחמה זאת ואם היתה למה לא ספר אותה הכתו' זהו דבר תימה אלא הנכון כמו שפירשנו: (יב) שני מלכי האמורי. פי' וגרשה שני מלכי האמורי גם כן והם סיחון ועוג וכן אמרו רבותינו ז"ל שתי צרעות

### רלב"ג

בזה הספר וזה ממה שיורה שכל אחד מהמלכים ההם היה לו חלק מה ביריחו כמו שזכרו רז"ל: (יב) והנה שלחתי לכם הצרעה. ר"ל שהדש

### מנחת שי

קריאה וסימן במסרה רבתא: (י) ואצל ברוב הספרים חסר יו"ד ונמסר עליו ב' חסרים וחד מלא ולא מסייעי וכ"כ בשופטים ו' על פסוק ואצל אתכם מיד מצרים

### מצודת דוד

א"כ נכתב במי היה אבל לפי שהלך בחשך לא ידע מכל זה וכאלו אחריהם היה מבלי דעת כי יה הוא וכבואו נכתב בו: (ט) וילחם בישראל. חוזר ומפרש שהמלחמה היתה במה ששלח אחר בלעם לקללם להלחם עמהם בזה: (י) לשמוע לבלעם. הספיק בידו לקלל כפי מחשבתו: ויברך. ועוד בכך אותם בברכה: מידו. מיד בלק שערך מלחמה בפיו של בלעם: (יא) בעלי יריחו. וחוזר ומפרש האמורי וכו' כי כל מלכי הפו"ג ההם היו אדונים ביריחו כמ"ש רז"ל שכ"א היה לו חלק מה ביריחו לגודל חשיבתה וכולם נתקבלו להלחם בישראל ונפלו בידם: (יב) את הצרעה. היא הטילה בהם

### מצודת ציון

(י) אביתי. ענין רצון כמו לא אבה יבמי (דברים כה): (יא) בעלי יריחו. אדוני יריחו כמו אם בעליו עמו (שמות כב): הצרעה.

## Commentary Digest

*cho is situated on the border, and it was the bolt and lock* (i.e. the fortification) *of Eretz Israel, and the heroic soldiers of all the seven nations assembled therein.*" — R[4] This battle was not mentioned previously.

12. *even the two kings of the Amorites* — i.e. Sihon and Og, on the east bank of the Jordan, in the days of Moses. This is mentioned separately, because there were two different species of "hornet," one aid-

the Jordan, and they waged war with you; and I delivered them into your hand, and you inherited their land; and I destroyed them from before you. 9. Then Balak the son of Zippor, king of Moab, arose and warred against Israel, and he sent and called Balaam the son of Beor to curse you. 10. And I did not want to hearken to Balaam, and he blessed you; so I delivered you out of his hand. 11. And you crossed the Jordan and came to Jericho; and the inhabitants of Jericho fought against you, the Amorites, and the Perizzites, and the Canaanites, and the Hittites, and the Girgashites, the Hivites, and the Jebusites; and I delivered them into your hand. 12. And I sent the hornet before you, and it drove them out from before you, even the two kings of

## Commentary Digest

were many, who, like Joshua, had been present at the exodus from Egypt and the crossing of the Red Sea. They were over sixty or under twenty at the time of the Exodus, and so were not destined to perish in the wilderness, since the decree included only those between the ages of twenty and sixty. — K

7. *And your eyes have seen what I have done in Egypt* — To see Israel avenged was an especial favor. "The righteous will rejoice upon seeing (Divine) revenge."[1] — A

*and brought the sea upon him* — "i.e. upon each individual among them, for if one escaped entering into the sea, a wave of the sea would pursue him and overtake him." — R[2] K explains "him" as referring to Pharaoh.

9. *and warred against Israel, and he sent and called Balaam ... to curse you* — i.e. he warred against Israel not with arms, but by calling upon Balaam to curse them. — K

10. *out of his hand* — i.e. out of the hand of Balak, who waged war upon Israel through Balaam's curse. — D

11. *and the inhabitants of Jericho* — J Z renders: the lords of Jericho. All the Canaánitish kings owned parts of Jericho. — D[3]

*and the inhabitants of Jericho fought against you, the Amorites, and the Perizzites etc. — All seven nations are mentioned here, since Jeri-*

הָאֱמֹרִי לֹא בְחַרְבְּךָ וְלֹא בְקַשְׁתֶּךָ׃
יג וָאֶתֵּן לָכֶם אֶרֶץ ׀ אֲשֶׁר לֹא־יָגַעְתָּ בָּהּ
וְעָרִים אֲשֶׁר לֹא־בְנִיתֶם וַתֵּשְׁבוּ בָּהֶם
כְּרָמִים וְזֵיתִים אֲשֶׁר לֹא־נְטַעְתֶּם אַתֶּם
אֹכְלִים׃ יד וְעַתָּה יְראוּ אֶת־יְהוָה וְעִבְדוּ
אֹתוֹ בְּתָמִים וּבֶאֱמֶת וְהָסִירוּ אֶת־
אֱלֹהִים אֲשֶׁר עָבְדוּ אֲבוֹתֵיכֶם בְּעֵבֶר
הַנָּהָר וּבְמִצְרַיִם וְעִבְדוּ אֶת־יְהוָה׃
טו וְאִם רַע בְּעֵינֵיכֶם לַעֲבֹד אֶת־יְהוָה
בַּחֲרוּ לָכֶם הַיּוֹם אֶת־מִי תַעֲבֹדוּן אִם
אֶת־אֱלֹהִים אֲשֶׁר־עָבְדוּ אֲבוֹתֵיכֶם
אֲשֶׁר בְּעֵבֶר הַנָּהָר וְאִם אֶת־אֱלֹהֵי
הָאֱמֹרִי אֲשֶׁר אַתֶּם יֹשְׁבִים בְּאַרְצָם

מעבר קרי

מִן קֳדָמֵיכוֹן תְּרֵין מַלְכֵי
אֱמוֹרָאֵי לָא בְחַרְבָּךְ וְלָא
בְקַשְׁתָּךְ׃ יג וִיהָבֵית לְכוֹן
אַרְעָא דִי לָא לְאֵיתוֹן בַּהּ
וְקִרְוִין דִי לָא בְנֵיתוֹן
וִיתֵיבְתּוּן בְּהוֹן כַּרְמִין
וְזֵיתִין דִי לָא נְצֵיבְתּוּן
אַתּוּן אָכְלִין׃ יד וּכְעַן
דְחִילוּ מִן קֳדָם יְיָ וּפְלַחוּ
קֳדָמוֹהִי בִּשְׁלָמוּתָא
וּבְקוּשְׁטָא וְאַעֲדוּ יָת
טַעֲוָתָא דִי פְלַחוּ
אֲבָהָתְכוֹן בְּעִבַר פְּרָת
וּבְמִצְרַיִם וּפְלַחוּ קֳדָם יְיָ׃
טו וְאִם בִּישׁ בְּעֵינֵיכוֹן
לְמִפְלַח קֳדָם יְיָ בְּחַרוּ
לְכוֹן יוֹמָא דֵין קֳדָם מַן
תִּפְלְחוּן אִם יָת טַעֲוָתָא
דִי פְלַחוּ אֲבָהָתְכוֹן
דִבְעִיבְרָא דִפְרָת וְאִם יָת
טַעֲוַת אֱמוֹרָאֵי דִי אַתּוּן
יָתְבִין בְּאַרְעֲהוֹן בְּרַם
אנא

ת"א יראו את ה'. כל הפרשה עד. כי את השם נעבוד עקדה שער פט:

## רד"ק

היו חדא דמשה וחדא דיהושע והצרעה הוא מין זבוב רע מטיל ארס ואמרו כי היתה הצרעה מכה בעיניה ומסמא עיניהם ולא היו יכולין לחלחם ובאין ישראל והורגין אותם כמו שאמר לא בחרבך ולא בקשתך ותרגום צרעה ארעיתא ואמר למה נקרא שמה ארעיתא שעומדת לקראת אדם ומכה בפניו כדמתרגמינן אשר קרך דיארעך: לא בחרבך. פי' אם לא היה עזר האל והוא על דרך כי לא בקשתי אבטח וחרבי לא תושיעני: (יד) בתמים. שם לא תואר וכן אם באמת ובתמים: והסירו את אלהים. פי'

## מנחת שי

ועל חברו דשמואל י' וכמלא היא דשמואל: (יד) ועתה יראו. האלף נחה וכמסורת יראו ג' וחביריו יראו את ה' קדושיו (תהלים לד) אך יראו את ה' (ש"א יב): (טו) את מי תעבדון. בחטף פתח העי"ן ובחולם הבי"ת לא כספרים משובשים

## רלב"ג

להם נזקין הוזקו בהן זולת חרב המלחמה: (יד) ואחר שזכר כל הטובות שחנן הש"י את ישראל לוה אותם לירא את ה' ולעבוד אותו ולהסיר את אלהי הנכר מקרבם: (טו) ולפי שידע מתכונתם אז שלא לעבוד ע"ג עם מה שמשך לבם אל זה בדברים אלו אמר להם שאם רע בעיניהם לעבוד את ה' יבחרו להם אלהי אבותיהם אשר מעבר הנהר שהרחיקם הש"י מזה בכל עז ולזה לקח את אברהם משם והוליכו אל ארץ כנען שלא לעבוד אלהי האמרי אשר הביאם הש"י לשבת בארצם כשהורישם את ארצם והנה אמונותיה' הכוזבות ומנהגותיה' הפחותים היו סבה שהקיאה הארץ אותם כמו שנזכר בתורה כי ברשע' הגוים ההם ה' מורישם מפניהם וזה היה ג"כ סבה להרחיק ישראל מאלהיה' לעבדם והודיעם גם כן יהושע עם זה שאם יבחרו לעבוד אלהים אחרים שלא יסכים עמהם אך הוא וביתו יעבדו את ה' כדי להרחיקם עוד מלבחור בע"ג. והנה היה ההשתדלות באלו כדי שיקבלו עוד סדור הבוא לפני האלהים שלא לעבוד ע"ג כי זה היה ראוי שירחיקם יותר מהמשך אחר ע"ג אחרי מות יהושע ועכ"ז לא נשמרו מזה כמו

## מצודת דוד

ארם ולא יוכלו להלחם וכאלו היא גרשה אותם ומזה ומפרש את שני מלכי האמורי סיחון ועוג: לא בחרבך. כי בדרך הטבע לא הייתה יכול לעמוד כנגדם: (יג) אתם אוכלים. את פירותם: (יד) ועתה. הואיל והרבה להיטיב עמכם: והסירו וגו'. ר"ל הסירו מהלב מכל וכל מחשבת ע"ג: ובמצרים. כי רבים מהם עבדו במצרים ע"ג כמ"ש ואת גלולי מצרים לא עזבו (יחזקאל כ'): (טו) בחרו לכם

the Amorites; not with your sword, nor with your bow.
13. And I have given you a land for which you did not labor,
and cities which you did not build, and you have settled in them;
of the vineyards and oliveyards which you did not plant, you
eat. 14. And now fear the Lord, and serve Him in sincerity
and in truth; and remove the gods which your fathers served
on the other side of the river and in Egypt, and serve the
Lord. 15. And if it displeases you to serve the Lord,
choose this day whom you will serve, whether the gods which
your fathers served that were on the other side of the river,
or the gods of the Amorites, in whose land you dwell,

## Commentary Digest

ed Moses in vanquishing Sihon and Og, and the other variety aided Joshua in the conquest of Canaan. — K[1]

*not with your sword nor with your bow* — Had the Almighty not aided you, your weapons would have been of no avail, as the Psalmist says: "For I shall not trust in my bow, nor will my sword save me."[2] — K

14. *and in Egypt* — Joshua makes only fleeting reference to this aspect of Jewish activity in Egypt. See Ezekiel XX for a further elaboration on this point.

15. *choose this day whom you will serve ... but as for me and my household* — Joshua gives Israel a complete freedom of choice in order that they accept of their own free will. He makes it clear, however, that this should not be done in a spirit of condescension and patronage, for there will always be those who recognize the truth and understand the privilege of serving the Lord. In the "generation of the wilderness," it was the twenty-two thousand of the tribe of Levi who remained loyal and did not worship the golden calf. In the Second Commonwealth it was the indomitable Hasmoneans, who were not dismayed by numbers. In the dark of Assyrian domination, it was King Hezekiah who burned the midnight oil of learning and was triumphant.[3] And, in the dark days following the

ואנכי וביתי נעבד את־יהוה: טז ויען
העם ויאמר חלילה לנו מעזב את־יהוה
לעבד אלהים אחרים: יז כי יהוה אלהינו
הוא המעלה אתנו ואת־אבותינו מארץ
מצרים מבית עבדים ואשר עשה
לעינינו את־האתות הגדלות האלה
וישמרנו בכל־הדרך אשר הלכנו בה
ובכל העמים אשר עברנו בקרבם:
יח ויגרש יהוה את־כל־העמים ואת־
האמרי ישב הארץ מפנינו גם־אנחנו
נעבד את־יהוה כי־הוא אלהינו:

אנא ואנש ביתי נפלח
קדם יי: טז ואתיב עמא
ואמר חס לנא מלמשבק
ית פולחנא דיי למפלח
לטעות עממיא: יז ארי
יי אלהנא הוא דאסיק
יתנא וית אבהתנא
מארעא דמצרים מבית
עבדותא ודי עבד
לעיננא ית אתיא וית
גבורתא האלין ונטרנא
בכל אורחא די הליכנא
בה ובכל עממיא די
עברנא ביניהון: יח ותריך
יי ית כל עממיא וית
אמוראה יתיב ארעא מן
קדמנא אף אנחנא
נפלח קדם יי ארי הוא
אלהנא

רלב"ג

מנחת שי

נשלם ביאור ספר שופטים: (טז) ויען העם וגו׳. וסימן העם כי … העברון : בספר … (יז) המעלה אתנו ואת אבותינו … [illegible]

מצודת דוד

וגו׳. הטיב כאשר יבחרו מי אז יכירו מעות לעשות אותם: ואנכי וגו׳. ולא נהיה כמשכים אחריכם: (יח) גם אנחנו. כמו אתם

## Commentary Digest

19. *And Joshua said to the people, "You will not be able to serve the Lord..."* — His intention was for Israel to maintain openly their resolve to serve the Lord in the face of his seeming dissuasion. — D Azulai explains that when the nation answered, "God forbid that we should forsake the Lord, to serve other gods," they did not negate the possibility of worshipping God through intermediaries, such as heavenly bodies or angels, as was done in the times of Enosh.[2] Upon this, Joshua rejoined, "You will not be able to serve the Lord, for He is a holy God; He is a jealous God; He will not forgive your transgressions or your sins." I.e. He will not tolerate polytheism in any form. In such a manner, you will not be able to serve the Lord. Furthermore, *"when you forsake the Lord, and worship strange gods,"* i.e. eventually, you will forsake the Almighty and worship pagan deities exclusively. Thereupon, they replied, "No, but we shall

but as for me and my household, we shall serve the Lord."
16. And the nation answered and said, "God forbid that we
should forsake the Lord, to serve other gods: 17. For the
Lord our God, it is He Who brought us and our fathers up
from the land of Egypt, from the house of bondage, and Who
performed these great signs in our sight, and preserved us in all
the way that we went and among all the peoples through whom
the Amorites who dwell in the land, from before us; we too
shall serve the Lord, for He is our God."

## Commentary Digest

fall of Betar in the year 120 C.E., it was R. Simeon b. Yohai who proclaimed the doctrine of unbending determination of the minority in the face of Roman rule.

17. *brought us and our fathers up from the land of Egypt* — This refers to the patriarchs, Abraham, Isaac, and Jacob. With the delivery of Israel from Egypt, it was as though the patriarchs had been delivered with them. — R[1]

Alternatively, our forefathers' redemption from Egypt is considered as though we ourselves had been redeemed from there. This is in accordance with the Rabbinic dictum *One is obliged to consider himself as though he had come out of Egypt.*[1a] — A

*and preserved us in all the way that we went and among all the peoples through whom we passed* — All roads are perilous, certainly when the neighboring peoples are hostile. — A

*and Who performed these great signs in our sight.* — I.e. the splitting of the Jordan, the siege of Jericho, and the battle of Gibeon, that we ourselves personally witnessed. — A

18. *And the Lord drove out* — For all these reasons we are obligated to serve the Lord. — A

*all the peoples and the Amorites* — The Amorites are mentioned specifically because they were the most powerful of all the nations, and represented the greatest threat to the conquest of the land of Israel.

יט ויאמר יהושע אל־העם לא תוכלו
לעבד את־יהוה כי־אלהים קדשים
הוא אל־קנוא הוא לא־ישא לפשעכם
ולחטאותיכם: כ כי תעזבו את־יהוה
ועבדתם אלהי נכר ושב והרע לכם
וכלה אתכם אחרי אשר־היטיב לכם:
כא ויאמר העם אל־יהושע לא כי את־יהוה
נעבד: כב ויאמר יהושע אל־העם עדים
אתם בכם כי־אתם בחרתם לכם את־

**תרגום**

אלהנא: יט ואמר יהושע
לעמא לא תוכלון
למפלח קדם יי ארי
אלהא קדישא הוא אל
קנא הוא מן קדם דין
דקשוט לא ישבוק
לחוביכון ולחטאיכון:
כ ארי תשבקון ית
פולחנא דיי ותפלחון
טעות עממיא ויתוב
ויבאש לכון וישיצי
יתכון בתר דאוטיב
לכון: כא ואמר עמא
ליהושע לא אלהן קדם
יי נפלח: כב ואמר
יהושע לעמא סהדין
אתון בנפשתכון ארי
אתון בחרתון לכון ית

**ת"א** אלהים קדושים (ברכות יג). מלא ואו

## רד"ק

אלהי כסף ואלהי זהב שלקחו בערים אשר כבשו ובמצרים כמו שכתוב ביחזקאל: (יט) אלהים קדושים הוא. קדושים לשון תפארת כמו אלהים וכן ישמח ישראל בעושיו איה אלהי עושי (כב) עדים אתם בכם. אתם בעצמכם תהיו עדים בכם כי אתם בחרתם לכם את ה' וי"מ עדים אתם בכם הנשמה והגוף וכן

## מנחת שי

פו בעינא לאודועי דהע"ג דבכימן י"ב היושב בחשבון נדפס חסר' טעותא הוא דמפסנא דפוסי ויניליאה ואמשטרדם וא"ל מלא ע"כ): (יט) אל קנוא. כתיב בחילופים ב"א אל קנא ב"נ אל קנוא נראה שהחילוף הוא בוא"ו קנא קנאתי לרוב הטעיות שנפלו בספרים כי בכל המקראות הוא מלא וכן ראוי ע"פ המסורת והפלוגתות שבין ב"א ובין ב"נ אינן באותיות רק בנקודות וטעמים כמה שכתב רבי אליה בהקדמה השלישית למסורת המסורת. וגם חילוף זה הוא בטעם בלבד. ולפי

## רש"י

ונתקבלו לתוכה מכל ז' האומות גבורי החיל: (יט) אלהים קדושים. ברוב מקומות נקרא כל לשון רבנות ל' רבים כמו אדוני הארץ אדוני יוסף אם בעליו עמו אשר הלכו אלהים לפדות לפי שהשם הזה שם שררה הוא (כב) עדים אתם

## רלב"ג

חלילה להם מעבוד אלהים אחרים עם ראותם הטובות והנפלאות שהגנם הש"י. (יט) והנה להרחיקם עוד מעבוד ע"ג אמר להם כי אחר שיכנסו לעבודתו יתברך תקשה להם מאד עבודתו כי לא ישא לפשעיהם אם יסורו מאחריו לעבוד ע"ג אך יכלה אותם אחר הטיב להם ולא אמר להם זה יהושע שיהיה הענין בבחירתם לסור מאחרי ה' כי כבר נקשרו בזה כל הדורות במעמד הר סיני אך אמר להם זה להוסיף להם הרחקה מעבוד ע"ג כמו שזכלנו שם שכבר היה יודע מטוב תכונת' בעת ההיא שהם לא יסכימו בשום פנים לעבוד זולתי הש"י ואחר זה אמר להם יהושע שהם עדים בהם כי הם בחרו

## מצודת ציון

ארז"ל שהוא מין סרן עוף שהטילה בהם ארם: (יט) קנוא. מתנקם ליפרע: ישא. ענין כפרה ומחילה כמו נושא עון (שם לד)

## מצודת דוד

וביתך: (יט) לא תוכלו. כוונת יהושע היתה שיגלו מלפוני באר היטב ולקשרם במוסרי הברית אומר דבריו להטעותם כאלו הבחירה בידם לבחור מי שירצו הם ולדעת מה ישיבו: אלהים קדושים. קדוש בכל מיני קדושות ומאד קשה להיות נזהר בעבודתו: אל קנוא הוא. נוקם הוא מעוברי רצונו ולא ישא הפשעים: (כ) כי תעזבו. וכאשר תעזבו אותו ישוב להרע להם ולכלות אתכם: אחר אשר היטיב לכם. ר"ל ותהיה א"כ הרעה כפולה כי האדם הרגיל בטובה כפול לערו ממי שלא ראה בטובה מעולם: (כא) לא. ר"ל לא נעזוב אותו כי את ה' נעבוד כל הימים ונהיה נזהרים בעבודתו: (כב) עדים אתם בכם. אתם היו עדים בעצמיכם שבחרתם לעבוד את ה' ויאמרו עדים. ר"ל נהיה עדים בעצמינו

19. And Joshua said to the people, "You will not be able to
serve the Lord, for He is a holy God; He is a jealous God;
He will not forgive your trangressions or your sins. 20. When
you forsake the Lord and serve strange gods, then He will
turn and do you evil, and destroy you, after He has done you
good." 21. And the people said to Joshua, "No, but we will
serve the Lord." 22. And Joshua said to the people, "You
are witnesses against yourselves that you have chosen

**Commentary Digest**

serve the Lord." We shall worship the Lord without any intermediaries of any kind. This statement pleased Joshua, and he called them to be witnesses of their acceptance of pure monotheism.—Also found in Akeidah

*a holy God* — Heb. אלהים קדשים, a plural form. *"In most places, every expression of lordship appears in the plural form, like: "The lord of the land* (אדוני),*"*[1] *"Joseph's master* (אדוני),*"*[2] *"if his master is with him* (בעליו),*"*[3] *"that God* (אלהים) *went* (הלכו) *to redeem,"*[4] *because this name* (אלהים) *is a name of majesty."* — R This is known as the plural of majesty.

*a holy God* — He is a most holy God, whose commandments are difficult to follow. — D You must serve Him by emulating His holiness. Joshua wishes the people to be fully aware of the grave responsibility that is theirs upon acceptance of the covenant. If they serve the Eternal only in good times, in the hope of receiving reward, they serve themselves, not the Eternal. — M

*a jealous God* — i.e. unrelenting to those guilty of idolatry. — Z

20. *after He has done you good* — i.e. it will be doubly difficult for you to accept your fate, after you have become accustomed to a comfortable life. — D

21. *"No, but we will serve the Lord."* — We insist that we will serve the Lord, despite any difficulties or hardships involved in His service. — D We will serve Him for *His sake,* not for the sake of receiving reward. — M

22. *"You are witnesses against yourselves..."* — *"Joshua foresaw that they would contest* (this covenant) *in the days of Ezekiel, and say, "Let us be like the nations."*[5] *Therefore, he made it more difficult now. He therefore, answered them in the days of Ezekiel, "And that which enters your thoughts, shall not come to pass, etc. As I live etc., surely with*

יהוה לעבד אותו ויאמרו עדים: כג ועתה
הסירו את־אלהי הנכר אשר בקרבכם
והטו את־לבבכם אל־יהוה אלהי
ישראל: כד ויאמרו העם אל־יהושע את־
יהוה אלהינו נעבד ובקולו נשמע:
כה ויכרת יהושע ברית לעם ביום ההוא
וישם לו חק ומשפט בשכם: כו ויכתב
יהושע את־הדברים האלה בספר

פולחנא דיי למפלח
קדמוהי ואמרו סהדין:
כג וכען אעדו ית טעות
עממיא די ביניכון ואפנו
ית לבכון לפולחנא דיי
אלהא דישראל:
כד ואמרו עמא ליהושע
ית יי אלהנא נפלח
ולמימריה נקביל:
כה וגזר יהושע קים
לעמא ביומא ההוא ושוי
ליה קים ודין בשכם:
כו וכתב יהושע ית
פתגמיא האלין
ואצנעינון בספר

ת"א ויכתוב יהושע. מכות יא:

**רש"י**

בכם. ראה יהושע שעתידין לערער בימי יחזקאל ולומר נהיה כגוים לפיכך הכביד עליהם עכשיו. ולכך השיב להם בימי יחזקאל והעולה על רוחכם היו לא תהיה וגו' חי אני וגו' אם לא ביד חזקה וגו' כבר קבלתם עליכ' בימי יהושע ולא תאמרו מה שקבלנו עלינו בימי משה כדי ליכנס לארץ שעינו הרי בימי יהושע כבר נכנסתם וקבלתם; (כה) וישם לו חוק ומשפט בשכם. סידר להם שם החוקים שבתורה וקבלו עליהם; (כו) ויכתוב יהושע וגו'. ת"י וכתב יהושע ית פתגמיא האלין ואצנעינון בספר אורייתא דה'. ובמסכת מכות נחלקו בו אמוראים חד אמר אלו ח' פסוקים מן וימת

**רד"ק**

האזינו השמי' ותשמע הארץ שמעו שמים והאזיני ארץ הנשמה מן השמים והגוף מן הארץ: (כה) וישם לו חק ומשפט. פי' לו לעם וענינו כמו שם שם לו חק ומשפט שסדר להם דרך כלל חקי התורה והמשפטים וקבלום עליהם או פי' וישם לו חק ומשפט יהושע שם לעצמו חק ומשפט: בשכם. על הברית שכרת להם והחק והמשפט האבן והאלה ששם לעדים ודברי הברי' שכתב בספר תורת אלהים וי"ת ויהושע כתב ית פתגמי' האילין בספרא ואצנע בספר אוריתא דה'. ובדברי רז"ל ר' יהודה ור' נחמיה חד אמר שמנה פסוקים שבתורה וחד אמר

**רלב"ג**

לעבוד את ה' להרחיקם יותר במה שאמר זה מעבוד ע"ג: (כג) ואמר להם שיסירו את אלהי הנכר אשר בקרבכם ויטו לבבם אל ה' אלהי יש' והוא אמר להם זה שאם נטתה לבם בסתר מאחת העבודות האלו אשר לאנשי הארץ יסירו מלבם הדעות הנפסדות בהם והם לא הודו שילטרכו לזה אך השיבו כי הם יעבדו את ה' אלהי ישראל ובקולו ישמעו: (כה) ויכרת יהושע ברית לעם. על זה להיותם עובדים את ה' ולהשאיר זכר לזה המעשה למען יבוא ישראל אם יסורו מאחרי ה' כתב יהושע את הדברים האלה בספר תורת האלהים והקים אבן גדולה תחת האלה אשר במקדש ה' להיות לזכר ולעדות על זה המעשה כמו שעשו יעקב ולבן במעשה הגל והמצבה להיות לעד ביניהם על בריתם את ה':

**מצודת דוד**

(כג) ועתה הסירו. הם לא הכיחו ליהושע לגמור את דבריו והשיבו עדים ואח"ז הזר יהושע לגמור דבריו ואמר ועתה הסירו מלב מכל וכל מחשבות עו"ג: (כד) ויאמרו העם. חזרו העם לגמור דבריהם שאמרו נהיה עדים בעצמינו אשר קבלנו לעבוד ה' ולשמוע בקולו: (כה) ויכרת וגו'. לקבל עבודת ה' מאהבה: וישם לו. סדר לישר' חוקי התורה ומשפטיה: (כו) את הדברים האלה. אשר דבר עם ישראל בשכם: בספר וגו'. ת"י ואצנעינון בספר אורייתא דה' ר"ל נתנה במקום שמונח בה התורה: במקדש ה'. היא שכם ולשעתו

## Commentary Digest

*However, there is a divergence of opinion between two Amoraim. One says: These are the eight verses from: 'And Moses died there,' until: 'To the eyes of all Israel,'[4] for the scroll*

the Lord for yourselves, to serve Him." And they said, "[We
are] witnesses." 23. "And now," [said he,] "remove the
strange gods which are among you, and incline your heart to
the Lord God of Israel." 24. And the people said to Joshua,
"The Lord our God we shall serve, and to His voice we shall
hearken." 25. And Joshua made a covenant with the people that
day, and set them a statute and an ordinance in Shechem.
26. And Joshua wrote these words in the book of

## Commentary Digest

*a strong hand etc."*[1] *You have already accepted upon yourselves in the days of Joshua. And you shall not say, "The covenant which we accepted upon ourselves in the days of Moses, we did only in order to enter the Land," for in the days of Joshua you had already entered and you* (nevertheless) *accepted* (the covenant)." — R[2]

23. *"And now,"* (said he) — These words are missing from the text. This is but the continuation of Joshua's statement in the previous verse. The people interrupted by replying, "We are witnesses." Now Joshua resumes his charge to the people. — D

*remove the strange gods which are among you* — Idolatry must be eradicated even from your hearts and innermost thoughts, even as from your words and deeds. — G and D This also refers to the removal of all idols found among the spoils of the Canaanites. — K

24. *"The Lord our God we will serve .."* — There is no need to remove any idolatrous thoughts from our hearts. We are prepared to obey the Lord and observe all His commandments. — G

25. *And Joshua made a covenant with the people* — to serve the Lord with all their heart and soul whether they receive favors or tribulations from Him. — P. Y.

*and set them* — lit. him, referring to the nation, — or "for himself." — K

*and set them a statute and an ordinance in Shechem* — *"He arranged for them there, the statutes of the Torah, and they accepted them upon themselves."* — R and K

26. *And Joshua wrote etc.* — *"J renders: And Joshua wrote these words and placed them in the Book of the Law of God.* (I.e. in the place where the scroll of the Torah was kept, in the Holy Ark. — D This was likely done so to keep a record of the Israelites' acceptance of the covenant to observe the laws of the Torah.) *In the Tractate Makkoth,*[3]

תּוֹרַת אֱלֹהִים וַיִּקַּח אֶבֶן גְּדוֹלָה וַיְקִימֶהָ
שָּׁם תַּחַת הָאַלָּה אֲשֶׁר בְּמִקְדַּשׁ יְהוָה׃
כז וַיֹּאמֶר יְהוֹשֻׁעַ אֶל־כָּל־הָעָם הִנֵּה
הָאֶבֶן הַזֹּאת תִּהְיֶה־בָּנוּ לְעֵדָה כִּי־הִיא
שָׁמְעָה אֵת כָּל־אִמְרֵי יְהוָה אֲשֶׁר דִּבֶּר
עִמָּנוּ וְהָיְתָה בָכֶם לְעֵדָה פֶּן־תְּכַחֲשׁוּן
בֵּאלֹהֵיכֶם׃ כח וַיְשַׁלַּח יְהוֹשֻׁעַ אֶת־הָעָם
אִישׁ לְנַחֲלָתוֹ׃ כט וַיְהִי אַחֲרֵי הַדְּבָרִים
הָאֵלֶּה וַיָּמָת יְהוֹשֻׁעַ בִּן־נוּן עֶבֶד יְהוָה
בֶּן־מֵאָה וָעֶשֶׂר שָׁנִים׃ ל וַיִּקְבְּרוּ אוֹתוֹ

**תרגום**

אוֹרַיְתָא דַיְיָ וּנְסֵיב אַבְנָא
רַבְּתָא וַאֲקִימַהּ תַּמָּן
תְּחוֹת אַלְתָא דִי בְּבֵית
מַקְדְּשָׁא דַיְיָ׃ כז וַאֲמַר
יְהוֹשֻׁעַ לְכָל עַמָּא הָא
אַבְנָא הָדָא תְּהֵי לָנָא
כִּתְרֵין לוּחֵי אַבְנָא קְיָמָא
אֲרֵי יָתְהוֹן עֲבַדְנָא לְסַהֲדוּ
אֲרֵי פִּתְגָמַיָא דִכְתִיבִין
עֲלַהּ מְעֵין כָּל פִּתְגָמַיָא
דִי מַלֵּיל עִמָּנָא וּתְהֵי
בְּכוֹן לְדִכְרָן וּלְסָהֲדוּ
דִילְמָא תְכַדְּבוּן קֳדָם
אֱלָהֲכוֹן׃ כח וְשַׁלַּח
יְהוֹשֻׁעַ יָת עַמָּא גְּבַר
לְאַחְסַנְתֵּיהּ׃ כט וַהֲוָה
בָּתַר פִּתְגָמַיָא הָאִלֵּין
וּמִית יְהוֹשֻׁעַ בַּר נוּן
עַבְדָּא דַיְיָ בַּר מְאָה
וַעֲסַר שְׁנִין׃ ל וּקְבַרוּ יָתֵיהּ

**רד"ק**

ערי מקלט ולא נראה לפי הפשט לא זה ולא זה והאמת הוא שת"י: (כו) תחת האלה. הדגש תמורת הנח אשר בתחת האלה אשר עם שכם. ובמדרש כי הוא האלה שטמן התחתיה יעקב אלהי הנכר כמו שכתוב ויטמן אותם יעקב תחת האלה אשר עם שכם ואין בן דעת המתרגם שתרגם אלה בוטימא ותרגם האלה אלתא יהיא מזוזות השער כמו האיל מזוזות השער ומדה אית לאלים שתרגם אלון אליא: אשר במקדש ה'. הבית שהיה שם הארון בשכם קראו מקדש לקדושת הארון שהיה שם לשעה: (כז) אשר דבר עמנו. ת"י הפסוק כן ואמר יהושע לכל עמא הא אבנא הדא תהי לנא כתרין לוחי אבן קיימא ארי יתה עבדנא לסהדו ארי פתגמיא דכתיבון עלה מעין כל פתגמיא

**רש"י**

משה עד לעיני כל ישראל שהיה ספר תורה חסר והשלימו וזהו אמר פרשה זו של ערי מקלט כתב בספרו כמו שהיו כתובים בספר התורה: תחת האלה. תחות אלתא היא מזוזות הפתח כמו כנאמר האיל מזוזות חמשית ומדה אחת לאלים. דים אומרי' זו האלה אשר עם שכם שכתוב ביעקב ויטמון אותם יעקב תחת האלה: אשר במקדש ה'. כלפי שהביאו שם את הארון כמה שנאמר למעלה ויתיצבו לפני האלהים: (כז) הנה האבן הזאת תהיה בנו לעדה וגו'. הא אבנא הדא תהי לנא כתרין לוחי אבן קיימא ארי יתה עבדנא לסהדו ארי פתגמיא דכתיבין עלה מעין כל פתגמיא דה' דמליל עמנא. וגם יש לפותרו כמשמעו כי היא שמעה את

**מנחת שי**

דעתי הוא אם יש חתיך במלא אל: (כו) ויקימה. בספרים כתיבי יד מדוייקים ודפוסים ישנים מלא יו"ד:

**מצודת ציון**

(כו) האלה. הוא שם אילן מה: (כז) לעדה. לשון עד בלשון נקבה:

**מצודת דוד**

קראו מקדש לפי שהיה שם הארון: (כז) כי היא שמעה. ר"ל במקום הזה נאמר וכאלו שמעה היא: אמרי ה'. כי כל הדברים האלה בנבואה נאמרו ולא מלבו:

## Commentary Digest

*We can also interpret this according to its simple meaning: for it has heard* (figuratively — K and D) *the words which I have spoken to you as a messenger of the Omnipresent.*" — R K explains: *the words of the Lord which He spoke to us* — on Mount Sinai, since these words had already been said at Mount Sinai. All these explanations are meant to reconcile two difficulties: (1) How did the stone hear? (2) There was no divine revelation at this point. How, then, does the Scripture say: "which He spoke to us?"

*to us* — lit. with us.

29. *and Joshua...died* — continued by Eleazar the priest.[8]

the law of God, and took a great stone, and set it under the
doorpost which is in the sanctuary of the Lord. 27. And
Joshua said to all the people, "Behold, this stone shall be a
witness against us, for it has heard all the words of the Lord
which He spoke to us; it shall be a witness against you, lest
you deny your God." 28. And Joshua sent the people away,
every man to his inheritance. 29. And it was after these things,
that Joshua the son of Nun, the servant of the Lord, died, being
a hundred and ten years old. 30. And they buried him

## Commentary Digest

*of the Law was incomplete, and he completed it. The other one says: This chapter*[1] *of refuge cities he wrote in his Book, as they were written in the Book of the Law."* — R The safeguarding of the rights of the individual, even one who had committed murder, the gravest of all crimes against society, was considered of sufficient importance to be singled out for a special chapter by Joshua. The latter opinion is easily understood. "These words" refers to ch. 20, which is shortly before this chapter. According to the former opinion, we explain: "these words" as referring to v. 5-7, which are similar to Deut. XXXIV:11, 12.[2] A explains according to J, that Joshua wrote "these words," i.e. this entire book, whose authorship the Talmud[2*] ascribes to Joshua.

*with* the book of the law of God, i.e. it was counted in the Holy Writ as following the Pentateuch, because it follows chronologically and because its sanctity is secondary only to that of the Pentateuch.

*under the doorpost* — Heb. תחת האלה, (J renders) תחות אלתא, *"This is the doorpost of the entrance, as it is stated:*[3] *'The doorposts* (האיל) *having five angles,*[4] *and one measure for the doorposts.' Others*[5] *say that this was the oak near Shechem, about which it is written in connection with Jacob:*[6] *'And Jacob hid them* (the idols and their ornaments) *under the oak* (האלה).'" — R and K

*which is in the sanctuary of the Lord* — This was not a permanent sanctuary, but it was called "the sanctuary of the Lord," *"because they brought the Ark there, as it is stated above*[7]*: 'And they presented themselves before God.'"* — R, K, and D

27. *"Behold, this stone shall be a witness against us, etc.* — J paraphrases: *"This stone shall be to us even as the two stone tablets of the covenant, for we have made it for a witness, for the words which are written thereon are similar to the words of the Lord which He spoke to us.*

בִּגְבוּל נַחֲלָתוֹ בְּתִמְנַת־סֶרַח אֲשֶׁר
בְּהַר־אֶפְרָיִם מִצְּפוֹן לְהַר־גָּעַשׁ: לא וַיַּעֲבֹד
יִשְׂרָאֵל אֶת־יְהוָה כֹּל יְמֵי יְהוֹשֻׁעַ וְכֹל
יְמֵי הַזְּקֵנִים אֲשֶׁר הֶאֱרִיכוּ יָמִים אַחֲרֵי
יְהוֹשֻׁעַ וַאֲשֶׁר יָדְעוּ אֵת כָּל־מַעֲשֵׂה
יְהוָה אֲשֶׁר עָשָׂה לְיִשְׂרָאֵל: לב וְאֶת־
עַצְמוֹת יוֹסֵף אֲשֶׁר־הֶעֱלוּ בְנֵי־יִשְׂרָאֵל

**תרגום**

בִּתְחוּם אַחְסַנְתֵּיהּ
בְּתִמְנַת סֶרַח דִּי בְּטוּרָא
דְּבֵית אֶפְרַיִם מִצִּפּוּנָא
לְטוּר גָּעַשׁ: לא וּפְלַח
יִשְׂרָאֵל קֳדָם יְיָ כָּל יוֹמֵי
יְהוֹשֻׁעַ וְכָל יוֹמֵי סָבַיָּא
דִּי אוֹרִיכוּ יוֹמִין בָּתַר
יְהוֹשֻׁעַ וְדִי יְדַעוּ יַת כָּל
עוּבָדָא דַּיְיָ דִּי עֲבַד
לְיִשְׂרָאֵל: לב וְיַת גַּרְמֵי
יוֹסֵף דְּאַסִּיקוּ בְּנֵי יִשְׂרָאֵל
מִמִּצְרַיִם

**ת"א** וימת יהושע. ב"ב טו: ויקברו אותו. שבת קה: בתמנת סרח. מגלה י"ד: וכל ימי. שבת קה: ואת עצמות יוסף. סוטה יג:

## רש"י

הדברים אשר דברתי לכם בשליחותו של מקום: (ל) בתמנת סרח. כך שמה ובמקום אחר הוא קורא אות' תמנת חרס על שם שהעמידו תמונת החמה על קברו. ר"ל זה הוא שהעמיד החמה וכל העובר עליה אומר חבל על זה שעשה דבר גדול כזה ומת. וי"א תמנת חרס שמה ולמה נקרא שמה תמנת סרח על שם שפירותיה מסריחין מרוב שמנן: להר געש מלמד שרעש עליהם ההר להורגם לפי שלא הספידוהו כראוי: (לא) האריכו ימים. ימים האריכו שנים לא האריכו שנעשו: (לב) קברו בשכם. משכם גנבוהו

## רד"ק

דה' די מליל עמנא וגו'. ולפי הפשט אשר דבר עמנו ר"ל כי מה שדברתי עמכם והברית אשר כרתי עמכם לא מלבי כי הם אמרי ה' אשר דבר עמנו בהר סיני. ופי' כי היא שמעה על דרך ותשמע הארץ אמרי פי: (ל) בתמנת סרח. ובספר שופטים בתמנת חרס ושניהם אחד כמו כבש וכשב ורבי' דרשו בו מהם אמרו סרח שמה ולמה נקראת חרס בשביל שנקבר שם יהושע שהעמיד חמה לישראל והחמה תקרא חרס כמו האומר לחרס ולא יזרח וי"א חרס שמה ולמה נקרא שמה סרח שהיו פירותיה מסריחין מרוב שמנן: מצפון להר געש. ר' ברכיה ורבי סימון בשם ריב"ל חזרנו על המקרא ולא מצאנו מקום ששמו הר געש אלא מה הוא הר געש ע"י שנתרשלו ישראל בו ולא הספידוהו כראוי רצה הקב"ה להגעיש עליהם ההר ר"ל שגעש ההר ביום קבורתו:
(לב) אשר העלו בני ישראל. אע"פ שכתוב ויעל משה את עצמות יוסף עמו הוא הזהיר את בני ישראל להעלותם כמו ויבן שלמה

## רלב"ג

(ל) אחר זה זכר שכבר מת יהושע בן מאה ועשר שנים וקברו אותו בגבול נחלתו: (לא) וזכר עוד שכבר עבדו ישראל את ה' כל ימי יהושע וכל ימי הזקנים אשר האריכו ימים אחרי יהושע ואשר ידעו את כל מעשה ה' אשר עשה לישראל והם יוצאי מצרים כי זולתם לא ידעו את כל המעש' וזכר אחר זה כי עצמות יוסף קברו במקום ההוא שהיה לבניו לנחלה וכי אלעזר בן אהרן מת וקברו אותו בגבע' פנחס בנו אשר נתן לו בהר אפרים ואם יאמר אומר איך היתה לפנחס אם לא היתה לאלעזר היה יורשו פנחס לפי שרשי התור' ולזה כשנקבר נקבר בגבע' פנחס בנו ואולם רבותינו ז"ל אמרו בפ' יש נוחלין כי פנחס ירשה מאשתו וזה דרך דרש ואמנם הפשט הוא לפ"מ שכתבנו: ואולם התועלות המגיעות מזה הספור הם אלו: הא' הוא לפרסם עוצם השגחת הש"י לישראל ושכבר קיים מה שנשבע לאבותינו ולזרעם שיתן להם את הארץ ולזה זכר מה שירשו מהארץ ע"י משה וע"י יהושע והמלכים הרבים אשר נפלו בידם: הב' הוא במדות הוא שראוי לכל אדם שלא יקלר מעשות מה שאפשר מהטוב בחייו הלא תראה כי יהושע מפני שלא יכול להשלים ירושת הארץ לישראל גם קלך לעשות מה שהיה אפשר לו מהטוב והוא הפלת הארץ בנחלה לשבטים כי בזה היה תועלת כי הוא היה נביא ולא תשלם זאת החלוק' בשלמות למי שאינו נביא כי ע"פ ה' היתה כמו שזכר עם שכבר נמשך מזה תועלת שאם חלקו הארץ הנכבשת לבד היו ישראל מתעצלים בירושת מה שאר מהארץ לדעתם שמה שיכבשו יגיע לכלל ישראל הנה לא יקום אחד מהשבטים אם לא יקומו כלם ואולי תהיה זאת העצלה סבה שלא תשלם להם ירושת הארץ אך כשידע כל שבט המגיע לו מזה יזדרז לכבוש הארץ ההיא לפי מה שאפשר ואם הולך אל העזר יבקש אותו מאח' השבטים או יותר והבטיחו שהוא יעזור אותו ג"כ לכבוש חלקו כמו שמצאנו שעשה שבט יהודה ושבט שמעון לפי מה שנזכר בראש ספר שופטים: הג' הוא בזכירה המגיע לשבט ושבט מהארץ וגבולים מהקצתה והמריבה אם ברוב הימים יפול מחלוקת ביניהם בענין הארץ הנה מה שנזכר בזה המקום מהמגיע לחלק מהם ישמרם מהקטט': הד' הוא להזכיר קיום מה שייעד הש"י לכלב באשר מלא אחרי ה' ולא הלך בעצת שאר המרגלים שהארץ אשר דרכה רגלו בה תהיה לו לנחלה ולבניו: החמישי הוא להודיע שכבר נתקיים ייעוד הש"י

## מנחת שי

(לא) ויעבד ישראל. סימן יהושע ויעבד ישראל (שופטי' ב) ויעבדו העם וסימן ישראל לא ידע עמי לא התבונן:

## מצודת דוד

(לא) אשר האריכו ימים. עד כלות כ"ח שנה מיום שעמד יהושע את ה' אשר ידעו מעשה ה' כי בעיניהם ראו ובזה היו מיסרי' את לבות ישראל לאביהם שבשמים: (לב) העלו בני ישראל. אף כי ר"ל בימי הזקנים האלה עבדו כ"כ בש"ע: ואשר ידעו וגו'.

in the border of his inheritance in Timnath-serah, which is in Mount Ephraim, on the north side of the hill of Gaash.
31. And Israel served the Lord all the days of Joshua, and all the days of the elders that outlived Joshua, and who had known all the works of the Lord, that He had done for Israel.
32. And the bones of Joseph, which the children of Israel had brought up

## Commentary Digest

30. *in Timnath-serah* — *"So was its name. Elsewhere the Scripture calls it Timnath-heres,*[1] *because they set up a figure of the sun upon his grave.* (חרם means sun, as in Jud. VIII:13, XIV:18, Job IX:7.) *I.e. this is the one who caused the sun to stand still.*[2] *And anyone who passes by it, says, 'Woe to this one who performed such a great feat and died.'*[3] *Others say: its name was Timnath-heres, and why was it called "Timnath-serah?" Because its fruits would rot* (מסריחין) *because of their great richness."*[4] — R I.e. if they were kept too long. — SM[4]

*of the hill of Gaash* — J Our rabbis say that Gaash is not a proper name, but the Scripture *"teaches us that the hill stormed forth* (געש) *upon them to kill them, because they did not eulogize him properly."*[5] — R and K This was probably an earthquake or a volcanic eruption which threatened to bury them because they hid themselves (מצפון) and did not attend the eulogy made for Joshua. The insufficient warmth shown for the loss of so great a leader and figure in Jewish history, was considered a grave sin.

31. *outlived* — Heb. האריכו ימים. lit. *"Their days were lengthened* (i.e. they were peaceful and enjoyable) *but their years were not lengthened* (only until the end of twenty-eight years since Joshua was appointed leader which was less than a year after his death. — D from Seder Olam[6]), *because they were punishsed."* — R[5] The elders were likewise guilty of not sufficiently emphasizing the enormity of the loss of Joshua to the people.

32. *which the children of Israel brought up* — Although Moses was the one who originally brought up the remains of Joseph,[7] and kept watch over them for the forty years of the journey through the wilderness, the children of Israel are credited with this deed because they com-

מִמִּצְרַיִם קָבְרוּ בִשְׁכֶם בְּחֶלְקַת הַשָּׂדֶה אֲשֶׁר קָנָה יַעֲקֹב מֵאֵת בְּנֵי־חֲמוֹר אֲבִי־שְׁכֶם בְּמֵאָה קְשִׂיטָה וַיִּהְיוּ לִבְנֵי־יוֹסֵף לְנַחֲלָה׃ לג וְאֶלְעָזָר בֶּן־אַהֲרֹן מֵת וַיִּקְבְּרוּ אֹתוֹ בְּגִבְעַת פִּינְחָס בְּנוֹ אֲשֶׁר נִתַּן־לוֹ בְּהַר אֶפְרָיִם׃

**תרגום**

מִמִּצְרַיִם קְבָרוּ בִשְׁכֶם בְּאַחְסָנַת חַקְלָא דִקְנָא יַעֲקֹב מִבְּנֵי חֲמוֹר אֲבוּהִי דִשְׁכֶם בִּמְאָה חוּרְפָן וַהֲווֹ לִבְנֵי יוֹסֵף לְאַחְסָנָא׃ לג וְאֶלְעָזָר בַּר אַהֲרֹן מִית וּקְבָרוּ יָתֵיהּ בְּגִבְעֲתָא דְפִנְחָס בְּרֵיהּ דְאִתְיְהִיבַת לֵיהּ בְּטוּרָא דְבֵית אֶפְרָיִם׃

ת״א ויהיו לבני יוסף . סוטה יג :
ואלעזר . ב״ב טו קיא קיב קיג
(ב״ב טו) : פנחס בנו ב״ב קיג :

**סכום הפסוקים** של ספר יהושע שש מאות וחמשים ושששה וסימנו **והרן** לשון אלם, וסדריו י״ד. היתה עלי **יד** ה׳ סימן. ופרקיו עשרים וארבעה. וסימנו **כד** הקמח לא תכלה. והציו ומחשבון עד רמת המצפה:

## רד״ק

**והדומים לו.** ובדרש כל המתחיל במצוה ואחר גומרה נקראת ע״ש האחרון ממי אתה למד מכשה דכתי׳ ויעל משה את עצמות יוסף עמו נסתלק משה במדבר ולא נכנס לארץ והכניסו ישראל עצמותיו לארץ וקברו אותם ונתלית המצוה בהם דכתיב **אשר העלו** בני ישראל ממצרים אשר העלה משה אין כתיב כאן אלא **אשר העלו**: קברו בשכם. דרשו בו משכם גנבוהו ולשכם החזירוהו ולפי השם לפי שהיה שכם בחלק אפרים ולכבוד יוסף קברוהו בנחלה הראשונה אשר היה ליעקב אבינו בארץ ישראל ולפי דעתי בפסוק **ואני** נתתי לך שכם אחד על אחיך רמז לו שיקבר שם בשכם זהו שאמר לך כי כבר זכר הגבורה שנתן לו שיטלו בניו שני חלקים: ויהיו לבני יוסף לנחלה, וחשבו להם העצמות לנחלה טובה שנקברו בנחלתם ודרשו בו על בני יוסף שהתעסקו בקבורת העצמות בנחלתם: (לג) אשר נתן לו בהר אפרים. אמרו רבותינו ז״ל מניין היה לו לפנחס שלא היה לו לאלעזר אלא מלמד שנשא פנחס אשה ומתה וירשה ומכאן סמכו לירושת הבעל ומהם אמרו כי אפשר שנפלה לו בשדה חרמים ויתכן גם כן לפרש כי ישראל נתנו לו כמו שנתנו לכלב ליהושע אבל לא על פי השם ית׳ כמו שנתנו להם וזהו שאמר אשר נתן לו ואילו היתה ירושת אשתו או שדה הרמים לא היה אומר אשר נתן לו ורבותינו ז״ל אמרו כי לא נוכל לומר שקנה פנחס אותה גבעה דאם כן נמצאת שדה חוזרת ביובל ונמצא אותו צדיק קבור בקבר שאינו שלו אבל לשון נתן לו לא הקשה להם כי מצאנו לשון מתנה במכר כמו ויתן לי את מערת המכפלה ואם תאמר לפירושינו קשה גם כן שהרי מתנת יחיד חוזרת ביובל אבל מתנת רעים אינה חוזרת וזאת הגבעה שבט אפרים נתנוה לו ולדבריהם שאמרו כי ירושת אשתו היתה הם אמרו גם כן כי ירושת הבעל אינה חוזרת ביובל וכן תדין:

## רש״י

לשכם החזירוהו: (לג) בגבעת פנחס בנו. מהיכן היה לו לפנחס הלק בארץ שירש אשתו:

## רלב״ג

בשבט שמעון ולוי במה שאמר יעקב אחלקם ביעקב ואפיצם בישראל כי כבר היו נחלותיהם מפוזרות כמו שזכרנו: הששי הוא להודיע שבכר קיימו ישראל מה שצוה בתורה להבדיל ערי המקלט ולתת ללוים ערים לשבת ומגרשיהן לבהמתם והנה קבלנו שתי המלות יחד כי ידמה שערי הכהנים והלוים כלם קולטות והנה התבאר מן התורה כי המזבח היה קולט ההורג בשוגג ולזה הולך ואומר בהורג במזיד מעם מזבחי תקחנו למות כמו שביארנו שם וידמה כי מפני שכלל ערי המקלט עם ערי הלוים הנשארות בזה המספר ואמר בסוף שהם ערים מ״ח ומגרשיהן שכבר הקישן זו לזו ולזה תהיינה כלם קולטות: השביעי יוהוא מה שלמדנו מהמזבח שבנו השבטים אשר מעבר הירדן כי כשילא האדם דבר אפשר שיתחדש ממנו הפסד או נזק ראוי שיתחכם להסירו קודם בואו ולא ימנעהו מזה ראותו שלא יתכן הגעת ההפסד או הנזק ההוא כי אם לעתים רחוקים הלא תראה כי אלו השבטים כשראו כי בארך הזמן יהיה אפשר שיסבב היות הירדן מספיק ביניהם ובין ארץ ישראל שישביתו בניהם מעבוד את ה׳ התחכמו להמציא דבר נשאר יורה שגם הם מעם ה׳ ולזה בנו שם המזבח ההוא שיהיה בתבנית מזבח ה׳ וקראו שמו כי עד הוא בינותינו כי ה׳ האלהים ויהושע כאשר ראה ג״כ אפשרות סור ישראל מאחרי ה׳ מלד מה שנשארו מן הגוים ההם שלא החרימום ג״כ לפי מה שאפשר להצילם מזה והביאם מזה אל שיקבלו עליהם שנית את האלהים לעבדו ולאהבה אותו ושלא לסור מאחריו להרחיקם יותר מזה הענין: השמיני הוא שלמדנו מענין שלוח פנחס והנשיא׳ לשבטים שהיו מעבר לירדן לחקור אמתת קודם עלותם עליהם לצבא והוא כי גם בענינים אשר יחשב שאין להמתין עליהם לעשות׳ כי אם תכף צריך להתישב ולחקור הענין הלא תראה כי לולא זאת התקיל׳ היה נמשך מזה נזק רב בעלות בני ישר׳ לצבא על אחיהם והנה יחשב שאין להמתין על אלו הדברי׳ שהם הם״י מפני הסבות שזכרו פנחס והנשיאים לשבטים האלו בזה המקום ולזה תמלא שלא המתון פנחס לקחת עלה ממשה רבינו בדבר זמרי אמרו רבותינו ז״ל כל מקום שיש חלול השם אין חולקין כבוד לרב ומזה המקום יותר הספק איך לא נמלכו ישראל בזה ביהושע שהיה נביא עם שהיה מהענינים הראוים לעשות לפי משפטי התורה בהשבעת הענושים ראוי שיהיה המעשה בהם לפי דרכי התורה באופני ההקירה המיוסדת בתורה לא שישאלו איך האמת בזה לנביא ואם באנו לבאר זה בזה המקום יארכו הדברים יותר מהראוי למה שאנחנו בו: התשיעי הוא מה שלמדנו שראוי לכל אדם שישתדל שיהיה נקבר בגבול משפחתו להשאיר שמו ולזה זכר בהקבר יהושע בגבול נחלתו והקבר יוסף בגבול נחלת בניו והקבר אלעזר בן אהרן בגבעת פנחס בנו ומזה המקו׳ למדנו התועלת שהגיע מזה הלד ליוסף כשנחלקו בניו לשני שבטים וזה כי בזה היה רבוי בגורלות לבני רחל ויתכן יותר שיגיע מקום קבורתה בנחלה לאחד מהם וכבר נתבאר שכן היה לפי מה שנזכר בספר שמואל:

## מצודת ציון

(לב) בחלקת. ענין אחוזת שדה כמו ויקן את חלקת השדה (בראשית לג) : קשיטה. מעה והוא מטבע מה: (לג) בגבעת. מלשון גבעה והר:

## מצודת דוד

משה העלם ממצרים אבל לפי שמת במדבר ולא הספיק להביאם והביאום הם לכך נקרא על שמם: ויהיו לבני יוסף לנחלה. כדוש החלקה ההיא היו לבני יוסף לנחלה ולזה קברו שם את יוסף אביהם. או יאמר שעצמות יוסף חשבו להם בני יוסף לנחלה טובה כי מאד נסנו והוטב להם במה שנקבר באחוזתם: (לג) אשר נתן לו. בני ישראל נתנו אותה לו במתנה עם שלא נתן נחלה לשבט הלוי:

out of Egypt, they buried in Shechem, in the parcel of ground which Jacob bought from the sons of Hamor the father of Shechem, for a hundred pieces of money; and they became the inheritance of the children of Joseph. 33. And Eleazar the son of Aaron died; and they buried him in the hill of Phinehas his son, which was given to him in Mount Ephraim.

## Commentary Digest

pleted it. A mitzvah is only credited upon its completion.[1] It is also possible that Moses did not personally care for Joseph's remains, but ordered the children of Israel to do so. — K

*they buried in Shechem* — *"From Shechem they kidnapped him;[2] therefore, to Shechem they returned him."[3]* — R Furthermore, Shechem was in Ephraim's territory. Also, it was the first parcel of land which Jacob possessed in Eretz Israel, and he promised it to Joseph[4] for his burial. — K[5] Moreover, burial in the Holy Land was a fitting reward for Joseph who never forgot his homeland, even when in the dungeon in Egypt[5]*: "For I was stolen from the land of the Hebrews."

*for a hundred pieces of money* — a coin usually called מעה. — Z[6]

*and they became the inheritance* — Joseph's bones were as precious to the children of Joseph as any worldly inheritance. — K, A, P, and D This may also be interpreted as referring to the lands or fields of Shechem, which became an inheritance of the children of Joseph.

33. *And Eleazar the son of Aaron died* — This last verse was written by Phinehas.[7]

*in the hill of Phinehas his son* — *"Whence did Phinehas receive a part in the Land of Israel* (if not from his father)? (The verse implies that he was the possessor independent of his father.) *He inherited it from his wife."* — R[8]

# BIBLIOGRAPHY

## I. BACKGROUND MATERIAL.

1. Bible with commentaries ("Mikraoth Gedoloth"), including Rashi, R. Abraham ibn Ezra, R. Elijah Gaon of Vilna, R. Isaiah of Trani, R. Levi b. Gershon (Gersonides), and R. David Kimchi.
2. Talmud Bavli or Babylonian Talmud. Corpus of Jewish law and ethics compiled by Ravina and Rav Ashi 500 C.E. All Talmudic quotations unless otherwise specified, are from the Babylonian Talmud.
3. Talmud Yerushalmi or Palestinian Talmud. Earlier and smaller compilation of Jewish law and ethics, compiled by R. Johanan, first generation Amora in second century C.E.
4. Midrash Rabbah. Homiletic explanation of Pentateuch and Five Scrolls. Compiled by Rabbi Oshia Rabba (the Great), late Tannaite, or by Rabbah bar Nahmani, third generation Amora. Exodus Rabbah, Numbers Rabbah, and Esther Rabbah, are believed by many to have been composed at a later date.
5. Midrash Tanhuma. A Midrash on Pentateuch, based on the teachings of R. Tanhuma bar Abba, Palestinian Amora of the fifth generation. The original Midrash Tanhuma was discovered by Solomon Buber. It is evident that this is the Midrash Tanhuma quoted by medieval scholars, e.g. Rashi, Yalkut, and Abravanel.
6. Midrash Shoher Tov, or Midrash Tehilim (Psalms). A homiletic exposition on the Book of Psalms, composed of the works of various Tannaites and Amoraim who lived in the Holy Land. It was completed sometime before the Gaonic period. New York 1947.
7. Yalkut Shimoni. Talmudic and Midrashic compilation on Bible, composed by R. Simon Ashkenazi of Frankfurt am Main. Earliest known edition dated 1308 in Bodlian Library Berlin 1926.

## II. MEDIEVAL COMMENTATORS AND SOURCE MATERIAL

1. Rambam. Rabbenu Moshe ben Maimon, also known as Maimonides. Leading medieval authority on halachah, philosophy, and medicine. After having fled Spain, his native land, he became court physician to the sultan of Egypt. His works include a commentary on the Mishnah, Sefer ha-mitzvoth, (a concise presentation of the 613

commandments of the Torah, together with comments of Ramban New York 1946) Mishneh Torah or Yad ha-chazakah — Rambam's "opus magnum", containing a decision on all problems of Jewish law, whether discussed in Talmud, Midrash, or later Gaonic writings, with glosses of Kesef Mishneh, Magid Mishnah, etc. New York 1946. 1134-1204.

2. R. Ishtori Haparchi. Kaftor Vaferach. Halachic treatise on the laws pertaining to the Holy Land and its boundaries, to Jerusalem and the Temple; by a thirteenth century sage, who spent seven years in the Holy Land in an extensive study. New York 1958.
3. Rabbi Isaiah of Trani. Commentary on Joshua and other books of the Bible. Published by Prof. Abraham J. Wertheimer, Jerusalem 1959.
4. Don Isaac Abravanel. Commentary on Joshua; by a renowned scholar, former finance minister of Spain. Lived 1437-1509. Jerusalem 1959.
5. R. Isaac Aramah. Sefer Akedah. Expositional studies on the Pentateuch and Five Scrolls. Author was a famous scholar in Torah and other fields. Lived in Spain in fifteenth century. Expelled in 1492. Warsaw 1911.
6. R. Hisdai Crescas. Ohr Ha-shem. Critical evaluation of Maimonides' philosophical system. Died in 1396.
7. R. Nissim, Drashoth (sermons). Collection of twelve essays on problems in Jewish thought, by a fourteenth century Spanish scholar.
8. R. Menahem Ha-me'iri. Beth Ha-bechirah, commentary to tractate Aboth. The writing of this fourteenth century luminary are one of the treasures recently discovered in Parma, Italy, and other libraries. Published by Rabbi S. Waxman, Jerusalem 1944.

## III. MODERN COMMENTARIES

1. I. R. Moses b. Joseph (MBIT) of Trani. Beth Elohim. Brilliant exposition of Judaic concepts by the sixteenth century Rabbi of Safed, Israel. New York 1961.
2. R. Judah Loew of Prague. Gvurot Hashem. Exposition on all aspects of Exodus from Egypt; by the famous "Maharal of Prague", sixteenth century leader of Jewry.
3. R. Elijah Gaon of Vilna. Commentary on Bible. Sinai Publishing, Tel-Aviv, Israel.
4. R. Chaim Joseph David Azulai. Birchai Joseph. Commentary on "Shulchan Aruch" by an 18th century Sephardic scholar and traveller, Vienna, (no year given).

   Chomath Anach on all parts of Bible. Leghorn 1803, Jerusalem 1965.

5. R. Meyer Laibush (MALBIM) Commentary on Joshua. Commentary combining ancient tradition with keen insight into nuances of meaning and richness of Hebrew language; by a leading ninteenth century scholar and saint. New York, 1951.
6. R. Meyer Simcha. Meshech Chochmah. Penetrating observations on Pentateuch as a mirror of complete panorama of Jewish thought; by world famous Rabbi of Dvinsk (4 Elul, 5686), Riga, 1927.
7. R. Sh'muel Laniado. K'li Y'Kar, Commentary on N'Viim Rishonim, containing comments on earlier commentaries and original exegesis. Venice (5363) 1603.
8. R. Rahamim Menahem of Trani. Me'am Loez, Anthology on many books of Bible. Written originally in Ladino. Translated into Hebrew, Jerusalem, 1972.
9. R. Moshe Alschich. Mar'oth Hazov'oth. Biblical exegesis by renowned scholar in Safed. Mikraoth Gedoloth, Jerusalem, 1964.
10. R. Chaim Rabinowitz, Daath Soferim. Biblical exegesis by contemporary historian, exegete, and educator, Jerusalem, 1975.
11. R. Enoch Zundel. Porath Yosef. Anthology by renowned author of similar works on Midrashim, prayers, etc., Jerusalem, 1970.
12. Judah Kil. Daath Mikra. Contemporary exegesis. Mosad Harav Kook, Jerusalem, 1977.

## IV. ARTICLES AND GENERAL WORKS

1. Bezalel Ben-Har. Concealed Biblical Maps and their Significance Jerusalem '61.
2. Meyer Ish-shalom. "Gvulot Eretz Yisroel Suria" (Boundaries of Israel and Syria), especially pages 71-97. Jerusalem, Vol. II.
3. R. Naftali Zvi Berlin. Introduction to "Ha-amek Shealah." Essay on manner of establishment and development of Jewish Law, by the renowned Dean of Volozhin Yeshiva. Jerusalem, 1948.
4. Essay by R. Aharon Kotler. Introduction to "Yalkut Midah K'neged Midah." Exposition of Biblical problems by the Dean of Beth Medrash Govoha (2 Kislev 5723). Lakewood, 1961.
5. Sinai, Tamuz 5724 ("Nachal"). Periodical published by Mosad Horav Kook. Rabbi J. L. Maimon, Editor. Jerusalem, 1964.

# ABBREVIATIONS USED IN THIS VOLUME:

**A** — Don Isaac Abarbanel or Abravanel
**AZ.** — Azulai
**D** — Mezudath David
**D.S.** — Daath Soferim
**E** — Rabbi Abraham Ibn Ezra
**E. G.** — Rabbi Elijah Gaon of Vilna
**El. R.** — Elijah Rabbah
**El. Z.** — Elijah Zutah
**E. R.** — Exodus Rabbah
**G** — Rabbi Levi ben Gershon or Gersonides
**G. R.** — Genesis Rabbah
**J** — Jonathan ben Uziel
**J.K.** — Rabbi Joseph Karo
**K** — Rabbi David Kimchi or Redak
**K.Y.** — K'Li Y'Kar
**M** — Rabbi Meir Leibush Malbim
**M.L.** — Me'am Loez
**M. Ps.** — Midrash Psalms
**M. S.** — Midrash Samuel
**N. R.** — Numbers Rabbah
**P** — Rabbi Jacob Pidanki
**P.Y.** — Porath Yosef
**R** — Rabbi Shlomo Izhaki or Rashi
**R. R.** — Ruth Rabbah
**S. G.** — Saadiah Gaon
**S. M.** — Rabbi Samuel ben Meir or Rashbam
**T** — Midrash Tanhuma
**T. P.** — Palestinian Talmud or Yerushalmi
**Y** — Yalkut Shimoni
**Z** — Mezudath Zion

**PAGE 1**

[1] Deut. XXXIV:10. [1*] Ibid., 8. [2] v. 10. [3] I Ch. VII:26:27. [4] Sotah 34b, N. R. and T. Num. XIII:16. [5] Mechilta Jethro s. 1. [6] SM, Tos. in Hadar Zekenim, Hizkuni ibid. [7] Lekah Tov Ex. XXXIII: 11, Num. XI:28. See also note 8. [8] Battei Midrashoth, Perek Zedakoth, ch. 1 s. 7. [9] Prov. XXVII:18. [10] N. R. s. 21, 15, cf. T Pinchas s. 11.

**PAGE 2**

[1] Beth Elohim p. 141. [2] Temurah 16a. [3] Deut. XI:24. [4] Num. XX:16. [5] Ibid., XXXIV:3. [6] Shev. 47b.

**PAGE 3**

[1] Sifre Deut. XI:25. [2] Ibid. [3] Ber. 32b. [4] Ibid.

**PAGE 4**

[1] Men. 99b. [2] Laws of Talmud Torah, ch. 1. [3] Deut. IV:9. [4] G.R. s. 6. [5] Deut. XXXIV:17. [6] Ps. XIX:15. [7] Is. XXXIII:18. [8] Hor. 13a.

**PAGE 5**

[1] Deut. III:28. [2] Cf. ibid., XVI:18. [3] Infra V:12 based on Kid. 38a, Tem. 16a, Y end of Deut. [3*] Y from El. R., ch. 18. [4] R Num. XXXII:24.

**PAGE 6**

[1] N Num. XXXII:33. [2] Sh'viith ch. 9, Mishnah 2. [3] San. 49a. [4] II Sam. XX:4, 5.

**PAGE 7**

[1] Infra v. 22. [2] Infra v. 23. [3] Infra III:1. [3*] Num. XXXIII:49, E Num. XXV:1. [4] Y from RR, s. 2. N R and Tan. beginning of שלח. [5] II Sam. II:30.

**PAGE 8**

[1] Kings XI:1. [2] Num. XXXI:6. [3] See R v. 11. [4] Meg. 15a Maharsho. [5] Ibid., 14b. [6] Job. XXXIX:29.

**PAGE 9**

[1] Tan. beginning of שלח, N.R. ibid. [1*] II:7. [2] Prov. XXVII:9. [3] Ginsburg. [4] Num. XIII:30. [5] Ibid., XXXI:6. [6] Deut. XX. [7] Alshich.

**PAGE 10**

[1] Based on Meg. 3a.

**PAGE 11**

[1] Ezek. I:1. [2] Y from MS s. 9.

**PAGE 12**

[1] Tos. Sotah 35b. [2] Ned. 65b, see commentaries. [3] Ibid. 22b.

**PAGE 13**

[1] Alschich. [1*] Zeb. 116b, R ad loc., Mechilta Jethro s. 1. [2] Ber. 54b. [3] Infra VI:22. [4] RR s, 2; 1, Sifrei Deut. I:24. [5] GR s. 56:1, M Ps. XXII:5.

**PAGE 16**

[1] Mechilta Ex. 12:22. [1*] Supra I:11. [2] Infra IV:19. [2*] Sabb. 30b. [3] II Kings III:14. [4] Gen. XLV:27. [5] Based on Kidd. 38a.

**PAGE 17**

[1] Sotah 33b. [1*] Taan. 9a. [2] Source unknown. The Talmud mentions 24 places. See Yeb. 86b. [3] Sefer Hamitzvoth, shoresh 3, 'asseh 34. [3*] Ps. CKLIX:2. [3**] Sotah 13.

**PAGE 18**

[1] Num. s. 9. [1*] El. R. ch. 18. [2] Probable meaning of K, cf. A. [3] Infra X:12, 13. [4] A. Z. 25a. [5] Num. XIX:10. G.R. s. 5:6, L. R. s. 10:8.

### PAGE 19

[1] Sotah 35a. [1*] See above p. 18, 5. [2] II Kings XVI:17. [3] Jer. XXXI:39.

### PAGE 20

[1] Suk. 39a. [1*] Y from Pesikta d'Rav Kahana, ch. 15. [1**] Infra IV:2. [2] Y from Sotah 33b. [3] Ps. XXXIII:7. [4] Is. XVII:11.

### PAGE 21

[1] As appears in "An American Translation." [2] Quoted by Mandelkorn. [3] Infra 14:15. [4] Yeb. 11b.

### PAGE 22

[1] Ex. XII:38. [2] Deut. XXVIII:10 R. [3] Hul. 7a. [4] Supra III:12. [5] Deut. XXVII:1-8. [6] Sotah 36a.

### PAGE 23

[1] Zeb. 119a.

### PAGE 24

[1] 35a.

### PAGE 25

[1] Num. XXXIII:51-2. [2] V. 18. [3] Sotah 35a.

### PAGE 26

[1] Cf. R. infra XXII:8. [2] III:15. [3] Ibid. 17. [4] II Sam. VI:6, 7. [5] Sotah 35a. [6] Ibid. [7] Ex. XVI:33, 34.

### PAGE 27

[1] Num. XVII:25, 26.

### PAGE 28

[1] Based on G.R. s. 68,13; s. 76. 4. [2] Ibid., s. 40,8. [3] Agadath B'reishith s. 8. [4] Deut. XXXIV:10.

### PAGE 29

[1] Jeb. 71b. [1*] Ps. LXXXIX:44. [2] Ch. 2, par. 1.

### PAGE 30

[1] E. R. s. 19, 6; S.R. s. 1, 57. Pirkei d'R. Eliezer, ch. 29. [1*] 71b. [1**] Tos. Jeb. 71b. [2] L.R, s. 25, 7; N R, s. 11, 6; S R, s. 3, 14; Ec. R, s. 11, 5. [3] Pirkei d'R. Eliezer, ch. 29. [4] Gen. XXVII:14.

### PAGE 31

[1] Ibid., XVII:8, 9. [1*] G R, s. 46, 8. [1**] XVI:7. [2] V. 6. [2*] IX:11. [2**] Y Ez. ibid. [3] E R, s. 19, 6; S R, s. 1, 57. [4] See above v. 2. [5] Ex. X:10. R. [6] Mars, See K'li Y'kar ad loc.

### PAGE 32

[1] See above v. 2. [2] Ex. X:10. R. [3] Mars, See K'li Y'kar ad loc. [4] Y, Greenhut, Mid. Song of Songs p. 15. [5] Ps. CXIX:22. [6] Gen. XXIX:10.

### PAGE 33

[1] Num. XIV:16. [1*] See Ex. XII:6, R. [1**] Mechilta, s. 12. See R Ex. XII:25. [2] Lev. XXIII:14. [3] Ex. XVI:35. [4] Should read: sixteenth Ex. XVI:1, 13, R ibid. [5] Kidd. 37b, 38a. [6] Tos. ibid.

### PAGE 34

[1] Men. 65a. [2] Ex. XVI:35. [3] Kidd. 38a. [3*] E R, ch. 18. [4] Tosefta Sotah, ch. 11, par. 6.

### PAGE 35

[1] Sifre "B'ha'aloth'cha," ch. XI:8. [1*] Absent in Y. [1**] II:2. [2] Ex. XVI:33. [3] Yoma 52b. [4] See R Gen. XII:6. [5] See Mizrachi, Gen. I:1. [6] Kaftor vo'Ferach. [7] Mechilta, Bo, s. 18. [8] Ned. 56b. [9] Guide to the Perplexed s. 2, ch. 42. See N Gen. XVIII:2. [10] Ex. XXXIII:15. [11] T Mishpatim s. 18.

### PAGE 36

[1] Dan. X:21. [1*] Meg. 3a.

### PAGE 37

[1] R.H. 26a. [2] Ber. 54b.

### PAGE 38

[1] Deut. XXXIV:20. [2] Num. XXXII:29.

**PAGE 39**

[1] P T Sab. ch. 1, hal. 8; Moed Katan ch. 2, hal. 4, N R s. 14, 5; T מסעי 5; T Buber נשא 31; S E ch. 11. [2] Maimonides, Laws of Sabbath, ch. 2, par. 25, Lehem Mishneh. Cf. Sab. 19a.

**PAGE 40**

[1] N R s. 14, 5; 23, 6; T Mass'ei s. 5. [2] T, Vay'chi 8; T Mass'ei 5. [3] Ch. II. [4] Infra ch. VII.

**PAGE 41**

[1] Num. XXXI:50. [2] Supra v. 5. [3] XXIX:1. [4] Rosh Hashana 34a.

**PAGE 42**

[1] T בהעלתך, s. 10, Sifre, Num. X:8. [2] Lev. XVIII. [3] Deut. XX:16. [4] Kol Bo. [5] Ex. XXXIII:11. [5]*v. 22. [6] V. 25. [7] RR, s. 2, 1; PT Ber. 4:4; San. 10:2. Mid. of Defective and Plene Spellings, Battei Midrashoth, Wertheimer, vol. II.

**PAGE 43**

[1] Yeb. 76a. [2] Tos. Meg. 14b, Sotah 35b. [3] San. 113a. [4] I Kings XVI:34.

**PAGE 44**

[1] Deut. XXXIV:17. [2] Y from GR s. 39, 11. [3] R ibid. [4] Jer. XL:3. [5] Deut. XIII:3. [6] PT Sab. 9:1. [7] X:5.

**PAGE 45**

[1] G R, end of S. 39. [2] Sifrei Deut. III:28, Mechilta d'R. Simeon ben Johai, Bo 37. [3] B.B. 121b San. 44a; — G R, S. 39, 24; L R s. 11, 7; intr. to Es. R. [3]* Sabb. 105b. [4] Meg. 22a. [5] O. H. 131:2. [6] Gen. XVIII:27. [7] G R, end of s. 39.

**PAGE 46**

[1] Deut. III:23-25. [2] Prov. XVIII:23. [3] San. 44a. [4] Maharsha and Iyun Jacob, Ein Jacob ad loc. [5] Ex. V:23. [6] P T Taan. 2:6. [7] Perush Hakotheb, Ein Jacob ad loc.

**PAGE 47**

[1] PT Taan. 2:6. [2] Num. XXVII:17. [3] Deut. XXXI:23. [3]* Ibid., III:28. [4] Sifrei ad loc. [5] San. 44a. [6] Ibid. b.

**PAGE 48**

[1] San. 44a. [2] Pirkei d'R. Eliezer ch. 38. T וישב s. 2. [3] Source unknown. [4] El. R. ch. 18. [5] Deut. XI:30 R.

**PAGE 49**

[1] II Sam. V:8. [2] XI:5. [2]* San. 44a. [3] N ad loc. [3]* Ex. XXVIII:21. [3]** Pirkei d'R. Eliezer, ch. 38; cf. supra v. 14. T Vayeshev 5:2. [4] San. 42b.

**PAGE 50**

[1] NR s. 23, 6; T Mass'ei, s. 5, Buber, s. 4. [2] Num. XXI:2. [3] San. 43b. [4] Num. XXXI:48-54. [5] Deut. XX:14. [6] Jer. III:19. [7] T Mishpatim s. 17. [8] Mandelkorn.

**PAGE 51**

[1] T Mass'ei 5, Buber 4, NR s. 23, 6. [2] II Sam. XV:24. [3] San. 44a. Cf. note 1. [4] Maharsha, Hidushei Aadoth, ad loc. [5] See R, Deut. XXIV:16, Rambam, Laws of Repentance, ch. 6. [6] San. 44a. [7] V. 15.

**PAGE 52**

[1] San. 43a. [2] T Mass'ei 5, Buber 4, NR s. 23. [3] San. 44a. Cf. note 2 Acc. to Mid., Achan was burned for violating the ban and stoned for profaning the Sabbath. [4] Yoma 54a. Cf. Sotah 46b R, Iyun Jacob ad loc.

**PAGE 53**

[1] A species of snake or lizard. [2] Ber. 33a. [3] Supra VII:3.

**PAGE 54**

[1] Jer. XII:3. [2] Gen. XII:18. [3] See VII:10, R.

**PAGE 55**

[1] Gen. XXVII:36. [2] See above V:14.

**PAGE 56**

[1] Supra I:8. [2] Supra V:14.

**PAGE 58**

[1] Deut. XIX:16, 17.

**PAGE 59**

[1] Deut. XXI:23.

**PAGE 60**

[1] Pes. 3a, Sotah 36a. [2] Deut. XXVII:2-8. [3] PT Meg. Ch. 1:14; LR, S. 22:9; NR, s. 14:1; M. Ps. ch. 27; MS, s. 13. [4] Sotah 36a. [5] Sotah 35b.

**PAGE 61**

[1] Maharsha Sotah 35b. [2] R Ex. XXIV:12. [3] Deut. XXVII:3. [4] Sotah 32a. [5] R. Deut. XI:29. [6] Ibid., XXVII:14-26. [7] Sotah 37a.

**PAGE 62**

[1] Sotah 33b; PT ibid., ch. 7:4. [2] PT Shviith, ch. 6:1; Mechilta, end of Bo; DR, s. 5:13.

**PAGE 63**

[1] Gen. XXXIV:2. [2] T ibid. [3] Obad. I:1.

**PAGE 64**

[1] Gen. XLIV:16. [2] Absent from Kara. [3] Dan. IV:30, V:21. [4] Pes. 40a. [5] Abodah Zarah 30a. [6] Deut. XX:17. [7] Mishneh Torah, Laws of Kings, ch. 6:5.

**PAGE 66**

[1] Ex. XXI:13, cf. R ad loc. [2] Num. XXVII:21. [3] Mishneh Torah, ch. 6:5.

**PAGE 67**

[1] Infra XVIII:25, 26. [2] Infra XV:9. [3] Gittin 46a, R ad loc.

**PAGE 68**

[1] Num. XII:9, Sifre ad loc. [1*] PT Kid. ch. 4:1. [2] I Sam. XXI:2. [3] Keth. 29a. [4] Tos. and R. Nissim. ad loc.

**PAGE 69**

[1] Source unknown. [2] See Zeb. 54a.

**PAGE 70**

[1] See Y. Also Gen. XIV:18, N ad loc.

**PAGE 71**

[1] NR, s. 8:14. [2] See II Sam. XXI:1-13.

**PAGE 72**

[1] Ex. IX:33. [2] Ber. 54b. [3] Ex. XV:1. [4] Y from T Aharei, ch. 9. [5] I Sam. XIV:9. [6] Ps. XXXVII:7. [7] Ec. Zuta, 1:5.

**PAGE 73**

[1] Infra XVII:25. [2] Infra XIX:42. [3] Pirkei d'Rabbi Eliezer, ch. 52. [4] Gen. XLVIII:19. [5] A. Z. 25a. [6] Num. XXII:9. [7] Deut. VI:18. See Maharsha A. Z. ibid. G.R. s. 6:8. [8] R ibid.

**PAGE 74**

[1] A.Z. 25a. [2] V. 13.

**PAGE 75**

[1] Ex. XI:7. [2] II Sam. V:24.

**PAGE 76**

[1] Deut. XXXIII:29. [2] Sifre, Targum Jonathan, Targum Yerushalmi, Malbim ad loc. M. S. ch. 21.

**PAGE 77**

[1] V. 29. [2] V. 32.

**PAGE 79**

[1] Above v. 16-18. [2] Ibid., 26.

**PAGE 80**

[1] Other editions: *This is the southern boundary of Eretz Israel.* [2] XIII:2. [3] Ibid., v. 3. [4] Infra XV:51. [5] Cf. Commentary Digest, XI:16.

**PAGE 81**

[1] Ber. 44a, Pes. 8b.

**PAGE 82**

[1] A. Z. 13a. [2] Deut. XVII:16-17, N ad loc. [3] Rabbeinu Nissim, Yad Ramah, San. 21b.

**PAGE 83**

[1] See Ecc. III:21 and Introduction of Maimonides to Tractate Aboth. [2] Supra VIII:28. [3] S. 81:4.

**PAGE 84**

[1] Deut. XIII:18. [2] MS s. 18:4. [3] Unknown. [4] Apparently another Targum, or another version of J.

**PAGE 85**

[1] Supra X:42. [2] Deut. XXXI:7. [3] מטות s. 4. [4] Num. XXXI:2. [4*] Infra 24:29. [4**] Ex. XIV:8.

**PAGE 86**

[1] Ibid., XXIII:33. [1*] Infra XIV:13, XV:14. [2] Ibid., v. 16, Jud. I:13. [3] Jud. ad loc. [4] Ibid., v. 18.

**PAGE 89**

[1] Y ad loc. from Sifrei 'Ekeb, s. 37, 76. [2] R ibid.

**PAGE 90**

[1] Y ad loc. from Sifrei, s. 37, 76. [2] Gen. XV, end of chapter.

**PAGE 91**

[1] Num. XXXIV:5. [2] Supra XI:17, X:41.

[1] Hulin 60b. [2] R ibid. [3] Tos. ibid.

**PAGE 92**

[1] Num. XXXIV:7, 8.

[1] Laws of Terumoth, ch. 1.

**PAGE 93**

[1] Gen. XIV:5. [2] Nidah 61a. [3] Infra XXI. [4] See especially Maimonides, Laws of Sabbatical and Jubilee Years, ch. 13.

**PAGE 94**

[1] Num. XXI:26. [2] Deut. III:29. [3] Num. XXI:21-35, XXXI.

**PAGE 95**

[1] Ibid., XXXI:8. [1*] Num. XXIII, XXIV. [2] Baba Bathra 15b. [3] San. 106a. [4] Num. XXIV:14, San. ibid. [5] Sirfei Num. XXXI:8. [6] XXVII:40. [7] Num. XXXI:8 from unknown source. [8] San. 106b, J Num. XXXI:8. [9] Num. R. s. 22:4. [10] Ibid., 5.

**PAGE 96**

[1] Deut. II:19. [2] Ibid., 37. [3] Jud. XI:12-23. Cf. Hulin 60b.

**PAGE 97**

[1] See supra XIII:14. [2] See Deut. XVIII:2, R. N, Maharal. [3] Maimonides, Laws of Sh'mittah, ch. 13, T. P. Bikkurim, ch. 1, Mishnah 8. [4] Yebamoth 89b, Rashal ad loc.

**PAGE 98**

[1] Erubin 56b, Sotah 27b. [2] Laws of Shemittah, ch. 13. [3] Num. XIV:24. [4] N R, s. 16, T Shelach s. 10.

**PAGE 99**

[1] Num. XIII:22, R ibid., from Sotah 34b. [2] Zeb. 118b.

**PAGE 100**

[1] Infra XXI:11-13.

**PAGE 101**

[1] G. R. s. 58. [2] Gen. XXIII:6. [3] Sifra Lev. XVIII:3. [4] Gen. XXXVI:15. [5] Num. XXXIV:12.

**PAGE 102**

[1] Jeb. 13b. [2] Succah 32. Cf. J. Num. XXXIV:3-4. [3] Zeb. 54a. [4] Infra v. 8. [5] Supra XIII:3. [6] Num. XXXIV:12.

**PAGE 103**

[1] Num. XXXIV:12. [2] See above v. 3. [3] See above VII:24, 26.

**PAGE 104**

[1] 54b. [2] Deut. XXXIII:12. [3] Is. XLIV:13. [4] Yoma 31a.

**PAGE 105**

[1] Gittin 8a.

**PAGE 106**

[1] I:20. [2] Temurah 16a. [3] Supra XIV:6. [4] Sotah 11b.

**PAGE 107**

[1] Num. VI:24, R. [2] Gen. XXXIII:11. [3] Ibid., VIII:14. [4] Temurah 16a. [5] Gen. XXXVII:4. [6] Jer. X:20. [7] I Kings XIX:21. [8] Jud. III:9, I Chron. IV:9, 10.

**PAGE 108**

[1] Source unknown. [2] Supra XI:11. [3] Infra XIX:1-9.

**PAGE 109**

[1] Infra XVII:7. [2] Gittin 8a.

**PAGE 110**

[1] V. 24.

**PAGE 111**

[1] Deut. XII:17. [2] R ad loc. [3] Yoma 12a. [4] XVIII:5. [5] Ibid., 11.

**PAGE 112**

[1] Gen. XXVIII:19. [2] XV:32, XVI:16, XVII:5, 14. [3] K II Sam. XV:32. [4] VII:32, 33.

**PAGE 113**

[1] Zeb. 118b, R. Cf. Yoma 39b and Maharsha's comment.

**PAGE 114**

[1] Deut. XXXIII:17.

**PAGE 115**

[1] 119a. [2] V. 2.

**PAGE 117**

[1] XII:23. [2] XI:2.

**PAGE 118**

[1] I:35. Perhaps this should read: "In the Sidrah Bamidbar," since both quotations are from the Book of Num. Furthermore, R never refers to this Book as Bamidbar, but as Va'yedaber. See R Sab. 116a, Yoma 68b. [2] XXVI:34. [2*] Y. [3] Gen. XV:5. [4] Num. I:33. [5] Ibid., XXVI:37. [6] BB 122a. [7] Cf. Num. XXVI:54, and comments of R, N. and Mizrachi; also A here as great length. [8] Ez. XXIII:47.

**PAGE 119**

[1] Gen. X:18.

**PAGE 120**

[1] B.B.118a. [2] 112b. [3] I Sam. I:24. [4] Ps. LXXVIII:60. [5] Ibid., 67. [5*] Zeb. 118a.

**PAGE 121**

[1] I Sam. IV. [2] Zeb. 112b. [3] Num. XXVI:53.

**PAGE 122**

[1] Supra XIII:5. [2] Ex. XV:1.

**PAGE 123**

[1] See above XV:3.

**PAGE 124**

[1] Gen. XII:8, XIII:3. [2] Ibid., XVI:2. [3] V. 22. [4] V. 28. [5] Ps. LXXVIII:67 [6] 118b.

**PAGE 125**

[1] Gen. XXXV:18. R, Kol Elijah, Vayishlach. [1*] Supra XV:6-11. [1**] Ibid., v. 9. [2] Ibid., v. 7. [3] Ibid., v. 6.

**PAGE 127**

[1] Mishnah, Kelim, chs. 1. [2] XVIII:5.

**PAGE 128**

[1] XV:28. [2] Ibid., v. 29. [3] Ibid., v. 30. [4] Ibid., v. 31. [5] Ibid., v. 32. [6] I:3, 17. [7] Gen. XLIX:7. [8] Supra XXI.

**PAGE 129**

[1] II Kings XIV:25. [2] V. 27.

**PAGE 130**

[1] Supra XVII:16.

**PAGE 131**

[1] See above XVII:5, Commentary Digest.

**PAGE 132**

[1] Cf. R supra v. 12. [2] Meg. 6a.

**PAGE 133**

[1] Supra XV:33. [2] Ibid., v. 45. [3] Source unknown. [4] Ch. XVII, XVIII. See R XVII:1. [5] XVIII:7. [6] Bechoroth 55a. [7] I Sam. III:20.

**PAGE 134**

[1] B. B. 122a.

**PAGE 135**

[1] Deut. XIX:1-2. [2] Makkoth 13a. [3] Ibid., 9b.

**PAGE 136**

[1] Sifrei Num. XXXV:25. [2] Makkoth 11a, cf. R Num. XXXV:25. [3] Deut. IV:43. [4] Makkoth 9b. [5] See above I:14, Commentary Digest.

**PAGE 137**

[1] See Maimonides, Laws of Kings, ch. 8, par. 10; Makkoth 9a. [2] Laws of Homicide, ch. 6, par. 4, 5. [3] Num. XXXV:6.

**PAGE 138**

[1] Ex. VI:18. [2] Num. XXXV:8.

**PAGE 140**

[1] I Chron. VI:45. [2] II Sam. XVI:5. I Kings II:8.

**PAGE 141**

[1] V. 25.

**PAGE 143**

[1] I Chron. VI:62. [2] V. 7.

**PAGE 144**

[1] Num. XXXV:4, 5.

**PAGE 145**

[1] Num. XXXII:24, R ad loc. [2] Bezah 5a.

**PAGE 146**

[1] R, Deut. XI:22, from Sifrei ad loc. [2] V. 7, 8. [3] Y from G R s. 35, 3.

**PAGE 147**

[1] Y from G R s. 35, 3. [2] Ibid., s. 43, 14. [3] I Sam. XXX:25. Commentary Digest.

**PAGE 148**

[1] II:28. [2] Jud. XX.

**PAGE 150**

[1] Zeb. 112b. [2] Above VII:5.

**PAGE 151**

[1] Ps. L:1. [2] Ex. XX:5. [3] From Y ad loc. GR s. 8, M Ps, 50, TP Ber. ch, 9, hal. 1, Shekalim ch. 3, hal. 2.

**PAGE 152**

[1] Jer. XXXVIII:19.

**PAGE 154**

[1] See Rabbenu Bechayah, Deut. VIII:10.

**PAGE 156**

[1] Rambam, ch. 1. Terumoth. [2] San. 63b. [3] Ex. XX:5.

**PAGE 157**

[1] II Sam. XXIII:8. [2] Moed Katan 16b. [3] Prov. XXVI:3. [4] Ez. XXIII:24. [5] Ps. V:13. [6] I Sam. XXIII:26.

**PAGE 158**

[1] Lev. XXVI:14-46. [2] Sab. 88a.

**PAGE 159**

[1] Gen. XXXV:2. [2] Below v. 23. [3] Gen. XXXV:5. [4] Ib., XII:6. [5] Ibid., XXXIII:19. [6] Ex. XX:3. [7] Pes. 116a.

**PAGE 160**

[1] T P, ch. 10, 5. [2] Gen. XXI:13. [3] Ib., XVII:18. [4] On Haggadah. [5] Gen. XXV:1-4. [5*] Ibid., XV:13.

**PAGE 161**

[1] Ps. LVIII:11. [2] Source unknown. [3] See above VII:21, Digest. [4] T B'ha-alothecha 10, N R s. 15, 15.

**PAGE 162**

[1] Sotah 36a. [2] XLIV:7. [3] II Kings XIX:35, Is. X:27 R.

**PAGE 163**

[1] Num. XX:15. [2] Rambam, Laws of Idolatry, ch. 1, par. 1.

**PAGE 164**

[1] Gen. XLII:30. [2] Ibid., XXXIX:20. [3] Ex. XXII:14. [4] II Sam. VII:23. [5] Ezekiel XX:32.

**PAGE 165**

[1] Ezekiel XX:33. [2] Source unknown. [3] 11a. [4] Deut. XXXIV:5-12.

**PAGE 166**

[1] XX. [2] Maharsha, Makkoth ibid. [2*] Baba Bathra 14b, 15a. [3] I Kings, VI:31. [4] Ez. XL:10. [5] Source unknown. [6] XXXV:4. [7] V. 1. [8] Baba Bathra 15a.

**PAGE 167**

[1] Jud. II:9. [2] Supra X:10-13. [3] Source unknown. [4] B. B. 122b. [5] Sab. 105a, Ecc. R. 7, 1; Introd. to Ruth R. 4; MS 23. [6] Ch. 12. [7] Ex. XIII:19.

**PAGE 168**

[1] Sotah 13b, T Ekev ·6, r Deut. VIII:1. [2] Gen. XXXVII:12-28. [3] Sotah 13b, G R s. 85, 3. [4] Gen. XLVIII:22. [5] Deut. P. S. 2. [5*] Gen. XL:15. [6] Rosh Hashanah. [7] B. B. 15a. [8] Ibid., 111b.

ZIDON
HERMON
ARAM
DAN
IJON
LAJISH
CANAANITE
TYRE
ABEL BETH MAACHA
KANAH
BETH REHOB
ASHER
ACHSIB
KEDESH
YIRON
ARGOB
BET HAEMEK
BETH DAGON
HORMAH
Hazor
MEROM
ACCO
KABUL
NAPHTALI
BASHAN
HANATON
ZEBULUN
RIMON
KINERET
ACHSAPH
KITRON
Sea of Kinnereth
Shomron
Nahalal
GATH CHEFER
ASHTAROTH KARNAJIM
Mt. Carmel
KISHON R.
RAKAT
DOR
YAFIA
HAMATH
YAKNEAM
SARID
Mt. TABOR
Aphek
YABNEL
EN DOR
KENATH
MEGIDO
SHUNAM
YARMUK R.
KEDESH
ISSACHAR
YISREEL
ANHARATH
EDREI
TANOCH
MANASSEH
MEDITERRANEAN SEA
LO DEBAR
RAMOTH GILEAD
BETH SHEAN
MANASSEH
BETH HAGAN
CHEFER
Yabesh Gilead
SALCHAH
TEBETS
MITZPAH
SOCHO
MAHANAIM
ZAPHON
TIRTSAH
SUCCOTH
PNUEL
Yabok R.
Mt. EBAL
SHECHEM
GILEAD